PARIS

the collected traveler

271340

COLLECTION PERMANENTE
ENTRÉE
Plein Tarif A

Edmund White, The Flaneur
—, Our Paris

Also in the series by Barrie Kerper

CENTRAL ITALY

The Collected Traveler

PARIS

the collected traveler

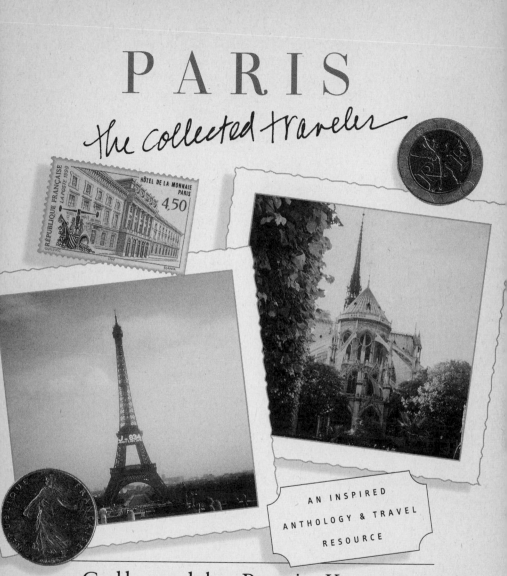

HÔTEL DE LA MONNAIE
PARIS

4.50

RÉPUBLIQUE FRANÇAISE
LA POSTE 1999

AN INSPIRED
ANTHOLOGY & TRAVEL
RESOURCE

Collected by Barrie Kerper

Three Rivers Press / NEW YORK

See page 614 for additional credits.

Published by Three Rivers Press, New York, New York.
Member of the Crown Publishing Group.
Random House, Inc. New York, Toronto, London, Sydney, Auckland
www.randomhouse.com

THREE RIVERS PRESS is a registered trademark and the Three Rivers Press logo is a trademark of Random House, Inc.

Printed in the United States of America

DESIGN BY LYNNE AMFT

Library of Congress Cataloging-in-Publication Data
Paris: the collected traveler: an inspired anthology & travel resource / collected by Barrie Kerper.
1. Paris (France)—Guidebooks.   2. Travelers, writings.   3. Paris (France)—Description and travel—Sources.   I. Kerper, Barrie.
DC708 .P328 2000
914.4'3604839—dc21   99-059313

ISBN 0-609-80444-8

10 9 8 7 6 5 4

For my mother, Phyllis,
who always believed my boxes of files
held something of value.

acknowledgments

Publishing a book requires a staggering amount of work by a team of dedicated people. An anthology, however, requires the participation of an even greater number of people, ensuring the project will be that much more complex. It is essential, therefore, that I extend my heartfelt thanks and deep gratitude to the following colleagues and friends: Alison Gross, Anne Messitte, Bonnie Ammer, Anthony Gambino, Jessica Schulte, Kristen Wolfe, Whitney Cookman, Teresa Nicholas, Jane Searle, Jay and Kathleen Goodfriend, Maha Khalil, Vivian Fong, Chris Warnasch, Amy Myer, Florence Porrino, Patty Flynn, Steve Weissman, and Martine Gérard and her colleagues at Maison de la France in New York. Special thanks are due to Steve Magnuson, who shares my passion for France and whose enthusiasm for this project resulted in it becoming reality; each of the individual writers, agents, and permissions representatives for various publishers and periodicals—especially Leigh Montville of The Condé Nast Publications and Rose Sorvino of *The New York Times*—without whose generosity and understanding there would be nothing to publish; Shaye Areheart, my editor, who I am honored to work with and am grateful to for a million reasons, most especially for her belief in the series and her firm but guiding hand; Amy Boorstein, Mark McCauslin, and Lynne Amft of Crown's production editorial and art departments, who after many missed deadlines and an initial manuscript of over 2,000 pages, somehow figured out how to pull everything together and get the thing published; Chip Gibson, the best boss and mentor I've ever had, who allowed me to spend much of my time at the office working on this (although there were many days he questioned the wisdom of that decision); and Lorraine and Luc Paillard, *mes amis intimes* and correspondents *par excellence*, who sent more notes, restaurant and hotel tips, postcards, and invaluable observations than I can possibly count. Lastly, my sincere apologies to the many friends, relatives, and colleagues not named here—you know who you are—who never failed to inquire about my progress but with whom I was out of touch for over a year, and to my husband, Jeffrey, and daughter, Alyssa. It was perhaps inevitable that Jeff would be left with baby duty more often than he imagined, but while I'm sorry for creating the burden, I believe the effort will prove to have been worthwhile. Alyssa is too young to realize it now, but I hope our home and, by extension, this series, will inspire in her a love of reading and travel, ensuring she will grow up to be a true *citoyenne du monde*.

contents

Paris is a city that might well be spoken of in the plural, as the Greeks used to speak of Athens, for there are many Parises, and the tourists' Paris is only superficially related to the Paris of the Parisians. The foreigner driving through Paris from one museum to another is quite oblivious to the presence of a world he brushes past without seeing. Until you have wasted time in a city, you cannot pretend to know it well. The soul of a big city is not to be grasped so easily; in order to make contact with it, you have to have been bored, you have to have suffered a bit in those places that contain it. Anyone can get hold of a guide and tick off all the monuments, but within the very confines of Paris there is another city as difficult of access as Timbuktu once was.

—Julian Green, PARIS

Introduction

A traveler without knowledge is a bird without wings.
—Sa'di, *Gulistan* (1258)

SOME YEARS AGO, MY HUSBAND and I fulfilled a dream we'd had since we first met: we put all our belongings in storage and traveled around the countries bordering the Mediterranean Sea for a year. In preparation for this journey, I did what I always do in advance of a trip: consult my home archives—a library of books and periodicals—and start researching. I have been an obsessive clipper since I was very young, and by the time I was preparing for this trip, I had amassed an enormous number of articles from periodicals on various countries of the world. After a year of reading and organizing all this material, I then created a package of articles and notes for each destination and mailed them ahead to friends we'd be staying with as well as to appropriate American Express offices. Although we had no schedule to speak of, we knew we would spend no less than six weeks in each place.

My husband wasted no time informing me that my research efforts were perhaps a bit over the top. He shares my passion for travel (my mother-in-law told me that, when he was little, he would announce to the family exactly how many months, weeks, days, hours, minutes, and seconds it was before the annual summer vacation) but not necessarily for clipping (he has accused me of being too much like the anal-retentive fisherman from an old *Saturday*

Night Live skit, the one where the guy neatly puts his bait, extra line, snacks, hand towels, etc., into individual plastic sandwich bags. In my defense, I'm not *quite* that bad, although I *am* guilty of trying to improve upon pocket organizers.

While we were traveling that year, we would occasionally meet other Americans, and I was continually amazed at how ill-prepared some of them were. Information, in so many different forms, is in such abundance now that it was nearly inconceivable to me that people had not taken advantage of the available resources. Some people we met didn't even seem to be having a very good time; they were generally unimpressed with their experience because they had missed the significance of what they were seeing and doing. Therefore, I was surprised again when these same people were genuinely interested in my little packages of notes and articles. Some people even offered to *pay* me for them, and I began to think that my collected research would perhaps appeal to other travelers. I also realized that even the most well-intentioned people were overwhelmed by trip planning or didn't have the time to put it all together. Later, friends and colleagues told me they really appreciated the packages I prepared for them, and somewhere along the line I was being referred to as a "modern-day hunter-gatherer," a sort of "one-stop information source."

While there is much to be said for a freewheeling approach to travel—I am not an advocate of sticking to rigid schedules—I do believe that, as with most things in life, what you get out of a trip is equal only to what you put into it. Learning about a place is part of the excitement of travel, and I wouldn't dream of venturing anywhere without first poring over a mountain of maps, books, and periodicals. I include cookbooks in my reading (some cookbooks reveal much historical detail as well as prepare you for the food and drink you will most likely encounter), and I also like to watch movies that have something to do with where I'm going. Additionally, I buy a blank journal and begin filling it with all sorts of notes, reminders, and entire passages from books I'm not bringing along. In other words, I completely immerse myself in my destination before I leave. It's the most enjoyable homework assignment I've ever had.

Every destination, new or familiar, merits some attention. The reward for your efforts is that you'll acquire a deeper understanding and appreciation of the place and the people who live there, and not surprisingly, you'll have more fun.

Every land has its own special rhythm, and unless the traveler takes the time to learn the rhythm, he or she will remain an outsider there always.
—Juliette de Baircli Levy, ENGLISH WRITER

Occasionally I meet people who are more interested in how many countries I've been to than in those I might know well or particularly like. If "well-traveled" is defined only by the number of places I've been, then I suppose I'm not. However, I feel I *really know* and have *really seen* the places I've visited, which is how *I* define "well-traveled." I travel to see how people live in other parts of the world—not to check countries off a list—and to do that requires sticking around for more than a few days and adapting to the local pace and rhythm. Certainly any place you decide is worthy of your time and effort is worthy of more than a day, but you don't always need an indefinite period of time to immerse yourself in the local culture or establish a routine that allows for getting to know the merchants and residents of your adopted neighborhood. One of the fastest ways to adjust to daily life in France, for example, is to abandon whatever schedule you observe at home and eat when the French eat. Mealtimes in France are generally well established, and if you try to find a place to eat at two in the afternoon, nearly every place will have stopped serving lunch by that hour.

Likewise, dinner is not typically served at 6 P.M. Adjust your schedule and you'll be on French time, doing things when the French do them, eliminating possible disappointment and frustration.

About fifteen years ago, the former Paris bureau chief for *The New York Times,* John Vinocur, wrote a piece for the travel section entitled "Discovering the Hidden Paris." In it, he noted the French word, not easily translated into English, *d'épaysement.* His translation of the word was "the feeling of not being assaulted by the familiarity of things, a change in surroundings where there is no immediate point of reference." He went on to quote a French journalist who once said that "Americans don't travel to be *dépaysés,* but to find a home away from home." This is unfortunate, but too often true. Some tourists can travel all around the world if they desire, but their unwillingness to adapt ensures they will never really leave home.

Similar are the people who endorse "adventure travel," words which make me cringe as they seem to imply that unless one partakes in kayaking, mountain climbing, biking, rock climbing, or some other physical endeavor, a travel experience is somehow invalid or unadventurous. *All* travel is an adventure, and unless "adventure travel" allows for plenty of time to adapt to the local rhythm, the so-called "adventure" is really a physically strenuous—if memorable—outdoor achievement. Occasionally I hear descriptions of a biking excursion, for example, where the participants spend the majority of each day in the same way: making biking the priority instead of working biking into the local cadence of daily life. When I ask if they joined the locals at the café for a morning croissant or an evening aperitif, shopped at the outdoor *marché,* went to a local *fête,* or people-watched in the *place,* the answer is invariably no. They may have had an amazing bike trip, but they do not know France—one has to get off the bike a bit more often for that sort of knowledge—and if a biking experience alone is what they were seeking, they certainly didn't need to fly to France: there are plenty of challenging and beautiful places to bike in the United States.

I believe that every place in the world offers *something* of interest. In her magnificent book *Black Lamb, Grey Falcon,* Rebecca West recounts how in the 1930s she passed through Skopje, Yugoslavia (formerly the Yugoslav Republic of Macedonia), by train twice, without stopping, because friends had told her the town wasn't worth visiting. A third time through she did stop, and she met two wonderful people who became lasting friends. She wrote, "Now, when I go through a town of which I know nothing, a town which appears to be a waste land of uniform streets wholly without quality, I look on it in wonder and hope, since it may hold a Mehmed, a Militsa." I, too, have been richly rewarded by pausing in places (Skopje included) that first appeared quite limiting.

Travel is fatal to prejudice, bigotry, and narrow-mindedness.
                                                    —MARK TWAIN

The world is a book, and those who do not travel read only a page.
                                                    —ST. AUGUSTINE

I would add to Mark Twain's quote above one by Benjamin Disraeli (1804–81): "Travel teaches toleration." People who travel with an open mind and are receptive to the ways of others cannot help but return with more tolerance for people and situations at home, at work, in their cities and communities. I find that travel also ensures I will not be quite the same person I was before I left. After a trip, I typically have a lot of renewed energy and bring new perspectives to my job. At home, I ask myself how I can incorporate attributes or traits I observed into my own life and share them with my husband and daughter.

The anthologies in The Collected Traveler series offer a record of people's achievements and shortcomings. It may be a lofty goal to expect that they might also help us realize that despite cultural differences between us and our hosts—in *any* country where we happen to be guests—we have much more in common than not.

About This Series

The Collected Traveler editions are not guidebooks in the traditional sense, yet they *may* be considered guidebooks in that they are books that guide readers to other sources. Each book is really the first book you should turn to when planning a trip. If you think of the individual volumes as a sort of planning package, you've got the right idea. To borrow a phrase from a reviewer who was writing about the Lonely Planet Travel Survival Kit series years ago, The Collected Traveler is for people who know how to get their luggage off the carousel. If you enjoy acquiring knowledge about where you're going—whether you plan a trip independently or with a like-minded tour organization—this series is for you. If you're looking for a guide that simply informs you of exact prices, hours, and highlights, you've got the wrong book.

A few words about me may also help you determine if this series is for you: I travel somewhat frugally, because I respect money and its value and I'm not convinced that if I spend $600 a night on a hotel room I'll have a better trip. I've been to some of the world's finest hotels, mostly to visit friends who were staying there or to have a drink in the hotel bar. With a few notable exceptions, it seems to me that the majority of these places are all alike, meant to conform to a code of sameness and predictability. There's nothing about them that is particularly French or Italian or Turkish—you could be *anywhere*. The cheapest of the cheap accommodations don't represent good value, either. I look for places to stay that are usually old, possibly historic, with lots of charm and character. I do not mind if my room is small; I do not need a television, telephone, or hair dryer; and I most definitely do not care for an American-style buffet breakfast, which is hardly what the locals eat. I also prefer to make my own plans, send my own letters and faxes, place telephone calls, and arrange transportation. Not because I think I can do it better than a professional agent (whose expertise I admire) but because I enjoy it and learn a lot in the process. Finally, I think you'll quickly ascertain that I do indeed enjoy many of life's little luxuries, when I perceive them to be of good value.

This series promotes the view of staying longer within a smaller area. Susan Allen Toth refers to this in her book *England as You Like It,* in which she subscribes to the "thumbprint theory of travel": spending at least a week in one spot that is no larger than what her thumbprint covers on a large-scale map of England. She goes on to explain that excursions are encouraged, as long as they're no more than an hour's drive away. As I have discovered in my own travels, a week in one place, even a spot no bigger than my thumbprint, is rarely long enough to see and enjoy it all. Not only does The Collected Traveler focus on one corner of the world—the countries that border the Mediterranean Sea—it also focuses on cities and regions rather than entire countries. This edition features a section on places within an hour or so of Paris to visit for the day, the weekend, or longer *("Île-de-France et d'Ailleurs").*

Each section of this book features a selection of articles from various periodicals and an annotated bibliography relevant to the theme of each section (the *"Renseignements Pratiques"* section is a bit different, with the books being a part of the A–Z listings). The articles and books were chosen from my own files and home library, which I've maintained for over two decades. The selected writings reflect the culture, politics, history, current social issues, religion, cuisine, and arts of the people you'll be visiting. They also represent the observations and opinions of a wide variety of novelists, travel writers, and journalists. These writers are authorities on Paris or France or both; they either live there (as permanent or part-time residents) or visit there often for business or pleasure. In some cases, their names are as linked with France as Balzac or Colette. I'm very discriminating in seeking opinions and recommendations, and I am not interested in the remarks of unobservant wanderers. I am not implying that first-time visitors to Paris have nothing noteworthy or interesting to share—they often do and are often keen observers; conversely, frequent travelers are often jaded and apt to miss the finer details that make Paris an exceptional city. I am interested in the opinions of people who want to *know* Paris, not just *see* it.

I've included numerous older articles (even though some of the specific information regarding prices, hours, etc., is no longer accurate) because they were either particularly well written, thought-provoking, or unique in some way, and because the authors' views stand as a valuable record of a certain time in history. Often, even with the passage of many years, you may share the same emotions and opinions of the writer, and equally as often, *plus ça change, plus c'est la même chose*. I have many, many more articles in my files than I was able to reprint here. Though there are a few pieces whose absence I very much regret, I believe the anthology you're holding is very good.

A word about the dining-out section, *"À Table"*: I have great respect for restaurant reviewers. Their work may seem glamorous— and it sometimes is—but it is also hard. It's an all-consuming, full-time job, and that is why I urge you to consult three good books: *The Food Lover's Guide to Paris* by Patricia Wells; *Cheap Eats in Paris* by Sandra Gustafson; and *The Paris Café Cookbook* by Daniel Young, all detailed in the *"À Table" bibliothèque*. My files are bulging with Paris restaurant reviews, and I could have included many, many more articles about restaurants, bistros, cafés, and brasseries; but it would be repetitive and ultimately beside the point. I tried to select a few articles that give you a feel for eating out in Paris, alert you to some things to look for in selecting a truly worthwhile place versus a mediocre one, and highlight some dishes that are not commonplace in America. I also did not feel it necessary to provide information about Paris's Michelin-starred restaurants as they are covered well in other books and articles (and in the red *Guide Michelin,* of course). My files are also bulging with hotel recommendations, but again I refer you to the experts and their books, featured in *"Renseignements Pratiques."*

The annotated bibliography for each section is one of the most important features of this book. Reading about travel in the days before transatlantic flights, I always marvel at the number of steamer trunks and the baggage people were accustomed to taking. If I had been traveling then, however, my bags would have been filled with books, not clothes. Although I travel light and seldom check bags, I have been known to fill an entire suitcase with books, secure in the knowledge that I could have them all with me for the duration of my trip. Each *bibliothèque* features titles I feel are the best available and most worth your time. I realize that "best" is subjective; readers will simply have to trust me that I have been extremely thorough in deciding which books to recommend. (I have read them all, by the way, and I own them all, with the exception of a few I borrowed.) If the lists seem long, they are, but the more I read, the more I realize there is to know, and there are an awful lot of really good books out there! I'm not suggesting you read them *all,* but I do hope you will not be content with just one. I have identified some books as "de rigueur," meaning that I consider them required reading; but I sincerely believe that *all* the books I've mentioned are important, helpful, well-written, or all three. I don't miss much; but there are surely some books I've not seen, so if some of your favorites aren't included here, please write and tell me about them.

I have not hesitated to list out-of-print titles because some excellent books are out of print (and deserve to be returned to print!), and because many, many out-of-print books can be found through individuals who specialize in out-of-print books, booksellers, libraries, and on-line searches. I should also mention that I believe the companion reading you bring along should be related in some way to where you're going. Therefore, the books listed in *"Des Belles Choses"* are novels and nonfiction books that feature characters or settings in Paris or France, or feature aspects of France and the French (such as *Les Misérables, A Moveable Feast, The Château, Travels with Alice,* and *Fields of Glory*). Also, biographies make up most of the books in the *"Personalités"* section. The selection isn't meant to be comprehensive—there are many more I could have included—but represents a variety of books about a variety of interesting people, one or more of whom may also interest you. The *"Musées, Jardins, et Monuments"* section, therefore, doesn't include biographies of artists, as I thought it better to separate art history books and museum catalogs—with their many reproductions of artworks—from memoirs and biographies.

Together, the articles and books lead you on and off the beaten path, and present a "reality check" of sorts. Will you learn of some nontouristy things to see and do? Yes. Will you also learn more about the better-known aspects of Paris? Yes. The Eiffel Tower and the little neighborhood park in the middle of the 20th are equally representative of Paris. Seeing them *both* is what makes for a memorable visit, and no one, by the way, should make you feel guilty for wanting to see some famous sites. They have become famous for a reason: they are really something to see, the Eiffel Tower included. Readers will have no trouble finding a multitude of other travel titles offering plenty of noncontroversial viewpoints. This is my attempt at presenting a more balanced picture. Ultimately, this is also the compendium of information that I wish I'd had between two covers years ago. I admit it isn't the "perfect" book; for that, I envision a waterproof jacket and pockets inside the front and back covers, pages and pages of accompanying maps, lots of blank pages for notes, a bookmark, mileage and size conversion charts . . . in other words, something so encyclopedic—in both weight and size—that positively no one, my editor assures me, would want to read it. That said, I am exceedingly happy with The Collected Traveler, and I believe it will prove helpful in the anticipation of your upcoming journey; in the enjoyment of your trip while it's happening; and in the remembrance of it when you're back home.

Paris was the undisputed capital of the nineteenth century. Writing in the early half of the 1900s, Gertrude Stein observed that "Paris was where the twentieth century was." The city unquestionably lost some of its luster by the mid to late twentieth century, but I have no reason to doubt that Paris will re-emerge as a city of grace, significance, and beauty in the twenty-first. In his book *Fragile Glory*, Richard Bernstein penned what may be the most apropos passage on Paris as we enter the new millennium:

> What makes a Parisian? A certain style? An intonation of language? A way of speaking? For the taxi driver, apparently, a Parisian can be distinguished from another sort of Frenchman by the way he looks and talks, by the way he spends his day, by a certain connoisseurship of life, an appreciation of the quaint charms of Paris's beauty . . . His nostalgia derived from an image of his city similar to one of those naive paintings that became the rage in the 1980s, showing a little Parisian square from the point of view of a child's innocent eyes, with all the ideal elements in place: the grouping of narrow houses with wrought-iron balustrades and gray slate roofs and dormer windows, clustered around a small green space with plane trees and a café, along with a *boulangerie*

and a couple of people passing by on bicycles. It is Paris as picture postcard . . . But that's just it. The Paris that the taxi driver imagines, the city he believes is disappearing (and they have all through this century believed that Paris was disappearing), is not Hugo's city of the world or Rilke's place that lives close to death. Many Parisians, like the taxi driver, have always been struggling against the essence of Paris, not realizing that what they saw as decline, as the growth of impersonality, as the increase of foreigners, as the sound of music that was not real music, was really their city's greatness, the thing that made it unique in the world. Paris, to be Paris, must be the place where the great moral dilemmas of mankind are identified and where the experiments in the life of thought—if not of action—take place at the highest register. Paris should be infuriating, as it must have been to millions when, for example, Edouard Manet painted a naked woman lunching on the grass . . . Above all, for Paris to be Paris, it has to be free. The question thus is not: Are there too many Arabs in Belleville, too many Chinese in the Thirteenth Arrondissement, too many neighborhoods that have lost their character? The question is: Will the fear that there are no longer any Parisians lead the inhabitants of the great village on the Seine no longer to fashion a place that matters to all humanity?

Tous mes vœux pour un bon voyage!

Renseignements Pratiques
(Practical Information)

If you are a prowler (and a good traveler is) you will often find yourself peering into a Paris courtyard and the lowering face of the concierge thereunto attached. As she emerges from her cell, call out in the lilting bird song you must learn imme-diately as you touch French soil, "Bonjour, Madame. C'est très joli, votre cour" (not hers at all but she insists it is and you must maintain the fiction with her). Ready for a fight, or better still, expecting to see you flee her Medusa head, this stuns her and may keep her speechless long enough for a good look around. If you need more time when she comes to, "Je suis artiste," a phrase which still evokes some respect in Paris. As you saunter out, "Au-voir, Madame. Merci mille fois. Vous êtes très gentille." She isn't nor need you be so grateful, but you can afford to be generous in victory.
—Kate Simon, PARIS: PLACES & PLEASURES

A–Z Renseignements Pratiques

A

Accommodations

IF YOU ARRIVE IN PARIS without a room, you can always take your chances at the Bureau d'Accueil (welcome bureau). The staff will find you a room for a small fee. I've only had to use this service once, and although it was the off-season, it was also the Easter holiday weekend, and rooms were in short supply. I ended up in a rather dingy place, so avoid being desperate if you can help it. There are Bureau d'Accueil offices at five train stations (Gare du Nord, de l'Est, de Lyon, Montparnasse, and d'Austerlitz) and the main tourist office (127 avenue des Champs-Élysées).

Apartment rentals might be a suitable choice depending on how long you'll be in Paris and the number of people traveling together. Organizations that arrange apartment rentals would fill a small book. Here are some sources that have come highly recommended or with which I have had a positive experience: Barclay International Group (well-established company offering worldwide rentals; Barclay also reserves cars, sight-seeing tours, rail passes, theater tickets, cellular phones, and laptop computers; the "Last-Minute Specials" feature of its Web site is a good deal; 3 School Street, Glen Cove, New York 11542; 516-759-5100 / 800-845-6636 / fax: 516-609-0000; www.barclayweb.com); Chez Vous (rental agency that offers apartments in Paris—for stays as short as three days—as well as accommodations in the French countryside; for a copy of its *Bonjour Paris* brochure and information, contact Chez Vous at 220 Redwood Highway, Suite 129, Mill Valley, California 94941; 415-331-2535 / fax: 415-331-5296); The French Experience (full-service travel agency/tour operator that represents apartments ranging from studios to five rooms in Paris, for stays of four days or longer; contact the agency at 370 Lexington Avenue, Suite 812, New York, New York 10017; 212-986-1115 / fax: 212-986-3808; www.frenchexperience.com); Paris Appartements Services (rents furnished studios and one-bedroom apartments, from one week or longer, in the Opera, Louvre, and Marais neighborhoods; 69 rue d'Argout, 75002 Paris; 01.40.28.01.28 / fax: 01.40.28. 92.01; www.paris-appartements-services.fr); Homebase Abroad Ltd. (features rentals of fine private homes, villas, and apartments in Paris and Italy only; its properties share "distinction, quality, and value," and indeed the lowest rate I found on its Web site was $1,440/week for a Paris apartment; 29 Mary's Lane, Scituate, Massachusetts 02066; 781-545-5112 / fax: 781-545-1808; www.homebase-abroad .com); At Home Abroad (405 E. Fifty-sixth Street, Suite 6H, New York, New York 10022; 212-421-9165 / fax: 212-752-1591); Ville et Village (agency offers rentals it personally inspects and selects in the cities and countryside of France, Spain, Portugal, and Italy; 2124 Kittredge Street, Suite 200, Berkeley, California 94704; 510-559-8080 / fax: 510-559-8217; www.villeetvillage.com).

Bed & Breakfast accommodations are available in Paris and some suburbs through an organization called Paris B&B. At its Web site (www.parisbandb.com), viewers can click on the name of a property and a color photo appears with a description running along the right side of the screen; dial 800-872-2632 in the United States to reserve or inquire about lodgings.

Camping (known as *campings municipaux* or simply *campings*): The European conception of camping is about as opposite from the American as possible. Europeans do not go camping to seek a wilderness experience, and European campgrounds are designed without much privacy in mind, offering amenities ranging from hot-water showers, facilities for washing clothes and dishes, electrical outlets, croissants and *café* for breakfast, and flush toilets to tiled bathrooms with heat, swimming pools, cafés, bars, restaurants, telephones, televisions, and general stores. If you find yourself at a campground during the summer months, you may notice that entire families have literally moved in (having reserved their spaces many months in advance) and that they return every year to spend time with their friends, the way we might return every year to a ski cabin or a house at the beach. It's quite an entertaining and lively spectacle, and camping like this is not really roughing it! There are several campgrounds in and around Paris. As always, the Tourist Office has specific information, or you can contact the Espace du Tourisme d'Île-de-France (99 rue de Rivoli, 1st; 08.03.81.80.00), which also provides information on campgrounds outside of the city. The campground in the Bois de Boulogne (01.45.24.30.00) is rather nice (three-star) and very international; another three-star choice is Camping du Tremblay (Boulevard des Alliés, Champigny, 94507; 01.43.97.43.97 / fax: 01.48.89.07.94), which is near the Bois de Vincennes and along the banks of the Marne. Paris is a twenty-minute ride away on the RER and EuroDisney is fifteen minutes away (private bus service is offered during the high season). It's been my experience that at *campings municipaux* during the off-season, no one ever comes around to collect fees. The campgrounds are still open and there is running water, but the thinking seems to be that it just isn't worth it to collect money from so few campers. (This will not hold true at privately run campgrounds.) Outside of Paris, you may see signs for *camping à la ferme,* which is a camping experience on a farm. Typically there are no facilities, but the setting is usually beautiful and quiet and often comes with the offer of a home-cooked meal or two. If you plan to camp for even a few nights, I recommend joining Family Campers and RVers. Annual membership (valid for one year from the time you join) is $25. FCRV is a member of the Fédération Internationale de Camping et de Caravanning (FICC) and is the only organization in America authorized to issue the International Camping Carnet for camping in Europe. Only FCRV members are eligible to purchase the carnet—it cannot be purchased separately—and the membership fee is $10. The carnet is like a camping passport, and since many FICC member campgrounds in Europe are privately owned, the carnet provides entry into these member-only campsites. A carnet offers campers priority status, and occasionally, discounts. An additional benefit is that instead of keeping your passport overnight—which hotels and campgrounds are often required to do—the campground staff simply keep your carnet, allowing you to hold on to your passport. One ICC membership is good for the entire family: parents and all children under the age of eighteen. To receive an application and information, contact the organization at 4804 Transit Road, Building 2, Depew, New York 14043; 800-245-9755 / fax: 716-668-6242.

Home exchange might be an appealing option: I've read wildly enthusiastic reports from people who've swapped apartments or houses, and it's usually always an economical alternative. Some services to contact include Vacation Exchange Club (the leading agency, which publishes multiple directories each year; P.O. Box 650, Key West, Florida 33041; phone/fax: 800-638-3841); Trading Homes International (P.O. Box 787, Hermosa Beach, California 90254; 800-877-8723 / fax: 310-798-3865); Worldwide Home Exchange Club (806 Branford Avenue, Silver Spring, Maryland 20904; 301-680-8950); a general home-exchange Web site is www.webhomeexchange.com. ~A good but out-of-print book to read is *Trading Places: The Wonderful World of Vacation Home Exchanging* (Bill and Mary Barbour, Rutledge Hill Press, Nashville, Tennessee, 1991).

Hotels: For our purposes here we are referring to hotels as accommodations, but note that the word *hôtel* in French has a number of meanings: it also refers to a private, aristocratic mansion (known as a *hôtel particulier,* such as the Hôtel de Sully); city hall (known as the *hôtel de ville;* every French town of any size has one); a hospital (known as the *hôtel-Dieu*); a general post office (known as the *hôtel des postes*); an auction house (known as a *hôtel des ventes*); and, in Paris, a home for wounded *(invalide)* war veterans, founded by Louis XIV (known as the Hôtel des Invalides). I feel the same way about books on hotels as I do about guidebooks: the right one for you is the one whose author shares a certain sensibility or philosophy with you. It's important to select the right book(s) so you can make choices that best suit you and your style. Once you've selected the book you like, trust the author's recommendations. It is completely unnecessary to continue seeking information about the hotel(s) you've chosen. Trying to validate your choice by searching the Web, for example, serves no good purpose: remember, *you don't know the people who are writing reviews, and you have no idea if the same things that are important to you are important to them.* The author of the book you've chosen has shared his or her standards with you and explained the criteria used in rating accommodations. Stick with the author and move on to the next step in planning. Following are some of my favorite books to use when searching for a Paris hotel: *Alastair Sawday's Guide to Special Paris Hotels* (edited by Ann Cooke-Yarborough, Alastair Sawday Publishing, Bristol, United Kingdom; distributed in the U.S. by St. Martin's Press). I have used two of Sawday's other guides—*French Bed & Breakfast* and *Special Places to Stay in Spain and Portugal*—and I have used all three with happy results. Some of his comments which won me over: "This book sets out to introduce you to some of the nicest, least pretentious, best-value hotels in the City of Light. We hope we have left out the very grand, the pompous, the poor value, the clinically modern, the unfriendly, the ordinary." And "Don't, please, go to a chain hotel; they destroy so much that you probably value. Don't spend your money on the big names, even if their radical price-cutting tactics seem seductive." Each listing in the book features two color photos and a description of the property, with symbols indicating such things as double windows, pets accepted, elevator, and air-conditioning. There are also four maps and a useful vocabulary of words and expressions. I last used the *Bed & Breakfast* guide (fourth edition) for a trip to Provence, and I could not believe I was sleeping in such old, beautiful *châteaux*, surrounded by vineyards and lavender fields, and not a single one was over $100 a night. One of the main differences between this guide and Karen Brown's (see below) is price—this one offers places that are every bit as charming but not always *luxe,* and the prices reflect this. There is a mileage chart plus sixteen pages of good maps that feature numbers corresponding to the various lodgings. New to this edition is the *bulletin de réservation* (booking form) at the back of the book to use as a guide in making reservations. *Cheap Sleeps in Paris* (eighth edition, Sandra Gustafson, Chronicle Books, 1998). A companion volume to Gustafson's *Cheap Eats in Paris,* this is a great resource for best-value places to lay your head. Lest you get the wrong idea about Gustafson's aim, she states that "if you are looking for a book about the cheapest beds in Paris, *Cheap Sleeps in Paris* is not for you. What you will find here is a highly selective guide to the hotels that I have discovered to be the best value in their category, be it a no-star with the shower and toilet down the hall or an antique-filled, three-star Left Bank hotel with a Jacuzzi in the marble bathroom." I have used this guide on three occasions and stayed at three completely different hotels, in three different price ranges, and each was wonderful. Listings appear alphabetically by arrondissement with a map for each one. What really separates this guide from others is the inclusion of both "Big Splurges" and "Other Options"—apartment rentals, camping, private hostels, residence hotels, and student accommodations, making it a book for *everyone*. Additionally, there is a "Cheap Chic" shopping section at the end of the book (which includes a useful shopping vocabulary) with listings for the best places to purchase cosmetics, perfumes, flowers, hats, jewelry, clothing, haircuts, handbags, and gifts at a discount, plus details on flea markets and the roving food markets. There are also special recommendations for people to contact for walking tours, private and group cooking lessons, and personalized travel itineraries. *Karen Brown's France: Charming Inns & Itineraries,* and *Karen Brown's France: Charming Bed & Breakfasts* (both Fodor's Travel Publications, Inc., 1999). My husband and I have found some of the most wonderful places to stay in France, Spain, and England with the help of Karen Brown's guides. In addition to the thorough descriptions of lodgings (some of which are in châteaux, old mills, and buildings of historical significance), *my* favorite features of these guides are ones no one ever mentions: the sample reservation-request letter (in French and English so readers can construct a letter or fax of their own) and the tips that appear in the introduction, such as how to say "Fill it up" at the gas station *(Faites le plein, s'il vous plaît)*. The itineraries are useful for planning your route and deciding if you want to travel by car, but the descriptions of individual towns and sites are not detailed enough to warrant bringing the book along—this is really a "before you go" book. I find the organization of the guides maddeningly cumbersome—the lodgings are listed alphabetically by individual city, town, or village, but maps are at the back of the book, so you end up constantly flipping pages back and forth to evaluate all the available choices in any region of the country. However, this frustration is really a small price to pay for the opportunity to stay in a memorable auberge or château. The Paris section in the *Inns & Itineraries* edition is *much* easier to use as the entries are listed by arrondissement. The *Bed & Breakfasts* edition offers a selection of *chambres d'hôtes* and *gîtes de France,* less expensive lodgings that are no less charming or special. Each entry includes all practical information, garage or parking availability, corresponding Michelin map, directions, and black-and-white illustration of the property. Paris aside, the B&B edition features twenty-five lodgings in the Loire Valley, fourteen in Burgundy, and twenty-one in Normandy. The inns edition features ten in the Loire Valley, nine in Burgundy, and ten in Normandy. *Fodor's Rivages Hotels of Character and Charm in Paris* (second edition, Fodor's Travel Publications, 1998). The French Rivages guides have been popular in Europe for years, and with Fodor's exclusive English-language translation, I think they are a welcome addition to lodgings literature here in the States. All the guides feature color photographs of the properties with one-page descriptions and good maps. Hotels in this Paris guide are presented alphabetically by arrondissement. There is a useful neighborhood index at the back of the book with hotels divided by *Rive Gauche* and *Rive Droite quartiers.* There is also a "Good Value" index and one for motels with restaurants. Some of the listings will be familiar to readers of other guidebooks, but many do not appear in any other books. Although "character and charm" is not exclusively equated with four-star luxury (there are numerous two- and three-star choices), this guide is also not for the serious budget traveler (there is only one one-star listing). Companion volumes include *Hotels and Country Inns of Character and Charm in France* and *Bed and Breakfasts of Character and Charm in France*. Both have listings for the Île-de-France and regions a bit farther out from Paris.

Youth hostels (auberges de jeunesse) are another choice for those seeking budget accommodations (and keep in mind that hostels are not just for the under-thirty crowd). I would take back in a minute my summer of vagabonding around Europe, meeting young people from all over the world, and feeling that my life was one, big endless possibility. I now prefer to share a room with my husband rather than five twenty-somethings, but hosteling remains a fun and exciting experience. Younger budget travelers need no convincing that hosteling is the way to go; however, older budget travelers should bear in mind that although some hostels offer individual rooms (mostly for couples), comparing costs reveals that they are often the same price as a room in a real (albeit inexpensive) hotel, where you can reserve a room in advance and comfortably keep your luggage (you must pack up your luggage every day when hosteling and you can't make a reservation); additionally, most hostels have an 11 P.M. curfew. Petty theft—of the T-shirts-stolen-off-the-clothesline variety—seems to be more prevalent than it once was, and it would be wise to sleep and shower with your money belt close at hand. There are about a dozen youth hostels in Paris as well as privately run hostels under the auspices of the French Youth Hostel Association and the Maison Internationale de la Jeunesse et des Étudiants. A complete listing of hostels can always be obtained from tourist offices both here and in Paris, so I am not including them here. There are no age limits or advance bookings, but many require membership in Hostelling International. The HI national headquarters are located at 733 Fifteenth Street, NW, Suite 840, Washington, D.C. 20005; 202-783-6161 / fax: 202-783-6171. Hours are 8 A.M. to 5 P.M. eastern standard time, with customer-service staff available until 7 P.M. An HI membership card is free for anyone up to his or her eighteenth birthday. Annual fees are $25 for anyone over eighteen and $15 for anyone over fifty-five. HI also publishes several guidebooks, including *Europe and the Mediterranean*. The price is either $10.95 or $13.95, depending on whether you purchase it from the main office or one of its council affiliates around the country (HI staff have addresses and phone numbers for affiliates nearest you). ~A better book to get is *Hostels France & Italy: The Only Comprehensive, Unofficial, Opinionated Guide* (Paul Karr and Martha Coombs, Globe Pequot Press, Old Saybrook, Connecticut, 1999). This is one book that lives up to its no-nonsense title. It's a funny yet practical guide. In "How to Use This Book," the authors state that "what you're holding in your hands is the first-ever attempt of its kind: a fairly complete listing and rating of all the hostels we could find in France and Italy." They invite you to take a quiz ("What is a hostel?") and they don't hesitate to tell it like it is, using such adjectives as *sedate, educational, hoppin', quiet, plain, dirty, chaotic, strict, okay, small*. There are fourteen listings for Paris. ~Note that student accommodations are also available on some college and university campuses in July and August. The organization to contact for these is CROUS, Académie de Paris, 39 avenue Georges-Bernanos, Paris 75005 (01.40.51.36.00). You don't need HI membership to take advantage of these rooms.

   Outside of Paris, other types of accommodations you'll encounter include *Gîtes de France*, a network of typically inexpensive accommodations in private homes, sort of the equivalent of bed-and-breakfasts in the States. In my experience the families or hosts have been very welcoming and the accommodations very basic. Towels provided tend to be thin and small, and sometimes there isn't any soap, so don't forget to pack your own. Breakfast is served either with the whole family gathered around a large table and café au lait presented in large bowls (which I hardly ever see in Paris nowadays) or completely separate from the household. There are fifty thousand *gîtes* accommodations throughout France and the Maison des Gîtes de France et du Tourisme vert office has over one hundred guidebooks classified by region, *département,* or theme. These books are available at the office (59 rue St.-Lazare, Paris 75439; Monday–Saturday, 10–6:30; metro: Trinite; 01.49.70.75.75 / fax: 1.42.81.28.53) or by mail. *Logis de France* is a chain of 3,706 hotels in rural areas. These modest, good-value hotels are found all over France— near villages, in the countryside, in the mountains, and on the coast—and each hotel has an average of eighteen rooms. The hotels also have a restaurant offering local cuisine. Each year, a guide is published (in five languages) describing all the *logis,* and it comes with a fold-out map indicating precisely where each hotel is. The guide costs approximately $15, but I've noticed that every January the French tourist offices here in the States will offer the previous year's guide free—assuming there are copies left over—and I don't find it at all limiting to peruse an older guide. Reservations can be made by calling a hotel directly or by calling the Logis de France central reservations service (011.33.1.45.84.83.84). The Fédération nationale des Logis de France offices are at 83 avenue d'Italie (13th); 1.45.84.70.00 / fax: 1.45.83.59.66; www.logis.de.france.fr.

Staying in a château is also an option. Both privately owned *chateaux* and *chateaux-hotels* accept guests in France. Readers might be surprised to learn that some of the most famous *chateaux* in France are privately owned (Amboise and Chenonceaux among them), and the Loire Valley holds the largest number of private *chateaux.* At private *chateaux* you are guests in someone's home, and the experience is more akin to a bed-and-breakfast establishment. Staying at *chateaux-hotels* is more like staying at a regular hotel (but in far more grand surroundings!), usually with maid service and reception desk and sometimes a swimming pool or tennis court. Some privately owned *chateaux* don't always welcome overnight guests but do offer private tours. Some sources of information include *Bienvenue au Château: French Bed & Breakfasts in Châteaux and Private Homes* (a guide to 124 châteaus, manors, and country houses in Brittany, the Loire Valley, Normandy, Poitou-Charentes, and the western Loire; phone the France on Call Hotline at 410.286.8310 for a copy); *Vacances en Campagne* (over one hundred personally selected villas, farmhouses, and châteaux in rural France; 22 Railroad Street, Great Barrington, Massachusetts 01230; 413-528-6610 / fax: 413-528-6222); *Châteaux et Hôtels de France* (Michelin-starred chef Alain Ducasse now owns the organization that publishes this annual listing of 480+ châteaux, chateaux-hotels, and restaurants in France; copies are available at the three French Government Tourist Offices in the U.S., and reservations can be made through DMI Tours—800-553-5090; directly with the châteaux; or on-line: www.chateauxethotels.com). Relais & Chateaux (U.S. reservations number: 800-735-2478; www.relaischateaux.fr; this prestigious organization represents many properties that are chateaux). See also the fall 1999 issue of *France Insider's News* for the article, "Spend the Night in a Chateau-Hotel."

~Note: Breakfast is rarely a good value taken at a hotel and is not usually a Parisian experience. Save some money—and get the same thing, often better—and join the locals at the corner café. ~When you first arrive at your hotel, ask to see your room first. This is a common practice in Europe, and it is understood that if a room is not to your liking, you may request a different one. This is also your opportunity to ask for a room upgrade; if the hotel is not fully booked (and it rarely will be during low season), you may end up with a significantly nicer room at the same rate. It never hurts to ask. ~Speaking of fully booked: If you've been told that you can't get a room, call again between 4 and 6 P.M. and double-check. This is the time of day when many establishments cancel the reservations of guests who haven't shown up. ~If a hotel you choose also has a reservations office in the U.S., call both numbers. It is entirely possible that you will be quoted different rates. Also, some of the more expensive hotels offer a rate that must be prepaid in full, in advance of your trip, in U.S. dollars, but which is lower than the local rack rate. ~Useful vocabulary: *oreiller* (pillow); *clef* (key); *draps* (sheets); *couverture* (blanket); *serviette de toilette* (hand or face towel); *serviette de bain* (bath towel); *l'eau chaud* (hot water); *compris* (included, as in: Is breakfast included in the price?).

African-Americans in Paris

Especially in the 1950s and sixties, but also for many years before that, there was an important community of African-American artists and writers in Paris. Richard Wright, James Baldwin, Chester Himes, Barbara Chase-Riboud, Henry Tanner, Langston Hughes, to name just a few, were all in Paris, a city where, as Richard Wright has written, "your color is the least important thing about you." One of the more memorable art exhibits I've seen was "Explorations in the City of Light: African-American Artists in Paris, 1945–1965" at the Studio Museum in Harlem in 1996. The artists featured were Lois Mailou Jones, Herbert Gentry, Harold Cousins, Ed Clark, Beauford Delaney, Larry Potter, and Barbara Chase-Riboud. The accompanying catalog is great, and includes essays and excerpts about the Paris art world in the twenties and thirties. It's published by the Studio Museum and is available in the museum's gift store at 144 West 125th Street, New York, New York 10027; 212-864-4500. A related work is *From Harlem to Paris: Black American Writers in France, 1840–1980* (Michel Fabre, University of Illinois Press, 1991), and a wonderful article to read, which I was unable to include here, is "Chez

Tournon: A Homage" (Paule Marshall, *The Sophisticated Traveler* edition of *The New York Times Magazine*, 18 October, 1982).

Airfares and Airlines

We all know that not everyone pays the same price for seats on an airplane. One reason is that seats do not hold the same value at all times of the year, month, or even days of the week. Recently, I was researching some fares to Paris for a long weekend. One of my calls produced a particularly helpful representative who detailed all available fares for the entire month of September. There were approximately fifteen different prices—based on a seemingly endless number of variables—within that month alone. The best way, therefore, to get the best deal for your needs is to check a variety of sources. If you think all the best deals are to be found on the Web, you're mistaken: airlines and consolidators offer plenty of good fares over the telephone and through advertisements. To know with certainty that you've got a good deal, you need to have fares to compare, which requires checking more than one source. I like flying a country's own airline—Air France, for example—and even though Air France fares are usually among the highest available, its off-season fares are among the lowest. Following are some sources I typically consult before I purchase anything (note that some of these have corresponding Web sites mentioned below, but I prefer calling): 800-AIRFARE (800-247-3273); Cheap Tickets Inc., 800-377-1000; Lowestfare.com, 888-777-2222; 800-FLY4-LESS; Air Europa (New York is the only American city this airline serves), 888-238-7672; New Frontiers, 212-779-0600; and The French Experience, 212-986-1115.

Booking travel on the Web works best for people with simple requirements and lots of flexibility. If you have a lot of questions (as I always do), you can't get them answered and are setting yourself up for potential headaches. In my experience with sky auctions, I never seem to be able to find a flight scenario that accommodates my schedule, and I don't like that I can't narrow the criteria or place another bid if my initial one isn't accepted. But if you have no parameters to work around and are just looking for a good fare, here are some Web sites to check for domestic and/or overseas tickets: www.skyauction.com; www.previewtravel.com; www.cheaptickets. com; www.priceline.com; www.expedia.msn.com; www.travelocity.com; www. economytravel.com; www.lowestfare.com; www.TRIP.com; www.travelscape.com; www.airfare.com; www.thefarebusters.com and www.itn.com.

If you're in Paris and you want to fly somewhere else within Europe, the French discount operator Nouvelles Frontières (New Frontiers) conducts on-line auctions to sell unsold tickets. The Web site is www.nouvelles.frontieres.fr. Once in, click on the word *enchères*. Also, Europe by Air (888-387-2479; www.europebyair.com) offers flights within France and Europe.

~Don't be afraid of reputable consolidators, but recognize that their lower fares come with more restrictions. If there are flight cancellations or delays, you have no recourse with the airline since it didn't sell you the ticket directly. If you want to make any changes, you have to pay a penalty. ~Reputable charter flights, too, should not be feared. I've had three good experiences on charter flights and encourage you to investigate them. The limitations are that most charters offer only coach class and tend to be completely full—in fact, a charter operator is legally allowed to cancel a flight up to ten days before departure if it doesn't fill enough seats. Although I did not experience any problems on my charter flights, I understand that delays are common, and—as with consolidators—passengers don't have any recourse. However, operators who organize charter flights are required to place passengers' payments for the flight in an escrow account, so if the flight is canceled or if the operator doesn't abide by its agreement, you receive a refund.

~Flying as a courier may be the best deal of all, if you're a light packer (luggage is usually limited to one carry-on bag). Couriers also can't usually reserve a seat for more than one person, although your traveling companion could purchase a ticket on the same flight. Air couriers are cogs in international commerce; they are completely legitimate and demand for them exceeds the supply. They are a necessity simply because companies doing international business send a large number of documents overseas, and those documents can get held up in customs unless accompanied by a person. Couriers are responsible for chaperoning documents through customs and then hand-delivering them to a person waiting outside the customs area. Several companies arrange courier flights in the U.S., but the one I'm most familiar with is Now Voyager (74 Varick Street, New York, New York 10013; 212-431-1616). To review more options, consider joining the International Association of Air Travel Couriers (P.O. Box 1349, Lake Worth, Florida 33460; 561-582-8320). Members receive a regular bulletin with a variety of international routes being offered by air courier companies departing from several U.S. cities. Reservation phone numbers are included so you can make inquiries and schedule your trip yourself. I have seen some *incredible* bargains ($150 round-trip to Paris, for example), and some fares were valid for several months.

~Note that airlines are not required to offer much to passengers due to flight delays or cancellations. If you have visions of free meals, hotel rooms, and flights, you may be in for a disappointment. Each airline has its own "conditions of carriage," which you can request from an airline's ticket offices or public relations department, but the legalese is not identical from airline to airline. From what I can tell, the employees who stand at the gates have the authority to grant passengers amenities, so if you *don't* ask them for something (a seat on the next flight, a long-distance phone call, a meal, whatever) you *definitely* won't get it.

~Technically, airlines no longer allow passengers to fly standby at a discount; but I've been told that seats are occasionally sold at reduced prices for flights that aren't full. I've also been told that one of the best days of the year to show up at the airport without a ticket is Christmas Day. I can't personally confirm this, and it's doubtful an airline employee can, either. Perhaps this is either a well-kept secret or a myth, but if you're able to be that flexible, it would be worth trying.

Airports

Paris is served by two airports: Charles de Gaulle (northeast of the city) and Orly (just south of the city and a little closer). The most economical way to get to or from the airports and the city is the suburban RER line, but if you have more than a carry-on bag, this might not be the best choice as you do have to carry luggage quite a distance just to reach the RER tracks. The Air France bus also makes the trip to and from each airport every twelve minutes, with stops at Montparnasse, Arc de Triomphe, Porte Maillot, and Les Invalides. I consider it an easier option than the RER, but I have still found myself carrying my bags a bit farther than I would prefer. A relative newcomer—and easier still—is Airport Shuttle, a door-to-door van service. You need to make a reservation if you're going *to* the airport, but if you're headed into the city, you only need to call before claiming any baggage. However, it's best to make a reservation at both ends, I've found, otherwise you may have to wait twenty minutes or longer. The price is about $18 per person, for two or more people in the van. From either airport, call 0-800-505-610; to reserve in advance from the U.S.: 011.33.1.45.26.27.05 / fax: 011.33.1.43.21.35.67; E-mail: ashuttle@club-internet.fr; www.airportshuttle.fr. Another door-to-door shuttle is PariShuttle, which seems to be better known among Parisians than visitors. To reserve: 01.43.90.91.91 / fax: 01.43.90.91.10

Alliance Française

With 1,085 affiliates in 138 nations worldwide (including 142 chapters in 45 states), the aim of Alliance Française—the official cultural arm of France—is to promote awareness, understanding, and appreciation of the French language and culture. French grammar and conversation classes are offered at all levels, and class size is typically small. Plus, members have access to a library of books, videos, compact discs, periodicals, and special events. I enjoyed my experiences with Alliance very much, and if there is a chapter near you, I encourage you to enroll in a language class before you go—and when you return! Or, consider enrolling at the Alliance Française de Paris, which offers classes monthly. To locate U.S. chapters or to enroll in classes here or in Paris, contact the Alliance Française at Délégation Générale de l'Alliance Française, 2819 Ordway Street, NW, Washington, D.C. 20008; 202-966-9740 or 888-9-FRENCH / fax: 202-362-1587; www.afusa.org. The Web site features a list of frequently asked questions, and accommodations in Paris and the costs for classes are addressed. Alliance Française schools are also located in other cities in France: Bordeaux, Dijon, Montpellier, Nice, Rouen, Lyon,

Toulouse, and Marseille. ~Note: see "Studying in France" for other French-language courses.

B

Biking

Paris has approximately eighty-five miles of biking paths, including a stretch along the Canal de l'Ourcq in the 19th. Many main streets and boulevards have bike lanes, and it's possible to see much of Paris *à bicyclette* without having to dodge too many motorists. Bicycles can be rented from almost any SNCF station in Paris, and it is possible to rent from one station and return the bike to another (inquire at the tourist office for station specifics). Some other places that rent bikes include Paris a Vélo, C'est Sympa! (37 boulevard Bourdon, 4th; 01.48.87.60.01 / fax: 01.48.87.61.01; also offers guided tours in English in Paris and outskirts); La Maison du Vélo (8 rue de Belzunce, 10th; 01.42.81.24.72); and Paris-Vélo (2 rue du Fer-a-Moulin, 5th, 01.43.37.59.22 / fax: 01.47.07.67.45). There is an IGN (Institut Géographique Nationale) biking map available at a scale of 1:100,000 (see "Hiking" for IGN address). For biking farther afield, two good books to consult are *Cycling in France* (Carole Saint-Laurent, Ulysses Green Escapes, Ulysses Travel Publications), which details routes in Alsace, Brittany, Burgundy, Franche-Comté, Loire Valley, Périgord, Provence, and Quercy. This is a small, spiral-bound guide with biking tips, glossary of bicycle terminology, and maps (prepared by the IGN), and each route is outlined on black-and-white diagrams showing only the roads you'll be using; and *France by Bike: 14 Tours Geared for Discovery* (Karen and Terry Whitehill, The Mountaineers, Seattle, Washington, 1993). And for guided biking tours, a few organizations to contact are Discover France Biking (self-guided and guided trips from value accommodations to luxury; Loire Valley, Burgundy, and more; 40 West Baseline Road, #115, Tempe, Arizona 85283; 800-960-2221; E-mail: loren@discoverfrance.com); and Euro-Bike & Walking Tours (its Normandy, Brittany, and Loire Valley trip is also an epicurean's delight; P.O. Box 990, DeKalb, Illinois 60115; E-mail: info@eurobike.com; www.eurobike.com). ~Note that a *vélo tout terrain* (VTT) is an all-terrain bike.

Boat and Barge Cruises

The waterways of Burgundy and the Loire Valley offer opportunities to meander through the regions at a wonderfully relaxed pace. The experience is not cheap, but is unforgettable. Here are some companies to contact: Abercrombie & Kent (1520 Kensington Road, Suite 212, Oak Brook, Illinois 60523; 800-323-7308 / fax: 630-954-3324; www.abercrombiekent.com); Etoile de Champagne (88 Broad Street, Boston, Massachusetts 02110; 800-280-1492 / fax: 617-426-4689; www.etoiledechampagne.com); European Waterways (140 East Fifty-sixth Street, Suite 4C, New York,

New York 10022; 800-217-4447 / fax: 212-688-3778; www.europeanwaterways.com); French Country Waterways (P.O. Box 2195, Duxbury, Massachusetts 02331; 781-934-2454 or 800-222-1236 / fax: 781-934-9048); Le Boat (10 South Franklin Turnpike, Ramsey, New Jersey 07446; 800-992-0291 / fax: 201-236-1214); Continental Waterways (800-323-7308); American Media Tours (16 West Thirty-second Street, New York, New York 10001; 800-969-6344 / fax: 212-465-1636); and Holidays on a Pénichette (U.S. agent: 800-992-0291; Locaboat Plaisance address: BP 150, 89303 Joigny, France; www.locaboat.com).

Bookstores

Like the French (and most Europeans in general), I prefer to buy whatever goods and services I need from specialists. "One-stop shopping" is a nice idea in theory but has not been very appealing to me, as convenience seems to be its only virtue. Therefore, I buy fish from a fishmonger, flowers from a florist, cheese from a real cheese shop, etc. And when I'm looking for travel books, I shop at travel bookstores or independent bookstores with strong travel sections. The staff in these stores are nearly always well-traveled, well-read, very helpful, and knowledgeable. A big quibble I have with chain stores is that travel guides tend to be shelved separately from travel writing and related history books, implying that guidebooks are all a traveler needs or wants. Stores specializing in travel take a wider view, understanding that travel incorporates many different dimensions. Following is a list of stores nationwide that offer exceptional travel-book departments. (I've also included a few stores specializing in art books and cookbooks, as some of these titles are mentioned throughout the book). Note that all of them accept mail orders, and some publish catalogs and/or newsletters.

~Additionally, I must mention my favorite mail-order book catalog: *A Common Reader,* which is issued monthly and offers an excellent selection of books for adults and children. James Mustich Jr. is the man behind the venture, and his reviews wander here and there and make you want to read every single book in the catalog (his writing was an inspiration to me for the annotated bibliographies in The Collected Traveler, although my reviews are not quite as eloquent as his). Not content to simply offer new books, Mustich even arranges to bring out-of-print books back into print by publishing them under his own Common Reader Editions imprint. A wide variety of travel, history, art, and cooking titles are regularly featured in the catalog (141 Tompkins Avenue, Pleasantville, New York 10570; 800-832-7323 / fax: 914-747-0778; www.commonreader.com).

~If your favorite bookseller can't find an out-of-print title you're looking for, try one of the following Web sites: www.abebooks.com (American Book Exchange, which I like, because you buy books direct from independent booksellers) or www.alibris.com (whose motto is "The Ultimate Source for Used, Rare, and Hard-to-Find Books."

CALIFORNIA

Black Oak Books
1491 Shattuck Avenue, Berkeley
510-486-0698

Bon Voyage Travel Books & Maps
2069 W. Bullard, Fresno
800-995-9716
www.bon-voyage-travel.com

Book Passage
51 Tamal Vista Boulevard,
Corte Madera
800-999-7909 or 415-927-0960 locally
www.bookpassage.com

The Cook's Library
8373 W. Third Street,
Los Angeles
323-655-3141

Distant Lands
56 South Raymond Avenue, Pasadena
626-449-3220 / 800-310-3220—
California only
www.distantlands.com

Pacific Travellers Supply
12 West Anapamu Street,
Santa Barbara
888-PAC-TRAV
E-mail: pts@maplink.com

Phileas Fogg's Books, Maps & More
87 Stanford Shopping Center,
Palo Alto
800-533-3644
www.foggs.com

Rizzoli—five locations:
Two Rodeo Drive,
Beverly Hills
310-278-2247

South Coast Plaza, Costa Mesa
714-957-3331

One Colorado Boulevard, Pasadena
626-564-1300

332 Santa Monica Boulevard,
Santa Monica
310-393-0101

117 Post Street, San Francisco
415-984-0225
Catalog orders: 800-52-BOOKS

The Travellers Bookcase
8375 West Third Street,
Los Angeles
323-655-0575
www.travelbooks.com

COLORADO

Tattered Cover
2955 East First Avenue, Denver
303-322-7727

WASHINGTON, D.C.

AIA/Rizzoli
1735 New York Avenue, NW
202-626-7541
Catalog orders: 800-52-BOOKS

Travel Books & Language Center
4437 Wisconsin Avenue, NW
202-237-1322 / fax: 237-6022
800-220-2665 (mail orders)
E-mail: travelbks@aol.com

ILLINOIS

Rizzoli
Water Tower Place, Chicago
312-642-3500
Catalog orders: 800-52-BOOKS

The Savvy Traveller
310 Michigan Avenue, Chicago
888-666-6200
www.thesavvytraveller.com

MASSACHUSETTS

Brattle Book Shop
9 West Street, Boston
617-542-0210 / fax: 338-1467
800-447-9595 (mail orders)
*Brattle's specialty is art books, but it
also stocks over 250,000 used, rare,
and out-of-print books.

Globe Corner Bookstore
500 Boylston Street, Boston
800-358-6013 / 617-859-8008

Rizzoli
Copley Place, Boston
617-437-0700

MINNESOTA

Books for Travel, Etc.
857 Grand Avenue, St. Paul
888-668-8006

NEW YORK

*Archivia: The Decorative Arts
Book Shop*
944 Madison Avenue, New York
212-439-9194
*Beautiful store with a beautiful
selection of decorating, garden, style,
and art titles, some in French.

The Complete Traveller
199 Madison Avenue (Thirty-fifth
Street), New York
212-685-9007
*In addition to a great selection of
current books, a separate room is
reserved for rare and out-of-print
travel books. Owners Harriet and
Arnold Greenberg and their superb
staff will do their very best to track
down your most obscure request.

Hacker Art Books
45 West Fifty-seventh Street,
New York
212-688-7600 / fax: 754-2554
E-mail: hackerartbooks@infohouse
.com / www.hackerartbooks.com
*John Russell, former art critic of the
New York Times, wrote of Hacker
that "for an all-round art bookstore,
this one is something near to ideal."

Kitchen Arts & Letters
1435 Lexington Avenue (between
Ninety-third and Ninety-fourth),
New York
212-876-5550 / fax: 876-3584

Rizzoli—five locations:
Manhattan:
31 W. Fifth-seventh Street
212-759-2424

3 World Financial Center
212-385-1400
454 West Broadway
212-674-1616

1334 York Avenue
212-606-7434

Manhasset:
The Americana
516-365-9393
Catalog orders for all: 800-52-BOOKS

Strand Book Annex
95 Fulton Street, New York
212-732-6070 / fax: 406-1654

Strand Book Store
828 Broadway (at Twelfth Street),
New York
212-473-1452 / fax: 473-2591
800-366-3664 (mail orders)
E-mail: strand@strandbooks.com

NORTH CAROLINA

Omni Resources
10004 South Mebane Street,
Burlington
800-742-2677
www.omnimap.com

OKLAHOMA

Traveler's Pack LTD
9427 North May Avenue,
Oklahoma City
405-755-2924
www.travelerspack.com

OREGON

Powell's City of Books
1005 West Burnside, Portland
800-878-7323 / 503-228-4651 locally
www.powells.portland.or.us

Powell's Travel Store
701 SW Sixth Avenue, Portland
800-546-5025
www.powells.com

PENNSYLVANIA

Franklin Maps
333 S. Henderson Road,
King of Prussia
610-265-6277 / fax: 337-1575
*Extraordinary selection of foreign
and domestic maps as well as books—
one journalist wrote, "What travelers
will find at the 15,000-square-feet
Franklin Map store are maps, charts,
and books covering almost every
square inch of earth and universe."

VERMONT

Adventurous Traveler Bookstore
P.O. Box 64769 (for mail orders)
245 South Champlain Street (for
visiting), Burlington
800-282-3963 or 802-860-6776 locally
www.adventuroustraveler.com

VIRGINIA

Rizzoli
Merchants Square, Williamsburg
757-229-9821

WASHINGTON

Wide World Books & Maps
4411A Wallingford Avenue, North,
Seattle
206-634-3453
www.travelbooksandmaps.com

And, because some books I recommend are British publications, I include two stores in London: The Travel Bookshop, 13–15 Blenheim Crescent, W11 2EE, 171.229.5260 / fax: 243. 1552, and Books for Cooks (a few doors down at 4 Blenheim Crescent, 171.221.1992 / fax: 221.1517).

ENGLISH-LANGUAGE BOOKSTORES IN PARIS

The Abbey Bookshop, 29 rue de la Parcheminerie, 5th, 01.46.33.16.24

Brentanos, 37 avenue de l'Opéra, 2nd; 01.42.61.52.50

Galignani, 224 rue de Rivoli, 1st; 01.42.60.76.07

Shakespeare & Co., 37 rue de la Bûcherie, 5th; 01.43.26.96.50

Tea & Tattered Pages, 24 rue Mayet, 6th; 01.40.65.94.35

The Village Voice, 6 rue Princesse, 6th; 01.46.33.36.47

W. H. Smith, 248 rue de Rivoli, 1st; 01.44.77.88.99

SPECIALTY FRENCH BOOKSTORES IN PARIS

Au Fil du Temps, 8 rue Saint-Martin, 4th; 01.42.71.93.48 (specializes in movies old and new)

FNAC—five locations throughout the city in the 1st, 6th, 8th, 9th, and 17th arrondissements

La Librairie Gourmande, 4 rue Dante, 5th; 01.43.54.37.27

Librairie Des Gourmets, 98 rue Monge, 5th; 01.43.31.16.42

Librairie Gallimard, 15 boulevard Raspail, 7th; 01.45.48.24.84

Buses

I have never found the Paris bus system as easy as the metro, but it really isn't difficult to follow and the *noctambus* (after-hours bus service) has really been a godsend on those nights when I stayed out late and missed the last metro. If you purchase a *carte orange, carnet, Paris Visite,* or *Mobilis* pass (see "Le Metro"), you don't need to buy anything additional as these cover both metro and bus travel. ~Check with the tourist office about bus #29: when I took it a few years ago, passengers could ride in the back in an open-air section, making the route from Gare St.-Lazare to the Louvre—passing by a number of monuments and through a variety of neighborhoods—especially memorable.

C

Car Rental

My favorite feature of travel publications is the section featuring readers' letters. I have probably learned more from these letters than any other source, and the largest number of complaints seem to be about renting a car. No matter what you read, hear, or assume, the only word that counts is the one from your policy administrator, be it a credit-card or insurance company. If you have any questions about renting a car overseas and what is and isn't covered on your existing policy (including collision-damage waiver), contact your provider in advance. Request documentation in writing, if necessary. It is your responsibility to learn about your coverage *before* you rent a car. I have never encountered any rental-car problems, but then again I make it a habit to state to the company representative, "When I return the car to you, I will not pay anything more than this amount" while pointing to the total on my receipt.

~Hertz offers a competitive rate with its prepaid car-rental voucher. The conditions are that you pay in U.S. dollars in advance of your trip, and vouchers are typically faxed to a U.S. fax number or mailed to a U.S. address. The prepaid rate does not include such things as drop charges, car seats, collision-damage waiver, or gas, and these must be paid for in local currency at the time you pick up the car. ~You don't need an international driver's license in France. Save the $10 fee for driving in less developed countries, where the absence of the license could open the door for bribery to cross a border, etc. ~For information on leasing a car (as well as rentals), contact Europe by Car (1 Rockefeller Plaza, New York, New York 10020; 800-223-1516 / in New York: 212-581-3040; 9000 Sunset Boulevard, Los Angeles, California 90069; 800-252-9401 / in California: 323-272-0424; www.europebycar.com). Factory-direct new cars from Peugeot, Citroën, and Renault are available for low daily rates with special rates for faculty members and students.

~*Kilometers:* If you'll be making excursions from Paris, it's helpful to begin thinking in kilometers instead of miles. I jot down sample distances to use as a ready reference as I'm motoring along the *routes nationales* or speeding along the *autoroutes:* 1 mile = 1.6 kilometers, so 12 km = 7½ miles; 16 km = 10 miles; 40 km = 25 miles; 80 km = 50 miles; 160 km = 100 miles; 320 km = 200 miles, etc. ~Driving in the fast lane on European roads can be a bit disconcerting as any car suddenly looming up behind you is closing in at a *much* faster speed than we're accustomed to in the U.S. These drivers usually have no patience for your slowness and will tailgate you and flash their lights until you get out of the way. So if you're going to pass, step on the gas and go and return quickly to the right lane. ~I've read conflicting advice on parking tickets, so I would not recommend taking a chance if you're in doubt. Rental agencies do have your credit-card number, and it seems to me they can eventually bill you for any tickets you've received and add a service charge if they're so inclined.

~Useful vocabulary: *essence* (gas); *sans plomb* (unleaded gas); *vous n'avez pas la priorité* (you don't have the right of way—seen mostly at traffic circles, where you give way to traffic already in the circle coming from your left); *passage protégé* (yellow diamond road signs indicating that you have priority over traffic on minor side roads); *déviation* (diversion); *rappel* (reminder of the speed limit); *cedez le passage* (give way to traffic); *tout droit* (straight ahead), not to be confused with *à droit* (to the right; *à gauche,* by the way, is "to the left"); *défense de stationner* (no parking); *location de voitures* (rental-car agency).

Chauffeur-Driven Cars

If you prefer that someone else do the driving, especially for excursions outside Paris, The French Experience offers private car service with English-speaking guides. Rates are good and include unlimited mileage, gas, service, insurance for the passengers, and tax (not included are tolls and admission fees to sites visited). Sample fares for a five-hour city tour are: $180 for one or two people; $270 for three to six people; and $340 for seven or eight passengers. Full- and half-day trips are also available to Versailles, Giverny, Fontainebleau, Chartres, and Mont-Saint-Michel, as well as airport transfers. Contact The French Experience at 212-986-1115 or www.frenchexperience.com.

Children

Although I have been unable to find a book devoted exclusively to traveling with children in Paris, some guidebooks—including many of those mentioned under "Guidebooks"—offer excellent suggestions for things to see and do with kids. Parents should note that some kid-friendly restaurants in Paris include Altitude 95 (on the first level of the Eiffel Tower; 1.45.55.20.04); Stade Jean Bouin (a real sports club with a restaurant; 26 avenue du General Sarrail, 16th; 1.40.71.61.00); Pavillon Montsouris (an extremely popular place with local families, plus there are playgrounds nearby; 20 rue Gazan, 14th; 1.45.88.38.52); and Justine (in the Hotel Meridien-Montparnasse, 19 rue du Commandant Mouchotte, 14th; 1.44.36.44.00). It is essential, however, to make a reservation, and remember that kids' menus are not offered every day of the week. There is not an abundance of books available on traveling with children in general (the most I've ever seen in one store is three), but even if there were a lot more, I still think the best one would be *Have Kid, Will Travel: 101 Survival Strategies for Vacationing with Babies and Young Children* (Claire Tristram with Lucille Tristram, Andrews McMeel Publishing, Kansas City, Missouri, 1997). It's loaded with good, concrete suggestions and tips, and I wish I'd discovered it before we took our ten-month-old on her first plane flight, from New York to Seattle. Claire Tristram has visited all fifty states and thirty countries, and Lucille, her daughter, has been named "the best baby in the world" by several strangers sitting next to her on long-distance flights (a great recommendation for reading this book!). Among the best words of advice: "Above all, don't let a bad moment become a bad day, and don't let a bad day become a bad week."

A few good books to read with young children before a trip to Paris are *The Giraffe That Walked to Paris* (Nancy Milton, illustrated by Roger Roth, Crown, 1992), *Bonjour, Mr. Satie* (Tomie de Paola, Putnam, 1991), and, of course, *Eloise in Paris* (Kay Thompson, drawings by Hilary Knight, Simon & Schuster, 1957). Also, if you *really* want to immerse a child, the first edition of *Eloise* is published in French by *Editions Gallimard* (1982). A wonderful book to share with high school students lucky enough to study abroad is *Postcards from France* (Megan McNeill Libby, HarperCollins, 1997). Libby wrote a monthly letter to her local New England newspaper while she spent her junior year of high school in Valence, in the south of France. A selection of those letters make up this collection, and come to think of it, the book would be great for college-age students as well.

Clothing

The way I see it, you can hardly talk about clothing without talking about packing, but there is a separate "Packing" entry under *P*. I pack light, and unless I have plans to be at fancy places, I pack double-duty items (stuff that can go from daytime to evening) in low-key colors that also mix and match so I can wear garments more than once. Remember that the French tend to dress up a bit more than Americans, so reserve your jeans for casual daytime wear and leave the color-coordinated jogging suits at home. Suits and ties are only necessary at the finest restaurants, and polo shirts and khakis will always serve men well. Although comfortable shoes are of the utmost importance, I never, ever bring sneakers—my husband is positively forbidden to bring them—and you might not either once you realize that they scream "American." I prefer Arche, a line of French walking shoes and sandals for men and women, but several other lines are available that are also stylish *and* comfortable. The following mail-order catalogs offer some practical clothes and gadgets for travelers: L.L. Bean Traveler (800-221-4221 / www.llbean .com); Magellan's (800-962-4943 / www.magellans.com); and TravelSmith (800-950-1600 / www.travelsmith.com).

Club France

Whether you're a frequent or occasional traveler to France, you may want to consider becoming a member of this club of Francophiles, sponsored by the French Government Tourist Office. *A lot* of benefits and privileges—too numerous to list here—come with membership, including VIP treatment, discounts, free passes, room upgrades at hotels, inns, and châteaux, priority reservations at restaurants, subscriptions to publications, cultural events in the U.S., etc. This is one club that offers good value! The annual membership fee is $65, and $15 of it goes to help support the American Center in Paris. Inquire at one of the three tourist offices nearest you (see "Tourist Office" for addresses).

Coins

If you have leftover francs in the form of coins, you can always save them for a future trip; but perhaps a better idea is to give them to a great cause: UNICEF's Change for Good program. A number of airlines pass out envelopes to passengers on flights back to the U.S., but if you've never received one and want to learn more, contact the U.S. Committee for UNICEF (333 East 38th Street, 6th floor, New York, New York 10016; 212-824-6972 / fax: 824-6969).

Cooking Schools

The best single source for cooking schools in Paris—and the entire world—is the *Shaw Guide to Cooking Schools: Cooking Schools, Courses, Vacations, Apprenticeships, and Wine Instruction Throughout the World* (ShawGuides, Inc., New York). All the familiar Paris schools are listed—including La Varenne and Le Cordon Bleu—as well as more intimate classes, and interested food lovers can also view updates to the guide at its Web site: www.shawguides.com. One of the newest and most interesting courses is *L'École des Chefs*. Annie Jacquet-Bentley, a Parisian who now lives in the U.S. and works as a restaurant consultant, created the program after she spent time studying with some French chefs and wanted to make the experience available to others. Classes are in two- and three-star Michelin restaurants, and although they're for nonprofessionals, applications receive a thorough review. A standard internship lasts five to six days (French restaurants are traditionally closed one or two days a week), and some of the participating chefs include Alain Senderens, Michel Rostang, Georges Blanc, Guy Savoy, Marc Veyrat, and Michel Troisgros. In the U.S., contact *L'École* at P.O. Box 183, Birchrunville, Pennsylvania, 19421; 610-469-2500 / fax: 610-469-0272; www.leschefs.com; and to read about *L'École* see "Gourmet Adventurism" (*Paris Notes*, March 1999) and "How Great Paris Restaurants Do It" (*Saveur* No. 35, 1999). A course I didn't see listed but which I've heard a good word about is *Cours de Cuisine*, taught by Françoise Meunier (7 rue Paul-Lelong, Paris 75002; 01.40.26.14.00 / fax: 01.40.26. 14.08; www.intiweb.com/fmeunier). Of related interest, see "The Making of French Chefs" (Catharine Reynolds, *Gourmet*, March 1999), which provides an in-depth look at the rigorous training for chefs in France and also reveals the addresses of three *restaurants d'applications* (training restaurants for chefs and waiters still in school). Reynolds notes that a meal at one of these restaurants is a good value, making it a bit more difficult than you might think to secure a reservation.

Customs

There seems to be a lot of confusion over what items can and positively cannot be brought into the U.S.—and not only on the part of travelers, but customs agents, too. The rules, apparently, are not as confusing as they might seem, but sometimes neither customs staff nor travelers are up-to-date on what they are. Some examples of what's legal and what's not include olive oil, yes, but olives, no (unless they're vacuum-packed); fruit jams and preserves, yes, but fresh fruit, no; hard cheeses, yes, but soft, runny cheeses, no; commercially canned meat, yes (if the inspector can determine that the meat was cooked in the can after it was sealed), but fresh and dried meats and meat products, no; nuts, yes, but chestnuts and acorns, no; coffee, yes, but roasted beans only; dried spices, yes, but not curry leaves; fresh and dried flowers, yes, but not eucalyptus or any variety with roots. If you think all this is unnecessary bother, remember that it was quite likely a tourist who carried in the wormy fruit that brought the Mediterranean fruit fly to California in 1979. Fighting this pest cost more than $100 million. For more details, call the U.S. Department of Agriculture's Animal and Plant Health Inspection Service at 301-734-8645 or view its Web site: www.aphis.usda.gov (click on "Travelers' Tips").

E

Eating Out and Taking Away

In October 1998, *Wine Spectator* devoted one entire issue to Paris. This edition included what I believe to be a good summation and some of the best advice for Americans dining in France today. Americans *are* welcome at the great restaurants of France—as long as they are small in number. The writer stated, "The maître d' at one three-star restaurant told me, 'When an American calls, I put him on the waiting list until I see how the reservations are balanced. The French don't like to eat in a dining room full of Americans, and neither do the Americans.'" The writer went on to say that Americans are often seated at the worst tables, and as many of us are unlikely to return to a particular gastronomic temple, and it's presumed we don't know much about food, we remain low on every restaurant's priority list. It helps to know all this, but as the writer points out, "Don't be intimidated; remember who's paying the bill."

To my mind, *haute cuisine* is not simply a dining experience: it's nothing less than an elaborate stage production of the highest caliber. True, it's very expensive, but properly executed, the experience is sublime and unforgettable, and worth every franc. Ruth Reichl, former restaurant critic for *The New York Times*, frequently reminded readers during her tenure to keep several points in mind when considering the price of fine dining in France: *haute cuisine* is extremely labor-intensive and requires enormously expensive ingredients; you never have to wait for a table in France because you effectively "buy" that table for the afternoon or evening. Economically speaking, French restaurants are completely different from American restaurants, which concentrate on turning as many tables as possible during mealtimes; and prices on French menus include tax and tip, both of which add up to a hefty sum.

~Useful vocabulary: *sur place* is how you say you're going to eat in, and *à emporter* means you'll be taking food away. Note that for eating in, the price for food and drink is different depending on where you sit. If you stand at the bar (*comptoir* or *zinc*) and order a beer (usually available as a *demi,* which is about a third of a liter, or *une pression,* a draft), the price is cheaper than if you sit in the *salle* (dining room) or *à la terrasse* (the prime people-watching spot, usually outside on the sidewalk).

Elderly Travel

The two best-known organizations for elderly travelers are Elderhostel (75 Federal Street, Third Floor, Boston, Massachusetts 02110; 877-426-8056 / fax: 877-426-2166) and Interhostel (University of New Hampshire, 6 Garrison Avenue, Durham, New Hampshire 03824; 800-733-9753 / fax: 603-862-1113; www.learn.unh.edu). I've listed them here instead of under tour operators because I wanted them to stand apart from the more general travel companies. For some good articles about these two educational companies and others, see "Senior Classes" and "Catering to Older Travelers," both of which appeared in *The New York Times* travel section, August 25, 1991.

The Euro

The euro is significant not only economically but symbolically: a single currency is believed to prevent the EU member countries from finding reasons to go to war. The eleven nations to adopt the euro equal the world's second-largest trading region with a single currency, after the United States. You still have nearly two years in which to spend your francs (the euro doesn't go into circulation until 2002), but you'll notice that prices are often posted in both francs and euros. The biggest benefits to travelers will be that you won't have to exchange currency when crossing borders, and with a single currency it will be easier to compare prices. By far the best article I've read about the euro is "Europe's Uncommon Currency" (Reginald Dale, *FRANCE Magazine,* Spring 1999), which details its impact on business, financial markets, stock exchanges, prices, corporate governance, financial services, jobs and wages, e-commerce, taxes, and currency reserves and trade.

F

Film

I'm aware that the FAA maintains that X-ray scanners won't harm film less than 1,000-speed; but my friend Peggy, a freelance photographer, maintains that multiple trips through the scanner will, indeed, harm the film. Also, if you pack your film in checked bags, the scanners that inspect them are stronger than those for carry-on bags and should definitely be avoided. ~I always keep rolls of film—no matter what speed—accessible and hand them to the security inspectors before I walk through the scanner (remember to retrieve them after you pass, however!). ~If you take a lot of photos, you might want to buy some lead-lined pouches from a camera store. They're inexpensive and will even protect film in checked bags.

~Professional film (which is very sensitive and must be kept refrigerated until used and developed a day later) aside, a general guideline for us amateurs is that the higher the film speed, the faster the film—and fast film requires less light. So, think about the situations in which you anticipate taking pictures: if it's off-season and overcast in Paris, select 400; if it's summer with bright sunlight, select 200; for indoor gatherings in restaurants, try 400 or higher (unless you want to employ the flash); if you'll be in France for the Tour du Monde or the Grand Prix, select 400 or higher; for approaching dusk and sunsets, select 400. ~I am fond of black-and-white photos, so I always include a roll or two of black-and-white film in my bag.

La France Profonde

Even though it has absolutely nothing to do with Paris, every visitor should be aware of this phrase, which is deeply important to the French. Here is one of the best expressions of la France profonde I've ever encountered:

> When the French start talking about la France profonde, stop and listen. They are telling you about one of the secret keys that open the heart of their country. The region they have in mind is somewhat remote, a very long way from Paris, and even farther from any coastline. It leans toward conservatism, prefers the past to the future, the small-town or rural to the urban, and is profoundly unimpressed by fashion. There may be just a whiff of xenophobia there, but this can usually be disguised as an exaggerated love for *la patrie*. Its values are traditional, its architecture small-scale, and the more extreme excesses of the modern world are held at bay—partly by design and partly by economics. It is the world of Balzac and Marcel Pagnol, not Françoise Sagan. It is *boeuf en daube,* not nouvelle cuisine. If it could be bottled it would be concentrated essence of France: parfum, not eau de toilette. It is France's center of gravity—and *gravitas.* It is also a region that most foreign travelers never venture into. It's not that it is hard to get there, or that you're not welcome once you arrive; it's just that tourists tend, lemming-like, to prefer the urban delights of Paris, the crowded coast, or the proven cultural uplift of Chartres or the Loire Valley.
>
> There are, of course, many *Frances profondes,* scattered all over the

country. The idea is supremely elastic, combining—as only the French could—philosophy and geography in one elegant, intellectual package. The trick for the traveler is simple. Abandon any notion of going to a part of France that you have been to before, or, more daringly, that you have *heard* too much about. And then just listen when the French start talking and slowly plan how to steal the key. (Gully Wells, courtesy *Condé Nast Traveler*, copyright ©1991 by Condé Nast Publications, Inc.)

Frequent-Flier Miles

From what I've read, airlines wish they'd never created this program, and there are now fewer and fewer seats reserved for frequent fliers *and* you need even more miles to earn these seats. Should you happen to have enough miles and want to fly to Paris, plan to redeem those miles about a year ahead *or* plan to fly in the off-season (it's also possible that airlines will reduce the miles needed for the flight in the off-season). Don't immediately give up if your initial request can't be confirmed. Apparently, the airlines fiddle with frequent-flier seats every day as they monitor the demand for paid seats. If the number of paying travelers is low as the departure date approaches, more frequent-flyer awards may be honored. Also, try to reserve your mileage for expensive flights, rather than those which you can get for a good price anytime.

G

General Travel

Here are some good books to consult about trip planning in general: *The New York Times Practical Traveler Handbook: An A–Z Guide to Getting There and Back,* Betsy Wade, Times Books, 1994; and *Wendy Perrin's Secrets Every Smart Traveler Should Know: Condé Nast Traveler's Consumer Travel Expert Tells All,* Fodor's Travel Publications, 1997. It might seem as if these two books cover the same ground, but in fact there is little overlap and I refer to both of them all the time. The *Practical Traveler* book really is an A–Z guide, organized alphabetically, and covering such topics as airline code sharing, customs, hotel tipping, closing up the house, etc. Perrin's book is divided into eight sections plus an appendix, and the anecdotes featured were all previously published in the "Ombudsman" column of the magazine. She covers the fine art of complaining, what to do if your luggage is damaged or pilfered, travel agents and tour operators, car rentals, etc., as well as the ten commandments of trouble-free travel, which I think should be given to every traveler before he or she boards the plane.

In a similar vein, I highly recommend *Traveler's Tool Kit: How to Travel Absolutely Anywhere!* by Rob Sangster, Menasha Ridge Press, Birmingham, Alabama, 1996. "Tool kit" really is the best description of this travel bible, which addresses *everything* having to do with planning, packing, and departing. Whom is this book for? Everyone, really, or at least people who are curious about the rest of the world; people who are thinking about their first foreign trip; budget travelers; business travelers; people who want to travel more independently; and people who know "that life offers more than a two-week vacation once a year." It's a *great* book, with lots of ideas, tips, and advice, and I've found Sangster's checklists at the back of the book particularly helpful.

Guidebooks

Choosing which guidebooks to use can be bewildering and frustrating. I have yet to find the perfect book that offers all the features I need and want, so I consult a variety of books, gleaning tips and advice from each. Then I buy a blank journal and fill it with notes from all these books (leaving some pages blank) and end up with what is the "perfect package" for me: the journal plus two or three guidebooks I determine to be indispensable (I don't carry them around at the same time). In the end, the right guidebook is the one that speaks to you. Place yourself in front of the Paris section of a bookstore and take the time to read through the various guides. If you feel the author shares your sensibility, and you think his or her credentials are respectable, then you're probably holding the right book. Recommendations from friends and colleagues are fine only if they travel in the same way you do and seek the same qualities as you in a guidebook. Also, if you discover an older guide that appeals to you, don't immediately dismiss it. Background information doesn't change—use it in conjunction with an updated guide to create your own "perfect package." Keep in mind, too, that guidebooks within the same series are not always consistent, as they aren't always written by the same authors.

Here are the guidebooks I consult before a trip to Paris (note that they are listed alphabetically, not in order of preference, and I have indicated which features I use the guidebooks for and which books I feel are essential to bring along; note also that I never recommend a guidebook on all of France—unless one is planning an extensive trip throughout the country—as the Paris section in such a book is entirely too condensed):

Access Paris, Richard Saul Wurman, Access Press (a registered trademark of HarperCollins Publishers). There's not enough historical background for me in Access Guides, and descriptions are too brief, but as with *Pariswalks* and *Around and About Paris* (see *"Paris Je T'Aime" bibliothèque*), the beauty of Access is that it enables you to *really* get to know neighborhoods. In fact, a perfect combination would be to bring along one volume of *Around and About Paris, Pariswalks,* and *Access Paris.* Each chapter of the *Access Paris* begins with a good map and an overall description of the *quartier.* Things to see and do are listed numerically, corresponding to the numbers on the map. Entries are color-coded, blue for hotels, red for cuisine, green for special finds, and black for cultural and historic sights. My favorite feature is the "Bests" suggestions, contributed by noteworthy personalities, which appear throughout the book—I've discovered some great tips and ideas here. A bring-along.

Baedeker's Paris, Baedeker Stuttgart (distributed in the U.S. and Canada by Fodor's Travel Publications). No book sums up the excitement and romance of travel to me like an old, hardcover Baedeker guide (if you're a nut for them like me, The Complete Traveller in New York always seems to have a good assortment—see "Bookstores" for address and phone). The first Baedeker guide appeared in 1844, and the series has been the authoritative leader ever since. Current guides are now paperback, with color photos and an easy-to-read format. The best feature of a Baedeker is the foldout map (in the old editions this was glued to the back cover; in the updated guides the map is completely separate from the book, housed in a plastic sleeve at the back). The book is divided into three, color-coded sections: "Nature, Culture, History" (blue); "Sights from A to Z" (pink); and "Practical Information from A to Z" (yellow). In keeping with Baedeker tradition, sites are described in alphabetical order and are rated with one star (especially worth attention) or two (outstanding). The features I like are practical information (because there are often details which aren't included in other books) and "Baedeker Specials," two-page essays on subjects such as "Hot Jam Sessions and Afro Beat," "Poet of the Camera," and "Town Planner of the 19th Century."

Blue Guide: Paris and Versailles, distributed in the U.S. by W. W. Norton. Perhaps because it is so authoritative, I always feel that I *have* to check in with the Blue Guide. In fact, the Blue Guide series has been around since 1918, and the original founders were the editors of Baedeker's English-language editions. Blue Guides are straightforward and practical with a no-nonsense approach to art, architecture, and landscape. As author Ian Robertson explains, in the preface to the Blue Guide: *France*, he provides the reader with "sufficient historical and cultural context, yet without being so exhaustive as to leave him with no opportunity of discovering additional pleasures for himself. He will find that there is almost always more to a place than the description specifies, for France offers an *embarras de richesses* that can never be encompassed in a single tome." Each edition features a thorough glossary of French art and architectural terms, and is a worthy bring-along.

Cadogan City Guides: Paris, Dana Facaros and Michael Pauls, Cadogan Books, London; distributed in the U.S. by Globe Pequot Press, Old Saybrook, Connecticut. Cadogan (rhymes with *toboggan*) guides are almost all written by the Facaros-Pauls team, and I consider their guides to be of the bring-along variety. Cadogan Guides are honest, witty, interesting, and discriminating without being snooty. The authors are not easily impressed, so when they enthuse about something, I pay attention. I'm most especially fond of the "History" and "Topics" sections in the front of the book, which reveal how perceptive the authors are and introduce the reader to their style: one of the essays in "Topics" is entitled "No Dog Poo, Please, We're Parisians," and in the "Getting Around" chapter they suggest holding on to your metro ticket until the very end of your trip for spot checks and because some big stations have automatic exit gates that eat the ticket. This has never happened to me, but they refer specifically to the Chatelet–Les Halles station, which truly is, as they say, "phenomenally complex"—I used to take visitors there just to see it. As there are two exit gates in a row at this station, they write, "So you'll spend the rest of your life down there, unless you ask an employee for a get-out-of-the-metro-free card, a *contremarque*. They're used to it." Included are lodging and dining recommendations for all budgets and good commentary on sights famous and little-known. The walking tours are good (but not as detailed as in *Around and About Paris* or *Pariswalks* (see *"Paris Je T'Aime" bibliothèque*), and there are metro maps, menu vocabulary, glossary, and bibliography. Definitely my favorite all-around guidebook.

Eyewitness Travel Guides: Paris, DK (Dorling Kindersley) Publishing. Like the Knopf Guides, the Eyewitness series features bold graphics, full-color photos, maps, and illustrations. Unlike Knopf Guides, there are lots of bird's-eye views of historic buildings and arrondissements, and a running timeline from prehistoric times to the present. I am crazy for the views and the timeline, as well as the pages of historical themes, such as kings and emperors in Paris, Gallo-Roman Paris, Paris in the Age of Enlightenment, the Sun King's Paris, the belle epoque, etc. Overall, however, I find Eyewitness Guides to be visually appealing more than they are substantive.

Fodor's Paris 1999, Fodor's Travel Publications. I typically crave more information than Fodor's guides provide; however, I think the entire line of Fodor's guides just keeps getting better and better every year. I *always* read them before I go and *always* discover a handful of useful tips. Once, my husband and I planned on having dinner at a particular restaurant in Antibes, which was recommended in numerous books. Out of the dozen guidebooks I consulted, only Fodor's stated that coat-and-tie attire was required for men. This is a small but important piece of information that I consider crucial for business and holiday travelers alike. It would not only be disappointing but embarrassing—and potentially offensive—to appear at a restaurant improperly dressed, all the more so if you had arranged to meet friends or colleagues there. The Rand McNally map at the back of the book; the wider range of choices for lodging and dining; the color photos; the boxed "Close-Up" essays; and the "Off the Beaten Path" suggestions throughout the book make the Paris gold guide more valuable than it's ever been.

Fodor's UpClose Paris and *UpClose France,* Fodor's Travel Publications. The UpClose series is aimed at travelers on limited budgets, but not necessarily the *Let's Go* crowd. There are lots of money-saving tips throughout the book as well as information on rail passes, youth hostels, and studying in France, but there is also a wealth of practical information for *all* types of travelers, not just students. The range of options for transportation, lodging, and dining is wide, there are numerous maps, and—my favorite feature—there are interesting "trivia boxes" all through the book. Historical background is too thin for my taste, but this series is particularly welcome because I believe this audience—intelligent travelers who want an authentic experience on a modest budget—more accurately reflects the majority of people traveling today.

Insight Guides: Paris, APA Publications, Singapore (distributed by Houghton Mifflin). I have been a fan of the Insight Guides for years. When they first appeared, about twenty years ago, they were the only books to provide outstanding color photographs matched with perceptive text. The guiding philosophy of the series has been to provide genuine insight into the history, culture, institutions, and people of a place. The editors search for writers with a firm knowledge of Paris who are also experts in their fields. I do not think, however, that recent editions are quite as good as they used to be. I can't put my finger on it, but something is missing. That said, I am still recommending that you take a look at this Paris guide and decide for yourself. I remain fond of the beginning features section (which has always been the best section, in my opinion), a series of magazine-style essays on architecture, food, markets, the Parisians, history, the arts, and politics.

Kate Simon's Paris: Places & Pleasures, Capricorn Books, New York, 1971. Sadly, this wonderful, wonderful book is out of print, but it does occasionally turn up. If you ever run across a copy, buy it without hesitation. There are no more travel writers quite like Kate Simon, except perhaps Jan Morris and Barbara Grizzuti Harrison. "An Uncommon Guidebook" is how the book is described on the cover, and indeed this is like no other guidebook ever published. Instead of approaching things to see and do in a predictable fashion, Simon's book is divided into chapters named as days of the week: "The First Sunday," "Make It Ten Days: The Second Sunday," etc. Within these chapters are essays, such as "How Come the Angry Parisian?" "Est-ce Que Vous Parlez Anglais?" "Parisian Contours and Stances," "Paris in the Fall." A very special book, which is, to quote from the back cover, "a three-dimensional portrait of the world's fabled city, presented with a novelist's acute observation and a poet's sensitivity . . . Kate Simon once again shows readers how to savor and know a city to the utmost."

Knopf Guides: Paris, Alfred A. Knopf, originally published in France by Nouveaux-Loisirs, a subsidiary of Gallimard, Paris. I'm fond of the Knopf Guides in general, and the *Paris* edition is no exception. I like the bold design and the various sections ("Paris as Seen by Painters," "Nature," "A City for Gourmets," "Parisian Scenes," etc.). I also like the foldout pages on the Seine, Musée d'Orsay, the Louvre, and underground Paris. Surprisingly, for such a *luxe* book, there are thirteen listings for budget hotels, plus four youth hostels and the campsite in the

Bois de Boulogne. The restaurant section is particularly useful with such categories as "Restaurants with Spectacular Views," "Where to Eat on Sundays," "Meals for Under 150F," "The Traditional Gastronomic Stars," and "Fish Delights" (although if restaurants are *really* your thing, you'll also want the Knopf Guides *Restaurants of Paris*—see the *"À Table"* section). But, especially for such a chunky book, the Knopf Paris guide is not as substantive as it appears. I enjoy reading it before I go, but I wouldn't necessarily feel the need to bring it along.

Let's Go: France, Bruce F. McKinnon, editor, St. Martin's Press. "The World's Bestselling Budget Travel Series" is the *Let's Go* slogan, which is hardly debatable. *Let's Go* is still the bible, and if you haven't looked at a copy since your salad days, you might be surprised: now, each edition contains color maps, advertisements, and an appendix that features a climate chart, international calling cards, time zones, measurements, national holidays, festivals, a phrase book, French-English glossary, and a distance chart. A team of Harvard student interns still offers the same thorough coverage of places to eat and sleep, and things to see and do. I think the presentation of facts and history is quite good in *Let's Go,* and I would eagerly press a copy into the hands of anyone under a certain age (thirty-five?) bound for France (there is not an individual book for Paris).

Lonely Planet Paris, Steve Fallon, Daniel Robinson, and Tony Wheeler, 1998. Lonely Planet guides have been among my most favorite for many years. Tony and Maureen Wheeler founded the series in Australia in 1973. Originally, the series focused solely on Asia; but about a dozen years ago they realized that the Lonely Planet approach to travel was not exclusive to any particular geographic area of the world. The series is aimed at independent travelers, and each book is organized by chapters such as "Facts for the Visitor," "Getting Around," "Things to See & Do," "Places to Stay," "Places to Eat," etc. I am fondest of the opening chapters covering history, politics, ecology, religion, economy, and practical facts—the information on sites to see is not nearly detailed enough. I like that hotels and restaurants are presented least expensive to most expensive, and I like the candid opinions of the contributing authors. The *Paris* edition features nine color maps at the back of the book, a twelve-page architecture section, and a chapter on suggested excursions outside of Paris to Parc Asterix, Disneyland, Chantilly, Fontainebleu, Chartres, etc. A percentage of each book's income is donated to various causes such as Greenpeace's efforts to stop French nuclear testing in the Pacific, Amnesty International, and agricultural projects in Central America. A bring-along.

Michelin Green Guide: Paris. A Michelin guide might be more trustworthy than your best friend. Its famous star-rating system and "worth a detour" slogan may have become a bit too formulaic, but it's a formula that works. The series was created in 1900 by André Michelin, who compiled a little red book of hotels and restaurants, which today is the Michelin Red Guide famous for the stars it awards to restaurants. The green tourist guides first made their appearance in 1926. Each guide is jam-packed with information and is easy to pack. It will come as no surprise to readers that I prefer even more detail than Michelin offers, but I find it an excellent series, and each guide I've used has proven exceptionally helpful. Some of the features I especially like about the *Paris* guide include the "ABC of Architecture," "A Different Perspective Over Paris," and the "Admission Times and Charges" for all sorts of sites. While it is tempting to think of other guides as being more hip, even the Michelin *Paris* edition informs readers of where they can go to hear Rai, a type of music from the Algerian city of Oran that combines Portuguese fado with blues. The *Paris* edition also includes an "Excursions" chapter with details on Cathédrale St.-Denis, Versailles, and Disneyland Paris. Each Michelin guide is complemented by a Michelin map, of course, and for Paris it's map no. 11.

Paris Inside-Out: THE Insider's Handbook to Life in Paris, David Applefield, Globe Pequot Press, 2000. The title alone reveals that this book is comprehensive and definitely de rigueur. Applefield covers *everything*—I wish I'd had this book when I was a student in 1979. As he writes in the introduction, "The information assembled here, both objective and subjective, is based on experience, and experience is the key to knowing a place . . . *inside out!*" Readers will learn about how to find housing or accommodations, banking, colloquial expressions and argot (slang), obtaining a carte de séjour, using a télécarte, finding au pair positions, what the *formules de politesse* are for letter writing, where taxi stands are, etc. I wouldn't think of going to Paris, for the first or the fiftieth time, without consulting Applefield's bible.

The Rough Guide: Paris, Kate Baillie and Tim Salmon. When the Rough Guides first appeared, in the early eighties, they had limited distribution in the U.S. Then, the guides were sort-of-but-not-quite the British equivalent of *Let's Go*. I sought them out because I found the British viewpoint refreshing and felt the writers imparted more knowledge about a place than was available in U.S. guidebooks. Now, since the Rough Guides opened a New York office in the late nineties, the series is broader-based but still appealing to independent-minded travelers who appreciate the Rough Guides' honest assessments, and historical and political backgrounds (these last are found in the "Contexts" section of each guide, and my only complaint is that I think this section should appear at the beginning of each book instead of at the end). As in its cousin *Let's Go,* readers will find specifics on working and studying in France, gay and lesbian clubs and discos, and hotels that are frequented both by the backpacking crowd and those who carry luggage with their hands. However, readers will also find specifics on driving in France, boating holidays, and gourmet groceries. Some features that I've found especially interesting or useful: how to walk back to Paris from St.-Denis via the Canal St.-Denis towpath; late-night shopping spots, bars, and cafés; contacts for travelers with disabilities; Paris for vegetarians, and hours for the Turkish bath at Hammam de la Mosquée. All in all, a dependable, hip guide.

The Webb & Bower DuMont Guide: Paris and the Île-de-France, by Klaus

Bussmann, translated by Russell Stockman, 1984, DuMont Buchverlag GmbH & Co.; first published in Great Britain in 1985 by Webb & Bower, Exeter; English language edition first published by Stewart, Tabori & Chang. This guidebook is hands down the best one I've seen for detailed historical and architectural background. Filled with photographs (179 in all, 25 in color), drawings, engravings, ground plans of churches and hotels, cross-sections, and maps from the Plan Turgot, this is indispensable, and I have yet to find another book published in the U.S. quite as good. It's a comprehensive work for those interested in more than just the basic facts about Paris's people, streets, squares, palaces, monasteries, monuments, and buildings. Even the "Practical Travel Suggestions" on the blue pages at the end of the book offer ideas and recommendations that are still useful after so many years. I recommend seeking this series out, even if you have to order it by mail from the U.K.

H

Health

Staying healthy while traveling in France should not be a challenge, but things do happen. A good general reference book is *Travelers' Health: How to Stay Healthy All Over the World* (Richard Dawood, M.D., former medical editor for *Condé Nast Traveler*, foreword by Paul Theroux, Random House, 1994). This thick, 600+ page book isn't for bringing along—it's for reading before you go. In addition to Dr. Dawood, sixty-seven other medical experts contributed to this volume, which covers everything from insect bites, water filters, and sun effects on the skin to gynecological problems, altitude sickness, children abroad, immunizations, and the diabetic traveler. It also features essays on such topics as "The Economy-Class Syndrome" and "Being an Expatriate."

Hiking

There are lots of opportunities for hiking in and around Paris (see articles in *"La Seine"* and *"Île-de-France et d'Ailleurs"*). France has an extensive network of long-distance footpaths called the *Grande Randonnée* and a network of shorter paths called *Pétite Randonnée,* which begin and end at the same place. Many routes take walkers across entire sections of the country. Several GR trails are within or pass through the Île-de-France, and the GR3 follows the Loire to the Atlantic. An important point to keep in mind about hiking in France is that what you walk on is a *route* not a trail. The network wasn't created at random; it connects old paths that have existed for a long, long time. Routes wind through the middle of villages, sometimes cross private property where you have to open and close a gate, and are often farm tracks where you'll encounter shepherds and farmers—there are even some patches of original Roman cobblestones. Walking a GR is not a wilderness experience, but there are few places in Europe—now or ever—where you can backpack into completely isolated places and not encounter roads, people, or towns. Conversely, there are few—if any—places in the U.S. where you can backpack and be assured of finding a place to sleep in a bed plus a meal with wine or beer at the end of the day.

You'll need a good map to hike the GRs, and there are really only two appropriate choices: *guide topographique* (topoguide) or IGN (Institut Géographique National) *série bleue*. Topoguides contain extraordinary detail, but are available only in French. Fluency is not essential to read topoguides, but a fairly good command of the language is. Topoguides also include locations of accommodations, usually *gîtes d'étapes*. The meticulous IGN *série bleue* maps indicate everything from bodies of water, landmarks, power lines, etc., and are available in English. Both types of maps can be obtained at the national headquarters and information center for the Fédération Française de la Randonnée Pédestre, Comité National des Sentiers de Grande Randonnée (14 rue Riquet, 19th; 01.44.89.93.93 / fax: 01.40.35. 85.67; www.ffrp.asso.fr); at Espace IGN (107 rue la Boetie, 8th; 01.42.25.87.90); at Au Vieux Campeur, 48 rue des Écoles, 5th; 01.46.11.43.53 / fax: 01.60.11.49.66); and at good bookshops in the city.

Additionally, Seven Hills Book Distributors in Cincinnati carries the English-language versions of topoguides, published in Great Britain by McCarta. They are called "Footpath of Europe Guides" in English, and I didn't mention them above because they are not exact translations of the French versions; they're condensed and because of this aren't always as reliable as the originals. However, I do think for shorter-distance walks they would be good. Seven Hills offers eight guides: *Normandy & the Seine; Paris to Boulogne; Walking the GR5* in three editions: *Larche to Nice, Modane to Larche*, and *Vosges to Jura; Walks in Corsica; Walks in the Cevennes;* and *Walking Through Brittany*. Each edition is five by eight inches, 190–250 pages, $19.95, and features sixty to eighty color topo-maps. Contact Seven Hills for a catalog or to order: 1531 Tremont Street, Cincinnati, Ohio 45214; 800-545-2005 / fax: 888-777-7799; E-mail: customerservice@sevenhillsbooks.com. The catalog also offers some other imported books that may be of interest, such as *The French Directory: The Complete Guide to Learning French in France* and *Trekking in the Pyrenees.*

~The very best book available on hiking in France is *France on Foot—Village to Village, Hotel to Hotel: How to Walk the French Trail System on Your Own,* Bruce LeFavour, photographs by Faith Echtermeyer, Attis Press, St. Helena, California, 1999. Travelers interested in walking a little or a lot will be well served as LeFavour has thought of everything: trail classification and markers, a typical day en route, maps and trail guides, equipment, lodging and dining, recommended books, costs, packing list . . . even a handy "Walker's Vocabulary," which you cut out of the back of the book and carry with you on the trail. He *really* won me over, though, for two reasons: for recommending that readers make their own "guidebook" in advance (I *always* make a book before I go on a trip, even when there is no hiking on the horizon; my husband wondered if the photo on page 190 of a map, glue stick, scissors, paper, and a glass of wine was taken in our house) and for emphasizing that a walking experience is not the same thing as a backpacking experience (you do carry a pack, but you sleep in hotel beds and eat in restaurants, eliminating the need to carry a tent, cooking utensils, and food). As LeFavour puts it, "Walking in France is a glass of good wine while backpacking is a tumbler of ice water."

Walking forces us to slow down and take notice, the reasons we go on vacation in the first place. Another important point LeFavour emphasizes is that the French make little distinction between sports and leisure, moderation being considered the key to living a good, healthy life. Therefore, exercise goes hand in hand with enjoying wine and food. Overachieving Americans may find it odd to break a sweat at some physical activity and follow it up with pâté, a baguette, and some wine, but it is perfectly normal to the French. (For a hilarious extreme of this, see Adam Gopnik's "The Rules of the Sport," *The New Yorker,* May 27, 1996, in which he tries, unsuccessfully, for four months to exercise at a health club in Paris.) When you walk from village to village in France, you stop for lunch and have the *plat du jour* and half a carafe of wine. The French way is to embrace a happy medium, which LeFavour endorses. He details numerous walks in Paris and the Île-de-France, the Loire, Burgundy, Champagne, and Normandy, as well as all the other regions of France. Even if you're only planning on taking short day hikes, you'll find LeFavour's enthusiasm infectious and his book to be indispensable, inspiring, and absolutely de rigueur.

Note: Two other good books to consult for walking in France are *The Independent Walker's Guide to France* (Frank Booth, Interlink Books, Brooklyn, New York, 1996) and *Short Escapes in France: 25 Country Getaways for People Who Love to Walk* (Bruce Bolger and Gary Stoller, Fodor's Travel Publications, 1996). I took an immediate liking to Frank Booth's book because he explains that although he has written a guide about walking in France, his book is also about escaping and avoiding the DROPS (Dreaded Other People). He details thirty-five walks in sixteen regions, with nine walks in Paris and the Île-de-France, two in the Loire Valley, four in Normandy, one in Champagne, and one in Burgundy. Each walk is a day hike between two and nine miles, and a map and trail notes accompany each one. *Short Escapes* details four walks immediately outside Paris (Auvers-sur-Oise, Chevreuse, Barbizon, Giverny) as well as four walks in Burgundy, four in the Loire Valley, and two in Normandy. Every walk can be completed within a few hours, but the authors also include places to stay and eat, scenic picnic spots, historic sites, maps, and the address, phone number, and hours of the local tourist office. Both paperback books are small and are meant to be bring-alongs.

If you're *really* inspired to experience the GR network, you might want to consider a more ambitious trip. A great book about just such a journey is *Walking*

Europe From Top to Bottom: The Sierra Club Travel Guide to the Grande Randonnée Cinq (GR-5) Through Holland, Belgium, Luxembourg, Switzerland and France (by Susanna Margolis and Ginger Harmon, Sierra Club Books, 1986). The book is, sadly, hard to find and may now be out of print, but is worth tracking down for its wealth of detail and practical tips on the authors' 107-day trek from the Hook of Holland to Nice.

I

Internet Access

I'm only including this here for business travelers. If you're traveling for pleasure and feel you need to surf the Web, perhaps you should save your money and stay home. (I take the view that vacations are for removing yourself from your daily grind—what the French refer to as *vélo, boulot, dodo;* visiting another country is about doing *different* things and putting yourself in unfamiliar situations.) Overseas telephone services are not as reliable as those in the U.S., ensuring that connecting to the Internet is also not as easy or inexpensive. Business travelers who need to check in with the office via E-mail should consider what it will cost for a laptop, power adapter, disk and/or CD-ROM drives, plus any other related accessories, as well as how heavy it will be to carry. You may conclude that cybercafés (or Internet cafés) are more economical (and easier on your back). Fees for access to the Internet vary, but when you compare a hotel's charges for the same access— often at slower speeds—cybercafés represent good value. I found nine Paris cybercafés by searching in www.cybercaptive.com and www.netcafes.com. Also, the last time I was at Charles de Gaulle airport, I noticed that some of the public telephone booths were equipped for Internet access.

J

Jewish History in Paris

France is home to the fourth-largest Jewish community in the world and the largest Jewish community in Europe. According to Lucien Lazare in *Rescue as Resistance* (see *"Le Kiosque" bibliothèque*), three out of four Jews present in France in 1940 survived the war. He also notes that not a single deported child survived, but approximately 3 percent of the deported adults returned. Today Jews represent 1 percent of France's total population, the highest percentage in Western Europe (note that after Catholicism, Islam is the second-largest religion in France). Paris has a great number of things of Jewish interest, and a good book to consult is *A Travel Guide to Jewish Europe* (Ben Frank, Pelican Publishing Company, Gretna, Louisiana, 1996). Almost forty pages of the book are devoted to Paris, and they offer a complete list of synagogues, places to eat, organizations, community centers, museums, memorials, and cemeteries. And Frank notes that kosher visitors need not worry about where to take their next meal: there may be more kosher facilities in Paris than in New York, Chicago, and Los Angeles combined! Also, Maison de la France (the French Government Tourist Office in the U.S.) publishes a great thirty-one-page brochure: *France for the Jewish Traveler,* which includes eleven pages on Paris.

K

Le Kiosque-Théâtre

Half-price theater tickets are available at two *kiosque-théâtre* booths in the city: one on place de la Madeleine and the other in the RER station of Chatelet–Les Halles. Tickets are sold on the day of performance only and no credit cards are accepted. A small handling charge is added to the price of each ticket. Hours of operation are somewhat sporadic—the booths are not open all day long—so be sure to inquire at the tourist office (in the U.S. or in Paris) for specifics.

L

Language

Somewhere, I once read an observation by writer Lawrence Durrell that if one really wanted to know and understand France and the French, one had to learn the language (I cannot for the life of me find this reference again, so if you know of it, please write and tell me). I think he is absolutely right, for the French language really does define so much about the French and about France. Everyone will tell you, of course, that it is essential to attempt to speak French when in Paris; this is true—the French warm to anyone attempting to speak their beautiful language— yet it is also true that the natives of *any* country love it when visitors try to speak their language. What people may not tell you is that French is still a nearly universal language. It has been my experience that *someone* always speaks French, even in such seemingly unlikely countries as Egypt, Portugal, Turkey, Greece, and Croatia. Spanish may be the second language in the U.S., but it won't serve you very well outside of Mexico, Central and South America, Spain, and the Philippines. A multitude of French words and phrases have made their way into English, and it would never be a bad investment of your time to either brush up on your high school French or begin learning for the first time.

~The best language course I've used is Living Language. There are others— Berlitz, Barron's, etc.—but Living Language has been around longer (since 1946), the courses are continually updated and revised, and in terms of variety, practicality, and originality, I prefer it. French courses are available for beginner, intermediate, and advanced levels, in either audiocassette or CD editions. The "Fast &

Easy" course (referred to as "virtually foolproof" by New York's *Daily News*) is for beginner business or leisure travelers and is a sixty-minute survival program with a cassette and pocket-sized pronunciation guide. The "Ultimate Course" is for serious language learners and is the equivalent of two years of college-level study. In a copublishing venture with Fodor's, Living Language also offers the pocket-sized *French for Travelers,* which is a handy book/cassette reference—designed for business and leisure travelers—with words and phrases for dozens of situations, including exchanging money, using ATMs, finding a hotel room, etc., and also including a two-way dictionary. And to help build excitement for young children coming along, there's the *Learn in the Kitchen* and *Learn Together: for the Car* series. These book/cassette kits are for children ages four to eight and include a sixty-minute bilingual tape; sixteen songs, games, and activities; a forty-eight-page illustrated activity book with color stickers; and tips for parents on how to vary the activities for repeated use.

~If you prefer learning by videotapes, a good course is "French in Action." Call 800-LEARNER for additional information, and see the September 1999 issue of *Paris Notes* for an article ("Paris 'In Action'" by Ellen Williams) about this respected series. ~An essential book to have is *501 French Verbs* (Barron's). In addition to really good descriptions of the various tenses, a full page is allotted to each verb, showing all the tenses fully conjugated, plus the definition and a useful selection of "Words and Expressions Related to This Verb" at the bottom of each page. As if this weren't enough, there are also chapters on "Verbs Used in Idiomatic Expressions," "Verbs with Prepositions," "Verbs Used in Weather Expressions," "Thirty Practical Situations for Tourists and Popular Phrases," and "Words and Expressions for Tourists." If you're serious about learning or brushing up on French, I really can't see doing it without this book.

~Some related books for French-language lovers are *Les Bons Mots: How to Amaze Tout le Monde with Everyday French* (Eugene Ehrlich, Henry Holt, 1997). Not a dictionary, but rather an alphabetical listing of idiomatic phrases, many of which have found their way into English. If you always wanted to know how to say the equivalent of "don't judge by appearances" *(l'habit ne fait pas le moine),* "seize the moment" *(il faut vivre dans l'instant),* "I couldn't care less" *(je m'en fous),* or simply "hangover" *(gueule de bois),* you need this book; *Je Ne Sais What?: A Guide to* de rigueur *Frenglish for Readers, Writers, and Speakers* (Jon Winokur, Plume, 1996). "Frenglish"—not to be confused with "Franglais"—is grammatically correct *French* that enriches the *English* language. This is a collection of French expressions, maxims, and literary phrases that have found their way into our vocabulary. One will find *nouvelle cuisine, mauvais goût, enfant terrible,* and *tant pis* and their definitions and related quotations. As Winokur states in the introduction, "Much of our political, military, artistic, and culinary vocabulary originated in France."

Luggage

I've read of a syndrome—really—called BSA (baggage separation anxiety), which you may at first be inclined to laugh at; but as reports of lost luggage have escalated in the last two years, I'm not at all surprised (all the more reason, I say, not to check bags, and *definitely* the reason to pack at least some essentials in a carry-on bag). Even if you are the sort of traveler who cannot lighten your load, you will still probably bring a carry-on. As I write this, the standard limit for carry-on luggage is nine by fourteen by twenty-two inches, otherwise known as forty-five linear inches to the airlines. Although not all airlines enforce this policy, it seems foolish not to comply—storage space is limited, and less baggage means more on-time schedules and better passenger safety. Some airlines have even installed sized templates at the security X-ray machines, so if your bag doesn't fit, you don't walk through. Many luggage manufacturers—including Tumi and Samsonite—have responded, turning out a variety of bags at varying prices, which are meant to hold enough stuff for about three days of traveling—about the time it takes for a misrouted bag to show up, assuming it isn't lost altogether!

M

Maps

Getting lost is usually a part of everyone's travels, but it isn't always a bonus. Happily, there are maps, and no shortage of good ones.

For Paris, there is no better map than the pocket-sized *Plan de Paris* book, which can be purchased in Paris at nearly every bookstore as well as at some travel bookstores here in the States. Also, available in English for the first time is the *Taride Paris Guide,* the oldest and original city map guide. *Taride* is not much different from the *Plan de Paris*—it also features arrondissement maps, alphabetical street listings, metro and bus maps, and a listing of significant offices and principal monuments—but it doesn't have the letter thumb-indexes or the large, foldout map of Paris. The *Taride* guide is color-coded with white pages for the street index, blue for addresses, and yellow for bus routes. It's not *quite* as comprehensive as the *Plan,* but is certainly *utile* and comes in two sizes: classic ($3\frac{3}{4}'' \times 5\frac{7}{8}''$) and a larger format ($5'' \times 7\frac{1}{8}''$). *Taride* guides can be found in some bookstores in the States or ordered directly from the publisher/distributor (Penton Overseas, Inc., 2470 Impala Drive, Carlsbad, California 92008; 800-748-5804 / fax: 760-431-8110; www.pentonoverseas.com).

For driving, there are three superb choices: Michelin's *Road Atlas of France* (hardcover); Michelin's *Motoring Atlas: France* (spiral paperbound); and the IGN (Institut Géographique National) *série verte,* which covers all of France in seventy-two sheets at 1:100,000 (1 centimeter for 1 kilometer). (IGN maps are the equivalent of Ordnance Survey maps in the U.K., and both began as tools for the military.

France, in fact, was the first European country to have a complete national survey, in 1793.) The IGN *série rouge* is a great companion set, which indicates the exact position of monuments, châteaux, scenic roads, viewpoints, etc. The *série rouge* is available in fifteen sheets at 1:250,000.

For walking and hiking or any sort of vacances vertes *(outdoor holidays): guides topographiques* and the IGN *série bleue. Série bleue* maps cover France in two thousand sheets at 1:25,000.

Markets (marchés) *and Flea Markets* (marchés aux puces *or* brocantes)

Outdoor markets are one of the unrivaled pleasures of France in general and Paris in particular. Refer to *The Food Lover's Guide to Paris* by Patricia Wells for a complete list of the picturesque roving and permanent *marchés,* which are devoted mostly to food and food products—and remember: *Ne touchez pas!* (don't touch the produce; if you forget, you'll be swiftly reminded). Paris's flea markets, too, are a lot of fun even if you're not a collector. Bargaining is, for the most part, the accepted method of doing business (dealers will tell you if it's not), and therefore you should not try to visit a flea market in a hurry. Take your time, remember to stop for something to eat or drink so your stomach (or companion) doesn't grumble, and enjoy searching for a unique *souvenir* or soaking up the atmosphere. An excellent book you'll want to have is *Exploring the Flea Markets of France: A Companion Guide for Visitors and Collectors* (Sandy Price, Three Rivers Press, 1999). Price highlights the markets of twelve regions of France—including a section on Paris—and includes practical advice on what to look for at markets; hours; bargaining; useful vocabulary; how to transport your goods home; and a bibliography.

The three major flea markets in Paris are the Puces de Saint-Ouen, better known as Clignancourt (just beyond the 18th; metro: Porte-de-Clignancourt); Puces de Montreuil (20th; metro: Porte-de-Montreuil); Puces de Vanves (14th; metro: Porte-de-Vanves). The markets aren't in operation every day, but on Saturday and Sunday they are in full swing all day long (inquire at the tourist office for hours or consult Sandy Price's book, above). While most of my own bargaining has occurred in Turkey and Egypt, here are some tips that work well for me in France, too:

~Walk around first and survey the scene. Identify the vendors you want to come back to, and try to ascertain what the asking prices are for the items you're interested in. If you don't have any idea what the general price range is, you won't have any idea if you're paying a fair price. Even better is if you learn the prices of what items sell for here in the States before you leave home—then you'll also know how much (or how little) savings are being offered. ~If you do spy an item you're interested in, try not to reveal your interest; act as nonchalant as you possibly can, and remember to be ready to start walking away. ~It's considered rude to begin serious bargaining if you're not interested in making a purchase. This doesn't mean you should refrain from asking the price on an item, but to then begin naming numbers is an indication to the vendor that you're a serious customer and that a sale will likely be made. ~You'll get the best price if you pay with cash. I prepare an assortment of paper francs and coins in advance so I can always pull them out and indicate that it's all I have. It doesn't seem right to bargain hard for something and pay for it with a one-hundred. ~Occasionally, I feign interest in one particular item when it's a different item I *really* want. The tactic here is to begin bargaining and let the vendor think I'm about to make a deal. Then, I pretend to get cold feet and indicate that the price is just too much for me. The vendor thinks all is lost, and at that moment I point to the item I've wanted all along, sigh, and say I'll take that one, naming the lowest price from my previous negotiation. Usually, the vendor will immediately agree to it as it means a done deal. ~Other times, I will plead poverty and say to the vendor that I had *so* wanted to bring back a gift for my mother from "your beautiful country . . . won't you please reconsider?" This, too, usually works. ~Finally, remember that a deal is supposed to end with both parties satisfied. If, after much back and forth, you encounter a vendor who won't budge below a certain price, it's likely that it's not posturing but a way of letting you know that anything lower will no longer be advantageous to him or her.

Merde (#$*?), as in, I-Don't-Think-This-Needs-to-Be-Translated

I use the word here to refer to doggie poop. Tip: survey the *rue* or *boulevard* you're about to walk down and check for dog poop. In this way, you can either walk straight ahead with abandon—and even look up if you want—knowing you won't soil your shoes, or you'll be prepared to dodge the little piles. Either way, you'll look more like a native and less like a tourist.

Le Métro

Franz Kafka wrote, "Because it is so easy to understand, the metro is a frail and hopeful stranger's best chance to think that he has quickly and correctly, at the first attempt, penetrated the essence of Paris." Mastering the metro, which is one hundred years old this year, does give one a sense of truly belonging in Paris. The Météor is the newest line, which runs from the Madeleine to the new Bibliothèque François Mitterrand and is computer-operated. It makes the trip *rapidement* and *tranquillement,* and there are no doors between cars so you can see from car to car, end to end. The RER (Réseau Express Régional) line is the regional rapid-transit line, created to serve the suburbs. The metro system divides the Paris/Île-de-France region into eight zones, which extend northeast to Charles de Gaulle airport, northwest to Pontoise, and south to Etampes. Nearly everything you would want to see and do is in zones one and two.

If you plan to use the metro at all, several *tarifs réduits* (reduced fares) are available: a *carnet* is a package of ten individual tickets; a *carte orange* is available in both weekly (beginning on Monday) and monthly passes and requires a passport-size, black-and-white photo, which you can have taken in designated booths in the bigger stations; a *Paris Visite* pass offers unlimited travel on the metro, buses, suburban trains, Montmartre funicular, and private buses from ADATRIF and APTR. It does not require a photo and is available for one, two, three, or five consecutive days of travel, beginning any day of the week. Children between four and eleven pay half price. You may select either zones 1–3, 1–5, or 1–8, the latter serving Disneyland Paris, Versailles, and the Paris airports. Additionally, *Paris Visite* holders are offered a number of discounts on other area attractions, such as Canauxrama, Parc Asterix, and Montparnasse Tower; a *Mobilis* pass was intended for residents of the Île-de-France, who often need to travel on more than one mode of transport in the same day. So if you're staying in the suburbs, this is the best pass to buy as it's valid on all types of transportation in all zones and includes the SNCF suburban train network (except Roissyrail and Orlyrail).

There are two types of ticket passes you can purchase here in the States before you go: *Le Paris Visite* and *Le Paris Visite Plus*. These passes, however, are not exactly the same as those you purchase in Paris: the *Paris Visite* offers travel in zones one, two, and three, while the *Plus* pass includes travel to the outskirts of Paris, including the airports and Disneyland Paris and Versailles. For questions or to order passes, contact Marketing Challenges International, Inc. (10 East Twenty-first Street, New York, New York 10010; 212-529-9069 / fax: 212-529-4838; www.ticketsto.com. Note that Marketing Challenges also offers a number of other passes that can be purchased in advance, including three different Seine cruises, a *télécarte* phone card, two different types of dining vouchers, and *La Carte*, which is valid at sixty-five Paris museums and monuments). No one likes to waste money: with so many options, you should really think about the logistics of your trip and decide which deal is best for you. It doesn't make sense to buy rides and perks you'll never use, so plan ahead. ~Reminders: On most of the metro's cars, you have to lift the handle or push a button for the doors to open, both on the inside and outside of each car. ~Keep your ticket or pass handy for spot checks by inspectors.

Money

The best way to travel is with a combination of local cash, American Express traveler's checks (other types are not universally accepted), and credit cards. If you have all three, you will *never* have a problem. How you divide this up depends on how long you'll be traveling and on what day of the week you arrive—banks, which of course offer the best exchange rate, aren't generally open on the weekends. If you rely solely on your ATM card and you encounter a problem, you can't fix it until Monday when the banks reopen. Overseas ATMs may also limit the number of daily transactions you can make, as well as place a ceiling on the total amount you can withdraw.

~Make sure your password is compatible with French ATMs (if you have too many digits, you'll have to change it), and if, like me, you have memorized your password as a series of letters rather than numbers, write down the numerical equivalent before you leave. Most European cash machines do not display letters, and even if they did, they do not always appear in the same sequence as we know it in the U.S. ~Call your bank and inquire about fees for withdrawals, and ask if there is a fee for overseas transactions (there shouldn't be, but ask anyway); check if you can withdraw money from both your checking and savings accounts or only one; and ask if you can transfer money between accounts. ~Though I think this is a bit anal retentive even for me, it's possible to view on-line in advance the exact street locations of ATM machines in Paris. To see where Plus systems are, type in *www.visa.com;* for the Cirrus network, type *www.mastercard.com/atm.* Once in, select "ATM Locator," and you'll be given an opportunity to select a country, city, street address, and postal code (it's not essential to provide the postal code, but for best results, enter a city and cross streets).

~Savvy travelers always arrive with some local currency in their possession (I feel most comfortable with about $100). While the rates of exchange and fees charged obviously vary, it is far more important to simply obtain the currency than to spend an inordinate amount of time figuring how much money you'll save—we are, after all, talking about a small sum of money, and it will be money well spent when you get off the plane with the ability to quickly make your way to Paris. After a long flight, who wants to then exchange money, especially while looking after luggage and/or children? And keep in mind that there are often long lines at the exchange counters and cash machines, and that cash machines are sometimes out of order or out of cash. (Once, I even had the admittedly unusual experience of going directly to a large bank in a capital city only to find a posted sign stating that the bank was closed because it had *run out of money!?*). Smart travelers arrive prepared to pay for transportation, tips, snacks, personal items, or unanticipated expenses. If you're too busy to get the cash yourself, call International Currency Express and request its Currency Rush mail-order service. With two offices, in Los Angeles and Washington, D.C., the company offers excellent rates. Call 888-278-6628 and request either UPS second-day or overnight service.

~Over the years, I have cashed traveler's checks at good rates at La Monnaie d'Or (9 rue Scribe, 9th), around the corner from the Opéra. ~Refrain from wearing one of those ubiquitous waist bags, or as my friend Carl says, "Make our country proud and don't wear one of those fanny packs!" A tourist + fanny pack = magnet for pickpockets. I know of more people who've had valuables stolen from these ridiculous pouches than I can count. Keep large bills, credit cards, and passport hidden from view in a money belt worn under your clothes, in a pouch that hangs from your neck, or in an interior coat or blazer pocket. And for the person who balks at the suggestion of a money belt in a fine restaurant, it is a simple matter to excuse yourself from the table, head for the WC, and retrieve your money in the privacy of a stall. It is doubtful you'll be robbed walking from the bathroom back to your table. ~If possible, don't keep everything in the same place, and keep a separate piece of paper with telephone numbers of companies to contact in case of emergency. ~Some advice from *Paris: Places & Pleasures* by Kate Simon: "Learn the sizes and denominations of coins . . . and count them out slowly and carefully. Avoid the tourist tendency to keep changing bills because he can't sort out and add up coins, thus accumulating a Gibraltar of coins which makes things even more difficult." (Reprinted by permission of International Creative Management, Inc., copyright © 1971, Kate Simon.) ~Useful vocabulary: *des pièces* (coins); *d'argent* (money); *billets* (banknotes); *chèques de voyages* (traveler's checks).

Movies
Plan a meal from one or more of the French cookbooks mentioned in the *"Saveurs Français" bibliothèque* and invite some friends and family over for dinner and a movie. Some suggestions: *Rendezvous in Paris, An American in Paris, Celestial Clockwork, Le Ballon Rouge, Hôtel du Nord, Funny Face, French Kiss, Delicatessen, Window to Paris, Les Enfants du Paradis, À Bout de Souffle,* and *Paris Blues.*

Museums and Monuments
~Remember that most are closed on *either* Monday or Tuesday. Be sure to check in advance to avoid disappointment. ~*La Carte* is a pass that offers unlimited entry to museums and monuments in and around Paris, including the Louvre, the Musée d'Orsay, l'Institut du Monde Arabe, Musée Carnavalet, Musée Conde—Château de Chantilly, Château de Fontainebleau, Basilique Saint-Denis, and the Musée de la Renaissance—Château d'Ecouen. *La Carte* covers your admission fee and allows you to go straight to the head of any lines without waiting; you can also revisit any of the museums or monuments as often as you want. A one-day pass is $20, two-day is $40, and five-day is $60, and they can be ordered through Marketing Challenges (10 East Twenty-first Street, New York, New York 10010; 212-529-9069 / fax: 212-529-4838; www.ticketsto.com). I think I might become a victim of Stendhal syndrome if I visited that many museums to make the pass pay for itself, but if convenience is important to you, then the price doesn't matter.

Packing

Most people, whether they travel for business or pleasure, view packing as stressful. It doesn't have to be, and a great book filled with excellent suggestions and tips is *Fodor's How to Pack: Experts Share Their Secrets* (Laurel Cardone, Fodor's Travel Publications, 1997). You might think it silly to consult a book on how to pack a suitcase, but this is eminently practical and worthwhile. Cardone is a travel journalist who's on the road a lot, and she meets a lot of fellow travelers with plenty of packing wisdom to share. How to buy luggage, how to fill almost any suitcase, nearly crease-free folding, the right wardrobe for the right trip, and how to pack for the way back home are all thoroughly covered.

~Some pointers that work for me include selecting clothing that isn't prone to wrinkling, such as cotton and wool knits. When I *am* concerned about limiting wrinkles, I lay out a large, plastic dry-cleaning bag, place the garment on top of it, place *another* bag on top of that, and fold the item up between the two bags—the key here is that the plastic must be layered in with the clothing, otherwise it doesn't really work. ~If I'm packing items with buttons, I button them up before I fold them—the same with zippers and snaps. ~If I'm carrying a bag with more than one separate compartment, I use one for shoes; otherwise, I put shoes at the bottom (or back) of the bag opposite the handle so they'll remain there while I'm carrying the bag. ~Transfer shampoo and lotions to plastic, travel-size bottles, which can be purchased at pharmacies—and then put these inside a Ziploc bag to prevent leaks. ~Don't skimp on underwear—it's lightweight, takes up next to no room in your bag, and it's never a mistake to have more than you think you need. ~Belts can either be rolled up and stuffed into shoes or fastened together along the inside edge of your suitcase. ~Ties should be rolled, not folded, and also stuffed into shoes or pockets.

~Some handy things to bring along that are often overlooked: a pocket flashlight, for looking into ill-lit corners of old buildings, reading in bed at night (the lights are often not bright enough), or, if you're staying at a hotel where the bathroom is down the hall, for navigating the dark hallways at night (the light is usually on a timer and always runs out before you've made it to either end of the hallway); binoculars, for looking up at architectural details; small travel umbrella; penknife/corkscrew (although it would be far more fun to purchase a new one, made by Lagouile—pronounced *lie-gyole*—that you'll have forever; many of the shops along the rue de Rivoli sell them, or you can view the best selection in the city at the Boutique Lagouile: 1 place Saint-Opportune, 1st; these beautiful knives also make perfect gifts); if I'm camping, plastic shoes—referred to in the U.S. as jellies, which the French have been wearing on the rocky beaches of Nice for years and years—for campground showers; an empty, lightweight duffel bag, which I fold up and pack and then use as a carry-on bag for gifts and breakable items on the way home; copies of any current prescriptions in case I need to have a medicine refilled; and photocopies of my passport and airline tickets (which should also be left with someone at home).

Passports

For last-minute crises, it *is* possible to obtain a new passport, renew an old one, or get necessary visas (not required for France). Two companies that can meet the challenge: Travisa (2122 P Street, NW, Washington, D.C. 20037; 800-222-2589) and Express Visa Service (353 Lexington Avenue, Suite 1200, New York, New York 10016; 212-679-5650 / fax: 212-679-4691).

Periodicals

Following are some newsletters and magazines not available at newsstands that you may want to consider subscribing to in advance of your trip—or upon your return if you decide you want to keep up with goings-on in France:

The Art of Eating: One of the best publications ever, of any kind—see the *"À Table" bibliothèque* for more details and my enthusiastic endorsement. Back issues pertaining to various aspects of French food include no. 27 ("The Goat Is the Cow of the Poor—Provençal Farm Cheeses, Open-Air Markets"); no. 30 ("Red Wine Vinegar of Orleans"); no. 32 ("Three Wines of the Loire—Bourgueil, Vouvray, and Sancerre"); no. 36 ("Dark Chocolate and the Best French Chocolatiers"); no. 37 ("Munster Cheese, Dry Muscat Wine, Choucroute, and Other Happinesses in the Haut-Rhin of Alsace"); no. 40 ("In the Region of Cognac"); no. 43 ("The Caves of Roquefórt"); no. 44 ("Two Strong, Sweet Wines of Mediterranean France"); no. 48 ("Champagne"); and nos. 45 and 46, entitled "Paris (or What Is French Food?)," parts I and II, which are described in the *"À Table" bibliothèque.* Back issues are $9 each or $7.50 each for any four or more. To order on-line, open www.artofeating.com or write to Box 242, Peacham, Vermont 05862.

FRANCE Magazine: this fine quarterly magazine is possibly the most eagerly awaited item in my mailbox. It's published by La Maison Française and is only available by subscription in the U.S. The collection of feature articles in each issue is timely, fascinating, and diverse. There is no fee to subscribe, but all requests must be made in writing to 4101 Reservoir Road, N.W., Washington, DC, 20007-2182. For more information: 202-944-6069 / FAX: 202-944-6072.

France Today: An oversize bimonthly jammed with lots of articles, book and music reviews, trends, and travel tips and stories. One of my favorite columns is "What the French Are Obsessing About," and the classifieds alone are worth reading for the rental listings. Published by France Press, 1051 Divisadero, San Francisco, California 94115; 415-921-5100 / fax: 415-921-0213; www.francepress.com.

France-USA Contacts (FUSAC): More of a directory than a periodical, this is the bible for anglophones who are planning to live, work, or study in France—but it's also incredibly useful for shorter-term visitors. *FUSAC* contains job and housing listings, classified ads for things to buy and sell, services, holiday travel information, apartment rentals, etc. Now in its eleventh year, *FUSAC* is published in France, in English and French, and subscribers choose either first-class ($10) or third-class ($7) postage. Contact *FUSAC* at P.O. Box 115, Cooper Station, New York, New York 10276; 212-929-2929.

Journal Français: For those who read French—or want to improve their French—this is perhaps the best and most pleasant way to feel connected with all that's happening in France. The *Journal* is a monthly covering all the topics of a daily newspaper—politics, features, business, travel, etc. Published by France Press, 1051 Divisadero, San Francisco, California 94115; 415-921-5100 / fax: 415-921-0213; www.francepress.com. Subscribers can also read the *Journal* on-line: www.journalfrancais.com.

La Belle France: Until I began my subscription, I was rather put off by the subtitle, "The Sophisticated Guide to France." But this monthly, eight-page newsletter (with holes for a three-ring binder) is not stuffy and always includes some useful tips. Hotels and restaurants are critically reviewed at length with a rating system. Published by Travel Guide Publications, P.O. Box 3485, Charlottesville, Virginia 22903-0485; 800-225-7825 / fax: 804-977-4885; E-mail: labelle@golftravelguide.com.

Paris Notes: "The Newsletter for People Who Love Paris" is the motto of this monthly, eight-page missive, which features a wide variety of interesting articles—more in the style of a magazine than a daily newspaper. My only complaint is, I wish it were longer! Subscribers are informed of a secret password each month, allowing them to peruse back issues on-line. Editorial office: P.O. Box 3668, Manhattan Beach, California 90266; subscription services: P.O. Box 15818, N. Hollywood, California 91615; www.parisnotes.com.

Photography

I would rather have one great photo of a place than a dozen mediocre shots, so I like to page through photography books for ideas and suggestions on maximizing my picture-taking efforts. Some books I've particularly enjoyed include *The Traveler's Eye: A Guide to Still and Video Travel Photography* (Lisl Dennis, Clarkson Potter, 1996). Dennis, who began her career in photography at the *Boston Globe,* writes the "Traveler's Eye" column for *Outdoor Photographer.* I like her sensitive approach to travel photography and find her images and suggestions in this book inspiring. After chapters covering such topics as travel photojournalism, shooting special events, and landscape photography, she provides an especially useful chapter on technical considerations, with advice on equipment, film, packing, the ethics of tipping, and outsmarting airport X-ray machines.

Focus on Travel: Photographing Memorable Pictures of Journeys to New Places (text by Anne Millman and Allen Rokach, photographs by Allen Rokach, Abbeville

Press, 1992). More of a tome than *The Traveler's Eye,* although this doesn't cover video cameras. The authors offer much more information on lenses, filters, films, and accessories, and there are separate chapters on photographing architecture, shooting subjects in action, and taking pictures in a variety of weather conditions. The appendix covers selecting and preparing your photos after the trip, fill-in flash guidelines, color correction chart, and a page-by-page reference to all the photos in the book.

Kodak Guide to Shooting Great Travel Pictures: How to Take Travel Pictures Like a Pro (Jeff Wignall, Fodor's Travel Publications, 1995). Unlike the books above, which should be consulted before you go, this is a handy, small paperback good for bringing along as a reference. Six chapters present specific photographic challenges—such as city vistas, stained-glass windows, close-ups of faces, mountain scenery, motion, lights at night, and taking pictures through frames—and each is dealt with in one page with accompanying photos. It's important to note that this guide is meant for experienced *and* point-and-shoot photographers, and many of the images featured in the book are from the Eastman Kodak archives, a great number of which were taken by amateurs. The final chapter is devoted to creating a travel journal.

R

Rungis (Paris's Wholesale Food Market)

A visit to the vast food market may be of interest to visitors who are serious foodies. Rungis's predecessor was the Les Halles market—referred to as the "belly of Paris" by Émile Zola in *Le Ventre de Paris*—which was a fixture in the city for some nine hundred years until the seventies, when it was razed for a far less interesting shopping complex. Rungis (located outside Paris near the Orly airport) may not have the history of Les Halles, but it *is* amazing. However, visitors are only able to see the complex on an official tour. American expatriate Stephanie Curtis arranges tours for from two to one hundred guests on Tuesdays, Thursdays, and Fridays. Tours begin at 5 A.M. and return to Paris at around 11 A.M. The fee is 490 FF (about $82) per person, which includes breakfast, market entry, uniforms, and transportation. Advance reservations are required: 10 rue de Richelieu, 75001; 01.40.15.04.57 / fax: 01.40.15.04.58. Or, if you happen to be with a group of fifteen or more, you can arrange for a visit with Société Semmaris, the company that operates the market. The fee is about $10 per person, but doesn't include transportation. Phone: 01.41.80.80.82.

S

Single Travelers

(As in those traveling alone, not necessarily looking for romance.) Singles might be interested in a great book, *Traveling Solo: Advice and Ideas for More Than 250*

Great Vacations (Eleanor Berman, Globe Pequot Press, 1997). Berman offers the names of tour operators for different age groups and different types of trips and asks all the right questions in determining if a proposed vacation is right for you. ~Female *and* male solo travelers should beware of revealing too many personal details about their travels. If you admit that you're traveling for an indefinite period, for example, the perception is that you are probably carrying a lot of money. I met an Australian man who had the bulk of his money stolen from a youth hostel safe, and he was certain it was taken by a fellow hosteler he had befriended (but who had disappeared by the time the discovery was made).

Stendhal Syndrome
Named for the sick, physical feeling that afflicted French novelist Stendhal after he visited Santa Croce in Florence, this syndrome is synonymous with being completely overwhelmed by your surroundings (my translation: seeing and doing way too much). Visitors to Paris who arrive with too long a list of *les incontournables* (must-sees) are prime candidates for the syndrome. My advice: organize your days, factor in how long it takes to get from place to place, and see what you want. There will be no quiz.

Storage
Regrettably, France (and Paris in particular) is occasionally the scene of terrorist attacks, and as a security measure, the storage facilities at the airports close during these times of unrest. If you plan on traveling around France or beyond for extended periods (say, a month or longer) and want to store some baggage or other belongings, you should first investigate the storage possibilities at Paris's train stations. A locker at one of the stations may prove to be the ideal location as you might be traveling by train anyway. A private company I learned about from a friend is Home Box, which I later found listed in the *International Yellow Pages: Paris Edition* (Mariposa Press, 1999). Home Box has two locations: 8 place Boulnois, 17th (01.44.40.23.50) and 29 boulevard Ney, 18th (01.44.65.05.05; this facility is near the Porte de Clignancourt metro, so you could take advantage of its proximity to the flea market and store any purchases you make on the same day). The *Yellow Pages* feature five other storage options, as well as four pages of options for international packing and shipping and mailing services.

Studying in France
There are dozens and dozens of American colleges and universities that sponsor study abroad programs in Paris. I am partial to those that have had a long-established presence there—my own experience was with Hollins University (formerly Hollins College), which founded its school in 1955. Some other schools that

were among the first to offer programs in Paris include Columbia University, Hamilton College, Middlebury College, and Sweet Briar College. My advice is to select a program that allows you to stay a year, or even longer, and change your major if you have to—you won't regret it! Alternatively, investigate attending a French college or university. The French Ministry of Foreign Affairs provides a complete list of public universities, by location, at its Web site, www.education. gouv.fr/sup/univ.htm. (I found this by looking at the Web site of the French embassy, www.info-france-use.org, which provides information on tuition, fees, etc.) Remember that studying in France isn't limited to language (courses are also offered in the fine arts, photography, painting, business, literature, etc.) or age (plenty of programs welcome adults, and plenty of adults attend).

The guide to get is the *Directory of French Schools and Universities* by Michael Giammarella (EMI International, P.O. Box 640713, Oakland Gardens, New York 11364-0713; 718-631-0096 / fax: 718-631-0316). The guide, $19, plus $3 for first-class shipping, details a wide variety of programs—not just language—at over forty schools in France, about a dozen of those in Paris. Giammarella also handles the bookings for the programs and also publishes directories for Spain, Italy, and England. ~A good source for both French- and American-sponsored abroad programs, in Paris and the rest of France, is the annual travel/study guide of *France Today*. This usually appears in February or March and is inserted into issues of *France Today* and the *Journal Français*. The guide can also be purchased separately ($5.50 plus postage) by fax (415-921-0213) or E-mail (fpress@francepress.com). ~Remember, too, that the Maison de la France offices have numerous brochures on language and cultural programs in France.

T

Talk
As in, don't talk loudly—in English *or* in French. It's simply not the custom. Parisians love to debate (sometimes at the expense of customers who are standing in a long line in a shop), but they rarely shout. If you're walking around or eating in a restaurant and you hear loud voices, they will invariably be American. In the U.S. we may operate on the theory that the squeaky wheel gets the grease, but it doesn't fly in France. Parisians converse softly, and so should you.

Telephones
Remember that France is six hours ahead of eastern standard time, seven ahead of central time, eight ahead of mountain time, and nine hours ahead of Pacific standard time. To call France from the U.S., dial 011 + 33 + nine-digit number (011 = the overseas line, 33 = country code for France, and the nine-digit number includes the appropriate city code). Paris and the Île-de-France are in the telephone zone

identified as 01, so all Paris numbers begin with 01. However, when calling Paris from the U.S. *do not dial the initial 0.* If you're dialing a number within Paris or France, you must include the 0. All phone numbers in this book include the 0. To call the U.S. from France, dial 00 + 1 + area code + number. Within France, to reach a French operator, dial 13. To reach French directory assistance, dial 12. To reach an English-speaking operator, dial 1933.

~Remember that almost all public phones in France no longer accept a *jeton* (token). *La télécarte* (phone card) is now the way of the future and is available in two types: *télécarte* (for making calls in France in either 50 or 120 units) and *télécarte international* (for making calls abroad and locally, in 60 or 120 units). *Télécartes* can be purchased in *tabacs*, post offices, and metro stations; or, order one before you go from Marketing Challenges (10 East Twenty-first Street, New York, New York 10010; 212-529-9069 / fax: 212-529-4838; www.ticketsto.com). Note that you can also use *la télécarte* to connect with an AT&T operator. ~Useful vocabulary: *annuaire* (telephone directory); *un coup de téléphone* (a telephone call); *ne quittez pas* (hold on, don't hang up).

Theft

Whether of the pickpocket variety or something more serious, theft can happen anywhere, in the swankiest neighborhoods, on the metro, in a park, on a street corner. It bears repeating not to wear a waist pack, which is nothing but a neon magnet for thieves. I read about a lot of incidences that could so easily have been avoided. In 1998, I read a lengthy piece in the travel section of the *Philadelphia Inquirer* about a husband and wife traveling in France who had a pouch with all their valuables in it stolen. What made this story remarkable was that they were shocked the pouch was stolen. *I* was shocked reading their tale because they seemed to think it was a good idea to *strap their pouch under the driver's seat of their rental car.* This couple had apparently traveled all over Europe and North America every year for twelve years, so they weren't exactly novices. I think it's a miracle, however, that they hadn't been robbed earlier.

~Rental cars are easily identified by their license plates and other markings that may not be so obvious to you and me but signify pay dirt to thieves. Do not leave anything, anything at all, in the car, even if you're parking it in a secure garage. My husband and I strictly follow one rule when we rent a car, which is that we never even put items in the trunk unless we're immediately getting in the car and driving away, as anyone watching us will then know there's something of value in the trunk. Also, hatchback cars are good to rent because you can back into spots against walls, making it impossible to open the trunk.

~Do not leave your passport, money, credit cards, important documents, or expensive camera equipment in your room (yes, American passports are still very much a hot commodity, and French law requires its citizens and visitors to provide identification if asked). The hotel safe? If the letters I read are any indication, hotel safes—whether in your room or in the main office—are only slightly more reliable than leaving your belongings out in plain view. Sometimes I hear that valuable jewelry was taken from a hotel safe, which I find baffling as there really is only one safe place for valuable jewelry: your home. No occasion, meeting, or celebration, no matter how important or festive, requires bringing valuable jewelry. *Leave it at home.* I also find it offensive to display such wealth.

~Pickpockets employ a number of tactics on unwary travelers. Even if you travel often, live in a big city, and think you're savvy, professional thieves can usually pick you out immediately (and they'll also identify you as American if you're wearing the trademark sneakers and fanny pack). Beware the breast-feeding mother who begs you for money (while her other children surround you looking for a way into your pockets), the arguing couple who make a scene (while their accomplices work the crowd of onlookers), the tap on your shoulder at the baggage security checkpoint (when you turn around, someone's made off with your bags after they've passed through the X-ray machine) . . . anything at all that looks or feels like a setup. For a look at some common tricks, you might want to see *Traveler Beware!*—a video directed by a seventeen-year undercover cop, Kevin Coffey. This is a real eye-opening program with all the scams used to target business and holiday travelers. Coffey was founder of the Airport Crimes Detail and investigated literally thousands of crimes against tourists. He's been a guest on *Oprah* and *20/20* and has been featured in *The Wall Street Journal* and *USA Today*. The seventy-minute cassette is available from Penton Overseas (800-748-5804; E-mail: info@pentonoverseas.com) and is $14.95.

~If, despite your best efforts, your valuables are stolen, go to the local police. You'll have to fill out an official police report, but this is what helps later when you need to prove you were really robbed. Also, reporting thefts to the police alerts them to a persistent problem. You need to call your credit card companies (which is why you have written down these numbers in a separate place), make a trip to the American Express office if you've purchased traveler's checks, and go to the U.S. embassy to replace your passport.

Tipping

Tipping in France is not the mystery some people perceive it to be. At most restaurants, cafés, and other types of eateries, the tip—known as *service compris*—is included in the total. You'll see this amount (usually about 15 percent) as a line item on your receipt. It is common to round up the bill, leaving anywhere from one franc to twenty; however, you are not obligated to do so. If you stand at the counter in a café, a tip is not typically included in the bill, so you should leave some change. If you're at a bar and end up in a deep conversation about vintages or fine spirits with the bartender, you might want to leave an extra ten francs. If you're in a three-star restaurant and the sommelier has chosen a special wine for you, it's considered appropriate to give him or her 10 percent of the price of the bottle. If you receive exceptional service at any establishment, or you want to return and be remembered, you should of course feel comfortable leaving a larger tip. Other tipping guidelines: taxis—10 percent; WC attendants—one franc; cloakroom attendants—five francs; tour guides—five francs; porters—five francs per bag; hotel doormen who call you a cab—ten francs; parking attendants who fetch your car—ten francs; concierges who obtain reservations or tickets—twenty-five to fifty francs; chambermaids—ten francs per night; hairdressers—10 percent; theater ushers—two francs; movie ushers—one franc. ~Be prepared to tip by putting some small change in your pocket *in advance,* before you arrive at the hotel, for example, or before you go to the theater.

Tourist (as in, being one)

Whether you travel often for business or are making a trip for the first time, let's face it: we're all tourists, and there's nothing shameful about that. I think the reason we all loathe the word *tourist* is that it conjures up an image of an obnoxious yet provincial person who only cares to see the obvious (and misses the significance of even that). Yes, it's true that you feel a real part of *la vie quotidienne* when you blend in and are mistaken for a native; but since that's not likely to happen unless you live there, it's far better to just get on with it and have a good time. I made the mistake of ignoring this good sense when I was in Paris with my husband for the first time. I was anxious to show him the city, and I was positively obsessed with not being a tourist. So, I refused his requests to inquire what was inside the pastries at the *pâtisserie* (generally, Parisians don't have to ask); how to find a particular *rue* (preferring instead to figure it out myself with my *Plan de Paris*); or to ask exactly what brand of beer he would receive if he ordered a *demi-blonde* (it refers to a light, draft beer, but I've never seen anyone ask about the brand). To my great disappointment he wasn't having a good time and didn't take an interest in anything I suggested. We only stayed a week, and he wasn't at all unhappy to be leaving. Lesson learned. (More recently, he has decided that Paris is a great city after all, but as a precaution he insists that our friend Luc be there at the same time.)

Tourist Office (Maison de la France in the U.S., Office du Tourisme or Syndicat d'Initiative in France)

I cannot stress enough how helpful it is to contact the French Government Tourist Office as soon as you learn you're going to France. Think of it as the ultimate resource: all the information you need is there, or the staff will know how to direct you elsewhere. At the New York office, I have never stumped anyone with my questions or requests, and I think readers have observed that I ask a lot of questions about a lot of little details. A word of advice for dealing with tourist offices in general: it is not helpful to say you're going to Paris and would like "some information." Allow the staff to help you by providing as much information about your visit as you can: Is it your first trip? Do you only need information about hotels? The offices are stocked with mountains of material, but unless you ask for something specific, it will not automatically all be given to you. Sometimes I am amazed at what's available, at no charge—but you have to ask.

I recently learned that there is a Meetings & Incentives Department within Maison de la France, which helps companies organize conferences, seminars, conventions, exhibitions, and product launches in France. Some particularly noteworthy booklets available at Maison offices are *France Discovery Guide,* which is published annually and includes articles about all parts of France by an impressive roster of journalists (some of whom are featured in this book); *Paris Mode d'Emploi—User's Guide,* which is as good as or better than a full-length guidebook and includes an extraordinary amount of practical information; *The Good Value Guide to France,* offering lots of tips to make a visit to Paris and France more affordable; *Walks Through Paris,* a foldout brochure detailing four walks around the city; *Gay Friendly France: Liberté, Egalité, Diversité,* a brochure detailing a variety of destinations in France with practical information tailored to gay and lesbian travelers; and the more specialized *Protestant Paris: Yesterday and Today,* a foldout brochure.

There are three tourist offices in the States: 444 Madison Avenue, New York, New York 10022; 212-838-7800 / fax: 212-838-7855; E-mail: info@francetourism .com; 676 North Michigan Avenue, Chicago, Illinois 60611; 312-751-7800 / fax: 312-337-6339; E-mail: fgto@mcs.net; 9454 Wilshire Boulevard, Beverly Hills, California 90212; 310-271-6665 / fax: 310-276-2835; E-mail: fgto@gte.net. Travelers can also call the France On Call Hotline, 410-286-8310, or visit the Web site www .francetourism.com.

Office du Tourisme or *Syndicat d'Initiative:* There doesn't seem to be much difference between these two types of offices, but *offices du tourisme* appear solely for tourists while *syndicats d'initiative* are often more like general chambers of commerce. The main tourist office in Paris is at 127 avenue des Champs-Élysées, 8th; 01.49.52.53.54 / fax: 01.49.52.53.00; metro: Charles de Gaulle–Étoile, George V; Web site: www.paris-touristoffice.com. In high season the office is open daily from 9 A.M.–8 P.M. (except May 1). Low-season hours are Monday–Saturday, 9 A.M.–8 P.M. and Sundays and holidays from 11 A.M.–6 P.M. Branch offices are located in the Gare de Lyon and the Eiffel Tower but are open only from May to September.

Tours
For tours of Paris in English, contact Paris Walking Tours (01.48.09.21.40 / fax: 01.42.43.75.51), organized by Peter and Oriel Caine. They offer walks through

numerous neighborhoods and monuments as well as farther afield to Versailles, Malmaison, and Vaux-le-Vicomte. Reservations are not mandatory, and their walks are listed in *Pariscope*. A list of full-service tour companies would fill a separate book, and it is not my intent to promote only one company or one type of trip. Following are some companies that have appealed to me and offer an authentic experience:

Alternative Travel Group (69–71 Banbury Road, Oxford, OX2 6PE, England; 011.44.1865.315678 / fax: 011.44.1865.315697; info@alternative-travel.co.uk). "The best way to see a country is on foot" is the ATG motto. Recent trips in France did not include walks around Paris, but I am so impressed with this group's philosophy and lengthy catalog that I include it here for those planning on traveling farther afield.

Cross-Culture: Foreign Travel Programs Designed for Travelers Rather Than Tourists (52 High Point Drive, Amherst, Massachusetts 01002; 413-256-6303 / fax: 413-253-2303; xculture@javanet.com; www.javanet.com). Its trips to France include Paris with excursions to Normandy and the Loire Valley; the food and wine of Burgundy; and the south of France.

France in Your Glass (814 Thirty-fifth Avenue, Seattle, Washington 98122; 800-578-0903 / fax: 800-578-7069; info@inyourglass.com; www.inyourglass.com). Offers exceptional wine and food vacations in the major wine regions of France, including Champagne, Burgundy, and the Beaujolais.

The French Experience (370 Lexington Avenue, New York, New York 10017; 212-986-1115 / fax: 212-986-3808; www.frenchexperience.com). Though it offers some guided tours, The French Experience is not technically a tour operator. However, it's a worthy group to know of as it arranges special packages, self-drive tours, hotels and apartments in Paris and other regions of France, car rentals, *gîte* rentals, rail passes, etc.

Friends of French Art (100 Vanderlip Drive, Rancho Palos Verdes, California 90275; 310-377-4444 / fax: 310-377-4584). FoFA—whose motto is "art de vivre for art conservation"—is an exceptional organization as the annual trips it plans each year raise money to restore public works of art in France. In its twenty-plus years, the number of works it has helped to restore is enormous, but includes the Brunetti staircase in the Musée Carnavalet; five paintings in the Musée Camondo; a variety of works in the châteaux of Chantilly, Blois, Malmaison, Ephrussi de Rothschild, and Chaalis; and the Renoir balcony at Maison Fournaise in Châtou. Each trip offers participants the opportunity to go behind the scenes at sites and monuments and to meet the owners of private châteaux.

The Wayfarers (172 Bellevue Avenue, Newport, Rhode Island 02840; 401-849-5087 and 800-249-4620 / fax: 401-849-5878; www.thewayfarers.com). Offers walking vacations in France and six other countries.

~If you do select a tour operator, ask a lot of questions so you get what you expect. For starters, ask if the operator employs its own staff or if it contracts with another company to run its trips. Remember, however, that standards differ around the world, and operators don't have control over every detail. For example, many beautiful, old châteaux and inns do not have screens in the windows, and many first-class hotels don't have air-conditioning. The price you pay for accommodations may not be the same as the posted rates, but you have to accept that you're paying for the convenience of someone else booking your trip. Tour operators also reserve the right to change itineraries, thus changing modes of transportation as well as hotels. If you have special needs, talk about them with the company in advance.

Trains (Société Nationale des Chemins de Fer Français [SNCF])

Paris has six train stations for travel to other parts of France and beyond, and each station is sensibly located to serve particular directions, as follows: Gare du Nord (the north, including the English Channel—known as La Manche—ports, Belgium, Holland, and Scandinavia); Gare de l'Est (the east, including Nancy, Strasbourg, Germany, Eastern Europe, Moscow); Gare d'Austerlitz (the southwest, including Bordeaux, Toulouse, Spain, Portugal, Orléans, Tours, Poitiers, Angoulême); Gare St.-Lazare (Normandy and Dieppe); Gare Montparnasse (the western part of France, including Bretagne); Gare de Lyon (the southeastern part of France, Switzerland, Italy, Greece).

In addition to rail passes, SNCF offers a surprising number of reduced-fare options—be sure to inquire as it's likely one will apply to you. Discounts are offered for seniors (sixty-plus, known as *troisième age;* two types of tickets are *carte vermeil quatre temps*—good for four trips—and the *carte vermeil plein temps*—good for unlimited travel), children twelve to twenty-five years old, and children under four, plus traveling with a child (one or more) qualifies for a discount. There is even a *découverte* discount of 25 percent given to two people traveling together on a round-trip journey, *and* I've read that a discount is offered for a certain number of miles traveled. Plus, days and times of travel are broken down into color-coded price categories: *jour bleu, jour blanc,* and *jour rouge*. And, of course, discounts are offered for traveling pets. It's also possible to travel with a car on certain lines.

Remember that any ticket imprinted with the words *à composter* must be validated before you board the train. This is done by inserting the ticket in one of the orange machines at the entrance to the platforms, and your ticket will either be stamped with the date or punched with a hole. If you don't validate, you may be fined once on board. As with train travel elsewhere, if you purchase your ticket on board, you'll pay a surcharge. ~Useful vocabulary: *aller simple* (one-way ticket); *aller-retour* (round-trip); *quai* (platform); *voie* (track; note that *quai* and *voie* are sometimes used interchangeably as it's possible to have two tracks on either side of a platform); *consigne des bagages* (left-luggage locker); *guichet* (ticket office or window); *horaire* (timetable).

A good book for planning train trips outside of Paris is *France by Train: Hundreds of Great Trips and All the Sights Along the Way* (Simon Vickers, Fodor's Travel Publications, 1994). This is not a book of train schedules, so its 1994 publication is not a deterrent—even if the book were brand-new, train arrivals and departures would still have to be confirmed. The SNCF network—like train networks in most other European countries—is quite extensive, and there are few corners of France one can't get to by train. For each destination, Vickers provides information about the number of trains per day, the duration of the trip (not likely to have changed drastically), brief descriptions of noteworthy sites to see, and a "Practicalities" section that includes specifics on the tourist office, railway station, buses, hiking possibilities, markets, festivals, hotels, and restaurants. The Paris section details all six of the city's train stations, and again, even though hours and rates may have changed, it is enough to know that such services as currency exchange, left-luggage lockers, showers, brasserie, restaurant, waiting room, and post office are available.

Travel Insurance

I have never purchased travel insurance because I have never determined that I need it, but it's worth considering if you think the risks to you are greater without it. Ask yourself what it would cost if you needed to cancel or interrupt your trip, and how expensive it would be to replace any stolen possessions. If you have a medical condition or if a relative is ill, insurance might be a wise investment. First, check to see if your existing health or homeowner's policies offer some protection. If you decide you need to purchase additional insurance, read all the fine print and make sure you understand it; compare deductibles; ask how your provider defines "preexisting condition" and inquire if there are situations in which it would be waived; and check to see if the ceiling on medical expenses is adequate for your needs.

V

VAT (Value Added Tax)

The VAT is known as *détaxe* in French. Visitors to France (except from EEC member countries) are entitled to receive a reimbursement of VAT paid. I have an entire file with conflicting information about the *détaxe,* so even if you meet the eligibility requirements, be prepared for a potentially confusing procedure. The best explanation I've read about the VAT is in Maribeth Clemente's great book *The Riches of France* (St. Martin's Press, 1997). She makes a good case for persevering;

however, she doesn't mention many of the pitfalls I've read about elsewhere. Frankly, I think the procedure is a lot of bother unless visitors are making a significant purchase, and I think it would be worth asking the retailer simply to not charge any tax. But for those who are determined, you must produce your passport at the time of the purchase; spend at least twelve hundred francs at one store (but retailers are not required to participate in the program nor to match the dollar amount, so ask first); and produce receipts *and* merchandise for inspection at customs. Note that some shops don't have the necessary forms, and that the paperwork must be stamped by customs officials *before* you enter the U.S. Problems seem to arise when the customs desk is closed, although if you'll be in any other country before you return to the States, a customs stamp from that country is also valid (if the officials are willing to validate your forms). Also, it seems customs officials are rather lax at some borders, vigilant at others.

~The VAT form is known as a *bordereau de détaxe*. ~For a 20 percent fee, Global Refund will handle your refund through the Europe Tax-Free Shopping (ETS) network; once your forms are stamped, you can receive a refund—in cash, check (in francs), or charge card credit—right away at an ETS counter (or you can mail the forms from home). ~If you have attempted to have your forms validated in France and were thwarted in your efforts, or if it has been more than three months since you applied for a refund, contact Global Refund (707 Summer Street, Stamford, Connecticut 06901; 800-566-9828 / fax: 203-674-8709; www.taxfree.se).

W

Weather

Paris is perhaps most beautiful in the fall (many places in the world are at that time of year), but each season offers its own delights. Picking the "perfect" time of year is subjective; when it's rainy and cold, you don't have the pleasure of picnicking outdoors, but prices drop and you'll have little trouble securing reservations at hotels and restaurants. Go when you have the opportunity and that will be your experience, your Paris. It's true that peak season means higher prices and more people, but if you want to be in Paris for Bastille Day, then the cost and the crowds don't matter. (I've visited Provence four times, only once in the summer, which was the best trip of all because that's when the lavender is in bloom. I will never again go off-season to Provence!)

If you're a weather maven, you'll love *Fodor's World Weather Guide* (E. A. Pierce and C. G. Smith, 1998; published in 1998 in Great Britain as *The Hutchinson World Weather Guide, New Edition* by Helicon Publishing, Oxford). As frequent business or pleasure travelers know, average daily temperatures are only a small part of what you need to know about the weather. It is not helpful learning that the average monthly temperature in Paris in April is sixty degrees without also knowing that the average number of rainy days is thirteen. (Besides, I can verify that "April in Paris" is often a myth; it rained and rained and rained in April the year I lived in Paris, and it even snowed on May 2, the day my parents came to visit.) This is not to say, of course, that there aren't gloriously beautiful April days, but to assume you'll be having a plethora of *déjeuners sur l'herbe* under blue skies would be a mistake. This guide features weather specifics for over two hundred countries and territories and also includes a map of the world's climate regions; humidity and windchill charts; a centigrade and Fahrenheit conversion table; rainfall conversion table; and a bibliography pointing interested readers to other sources.

Web Sites

I don't find a single one of the following Web sites better than the tourist office or the appropriate book, but a few offer some good features:

www.allthingsfrench.com—This bilingual site allows browsers to select products (such as Health & Beauty, Home & Gifts, *Les Enfants,* Foods, *Les Vacances,* and *Les Films*) or departments such as *Améliorez Votre Français* (Improve Your French), which I found to be the best feature: quick translations for everyday situations are offered, and each month a different situation is highlighted. You are then given basic verbs, expressions, words, statements, and questions that are useful in the given situation.

www.bparis.com—Some of the categories to search here include arts and entertainment, food and wine, life in France, Parisian hotels, personalities, travel tips, and French lessons, my favorite feature. There are also full-length articles, some of which I found particularly helpful.

www.enjoyfrance.com—Search here for a selection of accommodations, including hotels, B&Bs, and guest houses. Regional Web sites are also provided, which is useful for contacting smaller tourist offices.

www.france.com/travel/hotels—This site is operated by the French Hotel Reservation Center and offers listings for over four thousand hotels all over France. Users can select and book hotels free of charge. Of more interest to me is the rental-car feature, which claims to offer the best available rates and seems worth investigating.

www.info-france-usa.org—The Web site of the French embassy, this has eight divisions: France on the Internet; News and Magazine; Just for Kids; *Tapis Rouge;* France and America; Profile of France; Trade and Technology; and Culture, Language Study, and Travel. Links can be made to French government ministries, regions, cities, media, French consulates, French corporations in the U.S., Alliances Françaises, etc.

www.locaflat.com—Two thousand authentic hotels and guest houses in France—including apartment rentals in Paris—are offered at this site, a member of the tourism office and Congress of Paris. My favorite magazine, *Maisons Côté-Sud,* shares this site, I suppose to offer the numerous rental properties featured in each issue. Clicking on "Useful Links" turns up selections like bike rental, limousine rental, Cordon Bleu cooking classes, getting around town, dining out, electronic directory of white and yellow pages for all of France, weather, etc.

www.musexpo.com—Find out what's showing at museums and galleries all over France, plus read reviews from *Le Monde*.

www.paris-tourisme.com—I found this to be pretty pedestrian, but clicking on "Paris for Kids" produced four sources for baby-sitting services, plus good suggestions for parks, gardens, zoos, and puppet shows.

Women Travelers

Whether a woman is traveling solo or not, lots of great advice is offered in *Travelers' Tales Gutsy Women: Travel Tips and Wisdom for the Road* (Marybeth Bond, Travelers' Tales, San Francisco, distributed by O'Reilly & Associates, 1996). This packable little book is filled with dozens and dozens of useful tips for women of all ages who want to travel or already travel a lot. Bond has traveled all over the world, much of it *toute seule,* and she shares a multitude of advice from her own journeys as well as that of other female travelers. Chapters address safety and security; health and hygiene; romance and unwelcome advances; money, bargaining, and tipping; traveling solo; mother-daughter travel; travel with children, etc.

~Also, the Women's Travel Club may be of interest. Founded by Phyllis Stoller, this organization plans numerous domestic and international trips a year and guarantees everyone a roommate. Its great list of travel safety tips was featured on NBC's *Today* as well as in *Travel & Leisure* (August 1999). Membership is $35 a year, and members receive a newsletter (800-480-4448; E-mail: womantrip@aol.com; www.womenstravelclub.com).

Y

Yellow Pages

Sometimes, you just need the yellow pages, and here they are: *International Yellow Pages, Paris Edition: Thousands of the Most Useful Addresses, Valuable Tips, and Expert Advice for the Vacation, Business or Student Traveler* (Betsy Andronikof, Laurie Blum, and Don Guest, Mariposa Press, Santa Fe, New Mexico, 1999) . . . and the pages really are yellow! As de rigueur as many books are, I would bet that this one will be used the most. At first glance, it might seem to be only for English speakers living in Paris, but it is incredibly useful even for first-time visitors. Absolutely everything, including apartment rental agencies, relocation companies, emergency towing and repair, stockbrokers, beauty salons, translators, notaries, employment agencies, child care services and baby-sitters, computer rentals and repairs, electronics, fitness clubs, insurance, international packing and shipping companies, medical services, animal doctors and hospitals, camera equipment, watch repair, religious affiliations, accountant and tax services, squash courts, cellular phone rentals, golf courses, twenty-four-hour services, utilities, and used compact discs is listed, and helpful hints are featured throughout.

How to Make the Most of Your Speaking Engagements

BY KAY ELDREDGE

∽

editor's note

Many more people speak English in France these days, and to the disappointment of the Académie Française, some American English words have crept into the language—some that haven't include best-seller *(succès de librairie),* data bank *(banque de données),* popcorn *(maïs soufflé),* and fast food *(restauration rapide).* Still, studying French in Paris is an experience of a lifetime. There are, after all, over sixty corners of the world—countries and territories—where French is spoken, and although not *everyone* in these regions uses the language, French is still widely understood.

Writer KAY ELDREDGE was a regular contributor to the former *European Travel & Life* and is coauthor of *East Hampton: A History and Guide* (Random House, 1985).

Those who've tried the various methods agree that the best way to learn French, or any language, is "on the pillow"—preferably with a lover who speaks no English. You have both incentive and exposure, so to speak, and it will also take a long time for any basic differences to surface and begin to spoil things.

Barring that approach, for whatever reasons, the next best way is to spend as much time as possible in France, consoled by the thought that even a lifetime will not be enough to master the language if you did not grow up there. A journalist friend of mine, a Dutch woman who has lived in France for over a decade and is fluent, once interviewed the aged widow of Pissarro, who afterwards complimented her, "You speak very well," she said, *"mais c'est pas français*—but it's not French."

So don't aim for perfection. What you're looking for is someplace on the spectrum between muddling through and being able to handle a philosophical or, more likely, a political discussion. All the experts say that to achieve real fluency you must immerse yourself totally in the language. You must arrange to be only with the French. You must read French, listen to French, speak French until you don't have to think of a word-by-word translation before you do it. You must forget your own language to the point that you are dreaming regularly in French. Dreaming in French! To be sure.

You can go to France and plunge in, solitary and fearless, or hire a private tutor, or you can start with a class. The two best-known language schools, Berlitz and Alliance Française, have branches all over the world, but what better place to start than Paris?

The biggest and oldest of French-language schools is the Alliance, which also happens to be far less expensive than most of the other possibilities. This is in part because they are offering what they almost regard as a public service, their duty being to spread the beauty and civilizing influence of the French language throughout the world. I'd sent for the brochure and preregistered from the U.S., but to be assigned to a class I had to appear at the school's main building on the boulevard Raspail on the morning I got off my transatlantic flight from New York. I answered the questions on the written exam through a jet-lag fog, then waited my turn with hundreds of others for a brief interview. I'd taken two years of French in high school and another in college and had spent stretches of time in France since then, but when my interviewer looked at my test paper, she merely drew a long, scornful diagonal through it with her newly sharpened pencil and put me in a second-level beginners' class.

It turned out to be all I could manage. It was conducted entirely in French and at a galloping pace. My fellow students included a couple of other Americans, four Italians, two Brazilian nuns, two Japanese, a Spaniard, a German, a Swiss, a Korean, a Chinese, a Filipino, an East Indian, two Mexicans, and a Turk. Our only common language, no matter how execrable, was French. Most of my classmates were in their twenties, and though some were fulfilling college requirements, many were learning French to further themselves—in publishing, medicine, teaching, business, or love. I was the oldest and the only one doing it for the satisfaction of knowing more French.

We met for four hours a day, five days a week, just around the corner from the main Alliance building, on the rue de Fleurus, down the street from the house where Gertrude Stein held court for many years. From the beginning, our class seemed too big for anyone to get much practice in speaking. My goal was to improve my conversational skills, but I hadn't realized that the Alliance is very conservative in its methods. First come the basics: You learn the grammar and learn to read and write and understand what you hear. Only afterwards do you concentrate on learning to speak. Some say this is backwards, that French is easier to speak than to write, and you should start by listening and repeating what you hear. This, of course, is the way children learn, and my four-year-old son was being initiated in this method at the École Maternelle preschool. Teachers say that most foreign children spend their first three months simply listening, and then all at once, it seems, they are able to speak.

"There are two French languages, the written and the spoken," a French editor told me. "Many things that you can say are not correct if written that way. Written French is a very narrow path. If you step off, you are stuck in the mud. Even the French can't write it absolutely correctly." Even the choice of words must be exact. A cabaret singer I met said, "Classical written French is very beautiful, but it's a corset. It's very straitlaced, like the classic French gardens. Every word means just one thing. There's none of the suggestion, the evocation that you have in English."

Perhaps she was right. Each word may have only one meaning, but understanding what you hear can be a challenge, given the full-throttle delivery of many French. Our energetic instructor, Mme. Hélène Bordaz, believed in preparing us for reality, and during the first week, I could catch only about a quarter of what she was saying. I congratulated myself at the end of the three-week session when I was able to get nearly all of it.

She suggested we watch TV and go to the movies to help our comprehension, but for me, one of the best places to practice was at a playground. The imperatives called out by mothers to young children, the simple explanations, often repeated like instant replay, the basic vocabularies of eating and the temperature and the time and coming and going—all these gave me an exaggerated sense of being able to understand.

It's harder in the ebb and flow of adult conversation. "French is a very quick language," said my editor friend. "People understand what you're saying before you finish and are preparing their reply. Often they don't wait for you to finish. It's very different from German, for example, where you don't understand until the end of the sentence, because the verb is at the end."

We did get some practice in speaking, if not in holding our own. The first thing that came up was pronunciation. "It is impossible to speak French unless you make *une grande bouche,* a big mouth," said Mme. Bordaz.

She wanted us to enunciate instead of muttering self-consciously. She said Americans (but not the English) have a particular problem because they speak with the tongue held down and back from the teeth, making the sounds in the throat, while in French the tongue is pressing against the lower front teeth. This is the kind of thing that leads to confusion, as when one of the Americans explained that he'd met his girlfriend at the *guerre* (war) instead of at the *gare* (station).

There's also the issue of accent. As one Frenchman commented, "There's actually no such thing as a French race. They only know they're really French when they can criticize the accent of someone else speaking French."

Of course, it's not just a matter of pronunciation. There's also content. In French, for example, a question is never answered with a mere yes or no—that's simply not enough. It must be accompanied by a phrase. This same attenuation is part of most exchanges. In a practice dialogue in class one day, a young American was pretending to initiate a conversation with a French girl. He began with, "Where are you going?" followed immediately by, "Do you want to go out tonight?"

"Non, non, et non!" cried Mme. Bordaz. "That is too direct, like an American. You have to circle around or a French girl will close her mouth and walk away. You must *prends des gants,* put on some gloves, that is, pay attention to the conventions."

Then there are the technicalities. Using the verb *descendre,* "to go down," a classmate concocted the sentence, "I am going to go down to Paris." Mme. Bordaz smiled. "You will go to the hospital," she said. "You are saying you will fall into Paris from above. The only ones who can *descendre* to Paris are people arriving from the north of Paris."

And explaining the difference between the present and future tenses, she noted, "In France, *le train part,* 'the train leaves,' at eight o'clock. You can count on it. *Partira* means something will happen in the future. It implies the possibility that something will happen: 'the train *will* leave,' like in Italy."

This isn't the only difference between countries that crops up. When asked to tell what he did yesterday, one student said haltingly, struggling with the vocabulary, that he'd gone to a doctor to get a shot to protect him against a severe reaction to bee stings. "There are no bees in Paris," declared Mme. Bordaz. And both a German girl and an Italian man confessed they'd been taking taxis because they'd heard the métro was dangerous. Clearly they'd never been to New York.

One of the most obvious differences between Europeans and Americans these days is that Europeans don't seem to have heard of lung cancer. During midmorning breaks and when classes were adjourned, the hallways and lobby were jammed with students obscured in a haze of cigarette smoke and, despite the order to speak only French, rattling away in a dozen different languages. It

was a relief to escape into the April drizzle, where on Tuesdays and Fridays a stretch of the austere boulevard Raspail is turned into an open market. The merchants are patient and willing to listen to fractured French before closing a sale and bidding, *"Retournez,"* as they turn to the next customer.

But even with all the differences, there is much in common as well. Paris is filled with American movies, of course, and rock music, McDonald's and Levi's. And when it comes to mastering slang, an American can fall back on his own language with perfect aplomb. What did you think of studying French in France? *Super!* But mind your accent.

The Password

BY ALEXANDRA BOUTIN

～

editor's note

....

This piece, as well as the following passage from *Neither Here Nor There* by Bill Bryson, reminded me of the "Soup Nazi" episode on *Seinfeld*: "You would go into a bakery and be greeted by some vast slug-like creature with a look that told you you would never be friends. In halting French you would ask for a small loaf of bread. The woman would give you a long, cold stare and then put a dead beaver on the counter.

'No, no,' you would say, hands aflutter, 'not a dead beaver. A loaf of bread.'

The slug-like creature would stare at you in patent disbelief, then turn to the other customers and address them in French at much too high a speed for you to follow, but the drift of which clearly was that this person here, this *American tourist*, had come in and asked for a dead beaver and she had given him a dead beaver and now he was saying that he didn't want a dead beaver at all, he wanted a loaf of bread. The other customers would look at you as if you had just tried to fart in their handbags, and you would have no choice but to slink away and console yourself with the thought that in another four days you would be in Brussels and probably able to eat again."

ALEXANDRA BOUTIN, a freelance writer who's been observing the French for more than twenty years, is absolutely right about the proper vocal forms of *boulangerie* etiquette.

From grammar books the French student learns to form perfect sentences. Language tapes impart a "good accent." French lessons provide vocabulary. Literature contributes clues as to what type of behavior to expect from natives once you finally raise enough money to cross the ocean and spend a few months in THE COUNTRY . . .

Well, if you think you're all set for that European Adventure, think again. Teachers can lecture their hearts out on French civilization, but nothing REALLY prepares you for day-to-day life in France. Even the smallest details can seem complicated to a foreigner.

I ran into my first problem on a simple mission to buy bread. Venturing down to the corner bakery should have been a breeze. It wasn't. Join me in front of the old VCR for a quick rewind back to the early seventies . . .

I take my place in line and wait my turn to purchase a crusty baguette. The line winds out the door and down the boulevard. Carefully, I observe behavior in order to get everything right and not be labeled AN UGLY AMERICAN.

To my consternation, I immediately realize the other customers all know something I don't know. Everyone else is using—oh, horrors—A PASSWORD! They say it fast, nonchalantly, so I won't understand. I prick up my ears but can't quite make out what it is. The baker smiles and nods, doles out the change. The line is moving fast. It's almost my turn. I begin to sweat. Egads! I haven't figured out what the password is yet. I quake in my shoes, expecting the baker to say: "Hey you! No password, no bread!"

My turn. I inch up to the counter and say nothing. I have laryngitis: that's it! I point at my throat and grimace wildly. The baker glares. His hand hovers over the different types of bread. Irritated, he gestures toward the other customers. A little cough of exasperation comes from the end of the line. I indicate the stack of baguettes. The baker harrumphs with contempt and hands over a slender loaf, hot from the oven. I beat a quick retreat before he changes his mind.

Later in the day I wander back in and loiter by the bulletin board near the glass door, where the neighborhood classifies are posted, to eavesdrop. Three kids purchase bubble gum. Intently, I study the want ads. Out of the corner of my eye I see a pint-size dynamo—dressed in what looks like a Chanel—hustle past. The woman mutters something to the baker's wife, then withdraws, baguette in hand: "SYURDAM," she says with a polite nod. Hmmmm. A word I have never heard before. Perhaps it's the name of the baker's wife?

A construction worker lumbers through the doorframe, clutching a bottle of red wine. He purchases an armful of baguettes and lurches back outside, hiccuping, "SYURDAM." WOW! That's it! I've got it: the password is SYURDAM. But what does it mean?

I rush back to my apartment and pounce on the dictionary. No luck. No such word.

I rack my brain for similar spellings. *Sciure* means sawdust. Perhaps the Parisians are referring to the sawdust on the tile floor, which keeps customers from slipping? Doesn't make much sense. I search under several different spellings. No success. *Sciure* it must be, then.

I return to the bakery, wait my turn, solemnly point down at the floor. "Sciure down," I announce with a smug smile. Apologetic, the baker's wife runs for a broom and sweeps the sawdust up. Unfortunately, she is wearing a definite frown.

When my French husband comes home from work, I ask discreetly—so he won't be aware of the hours I've just spent wrestling with the problem—"Chéri, what is the password I should be using when I go out to buy bread?"

"Password?" Uh-oh. He's looking at me as if I were crazy. "There's no password."

"Oh yes, there is," I insist, nodding vigorously. "Everyone who goes into the *boulangerie* says it: "SYURDAM."

He scratches his head, stumped.

"SYURDAM? Never heard of it before." The mystery remains complete.

Only after insisting that my husband accompany me on one of my eavesdropping missions do I finally learn what the French customers are saying: "Messieurs, Mesdames," a formal greeting, which—when swallowed—contracts to "SYURDAM"!

Now I am *branchée*—plugged in. Whenever I go into the bakery, I know the password and can pass for one of the natives. Well, almost . . .

The bread is tasty anyway.

"The Password" originally appeared in the October/November 1992 issue of *France Today*. Brief text from *Neither Here Nor There* by Bill Bryson. Copyright © 1992 by Bill Bryson. By permission of William Morrow and Company, Inc.

According to Plan—Maps of Paris

BY CATHARINE REYNOLDS

editor's note

All Parisian households have at least one, well-worn *Plan de Paris,* and I cannot imagine, even for a second, being in Paris without my own well-worn edition. Even if you only have a few days in the city, investing in a *plan*—which presents the city *par arrondissement* in a compact book—is essential for moving about skillfully and understanding Paris. "For in Paris," as noted in this piece, which appeared in July 1990, "geography and history are inseparably entwined."

CATHARINE REYNOLDS, a contributing editor at *Gourmet,* has been writing the magazine's "Paris Journal" column—which won a James Beard Foundation Award in 1998—for over twenty years.

To err is human, to stroll is Parisian." The peripatetic Victor Hugo's bon mot requires a word of counsel: Visitors intent on enjoying Paris's endlessly captivating cityscape need select their maps as painstakingly as their walking shoes. A certain sort of traveler is compelled to seek out a map of a new city upon arrival, if not in advance; a self-abusive breed disdains such support. In Paris hardened cartophobes eventually capitulate if they wish truly to understand the city.

Only pseudo-sophisticates recoil at the sight of "site-seekers" squinting at unfurled foldouts, struggling to trace the path from picture gallery to supper. In Paris, map-toting is no newcomer's proclamation of ignorance. The most knowledgeable taxi drivers

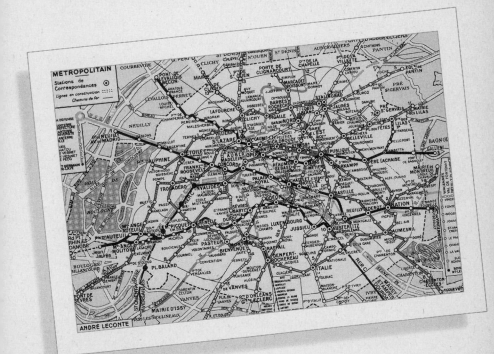

cannot know each of the city's 6,417 streets offhand; instead they pack copies of *Paris par Arrondissement* in their glove compartments. (Those who don't, warrant the curses of their hapless customers.)

But what constitutes a good map? Stationers and bookstores overflow with alternatives. Flat maps tend to be cumbersome, and so small map volumes, albeit more expensive, are a sound investment. A straightforward choice for a short stay is the classic *L'Indispensable,* a 7-by-4½-inch, navy volume that for the past fifty years has lived up to its name, with omnibus lists of government offices, embassies, schools, hospitals, museums, churches, department stores, theaters, movie houses, et cetera. *L'Indispensable* offers a thumb-indexed alphabetical list of streets followed by maps of each of the city's twenty arrondissements, with some of the larger ones meriting two maps, as well as plans of the bewildering Défense business complex. A large folded map at the back allows an overview of the city and suburbs.

The privately owned L'Indispensable publishing house brings out thirty-five different map formats in five languages, but its maps suffer on the whole from old-fashioned graphics, which, however evocative, can be less than easy to read, as are most of the maps produced by the firm of A. Leconte.

Many Parisians prefer the maps put out by the thirty-year-old firm of Ponchet, most of which wear practical black plastic covers. Ponchet produces a volume similar to the standard, midsize *Indispensable,* as well as a 12-by-8½-inch *Grand Paris,* ideal for those daunted by the challenge of map-reading in jackrabbiting vehicles. Their numbers must be growing, as this map has been a runaway success among Parisian motorists struggling to find either restaurants or friends living on obscure streets.

The beige ink favored by the firm of Plans-Guide Blay renders its maps less appropriate for walkers and drivers than for cipher clerks, who might also relish the challenge of the miniature type-faces and creative abbreviations in the staple-bound map booklets. These volumes offer the attraction of being compact, but they prove ultimately disappointing.

On the other hand, Michelin, whose yellow-clad road maps are models of the genre, puts out an exemplary if large 12¼-by-9¼-inch *Atlas Paris par Arrondissements* (number 15). Unhappily, Michelin's smaller Paris map book (number 11) does not divide its maps by arrondissement, which is slightly bewildering. The firm's other Paris *plans* are of the bedsheet variety: They may facilitate plain sailing on the open road, but their expanse sends puzzled pedestrians flying.

Visitors might welcome a few bits of information that a born Parisian is assumed to have learned at his or her mother's knee. For example, none of Paris's popular *plans* explains the disarmingly simple formula according to which buildings are numbered—a for-mula that can orient one in the most unfamiliar neighborhood. Since February 4, 1805, Parisian houses have been numbered seri-ally, with odd numbers on one side and evens on the opposite. On streets running at right or oblique angles to the Seine the numbers rise from the river; on streets running parallel to the river the num-bers start from the upstream, or eastern, side.

Nor do map books alert visitors to bear in mind that their street indices are alphabetized by the streets' full names. Thus the rue Edith-Piaf is found under *E* not *P.* But the rue Washington is called just that, so it is listed under W. Equally, a title is in some cases part and parcel of a street's name, as in the case of the avenue du Général-Leclerc, and is therefore alphabetized under G. Streets named for saints demand special attention as well: In some rosters the rue Saint-Yves is listed before the Rue Sainte-Anne; in others all the saints are heaped willy-nilly at the end of the *S* entries. Know your map—and, until you do, practice lateral thinking.

And don't try to make do with a dated map. Existing street names can no longer be changed, but an average of twenty-five additions appear each year, if only to honor deceased local worthies with tree-shaded crossroads. In a busy year Paris has been known to gain as many as forty-two new streets—and Murphy's Law decrees that the address you are seeking will be among the parvenus.

All of the maps here recommended rely on an arrondissement-to-the-double-page format that is both practical and culturally informative. The snail-curl of the arrondissements is easily grasped, but the character of each *quartier* must then be mastered. By focusing the map reader's attention on the individuality of each arrondissement—the haughty, established style of the 7ème, still known by its denizens as the Faubourg Saint-Germain; the *louche* air of much of the 9ème; the gritty charms of the 20ème, which set one to wondering how it came to be called Belleville; and the interminable turn-of-the-century sculpted masonry of the 16ème, largest of all the arrondissements—the maps offer a painless history lesson, for in Paris geography and history are inseparably entwined.

Geography provides Frenchmen another field in which to exercise their Cartesian heritage: Their earliest lessons teach them to call their republic the *hexagone* because the French land mass conveniently corresponds to that shape. This uncanny adherence to geometry applies to the capital as well, for Paris has managed to maintain a near-circular shape for more than two millennia. Settled on a damp island in the Seine, Lutetia initially relied on the river for defense. As Paris expanded along the adjacent banks, its citizens realized that topography offered little protection; where it failed, geology came to the rescue, providing abundant local limestone for walls.

The Romans built the first wall; the early Capetians are thought to have built a second. These seemed inadequate to King Philippe-Auguste on the eve of his departure for the Third Crusade, so in 1190 he began to girdle his capital's 625 acres with a thirty-foot rampart. It took twenty-three years to build but was very solid; vestiges still dot the older portions of the city.

A century and a half later the fortifications along the Right Bank were extended by Charles V to shield the city from the English; some three hundred years later additional works extended them to encompass more than twenty-five hundred acres until, in 1670, Louis XIV concluded that his victories were sufficient to guarantee Paris's security and ordered Charles V's walls demolished. The land thus freed was planted with trees, creating a "boulevard," a word deriving, ironically, from the Teutonic word for "bulwark."

But the kings of France had not had done with walls. Goods entering Paris had long been taxed at the gates of the city, but the new boulevards proved too permeable to fraudsters. In 1784 the tax collectors, or *fermiers généraux,* obtained royal permission to build a ten-foot wall around the capital:

> Pour augmenter son numéraire
> Et raccourcir notre horizon,
> La Ferme a jugé nécessaire
> De mettre Paris en prison.

> *To fill their coffers*
> *And lower our horizon,*
> *The taxmen have judged it necessary*
> *To imprison Paris.*

grumbled the wordsmiths of the Pont Neuf, who quickly assessed the popular resistance in near-palindrome, quipping that the fourteen-mile *"mur murant Paris rend Paris murmurant"* (the wall circling Paris renders Paris rebellious). Come the Revolution, no observer was startled when the forty-five strange and wonderful tax gates, designed by Claude-Nicolas Ledoux, figured among the mob's first targets.

The *fermiers généraux*'s wall was only a tax barrier. In 1814 Louis-Philippe, the Citizen King, was persuaded to build a twenty-five-mile fortification encircling the tax wall and encompassing twenty-four suburban villages. The annexation of these villages and their nearly twenty square miles in 1860 nearly doubled Paris's size.

In the twentieth century the walls finally came tumbling down (to the wrecker's ball), and the Bois de Vincennes and the Bois de Boulogne were incorporated into the city limits. Each successive wall had corseted the capital's growth. Having occupied less than five acres two thousand years previously, Paris had grown to a city of more than forty square miles, without much altering her rotund figure. Traces of each expansion, like the rings of a tree, can be seen in the street plan—in spite of Baron Georges Haussmann's radial thoroughfares. The nineteenth-century wall was demolished in the 1920s, but its circuit yielded the land for the *boulevards extérieurs* that speed (or fail to speed) traffic around Paris's periphery.

Baudelaire bemoaned the fact that "the shape of a city/Changes faster, alas, than the heart of a mortal." The historical maps of Paris chronicle those changes, reaching beyond language to recount their times; as a bonus they are often masterworks of the woodcut maker's and engraver's arts. Thus it is not surprising that those caught up in a passion for Paris are seduced by the siren charms of these historical maps, many of which have been reproduced and some of which can be purchased for reasonable sums.

The Archives Nationales, at 11 rue des Quatre-Fils, catalogs tens of thousands of maps, but the earliest recognized contemporary map of Paris is the Plan de Munster, which declares itself "The Portrait of the City." Produced, probably partially from memory, by a Franciscan monk named Sébastien Munster, this rather crude woodcut shows the Paris of about 1530, when François I was busy bringing the Renaissance to France. Like most maps in that era, Munster's map served as a kind of civic ego trip, enhancing the fame of the city and its monarch in both French and Latin.

A decade later an enormous tapestry incorporated a map of the late-medieval city in a style derived from illuminated manuscripts, with the place names inscribed on curious, beguiling banners. In the eighteenth century the tapestry, purchased by the city, was hung to adorn the facade of city hall on the Feast of Corpus Christi and was used to cushion the floor at a ball celebrating the advent of a dauphin in 1782. By 1787 it was in tatters. Fortunately the Plan de la Tapisserie had been copied, and engraving plates made. The latter are today part of the sumptuous collection of the Chalcographie, a unique department of the Louvre's Cabinet des Dessins, where fine engravings restruck from the original plates are available at quite affordable prices.

About 1551 another woodcut map appeared, the Plan de Truschet et Hoyau. This was an ambitious work covering eight sheets and cataloging the city's 287 streets and 104 churches—which served a population of roughly 350,000 souls. Like most sixteenth-century cartographers, Olivier Truschet and Germain Hoyau could not content themselves with two dimensions; they were forever trying to provide a third dimension, to limn the elevations and to add a human element. Guilt must have affected the cartographers' minds, because their cityscape included six cautionary gallows—occupied—not to mention plump-cheeked cupids blowing wind from the four corners of the map and drawing attention to the map's river axis rather than compass orientation. The precision sacrificed to figuration was almost always art's gain. The Plan de Truschet et Hoyau is often called the Plan de Bâle because the only extant original was discovered in the midnineteenth century in a library in Basel, where it had likely been carried by a traveler.

No modern chamber of commerce advised by the most go-go ad agency could outdo the purple prose of early map cartouche writers, as witness the etched Plan de Braun, published about 1572, on which a verse declares that "Paris is truly the royal house/Of the god Apollo." Even more naive, the Plan de Saint-Victor is usually attributed to the engraver of architect Jacques Androuet Du Cerceau. Only a single copy exists, but fortunately another engraver, Guillaume d'Heulland, copied it between 1755 and 1760 onto a copper plate that continues to yield purchasable restrikes at the Chalcographie. In 1609 both François Quesnel and Vassalieu produced *plans* for France's first urbanist king, Henri IV; each was long on praise for both the monarch and the "marvels" of his capital, and short on accuracy, often depicting construction projects that were still on the drawing boards. Many such projects progressed no further, due to Henri's assassination by the mad monk François Ravaillac, a crime that might never have succeeded—the king had eluded seventeen earlier attempts—but for the fact that the royal carriage was caught in a traffic jam on a narrow street.

Produced six years later, the splendidly engraved Plan de Mathieu Mérian includes an image of Henri's successor, the young Louis XIII, as well as a number of his subjects. Jacques Gomboust's 1647 nine-sheet map, peopled by 509 figures, decorated with engravings of six royal residences and the grander aristocratic seats, and framed by descriptive text, was a roll-up guide to the city and its environs. It omitted elevations of all but the most important structures and, over-all, was considerably more accurate than its predecessors.

The Plan de Bullet et Blondel, drawn less than two decades later, reveals the city's tremendous growth under Louis XIV and demon-strates the error in thinking that the Sun King neglected Paris in favor of Versailles. Drafted at the king's behest and surrounded with long-winded text, this map features its authors' own works, for architect François Blondel and his pupil Pierre Bullet had designed the triumphal gates at the Porte Saint-Denis, the Porte Saint-Martin, the Porte Saint-Antoine, and the Porte Saint-Bernard. Their architectural training is evident in their renditions of the gar-dens of the Louvre and Palais-Royal; these lacy engravings define the term *parterre en broderie*. An inset map of the environs of Paris points to the court's imminent transfer to Versailles.

The Plan d'Albert Jouvin de Rochefort is the most absorbing of all the seventeenth-century maps, alive with more than six hundred figures caught up in their daily lives: trudging to work, tilling the fields surrounding the city, hunting stag on the Plaine Monceau, dueling on Montparnasse, swimming in the river. For all its ani-mation, Rochefort's map, dated 1690, is remarkably scientific, ori-ented perpendicular to the meridian, that is, with the north at the top.

In the succeeding century, maps came into their own as admin-istrative tools. In 1714 Marc-René, Marquis d'Argenson, lieutenant general of the Paris police, commissioned the Plan de Jean de la Caille, which enumerates every feature, from the 896 streets and 22,000 houses down to the city's 25 horse troughs. This was the first map of Paris to divide the city into sections, illustrating each on a separate sheet.

The perceived value of such maps decided the city fathers to pioneer a municipal map office. The Abbé Delagrive, renowned for his devoted work with "rod, chain, and theodolite" and for the handsome geometric map that had resulted, was named Géographe de la Ville and quickly undertook studies of urban water distribution. Delagrive marketed his own map "in the Rue Saint-Jacques . . . at a wigmaker's"; today we can purchase a restrike of it at the Chalcographie.

The historic map of Paris best known to the world, the Plan Turgot, recalls to me the New York City of the seventies, when I frequented Le Cygne not only to feast on its raspberry soufflé but to thrill to eighteenth-century Paris, for the restaurant's walls were papered with blowups of the map.

The Plan Turgot is shrouded in misconceptions. First of all, unlike most maps of its time, it is known by the name of the man who commissioned it, Michel-Étienne Turgot, not the man who surveyed it, Louis Bretez. Descended from Norman nobility, Turgot was the capital's *prévôt des marchands,* a royal appointee responsible for administration, which office he held for an unusually long eleven years. Little surprise that he decided to blow his city's horn and commission a splendid *plan.* (Turgot's third son, Anne-Robert-Jacques, for whom Michel-Étienne is often mistaken, was to become Louis XVI's reforming minister of finance.)

The Plan Turgot was a map out of sync with its time, drawn in the great seventeenth-century tradition of the bird's-eye view. By 1734 Delagrive and his imitators had already accustomed the map-reading public to precise renderings on which one could number the very pillars of the churches. And the Cassinis, the family who put French cartography on the map, were just about to begin triangulating for their famed topographical map of the kingdom.

The purpose of Turgot's map—which it serves to this day—was as retrograde, and eternal, as its style: to broadcast the wealth and beauty of Paris. If Delagrive could draft sanitation plans worthy of the council chamber, Bretez would execute a vast plan worthy of the drawing room. Promised a fee of ten thousand *livres* and armed with a permit that granted him ready access to all the city's buildings to make sketches, Bretez, a member of the Académie de Sculpture et de Peinture and onetime professor of architecture and perspective, blazoned the capital across twenty sheets, which, end-to-end, measure 10½ by 8 feet. Bretez knew full well that he was bucking the trend and perhaps betraying his training in perspective, for he apologized in print for his license, explaining that without forcing the perspective he would have lost some of the most interesting monuments of the city. At a time when maps had come to be oriented perpendicular to the meridian, the Plan Turgot has the east at the top, to allow Bretez the bravura chance to detail the facades of the churches, almost all of which face east. Sadly, Bretez didn't live to see the final engraved product of his labors.

The Plan Turgot is the least rare of eighteenth-century maps because twenty-six hundred copies were run off. Some of them were mounted on linen; the remainder were bound. These were sent as presents to destinations as distant as Constantinople and China. Further copies have been (and remain) available, as the copper plates ended up at the Chalcographie. However inaccurate topographically, Bretez's map, which attempted to portray each and every building, makes this a fascinating architectural study—and enormously decorative.

Purists criticized the Plan Turgot from the moment of its appearance, but the public loved it, drawn in by the lack of topographical progression and left happily lost in the city. The map's popularity continues today, with reduced-scale facsimiles eagerly purchased from the Bibliothèque Nationale's shop in the rue des Petits-Champs, as well as from myriad souvenir shops.

But in the Age of Enlightenment scientific mapping necessarily had to triumph over figurative mapping, however artful. In Paris the apostle of the former was a Burgundian architect named Edme Verniquet, who, having purchased the venal office of road surveyor, discovered that none of the available maps was accurate enough to allow him to align buildings. He devoted half his adult life to devising such a mathematically exact plan. From 1783 until the royal purse grew too empty in 1788, Verniquet enjoyed Louis XVI's patronage in paying the sixty surveyors and two hundred helpers who charted the city at night by torchlight to avoid disrupting traffic. The project captured the imagination of *le tout-Paris,* who flocked to gape at the draftsmen laboring in the gallery of the Couvent des Cordeliers on a seventy-two-sheet map that, assembled, measures 16½ by 13 feet. The Plan Verniquet captures the last portrait of the Paris of the *ancien régime* before so many of its convents and churches were demolished and Napoléon's *gloire* was imprinted on the urban fabric.

Verniquet was a hard act to follow. His *plan* was the basis of almost all Paris maps in the first half of the nineteenth century until Baron Georges Haussmann commissioned a new survey in 1853. But that is not to say that nineteenth-century maps are not fascinating and charming. Engineer Aristide-Michel Perrot's 1834 *Petit Atlas Pittoresque des Quarante-Huit Quartiers de la Ville de Paris* offers alongside its maps delectable *aperçus* of the life of the city; the map of the 12th Arrondissement, the Quartier du Jardin du Roi, which became the Jardin des Plantes, is accompanied by an illustration of its caged giraffe, which drew all Paris in wonderment.

Haussmann definitively established the Office of the Plan de

Paris in 1853, appointing Deschamps to head it. The maps he and his colleagues produced were accurate and full of purpose, if perhaps less romantic than their predecessors. Literacy and cheap, colorful reproduction spread maps far and wide—but did not devalue them; as the Plan de Munster indicates, maps, regardless of design, production technique, or purpose, are "Portraits of the City."

Those bitten by the historical-map bug should repair to the Chalcographie, handsomely installed under the new Louvre's pyramid, for restrikes or to the Bibliothèque Nationale's smart new boutique at 6 rue des Petits-Champs, 2ème, for reduced-size facsimiles. Those seeking period maps might address themselves to one or another of the specialist map dealers, firms like Louis Loeb-Larocque, at 36 rue Le Peletier, 9ème; Fernand Martinez, at 97 rue de Seine, 6ème; and Sartoni-Cerveau, at 13 quai Saint-Michel, 5ème—all the streets of which they can locate in their *Paris par Arrondissement*.

Il connaît Paris comme sa poche (he knows Paris like the back of his hand or, literally, like his pocket) is high praise indeed. Those who merit such praise will have often whipped a map from pocket or pocketbook to find their way.

Le Kiosque—
Points de Vue
(The Kiosk—Points of View)

I lived in Paris for a long time without making a single French friend, and even longer before I saw the inside of a French home. This did not really upset me, either, for Henry James had been there before me and had had the generosity to clue me in. Furthermore, for a black boy who had grown up on welfare and the chickenshit goodwill of American liberals, this total indifference came as a total relief and even as a mark of respect. If I could make it, I could make it—so much the better. And if I couldn't, I couldn't—so much the worse. I didn't want any help, and the French certainly didn't give me any. They let me do it myself and for that reason, even knowing what I know, and unromantic as I am, there will always be a kind of love story between myself and that odd, unpredictable collection of bourgeois chauvinists who call themselves la France.

—James Baldwin, NO NAME IN THE STREET

National Memory

BY RONALD KOVEN

❧

editor's note

"History," writes Richard Bernstein in *Fragile Glory,* "stares down at the French like a bad conscience." Only recently have the French begun public debate on their World War II record of capitulation and collaboration—the "worst blots ever" according to Bernstein. The war may have officially ended fifty-five years ago, but the complicated issue of reparations by Swiss banks is still being addressed, as well as disputes over stolen artwork (an excellent book to read about Nazi art seizures is *The Rape of Europa* by Lynn Nicholas, Knopf hardcover, 1994; Vintage paperback, 1995) and, perhaps most disturbing, last year's report that American troops looted a train filled with valuables stolen from Hungarian Jews in May 1945. As historian Alan Schom notes in his monumental biography of Napoleon, "We may sometimes try to forget history, but it does not forget us." Doubtless other issues will come to light, reminding us once again that our history cannot be forgotten.

Once, while I was visiting the Memorial de la Deportation at the tip of the Ile de la Cité with my friends Jesse and Barbara, Jesse remarked that he felt the monument was moving but that it was really too little, too late to his way of thinking. He's right, of course, yet I've noticed that France has a significant number of memorials marking Nazi atrocities and Resistance efforts, more than I've seen in any other country. More than forty museums in France document the history of the Resistance and the deportation of French citizens to concentration camps (the largest is probably the Centre d'Histoire de la Resistance et de la Deportation in Lyon, the city that was headquarters for both Barbie and Resistance leader Jean Moulin) and on September 30, 1997, the Roman Catholic Church in France issued an apology to the Jewish people for the silence it maintained during Nazi occupation and Vichy collaboration. A report in *The New York Times* referred to the unequivocal language used in the apology as "remarkable." How and why it took decades to pronounce is perhaps best summarized by journalist Roger Cohen: "The two sides of French society clung to their divisive myths: the church to its immaculacy, the Republic to the illusion that it had nothing to do with Vichy's deportation to their deaths of 70,000 Jews" ("Week in Review," *The New York Times,* October 19, 1997). It would be difficult to argue that the apology didn't come too late, but I prefer to think that it is still welcome, if overdue.

Within the last decade a number of articles have appeared about France coming to terms with its history. However, as Adam Gopnik notes in his insightful "Paris Journal" column entitled "Papon's Paper Trial" (*The New Yorker,* April 27 and May 4, 1998), the French have been obsessed with Vichy for at least twenty-five years, and nearly every bookstore devotes a shelf to this chapter of French history. Gopnik observes that the French war-crimes trials of Klaus Barbie (1987), Paul Touvier (1994), and Maurice Papon (1998) "have been moving closer to the heart of the French identity." The following piece, which was sent to me by my friend Sarah, who in turn came across it in her work at National Public Radio, is the most thorough and thought provoking I've read.

The French are very quick to accuse one another of having a special aptitude for forgetting embarrassing episodes in their history, of having short memories. The real problem, however, is not forgetfulness. It is that different elements of the French nation simply can't agree on which parts of French history should be stressed. Yet these adversaries all seem to agree that there should be only a single, certified National Memory—their own, of course. This struggle over which memories should make up the French psyche reflects a hard-to-accept historical reality: Throughout much of its past, France, more than most other countries, has been engaged in actual or cold civil wars punctuated by more or less long periods of national reconciliation that have required a need to forget.

At least that is what a succession of recent French leaders, including four very different presidents of the Fifth Republic (Charles de Gaulle, Georges Pompidou, Valéry Giscard d'Estaing and François Mitterrand), have maintained, explicitly or implicitly. Their appeals to national unity, implying the sacrifice of certain grievances, have inevitably met with protests from groups who have felt that they were being asked to give up pieces of their collective memory. Hence a host of "Lest we forget"–style appeals to remembrance from Royalists, Gaullists, Communists, Catholics, Protestants, Jews, Algerians and so on.

Yet to observe these calls to remembrance essentially involves dwelling on painful recollections, not pleasant nostalgia. Even exercises in nostalgia seem to turn rapidly into references to collective trauma. A monthlong series of daily radio programs broadcast in Paris this summer, *Songs of the Liberation,* featured a detailed commentary on how all the expressions of joy or evocations of faraway places were nothing more than attempts to forget the horrors of the German occupation. The title of the memoirs of the late Simone Signoret, movie star and godmother of a generation of human-rights activists, sums it up nicely: *Nostalgia Is Not What It Used to Be.*

When memory is that painful, it is hardly surprising that people would sometimes simply prefer to forget. Another title, *Forgetting Our Crimes: National Amnesia, a French Specialty?* expresses the widespread perception that the French have not yet come to grips with certain aspects of their history. The book may be new, but the theme certainly isn't. For years, many foreigners, including a number of Americans, have gleefully joined French commentators in accusing the French of being unable to accept their past. The most recent debates concern the Vichy government's collaboration with Nazi Germany and the French army's commission of atrocities during the Algerian war.

Paradoxically, these debates come amid a series of high-profile commemorations ostensibly designed to celebrate national unity: the bicentennial of the French Revolution, the millennium of the French monarchy, the centennial of the birth of Charles de Gaulle and the fiftieth anniversaries of D day and the liberation of Paris.

This recent spate of commemorations has been accompanied by a cult of national heritage, known as *le Patrimoine,* in which even the Nazi bunkers of the Atlantic Wall have been classified as historic monuments. France now has some forty thousand officially listed historic monuments, with some nine hundred new sites added each year.

Places of Memory

This new sensitivity has produced a new concept—"places of memory"—which has been embodied in a seven-volume historical work of the same name. Conceived by historiographer Pierre Nora, this collection of essays is a solemn monument in its own right. For Nora, places of memory are not only the obvious sites and monuments—village war memorials, the prehistoric cave paintings of Lascaux, the Eiffel Tower or the Panthéon, the republican mausoleum serving as a pendant to Saint Denis Cathedral, the resting place of French kings. Places of memory are also defined as the famous moments in French history expressed in textbooks, proverbs, folktales and songs—including the national anthem, "La Marseillaise." Nora's definition even embraces the classic Tour de France bicycle race, the French language itself and culture-defining literature—above all, Marcel Proust's exploration of memory, *The Remembrance of Things Past.*

Nora notes that every French person is aware of the evocative powers that Proust attributes to the madeleine, regardless of whether or not they have personally tasted the cake or, for that matter, read the book. "It's like the metric standard—it is enough to know that it exists; people don't need to actually go see it." As a symbol of memory, Proust's novel has achieved totemic as well as literary value.

Nora concludes that memory is a synonym for national identity. He is concerned not with the spontaneous, natural memory of the individual, but with the memory inculcated in each generation and cultivated for later generations through an institutionalized approach to folk memory.

The Germans who occupied Paris during World War II must have had an instinctive understanding of the relationship between memory and national identity when they decided to melt down almost all the bronze statues in the French capital, except those of French heroes, such as Napoléon and Joan of Arc, who fought the English.

Few of the melted statues were replaced after the war, so squares such as the place Victor Hugo still have "memory holes" where statues used to be. Meanwhile, more recent statues made to honor men not universally accepted as heroes—Captain Alfred Dreyfus, the Popular Front's Socialist premier Léon Blum, leftist premier Pierre Mendès Blum, leftist premier Pierre Mendès-France—have been relegated to obscure locations that are surely not places of memory.

Besides, statues and larger monuments no longer seem to be the favored expressions of permanent commemoration. The latest trend runs to costly memorial museums with interactive electronic displays, notably the massive Memorial for Peace in Caen; the World War I Historical on the site of the Battle of the Somme; the World Peace Center in Verdun; the History Center of Resistance and Deportation in Lyon; the Resistance museum at Vercors; a new remembrance museum at Oradour, a village where the retreating SS systematically killed all the inhabitants they could find; and the Memorial Museum of Izieu, where the Gestapo arrested forty-four Jewish children for deportation to Auschwitz. None of these new places of memory commemorate happy events, a reminder of the truism that happy countries have no history.

Open Wounds

French self-flagellation over its modern history concerns episodes that proceed in a straight line from the beheading of King Louis XVI during the French Revolution to the present. Not that there aren't plenty of prerevolutionary events that remain unresolved in the French psyche, for example, medieval carnages such as the destruction of Provençal culture by the northern powers during the thirteenth-century Crusades against the Albigensian and Cathar heretics or the Saint Bartholomew's Day Massacre of Protestants, in 1572. In the 1930s, French political scientist André Siegfried demonstrated that the southern tradition of voting for the far left was traceable to the perhaps subconscious desire of Provençal people to defy a northern authority that had never made amends for the horrors perpetrated against their real or imagined ancestors.

Henry Rousso, author of *The Vichy Syndrome,* notes that the study of "the history of memory" in France stresses "profound crises of French unity and identity . . . those crises feed upon one another, with the memory of each preceding crisis playing a role in the next: the French Revolution in the Dreyfus Affair, Dreyfus in Vichy, Vichy in the Algerian war, and so on."

Indeed, it may be argued, French memories are not too short but too long. I recall meeting a descendant of Georges Clemenceau, the leading World War I ally of England, France's former hereditary enemy, against Germany, its more recent hereditary enemy. Speaking in the 1960s, he said he could forgive the English for a list of relatively recent affronts, including Mers el-Kébir (where the British Royal Navy destroyed a French fleet in 1940 lest it fall into German hands). "But for what they did to Joan of Arc—never!" In response to my laughter, the younger Clemenceau replied, "What's so funny? I'm very serious."

However old the historical grudges the French bear against one another or others, crimes committed with the tacit or overt blessings of the French state since the Revolution of 1789 have a special meaning. Since that date, France has considered itself a country with a universal message, contained in the Declaration of the Right of Man and of the Citizen and summed up by the French republican slogan *Liberté, Égalité, Fraternité*. The Declaration proclaimed the State of Law, equal for all, and abolished the legitimate exercise of arbitrary power. It notably inspired the European constitutional movement and the Latin American independence struggles. Since then, any actions by France that have contradicted that message—massacres, deportations, summary justice, invocations of "reasons of state" to justify illegal actions—have appeared as so many denials of that universality.

From the start, of course, many French rejected the message as a transgression of the eternal verities taught by the Church and the monarchy. For them, the French Republic was born in the original sin of the execution of Louis XVI. The guillotining of the deposed royal couple was a national trauma that still has not fully healed. Contemporary republicans discuss it defensively, and historical debate continues to rage over whether Louis and Marie Antoinette deserved to die. The debate has even been turned into a large-scale parlor game by actor-director Robert Hossein, who stages reenactments of Marie Antoinette's trial. The audience votes electronically from their seats; invariably, the verdict is overwhelmingly against putting the queen to death.

Ever since the decapitation of Louis and his consort, France has appeared to be a country living largely on the brink of civil war. Yet it was almost always recognized that beyond the internal passions of the moment, beyond the consecrated monarchy and the secular republic, the French nation was an underlying entity worthy of general defense against aggression.

So France reinvented the Athenian republican notion of amnesty—the effacement of political crimes. For the sake of national consensus, the crimes and their punishments were deemed no longer to exist. The word *amnesty* is rooted in the Greek word *amnesia*—loss of memory.

Amnesty, Amnesia

As Stéphane Gacon, a young historian of amnesty, notes, "All the Franco-French wars have had their amnesties: the Commune's in

1879–80, Boulangisme's in 1895, the Dreyfus Affair's in 1990, the collaboration's [partially] in 1951–53, the Algerian war's from 1962–68." It is a system for re-creating national unity.

The French press law of 1881, still in force, makes it illegal to publish, or discuss in public, any punishments, including those that have been amnestied. That the published facts are true is no defense in cases involving amnestied crimes, or for that matter, any legal punishments that are more than ten years old.

Each successive amnesty has different rules and case law to interpret it. But precedent is much weaker in the French legal system than in Anglo-American practice, and the general framework is still the 1881 law banning public discussion of amnestied crimes. That law has a chilling effect on editors, making them very cautious about printing historic facts that could involve them in costly, prolonged lawsuits, even if they are likely to win.

Although amnesty may have obvious advantages for society as a whole, it complicates dealing with national memory. At the very least, it makes it difficult to discuss recent history whose actors are still alive. There are prominent Frenchmen active today who are generally known to have been torturers in Algeria, but it is at least technically illegal to recall publicly that they have been accused of atrocities. And transgressors have regularly lost defamation suits in the courts.

Moreover, the ban does not end with the death of the amnestied person; the family may sue for harm to "the honor or the reputation of the living heir or spouses." In practice, nobody gets sued for discussing major historical figures such as Pétain, Pierre Laval or Joseph Darnand, the chief of Vichy's anti-Resistance force, the paramilitary Militia. But recalling the past or the postwar punishment of a simple Militiaman could lead to a lawsuit.

The loss is not merely to history. A sociology professor recounts how one of her graduate students was emotionally traumatized upon learning that his family had moved from one village to another to hide his grandfather's service in the Vichy Militia. "That family was living a lie," she said, "and my student was completely overwhelmed when he finally realized it."

Facing Collaboration

This makes it all too easy to perpetuate the myth that the French can't and don't deal with crimes committed in the name of France. There are countless articles that say, for example, that the French have never faced up to the reality that wartime collaboration was widespread. But thousands of suspected collaborators were publicly disgraced or executed by the Resistance at the Liberation, often without even the benefit of a kangaroo court. Such justice was often summary enough to be suspect. De Gaulle appealed to his compatriots: "Frenchmen, don't take it upon yourselves to administer justice."

Vichy premier Pierre Laval was tried, sentenced and executed by a firing squad, as was the writer/propagandist Robert Brasillach. The talented but openly anti-Semitic writer Céline escaped to permanent exile in Denmark. Pétain was condemned to death and the sentence commuted to internment on a small island off the Atlantic coast. Many collaborators were sentenced to periods of "national indignity" during which they were denied the right to vote or other civic rights.

Yet somehow the myth still persists that France did not deal with its collaborators. This is partly the work of de Gaulle himself. He had to erase the humiliation of France's defeat in 1940 and lead a vanquished but liberated nation to its seat among the victors. And he had to administer a country in need of reconstruction. Merely having worked under Vichy as a civil servant, plant manager, policeman or judge was not reason enough to be purged. Some administrators with dirty hands inevitably slipped through the nets.

Among the more disturbing cases were those of former high-level Vichy officials, such as René Bousquet and Maurice Papon. Both continued their careers—Bousquet in high finance, Papon in the government—before being charged with crimes against humanity (deportation of Jews), which, unlike war crimes, bear no statute of limitations. Bousquet was recently murdered by a deranged gunman. Papon, now eighty-three, still awaits a trial that Social Affairs Minister Simone Veil, a Jewish survivor of Auschwitz, and many former Resistance members—including President Mitterrand and former Gaullist prime ministers Michel Debré and Jacques Chaban-Delmas—have suggested is pointless fifty years after the event.

There was also obvious reluctance to try Paul Touvier, a Vichy Militia officer who ordered seven Jewish hostages executed in June 1944. He was actually pardoned in 1971 by President Pompidou, who defended himself against the outcry by asking, "Are we going to keep open the bleeding wounds of our national discords forever? Hasn't the time come to throw a veil over them, to forget those times when the French didn't like each other?" Later charged with crimes against humanity, Touvier was hidden for years by a network of Catholic clergymen. His eventual arrest prompted public soul-searching by France's horrified Catholic hierarchy.

The Resistance as Record

During the Cold War, there was a conscious effort to rally all non-Communists in France and elsewhere in the West against the Soviet threat. The political will to prosecute wartime collaborators dwindled. This fit in with De Gaulle's conscious attempt to wipe out the shame of the French defeat in 1940. De Gaulle's hostility toward U.S. President Franklin D. Roosevelt was in large part based on Roosevelt's refusal to accept Gaullist mythmaking.

In competition with the Gaullists, the French Communists pressed their own version of the Resistance, calling theirs "the party of the seventy-five thousand firing-squad victims," when, in fact, "only" thirty-five thousand Resistance members were executed, a large proportion of whom were not Communists.

No one can really say how many French citizens were collaborators and how many were in the Resistance. It is partly a problem of definition, degree and timing. Many early collaborators later joined the Resistance. Motives were mixed. Clearly, throughout much of the Occupation, it was Vichy—and not De Gaulle and the Resistance—that was considered the true representative of France. Many of the world's major powers, including the United States, maintained diplomatic relations with Vichy for as long as they could.

Far more numerous even than the *collabos* or the *résistants* were the fence-sitters, those whose main objective was survival or, perhaps, not to compromise the safe return to France of relatives held in German prisoner-of-war camps (2 million of them) or of the young men drafted into forced labor in Germany (600,000). Given this record, it is not really surprising that so many people went along with De Gaulle's implied urging to forget an inglorious era.

That said, it would be wrong to dismiss the Resistance as having made no meaningful contribution. Allied Supreme Commander Dwight D. Eisenhower, who commanded eighty-five Allied divisions in the Battle of Normandy, said that the Resistance was worth another fifteen divisions to him.

It also, of course, had the value that De Gaulle was so adept at exploiting—the creation of a record, of a socially and politically useful memory. It was just this kind of thing that General Henning Von Tresckow, one of the participants in the almost successful July 20, 1944, assassination plot against Hitler, had in mind when he said before the attempt: "It is no longer a matter of its practicality but a matter of demonstrating to the world and before history that the Resistance movement dared the decisive gamble. Beside that, everything else is a matter of indifference."

The official historians of postwar Germany used the commemoration of July 20 to create the founding myth of the new German democracy. They rejected, however, resistance by the German Communist Party. The memory of the Communists' role—as volunteers who fought the fascists during the Spanish Civil War and then in Germany—formed a competing myth, one used to found the German Democratic Republic.

Revisionist historians attack Roosevelt and Winston Churchill for insisting on unconditional surrender and for spurning feelers from the movement around the July 20 plotters, a vast, elite network going back to 1938 and embracing churchmen, jurists and intellectuals, not just the army officers accused of acting only to avert German defeat. But British and American leaders were vividly aware that the Nazis had come to power in part by riding the German nationalist movement's historical myth that Germany lost the Great War not on the battlefield but because of the "Stab in the Back" by socialists, liberals and Jews. The second time around, the Allies were determined to make the defeat unmistakable.

That made it much easier for the Germans to face up to their crimes. They had no choice. I recall, as a GI in Frankfurt in the early 1960s, taking part in a contact group between German university students and U.S. soldiers. During a discussion of the war, one of the young Germans said with great feeling, "We Germans want a holiday from history." Nobody granted them that.

Vectors of Memory

Exaggerating somewhat, French documentary filmmaker Marcel Ophuls, whose 1971 movie *The Sorrow and the Pity* set off the French public's reassessment of the French wartime record, says, "It is the same problem in France as in Germany, in different proportions to be sure. The French had to invent a victorious history. It was nonsense, but it was understandable. History was easier to deal with in Germany because they were the vanquished. They did rewrite their history books to acknowledge their guilt and so forth. But this problem remains at the center of French preoccupations, whether they admit it or not."

Ophuls, the French son of a prominent German Jewish moviemaker who took refuge in France, has devoted much of his career to the problem of memory. His latest film, *The Troubles We've Seen,* is about the role of memory in Sarajevo. And in 1976, he made *The Memory of Justice,* which opens with the Nuremberg trial of Nazi war criminals and wraps in such Allied crimes as the devastating firebombing of the German city of Dresden, an act that had no military justification, and continues through France's war in Algeria and the U.S. war in Vietnam.

Ophuls interviewed, among others, Albert Speer, Hitler's chief architect and a Nuremberg defendant released after a prison term, and former French premier Edgar Faure, an Allied prosecutor at Nuremberg. Speer dealt with questions about atrocities by escaping into disembodied abstract verbiage. Faure, however, spoke of the Nazi crimes in clear, direct, down-to-earth terms. Then Ophuls asked Faure about French actions in Algeria (admittedly a very different kind of war). The Frenchman's flight into abstraction was suddenly and hauntingly similar to the German's.

In France, a country with a major film industry, cinema is a key vector of national memory. Most French film producers, however, are loath to deal with historical controversy, an attitude that contrasts with Hollywood's willingness to tackle such subjects as the Vietnam War without waiting for the wounds to heal. Ophuls attributes this reluctance to commercial-minded "cowardice" and dependency on cofinancing by TV decision-makers who are even more prone to prudence. "It's self-censorship," he says. "Collectively speaking, French producers have been that way since the silent pictures. Look at the Germans; they've made lots of movies about the Nazi era. But what kind of country is this that hasn't made a real movie about the Dreyfus Affair, the most fantastic courtroom drama that you could imagine? My father tried to do things like that. But there was never any question of anyone allowing it, and there's still no question of it."

André-Marc de Loque-Fourcaud, spokesman for former Socialist culture minister Jack Lang, has a more complex explanation as to why the French have made minor movies about the Algerian war but not yet a big, honest movie like those the Americans have made about Vietnam. "Americans are ready to deal with things sooner than we are because they have a much shorter history," he says. "The Crusades and the Roman occupation are not part of their historical experience, but they are part of ours. The collaboration under Vichy wasn't anything new for us. It's the sort of thing we have dealt with throughout our history. Besides, for us, history is propaganda. So much of what was taught to us as history was pure invention, and it's still constantly being rewritten. What we were taught about Vercingétorix [the last leader of the Gauls] and Joan of Arc was invention, really."

Nonetheless, Loque-Fourcaud concedes that French governments have brought pressure against making movies about the reality of the Algerian war because "you shouldn't offend people's feelings." *The Battle of Algiers,* a 1960s Algerian-Italian coproduction made from the Algerian standpoint, was considered a masterpiece in the Third World but was banned for years in France.

"Take *Waterloo,*" Loque-Fourcaud continues, "a Soviet-American coproduction that was a failure in France. We've made practically no movies about our defeats. We don't want to be told we were not so great in Algeria or Vichy. The French don't like that. We were taught in history class that the French Empire was all about spreading civilization. We aren't going to make movies that call that into question, even if we know that what really happened was profoundly different.

"Americans don't have the same complexes about their history that we do. You went to the New World and forgot about the Old World. You grab hold of your history. Ours is full of taboos."

But, he notes, it is only recently that American moviemakers have started making films showing the savagery of the U.S. army during the Indian wars. "You Americans took almost no time to accept the reality of Vietnam, but you have taken far, far longer to accept how you settled your own country."

Martyrs and Victims

Despite their apparent reluctance to be entertained by their own defeats, the French do, paradoxically, like to think of themselves as victims or martyrs. Most of the great legendary heroes of French history have died tragically: Vercingétorix defeated by Caesar; Roland betrayed by his companion-in-arms while commanding Charlemagne's rear guard; Joan of Arc burned at the stake after being abandoned by the weak king she had enthroned; Napoléon exiled as a prisoner of the English enemy. This is psychological preparation not for self-examination but for La Revanche (as in Gambetta's dictum after Bismarck seized Alsace-Lorraine from France during the Franco-Prussian war: "Think of it always, speak of it never"). It is also preparation for the deep-rooted sense that the essence of history is tragedy.

Pétain's sense that the defeat of 1940 was a useful lesson in combating moral rot and encouraging national regeneration placed him firmly in the French tradition of heroic victims. Even his role as the victor of Verdun in World War I seems tragic because of the million men who died in history's bloodiest battle. De Gaulle's insistence that the French were victorious heroes thus appears to break with the image of the French as virtuous losers.

Perhaps it is because the French see themselves as victims in World War II that it is so difficult for them to admit that it was the French police, not the Germans, who rounded up seventy-six thousand Jews in France for deportation; that Pierre Laval went beyond Nazi demands by insisting that these Jews should be deported eastward, "without forgetting the children," and that it was not even Vichy but the democratic French Third Republic that created the first French internment camps for Spanish Republican refugees and later for German, Austrian and Italian antifascist refugees (including Jews) viewed as potential Fifth Columnists. Vichy only "inherited" such camps, noted a collaborationist trial defendant.

Yet those who try to paint the French as somehow sharing in Nazi guilt are obviously wide of the mark. There were 300,000 Jews in France before the war, and the 225,000 who survived did not do so by accident. Many non-Jews, including some of the police involved in the roundups, took risks to help them. The Jews in Germany and Nazi-occupied Eastern Europe were virtually wiped out, and they still don't find those countries congenial places to live. Today's French Jewish community is more than twice as large as it was before the war.

Erasing Folk Memory

France's colonial past is another chapter of French history that is still being digested. Endless ridicule has been heaped upon the classic French history manual used to teach black Africans about "our ancestors, the Gauls." There was nothing ridiculous about the intent: to assimilate the colonized elites as Frenchmen. France claimed to be bringing them culture and civilization. The colonized people's previous history could not be destroyed, but their memories could be erased or replaced with French history. It was an attempt to rewrite not History but Memory, a real-life example of George Orwell's fictional description of how Communist regimes shoved inconvenient history "down the memory hole."

In mainland France, this same policy of assimilation created a tense ambivalence between the centralizing French culture and the cultural identities of the Algerians, Alsatians, Armenians, Basques, Bretons, Catalans, Corsicans, Flemish, Jews, Poles, Protestants, Provençals and others who make up the French people. Assimilation meant a community had to give up its collective memory. Discrimination meant that the message of the Rights of Man was flawed.

France's attempt to turn immigrants and colonized peoples into Frenchmen made credible its insistence that the French were not racists—a policy that French spokesmen contrasted with that of Britain, which never tried to turn Indians into Englishmen. Now, of course, Britain returns the compliment by saying that it was more respectful of cultural identity.

Both approaches, however, beg the question of dealing with memories of colonial atrocities. The French public was far too focused on celebrating the German surrender on May 8, 1945, to notice that the French army was that same day massacring thirty thousand Algerian nationalists in Sétif to reassert French authority. Stirring of conscience over similar massacres in Madagascar in 1947, over the thousands who died in forced labor building the Congo railway and so on have still not been fully assimilated by official French memory.

Admitting Diversity

Today French national memory is no longer seen as the exclusive preserve of France's teaching corps. Under the Third Republic, these lay preachers instilled a new version of history, giving republicanism a near monopoly on virtue, while the priests taught rival memories of the massacre of two hundred thousand Royalist and Catholic counterrevolutionaries and the guillotining of nuns who would not renounce their vows.

Since the 1970s, starting with President Giscard d'Estaing's calls for *"décrispation,"* or *"relaxation,"* and continuing with President Mitterrand's acceptance of the rules of the game set by De Gaulle's Fifth Republic (the Socialists notably retreated from any idea of bringing parochial schools under central control), French society has grown more tolerant of cultural diversity.

The same fundamental debate about how much memory is good for a society is only just beginning in Eastern Europe (not to mention Argentina or Chile), with all the same competing principles—purge vs. pardon, social catharsis vs. consensus, justice vs. amnesty—in sum, remembering vs. forgetting. If the French experience is any indication, those questions will take a long time to sort out, and only much more history will settle them.

Perhaps the easing of the pains of memory really started in France back in 1959 with the birth of *Astérix,* the comic-book series that has sold hundreds of thousands of copies by mocking such official historical myths as "our ancestors, the Gauls." The French could finally make fun of themselves; laughter proved to be at least one useful complement to the "Duty to Remember."

Remembering the Righteous

Marek Halter is a Polish-born French human rights campaigner who has been on the front lines against oppression in Poland, the Soviet Union, Argentina and elsewhere. He has also been an ardent promoter of Israeli-Palestinian peace. His new film, *Tzedek* ("The Righteous"), is a documentary honoring those who saved Jews from Hitler's extermination program. He was interviewed in Paris by Ronald Koven.

RK: We are constantly told that it is our duty to remember certain things—things that are always horrors. But isn't it important to forget some things? It seems clear to me that memory is a two-edged sword that can also incite vengeance.

MH: Of course, forgetting is as important for humans as remembering. People who remember too much run the risk of going insane. We forget such things as physical pain very quickly. But people don't forget the harm their neighbors do to them. Those memories can become a kind of tribal memory unless they are transposed to the level of universal memory. Someone who has suffered an injustice may take it very personally unless he sees the episode objectively, as part of the evil inherent in mankind. That's where the notion of history as a lesson comes in. If we are to learn from history, we must recognize that the history of humanity is a reflection of all of us.

Palestinians have said to me, "The extermination of the Jews in Europe is none of our business. We had nothing to do with it." To them I say, "Why not? You are human. You are seeking my solidarity in the name of our common humanity. You should show your solidarity with my history too."

RK: When Palestinians say that to the Jews, don't they really mean: "Don't oppress me in the name of your misfortunes?"

MH: Yes, I think they do. And as I mentioned earlier, if misfortunes are not transformed into something universal, they may serve as a pretext for tribal warfare. As long as the Jews consider their misfortunes to be their exclusive property for which they demand an accounting, humanity won't want to share those misfortunes. I as well as many other people used to think that preserving the memory of the horror of what happened to Jews was the way to make the world stop and think, the way to ensure that that kind of atrocity would never happen again. Then I realized that the only ones maintaining the memory of the *Shoah* were the Jews. A thousand years from now, if we're the only ones who still remember

Auschwitz, then what will be the lesson for humanity? Six million people will have died for nothing.

RK: How does that idea relate to your film?

MH: People can't stand to be accused anymore. You can't say to a German skinhead today, "You're acting the same way your grandparents did." They couldn't care less. They think they're inventing their own crimes, against the Turkish immigrants.

If we are going to learn from history, Polish Catholics must start saying the same things I say. Perhaps they don't because we divided the postwar world squarely into two camps: all-good and all-bad, with nothing in between. There were the victims and the executioners. As far as individuals who just let the Holocaust happen, well, they were considered guilty, too.

Clearly, it was not that simple. There were people who risked their lives to save Jews. There were also people who knew about hideaways and didn't say anything. Half a million Jews were saved that way. It's not many, compared with 6 million dead. But as someone in my film says, "To save a Jew in Poland, there had to be one thousand Poles involved. To denounce one thousand Jews, it took just one Pole." To take in a Jewish family, there had to be an extraordinary network of complicity. Your neighbors, your concierge, the butcher who gave a little extra meat on a fake ration card, the local policeman, they all had to accept it, at least passively.

RK: Why did you make this film now?

MH: I felt a sense of urgency because many individuals who saved the Jews are very old now. Indeed, some of them have already died.

But there was another reason. At first, the Jewish survivors wanted to accuse everyone of having abandoned them, to give the world a bad conscience. I was told as a child in the Warsaw Ghetto that everyone had abandoned us. There were no demonstrations for us in the outside world, not even in America. But I continued to think that it just wasn't possible that in the whole wide world there was not a helping hand. The Talmud says that for humanity to continue to exist there must be at least thirty-six righteous individuals in every generation. That's the number of people I chose to interview in the film. But there were lots more who helped. Some were deported to Auschwitz, along with the Jews they tried to save.

I interviewed Catholics, Protestants, Muslims, people who didn't join the Resistance, people who didn't throw bombs but who saved the honor of humanity. Maybe young people are ready to share my memory because it reveals that a real generosity of spirit existed in their grandparents' generation.

RK: You did this for young people?

MH: Three years ago, I was speaking to a few hundred students at a French high school. Those kids wanted to work for good causes, against racism, against injustice, but I could feel they rejected my story about the war. Apparently, they thought my story was so horrible that nothing they could ever do would be as important. For them, I was putting the bar of heroism so high that they could never reach it. A fifteen-year-old boy essentially told me that I was discouraging the students instead of motivating them.

In the film I tried to show that alongside the evil in the war was the good, which was a form of heroism. Some individuals saved ten thousand Jews, others just one or two. I also show a man in Rome who saved no one but acted kindly toward neighbors he knew were in hiding. The neighbors were the family of the painter Modigliani. Today

Modigliani's son is a deputy in parliament, and for him that kind man, Gabrieli, who occasionally said a nice word or gave the children some candy, remains a symbol of human kindness. Modigliani has tears in his eyes when he talks about Gabrieli, who simply says, "I didn't do anything. I would have liked to, but I was afraid."

RK: In fact, he did do something.

MH: Yes, he made a very important gesture. He showed compassion, humanity, in a time when inhumanity was the law of the land. He knew where Jews were hiding and didn't denounce them. He ultimately helped save them.

"National Memory: The Duty to Remember, the Need to Forget" by Ronald Koven, *FRANCE Magazine,* Fall 1994.

Reflections: When the Old Wound Aches

BY NELSON BRYANT

editor's note

NELSON BRYANT was the outdoors columnist for *The New York Times* from 1967 to 1990, when he retired.

West Tisbury, Mass. When the barometer drops, and a cold, wet wind comes out of the northeast, my old wound aches and sometimes reminds me of when my fellow paratroopers and I jumped into Normandy a few hours before dawn on D day fifty years ago.

For many years I exploited that wound, made less than a week after my first combat jump by a machine-gun bullet that entered my chest and exited through my shoulder blade. Until I was in my late fifties, I would contrive to steer postdinner conversation around to the war, and then, if sufficiently unhinged by emotion and drink, I would tear off my shirt and invite guests to poke their fingers in the fore and aft indentations. There were times when I set fire to the hair on my chest to add a bit of drama to my antics and to better reveal the little entrance scar.

"Wear the silver badge of courage, drop like an eagle on your prey," the airborne recruiting posters had said, and the scars were symbols, albeit fading, of my having heeded that call.

Now having passed three score and ten, I have, I believe, put my participation in the Normandy and Holland jumps and the Battle of the Bulge in reasonable perspective. A decade ago, I wrote that taking part in those campaigns with the Eighty-second Airborne Division overshadowed all that followed, including love, marriage, career and children. That is no longer true. I have belatedly come to understand that slogging across the plain of everyday life with dignity and as much honesty as one can muster calls for as much heroism, if only because the struggle never ends, as assaulting a flaming hill.

Were it not for the old wound aching, months could pass before I thought of lying alongside a hedgerow, condoms taped over the holes made by the bullet, trying to swallow some of the soup a buddy was serving me from his fire-blackened helmet, or before I again recalled the first German soldier I killed as he walked along a dirt road in Normandy on the birdsong dawn of June 6 not knowing that I had him in my sights from the hillside above, slowly taking up the slack in the trigger and thinking all the while that the act was indecent, that it would be justified only if he was firing at me.

A few hours later, that dangerous reluctance departed in a short, fierce firefight that took the lives of several of my buddies.

There are also recollections of absurd encounters as when, the second morning after D day, I headed up a scouting patrol of three. I was given that task not because of my rank (I was a private first class) but because I had a smattering of French, enough to allow me to converse with the natives of the region. A mile or so from our own front line we came upon a farmhouse whose occupants greeted us warmly. The daughter of the household, a handsome, strapping six-footer, told me that there were no Germans in the vicinity. She then asked if they could have the silk parachutes (she had petticoats and such things in mind) that she had found in one of their pastures. I unhesitatingly responded, as befitted my lofty rank, that they were hers for the taking.

A big table was carried out into the dooryard, draped with white linen and laden with bread, cheese, cognac and wine, and the scouting patrol became a celebration of the invasion. I still wince as I think of what could have happened during our garrulous, lurching return to our little redoubt on Hill 30.

My Normandy endeavors ended the following day on a patrol led by Major Shields Warren Jr. The single bullet that hurled me on my back was one of a burst that riddled my fellow scout who whispered, "Help me, help me," then died.

The patrol surged on, encountered more resistance than it could handle, and returned under fire. Major Warren bent over me and said, "Nelson, if you don't want to be taken prisoner, you'll have to get off your butt and get the hell out of here."

I got off my butt, put my left arm over the shoulders of a fellow paratrooper and managed a stumbling trot back to Hill 30 where, draped with a parachute, I joined the other wounded. I don't remember whether we spent one, two or three nights there before a linkup with American assault troops from Utah Beach allowed us to be evacuated. I passed out as I was being loaded into an ambulance that took us to a tent hospital on the shore of the English Channel, and when I came to I was lying in the open on a cot and a fine rain was falling.

An older man's face, gaunt and compassionate, emerged from the dark clouds above me.

"Poor Nelson," he said. "How long have you been here?"

"I don't know," I replied, wondering how he knew my name, wondering if he was God. (A chaplain, he had looked at the metal identification tags that hung from my neck.)

My confusion ended when he told some passing GIs to take me into a large tent, where a weary surgeon glanced at me and cursed my chest wound.

Recuperating in a hospital in Wales, I was at first overwhelmed by the violation of my flesh, but by early July I was strolling, and, soon afterward, jogging, in the surrounding woods. I wanted to get back in shape, to erase the slumped-shoulder effect caused by my damaged right lung, and as my body mended, my desire to avoid further conflict began to fade.

When a rumor reached me that my outfit was preparing for another jump, I desperately wanted to take part in it. I cannot recall whether I left the hospital formally or informally, but by late summer I was back with my comrades—many new faces among them— in Nottingham, England, and on the sunny afternoon of September 17 I floated down to a soft, standup landing in a wide meadow on the outskirts of Nijmegen in the Netherlands. Part of the reason for the gentle landing was that, not yet being in top condition, I kept my gear to a minimum. My armament was a little M-1 carbine, a pocketful of shells for it and a couple of grenades. I soon regretted the choice of the carbine, which was useless at distances over 150 yards.

The Holland jump took the starch out of me, and when the Battle of the Bulge erupted a few months later I would have been content to sit on the sidelines, but that was not to be.

Rest after the Bulge campaign did wonders, however, and accounted for one more flare-up of compulsive behavior. A few days after Germany's unconditional surrender in May 1945, I marched down to company headquarters and requested permission to be transferred to the Pacific Theater, where the war had not yet ended. The company commander told me to go back to the barracks and read a good book.

The old wound aches, and most of the time the ache blends with all the other physical indignities to which my aging carcass has been subjected and reminds me of nothing save the attrition of the passing decades.

Of late, however, I have been dwelling on D day, and I am grateful that I was part of it.

I remember with some embarrassment the speech I delivered at my high school graduation in 1941. Laden with patriotic hyperbole, it brought tears to the eyes of the principal, but I cannot forget the sad and disapproving face of one of the town's ministers who sat in the front row. It was years before I understood his horror of all wars, however just.

I remember with gratitude the rifle range sergeant in basic training at Fort Benning who was bawling me out for shooting my M-1 from my left shoulder. I whispered to him that I had to shoot from that side because my right eye had been nearly blind since birth, that with a bit of chicanery—covering the bad eye twice, first with my right hand, then with my left—I had contrived to pass the airborne physical.

"If you want it that much, I'll say nothing," he said.

I am grateful to him because making the D day jump gave me emotional sustenance in the years that followed.

I had responded to the call as I heard it. In the dark watches of the postwar civilian night, I would lie listening to the measured breathing of our firstborn, whose cradle, because we were so poor, was a bureau drawer. And although frightened at the responsibility of caring for my family, I knew that fear alone was not enough to make me fail the gambit, that, in some ways at least, I was a man.

The old wound aches, and I am an old man filled with wonder at why I have been given so much time to wrestle with choices, to savor love, friendship and laughter, to dwell on the meaning of the long silence ahead while so many of the others with whom I drifted down through curving skeins of tracer bullets were so swiftly subtracted. Tomorrow evening, on the anniversary of D day, I shall sit on a boulder on the eastern shore of Lake Umbagog in the Maine wilderness as night falls, looking west over the hills, thinking of the brotherhood in which I have a cherished membership.

The French, Rude? *Mais Non!*

BY JOSEPH VOELKER

∽

editor's note

Lots of visitors to France have amusing language *faux pas* tales to tell. One of the most common mistakes is to say *"Je suis plein"* for "I'm full" after a meal, except that the phrase *Je suis plein* means "I'm pregnant" (*"J'ai assez mangé"* is a better way to say you don't want seconds). It is hard to speak French flawlessly. A more uncommon language mistake was related to me by my good friend Lorraine, an American who speaks French quite well. Her French in-laws once gave her daugher a red, wool cape, and in thanking them, Lorraine referred to it as a *capon rouge*. What she really thanked them for was a red condom (the in-laws blushed, but then had a good laugh).

Some French language trivia tips: Five exceptions to *liaison* (the practice of pronouncing the final *s* in a word when the next word begins with a vowel) are *les hors d'oeuvres, Les Halles, les haricots, les homards,* and *les hot-dogs*. The verb *chercher* translates as "to look for" (so you don't add *pour* after it); the verb *parler* is always followed by *à* and means "to speak to or with" (so you don't add *avec* after it). And the word for a conveyor belt at a grocery store is *tapis* (which is the word for carpet, rug, or mat).

JOSEPH VOELKER is associate dean of Franklin and Marshall College in Lancaster, Pennsylvania, and is the author of *Art and the Accidental in Anne Tyler*, University of Missouri Press.

It is funny that we Americans, in our current enthusiasm for cultural diversity, have collectively decided to be tolerant of all national and ethnic groups on the planet *except the French*. If a Bororo chieftain starts beating his wife in their hut, the visiting American anthropologist—though feminist to the core—will stand by and say nothing. But she'll tell you a story that vilifies the French waiter who refused to bring her a wine list.

No doubt there are complex historical reasons for this accept-ability of French-bashing: their arrogance as inheritors of a two-thousand-year-old culture, their irksomely deserved reputation for elegance and knowing how to live. And the fact that they are rude.

If we speak English, French waiters and hotel receptionists ignore us. If we try to speak French, they respond in English—and not always the best English at that. We are humiliated by this response. Why do they act so superior? Having recently spent a year living just outside Nantes, I venture a couple of amateurish expla-nations, in the spirit that *tout comprendre est tout pardonner*—to understand everything is to forgive everything.

First, the French language is simply much harder than the English. It certainly seems to have more tenses, moods and genders, and it's full of subtle and numerous irregularities. For instance, they don't pronounce the "f" in *oeufs* (eggs); for *deux oeufs* you have to say "duhz uhh." French is hard to articulate. The French mouth is far more tense than the English, and makes its sounds farther to the front, where seemingly minor errors can create major shifts in significance.

French people, from elementary school onward, learn their lan-guage in an atmosphere of intimidation. As corporal punishment was the medium in which our ancestors learned Latin, so humilia-tion is the medium in which the French learn French. As a result, they associate speaking badly with stupidity. At a dinner party recently, a French friend who is by no means pedantic told me she couldn't drink another glass of wine because it would cause her to make mistakes in the subjunctive.

Two of the best speakers of the French language in public life are François Mitterrand and Jean-Marie Le Pen, who correspond roughly in our political system to George Bush and Jesse Helms respectively. The two men are politically opposed on every count: Mitterrand is a socialist, Le Pen is a far-right xenophobe. But they share one attribute: They are able to employ the imperfect subjunctive spontaneously, in public speeches. It's a risky business; errors will be reported in the press. But doing it wins them respect and even votes.

In any given year, the French middle-schooler will have one course in French orthography, one in French grammar and one in French literature. All are hard, and all present the risk of humiliation. One reason the French are generally not good at foreign languages and avoid learning them is that they have no desire to suffer the agonies of French class all over again in another tongue. The vast majority—who by the way are not Paris waiters—are shy about speaking English because they fear they will sound funny.

A French academic I know (he's a Spanish professor) told me the story of a confrontation he witnessed in Paris. A retirement-aged American couple approached a Parisian and asked him where "Noder Daaame" was. The man responded by shrugging his shoulders and making a sound that I'm going to spell "PFFFFFT." Then he walked away.

Now, first of all, "PFFFFFT" is part of the French language. It means "I don't know" or "I don't understand." It is neither rude nor hostile. Children respond to teachers and parents with it. It is utterly unrelated to our "raspberry," which is spelled "PHGFPGHFPFR-RRT." The man made this gesture because he was a prisoner inside the difficult French phonetic system, in which *Noder Daaame* cannot by any stretch of the ear and brain be transformed into *"Nuhtr Dom-uh."*

"Okay," you answer. "He didn't understand and he said, 'I don't know.' But why did he walk away instead of trying to help?"

Well, France has been invaded a lot. Caesar arrived in 52 B.C. Then there were a half dozen Germanic and Hungarian migrations, followed by the Vikings, who stayed a century. And let's not forget three modern German invasions within a period of seventy years. Sometimes it is difficult for people whose country has never been invaded and occupied to understand people for whom that is a central fact of their national history. It is not admirable on the part of the French that they are not crazy about foreigners, but it runs very, very deep.

Hence, when the French insist on answering our noble efforts at their language by speaking English, we should be more forgiving. First, these are tired people trying to get through a day's work with dead-end jobs in the tourism industry. Second, they are sparing us from looking ridiculous, and thus embarrassing them in turn.

Early in my own sojourn in France, when I was by no means linguistically up to snuff, I found myself in the express lane of a grocery store. A tall young man challenged me—I didn't catch all the words—for being in the wrong lane. I stammered out an answer, to which he replied, *"Oh, M'sieur, vous ne parlez pas Français"* ("You don't speak French"). Instead of letting it go, I said, *"Mais, essayez-moi"* ("Try me"), unaware that the phrase is a standard homosexual come-on. Only his wife derived any enjoyment from the scene, and her *"Oh, Jean-Pierre, oh la la la la la la!"* will stay with me until I die.

Once I inadvertently told a French family gathered at the dinner table that my mother used to make wonderful jellies and she never put condoms in them *(les préservatifs)*. Once I phoned a neighbor to ask directions to a famous château and, wanting to know if she thought it was worth a visit, tried to ask, *"Vous l'avez vu?"* ("Have you seen it?") But the American phonetic system (and my untrained mouth) couldn't distinguish among the different French *u*'s, and so what I actually said was *"Vous lavez-vous?"* ("Do you bathe yourself?") She laughed inexplicably. An hour after hanging up, I realized what I'd said.

Just learning the body language to enter and order something in a bakery in France is a small challenge. Somehow we Americans never know where to stand. We end up dead center in the store, with everyone staring at us. I can offer some advice for negotiating small shops.

Begin with *"Bonjour,"* followed always by *"m'sieur"* or *"madame."*

(*"Bonjour"* by itself is rather abrupt—even, well, rude. In fact, I'd bet that that retired American couple approached that Parisian in a manner that seemed awfully brusque by his lights.) When you are handed your bag of croissants, say *"Merci, M'sieur,"* or *"Merci, Madame."* And always say *"Au revoir"* or *"Bonne journée"* or something equivalent when you leave. If that's all the French you ever speak, you'll be thought of as an intriguingly polite American.

And if you want to try the language, don't do it in the American Express office in Paris, for heaven's sake. That poor guy may have spent the last six hours in that cage. Get out of Paris, off the beaten track, where the people don't speak English, and where some of them will be delighted to chat with you. Try retired people: They've generally got the time, and therefore the patience, to let you practice.

If you need a subject, ask a question about food—or wine. Here's a sure thing. Ask if the region produces good asparagus—or, if you're near the coast, good oysters. These are questions so subtle, so complex, so rife with possibilities for a Frenchman to display a Cartesian clarity, that you will likely have a full hour in which you won't have to do anything but listen. If you want to say *"Ah, bon?"* ("Oh, really?") once in a while, go ahead. It's thought to be encouraging.

It pleases me to remember that the story I used to tell most often in conversation with new French acquaintances was the one about the grocery store, the *"essayez-moi"* story. I suppose I was shrewd enough to see that it endeared me to them. It was the sort of moment that they, as French people, feared the most. It is hard to explain, but it got me over a bridge. It made me human, rather than another bossy, abrupt American. *"Oh, le pauvre!"* they would say—"Poor thing!"— laughing in genuine sympathy.

We'll Always Have . . . Questions

BY ANN BURACK-WEISS

⤞

editor's note

I laughed out loud when I read this piece, especially when I got to the part about the handheld shower. I, too, have never been able to figure out what, if any, logic there is in this or how to use one without great difficulty.

ANN BURACK-WEISS, who claims to have never progressed beyond high school French, is the only contributor in this anthology who is not a writer by profession. She holds a doctorate degree in social work and teaches at Columbia University. In her work she has written for professional journals and academic books, but this effort was completely spontaneous. Her son, Kenneth Weiss, a professional harpsichordist living in Paris, is the reason for her frequent trips there.

The John Travolta character in *Pulp Fiction* had it right about Paris—things there are the same as here, "just a *little* bit different." His interest was piqued by the McDonald's special (a quarter-pounder transformed by the metric system and nostalgia for the monarchy into The Royal). Having just returned from a month in France, I share his quotidian observations. Mine, however, are awash in puzzlement. Would a French person take pity on me and answer the following:

Do you really save money on those timers?

Paris was probably dubbed the City of Light in irony—by a victim of the timer (aptly called a *minuterie*) that is attached to many lights in hallways and bathrooms. I picture this person midway up a winding staircase, or perhaps otherwise involved in a sealed six-by-six room, when the light clicked off. The French have combined their twin passions for privacy and frugality into the diabolical construction of Les Toilettes. The stall has a floor-to-ceiling door and a light that invites you to enter and fasten the intricate lock before the light suddenly turns off, leaving you to grope through a succession of awkward acts in total darkness.

Do you carry flashlights? Candles?

Doesn't it get expensive plastering up those holes in the wall?

Is there an expression for "penny wise and pound foolish" in French?

What do you do with the shower head while you soap and shampoo?

The French had to invent the shower *à deux,* not for its romantic possibilities but as a practical solution to an enduring national problem—the handheld shower. Alas, a shower partner is not always available. I have mastered the trick of never getting between the handheld shower and the wall in the curtainless tub. I accept that I will be standing in a foot of water, as tubs are short and deep and drains take their time. But I still don't know what to do with the shower head when I need both hands.

Do you hold it between your teeth? Under your neck?

Do you have special knee-toning exercises at the gym to work up your grasping strength?

Are you free mornings at seven?

Is attendance at scarf-tying classes mandatory in the public schools?

Every woman in France, nymphet to granny, wears a scarf. Squares, tiny and huge. Streamers, thick and thin. Silk, polyester, chiffon, wool—with everything from jeans to gowns—all tied with insouciant elegance. Not for them our continuous instructional videos at the scarf counter illustrating three obvious maneuvers: the shoulder triangle, the twice around the neck and the sailor's knot.

They intertwine two or more long scarves, they drape lightly and tightly, sling high and low. They wear scarves as hats, as belts, as hair bows. The men have only one style. And it is grand—very long, very trailing, very sexy.

Do you take off your scarves when you get home or do you keep them on till bedtime?

Are there any French people who just can't get the hang of it?

Are you free mornings at eight?

Is la caisse a cultural icon?

I am in a department store and see a soap dish that I like. I have the one hundred francs ($20) right here, the package will fit into my knapsack, and on to dinner—not. The salesclerk takes the dish from my hand and gives me a piece of paper. With it I go to the opposite end of the floor and wait as the empty-handed shoppers ahead of me converse earnestly and at length with La Caisse. The French are not a superficial people. Several modes of payment are possible and the meanings attendant to each must be explored. Payment concluded, claim ticket in hand, I cross the floor once again to the bath accessories department and these possibilities: the clerk who holds the dish is nowhere to be found, the clerk who holds the dish has never seen me before in her life and can't imagine what dish I'm talking about, the clerk who holds the dish remembers everything but where she put it. *Pas de problème,* here is another just like it. Well almost—it is a bit larger and twenty francs more. A notation on the chit, another trip to La Caisse, a return to her and . . . Voilà, the soap dish is mine.

Is this why the French dine late?

Are the motionless people in cafés recuperating from shopping expeditions?

How do you say "efficiency expert" in French?

Were the coquilles St.-Jacques *that Alice and Brad Hinkel of Des Moines enjoyed at Chez Claude (and asked* Gourmet *to get the recipe for) in fact . . . frozen?*

Don't deny that it is possible. The evidence is, as with Poe's pur-loined letter, hidden in plain sight—260 Picard stores full of frozen food lining the streets of France. Oh, they are wily. They have named the stores Les Surgelés—one glance through the window at the white-clad salespeople and low, long cases that you can't see into enhances the uneasy feeling that medical implements that you'd rather not think about are on sale there. Chef Claude may well have studied with Paul Bocuse—but don't tell me that when he has one of those nonstop days, he doesn't sneak into Picard for everything from *soupe* to *noix*. When the guests, ravenous from museum walk-ing, rush in asking, "What's for dinner?" he puts on his signature touch, a tomato rose, and produces the plate with a flourish. When they heap praises upon him, he stifles a knowing smile and thinks "just the way *I'd* do it myself, if I had the time."

Can a dish consisting of potato noodles, cheese, and ham (gnocchi-jambon-fromage) really be "Weight Watchers"?

What's the *real* story behind Croque Monsieur and Croque Madame?

Have you ever eaten a bad meal?

Can I come and live with you?

Your age, gender and appearance are, as they say in the person-als, not important. Oh, French person, I want to live your life. I want to walk kilometer upon kilometer every day—single file down narrow, curving streets and six abreast on large boulevards. I want to pay $3 for a tablespoon of coffee with a chocolate wafer on the side. I want to order a *tartine avec confiture* (bread and jam) at a different café every morning and notice how the bread is always a different length and consistency, the butter thick or thin, salted or sweet, the jam apricot or strawberry, already spread on or in a dish to the side, the price never twice the same. I want to pay confidently with money I no longer have to put on my glasses to check the denomination of. I want to shop where the bottle with the red cap is whole milk and the bottle with the blue cap is double *crème*. I want to go to a dry cleaner who calls a suit a costume and returns the pants done up in gift wrapping paper. I want to eat yogurt that sometimes tastes like sour cream and sometimes like sweet cream and is filled with fruits like rhubarb and figs. I want to stand in line for an ice cream cone where each scoop comes nestled in its own compartment.

I want to live where sitting is an activity that people get dressed up and go outside to do. I want to live where people who smoke don't cough and people who eat fat aren't fat and everyone looks as if they have secrets. I want to buy pierced earrings with those nifty European clasps.

I want to put my hand in my pocket and come up with a fistful of Métro stubs that were not required to leave the station last week and shuffle through them until I come up with the one needed for my release today. I want to stand midpoint on any bridge at any time of day, and store the sensations in every pore.

This piece originally appeared in the travel section of *The New York Times,* 2 June, 1996. Copyright © 1996 by Ann Burack-Weiss. Reprinted by permission of the author.

Bibliothèque

Europe

Europe: A History, Norman Davies, Oxford University Press, 1996. In the opening line to his preface, Davies states that "this book contains little that is original," but I would disagree. From the chapter titles ("Hellas," "Roma," "Origo," "Pestis," "Renatio," "Dynamo," etc.) to the manner in which ideas and material are presented, plus the useful appendices and notes at the end of the book, this *is* an original work, highly recommended.

The Civilization of Europe in the Renaissance, John Hale, Atheneum, 1994; first American edition, 1993. I picked up this book because the title was so similar to Jacob Burckhardt's *The Civilization of the Renaissance in Italy.* In the reviews on the back cover, the book was indeed compared not only to Burckhardt's classic but also to Fernand Braudel's *The Mediterranean in the Time of Philip II.* I needed no further justification to purchase the book. Featuring over one hundred black-and-white illustrations, this volume covers the period from about 1450 to 1620. Some of Hale's other works, which are ideal companion volumes to this one, include *Renaissance Europe, 1480–1520* (1971); *Renaissance War Studies* (1982); *War and Society in Renaissance Europe* (1985); and *Artists and Warfare in the Renaissance* (1990).

Fifty Years of Europe: An Album, Jan Morris, Villard, 1997. At last count, I discovered I'd read all of Jan Morris's books except three. Hers are among the very first books I distinctly remember as being responsible for my developing wanderlust. When I saw this volume, I thought, Who better to be a reader's companion on a tour of Europe on the brink of the twenty-first century? She's traveled to all of Europe's corners more than, I believe, any other contemporary writer, and one of the most appealing aspects of this book is that she often includes multiple perspectives, relating her observations on the first time she visited a place as well as more recently. The five chapters are sandwiched between ruminations on Trieste, which Morris refers to as "The cusp of Europe . . . where I can look one way toward Rome and Paris and London, the other toward Belgrade and Bucharest and Athens." The final chapter, "Spasms of Unity: Six Attempts to Make a Whole of Europe, from The Holy Roman Empire to The European Union," is perhaps the best.

The Penguin Atlas of Ancient History (1967; reprinted 1986), *Medieval History* (1968; reprinted 1992), *Modern History—to 1815* (1973; reprinted 1986), and *Recent History—Europe Since 1815* (1982), Colin McEvedy, Penguin Books. This is a brilliant idea: a chronological sequence of maps that illustrate political and military developments, which in turn illustrate history via geography.

Each individual volume is remarkably fascinating, and the four volumes as a whole present an enlightening read. Maps appear on the right-hand pages while one page of explanatory text accompanies them on the left-hand pages. Essential for history novices and mavens alike.

Travel Guide to Europe—1492: Ten Itineraries in the Old World, Lorenzo Camusso, Henry Holt and Company, 1992; originally published in Italy in 1990 under the title *Guida ai Viaggi nell'Europa del 1492* by Mondadori. This unique book, published to coincide with the five hundredth anniversary of the discovery of the Americas, deserves more than short-lived appreciation. Italian historian Camusso presents ten real (or probable) journeys, in chronological order, so that readers may imagine the passing of time and events. The first section of the book gives an overview of Europe in the fifteenth century and includes descriptions of what travel was like by horse, river, and seaworthy boats; the condition of roads; inns; money; royal families; artists and artwork; food and drink. Of the ten itineraries, Paris and cities nearby are featured in three. It was interesting to note that in a population chart of twenty cities on the itineraries, Paris was then the fifth largest after Istanbul (400,000) and Florence, Naples, and Venice (each 100,000).

France

Realms of Memory: The Construction of the French Past, Pierre Nora, English-language edition edited and with a foreword by Lawrence D. Kritzman, translated by Arthur Goldhammer, Columbia University Press; *Volume I: Conflicts and Divisions* (1996); *Volume II: Traditions* (1997); *Volume III: Symbols* (1998). Originally published in France in seven volumes as *Les Lieux de Mémoire* (memory places), this stunning collection is easily at the top of my de rigueur reading list. I would go so far as to say that if you only read these three volumes, you will have little need to read much else, and if you fancy yourself a knowledgeable Francophile and *haven't* read these, you just might be a poseur. This series is nothing short of a singular publishing event, hailed by *The Times Literary Supplement* in London as "a magisterial attempt to define what it is to be French." Not for the casual observer but for anyone seeking a deep understanding and appreciation of France and the French, this is a valuable trio of books.

The Identity of France, Fernand Braudel, in two volumes both translated by Sian Reynolds; *Volume I: History and Environment,* William Collins Sons and Co., Ltd., London, 1988; *Volume II: People and Production,* HarperCollins, 1988, first published in France under the title *L'Identité de la France,* 1986. This monumental work is phenomenal in its scope and originality. Braudel, who passed away in 1985, has been referred to as the "greatest of Europe's historians" and believed strongly in the necessity of world history. His genius was in his ability to link people and events across all time periods—in a single sentence. "Economic geography" was one phrase he came up with just before his death to describe his approach to history. And yet even he acknowledged that this was not quite right. In seeking to define the identity of France, he departs completely from any sort of chronological pattern. This is an unprecedented work, inexplicably out of print, but worth all efforts to track it down.

Fragile Glory: A Portrait of France and the French, Richard Bernstein, Alfred A. Knopf, 1990. To my mind, *Fragile Glory* is the best overall book about France since Braudel's *The Identity of France. Fragile Glory,* too, is inexplicably out of print, and I do not know if it was ever published in paperback, but I do see the hardcover frequently in used-book stores. Bernstein was the Paris correspondent for *The New York Times* from 1984 to 1987, and his book explores Paris and *"La France Profonde"* (this chapter is the best one I've ever read on the true definition of "deep France"), the concept of *le tout Paris,* naming French children, his unique "R5 complex," the myth of the anti-American, immigrants, French aristocrats, politics and parties, Jean-Marie Le Pen, *les affaires,* the French struggle with their past. By the final chapter, Bernstein has laid the foundation for two major but sometimes contradictory conclusions: that France is still a nation greater than the sum of its parts, but that the French people are becoming more like everyone else, losing many qualities that made them *different.* Another candidate for the de rigueur list.

Mission to Civilize: The French Way, Mort Rosenblum, Doubleday, 1988. When Rosenblum wrote this, he was senior foreign correspondent for the Associated Press in Paris (he is now a special correspondent to the AP and has also written two other wonderful books, *The Secret Life of the Seine*—see *"La Seine" bibliothèque*—and *Olives,* North Point Press/Farrar, Straus & Giroux, 1996). His career as a journalist took him to North and West Africa, the South Pacific, Asia, the southeastern part of the U.S., the Caribbean, the Middle East, Canada . . . all the former and present DOM-TOMs (*départements d'outre-mer* and *territoires d'outre-mer*). Yes, this book is about the French and France, but more specifically it is about the importance of *la mission civilisatrice* (read: colonization) to the French. Rosenblum explains the seemingly contradictory French foreign policy; the difference between a *mauvaise foi* and *mauvais caractère;* the *Rainbow Warrior bavure* (*bavure* being a hitch or foul-up, notably by officials or police, which is so common that a smooth operation is referred to as *sans bavure*); *beurs* and *beaufs;* the struggles in Algeria and Vietnam and the atrocities committed in both; and the presence of *"Faites mon jour"* (Make my day), *hypermarché* (super supermarket), and *le fast food* in the language. This book is by turns engaging, funny, and revealing, and though it's out of print, there are still copies out there. De rigueur.

France on the Brink: A Great Civilization Faces the New Century, Jonathan Fenby, Arcade Publishing, 1999. As excellent as the above-mentioned books are, an updated book on France was in order, and we now have Fenby's volume to provide us with thoughtful fodder for the early twenty-first century. Journalist Fenby—who has written for *The Economist, The Christian Science Monitor, The Times* of London and has been editor of the *South China Morning Post*—is married to a Frenchwoman and was named a chevalier of the French Order of Merit in 1990. He's been reporting on France for over thirty years, and in this work he presents a full array of the country's ills and contradictions, some of which are familiar (the Resistance was smaller than we like to think; high unemployment; immigration; government corruption) but nonetheless remain for us to reconcile. Readers who haven't kept up with the France of today may be alarmed to discover that some classic French icons— berets, baguettes, accordions, cafés, foie gras—are fading. In his review of the book for *The New York Times,* European cultural correspondent Alan Riding wrote that "the entire book serves as a valuable introduction to contemporary France." I would add that it is also de rigueur reading.

French or Foe?: Getting the Most Out of Visiting, Living and Working in France, Polly Platt, Culture Crossings Ltd./Distribooks, Inc., Skokie, Illinois, 1996; first published in 1994 by Culture Crossings, Ltd., London. Platt's on-the-mark book is without doubt the best one of its kind, and I consider it de rigueur for anyone planning to live, work, or study in France and anyone who really, really, really wants to understand the ways of the French. Platt's own company—Culture Crossings—which she incorporated in 1986, provides training seminars and workshops for corporate managers and executives and their spouses transferred to foreign countries. There is no other book as comprehensive as hers, covering such topics as perfecting the *mine d'enterrement* (funeral expression) and de-smiling; French time; the customer is automatically wrong; what *non* really means; what to expect at a dinner party; the French family; *se débrouiller* and le Système D; the logic of French management, etc. In addition to explanations, Platt offers her own personal tips, such as the Ten Magic Words (*Excusez-moi de vous deranger, Monsieur, mai j'ai un probleme*) and Persistent Personal Operating. Platt presents real people and situations in a clear and witty way. Irresistibly indispensable.

Culture Shock! France: A Guide to Customs and Etiquette, Sally Adamson Taylor, Graphic Arts Publishing Company, Portland, Oregon, 1990. Each Culture Shock! edition is authored by a different writer, and each is eminently enlightening. The France edition covers such topics as speaking and thinking in French, political parties, French film, the French attitude toward pets, the "no" syndrome, why things close for lunch, do's and don'ts in a restaurant, visas and work permits, queuing, being a guest in a French home, money and banking, and office and business relationships. The Culture Quiz at the end of the book is particularly helpful. Although some of the information is directed at people who plan to be in France for an extended stay, this is a really useful, basic guide that I consider de rigueur reading, even for a short visit.

The French Way: Aspects of Behavior, Attitude, and Customs of the French, Ross Steele, Passport Books, Lincolnwood, Illinois, 1995. One of my favorite books, this is a handy A–Z guide to eighty-five key traits of the French. Steele has compiled an interesting and useful list including abbreviations and acronyms tourists will need to recognize; the significance of the *bleu-blanc-rouge;* how *cartes de visite* (business cards) are used; *cocorico!* (not cock-a-doodle-doo); the French meaning of the word *extra* and other false friends of English; *gendarmes, agents de police,* and *les manifestations;* the deeper meanings of the word *grandeur; l'Hexagone;* high tech; holidays; *"La Marseillaise";* numbers; *la France métropolitaine;* politeness and directness; sports; time; xenophobia; and *yéyé. Absolument de rigueur.*

Creating French Culture: Treasures from the Bibliothèque Nationale de France, introduction by Emmanuel Le Roy Ladurie, edited by Marie-Helene Tesniere and Prosser Gifford, Yale University Press in association with the Library of Congress, Washington, and the Bibliothèque Nationale de France, Paris, 1995. The creators of the exhibit developed a theme for this project, which is to explore the relationship between culture and power in France; but I see this as nothing less than a history of France as told through its documents, manuscripts, books, orchestra scores, photographs, prints, drawings, maps, medals, and coins. Covering twelve centuries—from the time of Charlemagne to the present—you can imagine how extensive this collection is (the book runs to 478 pages). Some highlights include the "Letter of Suleyman the Magnificent to Francis I, King of France"; drawing of Catherine de Médici as a widow; first edition of *The New Justine, or The Misfortunes of Virtue,* by the Marquis de Sade; constitution of the Thirteen United States of America (French-language edition, printed at the behest of Benjamin Franklin); illustration of devices used to lift the two large stones of the pediment over the main entrance of the Louvre; map of the battle of Austerlitz; the handwritten *"J'accuse"* letter by Émile Zola in defense of Captain Alfred Dreyfus, which was then printed on the front page of *L'Aurore* on January 13, 1898; and five issues of *Resistance: Official Bulletin of the National Committee for Public Safety,* published from December 1940–March 25, 1941. I *love* this book. It's a masterpiece. Also included are a chronology of the history of France and good color maps.

Cultural Atlas of France, John Ardagh with Colin Jones, Andromeda Oxford Ltd., Oxfordshire, England/Facts on File, New York, 1991. Part of a great series, this edition is divided into four parts: geographical background, French history, France today, and a regional portrait of France. There are lots of maps and interesting statistics, and essay features covering such topics as cave art, hill towns of Provence, the Tour de France, the Dreyfus Affair, etc.

French Cultural Studies: An Introduction, edited by Jill Forbes and Michael Kelly, Oxford University Press, 1995. This volume, part of a Cultural Studies series (other titles cover Italy, Spain, and Russia), offers a variety of essays on French culture from 1870 to the present. The essays are grouped into three chronological chapters: 1870–1944; 1945–67; and 1968–95. If you are a serious Francophile, you'll want to add this to your library. The contributors are an impressive bunch (they're all British professors or lecturers), and there are a number of black-and-white reproductions of posters, drawings, photographs, and artworks throughout the book. There's also a chronology at the back of the book, and each chapter ends with "References or Suggestions for Further Reading." A valuable collection.

Portraits of France, Robert Daley, Little, Brown and Company, 1991. As a naive *étudiante,* I did not realize why the rue Lauriston, where Hollins Abroad Paris had its school for thirty-plus years, was referred to as *"sinistre"* until I read Daley's chapter, "The Gestapo of the Rue Lauriston," and learned that No. 93 rue Lauriston was the site of an infamous den of torture and inquisition during World War II—not by the Nazis but by a gang of French convicts organized by Pierre Bonny and Henri Lafont. (Happily—although I have nothing but fond memories of my classes at No. 16—Hollins has since moved its school out of the 16th altogether.) Daley has put together a miniature tour of French history and culture in this collection of twenty essays. The entry on drinking the 1806 Château Lafite in Les-Baux-de-Provence—even though it takes place far from Paris—is one of the best essays about a wine experience I've ever read. While his portraits take readers to all corners of *l'hexagone,* even dedicated students of France may find some surprises here as Daley has preferred to find his stories in places where most readers haven't looked before. There are, therefore, no sketches of the most typical French icons.

France: The Outsider, Granta No. 59, published by Granta Publications, United Kingdom, distributed in the U.S. by Penguin Books USA, New York, Autumn 1997. This edition of the hip, British literary magazine features modern France and *le malaise français* with essays by Patrick Chamoiseau, Luc Sante, Caroline LaMarche, David Macey, Assia Djebar, etc.; a selection of contemporary French slang from *Le Dico de l'Argot fin de siècle* by Pierre Merle; and a photo essay, "The Farm at Le Garet," by Magnum photographer Raymond

Depardon. As always, an insightful collection, and worth the effort to special order. (All *Granta* back issues are in print and can be ordered by sending $5 and the issue date to Granta USA, 1755 Broadway, 5th floor, New York, New York 10019; subscribers may order back issues—at up to 50 percent off— through the Web site www.granta.com.)

The French, Theodore Zeldin, Vintage, 1984, originally published in Great Britain by William Collins' Sons & Co. Ltd., London, and in the U.S. by Pantheon Books, 1983. Zeldin's book is referenced often as a classic. He is perhaps better known for his *France, 1848–1945* (Oxford), a monumental social history published in both a big hardcover and a five-volume paperback series. Nearly all the works listed in his bibliography in *The French* are in French, so he is not merely giving readers an exclusive British/American perspective. I feel the book is so witty because, as Zeldin explains on the first page, he puts a lot of stock in humor. As we know, comedians are often the only people willing to blurt out the truth, and Zeldin believes "nothing separates people more than their sense of humor." He found it interesting that the world knows so much about French cooking, wine, and the fine arts but little to nothing about French humor. Thus this book is filled with dozens of caricatures and cartoons, which help illustrate various points. There are six parts to the book, and throughout there are interviews with various French men and women, including Brigitte Bardot, Yves Montand, and Paul Bocuse. The concluding chapter, "What It Means to Be French," is alone a candidate for de rigueur reading.

The French: Portrait of a People, Sanche de Gramont, G. P. Putnam's Sons, 1969. Although published over thirty years ago, this book is still meaningful and truthful. Gramont is an astute binational observer (French-born, American-educated—at Yale and Columbia—and married to an American), and his book takes a different approach than Zeldin's. It's divided into two parts, "Data" and "Forms of Exchange," and Gramont manages to be both critical and fond of the French, going to great lengths to explain why they are simultaneously so imitated and so misunderstood. It's a shame this is out of print, but I see it often in used-book stores.

The Road From the Past: Traveling Through History in France, Ina Caro, Nan A. Talese (an imprint of Doubleday), 1994. What a grand and sensible plan Ina Caro presents in her marvelous book: travel through France in a "time machine" (a car), from Provence to Paris, chronologically, and experience numerous centuries of French history in one trip. I envy her and her husband, Robert Caro (the award-winning biographer of Robert Moses and Lyndon Johnson), for making such an unforgettable journey. I always plan my visits chronologically no matter *where* I'm going, so I am especially partial to Caro's method. Her route in this book takes travelers through Provence, Languedoc, the Dordogne, the Loire Valley, and ends in the Île-de-France. We not only progress chronologically, but the sites she has selected best represent a particular age and are also the most beautiful examples within each historical period. After seeing each period separately, and then to view all the periods together in Paris, is "an incomparable experience," as she concludes in her introduction. I would add that to see Paris alone in this fashion is also an incomparable experience, even if you've been there a dozen times. Caro's approach presents a unique way of looking at France, at history, and at travel.

Traveller's Literary Companion: France, John Edmondson, Passport Books, 1997. This is one book in a series that explores the relationship between writers and places, and it includes extracts from literary works; maps; biographies of the writers; a town-by-town guide to each *département* highlighting writers' houses and museums and anything of literary interest; and a list of recommended novels, plays, and poetry. Each chapter represents a region of France (Paris is allotted its own chapter and is divided into left bank, islands, right bank, and literary graves), and so the reader is led all around France and introduced to French writers and writers who wrote in France. With numerous black-and-white photos of writers, there is no other book like this for literary enthusiasts.

French Dreams, photographs by Steven Rothfeld, introduction by Richard Reeves, Workman Publishing Company, 1993. With writings by Edith Wharton, Balzac, Gérard de Nerval, Baudelaire, Henry James, Colette, Gertrude Stein, etc., to accompany the dreamy photographs by Rothfeld, this is a special treat to buy for yourself (but it also makes a nice gift for your favorite Francophile). The images—handmade Polaroid transfers—are not the Predictable Pictures of France one sees in so many other books. It's a beautiful package for those who appreciate beautiful things.

Citizens: A Chronicle of the French Revolution, Simon Schama, Vintage Books, 1990; originally published in hardcover by Alfred A. Knopf, 1989. I don't believe there is a better account of one of the major turning points in European history than *Citizens.* Schama is an interested and interesting writer (his *Landscape and Memory*—Knopf, 1995—might be the most beautifully written and unique book I've ever read) who strikes me as someone who covers a topic thoroughly or doesn't cover it at all. *Citizens* is not what I would call light reading, although it is entertaining, and it's not lightweight—at 948 pages it positively should not be packed in your bag—but if you are really interested in a complete, single-volume edition on the Revolution, this is it. Black-and-white illustrations, drawings, and photos throughout.

Dreyfus: A Family Affair—From the French Revolution to the Holocaust, Michael Burns, Harper Perennial (a division of HarperCollins), 1992; originally published in hardcover by HarperCollins in 1991. I've included this biography here, rather than in *"Les Personalités,"* because the Dreyfus Affair (1894–1906) remains one of the most significant events in French history. Even today, over one hundred years later, French scandals of one sort or another still command headlines of *"J'accuse,"* borrowing Zola's famous banner from his open letter in support of Captain Alfred Dreyfus. In *The Identity of France,* Fernand Braudel reflects on the remark of another historian, Julien Benda, who wrote that the history of France has in many ways been "a permanent Dreyfus affair." *L'Affaire* is also pivotal in the history of Judaism: Theodor Herzl, visiting from Vienna, attended the Dreyfus trial, recognized it as a sham, and shortly thereafter founded the Zionist movement. Michael Burns documents the Dreyfus family's beginnings in Rixheim, in eastern France, under Abraham Israel Dreyfuss. Treveris, a Roman village north of Rixheim on the Moselle River, provided the linguistic origin of the family name; Jewish families who remained after Germanic tribes pushed the Romans from the area in the fifth century borrowed the language of the new colonizers and used *drei* [three] and *fuss* [foot] to approximate the original Latin sound of Treveris), and takes us up to the present day, to the grandchildren of Alfred and Lucie Dreyfus. This is a shameful, extraordinary story firmly in the de rigueur category. With sixteen pages of black-and-white photos and a Dreyfus family tree.

The First World War, John Keegan, Alfred A. Knopf, 1999. As much of the war that changed the world forever was fought in France, it seems appropriate to include this work here. Keegan, distinguished author of fourteen books and a former military correspondent of *The Daily Telegraph* in London, is internationally respected as one of the best military historians. What I have found remarkable about Keegan's work is that he writes as if he had actually been there, but in fact he has never known combat—he contracted tuberculosis in his teens and was therefore disqualified from military service. This is a step-by-step, definitive account of the Great War, the end of which also marked the collapse of the Austro-Hungarian, Russian, and Ottoman empires. The war's effect on France immediately following the armistice and the coming catastrophe of its fall in 1940 cannot be overstated.

A Soldier's Story, Omar N. Bradley, introduction by A. J. Liebling—excerpted from a profile of Bradley entitled "Five-Star Schoolmaster," which appeared in *The New Yorker* on March 10, 1951—Modern Library War Series, 1999; originally published in 1951 by Henry Holt and Company. Modern Library recently introduced this war series (other volumes include Francis Parkman's *Montcalm and Wolfe,* Ulysses S. Grant's *Personal Memoirs,* and Theodore Roosevelt's *The Naval War of 1812*) with Caleb Carr as the series editor. In his overall introduction to the series, Carr makes several valid points about military history. He reminds us of the general attitude in this country during the sixties and early seventies, when admitting to an interest in human conflict was most unpopular. However, he counterargues that military-history enthusiasts are often among the most well-read people we'll ever meet, and that they are also usually quite knowledgeable in discussions of political and social history. "The reason for this," he writes, "is simple: the history of war represents fully half the tale of mankind's social interactions, and one cannot understand war without understanding its political and social underpinnings. (Conversely, one cannot understand political history or cultural development without understanding war) . . . military history is neither an obscure nor a peculiar subject, but one critical to any understanding of the development of human civilization. That warfare itself is violent is true and unfortunate; that it has been a central method through which every nation in the world has established and maintained its independence, however, makes it a critical field of study." Though Bradley's classic isn't exclusively about the war in France (Sicily, Tunisia, England, and Germany are also covered), the D day assault and the liberation of Paris are dealt with at length. Bradley—better known as the "GI General"— is often referred to as the greatest military tactician of our time.

D-Day: June 6, 1944: The Climactic Battle of World War II, Stephen Ambrose, Simon & Schuster, 1994. There are a plethora of books about the D day battles, but none are as good or as definitive as this one. Ambrose, author of over a dozen books—including a biography of Dwight D. Eisenhower—is a World War II historian and president of the National D-Day Museum in New Orleans. He is devoted to D day scholarship and has been referred to as the premier American narrative and military historian. For this project he drew upon fourteen hundred oral histories from the men who lived through it. This is really the story of the enlisted men and junior officers who freed the Normandy coastline, the twenty-four-hour story of their hard-won success. It's no exaggeration that Operation Overlord is referred to as "the most important day of the twentieth century." With two inserts of black-and-white photos and several maps.

The Collapse of the Third Republic: An Inquiry into the Fall of France in 1940, William Shirer, Simon & Schuster, 1969. I wasn't surprised to find that Shirer (*The Rise and Fall of the Third Reich*) had written this book, only that I didn't know he had until recently. It is, as you might expect, as thoroughly researched and revealing as *Rise and Fall*, and he carefully illustrates, point by point, how the fall of France was an absolute debacle. Until reading this I hadn't realized the extent of the utter chaos—the complete lack of communication between high government officials themselves as well as with the public—that followed the news that the Germans were en route to Paris. As French historian Marc Bloch recounts in the book, "It was the most terrible collapse in all the long story of our national life." No photos but good maps.

France Under the Germans: Collaboration and Compromise, Philippe Burrin, The New Press, 1996, translated from the French by Janet Lloyd. Robert Paxton referred to this book as "unsurpassed," and it is most definitely thorough and exhaustively researched. It's different from Paxton's book (below) in that Burrin, a Swiss historian, focuses on three sections of French society, each of which accommodated the Germans: French government, civil society, and a small but significant circle of journalists, politicians, and "ordinary" French people who voiced collaborationist opinions. Burrin seeks to dissect the meaning of the word *collaboration* itself, as it was first used by Pétain in October 1940 and which then passed into German as *Kollaboration.* It is important, as Burrin notes in his introduction, to understand how being occupied looked to the French then, and how they did not—perhaps could not—know what road they were going down and were not able to see the enemy for what he was. It may be too soon to refer to this work as a classic, but it already is to my mind. No photos, but a useful list of appropriate abbreviations and—best of all—a map clearly showing where the free and occupied zones began and ended.

Vichy France: Old Guard and New Order, 1940–1944, Robert O. Paxton, Alfred A Knopf, 1972. It doesn't take long to discover that, among the number of books about Vichy, the definitive volume is Paxton's. If you're only going to read one, read this. An internationally recognized authority on this subject, Paxton was an expert witness at the trial of Maurice Papon in 1997 (see his editorial, "Vichy on Trial," *The New York Times,* October 16, 1997). Understanding France during World War II is complicated at best, but is essential for understanding France at all today. Paxton documents the inner workings of the Vichy government, the politics between Philippe Pétain, Pierre Laval, and François Darlan, and the surprisingly slow growth of the Resistance. The fact that the Vichy government enjoyed such mass support came as somewhat of a shock upon the book's publication in 1972. It is accepted knowledge that the French wanted to avoid the destruction of France at all costs; Paris remains a beautiful city in part because of accommodation and collaboration. But the history of this period is certainly not as simple as that. As Paxton writes, "It is tempting to identify with Resistance and to say, 'That is what I would have done.' Alas, we are far more likely to act, in parallel situations, like the Vichy majority. . . . The deeds of occupier and occupied alike suggest that there come cruel times when to save a nation's deepest values, one must disobey the state. France after 1940 was one of those times."

An Uncertain Hour: The French, the Germans, the Jews, the Klaus Barbie Trial, and the City of Lyon, 1940–1945, Ted Morgan, William Morrow and Company, 1990. Morgan is a Pulitzer Prize–winning journalist who has also written biographies of Somerset Maugham, Churchill, FDR, and William S. Burroughs. He was a young boy in Paris at the time of the armistice, when he and his family left for Spain and then the U.S. He writes that he regrets they didn't remain in France to live through the occupation, as it was one of those times in history when people are faced with making a moral decision, and since he wasn't there, he's always felt like a deserter. Morgan came back to France in 1987 to cover the Barbie trial for *The New York Times Magazine,* and this work is the result of all the memories the trip brought back to him. It is also a record of the years 1940–45 in Lyon; he had access to thousands of pages of secret documents prepared for the Barbie trial, including hundreds of depositions that were never made public. Due to these documents, Morgan was able to provide much more detail about major events—and the everyday lives of residents under occupation. This is a moving, personal, and important account. Morgan notes that there were more journalists in Lyon for the Barbie trial than at the Nuremberg trials, and that younger people, mostly students, stood in line every day for hours hoping to get one of the one hundred seats set aside for the public. He wondered why, and he answered, "Because the French had to look into this particular mirror, however distorted. Because there was a generation of young people that was still picking up the tab for World War II."

Rescue as Resistance: How Jewish Organizations Fought the Holocaust in France, Lucien Lazare, translated by Jeffrey M. Green, Columbia University Press, 1996. This is not a book about the French Resistance, but rather French Jewish resistance groups who worked to rescue Jews. Lazare participated in Jewish resistance-group activity in France and is a Holocaust survivor and seems uniquely qualified to relate this important chapter in the German occupation of France. It's a significant and revealing study, and apparently the book's publication in France caused great public debate. Lazare's well-written and thoroughly researched book deserves a wider audience.

When Courage Was Stronger Than Fear: Remarkable Stories of Christians Who Saved Jews From the Holocaust, Peter Hellman, Marlowe & Company (Balliett & Fitzgerald Inc.), distributed by Publishers Group West, 1999; originally published as *Avenue of the Righteous,* Atheneum, 1980. In 1968, Peter Hellman visited Yad Vashem, the National Holocaust Memorial in Jerusalem. He was especially struck by the simplicity of the Avenue des Justes, better known as Avenue of the Righteous in English. The avenue is really a path lined with carob—and more recently, olive—trees, and under each tree is a small plaque displaying the name of a Christian (and in some cases a Moslem) who saved one or more Jews from Nazi persecution. Hellman recognized that this simplicity was deceiving, that behind each of these plaques was a dramatic story. He decided that very day that he wanted to learn more about these remarkable people. In this book he profiles five documented cases of the Righteous, each representing a different country (France, Italy, Belgium,

Holland, and Poland). His only criterion was that the Righteous person still be living and accessible, which obviously narrowed the field a bit. I include Hellman's work here both because it is inspiring and significant, and because the chapter on Raoul Laporterie gives a good account of life on both sides of the demarcation line (Raoul owned a clothing business on the occupied side but lived on the Vichy side, making it possible to offer his services as a *passeur*, someone who could slip Jews and others across the border). I consider this wonderful book de rigueur reading for everyone, but it comes with a warning: avoid reading it on any form of public transportation unless you don't mind others seeing your tears.

Your Name Is Renee: Ruth's Story as a Hidden Child, Stacy Cretzmeyer, Biddle Publishing Company, Brunswick, Maine, 1994. While Raoul Laporterie's story in Peter Hellman's book above is of a *passeur*, Ruth Kapp Hartz's story is of a refugee, written by a college classmate of mine. It is, obviously, a bit more dramatic: Ruth, only four years old in 1941, and her family were foreign Jews (originally from Germany) and as such were targeted to be expelled from the Unoccupied Zone. They had left Paris soon after the Nazis arrived in 1940, and their life since that time was one forced departure after another, moving from place to place in southern France, much of the time in hiding and several times nearly discovered. Ruth (alias Renee Caper) survived the war, and it wasn't until it ended that she realized she was wrong about how the French population had acted during the occupation. Because she was sheltered in the south, where she was treated kindly and protected by a number of citizens, she truly believed that 90 percent of the population had been involved in the Resistance. Upon her return to Paris in 1946, she was shocked and confused to confront anti-Semitism. In the afterword, she offers some thoughts on how to account for this difference.

PARIS ORSAY
15·2· 99
RUE DE COURTY 7è

271340
COLLECTION PERMANENTE
ENTRÉE
Plein Tarif A

PAR AVION

La Seine
(The River Seine)

The Seine, at Paris, is more than beautiful. Poets and neo-impressionists shift their attention to it as the mood strikes. But it is also the main character in the lives of eight million people. Three-quarters of Parisians' drinking water comes from the river. And a lot of their industrial poison and raw sewage empties into it. You do not have to jump off a bridge to commit suicide, one engineer observed. The backstroke is enough.

—Mort Rosenblum,
THE SECRET LIFE OF THE SEINE

The Well-Loved River

BY PIERRE SCHNEIDER

∽

editor's note

I know the *bateaux-mouches* are viewed as the ultimate tourist gimmick, but I love them all the same because I love seeing Paris (any city, really) from the river. It may be corny, but the vantage point can't be beat, and at nighttime, when many of the riverside monuments and buildings are illuminated, it's a breathtaking, romantic, and beautiful spectacle. The recorded commentary that accompanies the ride is completely worthless, so ignore it and just enjoy the view.

Some readers may remember the old *Horizon* magazine, where this piece originally appeared. *Horizon* was published in a hardcover, oversized format on beautiful paper and profusely illustrated with color and black-and-white illustrations. I collect them, and now have about thirty editions. I've found many of them at the Argosy Book Store in New York, but my biggest cache actually came from a neighbor's curbside refuse pile. Look for copies at used-book stores and tag sales—you won't be disappointed!

PIERRE SCHNEIDER contributed frequently to *Horizon* and wrote pieces on the artists Joan Miró, Pierre Bonnard, and Nicolas Poussin, among others.

The prestige of "the glorious river Seine," as Anatole France called her, is almost incomprehensibly disproportionate to her length: a mere rivulet when compared to the Amazon, the Nile, or the Danube. And yet, to those who know her, she—let us call her she, being all curves and, besides, the daughter of Bacchus—is the very paragon of rivers. When Dr. François Bernier reached the banks of the Ganges in 1665, on his way to the court of the Great Mogul to act as the latter's private physician, he "seemed," according to his companion Tavernier, "much surprised to find that the Ganges was no wider than the Seine in front of the Louvre." In that case, why go? The French are notoriously allergic to emigration. "We don't have Venice and its moon, nor its breeze, nor its lagoon, but we have the Seine," sang Parisian canoeists a century ago. Some people apparently did not even suspect the existence of other rivers. When Madame Grand, passing through Lyon, was shown the Saône, she exclaimed: "The Saône! Oh, how differently it is pronounced from Paris. In Neuilly we say 'the Seine'!" In a sense the frivolous lady was right, for through the centuries Paris has been the center of France, and Paris owes its predominance to the Seine. For what made the rulers of the Île-de-France, initially just a small medieval fief, prevail in the end over other, often stronger feudal lords was the key position they occupied on the river. Thus her course is not so short after all: she runs through five hundred miles of French countryside and twenty centuries of French history and civilization.

The way she runs provided her with her name and another key to the mystery of her importance. "Seine" comes from *Sequana,* which in turn is a latinized version of the Celtic word *skwan,* meaning "winding." In a straight line, the distance between spring and estuary is only 250 miles—just about half that of her actual itinerary. No other river shows such reluctance to reach the sea, and quite understandably: from Burgundy to Normandy she traverses some of France's most exquisite landscapes. In Paris she behaves like the American student who comes to visit, is conquered, and finds a pretext to stay: it is not until she has meandered three times through the city that she consents to move on.

Geologists, of course, have another explanation. Between spring and estuary, the difference in altitude is a paltry fifteen hundred feet, a fact that prevents her from rushing headlong to her end. Then too, the low quota of clay in her bed enables it to absorb sudden increases in the flow of water. Dramatic floods have occurred, but they are few and far between. Elderly Parisians still remember the winter of 1910 when several quarters were inundated. The worst flood took place in 1176. Bridges, houses, cattle, everything was carried away, until the Bishop of Paris, accompanied by the king and his court, came to the river and showed her the nail that had been used to pierce Christ's hand, saying, "May this sign of the Holy Passion return thy waters to their bed and protect this unhappy people!" They did. Our godless age has constructed dams and built up the banks. Anyway, it should be said that whatever floods occur are not the fault of the Seine but of her more torrentuous tributaries, the Marne and the Yonne: When you throw a big party, how can you prevent a few obnoxious strangers from crashing it?

On the whole, however, the Seine is smooth and slow. The virtue of that slowness has deeply impressed itself on the French spirit—how deeply can be sensed if we remember that the Seine's course is literally a demonstration of how a little can be made to go a long way. French vocabulary is extremely limited when compared to English, but every word is made to bear a maximum weight. Racine's tragedies seem narrow next to Shakespeare's, but they compensate in intensity for what they lack in extensiveness. A few apples, a small mountain, and some pine-covered rocks were all that Cézanne needed to revolutionize modern painting. An analysis of the mainstream of French culture must lead to the conclusion that its behavior parallels that of the Seine.

In reaching that conclusion so quickly, however, I have shown myself most disrespectful toward her message. So let me start again. But where? The answer seems simple: at the beginning. Unfortunately, the Seine has several. Is its source at Mount Tasselot, or near Saint-Seine l'Abbaye, or elsewhere? Specialists have long argued about it. The dilemma was finally bypassed, if not solved, when Napoléon III's government ordered the construction of a monument at the spring gushing near Saint-Seine. It is a fake grotto, with a basin, above which reclines a grotesquely academic female figure in stone. The responsible authorities have committed a twofold sin: against taste by perpetrating such a horror, and against truth by leading us to believe that greatness is a birthmark. Actually, nothing distinguishes this thin trickle of water from its numerous brothers in the neighborhood.

For the Seine's origins, we also have a choice between two legends. The pagan one relates how the nymph Sequana, relaxing on a Channel beach (no doubt the future site of Deauville), was espied and pursued by Neptune; she fled inland and, as her lecherous tormentor was about to catch her, implored the gods' help. They turned her into water and, much against his wish, Neptune had to wash his hands of her. In fact, this myth transcribes a natural phenomenon still observed today: the Seine's estuary is so broad that the sea's tide moves up along it, occasionally throwing up on the forefront of its progress a fierce-looking band of waves known as the *barre,* or the *mascaret.* The Christian legend, on the other hand, tells how the aged Saint Seine, returning one evening to the abbey he had founded, saw his donkey kneel down to make it easier for him to dismount and, more miraculous still, saw a spring welling up at the spot where the animal had kneeled. Different as the two stories are, they agree on one point: the curative virtues of the spring. Archaeological evidence, interpreted by medical authorities, shows that immersion in, or absorption of, Seine water was particularly effective against eye sores, sterility, imbecility, venereal disease, cellulitis, and hermaphroditism.

A few paces away from this spot a plank has been thrown across the rill; far downstream, at Tancarville, the Seine is spanned by a bridge nearly one mile long—the longest in Europe. Still, that plank deserves a pause: since civilizations grew up on the banks of rivers, bridges must have been one of man's earliest and most precious inventions. The last war, which destroyed so many of them, showed us how thoroughly their collapse short-circuits the current of community life. I do not know how many bridges there are on the Seine (more than thirty in Paris alone), but I do know that no public buildings are as deeply imprinted in the affections of Parisians. The earliest, the Petit Pont, has been destroyed and rebuilt sixteen times during the past thousand years. The Pont Neuf—which, by a quirk of history, is now the oldest surviving bridge—was the first not to be lined with houses and the first public thoroughfare to sport sidewalks. It quickly became an open-air salon where mountebanks, quacks, and barbers performed, watched by crowds of *flâneurs;* hence the saying, "At any time, on the Pont Neuf, you are sure to meet a monk, a white horse, and a whore." For a while it lost its role as Paris's promenade deck to the Pont des Arts, built by Napoléon Bonaparte on his return from Egypt. He lined it with orange and pomegranate trees, and with benches in the Roman style. Gone today are the fig and orange trees; gone, in fact, is Bonaparte's Pont des Arts; but on the present "temporary" bridge—in France temporary has a way of meaning permanent—the city's last organ grinder still performs.

The Pont Neuf's first stone was laid by King Henri III; the Pont de la Concorde, on the other hand, close by the spot where Louis XVI was beheaded, was built with stones from the Bastille, whose destruction ushered in the fall of royalty. But bridges are more essential than those who cross them. After Napoléon's defeat at Waterloo, the king of Prussia wished to blow up the Pont d'Iéna, named after one of his most resounding disasters. Upon hearing this, Louis XVIII, though Napoléon's lifetime enemy, had himself wheeled onto the bridge and declared: "They shall have to blow us up together." The bridge still exists but arouses no interest, whereas the Pont de l'Alma, though no more handsome, does—at least at times when the Seine is rising. Then every Parisian comes to inspect how far the water has mounted along the leggings of the Zouave, a statue on one of the bridge's piers. On the bridge's other pier another stone soldier stands frozen at attention, a no less convenient flood barometer—but no one has ever been concerned with him.

That kind of apparent injustice is quite in keeping with the Seine's character. When, at Marcilly, she meets her first important tributary, the Aube, the latter is the bigger of the two streams. Yet the Seine's name prevails. At this early stage the Seine is so inconspicuous as to be almost invisible, except from a bridge. You can tell her meandering course only by the trees that crowd her banks. Among them, poplars dominate, as they do along so many French roads. But then, Pascal has pointed out that "rivers are walking roads that carry us where we wish to go." Napoléon phrased this thought more matter-of-factly: "Paris, Rouen, Le Havre, are all one city of which the Seine is the main street." Nature invented the conveyor belt. Indeed, rivers are the world's earliest instance of automation, though it took men a long time to realize it: the earliest wills date back to the time of Augustus. It took man far less time to discover another use of the river: as washing machine. The Seine's early course is lined with countless *lavoirs,* where kneeling women clean the family linens and blemish their neighbors' reputations. As we move downstream, the washhouses disappear under the double impact of household appliances and pollution.

A different sort of pollution is first encountered near Anglure on the Aube: world history. The town's lord had been captured by Saladin during the Third Crusade. He had been allowed to return home on his word of honor in order to collect the money for his ransom and, having failed, he went back into captivity. Touched by such honesty, Saladin set him free on the condition that all the lords of Anglure were henceforth to bear Saladin as their (un)Christian name and that he build two mosques in his domains. One still exists at tiny Clesles on the Marne, but is now called the Fromage Tower, after the cheeses stored in it. The hostility to the exotic evident in this coarse anticlimax is a fundamental characteristic of the French spirit: the classic poet Boileau ends his enchanting description of the Seine at Haute-Isle, his rustic retreat, with this rather unexpected couplet:

> Its banks are lined with willows planted by nature
> And with nut trees oft insulted by the passerby.

It is my contention that the French invented the *vespasienne* to make it perfectly clear that this kind of insult is not the consequence of a pressing need but a gesture freely willed: a deliberate affront to sublimity. Restif de la Bretonne left another such footnote scratched into a parapet on the Île Saint-Louis, Paris's loveliest island. Commenting on an enchanting love affair, he wrote: "She made me happy, I made her pregnant, we are even."

With the absorption of the Yonne at Montereau, the Seine reaches adulthood, an age she inaugurates in the same manner as humans: with military service. At Montereau, Napoléon won his last big battle. The dangerously genial emperor is a splendid illustration of how closely the course of French history is entwined with that of the Seine: he abdicated at Fontainebleau and lived stormy days with Josephine at Malmaison: his first action after arriving in Paris—by riverboat—as a hungry Corsican youth was to browse along the quays; and had Europe's monarchs known the title of the battered book he purchased, well might they have trembled—it was *Gil Blas,* the story of a poor but ambitious boy who rose to absolute power. In his will Napoléon wrote: "I desire my ashes to rest on the banks of the Seine, amid the French people whom I loved so much." In 1840 the French government asked Great Britain for permission to make the transfer from Saint Helena. Lord Palmerston agreed to the request, though he thought it "very French." No record survives to show whether the throwing of Joan of Arc's ashes into the Seine at Rouen was regarded by the Dauphin as very English. Be that as it may, Napoléon's remains traveled solemnly up the Seine that year, to a great display of popular emotion, aboard the *Dorade III*, one of the steamships with the huge wheels and beanstalk chimneys introduced on the Rouen-Paris route only a short time before. Forty years earlier a certain Mr. Fulton, an American, had sought to interest Napoléon in an invention with which he was experimenting on the Seine, "a water-chariot moved by fire," as a contemporary described it. "Impostor," had been the emperor's curt reply.

Its eminent navigability was of course the Seine's chief quality from the outset. The Gauls had sailed and rowed on her and floated logs down her course; she was particularly precious in those troubled centuries when roads were few, bad, and dangerous. Even today, however, the traffic is intense. Rouen is eighty miles away from the sea, yet its importance as a port is equal to that of Le Havre; and cargo ships push as far inland as Paris, whose port, in terms of tonnage, is among the largest in France. Still, they are intruders, like the seagulls whose squeals are heard on certain days along the quays, or like the speedboats used by newspapers to deliver their latest editions more swiftly than the traffic-jammed streets would allow. Far truer to Sequanian style were the old river-coaches: distances were short, but the sluggish pace of these forerunners of the *bateaux-mouches* seemed like a real cruise. And, as on cruises, poignant idyls blossomed: the hero and heroine of Flaubert's *Éducation Sentimentale* meet on the ship that carried Napoléon's ashes, and Alain-Fournier made on a *bateau-mouche* the brief, hopeless encounter that was to inspire the most romantic scene of *Le Grand Meaulnes*. But really to understand the river's mentality and rhythm, we must turn to those surviving monsters of a less hectic age: the barges.

From north, east, west, and south, along tributaries and canals, they come puttering and creeping (towage by humans has disappeared, and the use of horses is on its way to extinction). It takes great strength of character to accept the excruciating slowness of barge life: barge people are a race apart, and the gap between them and landlubbers widens, if anything, as the tempo on the firm ground becomes faster and faster. Barge children feel uprooted when they are sent to school on land. Cases of landlubbers becoming successful bargemen are almost unknown, and few girls who marry a bargeman can bear fluvial life more than three or four years. Until recently, many river people could neither read nor write. Legislation has only lately ceased to treat them as nomads. They are wary of terra firma, venture on it only at certain bridgeheads, drink at their own *bistros,* shop at their own grocery stores (usually run by lockkeepers), and whenever possible, as at Conflans-Sainte-Honorine, pray in their own church—a barge, naturally. Between them and earth, the distance is but a few steps, yet they are worlds away, too busy holding the wheel and forging ahead to step ashore: a five-minute pause may mean a three-hour delay at the next lock.

Infinite patience, detachment, and preservation of customs that hark back to a quieter, saner universe—a universe still in touch with its wellsprings—are the presents the river lavishes upon those who approach her closely. Nowhere is the contrast more striking than in the heart of frantic Paris. To step down from the busy, car-jammed avenues along the Seine to the waterside quays is to regress into the past. Down here, grass grows between uneven cobblestones, poplars mirror themselves in the lazy current, the noise above is reduced to an agreeable hum. Whoever walks here is engaged in timeless activities: lovers embracing, old men chatting, a master walking his dog. The Seine is the natural ally of those who, temporarily or forever, have rejected the bonds of society: *clochards,* painters, and fishermen. One of the heartening things about Paris is to see how many fishermen are left in it and the fascinated attention with which their quixotic efforts are followed by passersby.

They are still exactly as Daumier sketched them. "Oh woe!" exclaims a rain-soaked lady shivering beside her husband who clings stoically to his rod, "Oh to have dreamt all my maiden years of a spouse who would share my taste for poetry, and to hit upon a husband who only likes minnows!" A poet he may not be, but a philosopher he is beyond doubt. "The fisherman," Daumier himself comments elsewhere, "is the truly independent, persevering, and resigned man; adversity does not discourage him." Indeed, I suspect him of being almost disappointed when he catches a fish: he is not doing it for profit.

At street level the browser is the intellectual equivalent of the fisherman down below. No less superbly indifferent to passing time and to social pressure, he plunges his eyes into the oblong green boxes of the *bouquinistes,* hoping to hook a rare and useless masterpiece amid the piles of dusty books. This affinity between words and rivers is the profound reason for their proximity in Paris where, as Guillaume Apollinaire nicely wrote, "the Seine flows between banks of books." The spectacle of so completely harmonious a conjuncture between the physical and the spiritual is one of the most satisfactory to be encountered in our world. Few French writers have remained unreceptive to it. "The air that comes to me from the river is lighter than elsewhere," wrote the poet Léon-Paul Fargue, who also claims a *clochard* assured him he slept on the quays facing the Louvre because he dreamt more distinguished dreams there. Anatole France would certainly have agreed: "Inasmuch as there are trees there," he wrote, "with books, and as women pass there, it is the most beautiful place in the world."

The quays are one of the points where the Seine's influence on French ways of thinking and literature is most deeply felt. "By frequenting those old, worm-eaten volumes," Anatole France remarked, "I gained, already as a child, a profound sense of the flowing away of things and of the universal nothingness." If that kind of wistful, resigned pessimism is so frequent in French literature, it is because of the Seine. Malherbe, Racine, La Rochefoucauld, Sainte-Beuve, Baudelaire, and countless others owe it a great debt, which Guy de Maupassant acknowledged for them all when he wrote: "Ah! the beautiful, calm, varied, and stinking river, full of mirages and filth. I believe I loved her so much because she revealed to me the meaning of life."

With time the proportion of refuse augmented until, a century ago, Théophile Gautier scoffed:

> The Seine, black sewer of streets,
> Loathsome river fed by gutters,
> Dirties my foot . . .

Was it while gazing at it that Verlaine came upon his definition of water, "that impure liquid, a drop of which is enough to spoil the transparency of absinthe"? But it has proved an insufficient deterrent to Paris's half dozen swimming establishments on the river. It is one of the best proofs of the Parisians' continuing faith in the pristine purity of their river—an obstinacy worthy of bargemen and fishermen—that they continue to jump into it by the thousands despite the fact that the proportion of filth to mirage is crushing. They do so without illusions. "Hey, old boy! Is the water good?" asks a character in a swimming establishment caricatured by Daumier (who lived right above one). "Young whippersnapper, if it were good, it wouldn't cost a mere twenty centimes."

The bond between bargemen, bathers, fishermen, and browsers is obvious: a certain insulation from the follies of modern life. Now insularity is an attribute of islands; hence Parisians have a veritable cult for theirs. Paris's nucleus, after all, is the Île de la Cité, and its most handsome district the Île Saint-Louis. In the eyes of Parisians, every island must be a desert island or a Cythera, and so they have long treated those that stud the Seine in the downstream suburbs as a combination of both. Today, mills and shanty-towns have all but conquered them; but here and there a rustic *guinguette*—where you can eat fried fish, drink *un petit vin blanc,* and promise eternal love to passing acquaintances—hangs on heroically, sandwiched between two factories. And I confess to being moved beyond words by the sordid tavern facing the Île Robinson, now turned into a grim coal dump, which continues to call itself with desperate bravura "The Balcony on the Islands."

The supreme attraction of islands remains yet to be mentioned: to reach them you must take a boat. Rowing and sailing attained, between 1860 and 1910, a popularity difficult to imagine at present. Maupassant was speaking for several generations that wore sailor shirts, straw hats, and mustaches, or twirled bright umbrellas, when he reminisced: "How many funny things and funny girls I saw during the days I spent canoeing! . . . a life of strength and carelessness, of gaiety and poverty, of robust and boisterous merrymaking."

The little boats often carried women—light women, so as not to weigh down unduly their frail hulls. But the fickle grisettes who trusted whatever was left of their virtue to the river should not be judged too harshly. Their lack of morals was more than compensated for by their warmheartedness and a disarming absence of snobbishness. Victor Hugo relates a charming example of these Sequanian traits. The Duc d'Aumale, son of King Louis-Philippe, was wont to walk home along the riverside from the camp where he was stationed as a captain. On the banks he met, day after day, a young girl, Adèle Protat, with whom he gradually began to flirt. One day, as she was canoeing on the Seine near Neuilly, she saw two young men bathing. "That's the Duc d'Aumale," the boatman told her. Adèle grew pale and said, "Bah!" And Victor Hugo concludes:

"Next day, she no longer loved him. She had seen him naked, and she knew he was a prince." She would certainly have felt more at ease in the company of Maupassant: "A woman is something indispensable on a boat. Indispensable because she keeps mind and heart awake, because she stimulates, amuses, distracts, lends spice, and completes the scenery with a red umbrella gliding against the green banks."

The picture evoked by these lines has, I am sure, brought a name to every reader's lips: Auguste Renoir. This is no coincidence. The very same places favored by Maupassant—Argenteuil, Bezons, Bougival, Châtou, *guinguettes* like La Grenouillère, and restaurants like Fournaise—were frequented and painted by Monet, Renoir, Manet, Sisley, and Pissarro. What attracted them to the river? The passion of the time for boating, to be sure. Sisley and Renoir sailed all the way down to Le Havre. Monet, taking a cue from his master Daubigny, spent long months on a studio-boat. They found both pleasure and inspiration in the gay life of the Seine. "I was perpetually at Fournaise's," Renoir recalled later. "There I found as many splendid girls to paint as I wanted. One wasn't reduced as today to follow a little model in the street for an hour, only to be called a dirty old man in the end."

But the Seine had something more important to offer them: impressionism. For some years, they had been trying to break out of the closed forms and the dark, compartmented colors prevailing around 1860. It was the Seine that furnished them the instruments: light and water. Under their twofold assault, forms were broken up into a myriad of brilliant reflections loosened by the tremulous atmosphere and reverberated across fluid surfaces. Stable facts gave way to fleeting "impressions." From his studio-boat Monet observed "the effects of light from one twilight to the other." He first studied the Seine at Bonnières in 1868; later he worked in the company of Renoir near Bougival; in 1871 he moved to Argenteuil; later to Vétheuil; finally, to Giverny, where he died, half a century later. Yet he continued to pursue those passing impressions on his pond strewn with water lilies, till he dissolved all objects and wed sun and water so indistinguishably that his ultimate paintings have been hailed as prefigurations of today's nongeometric abstraction. Line is the daughter of the solid, as color is the daughter of the liquid element: by drawing the impressionists to her bosom, the Seine had converted modern French painting to the latter, were it at the expense of the former. Quite logically, Vlaminck and Derain first tried their Fauve fireworks at Châtou; quite logically, too, Bonnard in search of a lighter palette moved to Vernonnet.

From Paris onward, the Seine belongs to painting. (Not upstream, strangely enough.) But it should not be inferred that the impressionists were the first artists to discover her. Others had worked on her banks before, and her lesson had permeated their work, though not as overtly. Corot often sojourned at Mantes: the moist tenderness and the prophetic lightness of his canvases are to be attributed to the Seine's influence. Farther down, at Les Andelys, Poussin was born and initiated into his art. True, he left his birthplace as a young man, never to return, but it is not excessive to recognize in his fondness for opulent verdure and for rivers an unconscious nostalgia for his native land. Flamboyant ornament ripples on Gothic structures in many places but nowhere as animatedly as at Rouen, where it comes as a response to the tireless play of light and shadow on the water. Finally, it is in Honfleur and Le Havre, the harbors on the Seine's estuary, that Jongkind and Boudin painted the delicate, fluid oils and watercolors that made them impressionism's precursors. How much the medium of watercolor is attuned to estuary conditions is apparent if we remember that Raoul Dufy came from Le Havre.

We have been moving along rather fast, but that is not surprising: since Paris, the Seine has grown considerably larger and events ashore more difficult to discern. Since 1850, when causeways were built to stabilize the final stretch of the Seine's course, Rouen has become a real sea harbor. Until then the river had had a most indecent way of changing beds from time to time. Lillebonne, Harfleur, and to some extent Honfleur have thus been stranded in the course of centuries—a fate as humiliating for a harbor as for a singer to lose his voice. Even within the existing bed, it used to take a clever pilot to pick out the navigable channels from the maze of treacherous shoals. Becoming stuck on a shoal could be fatal, especially at spring tides, when the *barre* would topple over vessels like bowling pins. The most famous ship to have suffered this tragic fate was the *Télémaque,* which sank opposite Quilleboeuf in 1790. Soon the rumor went round that it contained a fabulous treasure, some 85 million gold francs, which Louis XVI was trying to smuggle over to England. Time and again, people tried to raise the *Télémaque.* The last attempt was made in 1842 by a British engineer, Mr. Taylor, who convinced a number of gullible Frenchmen to sink their money into the undertaking. Then one night Taylor disappeared, leaving even his thirty-five British workmen unpaid. "The idea was too heavy, and the chains were too light," someone commented.

The moral is, never procrastinate in an estuary. Let us heed it. Already, Le Havre is visible on the starboard side. The water beneath our bow tastes of salt. The Seine yields to sea—but not before giving us, as a send-off present, one of the most beautiful stories ever told in honor of mankind. One day, while hunting in the forest of Roumare, which spreads in one of the Seine's last sweeping bends before Rouen, Rollo, Duke of Normandy, hung his gold bracelet on the branch of an oak. Three years later the bracelet was found, still dangling from the same branch.

Reprinted by permission of AMERICAN HERITAGE magazine, a division of Forbes, Inc. © Forbes, Inc., 1962.

A Poem of Paris

BY FREDERICK TURNER

✂

editor's note

FREDERICK TURNER has been a frequent and enamored visitor of France for thirty-five years, from the beaches of Normandy to those of the Camargue. But Paris is where his heart beats fastest. Since he took the river walk described here, the city has embarked on an ambitious plan to open the river's banks to walkers: 7.6 miles from Parc André Citroën in the 15th to Parc de Bercy in the 12th. Turner is currently at work on his eighth book of nonfiction, an account of his French adventures.

M ost visitors to Paris know that life there began on the river, and if they don't, they soon learn. Not only do they find themselves constantly crossing the Seine to get to the Louvre, the Musée d'Orsay, the great squares and shops of the Right Bank, the Eiffel Tower and famous cafés of the Left Bank, but images of it are everywhere: on postcards, in books of photographs and in impressionist paintings. Even the city's official logo of a sailing ship pays tribute to this river that is Paris's heart and soul, and that courses through it in a grand seven-mile arc.

This being so, visitors cheat themselves if they confine their experience of the Seine to hurried trips across it on the way elsewhere.

The *bateaux-mouches,* those delightful river cruisers that take you quickly past the monuments, can give you only a kind of TV version of Parisian life, packaged, sanitized and thin.

For a more authentic, full-bodied sense of what makes Paris Paris, you'd do a lot better walking a portion of the river from, say, the Île St.-Germain to the Pont d'Austerlitz. This is a distance of about four and a half miles, and to do it right would take you most of a day.

Because there are numerous streets and bridges to negotiate, and because of the ferocity of French driving habits, it is best to begin your walk after the morning rush hour. Take the branch of the R.E.R. rail network that hugs the Left Bank and get off at Issy-Plaine, about a fifteen-minute ride from the center of the city.

Emerging from that station you are on the Pont d'Issy, the first of the twenty-three pedestrian bridges you will encounter, where you can begin to practice the Parisian habit of using a bridge as a meditative viewpoint rather than merely a steel or concrete span.

There is a surprisingly bucolic feel to the riverscape down here, despite the huge smokestacks in the distance. The banks are wooded, fishermen sit along them with cane poles, and beneath you scullers and kayakers glide silently with the current.

The suburban riverscape the impressionists so loved has vanished, but this will give you a whisper of it, especially when you descend the bridge steps and walk out onto the green avenues of the park on the Île St.-Germain. Here you are likely to see children playing soccer, dog walkers, a juggler practicing his throws, and all of this watched over by Jean Dubuffet's huge, playful sculpture *Tour aux Figures*.

Passing over the bridge to the Right Bank onto the quai St.-Exupéry you must cautiously negotiate voie Georges Pompidou, a part of the late president's ambition to pave over the city to open it to unrestricted commerce. Fortunately, a tree-lined sidewalk rises above the freeway, and strolling under the branches you look out onto moored barges full of builders' sand, and the cement factories, warehouses and office buildings of working-class Paris on the river. Every now and again a barge slides by and gives a blast of its air horn. In the distance is the Eiffel Tower.

At the Pont Mirabeau the prospect changes as you begin to leave the Left Bank factories and warehouses behind and pick up glossy high-rise apartment complexes.

Next to you on the quai Louis Blériot are older, more stately apartments, and there are benches under the trees for those who want to sit and look at the Pont Mirabeau and its outsized statues, or the Pont de Grenelle, beneath which stands a small-scale copy of the Statue of Liberty flanked by willows.

As its plaque explains, the statue was a gift to the city from its American expatriates in 1889. Moviegoers might recall that it was here that the final scene was shot in the 1988 thriller *Frantic* starring Harrison Ford.

You get to the statue by walking to the middle of the bridge and descending the ramp, and now that you find yourself in the middle of the river, you also discover that you don't have to make a choice of banks, for the tree-lined allée des Cygnes runs up the middle of the river to the Pont de Bir-Hakeim. In good weather this offers one of the best viewpoints of Paris, with the Statue of Liberty at one end and the Eiffel Tower at the other.

At the Pont de Bir-Hakeim begins the monumental Paris of postcards, films and tourists' imaginings. In this landscape the river is itself the master planner, creating the majestic scale with its broad expanse and seigneurial bends.

Walk to the middle of Bir-Hakeim, and you can see how this is so from the strategically situated alcove in midspan that you will probably be sharing with an artist or two. A plaque on the railing explains that it was in Bir-Hakeim, in the Libyan desert, in the spring of 1942 that Free French forces engaged the German army under Field Marshal Erwin Rommel and so gave notice to the world that the French had not given up the battle.

Returning to the Left Bank you pass under the Eiffel Tower and continue along the narrow park of the quai Branly, perfect for either people- or river-watching. Beneath you are the moored *bateaux-mouches*.

On the Right Bank, at the place de l'Alma, there is a cluster of restaurants, ranging from the basic George V, where you can get a hot dog and a beer, to the pricey, stylish Chez Francis.

In the tiny place Reine-Astrid is a small bronze statue of a recumbent woman, the personification of the Seine, recalling the old song about the Seine's being a lover "and Paris lies in her bed."

Stay on the Right Bank to observe the increasing number of houseboats moored along there, many of them handsomely refitted barges. In good weather you will find families at lunch under awnings, sharing wine and laughter with the obligatory pride of cats. Before you are the Belle Epoque splendors of the Pont Alexandre III, the Seine's most ornate bridge, built to commemorate the Franco-Russian alliance of 1892.

At the Pont de la Concorde you begin to encounter the broad cobbled quays favored by strollers, university students, practicing musicians and *clochards,* and though it is occasionally necessary to climb to street level and then descend again on the other side of a thoroughfare, it is worth it to become a riverside stroller yourself.

Along here too are the *bouquinistes,* those secondhand booksellers whose stock-in-trade was once the naughty pictures now routinely purveyed in glossy magazines. Now the *bouquinistes* deal mainly in old advertising posters, hackneyed prints of city views and arcane volumes like *The Young Hegel* and *The Secret of Napoléon.*

Ahead of you lie the Pont Neuf, the city's oldest bridge (it was inaugurated in 1607), and the Île de la Cité, where the city began. At the island's prow is the willow-draped square du Vert Galant, honoring Henri IV.

Appropriately, the square features Henri's equestrian statue, since in 1605 he was the first to ride horseback across the bridge to the island. Behind the square is the place Dauphine, which Henri used as a royal orchard and occasional execution ground. In 1614 he ceded it to a developer who put up buildings but left the center open for plays and jousting. Today place Dauphine is one of Paris's most inviting, intimate spots, a tree-shaded haven with pigeons, benches and restaurants, including the friendly bistro Chez Paul.

It is a fitting entrance to the world of the islands, which on their own would take at least a week to thoroughly explore. A walk to the end of the Île de la Cité, over the Pont St.-Louis to the Île St.-Louis brings you to the Pont Marie, the Right Bank and the quai des Célestins. Here Parisians once watered and curried their horses, but there is no sign of that now.

There is history here, however: at the intersection of the quai des Célestins and the boulevard Henri IV is the tiny square Henri Galli, and, within it, half-buried in ivy, are stones from the towers of the Bastille. If you have been disappointed by the oddly unimpressive monument that a few blocks up marks the site of the storming of the infamous prison, these neglected old fragments might bring home to you the feeling of that revolutionary event.

The square Henri Galli provides a fine view of the Île St.-Louis and its delightful quai d'Anjou. But a better view can be had by walking over the Pont de Sully to the Left Bank and entering the out-door sculpture park on the quai St.-Bernard.

From a bench in front of the sculpture park, the view takes in the tip of the Île St.-Louis and the ivy-hung walls of its square Bayre, beneath which sun worshipers gather; the handsome apartment buildings of the quai Henri IV on the Right Bank, and, through the trees, the towers and buttresses of Notre Dame. On the river the long barges go past in steady procession, and the *bateaux-mouches* swing their sterns around to go up the Right Bank side of the islands.

In front of you is a beguiling cross-section of daily Parisian life: stylish women with small dogs; taut and straining middle-aged male joggers; a group of soignée women doing a dignified version of the Jane Fonda workout walk, their faces perfectly composed beneath their perfect makeup; pairs of elderly men who come to discuss the sculptures; solitary young men perched on the parapets, some with portable tape players, some with books; groups of students from the nearby University of Paris in their identifying uniform of scholarly black; off-duty policemen, kepis in hand, and, always, the lovers, managing somehow to stumble along while completely entwined.

When the mothers and the grandmothers descend into the park to put the children on the teetertotter and the swings of the adjacent playground, that is your signal that the afternoon is waning and that you should finish your walk with a leisurely stroll through the rest of the park to the Jardin des Plantes at the Pont d'Austerlitz.

During the siege of Paris from 1870 to 1871 in the Franco-Prussian War the citizens of this gastronomic capital of the Western world were obliged to eat the animals of the Jardin's menagerie, giraffes and all.

The current animal residents seem safe enough from such a fate but are in truth pretty shabby looking.

The gardens created by the great naturalist Georges-Louis Leclerc de Buffon, however, are surpassingly beautiful, especially in the late-afternoon sun that gilds the trees and flower beds and throws velvet shadows over the lush grass.

Here is a restful, fitting end to your adventure, and now you are in a position to assent to the lines of the French man of letters Blaise Cendrars who wrote:

> I could spend my whole life
> Watching the Seine flow by . . .
> It is a poem of Paris.

This piece originally appeared in *The New York Times* under the title "Paris Revealed, Down by the Seine." Copyright © 1993 by Frederick Turner. Reprinted with permission of the author.

Bibliothèque

The Secret Life of the Seine, Mort Rosenblum, A William Patrick Book, Addison-Wesley Publishing Company, 1994. "There is not a river like it in the world," Rosenblum writes of the Seine, and he reveals just how unique·it really is. Rosenblum, a special correspondent for the Associated Press and former editor in chief of the *International Herald Tribune,* traces the Seine (Sequana) to its source, in Burgundy, to Le Havre and provides us with a historical and present-day perspective on the river and the communities it serves. He informs us that the geographers' term for a river that flows into a sea is *fleuve,* but for the people who live and work on the Seine the river is *la rivière,* which generally refers to inland waterways. He should know, as he lives aboard a fifty-four-foot boat moored in the center of Paris (talk about a room with a view!), and he's written a truly marvelous book.

River of Light: Monet's Impressions of the Seine, Douglas Skeggs, Alfred A. Knopf, 1987; originally published in Great Britain by Victor Gollancz Ltd., London. Out of print but a beautiful and interesting book. Skeggs presents a portrait of Monet and his lifelong connection to the Seine, but this is nearly as much a story of the river as it is of Monet. As he writes in the beginning of the book, "The river Seine was Monet's landscape, his subject, and his home. The lessons that he learned from painting its water inadvertently altered the course of the arts. The vision that he imposed on it is still with us today." Chapters focus on different geographic points along the river, such as Sainte-Adresse, Paris, La Grenouillère, Argenteuil, Vétheuil, and Giverny, with nearly 150 reproductions of Monet's paintings and period photos.

Sundays by the River, Smithsonian Institution Press, 1999. Strolling or picnicking near water—oceans, rivers, lakes, streams, tributaries of any length—is a time-honored tradition in France. Sunday mornings and afternoons are still reserved for this activity, by residents and visitors alike. This favored *loisir* (leisure pleasure) is captured in this book by noted documentary photographer Willy Ronis. The forty-eight duotone images featured span nearly half a century, and they're reminiscent of scenes from impressionist paintings. A beautiful, evocative book.

Paris, Je T'Aime
(Paris, I Love You, and the World Admires You, Warts and All)

"On a corner the smell of fresh croissants wafts from a patisserie. Time to get dressed. In a greengrocer's shop two men are arranging fruit and vegetables as if they were millinery. An uncle in a cafe is looking through a magnifying glass at the stock prices in the morning paper. He doesn't have to ask for the cup of coffee which is brought to him. The last street is being washed. Where's the towel, Maman? This strange question floats into the mind because the heart of Paris is like nothing so much as the unending interior of a house. Buildings become furniture, courtyards become carpets and arrases, the streets are like galleries, the boulevards conservatories. It is a house, one or two centuries old, rich, bourgeois, distinguished . . . Paris is a mansion. Its dreams are the most urban and the most furnished in the world."
—John Berger, "Imagine Paris,"
KEEPING A RENDEZVOUS

La Ville Lumière

BY DAVID DOWNIE

~~

editor's note

I've often wondered how Paris came to be known as the City of Light,
so I was particularly pleased to read this thorough explanation. Nocturnal
Paris *is* magic—it's like seeing fireworks for the first time; it can take your
breath away. I remember once, as a student, I was given a ride in a car one
night, and I couldn't believe I lived in the same city as the one I was seeing.
I wanted to drive around all night until the sun came up. It was then I realized that by exclusively employing the metro to get around, I had missed a
beautiful spectacle! Remember to walk around at night, or take a taxi or ride
on a bus or a *bateau-mouche*.

DAVID DOWNIE has lived in Paris since 1986 and has contributed to
many travel guidebook series, including Gault et Millau, Fodor's, and DK's
Eyewitness Guides. He is also a contributing editor at *Appellation
Magazine,* Paris correspondent for the on-line literary magazine *Salon,* and
a regular contributor to the travel section of the *San Francisco Examiner.*
Additionally, he recently wrote his first thriller, *La Tour de l'Immonde,* published by La Baleine, an imprint of Seuil.

Webster's defines *cliché* as a "trite expression" and *trite* as
"worn out by constant use." Happily, the title *Ville Lumière*
or City of Light is neither a cliché nor trite. Though it is constantly
used in reference to Paris, it has become a nickname, a sobriquet,
an endearment.

For me, the images it evokes are rooted in history but remain
very much alive today.

Say *Ville Lumière* and some will see old-fashioned streetlamps
spilling pools of light along the Seine where lovers stroll hand in
hand. Others will think of the Champs-Élysées and Eiffel Tower

ablaze. Still others will envision night-lit monuments perched on hills—the Panthéon, Sacré Cœur, Trocadéro—and a cityscape bathed in an otherworldly glow.

Personally I've often imagined the expression had more to do with the welcoming lights of the city's cafés, its bookshops, museums and universities, where minds meet and tongues wag into the night. Certainly, for centuries, men and women from across the world have been drawn to Paris like the proverbial moth to a flame—or a light.

Professors and philosophers like to say that the appellation *Ville Lumière* isn't about physical sources of light at all. Rather it's a metaphor for political, spiritual, cultural and intellectual energy. Louis XIV, the enlightened despot, was known as the Sun King (though he abandoned luminous Paris for swampy Versailles). The eighteenth century's Enlightenment found fertile ground here for its philosophical, social and political ideals: empiricism, skepticism, tolerance and social responsibility. Voltaire, Diderot, Jean-Jacques Rousseau and other proponents were called *les lumières*.

In his writings on the French Revolution, historian Jules Michelet (1798–1874) was probably the first to call Paris *la Lumière du Monde*—Light of the Earth, a beacon for humanity. During Michelet's lifetime, Paris underwent radical change: its population more than doubled. By the second half of the nineteenth century (starting with the Second Empire in 1852), Paris had indeed become the most stimulating, the most modern and best-loved of European cities.

In some ways it was an ideal city, a military man's Utopia conceived by Emperor Napoléon III and built by his prefect Baron Haussmann. It was anything but ideal, though, for the nostalgic, romantic or visionary. In *Les Fleurs du Mal* and other works, Charles Baudelaire scented death and urban anguish in Haussmannization. "Old Paris is gone," he wrote in *The Swan*, "no human heart changes half as fast as a city's face."

Haussmann's was an ideal cosmopolis for those who believed in order, uniformity, and the hygienic properties of open air and sunlight. At Napoléon III's behest, the prefect demolished some twenty-five thousand centuries-old buildings in fewer than twenty years. Broad cannon-shot boulevards and regular street alignments with uniform facades rose where a tangle of dark medieval alleys had once been.

With few exceptions the impressionists and early photographers who documented this remade world were fascinated by its novel cityscapes and seemingly endless perspectives. They sought above all to capture the effects of a new kind of light that was at once physical and spiritual. It was the light that sifted through the trees planted on the new boulevards. Or the light cast by the hundreds of gas lamps erected in the 1860s on the sidewalks of those boulevards. Light streamed into the windows of modern buildings. Lights burned round the clock in the new cafés, theaters and train stations that sprang up all over town. And, by association, *la lumière* was also the enlightened attitude of the inhabitants of this marvelous new world.

The late nineteenth century's Universal Expositions, in particular that of 1889, which marked the centennial of the Revolution and the building of the Eiffel Tower, seemed at the time to herald a new age of technical progress and scientific reason flanked by the artistic flowering of the Belle Epoque. We may marvel today at their ingenuousness, but most of the spectators of all classes and walks of life who crowded around to watch the Eiffel Tower's inauguration in 1889 were astonished, transfixed and delighted. The world's tallest structure was lit by ten thousand gas lamps. Fireworks and blazing illuminations drew the spectator's eye to the tower's various levels. A pair of powerful electric searchlights— among the earliest of their kind—raked the city's monuments from the summit at a height of 984 feet. Some say it was this signal even that engendered the name *Ville Lumière,* but there are no records to prove this.

Admittedly not everyone was bowled over by the tower, its lighting display or what it stood for. Caricatures and political cartoons of the period show strollers shading their eyes at night, blinded by Paris's newfound modernity. One cartoon's caption noted that from then on, people would need to use Seeing Eye dogs to go out for an evening stroll. By the 1890s, most of the city's gas lamps had already been replaced by even brighter electric lighting (though the last gas *réverbère* was removed only in 1952).

It's no surprise then that at the height of the Belle Epoque (which coincided with the *Exposition Universelle* of 1900 and its further technical wonders), a novelist named Camille Mauclair wrote a book titled *La Ville Lumière.* This is the earliest documented use of the term as applied to Paris. The book was published in 1904 and has been out of print for decades. No one seems to remember precisely what it was about. Georges Frechet, *conservateur* at the Bibliothèque Historique de la Ville de Paris, has suggested that the book probably drew inspiration for its title and content from both the Universal Exposition (one of the exhibits, *La Fée Électricité,* was a celebration of the miracle of electricity) and the intellectual ferment generated by the period's artists, performers and writers, Stéphane Mallarmé foremost among them.

Though it has been modernized, Paris *intramuros*—i.e., the city within the boulevard Périphérique beltway—has changed relatively little since the Second Empire. Other than minor damage in 1870–71 caused by the Franco-Prussian War and Commune struggle, it was never bombed or burned.

But this changelessness goes beyond the physical. Jean-Paul Sartre described Baudelaire as a man who "chose to advance backwards with his face turned toward the past." In many ways the same can be said of Paris and the people who live here. This isn't a museum city—it is far from dead. But the sheer weight of its history, its institutions and above all its culture forces it and its inhabitants to constantly look back while moving forward.

This is particularly true when it comes to both the nuts and bolts of lighting the *Ville Lumière,* and the philosophy that lies behind the myriad of lighting-related technical and bureaucratic constraints.

For a down-to-earth example, consider the many light fixtures on Paris streets that were installed during the Second Empire. Haussmann-style lamps are still manufactured today. There are also Art Nouveau fixtures and others that were added in the 1930s. Are they obsolete? Of course. That's the point: no one would dream of removing them.

Why? In a word, *atmosphère.* The atmosphere these old-fashioned lamps create is warm, welcoming and infused with nostalgia. Nostalgia is both a state of mind and a cultural ID card. No other city goes to such lengths to create a "light-identity," an ambience that immediately says "you're in Paris, the City of Light." In many places you could be walking alongside Baudelaire or Brassaï or Sartre through a crepuscular time tunnel.

This is something most denizens and visitors alike take for granted. But behind the scenes, a score of *éclairagistes* and *concepteurs-lumières* (lighting designers)—plus architects, engineers and some four hundred technicians—are hard at work round the clock creating Paris's evening magic.

Glance up from anywhere in town and you'll see how lighting designer Pierre Bideau has illuminated the Eiffel Tower with hundreds of small sodium lamps. The tower's golden lacework glows from within, recalling the gas lighting of 1889. Louis Clair has turned the church of Saint-Eustache (at Les Halles) into a kind of magic lantern, with light tracing the flying buttresses and spilling outward through stained-glass windows. Clair's delicate lighting of the Rotonde de la Villette underscores the curves and colonnades of Claude-Nicolas Ledoux's fanciful eighteenth-century canal-side customs house.

Roger Narboni and Italo Rota—two other bright stars in the French lighting firmament—have worked together or separately to capture with lights the physical and spiritual essence of Notre Dame Cathedral, the Louvre, a handful of bridges over the Seine, and famous avenues like the Champs-Élysées. But there are dozens of other equally impressive nighttime scenes: the place Vendôme and its storied facades seem like a stage set; the fountains of the place de la Concorde or the boulevard Richard-Lenoir splash both water and light. . . .

What all of these projects share is the goal of bringing forth the history and symbolism of each site. Flamboyant or experimental lighting displays that might seem marvelous in America, for example, simply don't fit in here on anything more than a temporary basis. True, avant-garde French light-sculptors like Yan Kersalé do create works in Paris for special occasions (July 14 extravaganzas, bicentennials and so forth). And many French lighting designers rightly consider themselves artists or *créateurs*. But for them to succeed here, their talents must be solidly anchored to the city's multi-layered historical reality. To transpose Sartre's image of Baudelaire, they must light the future by illuminating the past.

"If you don't know exactly where you're going, at least you can look back to the past and form some ideas," says François Jousse, musing about the Parisian worldview in general and how it applies to lighting in particular. Jousse is the chief engineer of Paris's municipal lighting and street maintenance department, a title that describes only a few of his functions.

Modest yet contagiously jovial, the bushy-bearded Jousse is famous among French lighting professionals for his expertise on everything from the performance of electric bulbs to the philosophy of monument illumination or the history of lighting since antiquity. Indeed if any one person is responsible for setting the city's nocturnal mood, it's Monsieur Jousse.

Individual monuments, buildings and bridges may take on a beautiful sculptural quality at night, Jousse readily admits, but what most intrigues him is the night-lit city as a physical, spiritual and emotional whole—the grand display case of Paris and its lifestyles. "Drive into town at night from the suburbs and you feel the difference immediately," he tells me. "From the linear, traffic-oriented lights leading you through and out of the *banlieue*, you enter the floating blanket of Paris light—a destination, a place, the arrival point."

As far back as the Middle Ages, lanterns or candles marked the limits and strategic points of the city, Jousse explains. There were originally three. They were highly symbolic because they lit the Louvre's Royal Palace; the Tour de Nesle (a watchtower that once stood on the Seine); and the cemetery of the Saints Innocents, a favorite meeting place near Les Halles for thugs and lovers alike. Over the centuries, oil lamps were added here and there around town. But it was the Sun King who lived up to his title and in 1669 inaugurated the first systematic public lighting scheme (he even had a commemorative lantern medal minted to celebrate it). By the 1780s, a pulley system had been invented to hang new, elegant lamps over the streets. And then came *le déluge* of 1789. "The refrain in the revolutionaries' song *'Ah! ça ira'* is all about hoisting aristocrats from the lampposts," Jousse laughs. "And those new pulleys came in very handy."

~

Paris's nighttime identity as we know it today was largely defined with the advent of modern outdoor lighting in the mid–nineteenth century. Ever since then, the city's streetlamps have been erected at the same heights: six, nine or twelve meters (though the Champs-Élysée's new fixtures, designed by Jean-Michel Wilmotte, are exceptions at eleven and a half meters). Posts are staggered along the sidewalks on both sides of the street to create overlapping, gentle pools of light. The light laps at the buildings and hints at the roofline above the tops of the lampposts.

The overall effect is to give Paris a human dimension, making it an inviting yet safe place to enjoy after the sun goes down.

"It's the little things I like most," says Jousse, echoing the sentiments of many Parisians. "For example, there's a nineteenth-century wall fountain on the rue de Turenne not far from the place des Vosges that no one notices during the day. Even at night, drivers don't see it. But when it's lit with two small spots, it's a wonderful discovery for strollers. . . ."

Beyond the poetry and aesthetics, skillful lighting is one way to diminish vandalism in rough neighborhoods. Jousse is proud that since his technicians have illuminated a contemporary sculpture in the 18th Arrondissement's notorious Goutte d'Or quarter near Barbès, the locals have adopted it as their own: no more graffiti or damage. At the Porte de Clignancourt, under the spaghetti bowl of freeways where the city's main flea market is held, Jousse and his lighting technicians have lit a wall built there as a safety measure to divide a wide sidewalk. Now, instead of being viewed as an ugly obstacle, the wall is a noctambulist's landmark, a kind of luminous welcome mat on the city's edge.

Half a dozen other cities probably have more and brighter lights than Paris these days. New York is a forest of flaming skyscrapers and throbbing, colored bands. Parts of Tokyo and Berlin look like immense, garish outdoor advertisements, the objective correlatives of our age of consumerism. These three cities in particular also sparkle as among the world's great artistic, intellectual, and economic centers. Yet no one would dream of renaming them the City of Light. I don't think that's simply because Paris claimed the title a century ago. There's another, intangible reason. Something about the quality of life, the outlook of the people, and the essence of Paris makes the name *Ville Lumière* ring true. So even if it sounds like a cliché to the uninitiated, countless others—including me—will go on using it for as long as the city shines.

My Paris

BY SAUL BELLOW

~⌒~

editor's note

SAUL BELLOW is the author of over twenty books, including *The Adventures of Augie March, Henderson the Rain King, Herzog,* and *Humboldt's Gift,* all recently reissued in paperback editions by Penguin in 1996. This piece originally appeared in *The Sophisticated Traveler* edition of *The New York Times Magazine,* March 13, 1983.

Changes in Paris? Like all European capitals, the city has of course undergone certain changes, the most conspicuous being the appearance of herds of tall buildings beyond the ancient gates. Old districts like Passy, peculiarly gripping in their dinginess, are almost unrecognizable today with their new apartment houses and office buildings, most of which would suit a Mediterranean port better than Paris. It's no easy thing to impose color on the dogged northern gray, the native Parisian grisaille, flinty, foggy, dripping and for most of the year devoid of any brightness. The gloom will have its way with these new *immeubles,* too, you may be sure of that. When Verlaine wrote that the rain fell into his heart as it did upon the city (referring to almost any city in the region) he wasn't exaggerating a bit. As a onetime resident of Paris (I arrived in 1948), I can testify to that. New urban architecture will find itself ultimately powerless against the grisaille. Parisian gloom is not simply climatic, it is a spiritual force that acts not only on building materials, on walls and rooftops, but also on your character, your opinions and judgments. It is a powerful astringent.

But the changes—I wandered about Paris not very long ago to see how thirty-odd years had altered the place. The new skyscraper on the boulevard du Montparnasse is almost an accident, something that had strayed away from Chicago and come to rest on a Parisian street corner. In my old haunts between the boulevard de Montparnasse and the Seine, what is most immediately noticeable is the disappearance of certain cheap conveniences. High rents have done for the family bistros that once served delicious, inexpensive lunches. A certain decrepit loveliness is giving way to unattractive, overpriced, overdecorated newness. Dense traffic—the small streets make you think of Yeats's "mackerel-crowded seas"—requires an alertness incompatible with absentminded rambling. Dusty old shops in which you might lose yourself for a few hours are scrubbed up now and sell pocket computers and high-fidelity equipment. Stationers who once carried notebooks with excellent paper now offer a flimsy product that lets the ink through. Very disappointing. Cabinetmakers and other small artisans once common are hard to find.

My neighbor the *emballeur* on the rue de Verneuil disappeared long ago. This cheerful specialist wore a smock and beret, and as he worked in an unheated shop his big face was stung raw. He kept a cold butt-end in the corner of his mouth—one seldom sees the *mégots* in this new era of prosperity. A pet three-legged hare, slender in profile, fat in the hindquarters, stirred lopsidedly among the crates. But there is no more demand for hand-hammered crates. Progress has eliminated all such simple trades. It has replaced them with boutiques that sell costume jewelry, embroidered linens or goosedown bedding. In each block there are three or four *antiquaires*. Who would have thought that Europe contained so much old junk. Or that, the servant class having disappeared, hearts nostalgic for the bourgeois epoch would hunt so eagerly for Empire breakfronts, recamier sofas and curule chairs.

Inspecting the boulevards I find curious survivors. On the boulevard St.-Germain, the dealer in books of military history and memorabilia who was there thirty-five years ago is still going strong. Evidently there is a permanent market for leather sets that chronicle the ancient wars. (If you haven't seen the crowds at the Invalides and the huge, gleaming tomb of Napoléon, if you underestimate the power of glory, you don't know what France is.) Near the rue des Saints-Pères, the pastry shop of Camille Hallu, Âiné, is gone, together with numerous small bookshops, but the dealer in esoteric literature on the next block has kept up with the military history man down the street, as has the umbrella merchant nearby. Her stock is richer than ever, sheaves of umbrellas and canes with parakeet heads and barking dogs in silver. Thanks to tourists, the small hotels thrive—as do the electric Parisian cockroaches who live in them, a swifter and darker breed than their American cousins. There are more winos than in austere postwar days, when you seldom saw *clochards* drinking in doorways.

The ancient gray and yellow walls of Paris have the strength needed to ride out the shock waves of the present century. Invisible electronic forces pierce them but the substantial gloom of courtyards and kitchens is preserved. Boulevard shop windows, however, show that life is different and that Parisians feel needs they never felt before. In 1949 I struck a deal with my landlady on the rue Vaneau: I installed a gas hot-water heater in the kitchen in exchange for two months' rent. It gave her great joy to play with the faucet and set off bursts of gorgeous flame. Neighbors came in to congratulate her. Paris was then in what Mumford called the Paleotechnic age. It has caught up now with advancing technology, and French shops display the latest in beautiful kitchens—counters and tables of glowing synthetic alabaster, artistic in form, the last word in technics.

Once every week during the nasty winter of 1950 I used to meet my friend, the painter Jesse Reichek, in a café on the rue du Bac. As we drank cocoa and played casino, regressing shamelessly to childhood, he would lecture me on Giedion's *Mechanization Takes Command* and on the Bauhaus. Shuffling the cards I felt that I was simultaneously going backward and forward. We little thought in 1950 that by 1983 so many modern kitchen shops would be open for business in Paris, that the curmudgeonly French would fall in love so passionately with sinks, refrigerators and microwave ovens. I suppose that the disappearance of the *bonne à tout faire* is behind this transformation. The postbourgeois era began when the maid of all work found better work to do. Hence all these son et lumière kitchens and the velvety pulsations of invisible ventilators.

I suppose that this is what "Modern" means in Paris now.

It meant something different at the beginning of the century. It was this other something that so many of us came looking for in 1947. Until 1939 Paris was the center of a great international culture, open to Spaniards, Russians, Italians, Rumanians, Americans, to the Picassos, Diaghilevs, Modiglianis, Brancusis and Pounds at the glowing core of the modernist art movement. It remained to be seen whether the fall of Paris in 1940 had only interrupted this creativity. Would it resume when the defeated Nazis had gone back to

Germany? There were those who suspected that the thriving international center had been declining during the thirties, and some believed that it was gone for good.

I was among those who came to investigate, part of the first wave. The blasts of war had no sooner ended than thousands of Americans packed their bags to go abroad. Among these eager travelers, poets, painters, and philosophers were vastly outnumbered by the restless young, students of art history, cathedral lovers, refugees from the South and the Midwest, ex-soldiers on the GI Bill, sentimental pilgrims, as well as by people, no less imaginative, with schemes for getting rich. A young man I had known in Minnesota came over to open a caramel-corn factory in Florence. Adventurers, black marketeers, smugglers, would-be bon vivants, bargain hunters, bubbleheads—tens of thousands crossed on old troopships seeking business opportunities, or sexual opportunities, or just for the hell of it. Damaged London was severely depressed, full of bomb holes and fireweed, whereas Paris was unhurt and about to resume its glorious artistic and intellectual life.

The Guggenheim Foundation had given me a fellowship and I was prepared to take part in the great revival when and if it began. Like the rest of the American contingent I had brought my illusions with me but I like to think that I was also skeptical (perhaps the most tenacious of my illusions). I was not going to sit at the feet of Gertrude Stein. I had no notions about the Ritz Bar. I would not be boxing with Ezra Pound, as Hemingway had done, nor writing in bistros while waiters brought oysters and wine. Hemingway the writer I admired without limits, Hemingway the *figure* was to my mind the quintessential tourist, the one who believed that he alone was the American whom Europeans took to their hearts as one of their own. In simple truth, the Jazz Age Paris of American legend had no charms for me, and I had my reservations also about the Paris of Henry James—bear in mind the unnatural squawking of East Side Jews as James described it in *The American Scene*. You wouldn't expect a relative of those barbarous East Siders to be drawn to the world of Mme. de Vionnet, which had in any case vanished long ago.

Life, said Samuel Butler, is like giving a concert on the violin while learning to play the instrument. That, friends, is real wisdom. I was concertizing and practicing scales at the same time. I *thought* I understood why I had come to Paris. Writers like Sherwood Anderson and, oddly enough, John Cowper Powys had made clear to me what was lacking in American life. "American men are tragic without knowing why they are tragic," wrote Powys in his *Autobiography*. "They are tragic by reason of the desolate thinness and forlorn narrowness of their sensual mystical contacts. Mysticism and Sensuality are the things that most of all redeem life." Powys, mind you, was an admirer of American democracy. I would have had no use for him otherwise. I believed that only the English-speaking democracies had real politics. In politics continental Europe was infantile and horrifying. What America lacked, for all its political stability, was the capacity to enjoy intellectual pleasures as though they were sensual pleasures. This was what Europe offered, or was said to offer.

There was, however, another part of me that remained unconvinced by this formulation, denied that Europe-as-advertised still existed and was still capable of gratifying the American longing for the rich and the rare. True writers from St. Paul, St. Louis and Oak Park, Illinois, had gone to Europe to write their American books, the best work of the 1920s. Corporate, industrial America could not give them what they needed. In Paris they were free to be fully American. It was from abroad that they sent imaginative rays homeward. But was it the European imaginative reason that had released and stirred them? Was it Modern Paris itself or a new universal Modernity working in all countries, an international culture, of which Paris was, or *had* been, the center? I knew what Powys meant by his imaginative redemption from desolate thinness and forlorn narrowness experienced by Americans, whether or not they were conscious of it. At least I thought I did. But I was aware also of a seldom mentioned force visible in Europe itself to anyone who had eyes—the force of a nihilism that had destroyed most of its cities and millions of lives in a war of six long years. I could not easily accept the plausible sets: America, thinning of the life-impulses; Europe, the cultivation of the subtler senses still valued, still going on. Indeed a great European prewar literature had told us what nihilism was, had warned us what to expect. Céline had spelled it out quite plainly in his *Voyage to the End of the Night*. His Paris was still there, more *there* than the Sainte-Chapelle or the Louvre. Proletarian Paris, middle-class Paris, not to mention intellectual Paris, which was trying to fill nihilistic emptiness with Marxist doctrine—all transmitted the same message.

Still I had perfectly legitimate reasons for being here. Arthur Koestler ribbed me one day when he met me in the street with my five-year-old son. He said: "Ah? You're married? You have a kid? And you've come to *Paris?*" To be Modern, you see, meant to be detached from tradition, traditional sentiments, from national politics and, of course, from the family. But it was not in order to be Modern that I was living on the rue de Verneuil. My aim was to be free from measures devised and applied by others. I could not agree to begin with any definition. I would be ready for definition when I was ready for an obituary. I had already decided not to let American business society make my life for me, and it was easy for me to shrug off Mr. Koestler's joke. Besides, Paris was not my dwelling place, it was only a stopover. There was no dwelling place.

One of my American friends, a confirmed Francophile, made speeches to me about the City of Man, the City of Light. I took his rhetoric at a considerable discount. I was not, however, devoid of sentiment. To say it in French, I was *aux anges* in Paris, wandering about, sitting in cafés, walking beside the green, medicinal-smelling

Seine. I can think of visitors who were not greatly impressed by the City of Man. Horace Walpole complained of the stink of its little streets in the eighteenth century. For Rousseau it was the center of amour propre, the most warping of civilized vices. Dostoyevsky loathed it because it was the capital of Western bourgeois vainglory. Americans, however, loved the place. I, too, with characteristic reservations, fell for it. True, I spent lots of time in Paris thinking about Chicago, but I discovered, and the discovery was a very odd one, that in Chicago I had for many years been absorbed in thoughts of Paris. I was a longtime reader of Balzac and of Zola and knew the city of Père Goriot, the Paris at which Rastignac had shaken his fist, swearing to fight it to the finish, the Paris of Zola's drunkards and prostitutes, of Baudelaire's beggars and the children of the poor whose pets were sewer rats. The Parisian pages of Rilke's *Malte Laurids Brigge* had taken hold of my imagination in the thirties, as had the Paris of Proust, especially those dense, gorgeous and painful passages of *Time Regained* describing the city as it was in 1915—the German night bombardments, Mme. Verdurin reading of battlefields in the morning paper as she sips her coffee. Curious how the place had moved in on me. I was not at all a Francophile, not at all the unfinished American prepared to submit myself to the great city in the hope that it would round me out or complete me.

In my generation the children of immigrants *became* Americans. An effort was required. One made oneself, freestyle. To become a Frenchman on top of that would have required a second effort. Was I being invited to turn myself into a Frenchman? Well, no, but it seemed to me that I would not be fully accepted in France unless I had done everything possible to become French. And that was not for me. I was already an American, and I was also a Jew. I had an American outlook, superadded to a Jewish consciousness. France would have to take me as I was.

From Parisian Jews I learned what life had been like under the

Nazis, about the roundups and deportations in which French officials had cooperated. I read Céline's *Les Beaux Draps,* a collection
of crazy, murderous harangues, seething with Jew-hatred.

A sullen, grumbling, drizzling city still remembered the humiliations of occupation. Dark bread, *pain de seigle,* was rationed. Coal
was scarce. None of this inspired American-in-Paris fantasies of
gaiety and good times in the Ritz Bar or the Closerie des Lilas. More
appropriate now was Baudelaire's Parisian sky weighing the city
down like a heavy pot lid, or the Paris of the Communard *pétroleurs*
who had set the Tuileries afire and blown out the fortress walls. I
saw a barricade going up across the Champs-Élysées one morning,
but there was no fighting. The violence of the embittered French
was for the most part internal.

No, I wasn't devoid of sentiments but the sentiments were sober.
But why did Paris affect me so deeply? Why did this imperial, cere-
monious, ornamental mass of structures weaken my American
refusal to be impressed, my Jewish skepticism and reticence; why
was I such a sucker for its tones of gray, the patchy bark of its
sycamores and its bitter-medicine river under the ancient bridges?
The place was, naturally, indifferent to me, a peculiar alien from
Chicago. Why did it take hold of my emotions?

For the soul of a civilized, or even partly civilized, man Paris was
one of the permanent settings, a theater, if you like, where the greatest problems of existence might be represented. What future, if any,
was there for this theater? It could not tell you what to represent.
Could anyone in the twentieth century make use of these unusual
opportunities? Americans of my generation crossed the Atlantic to
size up the challenge, to look upon this human, warm, noble, beautiful and also proud, morbid, cynical and treacherous setting.

Paris inspires young Americans with no such longings and challenges now. The present generation of students, if it reads Diderot,
Stendhal, Balzac, Baudelaire, Rimbaud, Proust, does not bring to its

reading the desires born of a conviction that American life-impulses are thin. We do not look beyond America. It absorbs us completely. No one is stirred to the bowels by Europe of the ancient parapets. A huge force has lost its power over the imagination. This force began to weaken in the fifties and by the sixties it was entirely gone.

Young MBAs, management-school graduates, gene-splicers or computerists, their careers well started, will fly to Paris with their wives to shop on the rue de Rivoli and dine at the Tour d'Argent. Not greatly different are the behavioral scientists and members of the learned professions who are well satisfied with what they learned of the Old World while they were getting their BAs. A bit of Marx, of Freud, of Max Weber, an incorrect recollection of André Gide and his Gratuitous Act, and they had had as much of Europe as any educated American needed.

And I suppose that we *can* do without the drama of Old Europe. Europeans themselves, in considerable numbers, got tired of it some decades ago and turned from art to politics or abstract intellectual games. Foreigners no longer came to Paris to recover their humanity in modern forms of the marvelous. There was nothing marvelous about the Marxism of Sartre and his followers. Postwar French philosophy, adapted from the German, was less than enchanting. Paris, which had been a center, still *looked* like a center and could not bring itself to concede that it was a center no longer. Stubborn de Gaulle, assisted by Malraux, issued his fiats to a world that badly wanted to agree with him, but when the old man died there was nothing left—nothing but old monuments, old graces. Marxism, Eurocommunism, existentialism, structuralism, deconstructionism, could not restore the potency of French civilization. Sorry about that. A great change, a great loss of ground. The Giacomettis and the Stravinskys, the Brancusis, no longer come. No international art center draws the young to Paris. Arriving instead are terrorists. For them, French revolutionary traditions degenerated into confused leftism and a government that courts the Third World make Paris a first-class place to plant bombs and to hold press conferences.

The world's disorders are bound to leave their mark on Paris. Cynosures bruise easily. And why has Paris for centuries now attracted so much notice? Quite simply, because it is the heavenly city of secularists. "Wie Gott in Frankreich" was the expression used by the Jews of Eastern Europe to describe perfect happiness. I puzzled over this simile for many years, and I think I can interpret it now. God would be perfectly happy in France because he would not be troubled by prayers, observances, blessings and demands for the interpretation of difficult dietary questions. Surrounded by unbelievers He too could relax toward evening, just as thousands of Parisians do at their favorite cafés. There are few things more pleasant, more civilized than a tranquil *terrasse* at dusk.

A Bridge Too Fair

BY CHIP BROWN

~

editor's note

CHIP BROWN married the "she" of this piece and tags along when she has to go to Paris for *Vogue*. He might agree with the following quote I read in an old edition of *Paris Access:* "The view at night of the islands and the Left Bank, from the point where the Pont-des-Arts jumps over the Seine from the Institut de France to the Right Bank. Anyone who sees this and doesn't instantly agree that this is the most beautiful city in the world is a churl or a New Yorker, which is usually the same thing, anyway."

Brown was a contributing editor at *Esquire* for eight years and has written for over thirty national publications, including *Outside* and *The Washington Post*. He is also the author of *Afterwards, You're a Genius* (Riverhead, 1999) and is at work on his second book about dreams. Brown lives in New York, but when I spoke with him on the telephone he did not sound like a churl.

I knew I wanted to ask her in Paris, if only for the advantage of proposing in a place that makes it hard to say no. So many generations have seized on Paris as the epitome of romantic communion that the city sometimes seems to have the character of a wise old matchmaker for whom no obstacle to love is insurmountable. Is it the idea of Paris that predisposes the heart, or is there something in the water?

"Paris," you say, and people just sigh and fluff up their feathers. I know I was similarly affected—"undone," I should say, or is the word *unbound?* All over the world places advertise themselves as the Paris of this or the Paris of that. And then you're in Paris and it hits you: there are places in Paris that are the Paris of Paris. I knew it didn't matter where we went that night, as long as we ended up down by the Seine on the Pont des Arts.

And so we did. We had been the last to leave the restaurant, an out-of-the-way place on the Right Bank with checked tablecloths, extravagantly priced Margaux, and a proprietor who posted himself at the door to shake everyone's hand as if he were a host who'd had us all to his house. During dinner it had rained, and the streetlamps in the mist looked like little ringed moons. We wandered down the rue du Mail, past the colonnade of the Palais Royal, and then along the endless palisade of the Louvre where a pantheon of august stone personages coldly eyed traffic from their niches. At the quai du Louvre we walked upriver toward the bridge.

From afar the Pont des Arts is just a spindly footbridge, easy to miss. It takes its name from the passage it provides between the

Louvre, once known as the Palais des Arts, and the Institut de France, where Napoléon was thinking of housing the École des Beaux-Arts. The Bridge of Arts. It has none of the ostentation of the Pont Alexandre III, whose winged eagles were recently regilded with twenty-four-karat gold. It lacks the splendor of the Pont Neuf, whose stone archways the artist Christo swaddled in cloth more than a decade ago. It missed out on the expatriate cachet of the Pont de Sully, where Hemingway's beautiful losers stopped to assay the bittersweetness of exile.

But never mind. Set in the heart of the city just downriver from the Île de la Cité, where Paris emerged from the wilderness more than two thousand years ago, the Pont des Arts has a human scale and beauty that make it the most hospitable bridge in Paris. Its trestle boardwalk, free of cars, appears to float between the high embankments of the Seine; eight iron archways leap from pier to pier as gracefully as dolphins. At dusk tourists cluster at the rails holding maps they never seem able to fold right. Late at night young mademoiselles scuttle home from discos, trying to keep their heels from catching in the planking.

It's not what you see on the bridge so much as what you see from it, the phantasmagoria of nocturnal Paris. We walked out to the center and found a ringside bench. Here and there people were lingering, talking quietly or struggling with their infernal maps. The monuments were bathed in light; soon they would go dark. One of the long *bateaux-mouches* that ply the river glided upstream. Its wake sloshed against the stone banks, and its powerful searchlight swept the quay, illuminating the plane trees. When the boat slipped beneath us, it made the bridge seem much higher. It was as if we were suspended on an aerialist's catwalk above a gallery of circus-goers.

You could get dizzy just turning circles to take in the sights: the vaulting archways of the Pont Neuf, which form almost perfect circles when mated with their reflections; the place Dauphine; the spire of Sainte-Chapelle; the shadowy hulk of Notre Dame. North and south and west: gilded domes, zinc roofs, chimney thickets, slashing boulevards, the labyrinths of alleys and streets that by night seem not to have been cut into the city so much as insinuated. Even if your future wasn't hanging in the balance, you certainly could get dizzy looking down at the Seine, where the water is always murmuring to hulls and fish, and where it seems almost alive with shattered light, flowing forward, pushing on.

So we are pushed through the world, or push ourselves, and arrive at the moment where we feel the urgency of choice. A frozen life unfreezes. "Everything flows; nothing remains," Heraclitus once wrote, long before iron bridges spanned the Seine or the river even had its name. What I had come to understand was that if you do not write your destiny, it will be written for you. I had my grandmother's ring in my pocket, and conviction in my heart, and I was afraid only of my clown-self enacting some masterpiece of clumsiness and of having to watch the family diamond squirt out of my hands and into the Seine, never to be seen again. Or not to be seen for decades—not until a flabbergasted fisherman discovered it in the stomach of a freshwater pike. (These rings-recovered-by-fish scenarios have actually happened.)

Oh don't you know she said yes? She said yes, which I found almost impossible to believe, so I asked again, and she said yes again. In the rush of feeling I didn't notice when the city lights were turned off for the night, or when the sparse crowd dispersed, or by what art it was exactly that we came to find ourselves alone on the Bridge of Arts, sans tourists and mademoiselles. But we were alone. It seemed we lingered there forever on that bench above the Seine, lingered there midriver in the Paris of Paris, so that we might always remember the moment of this metamorphosis, and the water we had crossed.

Paying the Way

BY DEBORAH BALDWIN

~

editor's note

It's difficult to find an honest piece about the pros and cons of how Paris
spends its money, and I applaud Deborah Baldwin's efforts in revealing
some of them here. It is far too facile to say that the reason Paris seems a
cleaner, tidier, and more user-friendly city than many American cities is that
the French have different priorities than we do. Keep in mind that immigrants from former French colonies enjoy few of the city's amenities, and
that a seemingly democratic landmark such as the Panthéon (where Victor
Hugo, Voltaire, Zola, and Jean Moulin are buried) requires an admission
fee. There is no charge to visit Grant's Tomb in New York, or the Lincoln
Memorial in Washington, D.C. Also, the price of gas in France (about $4 a
gallon), an amount that makes Americans gasp, helps pay for some of the
services we so admire in the City of Light. (Another in-depth piece to read
that I was unable to reprint is "Why Paris Works" by Steven Greenhouse,
The New York Times Magazine, July 19, 1992.)

Before moving to Paris, DEBORAH BALDWIN was editor of the award-
winning *Common Cause* magazine. Since 1994 she has written about travel,
French culture, and cuisine for *The Washington Post, The Philadelphia
Inquirer, FRANCE Magazine, Paris Notes, France: A Quarterly Review of
La Vie Française, France Discovery Guide,* Discovery Channel Online, and
others. She has served as a part-time copy editor at the *International Herald
Tribune* and taught journalism at L'Institut des Sciences Politiques.

They've been working on our corner—for about five years. First
they dug up the sidewalk at the foot of the boulevard de

l'Hôpital to fix a sewer line. No sooner was the site paved over than the construction crew was back, this time to make a surgical attack on the curbstones. Soon the intersection had handicap-friendly pedestrian islands, several new traffic lights and the beginnings of a bike path.

Renovation of the century-old Pont d'Austerlitz took even longer, but now it, too, has a bike path and broad sidewalks that make walking over the Seine—which glows under the glittery new Charles de Gaulle bridge—even more pleasant. When the new Météor subway line opened on the far side of the river, piles of construction debris, makeshift offices, and lumberyards disappeared. Across the way emerged a manicured vest-pocket park.

Metro workers have sledgehammered and rebuilt the stairs leading into our station twice in the five years we've lived here, if I'm not mistaken, and last year they repositioned the bus stop across the street to bring it a little closer to our apartment. Shrubbery and flowers started appearing a few years ago as part of a city beautification program, and last summer the sidewalk was widened in parts and more new trees went in, making my weekly walk to the supermarket—itself the subject of recent renovations—more aesthetic.

And I can't fail to mention the best little capital improvement since we moved to this block: After years of dodging six lanes of traffic to reach the post office across the street, I awoke recently to find a new traffic light holding back the cars. In case I'd missed it, there was a note, personally signed by the mayor, in our mailbox. Here's something, I thought, as I cakewalked across the boulevard, I'd never expect to see back home.

This is a story about what happens when public property—the so-called commons—is treated with the same lavish attention as an investment banker's second home. Not that we live in some fancy part of town where the streets are trod by foreign dignitaries, wide-eyed tourists, and well-heeled residents. Indeed, our little patch of the Left Bank, hard by the sprawling Austerlitz train station and bereft of great bakeries and cheese shops, barely qualifies as a neighborhood. It is more like a way station, an area countless people pass through en route to the Bastille, Jardin des Plantes, Mosque or rue Mouffetard street market. Few are conscious of the myriad improvements, big and small, that contribute to the pleasure of their journey. And that's just the point.

The older you get, the more time and money you have to spend to look beautiful, and Paris is no exception. To maintain its handsome, well-scrubbed self, the city spent 28.6 billion francs in 1999 and the *département* Paris belongs to kicked in another 3.6 billion—all told, the equivalent of $5.3 billion. This doesn't include the billions that will flow out of state coffers and into city services—helping to fund everything from day-care centers and transit systems to parks and gardens, museums and riot police—or the countless billions in private spending that ultimately improve the physical environment.

Americans, said to be enjoying the greatest economic prosperity in history, can only stop and stare at what money can buy. Never mind *grands travaux* like the $1.3 billion Bibliothèque Nationale, or national library, whose immense glass towers rose up two years ago on a formerly forlorn tract beyond Austerlitz station. If God is in the details, consider Mayor Jean Tiberi's four-year plan, announced last March, to disperse $270 million on such refinements as overhauling the place de la Concorde to make it more pedestrian-friendly; sprucing up twelve kilometers (7.5 miles) of riverside between the Parc André-Citroën and the new Parc de Bercy; installing high-tech lighting under various bridges; and constructing a pedestrian *passerelle* (cost: $16 million) that will sail over the Seine between the Bibliothèque Nationale and Bercy Park. These embellishments, the urban equivalent of Martha Stewart writ large, are separate from the additional bike paths, off-street parking and other infrastructure projects that are also in the works. It's hard not to wonder what Tiberi would be doing if the economy was up instead of stagnant.

Nowhere is the contrast starker than between the capital of France and Washington, D.C., a city as renowned for its potholes, crime and decaying schools as it is for its cherry blossoms, great museums and bourgeoisie. A three-part CNN series in 1998 comparing the two capitals, *Tale of Two Cities,* dwelled on Washington's murder rate—twenty times that of Paris—and Paris's high-performance high schools, the envy of Washington's elite.

As CNN made clear, money makes a difference, and so does gun control. There are, however, other factors that contribute to Paris's well-being. I like to think of the culture gap this way: When the landscape is wanting, Americans pick up and move to greener pastures. Parisians, however, inhabit a city that was once hemmed in by stone walls. The city looks inward, and it invests downtown.

The underclass gets pushed to the edges, to neighborhoods delicately referred to as *quartiers difficiles.* And one hundred years after Napoléon III's urban planner Baron Haussmann rebuilt half of Paris, wiping out countless *quartiers difficiles* and others in the process, came a second era of sweeping renewal and big-ticket projects.

The edifice complex of the 1970s and 1980s yielded such startling visions as the Parc de la Villette, La Défense, the Louvre's glass pyramid, and the streamlined Parc André-Citroën, culminating with the creation of the hundred-acre spread at Bercy. Today, a mere two thousand years after construction began, Paris is largely "done," leaving only one megaproject still on the drawing board: a twenty-year, 20-billion-franc plan to flesh out the area around the Bibliothèque Nationale.

"We have fewer and fewer *grandes opérations,*" according to Michel Bulté, Mayor Tiberi's *adjoint chargé de l'urbanisme,* who oversees a Byzantine collection of thirty agencies. "Now it's more like a half acre here and a half acre there." Many of these "human-scale" projects—carried out, he maintained, with 1990s-style neighborhood input—are in the formerly overlooked eastern districts, where a peculiarly French merging of public and private interests is helping to recycle and retrofit historic and abandoned property and the rare vacant lot.

Despite problems associated with speculation and gentrification, "This is not a city just for tourists and the rich," he continued. "Fifty percent of the population is middle class. Twenty percent of the housing is low-income." A concerted effort is being made to lure offices out of apartment dwellings so they can be turned back into housing, and tax policies are designed to keep working-class families in the city and protect mixed-income *quartiers*.

By American standards, the system seems to work. Meanwhile, with its infrastructure largely in place, Paris has the luxury, as city hall elegantly sums it up, of moving "in the direction of the quality of services . . . their diversity, their imagination and their sense of adapting to the evolution of social needs."

Along with refining some social welfare programs (such as a debit card that gives large families entry at city museums and the like), Tiberi is making an "unprecedented environmental push." This translates into money for bigger sidewalks (and not a minute too soon; twenty-eight hundred pedestrians had run-ins with local drivers in 1997) and better controls on three Parisian bugaboos: noise, graffiti, and dog poop.

On the front lines are the platoons of men in green who ply a thousand sidewalks with pressure hoses, tricking me several times a week into thinking it's just rained. Many members of this unusual army come on foot, while others forge a path in fanciful vehicles custom-made to conform to Paris's unique needs: I caught one Dr.

Seussian contraption clamping its mechanical arms around the iron grates at the foot of the trees along our street and raising them so handheld brooms could get between the roots. Manned *caninettes* (also known as poop-mobiles) the size of Harley-Davidsons scurry down the sidewalks, vacuuming up some four tons of dog excrement a day, or about a fifth of what Paris's three hundred thousand pooches leave behind—for ultimate disposal I'm not sure where. Other vehicles have rotating brushes that work like carpet beaters, and some shoot out hot, soapy water. One person I know insists he saw two green trucks stop in the middle of the sidewalk *so they could scrub off each other.*

Garbage collection and street cleaning consume a stunning 10 percent of the budget, according to *Paris le Journal,* an absorbing little magazine distributed free by city hall. The city's obsession with the care and cleaning of pavements goes back a ways—to 1185—when Philippe Auguste introduced those tony granite blocks that look like sugar cubes. It's been build-and-clean ever since.

"Municipal sweeping" began in 1873, and in 1884 the city ordered residents to start using garbage cans. The next milestone appeared in 1978, with the introduction of those nifty green trash cans on wheels that can be hoisted and emptied mechanically. These days, the city deploys a rolling force of sixteen hundred vehicles, including not only dump trucks, which cart off some three thousand tons of household garbage a day, but two hundred specialized *engins,* nearly half of them *caninettes.* Asked how much the dog-poop control costs taxpayers, a city hall spokeswoman referred vaguely to the fact that a private contractor does the dirty work at some indeterminate fee that is folded into a nearly $1-billion budget for street, garden and park maintenance. Clearly, it's a lot, and wanton pooches provide much grist for the pages of *le Journal*'s letters page ("What a waste!" and so on). Articles politely suggesting that dog owners take advantage of city-sponsored dog-training classes—not to mention eighteen official doggie toilets recently installed in parks around town—haven't had the desired result, so the *cacamobiles* keep coming.

And so too, night and day, seven days a week, come the ranks of maintenance engineers—seventy-five hundred all told, including forty-five hundred who do nothing but sweep some 10 million square meters of sidewalks and street gutters. Cleanup artists "de-graffiti" some 129,700 square meters of vertical Paris a year and "de-poster" another 284,800; Tiberi announced they would strip every wall in town clean within "a few months." A team of 223 lumberjacks does nothing but trim the city's fifty thousand trees.

When Paris isn't giving its streets what-for, it is giving its parks and gardens the Versailles treatment. The city maintains around nine hundred acres of greenery; spending on green space will rise 34 percent this year, to $190 million, allowing the creation of six new gardens. The city employs one park worker for every fifteen residents, calculated Paris-based CNN producers James Bitterman and Patricia Thompson. The city's gardener in chief, Françoise de Panafieu, boasted at a press conference that city greenhouses cultivate 3 million flowers a year. "And five parks escape our supervision," Tiberi chimed in, including such biggies as Luxembourg, the Jardin des Plantes and the Tuileries.

Someone has to pay for all this, of course, and taxes are higher in France than in the United States—by about two-thirds, CNN calculated.

Indeed, there are so many line items on the typical French pay slip I had to be sedated when I was handed my first (the last in a long list: *autres charges patronales*). But you don't have to be on the payroll to help pay Paris's way. Visitors, who number more than 20 million a year, get a taste of the government's *savoir-taxer* at every store, theater, hotel, café or restaurant they walk into because a 20.6 percent VAT, or valued-added tax, is cloaked in the price of nearly all goods and services. Last year the VAT brought in $112 billion, according to the Finance Ministry, or twice the amount raised from income taxes.

Less obvious are the miscellaneous taxes on things like *habitation* (read: apartment occupancy), utilities and even TV ownership, all of which, directly or indirectly, help raise money for city services. According to one calculation, municipal taxes come to about $890 per person per year.

Then there's the do-it-yourself law that requires Parisian apartment owners to overhaul their building's facade every ten years—or face fines running as high as $6,600. Last year the owners of some non-descript low-rises near us spent several months scraping and repainting the exterior walls, going so far as to re-create a faded bootmaker's sign inscribed over the alley during some long-ago era.

Bitterman says he and Thompson, who co-own a 6th Arrondissement apartment building, coughed up $14,625 toward the *ravalement* of their ten-unit building, only $3,000 of it tax-deductible. Not that it was like throwing money out one of their lovely nineteenth-century windows. "It improves property values," Bitterman says of the *ravalement* requirement. "It improves the city's value. And it improves the way of life."

Not every corner of Paris gets regular face-lifts (or even a good sweeping, if the Stalingrad metro stop is any indication), and the turbulent close-in suburbs suffer from every kind of urban ill. Somewhere in all the municipal spending—which a mind-boggling forty thousand city hall employees handle—are surely examples of waste, fraud and abuse. Moreover, certain aspects of the city's well-being, most notably its low crime rate and competitive schools, cannot be explained in strictly financial terms. But nowhere else can a visitor get a better sense of what it means to tax and spend for the common good. Nowhere else can the payoff be so plain.

Live here long enough and you can begin to take it all for granted. Just recently, I got off the metro at Pyramides and was delighted to find spanking new walls and escalators and floors that shone like glass, all thanks to the new billion-dollar Météor subway line. I felt like an investment banker dropping in on her country estate after a long absence and being pleasantly surprised by the new marble floor and wrought-iron gate. Then thinking: "Hey, I'm so well-off other people take care of all this for me."

This piece originally appeared in the May 1999 issue of *Paris Notes*. Copyright © 1999 by Deborah Baldwin. Reprinted by permission of the author.

Bibliothèque

A *Traveller's History of Paris,* Robert Cole, series editor Denis Judd, Interlink Books, Brooklyn, New York, 1994. This edition is one in a great series for which I have much enthusiasm. Each edition gives readers a compact, historical overview of each place, highlighting the significant events and people with which every visitor should be familiar. Think of it as a mini "what you should know" guide, a minimum of milestones to help you really appreciate what you're seeing. The Paris volume features a five-page chronology of major events; a list of presidents and heads of government; detailed descriptions of monuments, parks, bridges, and cemeteries; and a section on the environs of Paris. Each book is small enough and light enough to carry around every day, and for a bigger picture, you may also want to consult the *Traveller's History of France* edition.

Paris, John Russell, Harry N. Abrams, Inc., 1983. This beautiful book by John Russell, former chief art critic of *The New York Times,* is one of the most valued in my library. Featuring over two hundred color and black-and-white reproductions of paintings and drawings, it's a veritable art history course between two covers. Yet it is quite a lot more, and quite substantive. It's a personal work—Russell knows Paris intimately—as well as a social and historical survey of Paris. Included also are photographs—of two generals about to be executed during the Commune, the rue de Rivoli in 1855, an aerial shot of the place des Vosges, and Picasso's studio in the rue des Grands-Augustins. This de rigueur selection is not one to bring along—it's a 350-page, coffee-table hardcover—but one to read before you leave and to take down from the shelf each time you return.

Travelers' Tales Guides: Paris, collected and edited by James O'Reilly, Larry Habegger, and Sean O'Reilly, distributed by O'Reilly and Associates, Sebastopol, California, 1997. I hope to meet the team who created the Travelers' Tales series one day because we seem to share similar ideas about travel. Each title in this series is a great mix of carefully chosen stories in the form of book excerpts and a few extracts from periodicals. For me, the best surprise of the Paris edition was that I learned about *Vie et Histoire,* the twenty-volume encyclopedia about the city of Paris, one volume for each arrondissement. I started my collection with the 1st Arrondissement and, due to the infectious enthusiasm of the Travelers' Tales contributor Jack Bronston, intend to eventually acquire them all (one shop where these volumes are available is the Librairie Caisse Nationale des Monuments Historique in the Hôtel de Sully, 62 rue St.-Antoine, 4th). This not very large, not very heavy paperback is a good choice for bringing along, and the *Travelers' Tales: France* edition makes a good companion.

A Place in the World Called Paris, edited by Steven Barclay, foreword by Susan Sontag, illustrated by Miles Hyman, Chronicle Books, 1994. For those who want a book of short passages, to be picked up at random, here is the *livre* for you: a collection of over 170 excerpts from twentieth-century fiction, poems, essays, and memoirs all having to do with some aspect of Paris. The excerpts are presented in twelve sections and some of the writers include Anaïs Nin, V. S. Pritchett, Djuna Barnes, Henry Miller, Ludwig Bemelmans, Kate Simon, Mary McCarthy, Edmund White, Maya Angelou, Mavis Gallant, and Frank O'Hara. Reading this collection led me to some works with which I was unfamiliar, which is really the most compelling reason for publishing an anthology of this sort.

Metropolitain: A Portrait of Paris, Matthew Weinreb and Fiona Biddulph, Phaidon Press (distributed by Chronicle Books), 1994. I like this photography book because none of the images are typical and Weinreb has focused on the smallest details, which, as he says, "are so often missed by the hurried walker in the street." Biddulph's accompanying text is engaging, and as well as I thought I knew the city, I made it a priority on my last visit to seek out some of these architectural details. The double-page spread photo of the l'Institut du Monde Arabe is especially nice as the structure is quite difficult for an amateur to capture on film. Also, the photo of Chagall's ceiling in the Opéra is magnificent—if you miss seeing the real thing, this is a good reproduction to have.

Paris: The City and Its Photographers, Patrick Deedes-Vincke, Bulfinch Press (an imprint of Little, Brown and Company), 1992. Louis-Jacques-Mandé Daguerre invented the daguerrotype in 1839 in Paris, so a book about Paris and the people who photographed it seems a natural. More than just a book of period photos, this is divided into four sections: the first looks at the history of photography and the role Paris played in its development; the second is devoted to the introduction of the handheld Kodak camera; the third explores how Marcel Duchamp, dadaists, and surrealists embraced the medium, as well as Lee Miller, Brassai, and André Kertesz; and the fourth includes the founding of the Magnum Agency and the works of Robert Capa, Henri Cartier-Bresson, Robert Doisneau, and Izis. The author chose to include no photographs taken later than 1968 because "with the student riots of that year and the ensuing disruption, and with the urban upheaval of the mid-1960s, came the end of an era." Different styles have evolved since then, and fill other, interesting photography books. The images he has selected "belong to that secret drawer of our imagination and of our dreams." I applaud his selectivity because you really remember these images long after you've closed the book.

À Propos de Paris, photos by Henri Cartier-Bresson, with texts by Vera Feyder and André Pieyre de Mandiargues written for the exhibition *Paris à rue d'oeil,*

Bulfinch Press (Little, Brown and Company), 1994. Here is a collection of over 130 photos of Paris by Cartier-Bresson, some well-known and a number never before published, taken over a span of fifty years. Paris has certainly been an inspiration to many photographers, but somehow it is virtually impossible to think of Cartier-Bresson without immediately thinking of Paris. There is very little text, allowing readers to simply view the elegant black-and-white plates.

Remembering Paris, text by Denis Tillinac, paintings by André Renoux, Flammarion, Paris, published simultaneously in French under the title *Je me Souviens de Paris*, 1998; English translation by David Radzinowicz Howell, 1998. Tillinac is a well-known author in France, and this is his beautiful "memoir" of Paris. He traces his life from childhood to the present by taking us to many known as well as unfamiliar corners of the city. Paired with the text are light and charming paintings by Renoux, who is an internationally known painter of Paris. This is a nice gift book, but I'd never be able to part with it.

The City as Work of Art: London, Paris, Vienna, Donald J. Olsen, Yale University Press, New Haven, 1986. In the preface, Olsen explains that the title of his work is a deliberate reference to the first chapter of Jacob Burckhardt's *Civilization of the Renaissance in Italy*, entitled "The State as a Work of Art." In much the same way that Burckhardt found parallels between the politics of Italians in the fourteenth and fifteenth centuries and their civilization, Olsen believes we can look at cities as credible documents that reveal much about the values and aspirations of the people who live there. In this unique work he examines three cities, London, Paris, and Vienna, during the period of their most significant growth: the century preceding 1914. (Paris, for example, before Haussmann transformed it in the 1850s, looked much the same as it had under Louis XIV.) Comparing these cities' approaches to urban planning is fascinating, but readers who choose to single out the chapters on Paris will not be disappointed. This book is also a celebration of city life in general and a critical discourse on urban policy.

Paris Was Yesterday, 1925–1939, Janet Flanner, edited by Irving Drutman, 1972; *Paris Journal, 1944–1965*, Janet Flanner, edited by William Shawn, 1977; *Janet Flanner's World: Uncollected Writings, 1932–1975*, edited by Irving Drutman, 1979; all Harcourt Brace Jovanovich. Janet Flanner—whose *nom de correspondance* was Gênet—wrote "Letter From Paris" for *The New Yorker* for fifty years. These collections of her pieces are both for those of us old enough to remember her missives and young Francophiles about to discover her. We are most fortunate, not only as readers but as human beings, to have such a vast and perceptive record of Parisian life and times. *She was there* for much of the twentieth century's momentous events. The entries gathered in the first two books cover an array of topics and personalities: Josephine Baker in *La Revue Negre;* the deaths and funerals of Claude Monet, Isadora Duncan, *La Goulue,* Marshal Foch, Sergei Diaghilev, and Edith Wharton; Marlene Dietrich's Paris visit; the Stavisky scandal; Sylvia Beach and Shakespeare and Company; *Le Lapin Agile;* "Peace in Our Time"; "War in Our Time" . . . the list is endless. *Janet Flanner's World* is mostly devoted to places other than Paris, or even France, but the entries on Cézanne, Colette, Picasso, the Mona Lisa, and Alice B. Toklas—and especially "The Escape of Mrs. Jeffries"—makes the entire work appropriate reading. All are highly, highly recommended.

Paris France, Gertrude Stein, Liveright, 1970; first published 1940. Stein's wonderful love letter to France, where she made her home for forty years, opens with the line "Paris France is exciting and peaceful." How ironic that her book was published the day Paris fell to the Germans. With black-and-white reproductions of artworks by Gris, Vlaminck, Picasso, and others, this is a special paperback, great for bringing along.

Paris, Julian Green, translated by J. A. Underwood, first published in a bilingual edition in the U.S. and Great Britain by Marion Boyars Publishers, New York and London; distributed in the U.S. and Canada by Rizzoli International Publications; first published in France in 1983 by Champ Vallon, reprinted in 1989 by Éditions du Seuil. A wonderful, brilliant little book printed in both French (on the left-hand pages) and English (on the right-hand pages). Julian Green may be the only author qualified to write such a work as he was born in Paris in 1900 and, except when he was forced to leave during the Second World War, has known the city more intimately and far longer than nearly anyone, ever. This is his very personal love poem to Paris, which begins with an inviting opening line: "I have often dreamed of writing a book about Paris that would be like one of those lazy, aimless strolls on which you find none of the things you are looking for but many that you were not looking for." "Dreamed" is a significant word because in fact you feel as if you're *in* a dream, or listening to a version of Green's dreams, when you read the book. It's a sensual work, to be read slowly and savored, and having the French text side by side with the English presents a unique language-learning opportunity. With twenty-four of Green's own black-and-white photos, plus a few pages of explanatory notes.

I'll Always Have Paris!: A Memoir, Art Buchwald, G. P. Putnam's Sons, 1996. I fully expected this second Buchwald memoir—his first was *Leaving Home*—to be funny (it was), but I was unprepared for it to be sad (it was, but I should explain: I am the sort of person who still gets choked up when the Tin Man tells Dorothy his heart is breaking at the end of *The Wizard of Oz*). So you may not get teary-eyed reading about his wife, Ann, who passed away before this book was published; she is present on nearly every page even when she's not part of the narrative. But you may very well laugh out loud at Buchwald's press-junket adventures with the *International Herald Tribune,* and the VIPs he met over the years. A very entertaining read, with eight pages of black-and-white photos.

Olympia: Paris in the Age of Manet, Otto Friedrich, Touchstone (Simon & Schuster), 1992, originally published in hardcover by HarperCollins. I *love* this slice-of-history book, which puts Paris of the late 1800s in the spotlight. Using Manet's succès de scandale, *Olympia,* as the centerpiece of the book, Friedrich presents Second Empire Paris under Napoléon III and Empress Eugenie and all the art, politics, and social unrest of one hundred years ago. Each chapter is great, but I was really taken with the one detailing how the succession to the Spanish throne resulted in the boondoggle of the Franco-Prussian War. *"Je nous considere d'avance, comme perdus"* ("I consider us, in advance, as lost") Napoléon wrote from his headquarters in Metz, and from there, of course, it was downhill, a debacle. I wish Friedrich would write an entire series of books like this, using various works of French art to define a particular period in French history. It's a creative idea for a book, and de rigueur for the time period.

Paris: City of Light, 1919–1939, Vincent Cronin, HarperCollins, London, 1994. This work follows Cronin's *Paris on the Eve, 1900–1914,* which I haven't yet read, and while they are obviously companion volumes meant to be read together, each book can certainly be approached individually. Paris at the time of the second volume was a city outwardly very confident, but, as Cronin notes, that confidence did not extend to fighting German aggression. Cronin relied on period writings from diaries and letters of various individuals, many translated for the first time. With two inserts of black-and-white photos, this is a great capsule of the political and moral struggles of the time, which simultaneously set the stage for struggles even more tangled and onerous.

The Fall of Paris: June 1940, Herbert Lottman, HarperCollins, 1992. Acclaimed historian and biographer Lottman (*Albert Camus: A Biography; The Left Bank: Writers, Artists and Politics from the Popular Front to the Cold War; Petain: Hero or Traitor; Flaubert: A Biography*) has lived in and written about Paris since 1956. This work is a dramatic account of the five weeks in the spring of 1940 when the Germans were approaching Paris. Even though we all know how it will end, the book reads like a fictional suspense story. Lottman had access to various archives and unpublished diaries, and he interviewed living survivors, so that we read a day-by-day and hour-by-hour report of the siege as told by native Parisians, diplomats, journalists, refugees, expatriates, and political figures. William Shirer was then a CBS correspondent, Simone de Beauvoir was a high school teacher, and Jean-Paul Sartre was at the front. Lottman's final chapter is "Sunday, June 23," but his epilogue is the true end of the book, and his last line may be the best ever written on the collapse of Paris: "The City of Light would become a dark and evil place for four long years. Nobody has been found to speak well of it."

Is Paris Burning? Larry Collins and Dominique Lapierre, Touchstone (Simon & Schuster), 1965. The title is a reference to an actual question Hitler asked on August 25, 1944. This is really two gripping stories, one of the liberation of Paris and the other of Von Choltitz's angst over being given orders to destroy Paris if it seemed inevitable it would fall into Allied hands. The Seine bridges were wired to be blown up also, but thankfully those bridges remain today. A photo of the swastika hanging from a window of the Hôtel Meurice on the rue de Rivoli is nothing short of horrifying. A good bring-along: nothing beats this for keeping you on the edge of your seat.

The Road Back to Paris, A. J. Liebling, Modern Library, 1997; originally published in 1944 by Doubleday. Just as wonderful a book as *Between Meals,* but very different. This is a collection of Liebling's dispatches to *The New Yorker* during the Second World War (he was sent to Paris in 1939). Liebling reported on what life was like at the front, and he interviewed soldiers of every rank. At one point he was forced to leave Paris and couldn't return until after D day; he was even shot at in North Africa. His passion for reportage is apparent in every piece, but so is his even greater passion: the freedom of *la Belle France.*

Paris in the Fifties, Stanley Karnow, Times Books, 1997. Karnow, best known as a Pulitzer Prize–winning historian and author and perhaps least known as a correspondent for *Time,* has written a memoir of a different sort. As he explains in the preface, he wisely saved carbon copies of his original dispatches sent from the Paris office to *Time*'s editors in New York, and what he saved is a chronicle of the 1950s in Paris. As one would expect, Karnow met an impressive number of personalities, including Charles de Gaulle, André Malraux, Albert Camus, Audrey Hepburn, Orson Welles, Pierre Mendès-France, and Christian Dior. I love the final paragraph of the book, "Toujours Paris," which makes me wish for the life of a habitué again, of either the student or professional persuasion.

Paris Dreambook: An Unconventional Guide to the Splendor and Squalor of the City, Lawrence Osborne, Vintage Departures, 1992 (paperback); originally published in Great Britain by Bloomsbury Publishing, 1990; first published in the U.S. by Pantheon Books, 1991 (hardcover). I am not aware of another book like this. In fact, Osborne's book isn't *like* any other book, period—it's decidedly in a category all its own. Chapters feature the metro, a Turkish *hammam,* the rue St.-Denis, graffiti, sex, food, various *quartiers* and *étrangers,* all of which Osborne cleverly links together. I wouldn't exactly call this a joy to read—for the most part, it's really an inside look at seedy characters and corners—but it is well written and interesting and true, and at least someone had the guts to write a book about aspects of Paris most people prefer to ignore.

Literary Paris, photography and commentary by Jeffrey Kraft, Watson-Guptill Publications, 1999. Initially, I thought this was to be another nice, run-of-the-mill collection of well-known passages by writers who've spent time in Paris. I was pleased to discover that the project is a beautiful marriage between lesser-known quotations and unique black-and-white photographs, in addition to Kraft's own observations. Text and photos are arranged in six thematic chapters. Kraft notes in *"Balades,"* "And the single best way to set about understanding the city is just to get out and go—*faire une balade*—stopping wherever you please. A *balade* is more a pilgrimage than a mere walk. Paris is for long, exploratory strolls—through her gardens, with their fat brown leaves, through courtyards, along grand boulevards and tiny, narrow streets—with your eyes wide open, taking in every detail." His uncommon photographs make you eager to begin the promenade.

Postmark Paris, Leslie Jonath, Chronicle Books, 1995. This little hardcover is an intimate picture of Paris viewed through old postage stamps and the eyes of a nine-year-old girl who lived there for a year with her family. Even though it's mostly fiction, Jonath really did collect all those beautiful stamps, attend the *école bilangue,* and watch *Wild Wild West* dubbed in French.

The Paris Review, No. 150, forty-fifth anniversary issue. For these milestones (150th issue, forty-five years of existence), the staff collected reminiscences and observations from writers who spent time in Paris after World War II, including Norman Mailer, James Dickey, Mordecai Richler, Mary Lee Settle, Alice Adams, Art Buchwald, Peter Matthiessen, and Ben Bradlee. Also, poets who contributed to the early issues (Robert Bly, Richard Wilbur, W. S. Merwin, and Donald Hall) were asked to submit new works for this one. All in all, a great cause for celebration and a great read. (To order this and any other back issues, contact *The Paris Review* at 45–39 171 Place, Flushing, New York 11358; 718-539-7085; tpranne@aol.com—once in the site, type "Attention: Nikki" in the space allotted; prices vary, as does issue availability.)

Walking Books

Walking the *quartiers* of Paris is the best way to get to know the city. While I believe a part of every visit should include some aimless wandering, I think an equal part should be devoted to structured walks. Visitors will feel they *really* know Paris, and they'll remember the details of their trip, by pounding the pavement (or the cobblestones). Crisscrossing the city a dozen times in search of the sights is just that: a blur of sight-seeing, not a feel for the people or the city. The best self-guided walking tours highlight things you might otherwise miss and also allow you to detour from the route whenever you want. They provide the perfect balance between too much structure and none at all. I enthusiastically endorse the seven books of walking tours described below.

Around and About Paris: From the Dawn of Time to the Eiffel Tower—the 1st, 2nd, 3rd, 4th, 5th, 6th and 7th Arrondissements (1995); *From the Guillotine to the Bastille Opera—the 8th–12th Arrondissements* (1996); *New Horizons: Haussmann's Annexation—the 13th–20th Arrondissements* (1997); all by Thirza Vallois, all published by Iliad Books, London. This three-volume, paperback British series is undeniably the very best I've seen. If—*mon Dieu!*— I was told I could only bring three books with me to Paris, I'd choose these. Vallois has lived in Paris for nearly forty years and, to quote from the jacket on volume one, "She knows Paris stone by stone and has read every book of note about its history and development." *This* is whom I want to accompany me around the city. Each volume in this informative series is organized numerically by arrondissement, representing the way the city grew. Each arrondissement is presented with an overall introduction, followed by a detailed walk through it. Readers and walkers will experience the major sights and out-of-the-way special places and will learn what makes each arrondissement distinct. I purchased these books here in the U.S., but they may also be ordered directly from the publisher. (Send inquiries to Iliad Books, 5 Nevern Road, London, England, SW5 9PG. Additionally, The Travel Bookshop in London—see "Bookstores" in *Renseignements Pratiques"*—will likely have them in stock.)

Pariswalks, Alison and Sonia Landes, Henry Holt and Company, New York, 1999. This has been a favorite of mine since the first edition appeared in 1981. The Henry Holt Walks series originated with this Paris edition, and there are now over a dozen in the series. This guide features walks through five of the oldest neighborhoods of Paris: St.-Julien-le-Pauvre, La Huchette, St.-Germain-des-Prés, Mouffetard, and place des Vosges. Each walk is about two and a half hours, which I like for those mornings or afternoons when I want *some* structure but not a full day of it. The walks are interesting and detailed (though not as detailed as those in *Around and About Paris,* above), and as the authors state in the introduction, after each walk you'll be "a friend and possessor of the *quartier* forever." I share the authors' enthusiasm for getting to know a part of the city intimately, what they call "close-up tourism." Two useful tips: morning walks are recommended because courtyard doors in both business and residential buildings remain open for mail and other deliveries, and sitting on the grass is not *interdit* in the square Viviani, next to little St.-Julien-le-Pauvre. At the end of the book there is a chapter on cafés, restaurants, hotels, and shops, but I don't find it very inspiring and these are covered better in other books. ~Note that this is also available on audiocassette (two tapes/three hours, maps included) from Penton Overseas, Inc.

The Impressionist's Paris (1997) and *Picasso's Paris: Walking Tours of the Artist's Life in the City* (1999), both by Ellen Williams, both published by The Little Bookroom. These two volumes represent what I hope will be a continuous series of beautiful little books. They're exactly the same shape and size and follow the same format, with color reproductions of the artists' works, maps, vintage and current photographs, period *cartes postales,* and detailed walks. They're also not just for first-time visitors: as Williams notes in the Picasso book, "Following in the footsteps of this one extraordinary inhabitant can reveal entirely new aspects of the city even to those familiar with it." The walks she offers in each guide include noteworthy sites and studios relevant to the artists' *oeuvres,* as well as the restaurants, bars, and cafés they frequented. The painters featured in the impressionist book are Manet, Degas, Monet, Renoir, Bazille, and Caillebotte (I wondered why Pissarro was not included, since many of his Parisian street scenes would seem to beg inclusion, but she notes in the afterword that he didn't begin painting his *grands boulevards* canvases until the 1880s and this book focuses on the 1860s and 1870s). Picasso lived in four neighborhoods in Paris—Montmartre, Montparnasse, Étoile, and St.-Germain-des-Prés—and happily, as Williams discovered, most of his Paris still exists today. The four museums in Paris that display his work are included in this volume. These small (approximately 5¼″ × 7¼″) hardcovers fit easily into a bag and are lightweight enough to carry with you all day long. Each book has a red-ribbon marker, a thoughtful touch for walkers who need to easily mark a page while looking around or stopping for a *vin ordinaire.*

Impressionist Paris: The Essential Guide to the City of Light, Julian More, Pavilion Books, London, 1998. This is a much bigger book than *The Impressionist's Paris* above, but is not as portable (it measures approximately 6½″ × 11″) and is not limited to the city of Paris. Author More has lived in France for more than twenty years, and the eight chapters he presents cover Fontainebleau, Les Batignolles-Pigalle, the Seine (St.-Germain-en-Laye, Marly-le-Roi, Louveciennes, Bougival, Voisins, Argenteuil, Île de la Jatte, etc.), Montmartre, the Oise (Pontoise, Auvers-sur-Oise), the Right and Left Banks of Paris, and Giverny. Walking is not the only method of following these itineraries—travel by car or public transportation is sometimes necessary. Each chapter includes detailed practical information with an itinerary, places to eat and sleep, museums, and the address and phone number of the nearest tourist office. The quality of some of the art reproductions is poor, but this doesn't take much away from the usefulness of the book; it is to be hoped, after all, that you'll be face-to-face with the originals. I wouldn't want to carry this book around while walking for several hours, but I would definitely recommend consulting it in advance of setting out.

Les Quartiers
(Some Neighborhoods of Paris)

There are of course several cities called Paris—the city of great monuments and the city of separate arrondissements, each with its own history and character, its social classes and cultural styles, each mirroring an element in the life of France itself. You could draw up a kind of map of the human geography of Paris, a list of the kinds of people one would see in different places. Like the imaginary tour of the perimeter of the entire country, the map would show, above all, variety.
—Richard Bernstein, FRAGILE GLORY:
A PORTRAIT OF FRANCE AND THE FRENCH

It isn't necessary to say that Paris is superbly beautiful. What you may not yet know is that it is not all beautiful, nor beautiful in the same way from place to place, nor beautiful in the same place, always, in the same way. . . . But Paris has been so beautiful for so long that, with few exceptions, every neighborhood has some treasure or other to show. It might be a well-designed antique water pump in a forbidding alley in the Glacière section of the 13th, a handsome fountain and a street of curiously designed apartment houses not far from the nondescript rue Monge, an old court, wrinkled and molten and still a grande dame, in the fur district—and everywhere, the rhythms of old streets meeting, proliferating, branching like the veins of a leaf.
—Kate Simon, PARIS: PLACES & PLEASURES

A Royal Haven in Paris

BY BARBARA GRIZZUTI HARRISON

✺

editor's note

BARBARA GRIZZUTI HARRISON is perhaps best known for her perceptive works on Italy, among them *Italian Days* (Ticknor & Fields, 1989)
and *The Islands of Italy* (Ticknor & Fields, 1991). However, she has written equally well about other parts of the world, and when I saw this piece
on one of my favorite corners of Paris, I knew that someone who wrote with
such care and passion about Italy would approach the place des Vosges with
respect and the eyes of a keen observer.

Midnight on the rue de la Bastille. At the table next to ours outside the glass-domed Bofinger brasserie, two tanned blond
lovers are fork-feeding each other oysters. Inside, amid lace and
stained glass, sinuous art nouveau wood and zinc-topped counters,
operagoers in opera finery are polishing off the piles of crustaceans
and the charcuterie served to them by orange-aproned waiters; outside, lean figures on motorized skateboards race by.

We can see, from our table, the gilded figure, the *génie* of Paris,
atop the monument to liberty and to those who died in the upris-
ings of 1830 and 1848. And we can see the curved facade of the
Bastille Opera, the brazenly white, brazenly modern, building
of marble and granite that has been compared to both a ship in
full sail and (because of its decorative black-and-white tiles) to a
pubic lav.

The Bastille and Bofinger form the eastern boundary of the
Marais, an area marked and anchored on the west by the glass and
metal Pompidou Center, with its blue, red and yellow innards outside (and rusting) for all to see.

It's what lies in between the Bastille and the Pompidou that is lovable. The Marais—the name means marsh or swamp—was, in the Middle Ages, a district of communal kitchen gardens; they belonged to the clerical orders who lived off their produce. The neighborhood became fashionable among the rich and noble at the beginning of the seventeenth century, when Henry IV moved there with court and courtiers.

In the heart of the heart of the Marais, the place des Vosges (designated, when it was created in the seventeenth century, the place Royale and generally acknowledged to be the most beautiful public square in Paris) combines friendly, distinguished houses with a severely geometrical park. Set behind great doors, the residences, far deeper than they are wide, stand between formal courtyards and mysterious back gardens; they are surrounded by a wide ribbon of sheltering arcades. The houses, nine on each side of the square, present a unified front to the world, all soft-pink brick and white stone and gray slate. Their slight variations are difficult, at first, to perceive. Some depend on trompe l'oeil—nearly perfect imitation bricks—but they have been assimilated into a harmonious whole. This immense rosy cloister is as relaxing and sociable as urban architecture gets to be, with cafés and restaurants and strolling musicians and antique shops that spill their lovely loot into the barrel-vaulted arcades. Inside the park, a square divided into four quadrants, each with a fountain, the trees are pruned into rectangles to tame the wilderness of leafage.

Dinner under the breezy arcades, a café called Ma Bourgogne. Three old friends are drinking kir—white wine mixed (in one case) with black-cherry liqueur and in another with cassis, and (mine) with scented peach liqueur. In the pale blue twilight the streetlights are on. Cold white ham, *haricots verts,* snails with crème frîche and butter and garlic noodles; sorbets and cold peach soup with raspberry *coulis,* strawberries and mint. Bold sparrows peck at our plates.

After dinner we do not have far to go. Our hotel, the Pavillon de la Reine, is one of the two tallest mansions on the place, a distinction it shares with its twin, the Pavillon du Roi, which faces it on the south side of the square. (The Pavillon de la Reine, on the north side, is in the 3rd Arrondissement and the Pavillon du Roi is in the 4th Arrondissement—it is hard to say why this fact tickles me, but it does—like rain falling on one side of the street and not on the other.) Without troubling to disguise their longing or envy, tourists stop to gaze at our beautiful hotel, its butter-creamy facade wreathed in swags and cascades of ivy, its courtyard full of pots of red geraniums; it is odd to be part of a tourist attraction.

The Marais declined when the court moved to Versailles in the late seventeenth century. In the nineteenth century, the magnificence of its mansions was disregarded; workshops defaced courtyards and gardens. By the 1960s, when the government took the district under its wing as a protected sector, it had very nearly become a slum. Now there are boutiques and perfumeries, tearooms and green, pleasant parks. Prowl: You will find garden oases and Gothic turrets and trellised courtyards and ancient wells, quiet streets of country houses and dark alleys suggestive of assassins. You will see, rising from its place of pride on the river, the slate roofs and sharp pencil tops of the Gothic towers of the Hôtel de Sens, one of the oldest secular monuments in Paris, and contrapuntally (at 13 rue de Sévigné), a kind of history of the Marais in layers of wood and stone, a series of what appear to be separate houses vertically placed one atop the other. At the corner of Vieille-du-Temple and the rue des Francs-Bourgeois, you will find a building unremarkable except for an anomalous early-sixteenth-century turret with lacy carvings that looks like it has been stitched to the corner wall and cries out for a princess.

To the south of the place des Vosges is the happily and domestically raucous rue St.-Antoine, which, as it winds its way westward, becomes the rue de Rivoli, home to the world's most elaborately pretty city hall, the neo-Renaissance Hôtel de Ville. The rue St.-Antoine is full of butchers and food markets, fruit-and-veggie stalls that make me want to set up house here. It is a street that used to stink of sewage and of fresh blood; it has seen its share of murders. Parisians are romantic but their history does not lead one to conclude that they are sentimental. Consider, for example, the murder of the Princesse de Lamballe, whose only crime was to have been a devoted friend and confidante to Marie Antoinette; having, while imprisoned, refused to swear against the king, she was delivered to the rabble and, near the corner of the rue St.-Antoine and rue Pavée, torn apart by a deranged mob. Her impaled head was paraded north through the streets of the Marais, to the Temple Prison where the queen was held, and exhibited under Marie Antoinette's window.

It's a curious thing to remember, the rending and dismembering of the princess, in this gentrified section of the Marais. Here, on the rue St.-Paul, in what used to be the garden of Charles V, is a self-conscious aggregation of zigzagging courtyards and short, winding flights of steps—a maze of antique shops too cute for me. The street is precious or charming, depending on one's mood or sensibility. It is certainly pretty.

I prefer to root for antiques—film posters, antique walking sticks, Tin Tin memorabilia—on and around the rue des Rosiers, the rue des Ecouffes and the rue Ferdinand Duval, the Jewish quarter of the Marais. *Rosiers* means "rosebushes," and rosebushes bloomed along the old city walls in this city-within-a-city, which still retains its medieval flavor. On this old, twisting street, buildings lean toward each other, a testament to survival, full of pleasures for the mind and body: bookshops (side by side with books by Primo Levi and by and about Anne Frank, are yellow child-sized yarmulkes decorated with pictures of Mickey Mouse and Donald Duck) and purveyors of Tunisian and Moroccan foods. From Finkelsztajn's 1851 deli and *boulangerie* and from Jo Goldenberg's deli: cheese-cake and challah, strudel, gefilte fish. The front wall of Finkelsztajn's establishment is made of *pique-assiette,* a result of that frugal and lovely French esthetic that puts to use pieces of broken porcelain and ceramics to make a charming mosaic surface. Bullet marks punctuate the wall of Goldenberg's, a sobering reminder of a 1982 act of terrorism in which six people were killed and twenty-two were injured. Not far away is an art nouveau synagogue, digni-fied and deliquescent, the work of Hector Guimard, designer of the entrances of the Paris metro stations.

We have lunch in a kosher Vietnamese restaurant *(poulet au cit-ron);* at the next table four men are, with great animation and equal goodwill, arranging a marriage.

The main thoroughfare northwest of the place des Vosges is the rue des Francs-Bourgeois; in the streets around it, whimsy reigns. The popular Loir dans la Théière—The Dormouse in the Teapot—is clubby and kitschy, quiche and tea among displaced Englishmen and leftover American hippies; diagonally across the street is Thanksgiving, a shop for food-nostalgic Americans that sells lime Jell-O. Cake mixes, too.

But for relaxed elegance in rooms that are both exotic and embracing, nothing measures up to Mariage Frères (30 rue du Bourg-Tibourg), since 1854 tea merchants to all of discerning Paris. Part museum, part bakery and part salon, Mariage Frères is full of Parisians fastidiously poking their noses into one or more of the 450 or so canisters stored in cubbies on open shelves. The tearoom com-bines the ambience of Southeast Asia (palms and rattan armchairs and handsome white-jacketed waiters) with ineffable Parisian chic. Rather against my will—I have never seen the point of tea ice cream—I accede to my Parisian friend Julie's prompting and order tea sorbet. Three kinds of tea, citrusy, sweet, smoky. Oh! Each mouthful lacquers the palate just long enough for you to plunge your spoon in for the next silky bite.

There is a cluster of museums in the Marais housed in magnificently restored hotels; they offer a soothing alternative to the rigors and crowds of the Louvre as well as a way to insinuate oneself into the gilded past.

In the seventeenth-century Hôtel Libéral Bruand, where the architect of the Invalides lived, there is the Musée Bricard, a museum of locks and keys. One might be inclined to think that the locks and keys exist merely to provide an excuse for tourists to visit the mansion; but French philosophers are singularly intrigued by the symbolic and metaphysical meanings of locks and keys—the philosopher Gaston Bachelard, for example, devotes a whole chapter to them in his *Poetics of Space*. How I wish it had been open. Alas, it was August, and the Hôtel Libéral Bruand was closed.

The Musée Carnavalet, the Museum of the City of Paris, is housed in a mansion where, at the end of the seventeenth century, Mme. de Sévigné lived for the last twenty years of her life. She owes her reputation as a writer of the first rank to her letters. Rushing home from dinner parties to scribble to her daughter in Provence, she conveyed the gossip that is a catalog of the absurdities of society: "For the pyramids of fruit the doorways had to be raised. Our forefathers never foresaw mechanics like these, since they didn't imagine a door had to be higher than themselves. A pyramid wants to come in (one of those pyramids that mean you are obliged to write notes from one side of the table to the other, not that there is anything upsetting about that—on the contrary it is very pleasant not to see what they conceal). This pyramid, with twenty dishes, was so satisfactorily knocked down at the door that the din drowned the violins, oboes and trumpets."

Mme. de Sévigné was a regular communicant at the purpledoored baroque Jesuit church of St.-Paul–St.-Louis on the rue St.-Antoine, a church of ten remarkable for its music and learned sermons—and for its trompe l'oeil dome, a copy of the theatrical Gesù in Rome, pained and sculptured souls tumbling out of the ceiling apparently into Hell.

I should love to have seen the desk at which Mme. de Sévigné wrote, "I have been satisfying the desire I had to tell a tale." But the rooms where her apartments are re-created were shut; and so we wandered around garden courtyards and the ground floor, regarding exhibits of documents from the Revolution and carved and painted shop signs. The rooms that housed these emblems for pork shops and locksmiths and spirits were grand and graceful and full of the kinds of architectural wonders Mme. de Sévigné lived with— wall panels of gilded animals (cobra, griffin, elephant, crocodile); immense glass chandeliers.

It is serendipitous that the paintings Picasso's heirs donated to the state are compatible with the gilded crimson glories of the seventeenth-century Hôtel Salé (named "the salty hotel" because the wealth of its original owner was derived largely from the salt tax imposed by the king). It is possible to look at the baroque as a deconstruction or reconstruction of the human form; and in that light the decorative elements of the hotel resonate well with Picasso's deconstructions. And with those of Braque, Cézanne, Rousseau and Matisse, paintings from Picasso's private collection that have found a home at the Hôtel Salé.

I have never loved Picasso so much as I have at the Salé. Why have I never seen so clearly his sweetness, his tenderness? It had never occurred to me before that the *Flute of Pan* had the massive simplicity and authority, the solidity and inevitability, of a Piero della Francesca. *"Qui regarde au fond de Paris a le vertige"*—he who looks into the depths of Paris grows giddy (Victor Hugo's dictum). Perhaps I am suffering from euphoric vertigo.

One night we made a circuit of the place des Vosges—past No. 6—the Victor Hugo museum. His rooms have been re-created—his walls of patterned velvet, the Louis XIII four-poster in which he died, and the interior of the cottage dining room on Guernsey, with the furniture he designed for his mistress, Juliette Drouet, and the chinoiserie panels he made for her "Chinese drawing room." One feels almost voyeuristic in these intensely personal and peopled rooms so solid and romantic (and only slightly pompous and melo-dramatic). He had a penchant for red (especially for a shade he had copied from a canopy in the Casbah of Algiers), and (in his study) for plump leather chairs, chandeliers from Murano, velvet and damask, striped rose-and-green wallpaper. Through these rooms passed Gautier, Balzac, Dumas, Berlioz, Liszt, Rossini; and in these rooms lived Léopoldine, his daughter, who drowned when she was nineteen. A spiritualist, Hugo claimed to have heard Léopoldine's voice while "table turning," also the voices of Joan of Arc and Shakespeare.

At No. 7 is the Hôtel de Sully. An orangery and a cobblestone courtyard with bas-reliefs of seasons and elements—Earth, Wind, Air and Fire, gilded and decorated to a fare-thee-well. On either side of the great entry door is a sphinx, one with its nose missing. You can make your way through the ivy-clad mansion, going through doors within doors through a magic garden, to the rue St.-Antoine. Or you could choose to loiter in the garden for the better part of your life.

At No. 9 is l'Ambroisie (closed in August), a three-star restau-rant. In it once lived a very busy courtesan, one of whose lovers was Cardinal Richelieu. (The *place* facilitated all kinds of social activi-ties. The cardinal's grandnephew, the Duc de Richelieu, claimed that he had made love to all the women of the *place*.) The École Maternelle is housed in what used to be Gautier's mansion; at No. 14 is a synagogue, the Temple des Vosges, easy to miss. Virgin Music has an office in No. 11, and Issey Miyake is at No. 3. No. 19 is Ma Bourgogne, and No. 25 is another restaurant, La Guirlande de Julie.

It is very late, and the double doors of our hotel are shut; we push the silver doorbell to gain admittance. A pale light shines on the verdigrised nymph in the interior courtyard I see from my Empire bed. In the ghostly hour, a little girl with long white-blond hair and long brown legs is playing an inscrutable game with her little brother in this patch of tidy forest, dodging and giggling behind sculpture and fountain and under trees and flowering bushes, safe in the heart of the city.

Neighborhood Retreats

Restaurants

Bofinger, 5 rue de la Bastille (telephone: 42.72.87.82). Specialties are seafood and brasserie fare.

Ma Bourgogne, 19 place des Vosges (42.78.44.64). Specialties include *tartare de saumon,* foie gras and crème brûlée.

L'Ambroisie, 9 place des Vosges (42.78.51.45). Gets three stars in the *Guide Michelin.* Specialties include *feuilleté* of truffles, lobster fricassee and a bitter-chocolate tart.

La Guirlande de Julie, 25 place des Vostes (48.87.94.07).

Coconnas, 2 bis place des Vosges (42.78.58.16).

Hotels

Pavillon de la Reine, 28 place des Vosges (42.77.96.40; fax: 42.77.63.06). Has thirty-two rooms and suites.

Bretonnerie is a ten-minute walk from the place des Vosges at 22 rue Ste.-Croix-de-la-Bretonnerie (48.87.77.63; fax: 42.77.26.78).

Place des Vosges, 12 rue Birague (42.72.60.46; fax: 42.72.02.64). Has sixteen rooms.

Paris When It Shimmers

BY MAVIS GALLANT

❧

editor's note

MAVIS GALLANT is a novelist and writer. Although Canadian-born she has lived for many years in Paris, and many of the characters in her fiction are Parisian. By 1996, she had contibuted 115 pieces of fiction and non-fiction to *The New Yorker* (following only John Updike and S. J. Perelman). Among her many works of fiction are *The Collected Stories of Mavis Gallant* (1996), *Across the Bridge* (1993), and *Overhead in a Balloon: Twelve Stories of Paris* (1985), all published by Random House.

How wonderful to see rainy streets once more, wrote the Goncourt brothers in their joint diary after a stay in intolerably sunny Rome. The Paris winter sky reflects wet sidewalks, or seems to, gray on gray. A photograph by Alfred Stieglitz, "A Snapshot, Paris," 1913, has it, exactly. There is a print of the photograph in the Musée d'Orsay. When you leave the museum and walk up rue de Bellechasse, you are still in the picture.

In November rain slants across a tone of daylight that does not vary from ten in the morning until three in the afternoon. It is an opaque gray sometimes, the gray you associate with older spiderwebs, or the floor covering at Beaubourg, or the outer walls of the Swedish embassy on rue Barbet de Jouy. (The attraction of northern taste to concrete the color of dirty snow deserves research.) The most truthful painter of the Paris winter is Pissarro. Not Utrillo; you will never see his particular kind of white, not even after a snowfall.

The branches of trees look wet and wild. People walk with their heads down. You can add to your repertory of useful remarks *"Quel sale temps!"* Unfortunately, it is like our own "How do you do?" and leads nowhere. The best one can do is answer the same thing, *"Quel sale temps!"* with a slightly different emphasis, a downward tilt, as if to mean "Indeed" or "How well put." If you learn to take part in this exchange, nodding your head, biting your lower lip, you will never be taken for a foreigner.

Christmas

Your Parisian friends will say they have not seen a winter like it since the Socialists were in power, or since the death of Charles de Gaulle. Actually, they saw the same rain a month ago and the same snow-fall the year before last. The collective memory is set for a span of five minutes; the collective future, fixed on next weekend. That is why every holiday is met by rapture and delight: if it is raining in Paris, it is bound to be fine just thirty miles away. Seasons are written in vanishing ink.

"Christmas in France isn't Christmas. To celebrate that particular Feast in a nightclub is absurd, wrong even. Still, it's what I did." That was Maurice Sachs, writer, actor and professional con artist, on December 26, 1919. He may not have been to a nightclub at all; he was a tireless liar. He may have gone to church. He was always in and out of some religious fantasy. Still, he was right in that first sentence, if one changes "France" to "Paris."

Parisians have never known what to do about Christmas except get out of town. Those left behind go to restaurants. In one Left Bank restaurant a few seasons ago, a table of diners who thought the serv-ings of the Venison Christmas Special were unreasonably skimpy sprayed the place with tear gas. While the other customers stood out-side in the sleety night drying their tears, the protesters made off with a painting dear to the owner and a clutch of unwashed cutlery.

They were lucky to have been offered the choice of venison. Christmas turkey is the only thing the French cannot cook. Avoid it, and the petrified chestnuts, and the disagreeable cake known as a *bûche de Noël*. It looks like a log, and it tastes like soft wood with butter frosting. The whole meal is repeated at the New Year, with only a week in between to recover. By January 2 it is quite forgotten, and you can begin to eat normal French food again.

Très Fatigué

Paris is the cleanest of winter cities. Snow lies on parked cars white and unsoiled, like the snow of childhood we think we remember. At night you notice a reddish light on snow clouds and on fallen snow, like a decanter of wine with a light behind it. From the Musée d'Orsay, the Tuileries are gray-white with a wash of pink. During the annual Christmas fair, on the rue de Rivoli side of the gardens, the Ferris wheel picked out in lights is like a constellation. You observe it through pristine winter air.

Parisians will not accept a word of this. They think their city is polluted, more poisonous than anywhere else. They are proud of the poison: it explains why everyone, in winter, is so fatigued. If you ask how someone is feeling, fatigue sets in at once. There is an anchored belief that winter pollution presses down, like a large and terrible hand, making one unfit to ride the escalator in a department store or stand in line for the bus.

Children are tired, too; they fall asleep at their desks. It is not because they have been up until all hours, watching television, but because of pollution and the winter season. Also, they may have been growing. As a rule, unless they are drastically undernourished, children do grow. In Paris it is accomplished at a cost of moral and physical strain. Parents measure the child, and measure the fatigue spent in that last quarter inch, and feel discouraged. A winter holiday is no help: the Alps are tiring because they are high; snow, because it is wet and cold. The return to sullied Paris drains whatever energy the child may have kept in reserve. If you say that the child seems fine, you will be told that it can't be so; he may not look it, but he is *très, très fatigué.*

For winter fatigue there are special candies and cookies in drugstores, about four times the price of similar things you can buy in a chain grocery. There are anti-exhaustion herbal and floral teas that taste of shredded dust cloths. If you compound your winter fatigue with other winter ailments—winter homesickness, winter perplexity, winter doubts—the pharmacist will send you away with a supply of homeopathic pills. They are no larger than the head of a pin and can be thrown down the drain without blocking the pipes, should you grow tired of antifatigue.

Mufflings

What did Balzac mean when he told his readers that the smart thing to eat was "mufflings"? He recommended it, or them, as part of a chic repast to be taken early in the day, served on a bare table, in "confusion and gracious disorder." On no account was this refreshment to be called a meal: in 1829 the word *déjeuner* was a thing of the past, and only rustics spread a cloth before six in the evening. Elegant nourishment consisted of eggs, salad, pilaf, strawberries, tea, soda water and mufflings.

"Mufflings" could be a winter dish, a mixture of muffler and whiting: *merlan en colère,* biting its own tail, on a bed that looks like wool—purée of sorrel, perhaps. It may just stand for winter food, dispensed in the confusion and gracious disorder of winter strikes, winter rain, unexpected snow (snow is never expected)— food that is remote from nouvelle cuisine, which is dying, but not fast enough.

Déjeuner, in spite of Balzac, made a rapid comeback, and before long another gracious collation had squeezed its way in: *le lunch. Un petit lunch, deux petits lunchs* [sic]. Even the pronunciation is disheartening, with the vowel close to the *ea* of *earth*. Before the twentieth century could get moving, *le lunch* had a chapter to itself in a book about correct behavior, *Le Guide des Convenances:* "There are *lunchs* where you sit, and *lunchs* where you stand. A standing *lunch* is not as comfortable." Granted.

Le Guide also deals with another source of worry, good for all seasons: "With Whom Should One Shake Hands?" Not as simple as you may think. "Generally speaking, the superior person of the two offers a hand. The only difficulty lies in establishing the superiority." A woman is always superior, it turns out, unless she is confronted with a man who is expected to do her a favor. In that case he automatically becomes superior, and will "extend a hand as part of his benevolence."

Is this helpful? Can you, visiting Paris, do a favor or expect one? Will you ever know anyone well enough to establish superiority or to acknowledge inferiority? The waiter who whistles up a cab wants a tip, not a hand with nothing in it. The best thing might be to visit a restaurant with a table d'hôte, sit with strangers and see who extends the first benevolent hand. A good place to try is the Ambassade d'Auvergne, at 22 rue du Grenier-St.-Lazare, in the Beaubourg area. It serves winter food—good, solid, sensible cold-weather mufflings from the heart of France, such as *pot-au-feu*, stuffed cabbage, potatoes cooked with garlic, *petit salé* and lentils.

The table d'hôte is to the left of the bar as you enter: a polished, handsome table, set for a dozen, where anyone may sit without a reservation, or when the other two rooms are crowded. It seems to be the domain of French out-of-towners. You will discover from them that in Tours, Lille, Marseille, Dijon, and Grenoble it is hard to park a car downtown, get children into a good school, or have a property-tax bill lowered. Comparing notes will make you equal, and you can shake hands all around, no discrimination, men and women mixed.

Priorities

Firemen are summoned to knock ice and frozen snow off rooftops. In Montparnasse, a ladder seven flights high crosses the facade of the Rotonde. Great slabs of ice smash onto the pavement. The *sapeur-pompier* at the top of the ladder sends them down, urban glaciers, with a single blow of an iron bar.

The radio warns pedestrians to be careful; the warning is part of the news bulletin, midafternoon, mid-February. Everywhere ice is falling with the most thunderous noise. In rue de Vaugirard, fragments of it rebound against parked cars. Walk close to the walls, says a policeman. Some pieces of broken ice are the size of grapefruit, but even a half lemon could stun a horse. Pedestrians set off, single file, like a duck with ducklings. The "duck" is a café waiter who works around the corner, in rue Blaise-Desgoffe. He seems to have known many forms of danger and strides off quite fearlessly.

The big fountain in the Luxembourg Gardens is frozen, the ice barrel-shaped, with a plume of water still blowing and splashing. The Panthéon looks soft and dark against a milky sky. Thaw is setting in; walkers are told to keep to paved pathways. The sunken gardens are fenced off with rows of park chairs that are held together with colored tape. It looks playful, improvised, but if you approach the barrier, a guardian blows a whistle. *C'est sérieux.*

It used to be the season for red plush bars, but they are empty now. The old Hôtel Crillon bar has become a restaurant, and the new one, along the hall, is decorated to resemble a bad dream of the 1950s. Better to walk. In the Champs-Élysées gardens, so-called, where Marcel played with Gilberte Swann, if you follow a muddy path called allée Marcel Proust, you soon come to the public convenience where Marcel's grandmother had her stroke and from which she emerged with her hat askew. It is a small, green chalet, with the polished wood and fittings of Proust's grandmother's time, and quite possibly the same attendant: a literary monument, the only one in the area, and one day it will undoubtedly be graced with a marble plaque.

The *guignol*—the puppet show—has been pushed back to a corner of the *jardin;* the noise of traffic along avenue Matignon all but smothers the voice of Guignol, opposite number to Punch. But the children, bundled up against the cold, sitting on benches, can shriek louder than anything. As Guignol fails to catch an impertinent mouse, they scream, *"Elle est là!"* From the back, rows of padded bottoms; from the front, runny button noses. They are children of immigrants—Asian, Arab, African—and their nursery-school French is already without flaw or accent. People old enough to know better continue to write and to announce that the children should go back where they came from. It has no meaning: they started off here, and some of the memories they are storing up are the same as Proust's.

The recent wave of pink winter coats like bathrobes has begun to abate, replaced by a craze for Mickey Mouse garments, made of undefinable synthetic stuff, with Mickey embossed here and there.

"I bought a Mickey Mouse coat for my little girl," says a man who is having his hair done in a unisex *salon de coiffure.* "She looks like a princess in it."

His attendant, Gisèle, says that it costs a lot of money to dress a child, more than she expected before she had one.

"C'est un choix de priorités." He will give up hot-towel treatments any day, should the cost of Mickey Mouse clothes start to climb.

Priorities. First things first. Mardi Gras before Easter.

Still Winter

No matter how late Easter falls, Mardi Gras counts as winter. Left Bank streets fill up with students trying to have a good time, but they've never had it—at least, not that way. They smear their own faces with flour, toss flour over people waiting at bus stops, open car doors and throw flour and trash inside. Parisians refer to this melancholy rollicking as "a demonstration," the term attached now to any kind of movement in the streets.

You can't be evicted before mid-March, even if you haven't paid any rent since the first rainfall of November. March is throwing-out time. Once, on a cold March day, a man saw an old woman crying in the street and paid what she owed. As the dollar then stood, it came to about $400. He wasn't rich, just an office employee who happened to have the money in the bank. He was treated with immense suspicion by the press. His voice in a radio interview became defensive.

"Do you realize," said the interviewer, "that you are never going to see that money again?"

Why had he done it? An impulse, he said. One imagined him slinking out of the studio to the damp street, wishing he could put the clock back, that it was still February, that the old lady was still waiting for her fate, and that he would never walk down that particular street.

The morning sky is whitish blue, a Sisley color, and the clouds have an iridescent shine. The whole sky seems to be moving along toward the outer suburbs, where Paris taxi drivers live and grow parsley and tomatoes and large pink roses. The afternoon weather may be gray, but different in texture and tone—thin and silky, Pissarro's gray. When you go out, you will see that some of the chestnut vendors have packed up their burners and are selling slices of fresh coconut. It is still winter, but near the end.

The 15th, a World of Its Own

BY ANN PRINGLE-HARRIS

∾

editor's note

A number of visitors to Paris never venture beyond the first seven or eight arrondissements, but as the writers of this piece (on the 15th Arrondissement) and the following one (on Passy-Auteuil) reveal, you'll be rewarded if you do. The 15th is the most populated arrondissement in Paris, and after this article appeared, some readers wrote to add a few details about the *quartier:* George Brassens Park was named after the popular singer/songwriter—somewhat the equivalent of Bob Dylan—who was a resident of the 15th and who died in 1981. The Tour Montparnasse inspires little affection among Parisians, who refer to it in the same way they once did the Tour Eiffel: the top floor is the most beautiful spot in the city because it's the only spot where one can't see the tower.

Although not stated in the text, the studio apartment the author rented for a month is owned by Wayne and Lydie Marshall. Readers may know Lydie as the author of *A Passion for Potatoes* (1992) and *Chez Nous* (1995)—which was published in paperback under the title *A Passion for My Provence* (1999)—all published by HarperCollins and HarperPerennial. Lydie and her husband operate the À La Bonne Cocotte en Provence cooking school, and her first book, *Cooking with Lydie Marshall* (Knopf, 1983), is based on the techniques and recipes she taught when her school was in New York. The Marshalls' studio apartment in Paris is available for a reasonable rent year-round. For detailed information—including photos and a map—and a brochure on the cooking school in Nyons, contact the Marshalls at Le Chateau Feodal, 26110, Nyons, France; 475.26.45.31 / fax: 475.26.09.31; or in the U.S. at 212-675-7736.

My love affair with Paris's 15th Arrondissement began, as love affairs often do, by mere chance. A studio was available there for this past July, the month I had chosen, at a price I could afford to pay. And it was within walking distance of the school where, in my continuing quest for fluency, I would again be studying French.

"The 15th?" murmured my Francophile friends, and I, too, had to spread out my Paris map to figure out just where I would be. A stone's throw from the Eiffel Tower in the 7th, a river's breadth from the discreet charm of Passy in the 16th, on the verge of Montparnasse in the 14th—the map told me exactly what the 15th was not.

I found out what it was as my taxi veered through a district that somehow put me in mind of Paris as it was on my earliest visits: a Paris of small neighborhoods not yet adopted by tourists; of blocks lined with shops displaying mouthwatering cheeses, glistening fruits and vegetables, exquisite baby clothes, bread in a dozen shapes and sizes; of tidy parks tucked into the midst of commercial and residential blocks; of pleasant cafés at virtually every significant intersection.

I regularly passed one of the small parks, off the rue du Commerce, and on weekends I always looked for the *boule* players, a fiercely concentrated group of men cheered on by their wives or female friends (women play *boules,* I was told, but I never saw one). On most days I also passed a café where a frail, elderly woman frequently sat, with or without a cup of coffee but always cradling her handbag and wearing lavender Courrèges-style boots, rain or shine.

Having settled into my light, spacious studio plus kitchenette and bath, I window-shopped for antiques and art deco treasures at upscale establishments in the Swiss Village off the avenue de la Motte-Picquet, lined up for bread baked in wood-fired ovens at Poilâne, and cruised among the stalls of exotic shellfish, gigantic mushrooms, cheap clothing and household supplies at the Wednesday open-air market under the elevated metro on the boulevard de Grenelle. I embraced and explored my new abode.

I quickly learned that the 15th doesn't always receive credit for its own history. For instance, Léger, Chagall, Soutine, Modigliani and other artists usually associated with Montparnasse spent their early, struggling years in the 15th, in a three-story octagonal building called, because of its resemblance to a beehive, La Ruche. The hive, fitted out with wedge-shaped studios, was originally a pavilion at the 1900 Paris World Exposition and was acquired, together with a neighboring structure, by the sculptor Alfred Boucher as a communal living-and-working space for needy artists.

Run-down and at risk of demolition by 1965, La Ruche was saved by a group headed by Chagall; its facade and roof were made a national monument in 1972. Today, visitors to 2 passage Dantzig (turn onto the rue Dantzig off rue de la Convention) will find at the entrance the high iron portals and stone caryatids taken from the 1900 exposition, and behind them, a tree-shaded garden and the studio buildings themselves, still occupied by painters and sculptors. Down the street is the Café Dantzig, where the original artists hung out.

Everyone goes to the Rodin Museum in the 7th—but the Antoine Bourdelle Museum in the 15th? I arrived on a drizzly day, one of very few visitors, and had a marvelous time admiring some of the late-nineteenth-century sculptor's finished works and plaster casts (for example, for the bronze panels that adorn the Théâtre des Champs-Élysées); examining his paintings—he was a gifted portraitist; and marveling at the variety of subjects he tackled. A student of Rodin's, he worked, as a rule, on a monumental scale, but his figures show a wide emotional range: Penelope looking rather bored as she awaits Ulysses' return, and Sappho full of quiet strength. The museum includes Bourdelle's studio and living quarters, plus a new wing and sculpture garden.

Now that the 15th was my quarter, I invested in a book, *Le Guide du Promeneur: 15e Arrondissement,* detailing nine walks there. I learned that it was one of the city's newer districts, having become a part of Paris proper only in 1860. Before that, the area embraced the villages of Vaugirard and Grenelle, both well cultivated in grain and vines. The rue de Vaugirard is Paris's longest street today, and the boulevard de Grenelle forms a convenient reference point for Left Bank walkers because of its elevated metro tracks.

In my walks, I was struck by how the architectural ambience of the 15th differs from that of older Paris districts. For seventeenth- and eighteenth-century mansions, or *hôtels particuliers*, one goes elsewhere; in the 15th, the emphasis is late nineteenth and twentieth century. There is joyous belle epoque excess here, in apartment buildings intended for the up-and-coming bourgeoisie. I passed one such building almost every day, a small jewel with flamboyant stone swirls and a rounded slate turret on the place Étienne-Pernet. There are riches from the art deco years, too: a series of matched 1920s houses with charming pointed roofs stretching along one side of the rue Santos-Dumont, named for the pioneer aviator whose villa stands at the end of the street.

On the boulevard Victor, near the Seine, an apartment building designed by the architect who was responsible, with Émile-Jacques Ruhlmann, for the interiors of the steamships *Normandie* and the *Île-de-France* typifies what my guide called the *paquebot* school of architecture. The architect of 3 boulevard Victor, Pierre Patout, did succeed in creating a strikingly original building. Long and sleek, its facade does indeed suggest a ship's hull, with tiers of decks and smokestacks (actually duplex apartments) at the top.

Clues to the 15th's history can also be found in its churches. The oldest one still maintaining its original construction, St.-Jean-Baptiste de Grenelle, was built in 1827–28, before Grenelle was officially a part of Paris. With a duchess and the daughter of a royal duke present to place the first stone, St.-Jean-Baptiste tells us that the local leading citizens, the businessmen for whom the rue des

Entrepreneurs was named, realized there was a need for a handsome new church in the district. It stands in a square where the rue des Entrepreneurs and the rue du Commerce meet.

A century later, between the two world wars, Paris saw an influx of White Russian émigrés. The artists and members of the impoverished Russian nobility living in the 15th and surviving as chauffeurs and factory laborers probably worshiped at St.-Seraphin de Sarov, at 91 rue Lecourbe.

Opening the doors of No. 91, flush with the street, I found myself in the first of two interior courtyards. St.-Seraphin was in the second one, along with a pretty, circular garden. The small Russian Orthodox church, constructed of natural wood, might almost be a hideaway in the forest except for its brilliant blue onion dome. Inside, it was ablaze with candles and icons. At one side was a large tree trunk, presumably left in place when the church was built. Periodically, a priest in gold robes entered the sanctuary from one of three doors behind the altar, said prayers in Russian, swung a censer that made a sound like the tinkling of sleigh bells, then left again through an altar door. A choir sang a cappella, and members of the congregation read long passages in Russian.

Not far from St.-Seraphin is the Pasteur Institute, where the distinguished scientist lived, worked and is buried. The story goes that when the Panthéon, resting place of France's greatest and most illustrious, was suggested, Pasteur's widow, who herself held a doctorate in science, replied that she thought he would prefer to be buried at home. And so, after visiting Pasteur's laboratories and the family living quarters—a spacious two-floor apartment furnished with antiques from various periods and featuring the doctor's pastel portraits of his family—one descends to the crypt. Far from being somber, its delicate mosaics in gold and floral colors, designed by A. Guilbert-Martin—pinks, blues, pale greens and yellows—are light and fresh. The motifs are animals and plants, the flora and fauna Pasteur worked with in devising methods to kill bacteria that spoil wine, beer, and milk, and in discovering vaccinations for anthrax and cholera in animals and rabies in human beings. Medical research is still carried on at this site and at the institute's branches in other parts of the world.

Thinking of covering several of my desired destinations in one walk, I headed one day for the Montparnasse-Bienvenue quarter and three museums there, the Musée de la Poste, devoted to the postal service, and the Jean Moulin and Maréchal Leclerc museums, dedicated to two heroes of the Second World War. One, the postal museum, was closed for restoration—perhaps just as well, because I would not have wanted to rush through the two others.

The Maréchal Leclerc Memorial, honoring Jacques Leclerc, the general who led a division into Paris at the time of the liberation, re-creates the events of the war through print, photographs, film footage and broadcasts. With the 15th in mind, I watched some footage on the gallant stand of the Free French forces at Bir Hakeim in North Africa, now commemorated in a bridge across the Seine and in the first metro station after crossing the river from Passy into the 15th. The Jean Moulin Museum adjacent to the Leclerc—both are in the Jardin Atlantique above the Gare Montparnasse—recounts the aims and accomplishments of the various Resistance movements during the war. Moulin, a leader and coordinator of those efforts, was eventually captured by the Germans and killed. His remains reside in the Panthéon.

One afternoon, as I strolled along the Seine at the quai de Grenelle, I came upon a group of young women sharing a picnic. Near them were other women, some with children, in bronze. They were part of a sculptural group memorializing the thousands of

Jews who were rounded up by French police in July 1942 and deported, most ending at Auschwitz. Awaiting deportation, they were kept at the Vélodrome d'Hiver (Vel' d'Hiv to Parisians), a building since razed, once used for bicycle races and other public events. A large bronze tablet tells their story.

A block or so from the river, at the corner of the rue Nélaton and the boulevard de Grenelle, I passed a smaller plaque, placed where the Vélodrome once stood. On the grassy square in front of the plaque there were wreaths of fresh flowers.

Where, I wondered, do children of the 15th play? Where do grown-ups lie in the shade and read? Besides the many neighborhood squares and public gardens, I found two large, relatively new parks. One, the André-Citroën, is a futuristic stretch of acreage occupying what used to be a Citroën plant along the Seine near the southwestern limits of the city. There are theme gardens here, planted in colors that accord with specific senses—red for taste, blue for smell, and so on—a white garden and a black garden, and lots of water, in canals, cascades and at least sixty-four jets (at that point I stopped counting) that spurt up seemingly at random, much to the delight of barefooted children. Guided tours are available, with dates posted at the entrance.

The Georges Brassens Park on the rue des Morillons, more traditional, also had an earlier life—as the Vaugirard abattoir. Very little suggests that bloody past now, except for the bronze bulls at the entrance, a campanile from which selling prices were once shouted, and a collection of stones from the original building, thoughtfully left for children to climb on.

Besides a pond and a large children's play area, the park offers lovely winding paths leading to arbors and secluded gardens, one of which, with signs in braille and plants chosen for their fragrance, was designed for the blind. Within the confines of the park are the hexagonal Silvia Montfort Theater, a beehive and a small vineyard. On Saturdays and Sundays, a used-book market is set up in an open-sided market building, the handsome nineteenth-century former Halles des Chevaux, along the edge of the park bordering the rue Brancion—just the place to find early Babar books and Sir Walter Scott's *Rob Roy,* in French.

One reason for having a kitchen in Paris is the sheer pleasure of shopping for food. In the 15th, one can do it in the time-honored French way—a visit to the *boulangerie,* another to the *charcuterie* and so on—or, if time is short, by making a one-stop foray into the enticingly stocked *alimentation* sections of Monoprix or Prisunic. But I didn't neglect my neighborhood eating places. Down the block, at a tiny Corsican restaurant called Le Beau Violet, I had *soupe de poisson* equal to any I have ever tasted: thick with chunks of mild fish and deliciously fresh crustaceans, with just enough anise to deliver a pleasant jolt. On my second visit I was tactfully given to understand that as a neighbor I might poke my head in from time to time to say hello. The next day, I did just that, charmed to have met the residency requirement.

When my month was up, I had by no means taken every walk. I will have to go back, and I know just when to do it. I'll go at a time of year when it gets dark by dinnertime, so I can watch all the lights of Paris go on as I sip an aperitif on the fifty-sixth floor of the Tour Montparnasse. In the 15th.

In general, parks and public monuments in the 15th Arrondissement are open every day, though most parks close at night.

Worth a Stop

La Ruche. For access, write to the Foundation La Ruche-Seydoux, 2 passage Dantzig, Paris 75015, for authorization, stating your telephone number.

Antoine Bourdelle Museum, 18 rue Antoine-Bourdelle, 33.1.49.54.73.73.

Pasteur Institute, 25 rue du Docteur Roux, 33.1.45.68.82.83.

Jean Moulin Museum and **Maréchal Leclerc Memorial,** 33.1.40.64.39.44; 23 allée de la Deuxième Division Blindée in the Jardin Atlantique above Gare Montparnasse (access from TGV Platform 3 or from the escalator at 25 boulevard de Vaugirard).

Tour Montparnasse, rue de l'Arrivée, 33.1.45.38.52.56.

Le Beau Violet, 92 rue des Entrepreneurs, 33.1.45.78.93.44.

Guide for Walkers

Le Guide du Promeneur: 15e Arrondissement, by Florence Claval (Éditions Parigramme). Available at most bookstores in the 15th and at FNAC stores.

On Île St.-Louis

BY HERBERT GOLD

~

editor's note

....

    This is certainly not the only piece written about the lovely Île St.-Louis, but it is my favorite. HERBERT GOLD is the author of over twenty books, including *Best Nightmare on Earth: A Life in Haiti* (Prentice Hall Press, 1991), *She Took My Arm As If She Loved Me* (St. Martin's Press, 1997), *A Girl of Forty* (Donald I. Fine, 1986), the forthcoming *Daughter Mine* (St. Martin's Press), and my favorite, *Bohemia: Where Art, Angst, Love, and Strong Coffee Meet* (Simon & Schuster, 1993). I share the following quote from *Bohemia* with you not because it is about the Île St.-Louis but because of the singular Parisian spirit that it portrays, which residents of the Île would appreciate: "A fellow Fulbright scholar, studying in Belgium, happened to arrive for his first visit to Paris on July 14, Bastille Day, when the entire city was strung with colored lights. Bands played on every corner, or at least on flutes and musettes; people were dancing, singing, embracing, inviting us and anyone else nearby to join them for their wine and food. It recalled the *soupers fraternels* of revolutionary times, when the people of Paris set their tables outside, lay extra places for hungry or convivial passersby who wished to share bread, wine, and cheese. This Bastille Day mood, after war and Nazi occupation, was one of spiritual orgy, a festival nourished by deep griefs. My friend saw only the gaiety. He looked about at the hubbub, sighed, and said, 'I always knew Paris would be like this.' Paris, of course, is not really like this. But we know it must be, therefore it is; the Paris of our dreams is a required course."

A n island prime, an island at the secret heart of Paris, floating in time and space across a footbridge on the shady side of the cathedral of Notre Dame de Paris, the Île St.-Louis may also be the most ambiguous orphan island there is—city and not a city, village and metropolis, provincial and centrally urban, serene and hyped by hundreds of years of noisy lovers of solitude.

Unique it is, possessed of itself, even self-congratulatory, yet available to all who choose to stroll from the population sink of contemporary Paris to a place that has no metro stop or depressed highway. One could live there forever and do it in a short span of time, and I did.

Just after World War II, I came to study philosophy amid the existentialists of St.-Germain-des-Prés. The first winter was bitter cold, with food rationing and no heat, and we philosophers—that is, admirers of Juliette Greco with her long nose, hoarse voice, black jeans and sweaters—had to find cafés to do our deep thinking in.

In existential pursuit of the largest café au lait and most tooth-rotting but warming chocolate, I bought a bicycle to widen my field of operations, showing a certain Cleveland shrewdness by paying $8 for the rustiest, most battered bicycle I could find so that I could leave it unlocked.

Behind Notre Dame, across the narrow footbridge of the Pont St.-Louis, on the tranquil Île St.-Louis, which did little business and did it negligently, I leaned my bike against a café that served large coffees, rich chocolate and few customers. I remember it as Aux Alsaciennes, because it served Alsatian sausage, corned beef and cabbage, *choucroute garnie* at lunchtime; but for many years, now that the place has been discovered, it has been called the Brasserie de St.-Louis-en-l'Île.

Somehow, here I couldn't think about Bergson and Diderot and the hyphen between them, a little-known idea-smith named Maine de Biran, my thesis. Maybe it was the action of pumping a rusty bicycle; maybe it was the red-faced waiters, the black-dressed postwar girls with bruised eyes; but on the Île St.-Louis I graciously allowed the history of philosophy to continue on its way without me.

My bike had no carrier for books; instead, I could stick a notebook under the seat. While warming myself at Aux Alsaciennes, I began to write a novel.

Nearly two years later, when the stationery-store lady wrapped the package for mailing to Viking Press, she figured out what it was and gave it a sharp slap, crying out, *"Merde!"* I was startled because I thought I knew what that word meant and took it as a judgment of my coffee-and-*choucroute*-fueled, eighteen-month creative frenzy, but she explained that it meant good luck!

(The book, *Birth of a Hero,* about a Resistance hero who happened to be stuck all his life in Cleveland, was published. I went home to Cleveland to buy the three-cent stamp with my picture on it but they were still using George Washington. I like that first novel now mostly because it instructed me that I had the right to do it.)

At some point in the creative process, I left a GI overcoat—the vestmental equivalent of my bicycle—on a rack at the brasserie. The waiters kept asking when I would take it again, but spring came, the birds sang on the Île St.-Louis, and other birds allowed me to buy them hot chocolate; I was too overwrought.

Later, I decided to see how long the coat would live on the coat-rack. As the years went by, I committed more novels, visited Paris as a tourist, and came to the Île St.-Louis to check on my coat. It was still there. "Soon," I promised the waiters.

One May in the early sixties, I noticed that the narrow, swaying footbridge across which I used to wheel my rustmobile had been replaced by a wider, stabler cement product, although it was still blocked to automobiles. And my coat was gone from the café, which had changed its name to the Brasserie de St.-Louis-en-l'Île. And that *tout Paris* had discovered the happy place that in my secret mustard-loving heart will always be Aux Alsaciennes.

Anciently, the Île St.-Louis was two islands, Île Notre-Dame and Île-aux-Vaches (Cow Island). You can buy old maps that show the walls of medieval Paris and this tiny pasture in the Seine, from which cows and milk were brought by dinghy into the city. In the seventeenth century the places were joined, and in a burst of elegant speculation, bankruptcies and re-speculation, a dense web of *hôtels* (fine mansions) were spun.

The Hôtel Lambert and the Hôtel de Lauzun are two noble examples, but the entire island, its narrow pre-Detroit and even pre-Citroën streets, its encircling quays for strolling and breeze-taking by the Seine, has a comfortingly unified classical pattern.

The decoration and architecture date from a single period of French elegance and are protected by fanatic preservationists, among whom was former president Georges Pompidou, who helped stuff other districts of Paris with freeways and skyscrapers. (Pompidou lived on the Île St.-Louis.)

There is an ice cream shop, Berthillon, with perhaps the best and certainly the most chic sherbets in France. Usually the lines stretch out onto the street—people waiting for their *glace café, sorbet, crème*—as others in other places wait in line to pay taxes or to see if their portrait is on the three-cent stamp.

There is but one church on the island, St.-Louis-en-l'Île—lovely, tranquil, softly flowing, with devout deacons scrubbing the stone with straw brooms from a stock that seems to have been purchased by some seventeenth-century financial genius of a priest who feared inflation in the straw-broom market.

Contemporary Paris discovered it could find quadruple use for the Île St.-Louis: as an elegant residential quarter of the 4th Arrondissement; as a strolling museum neighborhood, a sort of Tricolorland with no parking meters, no movie house or cemetery (if people die, they have to be taken to the Continent); as a quiet corner for small restaurants, antiquaries, bars, bookshops, hotels, Mme. Blanvillain's 160-year-old olive shop (she was not the founder), and a pheasant-plucker named Turpin in case you need your pheasant plucked; and the fourth use is optional.

On my most recent visit, the spirit of the place was expressed by the aforementioned Berthillon, the studio for ice cream masterpieces with the seventeenth-century aspect. It was early July. A cheerful sign said: "Open Wednesday, 14 September." Where else would an ice cream shop close for the hot months?

I was relieved by this assurance of little change in the weekend-maddened, vacation-crazed spirit of the French *commerçant*. No matter how greedy he might seem to mere mortals, plucking money from the air and sewing it into his mattress, the flight to seaside or country cottage remains sacred.

Throwing duffel on bed, not even glancing at the exchange rate, I seized a notebook in jet-lagged claws and made a quick tour of the few streets and circumnavigating quays of the island, trying to find what had changed, what had remained the same, and what might persuade my body that it was time to sleep. The fact that I had cleverly scheduled my visit to come near the July 14 celebration, when France dances and drinks and makes new friends in the street till dawn—all because their ancestors tore down the Bastille—did not induce thoughts of prudent shut-eye.

(In my student days, when an American friend studying in Belgium bicycled into Paris for the first time, he happened to arrive on Bastille Day and found colorful lights strung from everywhere, accordions, embraces, a fierce festival glitter in every eye. He fell upon my little room crying, "Oh, I always knew Paris would be like this!")

A street sweeper with the timid face of a peasant come to the metropolis was scrubbing down the stones in front of the St.-Louis-en-l'Île. No change here.

Libella, the Polish bookstore on the rue St.-Louis-en-l'Île, reminded me that Paris has always been everyone's other home. The wall above Libella bears a stone plaque telling us that in 1799 the engineer Philippe Lebon discovered, in this building, the principle of lighting and heating with gas—the word "principle" and past experience suggest that the French did not actually get around to doing it for a while.

The island is crowded with such notices—tributes to poets, advisers to kings, soldier heroes, men of God, and even a film critic immortalized on a plaque affixed to the place where he analyzed Jerry Lewis as *auteur*.

There is also a plaque on the wall of the Ferdinand Halphep Foundation in the rue des Deux-Ponts:

> To the Memory
> Of the 112 Inhabitants
> Of This Building
> Including 40 Children
> Deported and Killed
> In the Concentration Camps in 1942.

No island is entire of itself, exempt from history. Across the street, in the ice cream shops, bistros, the Bateau Bar—fifty brands of beer from all nations—gratification proceeds on its necessary course.

It was time to sit at a café table for the island equivalent of my typical San Francisco after-racquetball vitamin and health hi-pro yogurt shake; in this case, a coffee with "yak"—cognac.

Two helmeted Vespa people came skidding to a stop in front of me. Like space warriors, they were encased in huge plastic headgear. Evidently they knew each other, because they fell to kissing, their helmets thudding together. I peeked at their faces when they came apart. They were both about sixty years old and hadn't seen each other in hours.

A fisherman nearby, when I asked what he caught with all his equipment, assured me that trout hover near the fresh underground springs at the head of the island.

"And what else?"

"A moment of meditation. A view of Notre Dame. There are gargoyles, sir. At this season, there are roses."

During the morning, a fisherman was catching roses; that night in front of the footbridge leading to Aux Alsaciennes, the Communist Party sponsored a rock celebration of Bastille Day. A girl in a "Wichita University Long Island" T-shirt danced to a French knockoff of "Lady Jane" and other Rolling Stones' hits. Instead of a male partner, she held a contribution box for *Humanité,* the party newspaper.

The little park at the end of the island where the Pont de Sully links the Left and Right Banks of Paris—leading to the workers' quarter of Bastille in one direction, the Quartier Latin in the other—has a grand stone monument to "Barye 1795–1875" at its entrance. The sculptor seems to be telling a busy story, including naked lads, heroes, a foot on a screaming animal, a sword, a staff, a few less boyish youths. Who the heck was Barye 1795–1875?

He may be there to provide a little relaxation from all the really famous people who lived and live on the Île St.-Louis. (He turns out to have been a watercolorist.)

The square Barye, surrounded by the Seine on three sides, is quiet, peaceful, scholarly, artistic, with occasional summer concerts; kids sleeping on their backpacks, workmen with bottles of *rouge;* Swedish au pair girls watching the babies and sunning themselves with that passionate solar intensity only Swedish girls achieve—happy sunbathers when it's hot and moonbathing when it's not; haggard widows in black, wincing with their memories; birds chirping and barbered bushes and peeling-bark trees and neat cinder paths: all honor to Barye 1795–1875!

Three small hotels on the island located on the rue St.-Louis-en-l'Île, a few steps from each other, have been converted from seventeenth-century houses: the Lutece, the Deux-Îles and the St.-Louis.

When I telephoned the Lutece from San Francisco for a reservation, the place was booked, but the good madame leaned out the window and yelled next door to the Deux-Îles to ask if they had a place. Also booked. So was the St.-Louis. But on my arrival, I managed to persuade the daughter of the proprietor of the St.-Louis to find me a corner room.

On the short walk home—saying "home" comes quickly in this island universe—I noticed that Hippolyte Taine and Georges Sandoul did their work in the same building. Marc Chagall and Charles Baudelaire, Voltaire and Mme. Pompidou, dukes and barons, and *chanteurs de charme,* plus a stray prince or princess, an inventor or hero—who didn't have a connection with the Île St.-Louis?

The Île St.-Louis is like France itself—an ideal of grace and proportion—but it differs from the rest of France in that it lives up to itself. Under constant repair and renovation, it remains intact. It is a small place derived from long experience. It has strength enough, and isolation enough, to endure with a certain smugness the troubles of the city and the world at whose center it rests.

The self-love is mitigated partly by success at guarding itself and partly by the ironic shrugs of its inhabitants, who, despite whatever aristocratic names of glamorous professions, live among broken-veined *clochards* (hoboes) with unbagged bottles, tourists with unbagged guidebooks, Bohemians with bagged eyes.

The actual troubles of the world do not miss the Île St.-Louis—one doesn't string hammocks between the plane trees here—but the air seems to contain fewer mites and less nefarious Paris ozone.

The lack of buses, the narrow streets, the breeze down the Seine, help. And as to perhaps the most dangerous variety of Paris smog, the Île St.-Louis seems to have discovered the unanswerable French reply to babble, noise, advice, and theory—*silence.*

One can, of course, easily get off this island, either by walking on the water of the Seine or, in a less saintly way, by taking a stroll of about two minutes across the slim bridges to the Left Bank, the Right Bank or the bustling and official neighbor, the Île de la Cité.

Island fever is not a great danger, despite the insular pleasures of neatness, shape, control. Some people even say they never go to "Paris." (In 1924, there was an attempt to secede from Paris and France, and Île St.-Louis passports were issued.) Monsieur Filleui, the fishmonger, used to advertise: "Deliveries on the Island and on the Continent."

The Île St.-Louis, an elsewhere village universe, happens also to be an island by the merest accident of being surrounded by water. Its bridges reach inward to shadow worlds of history and dream; and outward toward the furor of contemporary Paris.

Shaded and sunny, surrounded by the waters of the Seine like a moat, it remains a kind of castle keep that is powerful enough in its own identity to hold Paris at bridge's length, a breath away. Amazingly, it has occurred to no one powerful enough to do anything about it that this place, too, could be high-rised, filthied, thoroughfared, developed. There is no metro station. The breezes down the Seine keep busy, sweeping and caressing.

Despite the claims of metropolis on all sides, the Île St.-Louis still expresses the shadow presence of the Île Notre-Dame and the Île-aux-Vaches. The ancestor islands make a claim to be remembered because they have been forgotten, and both the aristocratic and the chic who live here, and the *gratteurs de guitare,* who occasionally come to serenade the ghosts of counts and courtesans, know that they tread in a palimpsest of footsteps, including ancient Gauls, Romans and now, chirping and clicking beneath the willows, the occasional polyester-clad, camera-breasted tourist.

A more characteristic sight is that of the professional anguish of a French intellectual walking his dog. The rich tend to live like Bohemians here. (Only the poor, as Anatole France said, are forbidden to beg.)

The Île St.-Louis is one of the places where a postwar generation of Americans in Paris loosened its military discipline—if we happened to have any—studied peace and art and history and depravity (called it freedom, called it fulfilling ourselves), lived in awe before our fantasy of France (still do just a little).

We bought old bicycles and new notebooks. We pretended to be students, artists, philosophers, and lovers, and, out of our pretensions, sometimes learned to be a little of these things.

Remarks are not literature, Gertrude Stein said, and islands are not the world. But some remarks can tell us what literature is about, some islands can tell us what a sweeter, more defined world might be. In Spinoza's view, freedom consists of knowing what the limits are. I came to Paris as a philosophy student but left it as a novelist. On the Île St.-Louis, I am still home free, watching the Seine flow and eddy and flow again.

This piece originally appeared in the 9 August, 1987, edition of the *San Francisco Examiner.* Copyright © 1987 by Herbert Gold. Reprinted by permission of the author.

Joining Jefferson
on a Paris Walk

BY DIANA KETCHAM

ᖆᖇ

editor's note

"Were I to proceed to tell you how much I enjoy French architecture . . . I should want words," penned Thomas Jefferson in one of his many letters recounting his trip to France. Indeed, after this piece appeared in *The New York Times,* a reader wrote noting that the Hôtel de Salm in Paris was of great inspiration to Jefferson in the building of his Virginia home, Monticello. Jefferson wrote to a friend in 1787 that he was "violently smitten with the Hôtel de Salm," and he apparently visited it almost daily. As a result, Jefferson tore down Monticello as it then stood—a tall, two-story villa in the Palladian style—and rebuilt it as we know it today.

From the Champs-Élysées to the Left Bank, many of the buildings Jefferson knew remain in Paris, and this piece offers walkers an innovative itinerary.

Architectural historian and critic DIANA KETCHAM is a frequent contributor to *The New York Times* and a contributing editor at *House and Garden.* She is also the author of *Le Désert de Retz: An 18th Century French Folly Garden* (MIT Press, 1994), and coauthor of *The Architecture of the American People* (Oxford University Press, 2000).

Although two centuries have passed since Thomas Jefferson lived in Paris, today's visitor can see a surprising number of the buildings that enchanted this connoisseur of the city. Jefferson arrived in Paris in 1784 as American trade minister and stayed until 1789, succeeding Benjamin Franklin as ambassador. He explored the city on foot, walking to regain his health after being ill his first winter. With his pedometer strapped to his leg, Jefferson would travel as much as five miles a day through the Paris streets.

It was peculiar for a man of Jefferson's station to rely on walking to get about. The streets of late-eighteenth-century Paris were ill-lighted, rivers of mud in winter and dusty infernos in summer. But Jefferson was notoriously independent in his habits. Max Byrd's delightful 1993 novel *Jefferson* gives an appealing portrait of the American diplomat on his daily rounds, astonishing colleagues by walking home from Faubourg St.-Germain dinner parties and sending his two daughters ahead by carriage while he ambled along behind.

On his walks, Jefferson became well-acquainted with the construction sites that were changing the face of Paris. These pre-Revolutionary years saw the building of churches and bridges, a new city wall with tollhouses by the architect Claude Nicolas Ledoux, and the expansion of the Palais Royal. Jefferson was enthralled by the spectacle of the new architecture. He even took part in a small way, redesigning and furnishing two of the city's newest mansions (both gone) in the burgeoning residential quarters of the Right Bank.

To see Paris as Jefferson knew it, begin at the foot of the Champs-Élysées in front of the American embassy. Nothing is left of Jefferson's rented house, the Hôtel de Langeac, whose gardens once fronted on the Champs-Élysées at the corner of the present rue de Berri. But its atmosphere lingers today on the avenue Gabriel, where the embassy building by the same architect, Jean François Chalgrin, and other mansions from the period have retained their gardens. A fragment of Jefferson's neighborhood park, the Cours la Reine, exists on the south side of the avenue near the Restaurant Ledoyen, then a simple country inn. This was the site of his fateful stroll in September 1786 with the English artist Maria Cosway, who was the romantic companion of his Paris years. To impress her, the forty-four-year-old Jefferson tried to jump over a fence, breaking his right wrist. The result is our only love letter from the author of the

Declaration of Independence, the famous "Head and Heart" dialogue written to Cosway with his left hand.

The soul of Jefferson's Paris was Jacques Ange Gabriel's magnificent octagonal square, place Louis XV (now place de la Concorde), which he would have crossed every day going to and from home. (He calculated the familiar route from home to the square on his pedometer as 820 double steps.)

The *place* was the site of several key episodes in Jefferson's Paris education. In the center, where the obelisk now rises, stood the equestrian statue of Louis XV by Bouchardon. The power of this modestly sized statue ("probably the best in the world," Jefferson exclaimed, "and it is the smallest here") inspired his ideas for the statue of George Washington he commissioned from the French sculptor Houdon. The "modern front" on Gabriel's Hôtel de la Marine so impressed Jefferson that he wanted Pierre L'Enfant, the architect of Washington, to use it as a model for the presidential residence. In July 1789, on the eve of the storming of the Bastille, Jefferson entered the square to find the king's troops facing a crowd armed with stones. In 1792 his admired statue of Louis XV would be toppled and melted down—the right hand alone survived and is in the Louvre.

In happier times, Jefferson would have strolled across the square and into the Tuileries Gardens to the Terrasse du Bord de l'Eau. Here he would sit on the parapet to watch construction of his favorite new building, the Hôtel de Salm, across the river. Visible as the green dome to the right of the Musée d'Orsay, it is now the Palace of the Legion of Honor. The palace was gutted by fire during the Commune of 1871 and rebuilt to the original plans. Here Jefferson also watched the Robert Brothers ascend in one of the earliest manned balloons. To reach the Left Bank, he would have continued through Le Nôtre's gardens to the Pont Royal. Today it is more convenient to take the Pont de la Concorde (then under construction).

At the end of the bridge, turn left onto the rue de Lille (then the rue de Bourbon). At No. 119 stood the home of the Marquis de Lafayette, at the corner of what is now the boulevard St.-Germain, which had not yet been cut through the gardens and churchyards of the "noble" Faubourg. (The mate of the demolished Lafayette mansion can be seen in the courtyard of No. 121 rue de Lille.) Lafayette settled there when he returned from his exploits in the American Revolutionary War. His friend Jefferson became a regular of this colorful pro-American household, where the hall was hung with wild-animal skins and an Oneida Indian lived with the family. Continue along the rue de Lille with its mansions from the early eighteenth century, whose gardens once swept down to the Seine. At the rue de Solférino notice the grand street entrance of the Hôtel de Salm. Walk toward the river, to the north side, which Jefferson would have viewed from the Tuileries.

To reach his daughters' boarding school, Jefferson could have walked south along the rue de Bellechasse. At the rue St.-Dominique he would have seen a row of elegant seventeenth-century town houses, the present Nos. 1, 3, and 5. The last, the Hôtel de Tavannes, originally among the convents of the neighborhood, is open to the public. Farther south on Bellechasse is the school the Jefferson girls attended, the Abbaye Royale de Panthemont (or Pentémont), at No. 46, now occupied by the Ministère des Anciens Combattants (Veterans' Administration). Turn left onto the rue de Grenelle; at No. 106 is the convent chapel by Pierre d'Ivry. Now a Protestant church, its shadowy Ionic interior is little altered. Built in 1756, the domed chapel was one of the new classical churches of Paris when the Jefferson girls were there. Some have found it surprising that Jefferson the freethinker would have frequented this establishment, where he sent his oldest daughter, Martha (Patsy), at the age of twelve. On at least one occasion Jefferson attended services in the chapel, to observe two young women taking the veil. The legend that

Martha Jefferson wished to defy her father by becoming a nun is intriguing but unsubstantiated.

Panthemont was a worldly institution, presided over by an intellectual abbess. In addition to housing schoolgirl boarders, it was a fashionable residence for aristocratic women separated from their husbands, including Napoléon's future empress, Josephine, when parted from her first husband, Alexandre de Beauharnais.

Follow Jefferson's footsteps east to the Latin Quarter, then as now a center for publishing, where his only book, *Notes on the State of Virginia,* was issued in 1786. At the Croix-Rouge intersection, turn into the rue du Vieux Colombier, pass by the church of St.-Sulpice, whose classical tower was then being built, and turn right on the rue de Tournon. At No. 19 still stands the house where the American naval hero John Paul Jones stayed in Paris; he was involved in Jefferson's plans to subdue the Barbary pirates. At No. 12 lived one of the intellectual hostesses who admired Jefferson, the Comtesse d'Houdetot, immortalized as Sophie in Rousseau's *Confessions.*

Near the top of the rue de Tournon stands the Théâtre Français, now the Odéon, then one of the important monuments of the new architecture (the original, built in 1782 by Wailly and Peyre, burned and was replicated by Chalgrin). There on August 6, 1786, Jefferson attended Beaumarchais's *Marriage of Figaro,* which he much admired for its radical ideas. In the foyer he would have seen Houdon's bust of Voltaire, a version of which he installed in the hall at Monticello. Across the place de l'Odéon at No. 1 the celebrated Café Voltaire was a meeting place for the Encyclopedists.

To return to the river, Jefferson could have taken the rue de l'Ancienne Comédie. Molière's Comédie Française, which gave the street its name, had moved elsewhere by 1770, but he would have passed the popular writers' café Le Procope (still a restaurant) at No. 13 where Beaumarchais celebrated the premiere of *Figaro* in

1784. Taking the rue de Seine, cross the historic rue Jacob, where the present No. 56 is marked by the sign of the eighteenth-century printers Firmin Didot. Here the treaty recognizing American independence from England was signed by Benjamin Franklin, John Adams and John Jay in 1783.

At 14 rue Visconti remains a house that was part of the complex belonging to the Duc de La Rochefoucauld, a republican aristocrat who befriended Jefferson. Here he attended gatherings presided over by the duke's bluestocking mother, one of the many aristocratic women who were a little bit in love with Benjamin Franklin. The duke's beautiful, much younger wife, Rosalie, fell in love with Jefferson's secretary, William Short, a sad story well told in Max Byrd's *Jefferson*.

At 1 quai Voltaire, at the corner of the rue des Sts.-Pères (Voltaire died a few doors down, at No. 27) is the monumental Hôtel de Tessé. Madame Tessé, Jefferson's great admirer and fellow gardening enthusiast, gave him a marble pedestal to take home to Monticello.

Continuing east on the quai de Conti one can visit the Hôtel de la Monnaie (Royal Mint), the least changed of Jefferson's Left Bank haunts. Here he had medals struck of the heroes of the American Revolution and may also have visited his admired acquaintance, the mathematician Condorcet, who lived on the premises.

To the east of the Mint begins the medieval quai des Grands Augustins, then lined with the booksellers that Jefferson patronized. Barrois, his own publisher, was situated at the end, at the corner of Pont St.-Michel. Farther east is the rue St.-Jacques, the printer's alley of Jefferson's day.

Cross the Seine to the Right Bank by the Pont des Arts, looking toward the Pont Neuf, which Jefferson watched being stripped of its houses. Pass in front of the eastern end of the Louvre.

Its colonnaded facade by Perrault was one of the three "modern" building fronts that Jefferson wanted American architects to take as models. Inside the Louvre, Jefferson admired the paintings of Jacques-Louis David and Hubert Robert.

Cross the rue de Rivoli to the Palais Royal. Its gardens had opened the year Jefferson arrived, becoming the spot where all the fashionable delights and vices of Paris were for sale. Here Jefferson dined, bought books and ivory-handled knives, played chess (Nos. 57 to 60), attended the Variétés theater (rue de Montpensier), and, on April 22, 1789, had his profile drawn by a mechanical tracing device. We can imagine him at the Café Mécanique, No. 121, where food was elevated to the tables from a basement kitchen, eliminating the need for waiters. (He delighted in such labor-saving devices.) Perhaps his ghost haunts the Café de Chartres (Nos. 79 to 82), a political meeting place, today the three-star restaurant the Grand Vefour.

The walk ends where Jefferson's most romantic Paris adventure began, at Les Halles, where he first met Maria Cosway in August 1786. The artist John Trumbull had included Jefferson and the Cosways in a tour of the Halle aux Bleds (Grain Market), then the building with the largest dome in Paris, which inspired Jefferson's ideas for the Capitol in Washington but were never put into effect. Today's domed Bourse de Commerce is the replacement of the Halle aux Bleds. To one side is an architectural curiosity they surely saw that day: La Colonne Astrologique, the 1572 tower from which Catherine de Médici studied the skies with her astrologer.

After this meeting, Jefferson swept Cosway off on a round of excursions in and around Paris. They visited artists' studios, the châteaus of Marly, St.-Cloud, and St.-Germain, and the exotic garden of the Désert de Retz, now being restored and open to visitors, where Byrd's novel imagines them enjoying a romantic interlude. Recalling their Paris outings later, in a letter to Cosway, he wrote, "What a mass of happiness we traveled over."

Hôtel de Salm, now the Museum of the Palace of the Legion of Honor, 2 rue de Bellechasse, 45.51.87.05, is open daily except Monday and holidays from 2 to 5 P.M.

Hôtel des Tavannes, 5 rue St.-Dominique. The courtyard and entrance hall are open from August 20 to September 30 from 9:30 A.M. to noon and 2:30 to 4 P.M.

L'Abbaye de Pentémont, now Ministère des Anciens Combattants, 37 rue de Bellechasse, 44.21.10.00, can be visited with special authorization and is open to the public on the third weekend of September.

L'Église de Pentémont, 106 rue de Grenelle, 45.35.63.30, a chapel within the ministry, has services every Sunday at 10:30 A.M.

Le Théâtre de l'Europe, place de l'Odéon, 44.41.36.36. The lobby ticket office is open from 11 A.M. to 6:30 P.M. from Monday to Friday.

Le Procope, 13 rue de l'Ancienne Comédie, 43.26.99.20. Open every day and during the summer from 11:30 to 1 A.M. A moderately priced tourist restaurant.

Hôtel de la Monnaie, 11 quai de Conti, 40.46.55.33. Open from 1 to 6 P.M. The mint still produces collectors' coins, weights and commemorative medals. Workshops can be visited free of charge on

Tuesdays and Fridays at 1:15 and 2:45 P.M. The Coin Museum, the grand staircase, and exhibitions on the buildings' history are open every day but Monday from 9 A.M. to 5 P.M.

Near Chambourcy, ten miles west of Paris, the exotic English-Chinese folly garden the **Désert de Retz** (39.76.90.37) is open from March to October on the last Saturday of each month from 2 to 4 P.M.

A Little Light Reading

Some reading about Jefferson in Paris:

Jefferson, by Max Byrd (Bantam). A historically sound and psychologically penetrating novel of Jefferson's diplomatic career in Paris.

Thomas Jefferson in Paris, by Howard C. Rice (Princeton University Press). A masterpiece of narrative history and the most thorough retelling of Jefferson's Paris career.

Thomas Jefferson: The Scene of Europe, by Marie Kimball (McCann). A graceful anecdotal 1950s account of Jefferson's work and travels in Europe.

My Head and My Heart: A Little History of Thomas Jefferson and Maria Cosway, by Helen Duprey Bullock (Putnam's). A highly romantic interpretation of Jefferson's outings with the English artist Maria Cosway.

This piece originally appeared in the travel section of *The New York Times,* 5 March 1995. Copyright © 1995 by Diana Ketcham. Reprinted by permission of the author.

Bibliothèque

Surprisingly, there aren't many books devoted to single neighborhoods of Paris. I would really like to learn of others, so if you know of some titles, please share them with me.

A Corner in the Marais: Memoir of a Paris Neighborhood, Alex Karmel, David R. Godine Publishers, Jaffrey, New Hampshire, 1998. Alex Karmel is a novelist, not a historian, but he's very interested in history, especially the history of people no one's ever heard of before. In this beautifully written book, he traces the history of the apartment he and his wife bought in 1982, a pied-à-terre on the *cinquième étage* at the corner of rue Vieille-du-Temple and rue des Rosiers in the Marais. We learn of Philippe de Champaigne, Claude Bourgeois, Marie Lemaistre, and Étienne de la Porte, some of the "ordinary" people who owned, lived in, or otherwise had some connection to the nondescript building on the corner. While the history of the building is an interesting story by itself (it's six centuries old, after all), Karmel also reveals much about the neighborhood and the architectural and social development of Paris. Beautiful black-and-white photographs and engravings (including one of the house at 3 rue Volta, said to be the oldest house in Paris, and another of a preserved bullet hole in the window of Goldenberg's restaurant, a reminder of the tragic terrorist attack in the summer of 1982) appear throughout, and the final chapter, "Neighbors," is actually a walking tour of the Marais and Île St.-Louis, which highlights some rather obscure architectural details one might otherwise miss and reveals much about the people, famous and not at all, who made this *quartier* so picturesque.

~Some of the "Paris Journal" columns Catharine Reynolds has contributed to *Gourmet* provide more reading on various *quartiers* and *coins* of Paris. Some of these include "The 12th: Rebirth of a Neighborhood" (July 1996); "Hemingway's Haunts" (April 1992); and "Nouveaux Champs-Élysées" (April 1995). Additionally, a good article I was unable to reprint is "The Villages of Paris" (Larisa Dryansky, *Condé Nast Traveler,* February 1995), which highlights the neighborhoods of Auteuil, Montsouris, Passy, Plaisance, Butte-Aux-Cailles, Rhin-et-Danube, Batignolles, Charonne, Belleville, Menilmontant, La Goutte-d'Or, and Montmartre.

Apéritif artisanal

Apéritif aux Fruits rouges

séletion

La Coupe d'Or Avignon

04.90.82.18.31

5 cl

Produit de France Apértif à base de Vin
ingrédients: vin de liqueur, infusion de
cerises, sucre, alcool.

18%vo

Saint Nectaire
FERMIER

St. Nectaire
FERMIER

Saveurs Françaises
(French Foods and Flavors)

Everyone who has visited France knows that it is a nation of hardy, persistent individualists. The French simply refuse to conform to type, whether it be a question of dress, of manners, or of politics, particularly the last. This quality of independence manifests itself with unusual emphasis in the matter of food and wine. This may seem surprising to those who have formed a conception of typical French fare. The genuine French cuisine, however, is an absolute tapestry of individualism, varying abruptly from one province to another, to the fascination of food-minded travelers. There is nothing "typical" about it.

—Samuel Chamberlain, from the INTRODUCTION TO THE FOOD OF FRANCE by WAVERLY ROOT

A Saga of Bread

BY NAOMI BARRY

⤜∾

editor's note

The only baguette in all of France that Naomi Barry likes is *"La Flûte GANA"* from Ganachaud. After she first tried it, she immediately thought of a French advertising slogan of the time, *Voilà un préjugé qui m'a coûté cher,* which translates as "And that is a prejudice that cost me dearly." If she once thought all baguettes were alike—dull and tasteless—she didn't anymore. I happen to like the crispy, airy baguette, but I admit that the *"Flûte GANA"* is perhaps the most perfect baguette on earth.

My husband and I once had the supreme great fortune to meet Bernard Ganachaud before he retired, although it happened quite by accident. I mentioned to the cashier at Ganachaud that I was visiting from the States and had learned of the bakery from Patricia Wells's bo—but before I could say *book,* she excitedly summoned Bernard, who led us upstairs to his office, where we were served coffee and *bostock,* slices of brioche flavored with kirsch and almonds. All the while I was explaining that we didn't really *know* Patricia Wells, we had only read her book, but he didn't seem to mind, and shared his publicity clippings with us and chattered on about his recent venture with the Japanese.

There are a number of other outstanding *boulangeries* in Paris, but a trip out to rue de Menilmontant is still worth a detour. You could combine it with a visit to Père-Lachaise and Le Saint-Amour café—on the edge of the cemetery at 2 avenue Gambetta or 32 boulevard Menilmontant and recommended by Wells—making the trip a full-fledged excursion rather than a single-stop detour.

NAOMI BARRY lives in Paris and has been writing for *Gourmet* for over twenty years. She has also written for the *International Herald Tribune* and is the author of *Paris Personal* (E. P. Dutton, 1963) and *Food à la Florentine* (Doubleday, 1972).

C hristine, a bank of information about her city, gave me the address of "the best bread place in Paris." Of course I made the trip since you don't find great bread on every corner anymore, even in France where the national image used to be a pair of crossed baguettes under a Basque beret.

The bakery was at 150 rue de Menilmontant in the working-class district of the far-out 20th Arrondissement. Maurice Chevalier who had been a child of the neighborhood used to sing about Menilmontant and he infused it with a titillating glamour which has lingered.

The further we progressed up the steep hill on our first foray into the territory, the more unpromising it seemed as the site of "the best bread in Paris." I was mentally accusing Christine of a bum steer when up loomed Bernard Ganachaud's bakery with the sudden brightness of a big ferry station in an otherwise darkened landscape.

It was huge with six times the frontage of any shop in the vicinity. Breads of assorted shapes and sizes were artfully displayed behind the gleaming windows. Thirty varieties are available in a Tour de France of regional breads. Some are better than others because in the down-home original versions, some simply are better than others. A *pain d'Auvergne* had a real style but it turned out to be disappointing, for instance.

On one window a girl employee was writing in large white letters the hit parade of specialties due to come forth from the visible ovens. The odors tantalizingly evoked a glorious farmhouse kitchen even if your childhood had not been that lucky. Although the French are notorious for the way they jump queues, in Ganachaud's bread line they were a model of decorum, proving that good behavior is determined by what is worth waiting for.

Ganachaud refuses to deliver and he doesn't care who you are. The chef of the Crillon was crazy about the deluxe baguette baptized "Flûte Gana" and wanted it for the hotel. He was told to come and get it. Ganachaud insists on quality control of his product until the moment it is handed over to the customer. That means on the premises. Were it to spend a couple of hours in the back of a delivery van . . . he shudders. So the Crillon accepted to do its own fetch and carry. At the end of a year, the chef moaned, *"Mon cher,* do you realize that my taxi bill to get to you has been even greater than my bread bill?"

The complaint pleased Ganachaud no end. To go from the Crillon on the place de la Concorde to the rue de Menilmontant is like going from Eighty-first Street and Fifth Avenue in Manhattan to New Lots Avenue in Brooklyn. Individual customers from the chic arrondissements miles away have worked out a pool system. Whoever makes the trek is honor bound to bring back a supply for the others.

I immediately recognized the *maître-boulanger,* who was wearing the white work jacket with the tricolor ribbon collar and his name embroidered on the breast pocket that Bragard has made for most of the top chefs of France, giving them the uniformed look of an Olympic team. Despite a fluff of white hair and mustaches, Ganachaud's movements were quick and youthful and he was light on the balls of his feet like a bantamweight boxer. He interrupted a staccato monologue he was delivering to a young man in a corner, invited me to his organized little office, and *toc-toc* ordered me a coffee and a *flûte Gana.*

I have never been much of a fan of the baguette, the long skinny loaf usually known abroad as French bread, but I became a fanatic of Ganachaud's upmarket version. It is not only the best I have ever eaten but I am scared of it because once started I can't stop. It is twice the price of a regulation baguette which has been no deterrent to the sales.

There was a delicious chewiness to the crust and a pleasing consistency to the crumb and much as I love butter it didn't need any. The *flûte* was no mere support for cheese but could stand very nicely on its own.

"No serious artisan need ever worry about competition from the factory," said Ganachaud, "although if technology can make a bread with the same savor, I am not against it. However, the industrial bakery cannot furnish a bread that is really fresh."

He was referring mainly to the baguette whose short but happy life is responsible for those bread lines throughout France three times a day. The round loaf that was the peasant's staff of life could be counted upon to remain edibly fresh for several days. Big as a pillow, it took a while for all the moisture to evaporate from the crumb. The svelte baguette has comparatively little crumb and it goes dry in no time flat. Ganachaud's *flûte* has a crust porous enough for the moisture to come in as well as out and consequently it remains fresh for a few hours more than the average. As long as you don't ask the perishable to be forever, a quality baguette at its peak can be memorable.

The Japanese, anxious to acquire the best of the West, wanted to franchise his *flûte*. Ganachaud gave them his usual "On my conditions or No Go." Not only would the bread have to be made according to his rigorous specifications but the ovens had to be adjacent to every point of sale. They agreed and now there are sixteen outlets in Japan where you can buy an authentic *flûte Gana* thousands of miles from the rue de Menilmontant.

Meanwhile Ganachaud has created an artisanal network throughout France. Twenty independent young bakers have three-year contracts with him that allow baking and advertising the *flûte Gana* in their establishments. The contracts are renewable for another three-year period after which the bakers can go on producing the *flûte* with no more commitment to him. It is an odd financial arrangement and rather like six years in holy orders but profitable.

At breakneck speed, Ganachaud related a little of his past. He was born in southwest France in 1930. His father was a small farmer who plumped up the family income by baking and delivering big loaves of bread to other farm families around the countryside. Bernard supplied a helping hand from the age of eight, both at the kneading trough and on the delivery wagon.

While studying at a stern Jesuit academy in Bordeaux he continued to aid his father prepare the dough and make the dawn deliveries. He was an excellent student, wanted to become a lawyer and somehow found time to be active in the Scouts. But a daily schedule of 5 A.M. until midnight was too much for his health to sustain. He dropped his studies and concentrated on being a baker, applying all his intelligence and intensity to one of the oldest métiers in the world.

The real killer was lack of sleep. For the customer to have fresh bread in the morning, the baker must observe the fermentation at a fixed period in the night pretty much like a sailor on the watch who can sleep for a few hours only before the next stretch of duty.

Ganachaud decided to break the servitude by harnessing cold to slow down the fermentation and thus allow himself an eight-hour night without interruption. It was a freedom he had never known. At present he has twenty-three young bakers working under his rule but thanks to the scientific application of cold the deadly night shift is no longer necessary.

The harshness of his early youth had left a permanent toll and he felt he would have to sell his now flourishing business. His attractive young daughters, Valerie and Isabelle, were aghast. "Papa, you simply can't do it. We will carry on for you."

They enrolled in a professional school and finished the three-year course with top honors. As far as I know, Ganachaud's girls are the first professional women bakers in France and the first to earn the tough CAP *(Certificat d'Aptitude Professionnel)* in what is regarded as one of the most macho of the artisan trades.

Slender and full of grace, they admit to consuming at least a half pound of bread a day regularly, proof that it is not bread that makes you fat but what you put on it. Except for the respite offered by the slowing down of the night fermentation through cold, they watch the clock like hawks, for good bread-making demands chronometer precision.

In most other ways the Ganachauds work by the old-fashioned precepts. "A true baker," says Papa, "mixes his own flours." (Any loaf that disobeys his commands is rushed to a laboratory to find out the reason why.) The true baker chooses his combination of flours the way a great tea blender selects leaves of different strains. He uses natural leavenings instead of factory-produced yeasts and baking powders and shuns the preservatives that give added shelf life.

In Paris an alarming number of bakers are buying prepared mixes or frozen dough from industrial plants. With the latter they need but shape it into the desired form and slide it into the oven for baking. Bread from these terminal stations is rarely better than average. Bake shops are springing up with charming decors that suggest a world as it used to be but the decors are deceptive stage sets masking chain operations.

Lucien Pergeline, a director of the Grands Moulins de Paris, revealed that certain bakers have cut down on the traditional fermentation period with the astute use of commercial baking powders, thus saving themselves an hour or more of time. In addition, with the powders they can achieve a short-weight loaf of 200 grams that has the size of a 250-gram baguette and sell it for the price of the latter.

"Hmm," I said. "Sounds like watered stock when the drovers of upper New York State used to walk their cattle to market forcing them to drink a maximum on the long march, thus upping the price on the hoof."

The purists of the profession are up in arms and there are debates, symposiums and articles on saving the Good Bread of France. An alerted segment of the public passes around the names of honest bakers the way they pass on the name of a good bistro discovery. Jean-Michel Bédier, chef of the Chiberta in Paris, tells me there is a worthy baker in St.-Sauveur le Puisaye, the Burgundy town where Colette was born. We may drive down. It is only seventy-five miles away.

The more I learned, the more choosy I found myself becoming. Strolling in Paris, I noticed Gérard Mulot's sign at 2 rue Lobineau, a step from the rue de Seine in the 6th Arrondissement. *Fabrication Maison depuis 1976.* I liked this proud proclamation of the date as if it went back two centuries. What caught me, however, was the mention of *pain au Levain,* which meant that Mulot was using a starter dough as his leavening. His *pain de campagne* was excellent with a faint and pleasant note of acidity, more to my liking than any I have found in my neighborhood of the 7th Arrondissement.

On a recent Sunday afternoon I went to the big book fair at the Porte de Versailles because Paul Guth, whose *Me, Josephine the Empress* is one of my favorite biographies, was to autograph his latest work. The delightful Mr. Guth has written more than fifty books and is one of the few contemporary French authors who has been able to live by his pen.

He turned out to be a fervent partisan of honest bread. I went to see him a few days later in his 16th Arrondissement apartment where he writes with a pen at a small table looking out on what could be a small walled garden in the provinces.

At the request of other partisans, he had written a pamphlet entitled *Le Pain en Majesté,* or Bread Enthroned, in which he called bread "God's representative of his flesh and soul, born in the secret of the night during the night of time." Like a troubadour of old, Guth proclaimed the virtues of bread battling against our delirium for speed which was ruining our sensations and sentiments and leading to the downfall of the Occident. "With its eternal values, bread attaches us to the earth from which we are being torn by an industrial civilization."

In his childhood in a peasant house in the Bigorre, a pretending-to-be-asleep little boy watched his aunt Amandine knead the dough. "Writhing, she lifted it in strips, stretched it, threw it, punched it down. All the while, she groaned softly with the wails of love, of birth, of death."

After my next trip to Ganachaud, I dropped off a loaf at Guth's door.

My friend Maxine who eats out at a different Paris restaurant every night told me excitedly, "I found two great new ones. And they are baking their own bread."

Alain Passard, thirty-two, is the chef-owner of l'Arpège at rue de Varenne in the locale that used to be l'Archestrate. The youthful Passard has two stars from the Michelin. At Arpège, the bread is baked in the morning for the lunch service and in the afternoon for the evening service.

"Bread is very important in a restaurant and I love to make it. The customers are very surprised. Almost the first thing they say is, 'Where do you buy this bread? It is fabulous. We don't find it in Paris.' Some of the women ask me, 'Oh, if only I could have some with my coffee in the morning.' If any is left over, I give it to them for toast." His hundred clients a day manage to put away four kilos of Arpège's individual rolls and six kilos of country bread, which is a lot of bread for a fashionable crowd.

Alain grew up with the taste of good bread. It was made by a farmer friend of his father. When he was twenty and already trained as a pastry chef, he said to his father's friend, "May I spend two weeks and learn to make bread the way you do?" One of its secrets is sea salt from Guérande in Brittany, considered the Flower of Salt.

The fine bread accompanies a cuisine that is refined and restrained, genuine and unpretentious and never banal. An example is a simple and charming entrée consisting of cabbage leaves stuffed with crab meat in a light mustard sauce. The combination of rusticity and sophistication is characteristic of Alain Passard.

Like Passard, twenty-nine-year-old Gilles Epié of the Miravile, 25 quai de la Tournelle, is a Breton. His approach to food is much the same . . . imaginative and inventive without excess or affectation. His little restaurant was barely six months old when it received the accolade of a star from the Michelin.

He started baking bread while working in Brussels, and could find none that seemed suitable to partner his style of cuisine. The public's reception convinced him to do the same when he came to Paris. Not an insipid bread but a forthright loaf with the fermentation set off by beer and grapes. Into his dough goes a touch of honey and the honorable salt of Guérande. There is never any bread left over to give the customers to take home.

At Charenton le Pont on the edge of Paris, an address as unprepossessing as the rue de Menilmontant, is the small Musée Français du Pain. Occupying a floor in the head office of a flour-milling company that supplies most of the leading pastry chefs in France, it is an endearing place.

The museum is the dada of the company's owner, Jacques Lorch. For twenty-five years M. Lorch has been ferreting out artifacts pertaining to the subject that is his passion. The collection now numbers more than a thousand pieces, and to obtain some of them he had to beat out offers from big museums around Europe.

"The story of bread is the story of the life of man," said M. Lorch.

The oldest exhibit in the museum is a model of a granary in Egypt, dating back to approximately 2000 B.C. We know that the ancient Egyptians already had leavened bread because when the Hebrews fled the country they went in such a hurry they left their starter dough behind. As a result the Exodus had to be effected on matzos.

On a fourth century A.D. Roman mold of the Goddess of Victory are the letters DULC which according to Lorch was the abbreviation of the Roman confectioner Dulciarius. There are seals from many countries. During the ages when bread was brought to communal ovens for baking, it was the custom to mark the loaves. Thanks to these brands, an individual could claim his bread once it was baked.

Of the many documents on display, the one that captivated me most was a proclamation of November 15, 1793, announcing that only one type of bread could be sold, the *Pain d'Égalité*. Henceforth, there was to be no more white bread for the rich and black bread for the poor. The future did not promise Pie in the Sky but a compromise loaf for all alike.

"Can you find out more for me about the *Pain d'Égalité?*" I asked Lucien Pergeline of the Grans Moulins de Paris.

White flour is the ultimate refinement of the whole grain of wheat. According to the articles of the revolutionary decree, no more than fifteen pounds of bran could be extracted from one hundred kilos of any kind of grain. The order specified that all bread would be composed of three-fourths wheat flour and one-fourth rye flour. In localities lacking sufficient rye, barley flour was to be substituted.

In Article 9 the bakers were warned that they faced imprisonment if they made anything other than a single type of bread to be known as the "Bread of Equality."

The law didn't last for long. Under the empire of Napoléon I, the new aristocrats went right back to white bread. Society shifts. Now it is the well-to-do who cherish the virtues of the bread once spurned by the less-well-off. If it came to a choice today, the former would rather give up cake.

Whether it is white or black, leavened or unleavened, bread is the food common to all mankind.

In Turkey, a land of long-respected traditions, any piece of bread seen lying upon the ground is to be raised, pressed against the heart, the lips and the forehead and then placed on a high ledge. One does not walk upon bread. It would be a sacrilege to the Creator.

As the poet sang, "A jug of wine, a loaf of bread and Thou."

Why We Love French Wine

BY PETER HELLMAN

editor's note

I don't know why other people love French wine, but I know that *I* love it because in comparison with like wines from other countries, French wine is almost always, over 95 percent of the time, better, in any type of vessel from which it's drunk.

Journalist PETER HELLMAN is a contributing editor at *New York* and also writes frequently for *The New York Times, Atlantic Monthly,* and other publications. His book credits include *The American Wine Handbook* (Ballantine, 1987), *When Courage Was Stronger Than Fear* (Marlowe & Company/Balliett & Fitzgerald, 1999), and *The Auschwitz Album* (Random House, 1981).

The French insist that the unique glory of their wines originates in the soil—*le terroir.* For once, these rather immodest people are shortchanging themselves. The true source of French wines issues from their very own heads, hearts and finicky palates. Otherwise, any batch of happy peasants could have invented Champagne, or determined that it takes thirteen different grapes to make a proper Châteauneuf-du-Pape, or managed to classify the great red wines of Burgundy (all made from the same Pinot Noir grape, mind you) into more than 250 *grands crus* and *premiers crus*.

This last fact struck home years ago as I drove along a tiny country road that hugged the vine-draped Côte de Nuits—a first pilgrimage to the region of my favorite wine. A sign marked the spot where the commune of Morey-St.-Denis ended and Chambolle-Musigny began, fabled names to anyone who adores red Burgundy. The wine map in my head told me that the vines sloping gently upward to my right had to be the *grand cru* of Bonnes Mares, a thirty-seven-acre appellation that straddles the two communes. (Full yet delicate, meaty yet refined, a well-aged Bonnes Mares is my dream of red Burgundy.)

A woman was pruning vines near the road. I pulled over. "This must be Bonnes Mares," I said to her confidently.

"*Mais non, monsieur,*" she said reproachfully. "This is only plain commune wine."

I told her about the wine map in my head.

"Bonnes Mares is not here," she repeated firmly. "It's over there."

She pointed to a spot no more than half a dozen rows away. No undulation, dip or break of any kind that I could see separated the vines of the *grand cru* of Bonnes Mares from the communal stuff. Yet one wine fetches triple the price of the other. If you are lucky enough to drink a twenty-year-old bottle of Bonnes Mares from a good vintage, I'll lay odds that you won't find it overpriced.

How serious are the French about *le terroir?* It's said that the members of the INAO (Institut National des Appellations d'Origine des Vins et Eaux-de-Vie) entrusted with dividing the Côte d'Or into appellations as small as two acres (La Romanée) wouldn't hesitate to actually taste the soil. How else to detect subtle differences between similar-appearing plots? Perhaps such differences accounted for the otherwise undetectable boundary between Bonnes Mares and the lesser stuff.

Burgundy is the extreme example of the French compulsion to divide up territory. There are hundreds of appellations and an astounding number of place names. Charles de Gaulle once noted how difficult it is to govern a country that has a different cheese for every day of the year. How about a choice of wines for every cheese, *mon cher général?*

You'd think that so many wines would be a source of rampant confusion for the poor consumer. Actually, there's comfort in the rigidly monitored appellation system. That's because the French— an individualistic people in some ways—don't try to create an individual statement with their wines the way so many New World winemakers do. They are best satisfied when they make a wine that conforms to the standards of their appellation. On the Médoc peninsula of Bordeaux, for example, wines from the southernmost commune of Margaux are typically highly perfumed and delicate. Wines from St.-Estèphe, at the Médoc's northern end, tend to be hard edged and meaty. You might say that Margaux draws curves and St.-Estèphe right angles.

Here in Bordeaux, as in Burgundy, lines are sharply drawn in the soil. Just beyond the priceless vineyards of Château Lafite Rothschild in the commune of Paulliac, for instance, is land where no grapes deserving of the name Bordeaux may be grown. It's only a stone's throw from the most esteemed vineyard land in the world to the domain of reeds and bullfrogs.

If all French wines, Bordeaux in particular, were born beautiful, they'd be less wondrous when they come of age. In fact, there's nothing meaner in the mouth than young Bordeaux from a strong vintage. In my own cellar is a *cru bourgeois* called Château Marsac-Séguineau, from the intense 1975 vintage, bought when it was young. A brilliant royal purple, it ripped my gums with its tannin—the vinous equivalent of an assault rifle. The wine stayed that way for more than a decade, and I gave up hope that it would ever mellow. But then, after a long hiatus, I gingerly tried another bottle. Eureka! That snarl had turned to silk. Well, almost. At sixteen years of age, the wine was still angular enough to provide the classic contrast to the rich taste of roast leg of lamb.

As we get older, there's something deeply affirmative about the progress of well-aged Bordeaux. We hope that as the sap of our youth is left behind, we will show greater depth of character, soften our sharp edges and become more interesting people. In short, we want to believe that with age we can still bloom. That's precisely the path of a fine claret from youth to the fullness of age. We drink it overtly for pleasure. But we also drink it as a reminder that we can get not just older but better.

Usually it's red wines and such sweet wines as Sauternes that we save for aging. A very few dry white wines can also improve with age. My memory settles on a dusty case of 1964 Corton-Charlemagne, a *grand cru* Burgundy from the esteemed shipper Robert Drouhin, that a friend and I found forgotten in the back of a wineshop in 1977. The proprietor, happy to get rid of wine he presumed to be over the hill after thirteen years, sold us the case at a bargain. We'd planned to hold off until dinner before trying a bottle, knowing that the wine might indeed be over the hill. Instead, on the way home, we pulled over to a shaded roadside picnic table. Out of the glove compartment came clear plastic cups and a corkscrew.

The smell of that wine mingled oak, freshly toasted country bread and an elusive tang of lime. In the mouth came a rush of flavors and a texture that was simultaneously stony and unctuous. I'd be more specific, except that it is better to marvel at a great old white Burgundy—or red, for that matter—than to dissect it.

A year or so later, during a visit to Burgundy, I mentioned this marvelously youthful Corton-Charlemagne to a winemaker working in the Roman-era cellars of Drouhin located in Beaune. We were only a few miles from the hill of Corton.

His eyes lit up. "Ah, yes," he exclaimed. "In 1964, you know, the secondary aromas never really gave way to the tertiaries. It was most unusual."

The winemaker was alluding to the three phases into which French enologists divide a wine's evolution—as perceived by *le nez*. Primary aromas are those of the fresh juice of the grape. Secondary aromas develop with fermentation, the smell of young wine. The best wines go on to develop a bouquet in which multiple scents perform a dance as complex and as evanescent as a Balanchine ballet.

You needn't speak wine techno-talk to appreciate a wine like that '64 Corton-Charlemagne. But the precise terminology does drive home a point: the best French wines are not produced by happy little peasants. They are an expression of the unique French blend of sensuality and science. It wasn't by chance that fermentation was demystified by a wine-loving Frenchman named Pasteur.

We think of formal meals as the only way to properly honor a great wine in its prime. But that's not necessarily so. I once carried home from Paris a single magnificent bottle of Burgundy, a 1961 Musigny from the Comte de Vogüé. I don't mind saying that I have never, before or since, paid so much for a single bottle of wine. It awaited only a suitably lofty occasion to open it. For a long time, that opportunity never presented itself.

Then, for a birthday dinner, my wife prepared a favorite dish, potato and salt-cod puree, or what the French call *brandade de morue*. Its smell flowed from the oven and filled the house. As it came out of the oven, I heard a crash. Dashing in from the dining room, I found our beautiful old oval ceramic dish on the floor in shards, the *brandade* splashed everywhere and my wife in tears.

"This calls for the best bottle in the house," I said, as we cleaned up.

Our abbreviated birthday dinner consisted of a salad, some good country bread, a wedge of Gruyère—and that Musigny. It gave me the greatest pleasure of any wine I'd ever uncorked. Except, perhaps, for that Corton-Charlemagne drunk at roadside from a plastic cup.

Cooking *à la Pied-Noir*

BY JEFFREY ROBINSON

editor's note

The French left Algeria—its colony for 132 years—in 1962, after eight years of a nasty, complicated struggle to keep it. The *pied-noirs* (European white settlers) were, as Jeffrey Robinson notes in this piece (which appeared in December 1979), caught in the middle once France pulled out: staying meant certain death, and the countries they had left long ago (France, Italy, Spain, Malta, and Greece, mostly) were no longer home. But flee they did (they numbered over 1 million and found havens in France, Spain, Canada, and Israel), bringing not much else but the flavors and recipes from their kitchens.

JEFFREY ROBINSON is the author of eighteen books, including biographies of Princess Grace of Monaco and Brigitte Bardot. His investigative nonfiction credits include *The Laundrymen, The Merger, The End of the American Century, The Manipulators,* and *The Hotel: Backstairs at the World's Most Exclusive Hotel* (which is about Claridge's in London). A native New Yorker, Robinson lived in the south of France for twelve years, contributing short stories and articles to a number of American magazines. Since 1982 he has made his home in Great Britain, where he concentrates on writing books.

I t was 1960. Edmond Serfati was no longer alive in Fez, Morocco. More than a century before his ancestors had migrated from Reims, France, to Oran, Algeria, because that's where the work was. In Oran he met a woman named Perle Faruch whose family had left France at about the same time for Sidi-bel-Abbes. They were married in a strict Sephardic ceremony, and they lived in Fez, raising five children. Then Morocco gained independence, then Edmond Serfati died, and then Perle decided she had to go home to France—to a France that wasn't really her home. She brought with her everything she owned: Moroccan *pieds-noirs* like herself were the lucky ones.

It was 1962. The Algerians took their war to the streets. Antoine Colandrea was scared. His father had migrated from Naples at the end of the last century, a time when millions of Italians were looking for a better life. Waves of them went to America; but the Colandreas were shell fishermen and America was far away. Someone told them that there was plenty of shellfish in nearby North Africa. They settled in Bône, Algeria, and took on French nationality, one of the conditions of living in a French colony. Antoine married Victorine Fiengo, also a Neapolitan, in a small Catholic church, and they had two children. Then the Algerian war began. Some people left. Most of them, like the Colandreas, had no place to go, so they stayed. And most of them, like the Colandreas, stayed too long. When they went home to France, which wasn't really home, they brought with them only what they could carry on their backs: the Algerian *pieds-noirs* were refugees.

Perle Serfati's youngest son, Armand, went to medical school in Toulouse and eventually set up practice in a village not far from Nice. The *pieds-noirs* like the south coast of France because it reminds them of North Africa. He married a *métropolitaine*—a Frenchwoman who is not a *pied-noir*—moved his mother into a nearby apartment, and saw to it that she took his wife's culinary education in hand. "She's not a *pied-noir*," he says, "but she must cook like one."

The Colandreas arrived in Marseilles. Their son, who is called Coco by his friends, became a pharmacist. He *did* marry a *pied-noir*. Coco and his wife had a son, and they moved to the same village where Armand Serfati had started his medical practice. But Coco's wife was too young to have properly learned *pied-noir* cooking, and when he is angry with her he reminds her of that as he storms out of the house to his mother's, where he eats the way he did when he lived in Bône.

In essence, the *pieds-noirs* really have only their cookery left from a life that was very different from the way it is today.

The French took the colonies in North Africa during the early nineteenth century and protected their interests by sending in soldiers. The soldiers wore heavy black boots; the Arabs were shoeless. When the French landed, the Arabs pointed to the soldiers' boots and shouted, "*Pieds-noirs* [black feet]!" So goes one of the many stories relating the origin of the name. Immigration to North Africa was not exclusively French, however. There were Italians who went to Tunisia and the eastern part of Algeria. There were Spaniards, a good many of them Jews, who went to Morocco and the western half of Algeria. And there were of course the ruling French, who spread themselves over the three lands.

The French made everyone except the Arabs go to French schools and carry French passports. The melting pot worked, pouring forth a new breed of Frenchman: the *pied-noir*—a Frenchman who in many cases had never been to France. (Originally the term *pied-noir* referred only to the French in Algeria, but now it means all North African French.)

What you find then in *pied-noir* cuisine is a mélange: French, Spanish, Italian, Arab, and Jewish. Depending on the overriding influence in the particular village, the cooking changes slightly. The Colandreas cook with an Italian touch, the Serfatis, with a Jewish flavor.

Perhaps the classic example of this composite cookery is bouill-abaisse-couscous. Although couscous is a North African dish, the *pieds-noirs* made various refinements. The North Africans, for example, made their couscous with rancid butter. Then too, because most of them were poor and couldn't always afford mutton, they covered their couscous with vegetables such as cabbage, turnips, squash, zucchini, onions, tomatoes, celery, and chickpeas. The *pieds-noirs,* however, were considered the wealthy class and could afford lamb or chicken to cover their couscous. But most of them never used butter: first, because it didn't suit their taste, and second—at least in Morocco and the western half of Algeria—because many of them were Jewish and kept kosher homes. For their bouillabaisse-couscous they used a series of *bon marché* fish cooked in saffron stock and served atop the standard vegetables. The above variations are obvious examples of how the *pieds-noirs* mix up recipes to create their own.

Because life in North Africa was considerably slower than it is today in France, even the style of cooking was different. Women had more time to cook—and *pied-noir* cooking generally takes time. It's a cuisine based on fresh produce that can be bought in the morning at open markets and leisurely prepared, like this *tagine,* or stew.

stewed chicken with prunes

In a small bowl let 16 pitted prunes soak in water to cover overnight. In a large flameproof casserole brown in batches a 4-pound chicken, cut into serving pieces, in ¼ cup olive oil over moderately high heat and transfer it with tongs to a plate.

In the fat remaining in the casserole cook 4 onions, chopped, and 1 red chili pepper about 4 inches long, seeded and minced, over moderate heat, stirring, for fifteen minutes, or until the onion is light golden. Stir in 4 teaspoons sifted ground unblanched almonds, return the chicken to the casserole, and add the prunes, drained, ¾ cup water, and salt and pepper to taste. Bring the liquid to a boil over moderate heat, cover the casserole tightly with foil, and with a skewer punch 6 holes in the foil. Bake the casserole in a preheated moderate oven (350°F) for 1 hour. Remove and discard the foil and transfer the chicken with a slotted spatula to a heated platter. Reduce the sauce, if necessary, over moderately high heat, stirring, until it is thickened and pour it over the chicken. Serves 4.

There is a ritual to eating *à la pied-noir*.

In the center of the table there is always a pestle and mortar, usually of brass. And then you've got to surround the table with a dozen friends and all of their children. Unlike the *métropolitains*, whose homes are strictly private (a true Frenchman prefers inviting friends to a restaurant instead of his home because his home is only for family; no friends, no business associates, and certainly no tax collectors!), the *pieds-noirs* believe that the more people around the table, the easier the digestion. That may or may not be true, but I can gladly attest to the fact that when there's enough for five at dinner, there's enough for six, and Armand will ring me to ask if I have eaten yet. Even if I have I usually say no, because there's no sense in missing out on a great meal.

So the pestle and mortar (more about which later) are on the table, and next comes the *pastis* (anisette)—ice cubes in a tall glass, three fingers of *pastis*, and plenty of cold water.

That's followed by a tableful of *amuse-gueule* (literally translated: "make your face happy"), which are hors d'oeuvres. Olives, both green and black, shredded carrots, fennel, chickpeas, artichokes in lemon juice, hot sausages, stuffed pancreas—it takes a little getting used to—and a sardine preparation called *scabech*.

scabech (chilled sardines with garlic and vinegar)

Rinse 2 pounds fresh sardines, cleaned and heads removed, and pat them dry with paper towels. Sprinkle the fish with salt and pepper and dredge them in flour, shaking off any excess. In a stainless-steel or enameled skillet heat $^2/_3$ cup olive oil over moderately high heat until it is hot, add the fish in batches, and fry them, turning them, for 1 to 2 minutes on each side, or until they are golden. Transfer the fish as they are fried with a slotted spatula to a platter. Add to the skillet 6 garlic cloves, 1 red chili pepper about 4 inches long, seeded and minced, 2 tablespoons paprika, $1^1/_2$ tablespoons ground cumin, and salt and pepper to taste and cook the mixture over moderately low heat, stirring, for 2 minutes. Add 3 tablespoons red-wine vinegar, or to taste, and pour the mixture over the sardines. Let the mixture cool and chill it, covered, overnight. Serves 6 to 8 as an hors d'oeuvre.

Along with the *amuse-gueule* the Serfatis and the Colandreas serve *taïba*.

taïba (chilled tuna with chilies and tomatoes)

Arrange 4 tomatoes, halved crosswise and seeded, on the rack of a broiler pan and broil them under a preheated broiler about 2 inches from the heat for 2 minutes, or until the skins are blistered and charred. Let the tomatoes cool, remove and discard the skin, and chop the pulp. Roast 2 red chili peppers each about 4 inches long on a rack under a preheated broiler about 2 inches from the heat, turning them, for 1 minute, or until the skins just blister. Enclose the peppers in a paper bag, let them steam, and wearing rubber gloves, remove and discard the skins, seeds, and ribs. Mince the peppers.

In a stainless-steel or enameled saucepan cook the tomatoes, the minced pepper, and 3 garlic cloves in 3 tablespoons olive oil over moderate heat, stirring, for 5 minutes, or until the mixture is a coarse puree. If desired add 1 tablespoon tomato paste, or to taste. Add two 7-ounce tins solid white tuna, drained and flaked, 1 red chili pepper about 4 inches long, seeded and cut into thin strips, ¼ teaspoon ground coriander, and salt and pepper to taste and simmer the mixture, stirring occasionally, for 5 minutes, or until the liquid is evaporated. Let the mixture cool and chill it, covered, for 2 hours, or overnight. Serve the mixture with crusty bread. Serves 4 as an hors d'oeuvre.

Life in North Africa is hot-weather life. Probably because the *pieds-noirs* lived in a warm climate they are not soup eaters, the way the French are. There is, however, a souplike dish made of ham, beef, and chickpeas and somehow associated with Oran. There is also *shorba,* which is lamb, beans, and chickpeas. But no, Coco insists, the *pieds-noirs* are not soup people. "What we like better is a kind of brochette."

Shish kebab in some parts of the world, brochette *à la pied-noir* is thumbnail-size pieces of lamb heart, lamb liver, and lamb lung on a six-inch wooden skewer that are grilled and covered with cumin and *harissa* (hot pepper sauce).

Coco also claims that no one makes a better couscous than his mother: Her grain is mixed with slightly sugared milk and there are plenty of raisins. But the real secret of it is her *hasban,* a mixture of stomach, tripe, and lung that is cooked into the sauce and served over the grain. Needless to say, it's a very special dish and not suited to everyone's taste. The three Serfati children won't go near it, and

Armand's wife has learned that the hard way. So have I. Yet Armand loves it. On nights when Armand rings and asks, "Have you eaten yet?" and I suspect that *hasban* is a possibility, I beg off. If however my luck is any good on nights when Armand is feasting on *hasban,* I'll manage to bump into Coco, and his wife will be making *chouchouka*. For that I'm always available.

chouchouka (lamb chops and poached eggs with tomato and eggplant)

Spread a 1-pound eggplant, peeled and diced, in a colander. Sprinkle the eggplant with 2 teaspoons salt, toss it, and let it drain for thirty minutes. Pat the eggplant dry with paper towels.

Pat dry with paper towels six ¾-inch-thick shoulder lamb chops and sprinkle them with salt and pepper. In a large flameproof stainless-steel or enameled casserole sear the chops, 3 at a time, in 2 tablespoons olive oil over high heat for 1 minute on each side. Reduce the heat to moderately high and cook the chops, 3 at a time, for 4 minutes more on each side. Transfer the chops as they are cooked with a slotted spatula to a platter. In the casserole cook 2 pounds red sweet peppers, thinly sliced, in ¼ cup plus 2 tablespoons olive oil over moderate heat, stirring, for 10 minutes. Add 3 onions, chopped, and 3 garlic cloves and cook the mixture, stirring, for 5 minutes. Add 3 pounds tomatoes, peeled, seeded, and chopped, the eggplant, 1 red chili pepper about 4 inches long, seeded and minced, and salt and pepper to taste and simmer the mixture, stirring occasionally, for 1 hour.

Poach 6 eggs and keep them warm. Arrange the chops over the vegetable mixture, cook the mixture over moderate heat for 5 minutes, or until the chops are heated through, and top each chop with 1 poached egg. Serves 6.

Because of the Arab influence, dessert usually means some sort of pastry—lots of almond paste and dates, figs and sesame seeds. *Agua limón,* a tart lemonade, is often served with the pastry.

agua limón (tart lemonade)

In a stainless-steel or enameled saucepan bring 2 cups water with 2 tablespoons grated lemon rind to a boil over moderate heat, simmer the mixture for 10 minutes, and let it cool. In a large glass jar fitted with a lid combine 2 cups water with ½ teaspoon sugar, stir the mixture until the sugar is dissolved, and add the lemon rind mixture and ¼ cup lemon juice. Chill the mixture, covered, for 2 hours. The mixture should be tart, but add sugar to taste if desired. Strain the mixture through a fine sieve set over a pitcher and divide it among tall glasses filled with ice cubes. Makes 1 quart.

For something more exotic at the end of a *pied-noir* meal, there's always *vin à l'orange.*

vin à l'orange (orange-flavored wine)

In a large glass jar fitted with a lid combine 4 cups dry white wine or dry red wine, 1¼ cups sugar, and ⅓ cup each of light rum and grated orange rind, stir the mixture until the sugar is dissolved, and seal it with the lid. Chill the mixture, shaking the jar once a day, for at least 1 day, or as long as 3 weeks. Strain the mixture through a fine sieve set over a large pitcher and serve it immediately or pour it into dark glass bottles fitted with corks and store it in a cool, dark place. Makes about 5½ cups.

When the *pied-noir* meal is over, *eau-de-vie* is usually served while the table is cleared. Finally only the pestle and mortar remain. By this time the mortar is full, and both Perle Serfati and Victorine Colandrea can judge the success of their meal. During dinner, instead of putting ends and stems and skins and bones back on your plate, you're supposed to put them in the mortar. Depending on how much is served and how many people have sat around the table, the mortar should be filled and emptied several times. How many times? Neither Perle nor Victorine can say. They've managed to teach their daughters-in-law how to cook *à la pied-noir*—both Armand and Coco say they eat almost as well these days as when they were in North Africa and it was *maman* who did the cooking—but when it comes to the mortar the wisdom of mothers-in-law falls short. How many times for a successful meal? *"Assez,"* they say. Do they simply mean "Enough"? No, *assez* is simply *assez*. Maybe it means as much as it should be. Translations like this don't come easy.

Le Beaujolais Nouveau Est Arrivé!

BY GERALD ASHER

editor's note

Frank Prial, wine columnist for *The New York Times,* has written that Gerald Asher is "one of the few writers on wine whose timely pieces are a delight to read long after they first appeared." Asher has been writing about wine for *Gourmet*—from which this piece is reprinted—for many years, and some of his other *Gourmet* articles on wine from regions near Paris include "Chinon: Red Wine From the Garden of France" (April 1997); "A Glass of Muscadet" (November 1992); "Burgundy's Best" (October 1993); "Chablis: A French Classic" (June 1995); and "Paris by the Glass: City of Light . . . And Great Wine Lists" (October 1998), which is about Paris restaurants whose proprietors believe the wine list is as important as the menu.

I chose this piece, which appeared in November 1995, about Beaujolais Nouveau because even with all the hype every year, Americans seem not to know much about Beaujolais Nouveau or the Beaujolais *crus,* and because it is a piece that best exemplifies Gerald's ability to write about wine in a way that takes the reader off on various tangents but always returns to some simple, elemental point. The last paragraph of this piece offers one of those points to visitors (readers may also want to know that at press time the restaurants mentioned were all still in operation; additionally, the Villefranche Tourist Office—4.74.68.05.18/fax: 4.74.68.44.91—offers a free *carte touristique* for a self-guided tour along the forty-two-mile *Route des Vins,* and brochures on the *pays* Beaujolais and its twelve *appellations*).

GERALD ASHER is also the author of *On Wine* (Random House, 1986) and *Vineyard Tales* (Chronicle Books, 1996). He has contributed to several UK publications, including *Decanter, The Sunday Times,* and *Punch,* and for some years wrote a monthly "Letter From America" column for *Wines and Spirits.* Among the numerous honors he's received are the 1998 James Beard Award for articles on wines and spirits, and the Mérite Agricole, an award rarely given to foreigners, with which he was decorated in 1974.

E very year on the third Thursday of November, bars, cafés, and bistros all over Paris revel, with varying degrees of decorum, in the new harvest's Beaujolais. The cynical would say that the success of Beaujolais Nouveau—almost as great in Brussels, Amsterdam, Frankfurt, and New York as it is in Lyons—is a triumph of marketing and promotion. But commerce merely cashes in: The gaiety is spontaneous, and the joy a response to something beyond posters and bar streamers. A mouthful of wine that was grapes just weeks before, and earth, rain, and sunshine only weeks before that, is an exhilarating reminder of what really makes the world go round.

Well over half the annual production of Beaujolais and Beaujolais-Villages together is sold, shipped, and presumably paid for before Christmas. This is not an unhappy situation for the growers to find themselves in. Unfortunately, the intense but fleeting attention distorts our perception of the wine: It is more than a nine days' wonder. The phenomenon of Beaujolais Nouveau also means that wines of the ten Beaujolais *crus* are often considered stale news when released the following spring. (Brouilly, Côte de Brouilly, Chénas, Chiroubles, Fleurie, Juliénas, Morgon, Moulin-à-Vent, Saint-Amour, and Regnié may not be sold as *vin nouveau*.) They can hardly re-create the excitement generated the previous November, when the vintage made its debut. The result is that some of the region's best wines slip onto the market unannounced and unnoticed.

Once (and I mean centuries ago), when all wine was sold from the barrel and no one knew how to keep a part-empty container's contents from deteriorating, each new vintage was so eagerly awaited that it would be shipped off to market still seething its way through the final stages of fermentation. Most of those wines were boisterously rough; few could have been as delectable, drunk in their infancy, as wine made from the Gamay grape of the Beaujolais. Even without the help of controversial techniques to expand the wine's aromatic potential or boost its power, young Beaujolais, tender yet sprightly and, left to itself, redolent of peonies in full flower, is as seductive as any wine can be.

Growers were still shipping barrels of new (and probably fizzy) Beaujolais to Lyons as recently as the 1930s. The wine was set up on bistros' zinc counters and, once tapped, run off directly into the pitchers from which it was served. In Paris, too, there were bars known for the new Beaujolais that arrived each fall with much local fanfare. Such wine, with "beaded bubbles winking at the brim," brought to the shabbiest hole-in-the-wall a vision of distant countryside, of vines in sunlight, and, who knows, perhaps of Dionysus himself. Jubilant.

There was nothing either formal or official about the dispatch of these wines: no release date; no organized promotion; and, even when the machinery of controlled appellations had already been put in place, no trail of certificates. Eventually, however, bureaucracy stepped in to tidy things up. In 1938 the practice of selling a Beaujolais freely outside the bounds and documentation of the new appellation laws was curtailed, and then wartime measures that controlled the release of all wines broke the tradition altogether—at a time when it might have done most good.

The restrictions inaugurated under the Vichy administration (how fitting for that lot to have put paid to one of life's simple pleasures) were not revoked until 1951, when the authorities fixed December 15 as an annual date on which controlled-appellation wines of the new vintage could be released for sale. Growers in regions that had traditionally sold some of their new wine earlier immediately lobbied for appropriate exceptions. On November 9, 1951, permission was given for Beaujolais growers, among others, to release certain wines for sale *en primeur*—which meant, specifically, one month earlier than the standard date.

That, then, was when Beaujolais Nouveau (or Beaujolais Primeur, as some people prefer to call it) was first given official recognition. In 1985 the *primeur* release date of November 15 was changed, as far as Beaujolais was concerned, to the third Thursday of November so that arrival of the new wine in far-flung places could be tied to a weekend during which everyone could enjoy it. Sales of Beaujolais Nouveau, which had grown to almost half a million cases by 1960, now exceed 6 million cases a year.

The Beaujolais region lies west of the Saône, just above Lyons. Though now perceived as an appendage to Burgundy (at the northern limit, Beaujolais vines fraternize with those of the Mâconnais), the Beaujolais and Burgundy have never been, historically, connected. In fact, rivalry between the Beaujolais and the Mâconnais was so extreme in pre-Revolutionary France that it erupted regularly in drawn-out legal actions and appeals to the courts and councils of the crown.

The Beaujolais, protected by Lyons's powerful archbishops, had been allowed to sell that city its wine free of taxes, an advantage denied growers of the Mâconnais, regarded as denizens of the duke of Burgundy. This snub became all the more galling to Mâcon in the seventeenth century, when improvements to an ancient road west from Belleville, the small Beaujolais port on the Saône River, across the watershed to Pouilly-sur-Loire, gave Beaujolais producers easy access to Paris, a market the Mâcon growers had worked hard to open for themselves. On convoys of barges that passed through the newly constructed Briare canal, linking the Loire and the Seine Rivers, Beaujolais made its appearance in the capital.

The town councillors of Mâcon relied on the archaic configuration of the revenue system under the ancien régime in desperate attempts to crush Beaujolais with taxes. But in 1694, after years of squabbling, the mayor of Villefranche (the Beaujolais's own "capital") and his supporters were granted a ruling in their wine's favor. They won their case on a legal nicety but had suggested anyway that the crown's income would in fact increase at a faster rate if no additional taxes were imposed. It's the standard argument, of course, in such situations (*plus ça change,* and all that); but the Beaujolais growers gave weight to it by predicting that, left alone, they would be shipping to Paris at least eight thousand hectoliters of wine a year by 1700. Their claim proved to be incredibly modest: A report published in 1769 shows that Beaujolais growers were by then shipping to the city 160,000 hectoliters a year—equivalent to 1.75 million cases of wine. (This result eventually persuaded the growers of Mâcon to drop Pinot Noir in favor of the Gamay they had sneered at in their litigation.)

This growth of sales caused a dramatic expansion of vineyards in eighteenth-century Beaujolais and led to the spread of a system of sharecropping already prevalent in the area. Groups of a dozen or more small growers each held and tended ten to twenty acres of land—both vineyard and arable—for an owner with whom they were obliged to share their harvest. The system still exists on some large Beaujolais estates; I sometimes see the great casks the French call *foudres* lined up, each identified with the name of the grower whose crop is destined to fill it. As for the Beaujolais's privileged relationship with Lyons, that still exists, too, but in a different and curiously modern form: anyone driving down the autoroute from Paris to the Mediterranean discovers that there is no toll for using the stretch of road between Villefranche and Lyons.

The Beaujolais no longer has a political boundary. Partly in the administrative *département* of Saône-et-Loire and partly in the *département* of the Rhône, it is defined viticulturally by the French appellation laws. Villefranche is a convenient hub from which to explain the layout of the various appellations that make up the Beaujolais. More confusing than the article, which distinguishes "the" Beaujolais region from Beaujolais wine, is use of the word *Beaujolais* to refer broadly to the wines of the entire region; they include Beaujolais-Villages and wines of the ten *crus* as well as plain Beaujolais itself. As a result one often hears wine from the basic Beaujolais appellation referred to (as above) as "plain" Beaujolais, "simple" Beaujolais, or "ordinary" Beaujolais when it may not be plain, simple, or ordinary at all.

The twenty-two thousand acres of vineyard southwest of Villefranche where "plain" Beaujolais is produced form both the largest and the most varied of the appellations. Beaujolais-Villages is produced northwest of the town in a region of wide, undulating hills. Its fifteen thousand acres of vines lie adjacent to, and some-times surround, the vineyards of the ten *crus,* which vary in size from Chénas, with six hundred planted acres, to Brouilly, with three thousand. Together, the *crus* comprise some thirteen thousand acres of vineyard.

Those Beaujolais-Villages hills are the last outcroppings of the Massif Central, a granite formation far older than the Alps or the Pyrénées. Millennia of rain and wind, heat and ice, have reduced them to a coarse sand that now presents a deceptive softness of con-tour. Though never seeming so, the hills can be both high and steep. Their soils are less homogeneous than their common profile might suggest. Granitic sand predominates, but there are everywhere gra-dations and mixtures. In the Beaujolais-Villages, the sand, mostly gray-colored, is often mixed with clay. At Brouilly, Fleurie, and Regnié the sand, mostly pink, is fairly pure. On the Côte de Brouilly the vines are planted on a splintered blue-black rock (reputed to be among the hardest in France) that recurs, mixed with pink granite, at Juliénas. In Morgon, there's schist beneath the upper vineyards— notably its Côte de Py—and clay lower down, and Moulin-à-Vent has deposits of manganese so heavy that in the last century they were mined commercially. The relative toughness of Moulin-à-Vent wines is thought to be connected to this presence.

As might be expected, each *cru* has distinctive characteristics. One such might be no more than a particularity of aroma— Brouilly, it is said, is grapey, while Fleurie smells of violets, Saint-Amour of peach, and Chénas of spices. These differences are harder to pin down, however, than the sharper divisions based on body and structure. It's far easier to see that, whereas Brouilly, Côte de Brouilly, Regnié, Fleurie, Saint-Amour, and Chénas have in common their elegance and fragrant delicacy, Juliénas, Morgon, and espe-cially Moulin-à-Vent possess greater generosity, deeper flavor, and more lasting power. Chiroubles, of which there is very little anyway, stands apart from the others: Less aromatic than some, and without the fleshiness of others, it has a lacy texture and a sleek charm.

Markets usually show a marked preference for one *cru* over another. "Lyons traditionally prefers a Beaujolais with a firm edge," Paul Jambon of the Pavillon de Chavannes on the Côte de Brouilly told me. "The Lyonnais like structure, and they don't like the aroma to be too exuberant. Lyons drinks Morgon and Moulin-à-Vent. But Paris, which appreciates lighter red wines with fresh aromas, drinks Fleurie and Brouilly. The Swiss, too, have a passion for Fleurie, which is why it is now one of the most expensive of the *crus.*"

Site—*terroir*—is important everywhere in establishing the personality of a wine, but Claude Geoffray of Château Thivin, also on the Côte de Brouilly, feels it to be especially so in the Beaujolais because Gamay itself is such a low-key varietal. A Gamay wine expresses the character of the vineyard or it expresses nothing. Which is why, Geoffray says, the yield of grapes from each vine must be severely restricted and winemaking as nonintrusive as possible. With roughly four thousand vines planted to the acre, Geoffray expects to harvest no more than 1.5 pounds of grapes from each. In comparison, most California vineyards carry 650 vines to the acre, from which they rarely harvest fewer than four tons of grapes. That's about twelve pounds of fruit from each vine.

Château Thivin's *cuverie,* built against a hillside, was planned to allow its winemaking to flow without pumps but by gravity from the tanks—where the whole bunches are allowed to ferment and macerate in a manner unique to the Beaujolais—to presses below and then farther down into the cellar. Fermentation is completed in old wooden *foudres,* each with a capacity of about one thousand gallons.

In a tradition imposed, in fact, by the appellation regulations, the harvest must be brought to the *cuverie* in whole bunches. There they are dumped into reception tanks, preferably no higher than they are wide. The weight of the mass crushes the bottom bunches, which begin to ferment and release carbon dioxide. It fills the crevices between the rest of the bunches, stifles the yeast, and inhibits the spread of fermentation. But even in these conditions the warmth generated affects the uncrushed bunches in ways that extract color and flavor from the grapeskins without releasing tannin (not that the Gamay grape has much). Malic acid is also substantially reduced—a reason for the softness of new Beaujolais—and the grapes' sugars are freed for a more rapid and complete fermentation later, once the bunches have been removed from the vat and pressed. First, however, they spend from three to ten days in this state of anaerobic metabolism, a process basic to the universally appealing style of Beaujolais.

Each grower handles the maceration phase differently, of course, and distortions do occur. Usually they are the result of a grower's taking a shortcut, hoping to get quality results while boosting yields, or of his allowing the success of *primeurs* to influence the way he makes a *cru* wine. Or they are an exaggeration to attract star ratings from the more-is-more school of wine critics. One technique is to heat the grapes to sixty or seventy degrees centigrade, thereby increasing the extraction of color, before cooling them to a temperature at which a yeast culture can be introduced. Wines made this way are round and big but lack both vivacity and personality. Another technique is to push yields to the limit, despite the risk that the fruit will then not ripen fully. A heavy hand with chaptalization—adjustment of sugar levels from sacks held ready for the purpose—and the introduction of yeasts that generate powerful, if short-lived, aromas during fermentation mask the wine's inherent deficiencies. On the other hand there are many growers—young ones especially—whose approach to winemaking is practically in step with that of their grandfathers.

Olivier Ravier, of the Domaine de la Pierre Bleue and president of the Beaujolais growers' association, says that people accept clumsy wines made with exaggerated chaptalization and monster yeasts when they lose their ability to taste and appreciate subtlety.

"French children," he told me, "once went from water to water-and-wine, to wine-and-water, and eventually, to wine. It was part of growing up, and they learned to appreciate the taste—and the use—of wine. Now our children drink heavily advertised sugary soft drinks with phony fruit flavors. One day they learn from their friends to add alcohol to it. And eventually they leave out the soft drink. This has led to both social and economic problems. We winegrowers have difficulty tempting such impaired palates back to wine. But it's the same with food. Too much of what we eat is processed and tastes of manufactured flavors. How can we expect anyone to understand and enjoy the infinite range of tastes and aromas that real wine and real food offer? These are things one must learn in childhood."

To get to the root of the problem, Ravier and other Beaujolais growers started a program—*L'Univers du Goût*—for Villefranche elementary schools, which teaches children how to taste. One of the most basic lessons for very small children involves each child's bringing to school a particular vegetable—a carrot, a leek, and so on—which the class tastes and then puts in a pot for making, with the help of the teacher, a soup that they all get to eat. Gradually the lessons go deeper. A discussion on varieties of pears, for instance, will include a simple history of the fruit, an explanation of how it is cultivated, the uses for each variety, and of course, a chance to taste and compare them.

So far, forty-four of the town's schoolteachers have taken the voluntary training course for the program, which covers all fruits, vegetables, herbs, and spices. There is a Villefranche center for the program with its own reference library, but much of the teacher training is done in the well-equipped tasting room at Ravier's vineyard. There, each session ends with a wine tasting. Ravier just smiled when I asked if that might have contributed to the program's phenomenal success. The agricultural college of the next *département* has asked for his group's assistance in starting a similar program.

Food is important in the Beaujolais: The style of cooking has a solid, country quality. The serious reputation of the Auberge du Cep in Fleurie attracts a clientele from Paris as well as Lyons, whereas the Coq au Vin in Juliénas, with its slightly more flamboyant appeal, is presently popular with the local smart set. Other restaurants with excellent—and typical—food include Chez Christian Mabeau at Odenas, elegant and welcoming and with a large shaded terrace for lunching and dining in summer; Anne de Beaujeu, a small, reasonably priced hotel and restaurant in an attractively appointed former private mansion in Beaujeu; and Le Morgon, a simple-looking restaurant, up a lane away from the village of Villié-Morgon, with a wide selection of Morgon wines listed by producer.

Visitors to the area may also enjoy a tour of George Duboeuf's Hameau du Beaujolais, a transformation of the former railway station at Romanèche-Thorins. Its hour-long mixed-media overview of the region includes exhibits (as well as a slow-motion film of fermentation shot with an endoscopic camera, the kind surgeons use to take a look where the eye cannot go) on everything from geology to the history of making bottles. The show ends with a wine tasting accompanied by local bread and sausage.

The chalk-clay soil of the southern Beaujolais, rich in iron, has a golden color that has earned it the name of *terres dorées,* or golden lands. The terrain is precipitously abrupt and strewn with old castles, tawny Romanesque churches, and impossible legends. The clay and the iron, especially, lend the wines here—the plain Beaujolais—a natural rusticity. Good examples are the wines from

Jean-Paul Brun's Domaine des Terres Dorées and Pierre-Marie Chermette's Domaine du Vissoux at Saint-Vérand.

On this area's back roads a succession of villages, each prettier than the last, has cafés and bistros offering a simple country lunch and a carafe of wine from the vineyard outside the window. Those looking for more refined cooking will find that too, at restaurants like the Vieux Moulin at Alix and Les Marroniers at Lozanne. Everyone hopes, one day, to find a corner of France, true to itself, easily accessible, but overlooked by tourism. Here it is. Just turn right off the autoroute at Villefranche.

The State of Chocolate in Paris, France

BY NAOMI BARRY

editor's note

I rarely enjoy milk chocolate, so I suppose I'm not a true chocoholic, but I have no restraint when in the presence of very, very good dark chocolate, especially of the sort to be found at Paris's *haute chocolaterie*.

It was probably a mistake, therefore, to drag my husband, who is rather indifferent about chocolate, to La Maison du Chocolat in the rue François 1ᵉʳ (this branch of the chain has a café; not all of them do). For the rest of my life I will be reminded that I forced him to have the most expensive cup of hot chocolate on the planet (two cups and a plate of assorted chocolates cost about $25). It might indeed be the most expensive cup anywhere, but I'll never forget it, and it remains the best cup I've ever had (people may tell you that the best hot chocolate is at Angelina, in the rue de Rivoli, but that is only because they've never had one at La Maison). Thank God there is a La Maison outpost in New York, complete with a café, which also arranges mail orders (1018 Madison Avenue, New York, NY 10021; 212-744-7117).

Naomi Barry remembers that this piece, which appeared in March 1987, came into being over lunch one day with Jane Montant, former editor of *Gourmet*. Jane was lamenting that all anyone was interested in at that time was chocolate, and Naomi promised to write the "most glamorous chocolate piece there ever was." Here it is, and for the record, even in extremis, I have never eaten the baking chocolate.

I n Extremis, when nothing else is at hand, there is the baking chocolate. I didn't expect to find fellow weaklings among the All Gauls. Slim, sleek deceptive types who look as if they were nourished on a string bean.

Micheline Haardt, the neat-as-a-pin stylist, whispered that Sonia Rykiel, the designer, was also an unbridled fanatic of chocolate.

Generally speaking, chocolate in the French capital is seductive, refined, recherché, noble and expensive. The best part of this town is at the rarefied top. Haute Couture. Haute Chocolaterie.

The Paris passion for Haute Chocolaterie is shameless in contrast to my wholesome background of divinity fudge and frosted cupcakes where the "Can't Resists" who binged in private were advised to keep it a dark secret.

These people, on the other hand, extol a bash of indulgence as a *péché mignon* (an adorable little sin). For the past few hundred years they have been treating chocolate as a suave, voluptuous and amusing commodity.

Back in the eighteenth century a witty Parisian confectioner upped his business by numbering his chocolate truffles from one to ninety. The aristocrats bought big bags full for playing family lottery in their gilded salons. Win or lose, everybody had a consolation prize.

One of the most publicized meals of the 1970s was a lunch at the Élysée Palace prepared by three-star chef Paul Bocuse and a few of his Pen Pals for the then President Valéry Giscard d'Estaing. The crescendo was in chocolate.

The opening bang was an extravagant black truffle soup, all its heady perfume held captive under a dome of puff pastry. Chosen as the climax for the sophisticated menu was a chocolate cake dubbed Le Président. It too was a domed masterpiece, smothered under a froufrou of chocolate rufflettes. The cake—created by Maurice Bernachon, the famed Lyons chocolatier, and still a leader in his repertory—resembles a saucy dancer dressed for a can-can version of *The Black Swan*.

Bernachon, a specialist in the finesse that lifts frivolity to an art, occasionally decorates a cake with chocolate leaves. To obtain them, he paints melted chocolate over a fresh leaf to capture the veined imprint. Once the chocolate hardens the leaf is thrown away.

In Paris the contemporary taste is for a chocolate that is dark, unsweetened and intense. Lovers of The Chocolate Kiss won't like it. They are not yet ready for The True Bite.

Christian Constant's small shop and tearoom at 26 rue du Bac in the stylish 7th Arrondissement concentrates on his own artisanal production. Constant is revered as The Chocolate Prince. He is an affable, attractive man, qualities that help quiet the tantrums of exigent hostesses on a day when supplies fall short of the demand.

Most of the professionals in Paris for their pastries and candies buy blocks of chocolate from Valrhona, an exacting little factory in Tain l'Hermitage in the department of the Drôme. Constant is such a fanatic that he has Valrhona send him the beans themselves. In the laboratory behind his shop he blends the cocoas from Venezuela, Indonesia and Trinidad to fabricate his own tablets. Part of the result is sold to the public in hundred-gram weights.

Constant's goal is a chocolate stripped of sugar, yet still palatable. He crashed through with Bitter Plus, a tablet with the high ratio of 80 percent chocolate. A cult of devotees sprang up immediately.

Constant ventured even further to achieve a Pure Pâte Sans Sucre. For straight-out eating, this last is beyond me but I may come to it yet.

Recently a woman doctor at the Hôpital Bichat engaged in some research on chocolate discovered that in its unadulterated state it was capable of producing a gentle high. She announced her felicitous findings on a television program with Constant.

The immediate reaction was a rash of customers to the rue du Bac shop furtively asking from behind the back of a hand for some Pâte Pure.

"To get the high," laughed Constant, "would require more chocolate than anybody could stomach."

Constant serves a Sorbet du Chocolat Amer, which is one of those marvels that isn't supposed to be. He wanted no sugar but found that the Pâte Pure didn't work. In the end pure cocoa did. He incorporates raisins which have been soaked in Scotch. The whisky cuts any possible cloy from the intensity of chocolate. It is a darkly delicious sherbet with a texture smooth and rich as an ice cream.

Constant is full of praise for America's wine and food but feels the country has not yet grown up to chocolate.

"America looks upon it as a bonbon. France has always regarded it as a jewel."

"*Vive la différence,*" I sighed and set off to investigate more.

La Maison du Chocolat, 225 Fbg. St.-Honoré, hit Paris in 1981. It didn't take long to become an establishment. Something like three weeks. The faces staring in the windows are a study in anticipation.

The chocolates are made below in what used to be a wine cellar.

Robert Linxe is less interested in chew than in flavor and melt. The marriages made in heaven are his forte . . . chocolate and coffee, chocolate and rum, chocolate and orange, an occasional flirt with Kirsch.

For a more indissoluble union with a well-defined personality, Linxe frequently has his coffee and cocoa beans ground up together.

"Good chocolate won't make you sick," he said as he urged us to taste a Romeo, a Bohème, a Rigoletto. "It won't even make you fat. Look at me and I eat it all day long."

True, he was svelte and active as a live wire and persuasive as a faith healer.

"Bitter chocolate is full of potassium and magnesium."

Convinced that it was so good for me, there was no point in refusing a Bacchus.

"Extraordinary subtlety, this one," said Linxe. "It contains Smyrna raisins that have been macerated in rum and flambéed before going into the chocolate."

La Maison du Chocolat is located near the Salle Pleyel. An enormous amount of energy is expended in the making of good music. Quite right that all these upper notes of the range should get together and that serious clients of the *chocolat amer* in various forms happen to have names like Daniel Barenboim, Itzhak Perlman, and Barbara Hendricks.

"I always know when Zubin Mehta is expected, I get so many orders to be sent to his hotel. Mehta goes through a kilo of my chocolates in a day and a half," said Linxe proudly.

Opéra seemed to be a popular number in quite a few restaurants and pastry shops. It is a flat cake, square or rectangular in shape, with alternate fillings of chocolate and coffee and a satin smooth chocolate *couverture*. Some of the pâtissiers averred that it was a favorite at the court of Louis XV. Others assumed it had been invented to coincide with the opening of the present Paris Opera in 1874.

The confusion of origin is an indication of its settled position in society. Actually it is a modern classic. In January 1986, Dalloyau—the celebrated pâtissier at 101 Fbg. St.-Honoré—held a huge fete for the thirtieth birthday of its famous creation. It was a neat twist of a party given for a cake instead of a cake being produced for a party.

"We do not let out the recipe. We often are imitated but it is never quite the same. Even we insist on our own daily controls," said Mme. Andrée Galavin, *présidente directrice générale* of this temple of gastronomic temptations that has been flourishing at the same address since 1802.

The Dalloyau version of Opéra is flecked with twenty-four-karat gold supplied by one of the last two artisans of France still working the precious gold leaf. It can be bought in any size from "petit four" to reception piece good for forty generous portions.

"This is patisserie as I respect it," said Mme. Galavin, an impressive woman of the old school. "Rich and with butter. I am anti-mousse," she said dismissing the current vogue for cakes that pretend to be lighter than air because of mousse fillings between the layers.

The original Dalloyau opened his catering establishment in 1802, the year Paris began to recover its brilliance after the Revolution. The foreigners and the émigrés were returning. Parties were being given again. Monsieur and Madame Bonaparte, the first consul and his wife, were holding court at the Palais des Tuileries. The year saw new lighting in the place Vendôme, the Temple of Mars transformed into the Église des Invalides and the institution of the lycée system of secondary education.

Monsieur Grimod de la Reynière, the first gastronomic chronicler with his *Almanach des Gourmands,* praised the confectioner Berthellemot for using as mottoes on his bonbons citations from the work of the most celebrated poets of the New France.

Questing chocolate in Paris became a fun foray into social history. The conquistadores brought the cocoa bean to Spain in their curio bags from the New World. The Spanish princess Anne d'Autriche, who married Louis XIII, brought chocolate to France.

According to Alexandre Dumas who recounted the hegira with his usual gusto, Spain went mad for the new cocoa drink, particularly the women and the monks. The señoras even carried it to church with them, mollifying their reproachful confessors with a proferred cup from time to time. Both sides were absolved from sin by the Reverend Father Escobar who with metaphysical subtlety formally declared that drinking chocolate prepared with water was not to be considered as breaking a fast.

The monks of Spain and France were a sharing community. During the fifteenth century they busily exchanged the savant theories that helped Columbus make his first trip west. Later the Spanish monks sent samples of chocolate as presents to their brethren north of the border.

The French made chocolate fashionable. The gift containers are of hand-painted silk or delicate porcelain. The Maison du Chocolat's cardboard boxes are as chic as those of Hermès. Both come from the same supplier.

One of the first references to chocolate in French literature was made by Mme. de Sévigné. In February 1671 she recommended it to her daughter Françoise as a cure for insomnia.

The ever-anxious-to-be-modish marquise probably overdid the chocolate because soon after she complained that although the stuff flattered you for a while, it caused dizziness, palpitations and a burning sensation. Apparently she couldn't keep away from it for long, however, because in October of the same year she wrote Françoise that she tried some as an after-dinner digestive and "it acted as it was supposed to."

Brillat-Savarin (1755–1826), the erudite lawyer-gastronome from Belley, took up the torch from Sévigné and touted chocolate as a stimulant and restorative for night workers, intellectuals suffering from a mental block and for any soul in torment.

His personal recipe for combatting old-age lassitude was a cup of strong chocolate well dosed with ambergris (a waxy substance from the sperm whale) and prepared according to the precepts of Mme. d'Arestrel, mother superior of Belley's Convent of the Visitation.

A good chocolate should be made the day before in an earthenware coffeepot, she counseled. "The overnight rest provides a velvety concentration which makes it only better. The Good Lord can't be offended by this little supplement for He Himself is 'all excellence.'"

No doubt it was in deference to the good gourmand Sisters of France like Mme. d'Arestrel that the pâtissiers of Paris created an éclair in the form of a brioche and baptized it "Une Religieuse."

Early in the nineteenth century a clever Parisian pharmacist, Sulpice Debauve, allied himself with a confectioner named Gallais to produce a line of "agreeable medicaments."

Chocolate with an additive of iron salts became the recommended tonic for those whose pallor indicated circulation problems. Chocolat des Dames, bonbons injected with orange-blossom water, promised relief from migraines and shocks to the morale. Chocolate incorporating almond milk was prescribed for sore throats, gastritis and indispositions resulting from overheated temperaments.

Debauve & Gallais were endorsed by Brillat-Savarin for their excellent chocolate at moderate prices. The premises at 26-30 rue des Sts.-Pères became the rendezvous of chic Paris. The stylish shop with the elegant fan windows and impressive horseshoe-curved oak counter has been attributed to Percier and Fontaine, the architects who shaped the taste of all Europe and were also responsible for the design of the Arc du Carrousel in the Tuileries.

The shop is classed by the Beaux-Arts. Although now reduced by half, Percier and Fontaine's original concept is clearly evident when viewed from across the street.

For a taste of Paris Past, Debauve & Gallais is an endearing place to visit. The chocolates are made up to their specifications although the "medical additions" have gone by the boards. Students from the École de Médecine across the way drop in regularly to see Mme. Geneviève for a sachet of "orangettes" or the fix of a nougat enrobed in dark chocolate.

The *bouchée* is a Paris habit. Generally it refers to a piece of candy, bought in a single unit. It is somewhat larger than the bonbon, priced at approximately $1 for one, and is a marvelously satisfying pickup and munch en route to the next appointment.

The Hédiard shop in the arcade at the rond-point des Champs-Élysées has a *truffe au café* that merits serious attention. Jadis et Gourmand, nearby on the avenue Franklin Roosevelt, is run like a fashion boutique with novelties presented regularly. Preposterously appealing are the *nattes* and the *tresses*. The chocolate has been braided into thick, long plaits studded either with mixed nuts or mixed dried fruits.

Not long ago I made a trip to Japan. Advised that the Japanese liked to receive small presents, I bought a dozen tiny boxes from Jadis et Gourmand. Each contained seventy grams of chocolate coffee beans, which I find one of the most alluring *péchés mignons* on earth. The Japanese, who have their own refinement, averaged three bites to a bean and loved them. My status was saved.

Similar chocolate Grains de Café are available at the Maison du Chocolat, the Marquise de Sévigné, Fauchon and other good *confiseurs*. For me they are the perfect *péché mignon*, a dainty little deviltry combining the arm-in-arm flavors of chocolate and coffee in a manner for a *petite marquise*.

L'Épicerie is a grocery boutique at 51 rue St.-Louis-en-l'Île with a strong concentration on chocolate specialties. Because a little knowledge is a lot of fun, l'Épicerie provides a genealogy of the beans that went into the various bonbons. This is an amiable manner of becoming comparative in the virtues of Venezuela, Trinidad and Indonesia versus Ivory Coast, Madagascar and Ceylon.

I've long been convinced that a touch of Sybaris is a therapeutic thing for everybody. One way to get it without cutting yourself off at the socks is a grand high tea at the Ritz, the móst Ritz of all Ritzes. Jean Marie Osmont the pastry chef has the elite distinction of being a Meilleur Ouvrier de France and his chocolate desserts on the trolley are sublime.

The hour of tea is a grace note of the day. One of the most sumptuous "tearooms" in the world is the Salon Pompadour of the Hôtel Meurice. Gilded *boiseries,* crystal chandeliers, sparkling mirrors, the portrait of the marquise de Pompadour, a pianist playing in the background for the fortunate few at the marble-topped tables. The pièce de résistance on the trolley is a rich chocolate mousse cake. The discreet and unsuspected retreat is one of the treasures of Paris classed by the Beaux-Arts.

I never pass through the place de la Concorde without thinking of Mme. Lafarge with her knitting needles and her folding chair. On the place de la Concorde is the Hôtel Crillon. Here on chairs far more comfortable than the folding chairs that still are a fixture in the gardens of the Tuileries I can forget all about Mme. Lafarge as I enjoy a beautifully served four-o'clock with a few of the Crillon's chocolate caprices.

My self-styled Route du Chocolat led me through a galaxy of restaurants I love for the imaginative way they handle fish and fowl, vegetables and meat.

"You're just as marvelous with chocolate," I said to the multi-starred chefs of Chiberta, Le Divellec, Gerard Besson, le Petit Bedon, and Tan Dinh.

Chocolate is a theme with a myriad of variations. Sweetly the chefs gave me the recipes of the desserts that are the running favorites with their exacting customers.

But for a quintessential interpretation of the rule of opposites, I paid a visit to the sixth-floor quai Voltaire apartment of Nena Prentice, one of the most gifted young American painters in Paris.

Here looking out over the subtly dramatic skies of the Île-de-France, she served me the traditional afternoon *goûter* of the French schoolchild . . . chocolate on good honest bread. It is one of the Great Simplicities.

Marrons Glacés: A French Chestnut Confection

BY JOAN NATHAN

〜

editor's note

Before I went to Paris, the only time I encountered chestnuts was when they were roasted in carts on the street corners of New York and Philadelphia. (I still love to smell those chestnuts roasting, a sure sign that colder weather is on the way.) But in Paris there are crepes filled with *crème de marrons*, fresh *châtaignes* in the markets, and of course, the precious *marrons glacés*, the subject of this piece, which was featured in December 1994.

On the occasion of the ninth birthday of Gaultier, the oldest child of the French family I lived with, Madame de Curel made a splendid birthday cake: four chocolate layers with *crème de marrons* spread between each, enrobed in dark chocolate with round, colored candies on top. One of Gaultier's gifts was a package of *marrons glacés*, so it seems Joan Nathan is on to something with this chestnut-birthday connection.

JOAN NATHAN writes often about food for a number of magazines and newspapers and is also the author of *Jewish Cooking in America* (Alfred A. Knopf, 1994; the 1998 expanded edition was the companion volume to the PBS series *Jewish Cooking in America with Joan Nathan*), *The Jewish Holiday Baker*, *The Jewish Holiday Kitchen*, and *The Children's Jewish Holiday Kitchen*, all published by Knopf.

S ome people go to France in search of vintage Bordeaux; others, to see how many three-star restaurants they can enjoy in a week. One of my trips led to yet a different pursuit—uncovering the story behind France's magical *marrons glacés*, the chestnut confection that rivals in cost—and desirability—the finest hand-dipped chocolates.

My romance with *marrons glacés* has not been a passing fancy. It started when I was in college during my junior year abroad, when a young Frenchman offered me a gold-paper-wrapped *marron glacé* at Christmas. I have been hooked ever since. In Washington, D.C., many years later, my husband celebrated the birth of our first child by bringing me a meal of my favorite things: a Moroccan couscous, a bottle of good champagne, and a box of imported *marrons glacés*.

My search for the story behind *marrons glacés* grew out of a mid-October trip to the Haute-Savoie for a few days of hiking. On one of our daily rambles in the Alps, we stopped in a tiny village near Megève for picnic fare. Having bought fresh walnut bread and some local Reblochon and Tomme de Savoie cheese to go with our Savoyard *vin nouveau,* we went to the village *pâtisserie* and asked for *marrons glacés*. The woman behind the counter stared. "*Marrons glacés!*" she said. "*Mais non!* We don't sell them until the winter—they are for *Noël!*" I needed to know more.

My journey would take me from the Alps to Annecy and then down the back roads near Saint-Pierre-de-Chartreuse. I wended my way through the mountains, crossing the Rhône in Valence, and finally reached the ruddier terrain of the Ardèche, a culinary border between the earthiness of Provence's cuisine and the sophistication of the Lyonnais kitchen. Seventy percent of French *marrons glacés* are made in this *département,* and before leaving the Alps I had set up an appointment with the president of the Ardèchois company Clément Faugier, France's oldest producer of the confection.

At one point on my drive I passed chestnut and walnut stands where men outfitted in royal blue jumpsuits encouraged prospective buyers to sample the nuts with *vin nouveau* poured from a wooden keg. I stopped and tasted the offerings—tiny chestnuts, the kind for cooking, not for candying; and walnuts of that and the previous year's harvest. Comparing the dry to the still-damp-with-freshness nuts was the game played here.

At noon I stopped at a tiny restaurant on the side of a winding Ardèche road, the likes of which make this area a testing ground for sports-car drivers. The restaurant had no name, merely a simple wooden sign reading "Restaurant Rural." Inside, the one waiter (husband of the chef, I later found out) ushered me to a table where three other people were already seated. Food was served family-style, and on the table was a *baguette* and a carafe of red wine. I broke off a piece of the bread and set it down so that it rested on its top, not its base, only to be cautioned by my eating companions. "That is bad luck!" they advised. "Keep the bread right side up!"

My faux pas broke the ice, and we started talking. Two of the diners, a couple, worked on an assembly line in a factory in nearby Privas, the industrial town that is the center of the *marron glacé* industry. The other diner was a chef who had been out picking *cèpes* for his small restaurant near Valence. When I told them of my quest, the three began talking about *marrons glacés.*

As we ate our way through the local *charcuterie,* a *daube de boeuf,* and a crisp, paper-thin potato pancake called *crique,* my new acquaintances explained that *marrons glacés*—made from the largest and most toothsome chestnuts—had been affordable only for the very rich until the last century. The smaller chestnuts were ground into flour and used in a dense, heavy bread called *le pain de bois,* the bread of wood. From the twelfth up to the twentieth century, chestnuts, not potatoes, were the staple starch in French purees and soups. *Cousinat,* a rich soup made of cooked chestnuts and cream, was a basic dish of the poor until well into this century, and many a Frenchman recalls enjoying it as a child.

Coffee drunk and the less-than-six-dollar bill paid, I bade my dining companions adieu and continued down the hairpin curves to the spa town of Vals-les-Bains. Here I met Claude Boiron, president of Clément Faugier, and furthered my education in the matter of *marrons glacés.*

A six-foot-plus man with firm chin and short-cropped, slightly graying hair, Boiron was born into the chestnut business. Before his family bought control of Clément Faugier, they had been chestnut merchants, at least as far back as 1804 and probably earlier.

Before permitting me to visit the Faugier factory, in Privas, Boiron whisked me off in his Peugeot to the tiny village of Vesseaux, a forlorn place with beautiful yet ailing chestnut trees growing in red-earthed fields where an occasional goat chomps on low leaves. "Here the commercial *marron glacé* business began," said Boiron as he jumped out of the car and picked up a large, flat nut that had fallen from a tree. "This is a *bouche rouge,* or red-mouthed *marron,* the finest chestnut in France and the one reserved for *marrons glacés.* These trees are hundreds of years old."

Boiron explained that a *châtaigne,* or ordinary sweet chestnut, comprises two or three nuts growing together in one shell. The *marron* is a variety with a shell containing only one large nut. "It will be a good year for chestnuts," he said, smiling. Warm and dry weather had aided pollination and flowering in spring and early summer, and lightly humid weather in August and September had resulted in unusually large nuts.

As we walked among the trees Boiron continued with the story of *marrons glacés* in the Ardèche. Until the late nineteenth century, when a plague wiped out the silkworm, the Ardèche-Lyons area had been a center of the silk industry in France. Nimble-fingered peasants unwound the silkworms' cocoons and spun and wove the silk in factories.

In 1882 Clément Faugier, a twenty-three-year-old public-service engineer, watched the former silk workers harvesting chestnuts and came up with an ingenious idea. Why not employ these agile people as chestnut peelers and mass-produce *marrons glacés?* Faugier abandoned his slide rule and logarithm tables to join forces with a candymaker, and they constructed the first factory in the world for candying chestnuts. From the beginning Faugier purchased *bouche rouge* chestnuts from the Boiron family, and the relationship endured. In the early 1960s the Boirons bought controlling interest of the company from Faugier's heirs.

For years the former silk workers peeled the chestnuts. Later, prisoners in the local jails were relieved of the duties that occupied their counterparts elsewhere in France—making shoes and weaving baskets—and obliged to peel chestnuts instead. But at the turn of the century the *maladie de l'encre,* or ink disease, hurt the chestnut trees of the Ardèche, and the Faugier company began buying frozen peeled chestnuts from Italy.

"People keep saying that the *maladie de l'encre,* which came from Portugal, is what destroyed our chestnut trees," explained Boiron. "I believe it was something else." He pointed to the goats in the distance. "The Ardèche was once an agricultural area with many goats, the source of our famous *chèvre.* These goats would eat the low branches of the chestnut trees, keeping the trees pruned and healthy. The farmers left, taking their goats with them. With no goats to trim the trees, diseases hurt the trees more readily."

Boiron then shared a bit of the more distant history of *marrons glacés*. The first written mention of the confection comes from the court of Louis XIV: *Marrons glacés* were served in the Galerie des Glaces at Versailles. But candied chestnuts, like candied fruits, were almost certainly eaten earlier, as far back as the 1500s. For centuries at Christmastime French candymakers would provide house-made *marrons glacés* for their wealthy clientele.

It was the Romans who brought chestnuts to France. Charlemagne, it is said, often enjoyed roasted chestnuts along with *vin nouveau*. The custom of pairing the two seasonal offerings continues to this day in the Ardèche, at roasting parties in the late fall and early winter.

As we drove through the countryside on our way to the factory in Privas, Boiron recalled tales his father had told of peasants from Vesseaux and the nearby Massif Central bringing their chestnuts to Paris and selling them, roasted, on the sidewalks. The nuts were delicious—and great hand warmers. The vendors often slept on street corners in the capital but would return to their villages with small fortunes.

The oldest written recipe for *marrons glacés,* from 1717, includes sixteen steps. All but the first of these steps—peeling the nuts—are still performed today in the Faugier factory. (The company continues to purchase frozen peeled chestnuts from Italy.)

When the nuts arrive at Faugier they are wrapped, five or six at a time, in very fine gauze. This protects them from breakage during confectioning. They are then simmered for three to seven hours in vast vats in order to cook the flesh and make the exteriors more receptive to being coated with the sugar syrup.

The cooked nuts are immersed in a vanilla syrup for forty-eight hours. Osmosis occurs, with the syrup progressively replacing the nuts' cellular juices. It is necessary to keep careful watch over this process so that the concentration of sugar in the syrup remains constant and crystallization does not occur. Finally, the *marrons glacés* are placed on a rack to dry before being gently wrapped and boxed.

Even with careful handling, some nuts are broken in the confectioning process. It was Clément Faugier, the engineer and practical businessman, who thought of a by-product for the broken *marrons.* In 1885, three years after his factory opened, he invented *crème de marrons,* basically a puree made from the broken glazed nuts. This is the key ingredient in the famous dessert Mont-Blanc: *Crème de marrons* is put through a ricer, and the resulting spaghetti-like strands are pressed into a round mold, which is then filled with Chantilly cream.

Faugier also thought of a way of packaging his *marrons glacés* in shock-resistant, virtually airtight containers for export. In 1890 he bet a friend that his product would not be damaged in taste or appearance after shipment to a distant place. He sent a few containers to an acquaintance in Zanzibar, who then returned them to Faugier. The candied nuts arrived in perfect condition. Thus began a worldwide export business, which boomed until World War I. Recovery was slow after the war, but in 1924, in response to Prohibition, the Faugier company started exporting cans of chestnuts in cognac to the United States and experienced a second peak.

Today there are seven major producers of *marrons glacés* in France, with Faugier claiming the largest market share. French *marrons glacés* are sold to fifty-eight countries, including Japan, where the confection is relished year-round.

"In choosing the costly candy," explained Boiron, "just remember that the high price should be justified by good quality. The skin of the *marrons glacés* should be translucent, and the glaze should be thin enough so that you can see the lines of the chestnut through it. The color should be uneven; an even color means the *marrons* have been sulfurized or otherwise treated."

My daughter—the child whose birth was celebrated so deliciously—is now approaching her seventeenth birthday, and as she spent last year abroad expanding her culinary horizons, it seems the perfect time for her to taste her first *marron glacé*. I hope that she savors this holiday treat as much as I did so many years ago.

Marrons glacés are available by mail from the following sources:

Balducci's Mail Order Division, 42-25 Twelfth Street, Long Island City, NY 11101. Tel.: 800-225-3822.

Dean & DeLuca, 560 Broadway, New York, NY 10012. Tel.: 800-221-7714.

Maison Glass Delicacies, 111 East Fifty-eighth Street, New York, NY 10022. Tel.: 212-755-3316.

Bibliothèque

The Food of France, Waverly Root, Vintage, 1992, originally published in hardback by Alfred A. Knopf in 1958. Root says in the first chapter that "Eating habits are part of our social habits, part of our culture, part of the environment, mental and physical, in which we live." He proves exactly that as he makes his way around France, revealing the ways in which French food has shaped the French character. There are individual chapters on Île-de-France, Normandy, Burgundy, and Champagne. I could go on and on about the excellence of this book, but Samuel Chamberlain's words in the introduction say it much better: "This is a work for posterity. It will be entirely reliable decades from now. Present and future generations will rejoice in this definitive treatise."

M. F. K. Fisher, Julia Child and Alice Waters: Celebrating the Pleasures of the Table, Joan Reardon, Harmony Books, 1994. Although this book is a tribute to three women who changed the way Americans think about food and cooking, it is also a book about the common thread that inspired and united them: France and *la cuisine française.* I found it absolutely fascinating, and while I already greatly admired each of these writer-cooks, I was surprised to learn the degree to which they were pioneers in the food world. I do not think it's an exaggeration to state that due to Julia Child's PBS television series the Food Network exists and thrives today; that due to M. F. K. Fisher's passionate writing on gastronomy, cookbooks and food publications are more popular than ever; and due to Alice Waters's insistence upon fresh, seasonal food, we have more farmers' markets across the country (twenty-eight in New York City alone!). De rigueur reading for anyone interested in food, France, and America.

Absinthe: History in a Bottle, Barnaby Conrad III, Chronicle Books, 1988. Filled with old photos, drawings, and reproductions of artwork, posters, and bottle labels, this is an alluring history of the infamous, anise-flavored libation also known as *la fée verte* (the green fairy). On March 16, 1915, the production, distribution, and sale of absinthe was banned in France. Various groups had tried to ban it years earlier (absinthe was believed to be the cause of alcoholism, suicide, general insanity, epilepsy, etc., and that wormwood and its essence, thujone, was the ruinous and dangerous ingredient), but not until the beginning of the First World War was the law made official. Absinthe also had its supporters, but they had no sway over the army: it was determined that absinthe promoted drunkenness among soldiers, and it was crucial for the troops to be completely sober and united against Germany. In 1922 the government allowed the sale of wormwood-free absinthe, known today as *pastis,* available from producers such as Pernod, Ricard, and Henri Bardouin. Conrad uncovers a trove of details about this controversial drink, including a molecular structure comparison of thujone and THC, the psychoactive ingredient in marijuana. An unusually entertaining read.

Cheese Primer, Steven Jenkins, Workman Publishing Co., 1996. Though not exclusively about French cheeses, cheeses from France figure large in this excellent cheese bible. Jenkins—the first American to be awarded France's *Chevalier du Taste-Fromage*—created and/or revitalized the cheese counters at such New York food emporiums as Dean & DeLuca and Fairway. In addition to presenting the cheeses of France and twelve other regions of the world, he explains how cheese is made, the basics of butterfat, and the seasons that are best for making and eating cheese (yes, most cheeses have a season, which is determined by pasturage—vegetation that cows, goats, and sheep have been eating at the time of milking). For travelers, Jenkins provides the names of cheeses—most never exported—to try. This is the most comprehensive book on cheese I've ever seen.

The Joy of Coffee: The Essential Guide to Buying, Brewing and Enjoying, Corby Kummer, 1995, hardcover; 1999, paperback, both Chapters Publishing (Houghton Mifflin Company). A comment I hear often from people who visit France is that the coffee is so much better there. It's my opinion that it's not the coffee that's better but the quality of the dairy products. Anyway, if you're a coffee drinker, you can judge for yourself, and I've included this book here for those who want to know more about the elixir they love. I find this to be the best volume on coffee ever published. Food journalist Kummer is a senior editor at *The Atlantic Monthly* and has contributed to *Martha Stewart Living, New York, Food & Wine*, etc. He covers coffee plantations, cupping, roasting, grinding, storing (the best place, if you drink it every day, is not in the freezer, as many people mistakenly believe), and brewing, plus separate chapters on espresso, caffeine vs. decaf, and a country-by-country guide. There are also recipes for baked goods that pair particularly well with coffee (I've made almost all of them and can vouch that they are especially yummy; the Unbeatable Biscotti are the best ones ever, and I've baked a *lot* of biscotti).

Cookbooks

It seems to me that one cannot separate food—especially French food—from the rest of French history. Really good cookbooks—ones that offer tried-and-true, authentic recipes, as well as detailed commentary on the food traditions of the country or region and the history behind the recipes and the ingredients unique to the cuisine—are just as essential to travel as guidebooks. I read these cookbooks the way other people read novels; therefore, the authors have to be more than just good cooks, and the books have to be more than just cookbooks. All of the authors and books listed below fit the bill. These titles stand quite apart from the multitude of general French cookbooks crowding bookstore shelves.

The Cooking of Provincial France, M. F. K. Fisher (with Julia Child as consultant), Time-Life Books, 1968. The collaborative effort to produce this book (one of the volumes in the Foods of the World series) was extraordinary, the likes of which we'll probably never see again (a separate, spiral-bound recipe booklet accompanied each hardbound volume). This is long out of print and hard to find, but it does turn up at tag sales and in used-book stores.

The Taste of France, Robert Freson, Stewart, Tabori & Chang, 1983. This is my most favorite overall French cookbook. Fabulous photographs by Freson (who also took the photos for *Patricia Wells at Home in Provence*) are paired with text by leading food writers including Anne Willan, Alan Davidson, Jill Norman, and Richard Olney.

French Country Cooking, Elizabeth David, A Jill Norman Book (Dorling Kindersley), London, 1987; originally published by John Lehmann, 1951. Although I don't cook much from this book, I've learned a lot from it, and with the beautiful, color reproductions of food artworks by Bonnard, Gauguin, Chardin, Signac, Monet, Renoir, etc., it is one of my most treasured volumes.

French Cooking en Famille, Jacques Burdick, Fawcett Columbine (Ballantine Books), 1989. *En famille* refers to ordinary French households and the simple, good, and economical meals they cook and eat every day. Burdick adds dollops of social and cultural history as well.

The Cook and the Gardener: A Year of Recipes and Writings From the French Countryside, Amanda Hesser, W. W. Norton & Company, 1999. Hesser is a reporter for the "Dining In/Dining Out" section of *The New York Times,* and this is an account of her year in Burgundy when she cooked for Anne Willan, cookbook author and founder of École de Cuisine La Varenne. It's also the story of the gardener and his wife on the château property, and it brings readers and cooks a reminder that the stuff of a garden—our own, from a farmers' market, or the supermarket—should never be very far away from a kitchen.

For the very best in French techniques and classic recipes:

Larousse Gastronomique: The New American Edition of the World's Greatest Culinary Encyclopedia, edited by Jennifer Harvey Lang, Crown Publishers, Librarie Larousse, 1984; English text, 1988; reprinted 1995. The ne plus ultra of encyclopedias but also a cookbook, with four thousand recipes. With the exception of fiddleheads and ramps, absolutely everything I've consulted this gigantic book for I've found.

La Varenne Pratique, Anne Willan, Dorling Kindersley, London, 1989; first published in the U.S. by Crown Publishers, 1990. With over twenty-five hundred color photographs.

Mastering the Art of French Cooking, Volume I, Julia Child, Louisette Bertholle, and Simone Beck, Knopf, 1961. *Volume II,* Julia Child and Simone Beck, 1970.

Not a cookbook, but a very special culinary classic:

The Physiology of Taste or Meditations on Transcendental Gastronomy, Jean Anthelme Brillat-Savarin, translated by M. F. K. Fisher and with illustrations by Wayne Thiebaud, Counterpoint (by arrangement with Arion Press), 1994, distributed by Publishers Group West; original translation copyright 1949, The George Macy Companies, Inc.

And for baking, these are some authoritative volumes:

Paris Boulangerie-Pâtisserie, Linda Dannenberg, Clarkson Potter, 1994. The recipes I've made from this book are great (in particular the *pain d'épices* honey cake from Pâtisserie Lerch), and they're from thirteen legendary Paris bakeries such as Stohrer, Ladurée, Dalloyau, and Ganachaud. Also included is a directory of mail-order sources and stores in the U.S. and restaurant supply stores in Paris.

A *Passion for Chocolate*, Maurice and Jean-Jacques Bernachon, translated and adapted for the American kitchen by Rose Levy Beranbaum, Morrow, 1989. Fabulous recipes from the famous Bernachon chocolatier in Lyon.

The Pie and Pastry Bible, Rose Levy Beranbaum, Scribner, 1998. Though a definitive volume on pies and pastries of *all* types, there are many recipes for French and French-style creations.

Great Pies & Tarts, Carole Walter, Clarkson Potter, 1998. Another very good overall baking book with many recipes for open fruit tarts, French fruit tarts with pastry cream, etc.

Martha Stewart's Pies & Tarts, Clarkson Potter, 1985. Nearly all the recipes in this classic book are in the French style.

About French Wine

Larousse Wines and Vineyards of France, Arcade Publishing, Little, Brown and Company, 1991. Both a dictionary and an encyclopedia, this tome (639 pages) is, in my opinion, the best single volume on French winegrowing areas. This comprehensive work covers every topic relevant to French wine and was written by sixty-eight authors, each one an expert in his or her chosen field. Maps, over five hundred color photographs, charts, in-depth entries on vinification, glasses, soil, tasting, champagne secrets, etc., and two glossaries—one of French tasting terms and the other of technical terms—complete the package.

Adventures on the Wine Route: A Wine Buyer's Tour of France, Kermit Lynch, Farrar, Straus & Giroux, 1988, hardcover; North Point Press, 1995, paperback; preface by Richard Olney. Kermit Lynch, a Berkeley, California, wine merchant, is a wonderful storyteller, especially when he's talking about wine, which he is, of course, in this book. Besides being entertaining, readers will learn a lot about French wine—and the men and women who make this wine—while reading of Lynch's journeys. His is a unique book, and for visitors who want to read about wine regions close to Paris, there are chapters on the Loire, Beaujolais, Côte d'Or, Chablis, and Maconnais-Chalonnais. Every chapter is great, but the one I remember most is "Southern Rhône," in which he goes to a renowned restaurant, on two different occasions, and causes an (unintended) scene, the first time about credit cards (they weren't accepted, and he didn't have enough cash) and the second about a wine that was off (and—*quelle surprise*—it was an expensive wine). M. F. K. Fisher called this "one of the pleasantest and truest books about wine I've ever read," and I call it a candidate for the de rigueur list.

Wines and Vineyards of Character and Charm in France, Fodor's Rivages (Fodor's Travel Publications), 1998. *Finalement*, an English translation of this Rivages guide, popular for years among Europeans. French-wine enthusiasts will find this an indispensable guide, and wine regions close to Paris are included. Each section includes detailed road maps, color photographs, and practical information. Also indicated are languages spoken by the vintner (this is worth noting; unlike at wineries in the States—especially in California—you will almost always meet the vintner/owner or a family member, not a representative). Most of the vineyards included are privately owned, and negotiants and cooperative cellars that sell wines direct from the property are also included.

Alexis Lichine's Guide to the Wines and Vineyards of France, Alexis Lichine, Alfred A. Knopf, 1989, fourth edition. Lichine—former wine exporter, grower and winemaker (Château Prieuré-Lichine), author, and all-around wine authority—really knew how to bring wine to life. Even though this wonderful book is out of print (Lichine passed away in 1989, and Prieure-Lichine was sold in 1999), it can still be found at some wine shops and bookstores. This is a book for both travelers—with chapters on suggested tours, hotel and restaurant recommendations (though these can't be relied upon due to the passage of so many years, some of this information is still accurate)—and wine buyers, with lengthy profiles of each winegrowing area (twenty-one in all, including a chapter on cognac, Armagnac, and calvados) and chapters on storing and serving wine, tasting wine, wine and health, and buying wine (which includes a vintage chart).

About Wine in General

The Oxford Companion to Wine, edited by Jancis Robinson, Oxford University Press, 1994.

Jancis Robinson's Wine Course, BBC Books, London, 1995.

Tasting Pleasure: Confessions of a Wine Lover, Jancis Robinson, Viking, 1997. French wines are mentioned or featured throughout the twenty-four essays.

Vineyard Tales: Reflections on Wine, Gerald Asher, Chronicle Books, 1996. Six of the twenty-nine essays are about a variety of French wines.

Making Sense of Wine, Matt Kramer, Quill (William Morrow), 1989.

À Table!
(To the Table! Dinner Is Served)

I can hear the glass door of the café grate on the sand as I open it. I can recall the smell of every hour. In the morning that of eggs frizzling in butter, the pungent cigarette, coffee and bad cognac; at five o'clock the fragrant odor of absinthe; and soon after the steaming soup ascends from the kitchen; and as the evening advances, the mingled smells of cigarettes, coffee, and weak beer.

—George Moore,
CONFESSIONS OF A YOUNG MAN

A Clean, Well-Lighted Café
in Montparnasse

BY ADAIR LARA

~~

editor's note

To my knowledge, Adair Lara has never entered one of those annual "Write like Hemingway" contests, but if she ever did, she'd be a contender for first prize if this piece was the submission. A staff columnist for the *San Francisco Chronicle* since 1989, Lara writes a popular (and often very funny) personal column twice weekly for the back page. Her award-winning columns have been published in several collections: *Welcome to Earth, Mom* (1992) and *At Adair's House: More Columns by America's Formerly Single Mom* (1995), both published by Chronicle Books, and *Slowing Down in a Speeded-Up World* (Conari Press, 1994). She has also contributed pieces to numerous magazines, including *Cosmopolitan, Reader's Digest, Parenting, Glamour, Redbook, Ladies' Home Journal, Departures, Westways,* and *Good Housekeeping,* and teaches first-person writing.

Lara has traveled to France frequently, often with the Bill of this piece. At the time she made this trip to Paris, Bill was her friend (and my publishing colleague), but a short while later he became her husband. He still is, and they travel whenever they can.

Paris—It was a pleasant café in Montparnasse, the famous artists' quarter of Paris. An American sat at a small table, took out a yellow pad and began to write. A cup of coffee steamed at her elbow. It was good to sit in a café and watch the people go in and out.

Before coming to Paris, she had read *A Moveable Feast* by Ernest Hemingway, who lived here in the 1920s and wrote in the cafés. Her friend Bill had hated the book, in which Hemingway wrote terrible things about people who were nice to him in Paris but had the poor timing to die before he did. Bill was afraid she would start stringing all her sentences together with *and* too, but it was Paris in the warm summer, and she did not care what Bill said. He had gone to the American Library without her and would stay carefully away all morning to let her write.

She had chosen her café after some deliberation. It was a clean, well-lighted place on the avenue Julien LeClerc, near where Hemingway had penned his short stories at the Closeries de Lilias, where F. Scott Fitzgerald had written at the Dôme, and where stacks of other authors had written at the Deux Magots.

All the writers had horrid cheap flats—that's why they went to cafés. The American and her friend had a cheap flat too, owned by a depressed Frenchwoman named Marie-Claude, who nailed all the shutters closed, turned off the gas, took the TV and told a friend to rent it if he could.

So conditions were perfect to nudge the American with the very overdue novel and the tiny, dark flat into the cafés, where, she thought, if she sat where Hemingway sat and drank what he drank (though it seemed a tad early for a rum St. James), she might write a novel too.

She would sip the good Parisian coffee and watch the French hurry to the metro to work, and write about the way the ladybugs had swarmed on the bush in the sea-damped hollows of Lagunitas when she was eight and afraid of her father.

"Write one true sentence," Hemingway said, and the American thought, then wrote, "I hate that kind of advice."

She liked better what Steinbeck said: "Don't start by trying to make the book chronological. Just take a period. Then try to remember it so clearly that you can see things: what colors and how warm or cold and how you got there. Then try to remember people. And then just tell what happened. It is important to tell what people looked like, how they walked, what they wore, what they ate."

Next to her an elegant young couple were chatting and smoking. The French know that smoking is bad for you, but they don't care. The American, temporarily at a standstill with the ladybugs, wrote down everything they were wearing, her shiny black flats and his pink tie, and everything they ate and drank. Then she nibbled the end of her pen.

After a while the American put away her yellow pad. She was tired and sad and happy, as she always was after trying to write, and though she felt she had done some very bad writing indeed, she would not know how bad until she read it over the next day.

She sipped her cold coffee and looked around. Mozart and jazz played softly in the background, and a good cup of coffee cost four francs, and they left you alone, not even coming to wipe the table, but maybe it was not the right place for inspiration to come. She frowned. What was wrong?

It was pleasant. It was clean. It was in the heart of Montparnasse. It was McDonald's.

This column originally appeared in the August 20, 1991, edition of the *San Francisco Chronicle*. Copyright © 1991 by Adair Lara. Reprinted with permission of the author.

Par for Paris

BY PETER HELLMAN

∽

editor's note

When Peter Hellman first brought this piece to my attention, I had my doubts about its inclusion in this book. "An entire piece," I asked, "on a nondescript, unknown little restaurant you stumbled upon in 1990?" But when I reached the last page, I knew he really understood the spirit of The

Collected Traveler series. You will, of course, make your own discoveries, find your own versions of *Au Regent*. And even if they shut their doors in time, they will occupy a special place in your memories of Paris.

PETER HELLMAN is a contributing editor at *New York* and *Metropolitan Home* and has also written for *Travel Holiday, The New York Times, Esquire, Redbook, Food & Wine, Saveur,* and *Garden Design.* Additionally, he is the author of *When Courage Was Stronger Than Fear* (see *"Le Kiosque" bibliothèque* for details), *The American Wine Handbook, The Auschwitz Album,* and *Heroes: Tales From the Israeli Wars.*

I t had been three years since my last visit to Paris—that long, too, since I'd lunched at a species of restaurant that doesn't exist back in the food capitals of America. It's a step up from a café, bistro, or brasserie. Good as those places can be, the menu is often a bit too casual, the style too raffish. On the other hand, the place I had in mind was a full step down from a "fancy" restaurant. Even a single Michelin star would put it out of range. No, I was after lunch at a modest restaurant unknown outside its immediate neighborhood, where the chef was neither lionized nor aspired to be, where the price of an unabbreviated, prix-fixe lunch would be low, yet where the precise standards of French dining are upheld—perhaps even more so than at those famous French restaurants where tourists flock. A place where spirit and skills are taken for granted, not put on display. I was looking for the sort of little restaurant, in short, at which we Americans marvel the way the French marvel at our jazz. We do what comes naturally, and so do they.

So there I was on the Left Bank, at one o'clock on a magnificently gentle winter afternoon, turning onto the rue du Cherche-Midi (a street unfamiliar to me) for no other reason than it stretched long and narrow, its stately yet warm nineteenth-century facades receding to blue sky.

A blackboard stood outside the first prospect I came upon.

Instead of the usual three or four scribbled plats du jour, this one was ambitious enough to list eight—including *raie au beurre noir* (skate in black butter), an old standard that you can forget about finding stateside at any price. The place looked okay. But only one table was taken and the matron, standing by the bar, struck me as a bit too severe, her hair pulled back tightly, her makeup a shade strident. I was certain that were I to drop a fork, she'd make me feel guilty—the uncouth American with jittery fingers.

Half a block farther, I peeked through the curtains of a grander establishment. Tables were distantly spaced and great vases of dried flowers and reeds sounded a note of autumnal splendor. A dark-suited clientele reigned here. In my red-wool cardigan and open collar, I would have made myself uncomfortable, even in the unlikely event that nobody else did. In any case, the least expensive prix-fixe menu was $27—hardly an outrageous sum for a good lunch, but more than I cared to spend.

Farther along the rue du Cherche-Midi, I came upon Au Regent, a rather too stately name for a small restaurant with a bright blue-enameled facade. A few reprints of good critical notices posted in the window didn't impress me. Raves can be bought. Even if deserved, they often signal a decline in the kitchen: A rash of attention can flood the place with eager diners, overwhelming the chef and the dining-room staff. A peek through the lace curtains, however, filled me with optimism.

The matron of this place seemed correct but not haughty. Behind her, the door to the kitchen was propped open, a sign to me that nothing needed hiding. I glimpsed the chef, resplendent in his toque and whites, a midfiftyish man moving quickly, yet unrushed. The clincher, in this quick perusal, was the clientele: one table of businesspeople, one at which a very old couple was finishing lunch, and one where a father sat with his two near-adolescent daughters on best behavior. That mix, so typical of French society, was where

I wanted to ease in. At less than $20 for a full meal on the posted menu, the price was right.

As I'd guessed, Madame did not make me feel uncomfortable for arriving without a reservation or business dress. She seated me by the window, next to those two decorous girls and their father. Now I began to observe the little things that make a superior French restaurant tick: My large linen napkin was spotless, butter arrived in a covered tub, and the bread was fresh and of good character. A young waiter, immaculately groomed, swiftly cleared an empty table, while at the same time scanning adjoining tables to see what might be needed. His fast eyes reminded me of the first time, as a bumpkin in Manhattan, I had been aware of real service: At the precise moment I realized I was thirsty, a waiter appeared to fill my glass. He'd been watching. That, too, was in a French restaurant.

Having ordered *terrine de volaille* (chicken pâté) to start, I was surprised to be served instead two tiny quenelles of salmon set in red lobster sauce. I was about to call the waiter to point out the mistake, when one taste stopped me. The quenelles were egg-white light, their sauce pitting a slight tomato tang against the gentler assertiveness of the lobster.

Only when the pâté arrived did I realize that the first dish had been an opening teaser from the chef. The pâté delivered the flavor of a real bird, a reminder that every French market carries a variety of chickens (including the individually numbered *poulet de Bresse*), which may cost more than our supermarket counterparts but which also deliver more flavor.

The two scoops of pâté were mounded on slices of grilled white bread infused with butter and a few dark raisins. (When was the last time you were served bread that was grilled rather than toasted?) The plate was garnished with carrot and beet shavings, lettuce, and parsley, running in a bright ribbon between the two portions of the appetizer. A cross-hatching of jellied chicken-broth strips topped the two mounds of pâté.

The presentation of the appetizer was far more refined and beautiful than the rather plain decor of Au Regent would suggest. In fact, I can barely remember the interior, except for a few old champagne bottles along the walls and some undistinguished plants. But I do vividly remember that pâté. ("The memory of a good French pâté," Julia Child once wrote, "can haunt you for years.") Too often, it's the decor of a restaurant that's more memorable than what's on the plate.

Grilled *rascasse,* my main course, was a Mediterranean fish we don't see back home. With its bulbous eyes, it's a sort of Peter Lorre among fishes. Today, though, the *rascasse* was filleted, without eyes, and the flesh was so firm I could feel where it had been separated from the bones—a sign of exceeding freshness. The spray of baby vegetables enrobing the fish, I must say, gained no flavor benefit for being so small, putting them exactly on par with their American mini-brethren. The fresh spinach, on the other hand, nipped the palate with a tang that is lost when the delicate leaves are frozen.

I'd pledged to forgo wine at this lunch, hoping to walk more briskly afterwards. But the meal deserved more than water. Was there a recommended glass of house wine? I asked the matron. In true French fashion, where such a question gets the same weight as a game-deciding football play in the Rose Bowl, she didn't answer directly but went back to huddle in the kitchen with the chef. Out came a generous glass of a *Bourgogne aligoté* from St. Bris-le-Vineux—an obscure name to me, but fresh, lemony, and pinpoint perfect in complementing the *rascasse.* Scoops of fruit sorbets ended my lunch, or so I assumed until the arrival of a pair of tiny fruit tartlets, as if the kitchen knew that I'm most satisfied when a meal ends with a crunch.

The bill, including Perrier, wine, coffee, and tip, came to a mere $19, even when figured at a relatively weak six francs to the dollar.

On the way out, I had a word with the chef, Robert Benoist. For many years, he told me, he'd worked in a large restaurant in the Chablis region, where every customer order was an "impersonal number." He wanted to cook on a personal scale. Au Regent, with its ten tables, fulfilled that dream. As we chatted, I observed one more sign of a tip-top establishment: The lunch service just finished, two teenage apprentices were already vigorously scrubbing down the kitchen floor.

It would be missing the point about Au Regent to blow the trumpet too loudly. Thousands of restaurants just like it are to be found nestled on small streets off the great avenues of Paris. What would be a find in New York, Los Angeles, or Atlanta was merely the norm here—just taken for granted, on this particular afternoon, by a foursome of businesspeople, an elderly couple, a father, and his two daughters.

A moment's stroll from Au Regent I mentioned to the proprietor of a children's boutique how well I'd just lunched at the restaurant up the street. She stared at me blankly. The name meant nothing to her. Then, when she realized it was the place with the bright blue facade, her eyebrows arched.

"Oh, you could have done better," she said. And she proposed two small restaurants on her block. "Cheaper, too," she sniffed.

Carry on, Parisians, carry on.

This piece originally appeared in the February 1990 issue of *Travel Holiday*. Copyright 1990 © by Peter Hellman. Reprinted with permission of the author.

Café Do's and Don'ts

BY DANIEL YOUNG

~

editor's note

DANIEL YOUNG is the restaurant critic for the *Daily News* in New York and is also the author of the very excellent *The Paris Café Cookbook* (see *bibliothèque* for more details). Young's fascination with Parisian café culture stems from his love of French films. Growing up in New York, he idolized Truffaut, Godard, and Rohmer, and when he lived in Paris in 1996, he developed a deep appreciation for their descendants, among them Christian Vincent, Olivier Assayas, Arnaud Desplechin, and Cédric Klapisch. His ongoing exploration of the café landscape has proven to be a personal quest to determine if what he had seen—and indeed is still seeing—in French cinema is real or merely romanticized fiction. Happily, he reports that the "cinema" of the café is even better than what's portrayed on the screen. As he says, "The café game of conversational Ping-Pong is infinitely more interesting when you're holding one of the paddles." Young once asked his Parisian friend Juliette, an editor at Flammarion, why she detested the films of Rohmer so much. "Why should I see Rohmer and sit through all that talk," she replied, "when I can go to a café?"

To Young's guide to Parisian café decorum, I would add the following reminders: ~Waiters command respect in France, even at cafés, and men and women typically enter the field as a profession. ~Consult the menu posted outside the café before you sit down. Parisians usually know what they want before they take a seat. ~If you see tables set with napkins and silverware, don't sit at one unless you plan on eating a meal. ~Don't expect *service rapide*. Allow at least thirty to forty-five minutes to place your order, eat or drink, and pay. If you're really in a hurry, stand at the bar, where it will be faster and cheaper. ~If your waiter asks you to pay the bill before you've finished, it's because he or she is going off duty and is required to settle the bill first. ~Finally, don't complain about the price of your thimble-sized cup of espresso. You're in Paris, after all, and you're paying for the pleasant privilege of obtaining a seat at a table where you can linger—even if your tiny cup of coffee is long drunk—for hours.

I n the most richly rendered portrayals of Parisian café life you can practically taste the flavors of a favorite hangout. My raison d'être as I explored the foods, moods and rendezvous compiled in *The Paris Café Cookbook* was to trim off the "practically," to capture the character and taste, down to the last ingredient, of the French capital's fifty best cafés.

This glorious and, you might assume, enviable quest was marked by a series of humiliations. Indeed, although I initially viewed the role I was to play in the *salles* and on the *terrasses* of the City of Light's most adored haunts as that of a sophisticated café romantic, my true calling was that of a *cobaye*—a guinea pig.

Instead of entering Paris café society like the hero in a Truffaut film, I started out as the neophyte who invariably picks a café *terrasse* polluted with bus fumes and sits at a sunny table that one minute later is hidden in shade. I was the guy who believes that the Juliette Binoche look-alike seated a few chairs away is giving him the eye when she's really perusing the plats du jour listed on the slate menu positioned above and behind his head.

Happily, these humbling experiences led to a fuller appreciation of café flavors and behaviors. Only through those failures was I able to accumulate an essential catalog of café do's and don'ts like the ones below. *Do* put the list to use the next time you stop by a Paris café. *Don't* take a seat positioned in front of the slate menu that lists the plats du jour.

Don't order a café au lait at any Parisian café, brasserie, bistro or tabac. Do order a café crème *or, better yet, a* petit crème.

Though sentimental foreigners may regard a café au lait as the defining breakfast beverage of the Paris café experience, you'll rarely hear a resident of the French capital order the classic drink adored by Marie Antoinette and deplored by Balzac. Ordering a café au lait immediately pegs you as an outsider with little knowledge of the local customs. Now that espresso machines are omnipresent, a coffee with hot, frothy milk is ordered as a *café crème*, or, for short, *petit crème* or *grand crème*. Important: the words *petit* and *grand* are in the masculine form (and thus the *t* and *d* are silent) because they modify the implicit word *café*, as in *petit café crème*.

Don't use one of those newfangled sugar packets if you want to be seen as a traditionalist. Do use them if you want to be hip or up-to-date.

Paris café society has been sharply divided in its response to the *bûchette*, a paper tube of granulated sugar that may be the century's boldest new design in single-serving sugar packaging. Since northern France remains among the last bastions of the sugar cube, most traditionalists and conservationists are vehemently opposed to the new packets. Radicals and trendies, however, love these groovy, user-friendly tubes.

Independent thinkers may care more about the practical merits of these warring sugar packages. The sugar cube has the following advantages: the temperature of a coffee may be gauged by how fast a sugar cube dissolves; sugar cubes may be dunked into the coffee to make a candy; a premeasured sugar cube is a source of reassurance in an uncertain world.

The advantages of the *bûchette* are: granulated sugar leaves the golden mousse that floats atop an espresso unharmed; its narrow shape allows for greater control of sugar flow; granulated sugar dissolves more easily in milk-added drinks.

Don't assume a café that carries pain Poilâne *has good food. Do ask for* pain Poilâne *when you order a* croque-monsieur.

The sign *Ici, Pain Poilâne* is proudly displayed in café windows throughout the city as if possession of that sourdough country bread alone were a surefire sign of quality. Yet hundreds of establishments that carry the world-famous bread serve food that is otherwise disgusting.

That said, you definitely should pay the premium, usually five francs, to have your croque monsieur, *tartine* or *charcuterie* plate served with bread cut from Poilâne's crusty round loaf.

Don't sit upstairs at Brasserie Lipp. Do sit upstairs at Café de Flore.

The upper level of Lipp is that legendary haunt's Siberia. And since you go to Lipp to see and be seen rather than for the overpriced food, there is no reason to sit among the same sort of people you'd encounter back home at the local Sizzler. You can avoid such a fate by reserving a table in advance and *not* showing up in shorts, sandals, a Busch Gardens T-shirt and a Home Depot baseball cap.

One flight up at Flore, however, you find a bastion of reverse snobbism. White-collar intellectuals eschew the heady excitement of the famous room and Saint-Germain terrace below for the stuffy, quiet seclusion of a space they employ as an office or a private club.

Don't look to meet too many artists at the Deux Magots. Do expect to meet artists at Café Beaubourg.

During the 1920s, the predominant "ism" at the Deux Magots was surrealism. Now it's tourism. Today, if you see a young man wearing jewelry, it's most certainly cuff links and not nose rings.

Café Beaubourg, the starkly modern café designed by Pritzker Prize–winning architect Christian de Portzamparc, is a serene habitat where not-so-starving artists, designers, bookish professionals, and intellectual foreigners and poseurs hang out and hang low.

Do order a lightly chilled Loire red in place of a cold rosé or white wine. Don't order a lightly chilled red Bordeaux or Bourgogne under any circumstance.

Within the café counterculture, the refreshingly fruity reds from the Loire are as perennially fashionable as black turtleneck sweaters and Albert Camus paperbacks. While the Loire reds—Bourgueil, Saumur-Champigny, Chinon, Sancerre and Gamay de Touraine—

are commonly chilled, it's rightly regarded as a felony to demand that a red Bordeaux or red Bourgogne be put on ice.

Do ask if the tarte tatin is served hot before you order it. Don't assume that it will be served with crème fraîche.

As incredible as it sound, many cafés will not serve their *tarte tatin* warm or with crème fraîche unless so requested.

Do ask if the chocolate sauce is served hot before you order profiteroles. Don't be surprised if the waiter gives you a mean look.

The waiter may regard this inquiry as insulting. Still, it's the best method to ensure that he gets the sauce to you from the kitchen in under thirty seconds. Profiteroles with lukewarm chocolate sauce can rank with the fallen soufflé among the great tragedies in the French dessert experience.

Don't order a decaf espresso when you're trying to avoid a sleepless night. Do order a verveine menthe when you're avoiding caffeine.

Order a decaf in Paris and you're likely to get one of two things: a foul-tasting brew (truly decaf) or a decent one (a fake). Better to have an infusion (herbal tea) like *verveine menthe,* a popular and soothing blend of verbena (70 percent) and mint (30 percent).

Do carry a cigarette lighter whether you're a smoker or not. Don't seek out the nonsmoking section if you want to sit among the Parisian habitués.

Sometimes a request for a light is just a request for a light. But often it's a stranger's way of initiating a conversation and—who knows—a romance. That's why even Parisians who don't light up eschew the nonsmoking sections.

Don't plan a café lunch for noon. Do plan a lunch at a popular café for 12:55.

Few Parisians eat lunch before 1:00. But since office workers pour into the best cafés between 1:00 and 1:15, the surest way to get a table and still sit among locals is to show up at 12:55.

Do have developed thoughts and opinions about fate, coincidental encounters and synchronicity. Don't admit you've never heard of, much less read, Diderot's Jacques the Fatalist and His Master.

The subject of fate is a café obsession and Diderot's rambling novel is the best loved—and best hated—text on the subject. Even if you don't read the book, you can wow any philosophical Parisian by quoting its most famous line about destiny: *Tout ce qui nous arrive en bas était écrit là haut* (everything that happens to us down here was written up there).

Don't go to the Clown Bar and ask owner Joe Vitte to juggle wine bottles or perform pratfalls. Do go to the Clown Bar and tell Joe how much you like his newest Rhône wines.

Joe Vitte wants it understood he's nothing like the frolicking clowns depicted in the wondrous strip of ceramic tiles that adorn his breathtakingly restored café beside the Cirque d'Hiver theater. "We're not the smiling type," he warns potential customers. "We scowl when we feel like it."

As such, the second-best way to win over Joe is to ask him about his expanding collection of clown collectibles and memorabilia. And the very best way to put a half smile on this cantankerous café keeper's face is to first sample and then praise his latest wine selections, notably those from the Loire, Beaujolais and the Rhône.

Do wear a short skirt even if you're going to be sitting outdoors on a caned chair. Don't wear panty hose.

Having a grid pattern impressed on the back of your bare thighs is the lesser of two evils. Those adorable chairs will tear up your panty hose.

Do order œufs mayonnaise without apologies. Don't order céleri rémoulade unless you have confidence in the kitchen.

As humble a cold appetizer as it is, *œufs mayonnaise*—hard-boiled eggs and made-from-scratch mayo—ought not be snubbed.

I've met bistro connoisseurs of considerable financial and gustatory means who order the dish every day.

Another classic, *céleri rémoulade* (slawlike celery-root salad with spicy mayo), is more problematic. If the celery root is shredded too finely or the salad is prepared too far in advance, the result is mushy and unappealing. Look for celery root with the cut and texture of al dente linguine.

Don't order a composed salad (salade composée) *as an appetizer. Do order a composed salad as a meal, except at Brasserie Lipp.*

Composed salads are regarded as a meal in every Paris café except Brasserie Lipp, which prints "No salad as a meal" in English on its menu. Lipp's refusal to serve Coca-Cola also seems to target Americans.

Do make a reservation for a Sunday dinner at Brasserie Balzar. Don't act impressed if someone famous walks in.

While the City of Light goes dark on Sunday nights, Balzar is invariably packed with a chic and literary crowd. But insiders express nothing but ennui toward any celebs who walk through the door, with exceptions made only for internationally famous playwrights who are also the presidents of their countries. The Balzar contingent gave Czech leader Václav Havel a standing ovation when he came in for lunch.

Do go to Brasserie de l'Île Saint-Louis in the dead of winter. Don't let the ribbing from the brasserie's jovial staff go unanswered.

Though best known for its glorious terrace, Brasserie de l'Île Saint-Louis' charms and its robust Alsatian specialties are best appreciated in the dead of winter. It takes on the comforts of an old tavern only when the rest of the island has shut itself indoors.

Just don't let the incessant teasing of Gino the waiter and Yvan the barman go unanswered. The duo has over sixty-five years of combined experience at the brasserie. Should either man ride you too far, ask him rather innocently what apparatus he personally used to brew coffee before the Paris Express copper coffeemaker was installed. The machine, said to be the oldest still-functioning one of its kind, was put in place in 1913.

Do schedule a business meeting or clandestine rendezvous at Le Café Marly between 8 A.M. and noon. Don't under any circumstance move a single piece of Marly furniture.

Even during its quietest period, Marly's punctilious staff won't let you move so much as a stool from an adjacent and unoccupied table. Regardless, this fashionable café overlooking the Louvre's Cour Napoléon is where the elite come to meet and eat.

Do request a vue-sur-la-mer table at La Coupole's La Centrale. Don't expect to get in.

The central tables under La Coupole's cupola are the most desirable. The preferred café option of sitting as collaborators side by side on a banquette, rather than as adversaries opposite one another, is referred to as *vue-sur-la-mer*—seaside view. As such, an American requesting such a table location and arrangement will surely impress the headwaiter, though perhaps not enough to land a choice table in place of a regular customer long in years and money.

Do visit a café-tabac if you're feeling oppressed by local nonsmoking laws. Don't look for a nonsmoking section in a café-tabac.

Most tourists will enter a *tabac* (tobacconist) only to buy a phone card or stamps. Few stick around long enough to appreciate it as a hub for the exchange of secondhand gossip and smoke. The red *carotte* that hangs proudly outside every *tabac* is a diamond-shaped beacon granting instant access to the source of Paris's nicotinic, caffeinated pulse.

Do meet your illicit lover for lunch at the Dame Tartine (formerly Café Véry) in the Tuileries. Don't look guilty or act defensively if you get caught.

The modern cherrywood-and-glass pavilion designed for Dame

Tartine's outpost in the Tuileries makes for an inconspicuous presence in the northwest corner of the gardens. This is ideal for government ministers meeting their mistresses for lunch. In the unlikely event they are spotted, the wide-open location in a park visited by thousands gives their secret trysts the illusion of innocence.

When the Sun Shines in Paris, Dining Moves Outdoors

BY PATRICIA WELLS

editor's note

Food maven PATRICIA WELLS hardly needs an introduction, but for the record she is the author of *The Food Lover's Guide to Paris* (fourth edition, Workman, 1999), *The Food Lover's Guide to France* (Workman, 1987), *Bistro Cooking* (Workman, 1989), *Patricia Wells at Home in Provence* (Scribner, 1996), *Simply French: Patricia Wells Presents the Cuisine of Joël Robuchon* (Hearst Books, 1995), and *Patricia Wells' Trattoria* (Morrow, 1993). With her Paris guide in hand, you will surely *mange bien* and learn a lot about French food and drink along the way. Her book is so complete, and the articles she's contributed to American publications so varied, that it was difficult to make a selection for this book. I decided to choose articles with a unifying theme rather than those about a wide variety of unrelated restaurants—it seemed unimaginative to simply present a list of restaurants at random, wonderful as they may be. Readers can, after all, use Wells's book to find any type of restaurant—Paris is home to restaurants offering food from all the provinces of France, and beyond. The following two pieces highlight restaurants arranged by themes many visitors to Paris appreciate: places to eat outside (providing a better vantage point to see the city you came to see) and places where game is always on the menu in the fall (duck, pheasant, partridge, hare, venison, and wild boar not being as common on menus in the U.S., and autumn being a wonderful time of year to visit Paris).

Wells is also the only foreigner, and the only woman, to have held the post of food critic for the French newsweekly *L'Express* and is currently the restaurant critic for *The International Herald Tribune*. For new restaurant finds, information on her cooking classes, to be added to her mailing list, or to read her *Herald Tribune* reviews, consult her Web site at www.patricia-wells.com.

When I moved to Paris sixteen years ago, I marveled at the Parisian appetite for the sun. Even in the dead of winter, at the sight of the slightest patch of blue sky, tiny marble-topped café tables tumble out onto crowded sidewalks, as Parisians toss back their heads to expose faces to the sun. The practice no longer astonishes, for the always fickle, often gray northern skies make all of us cherish sunshine.

To assuage this passion, the city offers literally hundreds of outdoor spots—ranging from a few square feet of sidewalk in the direct line of auto exhaust, to full-fledged gardens, where the city can be left behind.

The problem with dining outdoors in Paris is that opportunities are rare, and chancy at best. At the first threat of rain, many restaurants have to move business indoors. And once the weather turns fair, outdoor tables at the few choice spots fill up faster than you can dial the numbers for a coveted reservation. That said, it's all worth the effort. Here is a personal guide to the best, the newest, the sunniest, the most gastronomic terraces in town. Just remember, you're paying for the sky and the real estate.

Laurent

Certainly the most romantic and most gastronomic of the city's outdoor dining experiences can be found on the protected terrace of Laurent, a pastel pink, nineteenth-century hunting lodge set in the gardens of the Champs-Élysées. Dining under enormous chestnut trees and giant white umbrellas as the sun begins to set is akin to watching an elegant ballet: waiters in crisp white jackets and sommeliers in bright red all but waltz about the terrace, as the sky changes from bright to midnight blue. A tall hedge of shrubbery surrounds the twenty or so well-separated tables, providing a fine buffer from urban clamor.

Laurent offers a classic, elegant meal of the first order, as it should with the team that's in place. The chef, Philippe Braun, is one of the top protégés of the chef Joël Robuchon, and the cuisine reflects the master's influence in its character, polish, technique and attention to detail. The extensive wine list, expertly selected and attentively served by Philippe Bourguignon and Patrick Laïr, helps properly round out the meal.

Indoor dining is only a touch less magic, with live piano music creating a delicate background to the large, elegant dining room, decorated in flowery tones of red and green. While the atmosphere here might easily turn stuffy, the mix of old and young diners, and discreetly attentive service, puts diners at ease.

Laurent is where wealthy businessmen go for their power lunches, so it's not surprising that the à la carte menu is likely to break the bank. A per-person bill could soar to $254 without wine, calculated at 4.72 francs to the dollar. Fortunately, for those of us who are paying with real money, the $80.50 lunch and dinner menu falls well within bounds of a fine gastronomic experience. The current menu includes the chef's signature foie gras and spicy black beans—*foie gras de canard aux haricots noirs pimentés*—a lively dish that marries soft and soothing sautéed duck liver and highly spiced beans. Another comforting first-course combination pairs tiny disks of warm potatoes with delicate morsels of gelatinous *pied de porc,* or pig's feet, arranged on a plate like an elegant *galette.* Filets of shining, fresh sardines marinated in thyme;

araignées de mer en gelée (jellied spider crab); and eggplant caviar in a lightly acidic tomato sauce round out first-course offerings.

Popular main courses include filets of fresh marinated mackerel on a bed of rosemary-infused tomato *coulis;* grilled pigeon; roast rack of lamb sliced tableside with true elegance; and for warm weather, a classic serving of *boeuf mode en gelée*—cool, jellied beef—with sautéed potatoes and watercress salad. Desserts range from a light, chilled peach soup to a vibrant, seasonal red fruit tart.

Wine lovers will delight in the textbook-sized wine list (with Bordeaux dating back to 1921 and Burgundies to 1929), even if it's just for reading. While a 1959 Haut Brion will set you back $1,440, the under-$53 selections include a 1990 red Bordeaux, Château Puygueraud, J. M. Raveneau's 1992 Chablis Premier Cru Montée de Tonnerre, and from the Languedoc, Gilbert Alquier's 1991 Faugères "Les Bastides."

A chilled bottle of André Roméro's splendid *vin doux naturel,* 1990 Rasteau from Domaine La Soumade, is a perfect match with cheese, particularly if you select an assortment of *bleus.*

Restaurant du Palais Royal

Combine excellent bistro food, a touch of history and a setting of calm and greenery, and you have one of Paris's newest and most pleasing outdoor dining spots, the Restaurant du Palais Royal.

At the end of the Palais Royal gardens (just a few steps from the famed restaurant Le Grand Vefour) one dines looking out on the elegant gardens, where schoolchildren romp and fountains play, the double rows of linden trees aligned in military order. This is pure calm in the heart of Paris.

The Palais Royal menu, as conceived by the chef and owner, Bruno Hees, is a model of modern French bistro fare, offering green salads, fish and beef tartares, varied fresh fish offerings, grilled chicken and daily specials.

During a recent sun-filled lunch we sampled ultrafresh new-season lentils paired with a generous serving of light, batter-fried *gambas,* or shrimps; sparkling fresh roasted turbot on a bed of varied vegetables; and a warm, meltingly tender chocolate cake with a refreshing scoop of *fromage blanc* sorbet. The brief wine list includes the always dependable, fruity Loire Valley red, the Saumur Champigny from Domaine Filliatreau; and Vincent and René Dauvissat's 1993 Chablis Premier Cru "La Forest."

The dozen or so terrace tables are elegantly covered in crisp white linens and shiny silver, shaded with umbrellas. Service is attentive, but far from hovering. Indoors, the decor is simple and bistrolike, with several charming private rooms. Note that the gardens close at ten-thirty in the evening, so the last dinner reservation accepted for the terrace is 8 P.M.

La Maison de l'Amérique Latine

The Left Bank harbors many hidden, secret gardens, but few are as spacious, airy, or classic as that tucked behind the two eighteenth-century mansions that house La Maison de l'Amérique Latine, a cultural center on the boulevard St.-Germain.

Diners enter through huge iron gates into the paired stone mansions that now serve as a center of art and contact for the nations of Latin America. The center has turned the large, white-tented terrace into a bona fide restaurant, with a Japanese chef, Yasuo Nanumi, at the helm. The atmosphere here is much like that of a very fine country club, with excellent service and better than average food.

On the carpeted terrace set with pale pink linens, shiny silver and cozy wicker armchairs, the setting is serene and romantic. A dozen choice tables under white tenting overlook the formal, well-ordered garden, a careful mix of ancient trees, shrubs, well-clipped lawn and pale pink roses in pots.

On a recent evening, even a flash rain shower couldn't dim diners' spirits. To the contrary, there are few experiences as exhilarating as dining in Paris, cooled by the rain, yet sheltered from it.

Mr. Nanumi's cuisine is light and classically modern, with a delicious starter of crispy, light, shrimplike langoustines, a batter-fried tempura set on a bed of sautéed mixed vegetables.

Main courses vary from a perfectly grilled, moist baby *bar* (sea bass) set on a bed of fennel, served with a well-dressed mixed-green salad on the side, to saddle of lamb paired with fresh mint and served with a mix of red peppers and eggplant.

The wine list includes selections from Argentina, Chile, Peru and Mexico. A good choice from France is a fruity red 1990 Saumur Champigny from Lomaine Rebeilleau.

Desserts include a refreshing, warm-weather assortment, such as a chilled gelatin-like peach dessert paired with a pleasantly tart yogurt cream, and a brilliant bowl of strawberries in a syrup seasoned with balsamic vinegar.

The small indoor dining room retains the same elegant, old-Paris charm as the rest of the building, with a dozen or so tables that look out onto the terrace.

Café des Feuillants

Few places in Paris are more seductive than the newly restored Jardin des Tuileries, now an elegant, fountain-filled swatch of land stretching from the Louvre to the place de la Concorde. At the Concorde end, strollers now find a quiet kiosk-style café for resting weary bones, the Café des Feuillants (no relation to Alain Dutournier's nearby restaurant, Carré des Feuillants.)

The pleasant, polished kiosk tucked between two forestlike stands of chestnut trees is run by Robert Petit, who owns two cafés named Dame Tartine. The café makes absolutely no pretense to gastronomy, so better to gaze at the blue skies than what's on your plate.

Inside, a few dozen tables are scattered beneath the skylighted kiosk, while outdoors, there are several dozen bare wooden café tables on the gravel terrace.

On a sunny day, it's a heavenly spot for sipping a chilled glass of Mâcon red, tucking into a warm *croque-monsieur* (a grilled ham-and-cheese sandwich) prepared with good-quality *comté*, a kind of Gruyère cheese. An assortment of open-face sandwiches, or *tartines*, can be ordered.

Warm main courses vary from chicken with morel mushrooms to poached salmon with cucumbers, while an assortment of sorbets (try the lime, or *citron vert*) and ice creams are the best choice for dessert.

If You Go

Laurent, 41 Avenue Gabriel, 8th Arrondissement; 42.25.00.39.

Restaurant du Palais Royal, 110 Galerie de Valois, 1st; 40.20.00.27.

La Maison de l'Amérique Latine, 217 boulevard St.-Germain, 7th; 45.49.33.23.

Café des Feuillants, Jardin des Tuileries, 1st; 47.03.94.84.

In Paris, It's Time to Name Your Game

BY PATRICIA WELLS

༄

E ven before autumn has transformed the city's leaves to a brilliant golden orange, the markets and menus of Paris take on a seasonal air. Wild cèpe mushrooms sautéed with garlic, trim and tender roasted filets of wild boar, or a crispy roasted wild duck set upon a bed of crunchy cabbage become the standard feast as the game season gets under way.

Few Paris restaurateurs choose to ignore game: whether it's a local café catering to the busy office crowd at lunch; the staunch family bistro that attracts gastronomes from all corners of the city; a brasserie that draws diners all the way from Belgium to feast on nothing but game and wild mushrooms; or an elegant establishment near the place Vendôme, where a well-heeled international crowd tucks into chestnut soup or a flavorful wild partridge.

Game season in France unfolds slowly, with local wild duck in mid-August, pheasant, partridge and wild hare in late September, then finally the arrival of *gibier à poil,* or such furred game as wild hare, venison, wild boar in October and November. The season runs to the end of January, sometimes early February. Although the French have always considered game hunting a birthright, pressures from ecologists and more stringent European Community controls have shortened the hunting season. Yet larger quantities of game are being imported from countries in Eastern Europe. What's more, even the chauvinistic French agree that there is nothing equal to the intensity of Scottish grouse, and both German and Austrian venison find their way to French tables. A proportion of French game is raised on farms, which is not necessarily a drawback. The meat of farm-raised wild boar remains firm and strong, while farm-raised partridge will still have far more character than chicken or guinea hen. And while years ago the style was to hang game for days after it was killed to allow it to "ripen"—a practice called *faisandage*—modern connoisseurs generally agree that when it comes to game, the fresher the better.

Here, then, are four reliable restaurants that offer a good choice of game, in a range of prices. Weather conditions and seasonal variations will determine availability. If your heart is set on a certain dish, be sure to call and verify that game is still available. Prices include service but not wine.

Carré des Feuillants

Alain Dutournier is a child of France's southwest, where wild mushrooms abound and game birds—duck, pheasant, the now-forbidden tiny birds, known as ortolans—are essential to the local heritage.

As chef and owner of the elegant Carré des Feuillants just steps from place Vendôme, Mr. Dutournier manages to keep one foot in Paris, the other in the southwest, marrying rustic farm fare with creations aimed at cosmopolitan palates. A recent visit to his dark green and gold restaurant, which has two stars in the Michelin guide, unearthed some seasonal treasures, including a soothing cold-weather soup—a velouté of chestnuts studded with chunks of pheasant breast—and an earthy yet elegant terrine that combined venison, chestnuts and foie gras, surrounded by apples, figs and cranberries.

Seasonal main-course specialties include his own rendition of *lièvre à la royale,* the most classic of game dishes, an elaborate affair that generally consists of wild hare with red wine, shallots, onions, and cinnamon, then rolled and stuffed with foie gras and truffles. Mr. Dutournier's version was light and refined, in which the hare is marinated for twenty-four hours in red wine and a complex blend of spices, then boned, stuffed with foie gras, and cooked slowly over low heat, in a stock of red wine laced with truffles. All was served with a welcome cornmeal puree, dotted with minced black truffles.

Mr. Dutournier specializes in spit-roasting, and on one visit the menu included wild partridge wrapped in paper-thin folds of salted pork. The tiny birds are tamely flavored and served with a mound of *pommes allumettes,* or matchstick potatoes.

If it's on the menu, sample one superb nongame dish: fried eel paired with a wild salad of fresh and fried greens and herbs, including basil, tarragon, parsley and thin wafers of garlic and black pepper.

Au Petit Marguery

The cuisine of the Cousin brothers—Alain in the dining room and Michel and Jacques in the kitchen—is directly inspired by their grandmother's kitchen near Poitiers, where, as children, mushroom hunting and cooking were favorite pastimes. They seem to have learned their lessons well, for Au Petit Marguery, a brasserie-like 1930s restaurant in the city's 13th Arrondissement, remains one of the city's citadels of game cuisine.

Game begins appearing on the menu in late September, when the first-of-season wild duck makes its appearance upon a bed of cabbage laced with tiny cubes of foie gras. A cold-weather dish if ever there was one, the wild duck is presented in thin slices that combine well with the crunchy texture of the cabbage and the rich taste of the foie gras.

Through much of the season the Cousin brothers try to have available their famous mixture of wild cèpes and *lactaire* mushrooms, sautéed with a generous touch of garlic. Their extravagant collection of game pâtés includes a pairing of wild hare and foie gras; pheasant and foie gras; a puree of partridge seasoned with juniper berries, and a lush wild-boar terrine. Generally, one also finds roast wild partridge, along with their own variation on *lièvre à la royale*.

À Sousceyrac

If one was building a stage set for a Parisian neighborhood bistro, the one-star À Sousceyrac would make a terrific model. For more than forty years, Luc Asfaux has held court in the warren of rooms that make up his restaurant not far from the Bastille.

He is now seconded by his son, Patrick, and together they continue a long tradition of serving their rich, nourishing portions of *lièvre à la royale* each Friday and Saturday from October to January.

Here you will be offered the most classic version, a two days of cooking affair that arrives in a pool of chocolate-colored sauce, rich with foie gras, and served with tiny toast points dipped in minced parsley and a pair of boiled potatoes.

Sousceyrac's fare is earthy and prepared with love.

You finally realize that some flavors—such as the wild-hare stew, which is not served every day—only reveal themselves after years of repetition and constant fiddling.

Don't leave without sampling their rustic terrine of wild duck and foie gras, where a thick slice of foie gras becomes "sandwich filling" for two layers of flawlessly seasoned terrine. A bitter green salad is a perfect foil to the rich, meaty fare. Grouse lovers will enjoy the Asfaux's mousse of grouse and foie gras, an almost frothy, whipped mixture served in small ramekins with grilled bread.

Les Fontaines

Les Fontaines—a popular café conveniently situated between the Panthéon and the flourishing fountains at the entrance to the Luxembourg Gardens—does not draw you in on esthetic grounds. The garish neon lights, the lack of any sign, the banal paper tablecloths, and nondescript decor offer no hint of the riches inside.

Come hungry, starved if you can, for whether you order a simple green salad or a virile portion of wild-boar filet mignon, your cravings will be sated.

Here the food is served on platters, not plates. The owner, Roger Lacipière, was formerly a butcher, and game, meat and cheeses from his native Auvergne are prized ingredients.

You will sit elbow to elbow with a young Parisian crowd, as you sample his grilled *sanglier,* or wild-boar filet mignon—a huge strip of meat cooked beautifully rare—served with a medley of wild mushrooms; the crunchy little tubers known as *crosnes,* or Japanese artichokes, and a finely seasoned celery-root puree.

Other regular offerings include a whole roast partridge paired with chanterelle mushrooms, pheasant and medallions of venison with wild wood mushrooms.

What It Will Cost

Carré des Feuillants, 14 rue de Castiglione, 1st; 42.86.82.82.

Au Petit Marguery, 9 boulevard du Port Royal, 13th; 43.31.58.59.

À Sousceyrac, 35 rue Faidherbe, 11th; 43.71.65.30.

Les Fontaines, 9 rue Soufflot, 5th; 43.26.42.80.

Paris's New Breed of Bistro

BY ANDREA PETRINI

~∾~

editor's note

An article about Parisian restaurants in a serious Italian food magazine? A valid question, perhaps, but not when the magazine is *Gambero Rosso,* one of the very best (and one of my most favorite) food publications. Though dedicated to wine, travel, and food in Italy, *Gambero Rosso* devoted two issues in 1998 to new French chefs and Parisian restaurants,

wine bars, and *néo-bistrots* (described as updated versions of small, unpretentious neighborhood places that have been spiffed up a bit, with the food
improved but the prices kept down). The magazine's editorial staff were bet-
ting that its readers would not be content to view Italian food and wine in a
vacuum, and that they would appreciate what was new and original in what
is arguably the world's finest cuisine. It was a worthwhile gamble, and the
following excerpt guides travelers to a variety of places the critics enjoyed,
most within the reach of ordinary food enthusiasts.

To read this article in full—recipes from some of the restaurants were
included, as well as some suggestions for Asian restaurants—and/or to subscribe, contact the magazine's U.S. distributor: Speedimpex USA Inc., 35-02
Forty-eighth Avenue, Long Island City, New York, 11101; 800-969-1258;
fax: 718-361-0815. To subscribe to the Italian version of the magazine, contact the main office in Rome: 53 Via Arenula, 00186, Roma, Italia;
39.06.68300741; fax: 39.06.6877217; E-mail: gambero@gamberorosso.it;
Web site: www.gamberorosso.it.

A t the peak of the consumer spree in Paris, just after the Gulf
War, a new generation of restaurateurs seemed to spring up
overnight. They were the ones who noticed that the wind was
changing, that the recession was on its way. And when the spending
had to stop, when the most modish dishes suddenly seemed old hat,
and sticker shock became a health hazard, the moment came for
reconsidering the attractions of sanity. Typical regional dishes, like
those that *maman* used to make, suddenly seemed as soothing as a
baby's smile. Nostalgic, hearty, friendly dishes were in demand,
food to eat crowded together around a checkered tablecloth, elbow
to elbow. Stews, pot-au-feu, soups, casseroles. Terrines, sausages,
fricassees, roasts and retro desserts. No sole, no lobster, not even a
truffle. And caviar? Only the kind the peasants ate: lentils, a familiar presence on the omnipresent prix-fixe menus. The prix fixe took
a starring role in these moderate-priced restaurants, commonly
known as *néo-bistrots*. It was the ideal formula: for 150–200 francs,
about $30–35, there was even a choice of dishes. Wine was often
sold close to cost, so it flowed freely.

But who were these culinary knights in shining armor, ready to defend the people's right to excellent food at affordable prices? Clearheaded young revolutionaries. Raised in the kitchens of the *grandes maisons,* trained in the most advanced and modern techniques, connoisseurs of top-level food, experts in the economics and organization of restaurants, they put their knowledge to work to make great eating accessible on a daily basis and not as a once-in-a-lifetime peak experience. Without much money backing them, they put abundant good sense and enthusiasm to work. Within a few seasons, they conquered Paris. Of necessity they ignored the chic quarters and went into neighborhoods that were just being gentrified. Food lovers began to jump into taxis or take long subway rides to the southernmost corner of the city to seek out a modest little place away from everything famous about Paris. Soon it became difficult not only to find the restaurant, but to get in once you were there. Now their tables are completely reserved both for lunch and dinner for weeks at a time. The new bistros have become willing victims of their own success, obliged to place their clients on waiting lists. Weekends are even worse. Three-star Michelin restaurants that cost seven and eight times as much would love to have such problems.

If you can eat well, drink even better, and spend very little, what more could you ask for in a restaurant? Creativity. Daring. An adventurous spirit willing to experiment with new tastes, new flavor pairings. Fine cooking with ordinary ingredients such as vegetables, clams, fresh sardines, long-ignored legumes. A cook who takes into account all the changes in the way we eat at the end of the millennium. But it is still easier for a camel to pass through the eye of a needle than it is to find a fearless vegetarian menu in Paris.

The best among these *néo-bistrots* have understood that their ultimate goal is not a return to the dishes that mother made, but to conquer the hearts of a new young public. This is a generation open to new ideas, sensitive to the pleasures of the palate, but necessarily cost-conscious. In this, at least, the French are just like the rest of us.

Yves Camdeborde

The phone never stops ringing. Everyone wants a table at La Regalade. If we can describe Christian Constant, ex-sovereign from the Hôtel du Crillon, as the spiritual leader of the new bistro movement, then Camdeborde is its biological father. At the beginning of the nineties, right after the Gulf War, Camdeborde had what felt like a revelation, and it completely changed his life. "I saw recession around the corner. I understood that we had better think up a new kind of restaurant that was within everybody's reach." And that appealed to everyone's appetite. A succulent *terrine-maison* brought to each table sets the rustic mood at La Regalade. The rest of the meal confirms the happy first impression. Tables crowded together, kitchen-style wooden chairs, hurrying waiters carrying merrily teetering trays, a busy counter for wine by the glass and aperitifs: the bistro is bustling. The 170-franc (about $30) prix-fixe menu permits a choice among twenty dishes, many of them regional—Camdeborde is from the southwest of France—and all of them seductive. After reserving fifteen days ahead, we ate a creamy *velouté* of scrambled eggs with basil, celery *rémoulade* with mustard and braised veal trotters, roast goose liver with dried fruit in a sherry sauce, cooked foie gras with spice bread, rice pudding with bitter orange peel, truffle and caramelized walnut ice cream, plum and apple tart with Armagnac ice cream, all matched with lovingly chosen bargain-priced wines. Everyone, from left-leaning proponents of social welfare to conservatives nostalgic for old-style dishes, finds solace in La Regalade's cheering menu. And everyone wishes that Yves Camdeborde's bistro was a well-kept secret, especially those who fruitlessly try to reserve for weeks and even months (weekends are hopeless) only to be told, *"Désolé, nous sommes vraiment complets."* But Camdeborde has only himself to blame for his astonishing success.

Christian Constant

Who would have guessed? Two Michelin stars can mask bucolic yearnings. For years Christian Constant constructed his image as an expert cook of exceptional products, faithful to the traditions of the most classic haute cuisine but with occasional hints of rustic, peasant flavors. The appeal of Ambassadeurs, the restaurant in the Hôtel du Crillon at place de la Concorde, was exactly that. The food was modern yet respectful of the past, a sort of culinary Janus, looking forward and back at the same time.

A master teacher and articulate, gifted talker, Christian Constant generously shared his expertise with those who knew how to listen. He taught both respect for a good product and economy in creation. He preached the art of reducing sauces and the graceful seesaw between olive oil and butter. He understood complexity in method and strategy with linear simplicity as the ultimate goal. It's no accident that among the disciples he influenced at the Crillon were Yves Camdeborde (La Regalade), Eric Fréchon (Le Verriere), and Thierry Fauché (L'Os à moelle). (You'll find descriptions of their restaurants in this section.) When he left the Hôtel du Crillon, Christian Constant opened Le Violon D'Ingres "with all the recipes and the copyright of my book." He planned the restaurant down to the smallest detail: elegant decor, discerning clientele, dishes delicious to the last drop of sauce. His recipes are not wildly inventive, but not for the fainthearted. We enjoyed scallops and escarole flavored with bitter oranges, braised sweetbreads in *vin jaune*—a sherrylike wine of the Jura region—praline napoleons, puff pastry with pears and tea-flavored cream. His wine list was sure-handed, his prices unthreatening. Result: Constant's tables are booked at lunch and dinner, year-round. And why not? At a fraction of the price, the food is just as it was at the Crillon. Word gets around.

Eric Fréchon

In little more than a year, this young cook has turned a small place on an anonymous street into the most sought-after reservation in Paris. Go by car, take a taxi, or arm yourself with a book for a good hour's ride on the subway, but above all, don't forget to reserve at least a week ahead. Otherwise you won't get the chance to choose among the twenty or so options on the Fréchon menu. Fréchon worked and learned in the very special school that the Hôtel de Crillon became under the guidance of Christian Constant. He searches for the right taste and impeccable preparation while paying homage to lightened and updated classics of the bistro tradition. But more precisely, Fréchon's cooking is based on what the food market offers, and he glorifies the lively earliest produce of the season. For example? Tiny chili peppers stuffed with dried cod; layered eggplant, tomato and fresh goat cheese with olives and basil; morel mushrooms and asparagus served with tender, milk-fed veal. The desserts are a delight. Cooked apples and raisins are served with a caramel and butter sauce.

What is the secret of Fréchon's touch? "I think about dishes in terms of the season's best products. Create, yes, but without technical extremes or excess fat. The wonderful spring morels, for example, are messengers, and it's the cook's job to underline, clarify, or even argue with this message by using spices and herbs. But we mustn't betray our ingredients." For Eric Fréchon, 1996 was a year of sudden success, while 1997 was the year of recognition: he was elected *Cuisinier de l'année* by GaultMillau. Now he is waiting patiently for the arrival of those eternal latecomers from Michelin, but we suggest that he start chilling the champagne.

We tried everything. Here's the list of the best we found, either because the food delighted us or was especially interesting, or perhaps because the atmosphere was just right and the price bearable. Paris isn't just expensive, it's exorbitant, so the names of reasonable restaurants are to be treasured.

Le Bamboche, 15 rue de Babylone, tel.: 01.4549.1440. Many of David Van Laer's dishes have a northern inspiration: turbot with spices, *rémoulade* of raw shrimp and parmigiana, duck foie gras with rhubarb compote, pork head with sage and braised lettuce. Intimate romantic-chic decor, well-chosen wines, skilled and courteous service. Prices within reason.

Au Bascou, 38 rue Réaumur, tel.: 01.4272.6925. The relaxed atmosphere, fragrant cuisine, and cheerful smile of Jean-Louis Loustau make this one of the pleasantest bistros in Paris. The dishes are southern, even Basque, in inspiration. Veal with Espelette chili peppers, black risotto with cuttlefish, excellent dried cod.

Le Bistrot de l'Étoile, 13 rue Troyon, tel.: 01.4267.2595. This is Guy Savoy's bistro for friends. Knee to knee you eat cheerful dishes: caramelized veal shin, tagliatelle al parmigiana, pig's feet terrine with basil, cod with puree of Jerusalem artichoke. Serious and not-so-serious wines.

Les Bouchons de François Clerc, 12 rue de l'Hôtel-Colbert, tel.: 01.4354.1534. The wine here is more important than the food. Customers come for the wide selection of both simple and world-class bottles, sold practically at cost. And when you drink Pichon-Longueville priced at little more than one hundred francs, it hardly matters if the monkfish is a little overcooked or the chocolate dessert a bit wrinkled.

Cap Vernet, 82 avenue Marceau, tel.: 01.4720.2040. In this chic brasserie run by Guy Savoy we can never resist the enormous display of fresh, sea-perfumed oysters from Brittany or the temptations of the beautiful wine list, with bottles at all prices.

Cercle Ledoyen, Carré des Champs-Élysées, tel.: 01.5305.1002. If it weren't for the killer bill, we'd like to eat more of the intelligent northern cuisine in the handsome room on the second floor of Ledoyen. But since we're not millionaires, we head for the ground floor, to the Cercle Ledoyen, a luxurious brasserie where the food is good and the bill is predictable. The appetizers (60F) and the main dishes (110F) are one price, the wine list intelligent. A view of the Champs-Élysées comes on the dinner.

La Dinée, 85 rue Leblanc, tel.: 01.4554.2049. It's worth crossing all of Paris for Christophe Chabanel's red mullet with citron and asparagus, shrimp and cream of oyster tartar, sweetbreads with oranges and escarole. The desserts are appealing, his ultrareserved waiters less so. A cheerful wine list, with sensible prices, adds to the fun.

Graindorge, 15 rue de l'Arc-de-Triomphe, tel.: 01.4754.0028. Had enough of the Mediterranean? Then try the beer-based cuisine of Bernard Broux. Dishes from his native Belgium are spotlighted in his place near the Arch of Triumph. Cooked without excessive fat or starch are lobster, eel aspic with leeks, pheasant and porcini-mushroom pie, beef stew with beer and juniper berries. An excellent wine list and an impressive selection of beer from small producers.

Guy Savoy, 18 rue Troyon, tel.: 01.4380.4061. If it weren't for the prices, we would haunt Guy Savoy's. His lush modern dining room is decorated with paintings by jazz drummer Daniel Humair. The kitchen turns out enthralling dishes: artichoke soup with truffles, puff pastry brioche with mushrooms, black radishes in herb salad, red mullet fillet, deep-fried herbs, lamb cooked in three ways, mustard-seed stew. The wine cellar, directed by his excellent sommelier, Eric Mancio, is extraordinary.

Jamin, 32 rue de Longchamp, tel.: 01.4553.0007. Benoït Richard took over the old Joël Robuchon restaurant where he had been right-hand man for many years. He changed nothing, not the position of the furniture, not the color of the bathroom towels. A series of bourgeois dishes with a bistro beat—terrine of jellied rabbit with herbs, lentil puree with smoked tuna, veal scallops with candied onions—all skillfully carried out except for the lavish quantities of butter.

L'Os à moelle, 3 rue Vasco-de-Gama, tel.: 01.4557.2727. Thierry Fauché is another one of the great Christian Constant trainees in the *néo-bistrot* style. The menu is written on a blackboard and changes every day, the wine costs little more than a bottle of mineral water in a three-star restaurant. Come on an evening when the chef prepares squab with cabbage.

L'Osteria, 10 rue de Sévigné, tel.: 01.4271.3708. This restaurant is so popular it doesn't even have a sign outside. Regulars order grilled Treviso radicchio, tagliolini with veal sauce, gnocchi with morel mushrooms or Gorgonzola (forget the ones with lobster!). The tiramisu really tastes homemade.

Paolo Petrini, 6 rue du Débarcadère, tel.: 01.4574.2595. The owner of this restaurant is no relation to either of the writers of these reviews, so we can unabashedly comment that Paolo Petrini makes the best Italian food in Paris. The wine list, heavily Tuscan, has no rivals in the city although the markups are often too high.

À T a b l e !

Le Relais Louis XIII, 8 rue des Grands-Augustins, tel.: 01.4326.7596. Manuel Martinez is back in the restaurant where he made his debut before taking charge of the Tour d'Argent for nine years. The menu resembles the Tour's—crustacean ravioli with herbs and porcini mushrooms, sweetbreads with *vin jaune,* guinea hen with mushrooms—alongside a few less calorie-rich additions. But everything, including the dishes we've mentioned, could be lightened up a bit.

Le Saint-Amarante, 4 rue Biscornet, tel.: 01.4343.0008. Near the Bastille, this bistro is always a pleasure to go back to. It has good dishes at reasonable prices and simple wines to drink without moderation.

La Table d'Anvers, 2 place d'Anvers, tel.: 01.4878.3521. The Conticini brothers write books and lecture on television. One prepares the main dishes, the other the sweets. Their cooking is ironic and playful, educated and joyful, but also determined to surprise no matter at what cost. Lobster salad; sugared eggs with banana; shrimps with bergamot; puff pastry with scallops, leeks, saffron, and balsamic vinegar; kidney with lavender honey. The service, a little like the cooking, doesn't feel very natural.

Vin et Marée, 106 avenue du Maine, tel.: 01.4320.2950. When you want straightforward fish prepared without any fuss, or crustaceans and mollusks as fresh as the morning dew, this is the place. We can warmly recommend it to everyone, from tough-talking journalists to innocent maiden aunts, from the budget-conscious to the big-time spender.

This excerpt originally appeared in *Gambero Rosso* No. 12. Reprinted with permission.

Bleu Plate Special

BY MARK BITTMAN

∽

editor's note

Six years ago, headlines first began appearing proclaiming the death of French bistros. While it is regrettably true that thousands of bistros have been forced to close their doors, many haven't, and many more have opened. While it might be an exaggeration to say they're thriving, bistros (or *bistrots*—allegedly derived from Russian soldiers who, in Paris following Napoléon's defeat at Waterloo, shouted the word impatiently to indicate they wanted their food and drink in a hurry) remain popular with the French and foreigners alike. Generally speaking—and including those associated with venerable Paris restaurants—bistros represent good value (though some are more tony than others); are small establishments, often family owned and operated; feature a simple menu most often based on Lyonnaise cuisine (as distinct from the cuisine of Alsace, traditionally featured at brasseries, the cousins of bistros); offer meals both à la carte and prix fixe, which almost always includes a half carafe of wine (not beer, which is, again, the specialty of brasseries); and are open for lunch and dinner but not at hours in between (unlike brasseries, which welcome drinkers or diners all day long).

MARK BITTMAN is the creator and author of the popular column "The Minimalist," which appears weekly in the "Dining In/Dining Out" section of *The New York Times*. His work has appeared in nearly every major American newspaper, in food magazines, and in general-interest publications ranging from *Business Week* to *GQ*. Bittman was a founding editor of *Cook's Illustrated* magazine and is also the author of several noteworthy cookbooks: *How to Cook Everything* (Macmillan, 1998), which won the Julia Child and the James Beard general cookbook awards for 1998, the only book to win both; *Jean-Georges: Cooking at Home with a Four-Star Chef* (Broadway, 1998), which won a James Beard chef cookbook award; and *Fish: The Complete Guide to Buying and Cooking* (Macmillan, 1994), which was the recipient of a Julia Child award. That same year he was honored with the coveted IACP (International Association of Culinary Professionals) Bert Greene Memorial award for Best Food Journalism.

For Americans visiting Paris twenty years ago, dinner at a bistro was an adventure. If the special of the day wasn't pig's feet, it might have been veal's head—offerings that had many people begging for steak *frites*. But today's bistros have taken a cue from the lighter, French-born nouvelle cuisine: You're likely to encounter olive oil in place of butter or duck fat, tuna rather than traditional steak tartare, and reduction sauces instead of cream.

Some of these restaurants have been around for nearly a century, and new ones open routinely. The model Paris bistro once was a family-run neighborhood place that offered locals an alternative to home cooking (which, of course, is better in France than in most countries). The menus changed daily, but there was always a special house dish, along with French provincial standards: veal stew, coq au vin, or cassoulet.

The best bistros still offer honest food at good value. They belong to their neighborhoods and are patronized more by natives than by tourists (most of these restaurants are downplayed in guidebooks or never make it into them at all). There are those where a meal seems impossibly cheap, not much more expensive than fast food, and yet it's startlingly good. The following four bistros range from funky upstarts to plush legends, and dinner costs anywhere from $25 a person up to $100. It's worth booking ahead, especially for weekend dinners (and reservations often mean a better table). Still, you can usually get seats for two at the last minute. Best of all, you could hit all four in two days and never repeat a dish.

Generation Excellent

Only two years old, L'Ardoise has an energy typical of a new bistro. Just a few minutes' walk from both the Louvre and the Plaza Athénée (where Roman Polanski was filming Johnny Depp for the upcoming film *The Ninth Gate* when I strolled by), it's bright and airy, with soft yellow walls, fewer than thirty seats, and a young, hip crowd. The dining room stays quiet, however, even when it's full, and the air always smells of good cooking, fresh and inviting.

L'Ardoise's youth shows most in its menu, with its emphasis on vegetables, fish, and herbs rather than old-fashioned bistros' bacons, stews, and organ meats. And the $30 prix fixe is a bargain. Start with mussels and clams poached in foil with thyme and butter, eggplant beignets, or poached langoustines served with fresh mayonnaise. Second courses include monkfish with zucchini and chorizo, lobster and fresh mushrooms (varying by the season), or rich, meaty squab with roasted fava beans in a dark, slightly sweet sauce. L'Ardoise has a great wine list, with many selections for less than $15, and wonderfully fresh, simple desserts, like light cherry soup topped with cherry ice cream (28 rue de Mont Thabor; 011.33.1.42.96.28.18; dinner for two is about $60).

Greasy Spoon, à la Française

With its vast and inexpensive menu, Les Fontaines is the Parisian equivalent of a New York City coffee shop. Down the street from the Jardin du Luxembourg, it has cheap furniture and even sickly looking plants. With about thirty tables, it may be too big to be considered a true bistro, but it's enormously popular with locals (working men eat their dinners standing at the bar), and rightly so—the food's about forty times better than any diner fare you've ever had.

Plus, you'll have trouble spending much more than $25 for two or three solid, good-tasting courses and a couple glasses of wine (especially if you come for lunch). The price goes down even more if you share appetizers or main courses, which, given the generous portion sizes, is a good idea. Artichoke ratatouille, for example, includes three large artichokes; the duck salad, though officially an appetizer, would make a meal for most people.

Main courses tend toward the traditional, from veal heart braised with carrots to roast quail with prunes (served with three kinds of potatoes) to duck confit. The desserts, all priced at thirty francs ($5.50), are standard—crème caramel, floating island, or chocolate mousse—but decent (9 rue Soufflot; 011.33.1.43.26. 42.80; dinner for two is about $60).

Cassoulet with Cachet

People used to go to the 11th Arrondissement only to see the place de la Bastille or Père Lachaise, but the neighborhood has recently taken a turn for the funkier and now has a wide selection of dining and nightlife options vaguely reminiscent of New York's TriBeCa. The two-year-old Zygotissoire fits in well: The artwork is ultrahip, even if the service is a little uneven and the tablecloths plastic. But just about everyone knows each other, and wonderful food comes out of the tiny upstairs kitchen. And at eighty francs (about $15), the straightforward, two-course menu is just the thing after eating the outrageously complicated cuisine served in many Parisian restaurants.

Like older bistros, the choices are few—just three or four per course—but they vary daily and are always tasty. First, try the salad topped with grilled chicken wings, or the ravioli stuffed with tomatoes, cream, and langoustines. You can follow them with a huge steak in a delicious shallot sauce, grilled Mediterranean sea bass on greens, or rabbit stew. The potatoes, in all their varying forms, are delicious—especially those with salt-pork lardoons—and for a place with only twelve tables, the wine list is extensive and even quirky. For dessert, my apricot tart was strikingly fresh, which brings to mind the bistro's name (everyone asks): Zygotissoire comes from the French word—*zygos*—for the muscles that allow you to smile (101 rue de Charonne; 011.33.1.40.09.93.05; dinner for two is about $70).

Magnificent Mainstay

Benoît is hardly a discovery, because it has long been a favorite destination of the well-heeled cognoscenti (even more so since it was supposedly the destination of Diana and Dodi that fatal night). Opened in 1912, it has seen the neighborhood (once the home of the fruit and vegetable market Les Halles) grow up around it. But the mirrored walls, wooden booths, faux marble, and intensely personal service still typify the authentic, old-school bistro.

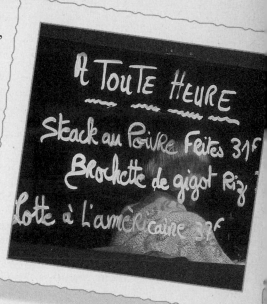

Still, if the food didn't deliver, few would eat at Benoît. But it does. There's a prix-fixe menu of about $35 at lunchtime, but everyone ignores it, opting instead for the recommendations of the *patron*—which, of course, boost the bill significantly. Nevertheless, you can sample a wide variety of the gorgeous, perfectly displayed dishes by asking for split portions (graciously done in the kitchen). Or you can eat simple dishes, such as the huge portion of smoked salmon, which, marinated with vegetables and served with warm potatoes and salmon caviar, makes a full meal.

For a grander experience, start with the crab soup with melba toasts and rouille (a super-garlicky mayonnaise) or the veal tongue with lentils; move on to bouillabaisse or chicken roasted in salt, then end with the perfect profiteroles (20 rue St. Martin; 011.33.1.42.72.25.76; dinner for two is about $175).

Spirited Wine Bars:
An Insider's Guide

BY FRANK PRIAL

editor's note

I love *bars à vin* and *bistros à vin* and wish they were as popular a concept in the States as they are in Paris. I have yet to set foot in one that I didn't like, but I have a soft spot in my heart for Jacques Mélac, if only because of a sign displayed there that states that water is for cooking potatoes.

A festive atmosphere seems to prevail at wine bars, as if every day is an occasion to celebrate wine. Wine bars are also a more economical alternative to traditional restaurants: with glasses of wine ranging in price from about $1.50 to $10, I have been able to taste wines that I otherwise could not afford by the bottle; and the uncomplicated dishes at wine bars are reasonably priced. An additional bonus is that diners end up with perfect pairings of wine and food, since the food offered is meant to complement the wine. (For some other good wine bar recommendations, see Jacqueline Friedrich's "In Paris, Finding the True *Bistro à Vin*," *The New York Times Magazine*, September 13, 1998.)

FRANK PRIAL has been writing about wine for many years and is the wine columnist for *The New York Times* as well as an author (*Wine Talk*, Times Books, 1978; and *The Companion to Wine*, which he coauthored with Rosemary George and Michael Edwards, Prentice-Hall, 1992).

I live in Paris part of the year and, like most Parisians, I tend to stay close to home. Every *quartier* has decent restaurants, fine markets and specialty shops. More important, perhaps, is the human scale of the neighborhoods, which the touristy areas tend to lack. Maybe that's why the best Paris wine bars are usually not around the corner from your luxury hotel. A good wine bar is, at heart, a neighborly place.

Like so many things that seem quintessentially French, the wine bar is an import, from England in this case. Cafés in France have always sold wine by the glass, but these upgraded versions of the old *café du coin* (corner café) are relatively new. They combine the stop-in-for-a-beer informality of the café—without, thank God, the pinball machine—and the quiet linger-all-afternoon intimacy of the bistro. Here are my favorites.

Jacques Mélac

The perfect Paris wine bar may be Jacques Mélac, named for its owner. Mélac, he of the infectious grin and handlebar mustache, holds forth over a mixed clientele. Local shopkeepers and repairmen from the garage next door mingle at the bar with copywriters and journalists from the center of town and wine buffs from the ends of the earth. They're greeted by a sign over the bar proclaiming: "Attention! Water is used here only for cooking potatoes."

Mélac, who is a native of southwestern France, is proud of the region's cheeses and charcuterie. A mixed plate of the latter—*jambon cru* (raw ham), *pâté aux cèpes* (mushroom pâté), *pâté de campagne* (country pâté), *saucisson* (sausage), pork and goose rillettes—served with an endless supply of country-style bread costs about $8. (All prices in this article have been calculated at an exchange rate of 5.9 francs to the dollar.)

Mélac has a vineyard, Domaine des Trois Filles, in Lirac, in southern Rhône, and he sells his wine for about $15 a bottle. The selection of other wines at Mélac is enormous, covering most of the *cru* Beaujolais, like Fleurie and Juliénas, and wines from the Rhône.

These and just about every wine Mélac offers are available by the glass. The waiter may pour you some or leave the bottle on the table and charge you later for what you have consumed. Most wines sell for about $2.50 a glass.

Mélac founded the Association of Paris Winegrowers, an organization that brings together everyone in the city who nurtures a few vines in a backyard or on a terrace. When the grapes on his own vines are ripe, Mélac cordons off the street outside his bar and holds a harvest festival, much as wine-country villages do all over France.

A small band plays while Mélac and his friends pick the grapes, which are quickly stomped—to much applause—by pretty girls in bare feet. After the "harvest," the crowd spends the afternoon in the street, dancing, drinking wine and feasting from hefty platters of charcuterie. Mélac has even been known to don a bear costume as part of the festivities.

Au Limonaire

Au Limonaire was named in honor of Les Frères Limonaire, who made the best hand organs in the nineteenth century (the bar's former owner had once been an organ-grinder). In keeping with its music-related heritage, Au Limonaire pushes back its tables several nights a week and becomes a showcase for musicians and folksingers, guitarists, ensembles and balladeers of every stripe.

Au Limonaire specializes in Rhône wines, dozens of which are available by the glass or by the bottle. Gigondas, Châteauneuf-du-Pape, St.-Joseph, Cornas and Hermitage are just a few. A rich, young 1988 Gigondas is about $20 a bottle. Cheeses and charcuterie and simple plats du jour like *saucisson de Lyon* (the famous sausage of Lyon) are featured. Prices for these dishes range from $11 to $13.

The inimitable Le Rubis, one of the most successful wine bars in the city, is in the neighborhood around the place du Marché St.-Honoré. At lunch hour, patrons spill outdoors, sometimes balancing their plates of Camembert or lamb stew on the roofs of cars.

Le Rubis veterans hark back to the days of Leon Gouin, who ruled the tiny bar and restaurant for thirty years before his retirement in 1980. Gouin would note the return of a client who hadn't been in for ten years not with a voluble greeting but with a barely perceptible nod and a glass of Beaujolais on the house.

Le Rubis regulars feared for the future when Gouin hung up his apron, although they need not have worried. Albert Prat, the current owner, carries on in the grand Gouin tradition with good Beaujolais (about $2.50 a glass), excellent charcuterie, a fine selection of cheeses and such tasty plats du jour as *saucisson chaud* (warm sausage) and tripe (all are about $8).

Le Passage

Le Passage, which opened four years ago, is one of the more refined wine bars in town. The wine bar's name refers to its location on one of the intriguing passages that snake through some of the city's older neighborhoods. Many of the passages are charming, others ominous. This one, the passage de la Bonne-Graine, connects the rue du Faubourg St.-Antoine and the avenue Ledru-Rollin. It can best be described as a cross between a London mews and a New York City back alley. The restaurant occupies a rehabilitated café and seats only about forty, but it is handsomely designed with a small bar and French doors that open onto the street.

Le Passage's menu offers seventy-seven items, including thirty desserts. You might begin with a duck rillettes appetizer (about

$6.50) or four marinated Iceland herrings with a salad of warm potatoes ($8.50), followed by calf's liver *à l'anglaise* ($16.50) or a confit of duck on a bed of sauerkraut and chestnuts ($16). A separate menu lists eight andouillettes, pork sausages ($13 to $15), each made by a different supplier from a different part of France.

The wine list ranges from bottles that cost about $10 to a 1990 Le Montrachet from Ramonet for about $260. The house wine, made by Robert Michel, a respected producer in Cornas, in the Rhône, is Le Pas Sage. A play on the restaurant's name, it means "a smart move."

In fact, Le Pas Sage is not a bad way to acquaint yourself with Le Passage. Its wine list is long, and there are some uncommon Rhône labels. This is a place where you should rely on the guidance of your waiter or the owner, an attractive young woman with a typical Breton name, Soizik de Lorgeril.

L'Écluse des Grands-Augustins

Just across the Seine from the Île de la Cité, on the quai des Grands-Augustins, is L'Écluse. (*Écluse* means canal lock, but there is no canal nearby.) L'Écluse has become one of the best-known names in Paris wine bars. There are five in the L'Écluse group in the city now, all much the same in decor and philosophy. They concentrate on Bordeaux wines by the bottle and the glass and offer uncomplicated yet well-prepared fare to complement them: carpaccio, for example, or steak tartare or lightly smoked salmon. Most dishes are about $13. A platter of mixed cheeses is about $9.

Among the interesting Bordeaux at L'Écluse are a 1986 Château d'Issan, about $7 a glass, and a 1990 Château Lasalle Médoc, about $32 a bottle. There are always at least thirty Bordeaux by the glass, including dry whites like a 1992 Château Reynon, about $3.50 a glass, as well as *vins liquoreux* (sweet whites), such as a 1984 Château Coutet, a most appealing sauternes, at about $7 a glass.

Taverne Henry IV is set on the Île de la Cité in close proximity to the Palais de Justice and so to many of France's most prominent lawyers. And the *préfecture de police* is just down the quai des Orfèvres. While the fictional Inspector Maigret preferred a café on the Left Bank, many genuine police officials stop by for the sandwiches and fresh young wines Robert Cointepas serves at Henry IV.

With its vaulted ceilings and refectory-style tables, the place seems suited to the lawyers who sometimes stand at the counter and gulp Beaujolais before hurrying back to face some ornery judge. Other customers, most of them tourists, linger, but the pace here basically conforms to the always frantic judicial calendar.

The sandwiches—pâté, Camembert, *jambon* from the Landes region—cost about $5 and are excellent. The plates of cheeses from the Auvergne and the charcuterie from Quercy are reasonable, for Paris, at about $4 to $10.

Cointepas offers Bordeaux but is not so secretly a Burgundy man, and Beaujolais is his true love. A *cru* Beaujolais, such as Chiroubles or Morgon, is about $4 a glass.

Willi's Wine Bar

Paris's first authentic English-style wine bar was Le Bistrot à Vin, which Steven Spurrier opened in the late seventies. Le Bistrot à Vin is in French hands now, and Spurrier's second wine bar, the Blue Fox, was demolished recently to make way for a new hotel. All of which means that Mark Williamson's Willi's Wine Bar is the most British in Paris. It is certainly a mecca for young Englishmen and Americans happy to hear their language spoken.

Willi's, hard by the Bibliothèque Nationale and just around the corner from the Palais-Royal, is located in a once-drab business section that has become more lively with the newfound popularity of the nearby place des Victoires. Willi's espouses an understated, almost spare decor: half London pub, half San Francisco fern bar. Its long bar leads to a pleasant, airy dining room in the rear.

Willi's wine list is as extensive as it is intelligent. There are selections from Australia, Bordeaux, the Loire, and especially, the Rhône. Cornas is a house specialty.

The kitchen here is considerably more ambitious than those at most wine bars. Williamson, who began his career in Paris with Spurrier, is justifiably proud of his seasonal confit of hare with braised celery, which costs about $16. A good companion wine would be André Perret's 1992 Condrieu, which is not inexpensive: about $9 a glass or $48 a bottle. There are always fifteen wines available by the glass at Willi's, starting at about $3.

Au Franc Pinot

The Île St.-Louis is among Paris's trendier neighborhoods. It is home to one of the better-looking and one of the oldest wine bars in the city, Au Franc Pinot, which has a high, timbered ceiling and stained-glass windows that overlook the Seine.

Understandably, the wines here emphasize their Pinot Noir heritage, from both the Côtes du Rhône and Burgundy. Good non-Pinot buys on recent visits have been a 1990 Côtes du Jura, about $6 a glass, and a light but intense 1992 Anjou red, about $5 a glass. There is also a selection of excellent sherries. A glass of wine costs about $3 to $13; a cheese platter is about $9; and the chef can make up an assortment of delicious sandwiches for about $11.

The French have a way of borrowing things from other cultures and making them their own. The wine bar may be a British contribution, but it's thoroughly French now and all the better for it.

Au Franc Pinot, 1 quai de Bourbon (Île St.-Louis), 4th Arrondissement; 43.29.46.98. Closed Sunday.

Au Limonaire, 88 rue de Charenton, 12th Arrondissement; 43.43. 49.14.

Jacques Mélac, 42 rue Léon-Frot, 11th Arrondissement; 43.70. 59.27. Closed all day Sunday and at dinner Monday.

L'Écluse des Grands-Augustins, 15 quai des Grands-Augustins, 6th Arrondissement; 46.33.58.74.

Le Passage, 18 passage de la Bonne-Graine, 11th Arrondissement; 47.00.73.30. Closed Saturday at lunch and all day Sunday.

Le Rubis, 10 rue du Marché St.-Honoré, 1st Arrondissement; 42.61. 03.34. Closed Saturday at dinner and all day Sunday. No credit cards.

Taverne Henry IV, 13 place du Pont-Neuf (Île de la Cité), 1st Arrondissement; 43.54.27.90. Closed Saturday at dinner and all day Sunday. No credit cards.

Willi's Wine Bar, 13 rue des Petits-Champs, 1st Arrondissement; 42.61.05.09. Closed Sunday.

Bibliothèque

The Food Lover's Guide to Paris, fourth edition, Patricia Wells, Workman Publishing Company, 1999. The day I first saw this book, I felt I had discovered someone who, like me, found not only that the experience of Paris changed her life, but also recognized that in learning about food one would also learn about history, language, people, and customs. Wells is sincerely passionate about food (she wrote in the introduction to the third edition that "The sure way to stamp out gastronomic mediocrity is to highlight and to encourage excellence") and seeks out the truly worthwhile in Paris. Even the French recognize her expertise, calling her an ecologist for French gastronomy. Similarly, she is for me a food trailblazer *par excellence*. Follow her along any *rue* in any arrondissement and you will find the journey well worth the occasional detour. She tells us where to find *pain au chocolat* that is made with three bars of chocolate instead of two; how to differentiate between a brasserie, bistro, and *brûlerie*, as well as between a *café noir, café crème,* and *café filtre;* and which eating establishments offer the best *qualité prix* (good value). One of her recommendations that proved particularly rewarding for me was a visit to Le Furet-Tanrade in the 10th, where I purchased a jar of *confiture de poire passée*, a smooth, unbelievably delicious pear concoction you stir into plain yogurt. There are chapters on *everything* to do with food—from restaurants, cafés, and *salons de thé* to *bistros à vin,* charcuteries, *fromageries,* and *pour la maison* (kitchen and tableware shops). New to this edition is the "Markets at a Glance" schedule for the *marchés volants* (roving food markets). I also use this book as a cookbook, and I still think Patricia's recipe for madeleines is the best one around (though I use slightly less lemon peel). The French-English food glossary alone is worth the price of the book, because as we all know it's *how food is prepared* that poses the most vocabulary problems: is the dish *bien cuit* (well done), *Bordelaise* (Bordeaux style), or *fourré* (stuffed or filled)? Don't think about getting on the plane without this book.

The Art of Eating: Paris (or What Is French Food?)—Part I: Posing the Question and the Classic Parisian Baguette and *Part II: More Answers and Places That Are Truly French.* Some readers may already know of this absolutely excellent, critical, and superbly written quarterly newsletter by Edward Behr. Although not exclusively about France, Behr has devoted several issues to various aspects of French food and restaurants over the years, and each of them is worth the effort to special order. Part I above (No. 45, winter 1998) poses the question "What today remains distinctly French about the food in Paris?" and also presents a search for real French bread. Part II (No. 46, spring 1998), as promised, offers recommendations for some good French addresses in Paris and poses a final question, "How long will French food last?" This is really de rigueur reading, so don't wait until the last minute to order these back issues ($9 each, $7.50 each for four or more). Further, if you really want to learn about the food traditions of France, other regions and countries, and care about the food you eat and its future, you'll definitely want to subscribe to this stellar periodical, which has been described as "one of the most respected publications in the food world" by *Chef's Edition* on National Public Radio. Some cookbook and cookware stores sell individual issues (Kitchen Arts & Letters in New York stocks it regularly), but to receive it in the mail you should subscribe: Box 242, Peacham, Vermont 05862; 800-495-3944; www.artofeating.com.

Cheap Eats in Paris, eighth edition, Sandra Gustafson, Chronicle Books, 1998. Gustafson offers many practical hints in the introductory section of the book, including a list of fifteen "Tips on How to Have the Best Cheap Eats in Paris." A word about the title: Gustafson's goal is to find good-value restaurants, what the French refer to as *qualité prix*. This book, as well as her *Cheap Sleeps in Paris,* does not aim to provide a listing of the cheapest places . . . "Those are left to books where quality and value are sacrificed for saving a franc, no matter what," as she states. Restaurants are presented alphabetically by arrondissement with an accompanying map. At the end of the book there is a handy reference guide, with restaurants listed by categories (big splurges, non-smoking, *boulangeries* and *patisseries,* non-French food, vegetarian, tearooms, and wine bars).

The Paris Café Cookbook: Rendezvous and Recipes from 50 Best Cafés, Daniel Young, William Morrow and Company, 1998. I like this guide-cookbook not so much for the recipes (though the ones I tried were good, especially the *tarte au citron et pruneaux*) but for the histories of and stories about the cafés. It's always fun to read of familiar spots—for me these include Ma Bourgogne on the place des Vosges, one of my favorite cafés in all of France, and Café Marly at the Louvre—but I was intrigued by the unfamiliar places, such as the Café de la Place in the 14th, which apparently sits in the middle of a Parisian triangle that has an inexplicable microclimate like that of the Mediterranean. Young was once at this café on a cold afternoon—complete with wind and freezing rain—and watched in amazement while a woman in sunglasses, seated nearby, coated herself with sunscreen. How positively *bizarre* . . . I cannot wait to investigate! Recipes are arranged by appetizers, sides, main dishes, and desserts, and there are black-and-white photos and charming color illustrations throughout. Interspersed between the recipes are great essays with titles like "Whatever You're Drinking, It's All *Limonade,"* "The End of Sugar Cubism?" "Le Café Tabac," and "Café Wines," which focuses on the less pricey wines typically offered at cafés.

À Table! 377

Restaurants of Paris, Knopf Guides, 1994. This is not a book of restaurant reviews but more a pictorial history of typical French ingredients and wine, and the great restaurant tradition in Paris. Just as in other Knopf Guides there are a number of themes: "Restaurants as Seen by Writers," "Restaurants as Seen by Painters," "Gastronomic Itineraries: 100 Memorable Restaurants," "Foreign Cuisine," and "French Specialties," etc. Within the "Practical Information" section there are chapters on "Wine with Meals," "Riverside and Floating Restaurants," and the Rungis wholesale food market. My favorite parts of the guide are the glossary; "Ten Specialties and Where to Find Them"; the itineraries with maps at the end of the book; and the foldout of *Le Train Bleu* in the Gare de Lyon, which to my mind is the epitome of a grand belle epoque restaurant.

Boulangerie!: Pocket Guide to Paris's Famous Bakeries, Jack Armstrong and Delores Wilson, Ten Speed Press, Berkeley, California, 1999. According to the authors, on January 1, 1997, the Small Business Ministry of the French government stipulated that only bakeries that select their own flour, knead their own dough, and bake loaves on the premises are permitted to call their establishments *boulangeries*. So, Armstrong and Wilson set out to identify true *boulangeries* in each of Paris's twenty arrondissements. They came up with 223, and no bakery is listed unless the answer to the question *"Faites-vous le pain vous même?"* (Is your bread baked here in your shop?) is yes. This is not, however, a discriminating guide— the featured bakeries are not rated because, as the authors note, "your individual tastes and interests may be different from ours." Therefore, I find this little book helpful for those times when you plan to be in a certain neighborhood and want to know where a handful of bakeries are located and what their specialties are, not necessarily the best one in the area. The address, phone number, nearest métro stop, hours, and autobus routes are provided for each entry. This little— approximately four by six inches—paperback fits easily in a pocket or a bag.

Between Meals: An Appetite for Paris, A. J. Liebling, North Point Press, San Francisco, 1986 (paperback), with an introduction by James Salter, and Modern Library, 1995 (hardcover). *Between Meals* was one of those books that had reached legendary propotions in my mind before I even read it. It seemed to be mentioned in nearly everything I read about Paris. I was thrilled to finally come across the paperback North Point edition featuring a black-and-white photo of a café on boulevard Montparnasse by Eugene Atget on the cover (the Modern Library edition is handsome but not nearly as era-evoking). Predisposed as I was to like this book, it exceeded my expectations. I've reread it three or four times because there are few other accounts of 1920s Paris that really make me feel that I'm right there with the author. With Liebling as a guide I can taste the wine, hear the cutlery clanking, smell the *gitanes,* and believe I'm sitting in a cane wicker chair at a sidewalk café.

Burgundy Stars: A Year in the Life of a Great French Restaurant, William Echikson, Little, Brown and Company, 1995. I had only read a few pages of this book before I became fascinated by the story of Bernard Loiseau and his La Côte d'Or, one of the few three-star restaurants in France (the 2000 *Guide Michelin* listed over four thousand restaurants in France, and only twenty-two were honored with three stars), in the Burgundian village of Saulieu. Part of the reason the book remains so captivating is that Echikson devotes each chapter to a single element of the restaurant, e.g., the cheese course, the wine (I was especially fond of Lyonel the sommelier), "The Michelin Mystique," the kitchen staff (including a few American *stagiaires*), etc. Loiseau is a public relations pro, appearing often on television and in the pages of newspapers and magazines. He recently took his enterprise public, becoming Bernard Loiseau, Inc., which enabled him to make a dent in his considerable debt. I was exhausted after reading about the extraordinarily hard work it is to own a restaurant, let alone maintain three Michelin stars. The story of La Côte d'Or gives a whole new meaning to appreciation of fine dining, emphasizing that even with every seat at every table occupied every day of the year, the cost of haute cuisine is staggering, and chefs must also be creative businessmen to survive. (A related article to consult is "Straight to the Source: A Journey Along the Byways of Burgundy, Armed With Michelin Three-Star Chef Bernard Loiseau's List of Suppliers," by Christopher Petkanas, *Travel & Leisure,* October 1998, which traces La Côte d'Or's ingredients to their sources. Included are restaurant and inn recommendations and the names, addresses, phone numbers, and specialties of vegetable, cheese, bread, honey, tea, snail, and jam suppliers, most of whom welcome visitors, offer tastings, and sell their products. To order a back issue, call *Travel & Leisure* at 800-888-8728 or write to P.O. Box 2094, Harlan, Iowa 51593; issues are $5.50.)

Les Personalités
(Natives, Expatriates, and Passionate Visitors)

"Parisians are in no doubt that they live in the most fascinating city that ever was: why should they stoop to argue the case? The history of Paris has a luster more continuous than that of any other European city—so much so, in fact, that no Parisian feels bound to hold on to the past in the way that the Athenian holds on to Plato and Pericles, the Venetian cleaves to Titian, the Viennese remembers Schubert, and the Florentine can hardly shave himself without thinking how Leonardo da Vinci would have designed a better razor."
—Rosamond Bernier, FROM THE INTRODUCTION TO *PARIS* BY JOHN RUSSELL

Astérix: Cartoonland's
Improbable Success-Storix

BY PETER MIKELBANK

〜

editor's note

In 1996, it was reported in *The New York Times* that Albert Uderzo's books had sold better than all others by any other French writer. His name, however, is not known in every household—he claims that next to no one recognizes him—but the comic-strip character he helped create is: Astérix, the mustachioed Gallic warrior who is sort of the French equivalent to Mickey Mouse.

Though he has been slow to catch on in the U.S., Astérix is popular around the world and has been translated into over seventy-five languages. Parc Astérix, about an hour from Paris, receives over a million visitors a year. On the surface, the appeal of Astérix may seem difficult to explain, but the French see aspects of themselves—both endearing and irritating—in the characters.

Sometimes, the best ideas are 10 percent inspiration, 90 percent desperation. Consider this story of two cartoonists: Sitting on a Bobigny balcony, working against deadline after several futile weeks, one artist wearily leans over a mountain of cigarette ashes and empty glasses. "Well, what if . . . ," he remarks casually, "what if when Vercingétorix laid down his arms . . . what if . . . *not* everyone surrendered?" Like a sudden downpour, the suggestion clears the late-August air. Ideas rush back and forth, and within moments furious pencil sketches depict a diminutive warrior wearing an outsize mustache and a cap of Pegasean wings. Beside him, another character—a braided warrior of greater waistline and a slightly puzzled expression—is hastily drawn. Realizing the pair's resemblance to Laurel and Hardy, the cartoonists laugh and agree that, yes, it's just conceivable that historians actually overlooked one small Breton tribe's continued rebellion—and that history books should at least record their fight with a small acknowledging mark. "Something like an asterisk?" they wonder.

Mulling over the sketches' potential, both artists fall quiet until one, with a playwright's love of comic wordplay, smiles slyly. "No, not an asterisk," he says, "an *Astérix!*"

The year is 50 B.C. Gaul is entirely occupied by the Romans. Well, not entirely . . .

"The Gaulois idea was René's," says Alberto Uderzo, the cartoonist who created Astérix the Gaul with René Goscinny in 1959. A friendly bear of a man with more than a passing resemblance to Astérix's partner, Obélix, Uderzo admits that neither he nor Goscinny anticipated the public's response to their creation. "This was a comic strip for children, appearing in a children's magazine," he says, glancing at the traffic below his studio windows. "In the first months, we worked all the time to meet deadlines—we never got out. The first time I realized what *Astérix* was becoming was one night at a cocktail party in early 1960. People kept coming up to me, adults, you understand, saying: 'Oh, so you are the one who draws *le petit Gaulois. C'est formidable!*'"

His grin widening into a crescent, Uderzo says he is "sometimes just bewildered" and still hard-pressed to explain the runaway success of the cartoon, especially in countries as different and as distant from France as chalk is from cheese. "The moment a character becomes 'universal,' I suppose, is when he touches something in people everywhere, when he is embraced in Mexico and Sweden." In fact, *Astérix* is most popular, in terms of per capita sales, in Finland. "And frankly," he adds, laughing, "what interest the Finns might have in the history of the Gauls versus the Romans is still beyond me!"

Astérix's appeal may simply come from its magic formula: the perfect marriage between partners in crime. A self-taught artist who debuted in the French press at age thirteen (despite parental warnings that comic books were a waste of time), Uderzo served as apprentice to the illustrator Edmond Calvo during the Occupation. He emerged a prolific journeyman working as both an advertising illustrator and a contributor to children's publications in postwar France and Belgium. Churning out dozens of strips, he soon came to the attention of cartoonist Goscinny, a half-Polish, half-Russian Jewish orphan born in Paris and raised in Argentina. Goscinny had spent the postwar years bouncing back and forth between New York, Brussels and Paris and writing comic story lines with Sempé *(Le Petit Nicolas)*, Morris *(Lucky Luke)* and Peyo *(The Smurfs)*.

With talents as diverse as his background, Goscinny shared Uderzo's slyly wicked sense of humor. The pair spent the 1950s together honing complementary skills for a variety of emerging journals. They were, in fact, already earning passable wages from Belgian publishers with *The Adventures of Oumpahpah the Indian* when they were asked to come up with an essentially French cartoon strip for the new magazine *Pilote*. The publishers' idea was to restart the French cartoon industry, which had suffered from wartime printing restrictions. Uderzo and Goscinny complied, submitting *Astérix,* which they described as "the mischievous incarnation of all the virtues of our Gallic ancestors."

The rest, as they say, is cartoon history.

One small village of indomitable Gauls still holds out against the invaders. . . .

Since his debut in the premier issue of *Pilote* on October 29, 1959, Astérix the Gaul has been unstoppable. The pint-size warrior, whose strength derives from a Druid's magic potion, and a host of cleverly named characters inhabiting the outpost of Ordralfabétix have traveled far beyond their Breton forest. In a series of adventures, they've brought their fight against the Romans to Spain, Britain, Switzerland (a story line suggested by former French president Georges Pompidou), Egypt and the Holy Land, Rome itself, and then far beyond the Empire's borders to the New World and India.

As modern mythology, however, Astérix and his battalion have traveled even farther, becoming French patrimony with a realm all their own. In essence, Uderzo's first pen-and-ink sketches were the genesis of a multimedia empire that now attracts enough corporate partners to rival the Olympic Games.

Since Goscinny's death in 1977, Uderzo has produced *Astérix* alone, writing as well as illustrating an additional five volumes, which have proven to be the character's best-sellers. Uderzo has also set a pattern: He spends three months working on the script, six months on drawing, then allows two years between projects. It's a permissible indulgence, considering that each release is accompanied by a carefully orchestrated promotional campaign. When the last album—*Astérix and the Secret Weapon*—was released in 1991, it set new records with 7 million first-run copies sold across Europe.

All told, more than 260 million books have been sold in nearly sixty languages—from Afrikaans to Hindi, Chinese to Latin. By conservative estimates, *Astérix* brings in $60 million annually—with only one-third of that amount related to book sales and author's royalties. The remainder derives from film and video sales of seven animated features and a diverse international portfolio that includes some six hundred endorsement contracts and product licenses. Along the Champs-Élysées, Astérix decorates McDonald's Happy Meals. In England, he's Renault's official spokesman. In Canada, Obélix drinks diet Coke. The feisty Gaul appears on items ranging from breakfast mugs to underwear, not to mention computer games (his Game Boy sold twenty-five thousand copies in its first week on the market) and interactive CD-ROMs that teach English and French. Another popular spin-off is Parc Astérix. Now in its seventh year, the amusement park north of Paris emerged from red ink in 1994, posting net profits of $3 million and welcoming a record 1.5 million visitors. With debt now down to a manageable $30 million, the park looks as if it may just fare better than its huge but debt-plagued rival, Disneyland Paris.

Year after year, in all of cartoonland and its ancillary businesses and product licensings, Astérix is number two in terms of revenue. Only Mickey Mouse brings in more money. And although Uderzo has become one of the richest men in France, he is ambivalent about being compared with Disney. "I have tremendous respect for Walt Disney. The man built an empire. Along those lines, in France, we had Marcel Dassault, who built airplanes. In Italy, there was Ferrari, who built race cars. Neither man was an engineer, and Disney was no artist. But all three men had a talent for organizing others. I'm not *le Disney français* at all. I'm just a little artisan who works alone."

And life is never easy . . .

Éditions Albert René, the publishing house Uderzo launched in 1979, is located in an elegant office building on the posh avenue Victor Hugo. Inside, however, the editorial enclave is a riot of color, with bright showcases displaying cartoon merchandise. Offices bustle with the ring and whir of telephones and faxes that mark a successful international business. Down a corridor, Uderzo's sparsely decorated office is a divided territory, where desk and drawing board occupy opposite corners. In a sense, this setup conveys the artist's conviction that in order to stay independent after Goscinny's death "I had to organize my own house and assume responsibility for all business decisions." When Goscinny passed away, *Astérix* was a successful but largely European phenomenon, earning its creators 10 percent royalties. Alone, Uderzo followed the path that both men had planned, founding his own publishing house and assiduously turning *Astérix* into an international success-storix.

"I don't really think of myself as a businessman—I'm simply an artist who wanted to remain independent," says Uderzo. He launched Éditions Albert René with only two employees; now he has ten people responsible for licensing alone, a studio that creates advertising designs, and another that produces animated features. Although Uderzo continues to pencil, ink and color Astérix's adventures himself, he minimizes his role in the company. "Me? I sign the contracts. Thank God, there are other people more competent to handle the negotiations."

. . . for the Roman legionnaires.

It is a corollary of popular culture that success breeds criticism. During the past thirty-five years, enough ink has been spilled to script an adventure entitled *Astérix Versus the Critix*. Critics and writers have engaged in endless intellectual gymnastics in defense of Astérix's appeal, vigorously exercising comparisons to Rabelais, Cervantes, Robin Hood, Napoléon, and the French Resistance to justify the character's appeal. In fact, one writer recently declared *Astérix* "the sole unifier between the Holy Alliance of *pétanque* and Heaven." Now honestly, not even Charlemagne managed that feat!

Similarly abandoning reason, other critics have branded *Astérix* "reactionary" or dismissed it as "a fantasy of middle-class France sold like Camembert or yogurt." Says Uderzo, "The strip was first criticized for its 'patriotic spirit'—but that's not what we meant to convey. It was only a comic strip, and we just wanted the pleasure of amusing readers. That explanation, however, didn't stop the daggers from being drawn. Success brought enemies who saw politics in *Astérix*. And the French are very Cartesian: If something is successful, it must be explained. But who can explain success?

"Even the French press refused to accept the notion that something could be successful on its own, and it began criticizing the strip as veiled political commentary," continues Uderzo. "Fortunately, its German popularity came almost instantly, so we were able to respond: 'If it's a comic strip celebrating French patriotism, why is it so popular in Germany?'" More recently, attacks have bemoaned Goscinny's absence and faulted Uderzo's texts. Yet critics rarely acknowledge the fact that millions of readers are ready, willing and able to refute these attacks.

Last year, following a setback in his legal wranglings with his former publisher, Uderzo announced his retirement. Public reaction ranged from disbelief to concerted protest. Briefly sketching his lengthy, *Astérix*-like legal battle, Uderzo says, "I had fought for years and finally won a court decision. Then the decision was reversed last year on appeal, and I said to myself, 'Enough. I'll just stop drawing *Astérix*.'

"But ah! The game is not up!" Uderzo exclaims, explaining that he has decided to challenge the appeal and resume drawing *Astérix*. "I was forced to reconsider after letters began arriving from fans, saying, 'You can't abandon us!' Readers of all ages love the characters. Most of the letters came from the first generation of readers who discovered the stories at age ten and now share them with their children. But there were many letters from children, including one from an elementary school where all the students had signed a petition. That was very touching."

Since returning to his drawing board last September, Uderzo has been busy celebrating *Astérix*'s thirty-fifth anniversary, launching the animated feature *Astérix and the New World*, arranging the sale of *Astérix*'s previous animated films to French public TV station FR2, and planning Astérix's thirtieth adventure. "Just now, I don't have any ideas. But I have to come up with something because readers are already waiting and I have employees who expect to keep working. I enjoy writing when I have ideas, but when I don't," he twists his face into a comic grimace, "I feel like killing myself!

"There is no magic potion, no formula for finding the right idea. I remember Goscinny saying that an idea had come to him once while he was in the metro, so the next time he needed an idea, he took the metro again. But nothing came to him the second time. Later, he explained, 'That's why I bought my first car!' You see, that's the spirit of Goscinny. I still get mail from young readers addressed to Goscinny and Uderzo. It's comforting to know that his spirit lives on and that René is still a success."

Meanwhile . . .

We all tend to slow down a little as we age, so, naturally, the question arises: Is Astérix in danger of slowing down now that he has reached middle age? Is he finding his battle against the Romans any easier? To borrow a phrase from each story's opening caption: "Well, not entirely . . ."

As evidence, Uderzo talks about the few female characters in the comic strip. "We were a generation of artists whose works were censored, and sensual figures of women were forbidden," he says. "So the earliest drawings of women were caricatures. Even after censorship was lifted, we were still governed for a long while by self-censorship because our books were for children.

"I was heavily criticized for featuring women in *Astérix and the Secret Weapon*. When I was in Canada promoting the album, a journalist confronted me, saying there was a connection between *Astérix* and domestic violence. This issue is a great problem in

Canada, and I admitted that I could see her point but that I had not made the connection before.

"Still, the journalist continued to argue. Luckily for me, she was accompanied by her fourteen-year-old daughter. Finally, the daughter spoke up and said, 'Give it a rest, Mom. Get a sense of humor. After all, it's only a comic strip!'"

"Astérix: Cartoonland's Improbable Success-Storix" by Peter Mikelbank, *FRANCE Magazine*, Spring 1995.

Julia: America's Favorite Cook

BY FRED FERRETTI

ᔐ

editor's note

Julia Child arrived in France with her husband, Paul, on November 3, 1948, and her culinary education officially began. She has written of her early years in Paris that "I was hysterical with pleasure just to be there."

I have framed in my kitchen a portion of the introduction she wrote for her monumental book *The Way to Cook* (Alfred A. Knopf, 1993), which I include here because I think it is a perfect summation of the way she has chosen to live her life, and the way the French live theirs: *"Fear of food, indulgences, and small helpings.* Because of media hype and woefully inadequate information, too many people nowadays are deathly afraid of their food, and what does fear of food do to the digestive system? I am sure that an unhappy or suspicious stomach, constricted and uneasy with worry, cannot digest properly. And if digestion is poor, the whole body politic suffers . . . *Final words.* The pleasures of the table—that lovely old-fashioned phrase—depict food as an art form, as a delightful part of civilized life. In spite of food fads, fitness programs, and health concerns, we must never lose sight of a beautifully conceived meal."

FRED FERRETTI has been a contributing editor of *Gourmet* for many years. This piece was featured in February 1995.

It must be burdensome for Julia Child, the thought occurs, to be looked upon often less as a person than as an enduring and accessible monument, particularly so for one who lives, eats, and drinks with such relish and exuberance as she does; for one who is a font of strong sentiment, smiling easily when pleased and bluntly declaring her dislikes when not—all of this in the communal eye. She manages, however, to wear her eminence with an innate ease and surefootedness, the accumulation of her decades as America's favorite cooking teacher.

A monument she surely is, this Julia—for it is Julia, never Mrs. or even Ms. Child—this candid, larger-than-life woman who created the world of television cookery and spawned, as so often happens in America, a gaggle of imitators. Nevertheless, as she has moved into her eighties, she remains best of show, an elevation from which she can, and does with regularity, send forth pithy epistles on such topics as her fear that our preoccupation with the salt and fat content of food is overwrought. An outspoken, unrelenting exponent of classic French cookery and its techniques, Julia bemoans the relatively low esteem in which this sauce-bound cuisine is held these days.

"What is wrong with a wonderful *blanquette de veau,* perfectly cooked?" she asked rhetorically during lunch recently at a table at the Hotel Cipriani overlooking the lagoon in Venice. She speared little daubs of butter from a pat with one *grissino* after another. "Cream? Egg yolks? I absolutely loathe people who are afraid of food. You see them everywhere. A person reduces his fat, and soon he has stringy hair, flaky skin, and he's not having any fun."

Julia loves red meat, adores eggs fried slowly in bacon drippings and finished off in the oven, and at lunch was ecstatic over her recent discovery and first taste of that layer of salted-pork fat known in Italy as *lardo.* Nor will she do without butter, "good butter, an idea we seem not to take seriously in the United States. Why not? Do you know that in France there are *crus* for butter?"

We're all familiar with Julia's gastronomic preferences, her prejudices, even those of us who might regard the above litany as so many coffin nails. We understand, because she is Julia, our Julia, with that high warble in her voice, who made us laugh as she spanked a suckling pig on camera and warmed our hearts as she trilled *"Bon appétit,"* poured herself a goblet of red Bordeaux, and wished us good-night. When we listen to her, when we watch her, we are happy to forget, for a while, the dieticians, the calorie and . carbohydrate counters, and our accumulated fats—be they poly- or monounsaturated or completely saturated.

Julia is an imposing preacher, though her big frame is slightly bent these days. As she speaks, her reddish hair, curled and frizzed, bounces upon her forehead and her blue eyes twinkle or narrow, depending on the subject at hand. Abstinence is folly, as is blind obeisance to culinary fads, she will say. Rather, we ought to be governed by moderation and the purity of what we eat. "I am for careful cooking, *cuisine soignée,*" she says. "Eat moderately, sensibly, with small helpings, but with *great* variety. Children should be taught not to have a great hunk of cake as lunch but to eat well and properly. Time at the table should be glorious. It is distressing that we have so many fat people. There are simply too many couch potatoes. I grew up with good, decent food. I believe you should try food as you try wine. Taste it, savor it, talk about it. That is the joy of food. It is marvelous to go to France and to watch the people in restaurants. They care about what has been cooked, what is offered. They have conversations about what they should eat that day. They are *interested*. It is important to them, not pretentious, not something chic."

Julia's musings recurringly roll back to France, for it was there that she bloomed as the cook who would become a proselytizer. Born Julia McWilliams in Pasadena, she grew up in a home in which "we enjoyed ourselves to the full at meals. This is what opened my eyes to food." But the urge to get to the stove did not come upon her until later, in France. She had been graduated from Smith College and with the outbreak of World War II joined the Office of Strategic Services, or OSS, which presaged the CIA (*not* the Culinary Institute of America). She was assigned to Ceylon, where she met fellow OSS volunteer, and future husband, Paul Child. Both were subsequently dispatched to China, where they remained until the end of the war. They were married upon their return to the United States and in 1948 moved to France when Paul, now a member of the United States Information Agency, was assigned to the Paris embassy.

"I came to cooking late. Paul was interested in eating good food, as I was, and I wanted to learn so I could cook for him, for us." Her first teacher, the man she calls her *maître,* was Max Bugnard, a chef and instructor at the Cordon Bleu. "He had come from Belgium, had worked with Escoffier, and was teaching a 'ladies course.' I wanted a serious cooking class, and he agreed to teach me privately from his wonderfully classical background." Other teachers she remembers well and fondly from those days are Claude Thilmont, "a fantastic *pâtissier,*" and Pierre Mangelotte, a "demonstration chef who taught afternoons in Montmartre."

Julia kept dutifully to her classes, she says, and began her habit of buying pots and pans and kitchen gadgets at Dehillerin in Les Halles: "It became an obsession I've never been able to break." Through a mutual friend she met Simone Beck, her "Simca," who in turn introduced her to Louisette Bertholle. In 1949 the three women opened their own cooking school, L'École des Trois Gourmandes, on the third floor of an old apartment house on rue de l'Université. "We had six students in the mornings, and then we would have guests for lunch. We cooked pleasant and elaborate haute cuisine—it was French cooking in a French atmosphere."

Paul Child was transferred to Marseilles, and Julia went with him, there to cook and to begin tentative work on the recipes she and Simca and Louisette had devised, recipes that were to be the core of *Mastering the Art of French Cooking,* which was eventually published in 1961. The book was ten years in the making: "I did two chapters, on poultry and sauces, and sent them off to publishers. Most of them, I must tell you, thought the recipes were too detailed." The proposal went to publishing houses in the United States and elsewhere, always to be returned with the response that its recipes were "too esoteric, too much work," Julia says. The manuscript ended up, finally, on the desk of Judith Jones, a young editor at Alfred A. Knopf, who told Julia, "This is what I want."

Following the book's publication, it was reviewed warmly by Craig Claiborne of *The New York Times,* and the then somewhat small food universe opened up for her. "Judith introduced me to James Beard. Dionne Lucas asked me to her restaurant for an omelette. Later, she gave a reception for the book. We wanted our own book tour, however, and we bullied until we got one. Simca and I toured, making madeleines and Roquefort quiches. We went to newspaper food departments, women's clubs—wherever we could demonstrate. One time I recall Simca and I had demonstrations one after the other, but we had only one set of dishes. Paul took them into the ladies' room and washed them between our appearances.

"That tour started us off. Still, I had to make a living somehow. Paul was retired. I began giving lessons in our home in Cambridge. Because of them, and the book, I was invited to appear on a WGBH program—it was 'educational television' then—called *I've Been Reading.* As part of the interview I whisked up an omelette in one of my copper bowls. They loved it, I guess, and I was asked to do three programs on French cooking, as a pilot. French cooking was the thing then. There was a demand for it. The programs were a lot of fun for me."

It turned out that there was indeed an audience for Julia's free-wheeling cooking instruction, and she was booked for thirteen programs. *The French Chef* went on the air February 11, 1963, the first of a series of shows (initially black-and-white telecasts, later in color) that have been broadcast somewhere, on some television station, ever since. What followed was *Julia Child & Company* (1978), *Julia Child & More Company* (1980), and *Dinner at Julia's* (1984). The books followed as well. *The French Chef* was published in 1968 and the second volume of *Mastering the Art of French Cooking,* written by Julia and Simca, two years later. Subsequently came *From Julia Child's Kitchen, Julia Child & Company, Julia Child & More Company,* and six years ago, an oversize book of kitchen techniques, *The Way to Cook.*

Through these very public years Julia became a popular icon, the recipient of both an Emmy and a Peabody Award for her television programs. The bakers of France elected her a member of the Confrérie de Cérès for her writings on French breads, and the French government awarded her both the *Ordre de Mérite National* and the *Ordre de Mérite Agricole.* All of which have given her the opportunity to do what she says she truly enjoys, "bringing people together to comment, to talk about cooking."

This was the idea behind the formation of The American Institute of Wine & Food, of which she was a founder: "to become serious and knowledgeable about the food we eat." She has encouraged Boston University, across the Charles River from her Cambridge home, to create a master's degree in gastronomy that would encompass the history and anthropology of food as well as its marketing and communication. "If you can get a degree in architecture, in dance, in business, or art, why not gastronomy? I am very interested in people who go into food as a career, often late in life, but with passion. I am thrilled with many of our young chefs in this country, those who delight in their profession, who have a passion for what they do."

She remains quite disturbed though, she says, by the increased consumption of processed and frozen foods. "They prevent us from *knowing* about food. When people get together to talk about food they should be aware of what good food is. If you don't know how something is supposed to taste how will you know if it is good? How will you know good cooking from bad cooking? I *hate* badly cooked food. I *love* food cooked with care by someone who knows what it's all about."

Cooking has changed so much," Julia said. "Techniques haven't changed, but attitudes have. Classics are classics. Some are old hat, but others have come into disrepute undeservedly. Take my favorite, *blanquette de veau*. I have tried it with some of that free-range veal. It's not veal at all. It's baby beef. I love real veal. It has to be milk fed, about three months old, and carefully raised. I get fed up with those doe-eyed animal rightists who have never been on a farm and don't know anything about animal husbandry."

Julia seldom minces about.

"I detest diet foods. You can get cake down to 230 calories a slice with flour, egg whites, and vegetable oil, but why would you want to eat it? Why not eat a piece of something good? I can't stand anything touted by the health mavens. There is nothing like a good piece of American bacon. I don't like low-salt, diet bacon. I am often disappointed in our beef today. And it becomes harder to get a decent piece of beef, beautifully marbled. Instead we get what I call 'diet beef,' lean and without taste. And isn't it difficult to get a good chicken?

"I remember in France, we would cook a Bresse chicken hanging by a string in the oven, with mushrooms and potatoes below to catch the fat drippings. Today we have so-called fresh chickens that aren't fresh at all. They have been frozen, defrosted, and frozen again."

After a lifetime of reveling in the foods of the French kitchen Julia still eats what she wishes, "not too many desserts though, and I eat between a quarter or a third of a portion. You *must* be tough about that." The luncheon we shared, at that table in the Hotel Cipriani, was her sort of meal, a substantial sampling of many tastes.

Following a salad of greens and tomatoes, Julia was served a fillet of turbot dressed with a Savoy cabbage leaf in a light tomato sauce, which she ate between tastes of the foods of others at the table: a *pasta e fagioli,* thick with beans and olive oil; a risotto with pumpkin flowers and scallops flavored with rosemary; a *saltimbocca* of veal covered with slices of prosciutto and round chips of fried zucchini, as well as an extra portion of *zucchini fritti* for the table. All these accompanied by glasses of a decent cold Verdicchio. "The chocolate gelato is wonderful here," someone said.

"By all means," said Julia.

Monuments must, after all, keep up their strength.

Royal Gardener's Treasure

BY OLIVIER BERNIER

editor's note

It turns out that the great Le Nôtre was even more talented than we suspected: I was completely unaware that he was a serious collector of art until

I read this piece, nor was I aware that he was quite accomplished at drawing and painting.

OLIVIER BERNIER is a writer and lecturer, and his many books include *Words of Fire, Deeds of Blood: The Mob, the Monarchy, and the French Revolution* (Little, Brown, 1989), *Fireworks at Dusk: Paris in the Thirties* (Little, Brown, 1993), *Louis the Beloved: The Life of Louis XV* (Weidenfeld & Nicolson, London, 1984), and *The Secrets of Marie Antoinette* (Doubleday, 1985).

P aintings by Poussin, a sculpture by Michelangelo, even a pair of Egyptian sarcophagi, all of irreproachable quality—it was the sort of collection that only a wealthy connoisseur could put together, a collection worthy of a king. Yet it belonged to a man who called himself a "poor gardener."

André Le Nôtre was, of course, far more than a gardener. The son and grandson of supervisors of the French royal parks, he was a genius, the creator of what we know today as the French garden. Vaux-le-Vicomte, Versailles, and Chantilly attest to his inventiveness and his feeling for light, color, and water. What is often forgotten is that he was also a distinguished art collector.

In an era when collecting was reserved for the most privileged, it is surprising that even this greatest of garden designers should compete with the likes of Louis XIV and Philip IV of Spain, especially given Le Nôtre's lack of pretension. He "had an honesty, correctness, and rectitude which made everyone respect and love him," wrote Louis de Rouvroy, duc de Saint-Simon, in his memoirs. "Never did he try to rise above his station. . . . He had a charming naïveté and truthfulness." At one point Louis XIV lent Le Nôtre to Pope Innocent XI for a few months. According to Saint-Simon, when Le Nôtre met the pope, "instead of kneeling down he ran right up to him. 'Well, hello, Reverend Father,' he said, hugging him and kissing him on both cheeks. 'You really look well. How glad I am to see you in such good health.'"

However naive Le Nôtre may have been in matters of papal etiquette, he was a model of sophistication once he started to look at art. Indeed, one of his tasks in Rome was to make purchases for the French royal collection, and while he was at it, he acquired several ancient Roman marble and bronze figures for himself.

As a boy, Le Nôtre had shown a striking aptitude for drawing and painting. His admiring father, Jean, seems to have thought he might forsake his family's profession, an unusual occurrence in an age so inhospitable to change. It is a mark of his talent that the artist to whom he was apprenticed at an early age was Simon Vouet, then the most illustrious painter of the French school and a favorite of Louis XIII. In Vouet's atelier Le Nôtre met Charles Le Brun, who became a lifelong friend and a member of the great trio—Jules Hardouin-Mansart, Le Brun, and Le Nôtre—who designed the palace, interiors, and gardens of Versailles.

We don't know why Le Nôtre decided to return to the vocation of his father and grandfather; his later career is proof enough he made the right choice. But we do know that Le Nôtre never lost his eye for art and that he soon had the means to indulge himself. By 1637 the twenty-three-year-old was in charge of the Tuileries parterres, jointly with his father; by the time he was thirty he was chief designer of all the royal gardens. His royal commission allowed him to work for private patrons as well, and in 1656 Nicolas Fouquet, superintendent of finance under Louis XIV, selected him to create the gardens at Vaux-le-Vicomte. From there it was straight to Versailles. At the height of his career he was earning thirty-five thousand livres a year, the equivalent of perhaps $250,000 today.

With that kind of money Le Nôtre could do quite well in the art market of the mid–seventeenth century, especially since he sometimes found less fashionable paintings appealing. This was true of his five splendid Poussins—one, *The Woman Taken in Adultery Presented to Jesus by the Scribes and the Pharisees,* was bought directly from the artist after the great French classicist had moved to Rome and was falling out of favor at home—and of his three paintings by Claude Lorrain. Firmly bucking the trends of the day, Le Nôtre also acquired Jan Brueghel the Elder's *Battle Between Alexander and Darius,* now called *The Battle of Issus,* and a Rembrandt portrait of a young girl. Three of his Poussins, two of his Claudes, and the Brueghel now hang in the Louvre.

All this is not to say Le Nôtre was unmoved by the taste of his time. He owned at least one important work by Pierre Mignard, whose rich color and ingenious compositions greatly appealed to Louis XIV, and about eight canvases by Francesco Albani, an occasionally insipid and now largely forgotten painter whose slightly etiolated classicism was once considered proof of his genius. (Four of his Albanis are now in the Louvre.) And like many of his contemporaries, Le Nôtre had several copies of famous paintings. Even demanding collectors of the seventeenth century did not distinguish as sharply as we do between originals and replicas.

Le Nôtre also purchased seventy-nine large portfolios of engravings. The list makes dazzling reading: the principal engraved oeuvres of Le Brun, Poussin, Mignard, and Antoine Coypel as well as significant works by the Carracci, Rembrandt, Rubens, Van Dyck, Vouet, and Jacques Callot. When Le Nôtre wanted to look at his prints, he could do so in great comfort, on a vast marquetry desk supported by bronze columns. (Known from an inventory of his possessions, the desk has vanished.) When he was tired of looking at his engravings, he could contemplate his rare Chinese porcelains, busts and statues of bronze and marble, gold and silver medals, or, perhaps the crowning glory of the collection, a sculpture described in the inventory as "one of Michelangelo's *Slaves,*" which may well have been a study for or a copy of one of the figures originally intended for Julius II's tomb.

Having accumulated all this, Le Nôtre decided in 1693, toward the end of his life, to give the best pieces to the king. It says a good deal about their relationship that Le Nôtre was confident the king would appreciate these great works of art and that Louis XIV felt honored by the gift. For the rest of the Sun King's life, these paintings and sculptures were arranged in his private gallery at Versailles. It surely would not displease the great gardener to know that three centuries and several revolutions later, his collection is still admired by crowds in one of the world's finest museums.

Two Americans in Paris

BY WALTER WELLS

❧

editor's note

Patricia Wells has been interviewed by writers from countless newspapers and magazines; but I always wondered whom someone with so much energy and talent had married and was delighted when this piece appeared by Walter himself.

Their life together in Paris (and Provence) may only be "mostly" peaches and cream, but it is impossibly hard not to be mostly green with envy.

WALTER WELLS joined the staff of the *International Herald Tribune* in 1980 and is now managing editor.

❧

"It's not all peaches and cream," one of us will say. Then, as though we're a meager but enthusiastic congregation on Sunday morning, we give the response in unison: "But it's *mostly* peaches and cream."

I't's not church, it's our hometown, Paris—not an address that elicits great pity. Curiosity, perhaps. Maybe puzzlement. But mostly what it feels like is envy.

It has been that way for fourteen years—considerably more than the two or three we intended to stay. Certainly we'd be away from the United States no more than that, we assured friends when we left New York at the end of 1979, so certain of our return that we didn't even bother to pack up our furniture. Except a lot of books.

It was a relaxed pace that we envisioned for our lives as we left New York, a sort of full-time vacation with many free hours to catch up on reading, to learn French and maybe Italian, too, and to enjoy leisurely strolls around Paris, long twilights at outdoor cafés, great meals in grand restaurants. The relaxed-vacation part was not to be, of course, and the books are mostly still unread.

Our family joke is that we moved here for my job, and we stay for Patricia's. While mine at the *International Herald Tribune* offers a full plate of daily challenges, it's not peaches and cream that I associate with the place. No, we've stayed because it is here that Patricia has flourished. She spoke not a word of French when we came, and now she's got a stint on her résumé as the restaurant critic (the first foreigner and the only woman) for *L'Express*. If the pace of our life is rapid, and if there hasn't been time for all the reading we counted on, there has certainly been no shortage of great meals. And still and all, it's a wonderful way to be jaded.

"Mr. Wells," my Southern housekeeper once scolded me, "you sure do like the high life." I don't know what it was that enabled Lucille Coles to define me so succinctly all those years ago in Richmond, Virginia. But she was right. And, frankly, in Paris we find about as much of it as a couple of small-town Americans can stand.

It's not quite like Zelda and Scott during *les années folles;* it's more like the title of Barbara Gordon's autobiography, *I'm Dancing As Fast As I Can,* except I'd probably say, "I'm chewing as fast as I can."

Our days are very full (and often our stomachs, too, given Patricia's line of work), mine determined by *Herald Trib* deadlines and Patricia's packed from beginning to end by her own head-spinning industriousness. When I struggle from bed at nine o'clock, she will already have run for an hour. The bread she's kneaded and left to rise the night before goes into the oven when she goes into the shower. By the time I head for the metro at eleven-thirty, she's logged on to her PC and is juggling paragraphs and phone calls. She keeps that pace up throughout the afternoon, working in the spare bedroom, her only staff the computer, fax, and photocopier.

Working at home and alone allows her to stop whenever she wants to, when other duties call or muses fly away. Chances are that those interruptions will lead her to our neighborhood market on the rue Poncelet, a source of inspiration as well as nourishment.

While we do more things together than a lot of couples, marketing is not among them—that remains solidly Patricia's domain. Sometimes on Sunday mornings I go with her, just for the companionship and the folklore. The incredible array of fresh produce so enticingly presented at every stall is a heady aperitif, and I need no encouragement when it comes to eating.

I find that shopping sets off the same kind of anxiety that overwhelms me in a really terrific bookstore. There's so much there; how can you possibly know where to start? And besides, my wife is Patricia Wells—I've been with her often enough that her merchants recognize me—and if I go to the wrong one or make a bad buy, tongues will wag.

For Patricia, though, a trip to the market frequently turns into an adventure. She heads out for a half dozen eggs and a pound of coffee and doesn't come home for hours. She's been kidnapped by M. Alléosse, the cheese merchant, and taken on a tour of his newest aging cellars, under the streets of the 17th Arrondissement, or for a tonic *double express* at the corner café. Besides the eggs, she returns with a Camembert so ripe it won't wait another minute or a chèvre so fresh that it's still within hours of being goat's milk.

Sometimes it's M. Romieu or his sister-in-law, Mme. Christian, who has detained her with a demonstration of their latest coffee-roasting equipment at the market's Brûlerie des Ternes. They used to try to break a very old habit of ours and would propose new roasts and new combinations of flavors—all of them delicious. But nothing seems to satisfy us as much as their Maragogipe, a full-bodied Guatemalan coffee that is naturally low in caffeine. Now when Patricia walks into the shop, they automatically open the Maragogipe bin and begin scooping, without saying a word.

What Patricia brings home depends on what she's working on, and her assignments always determine the time we spend at table. If she has, as she puts it, her battle helmet strapped on and is trying to wrestle an article or manuscript into shape against a dead-line, those trips to the market can be rare. She goes with a string bag, not a grocery cart, and comes home with coffee, maybe some yogurt, vegetables for salads and crudités. "How can Patricia Wells have a totally empty refrigerator?" I have muttered more than once.

But if she's in testing mode, we eat bountifully and well—if sometimes slightly bizarrely. A difficult recipe might require testing over four or five days, so we'll have the same thing four or five meals in a row.

Testing time is also one of the occasions when we entertain at home, something that both of us love to do but that our schedules rarely permit anymore. We invite another couple to join us for dinner, and we make it festive. We load up the tiny, round dining table (the big ones are all desks now) with enough china and crystal and silver for four, light the candles, and Patricia serves one of her unforgettable dinners.

The meal might be a one-dish wonder—a cassoulet or a Provençale daube—followed by a salad and a dessert, or it might be a more elaborate menu.

This dinner starts with a salad that combines the crunch of pear with the pepperiness of watercress. The main course is quail, which has long been a favorite. Years ago during visits with my parents in the South, we always prepared a meal using fresh quail we bought from a neighboring farm. Those were what Patricia calls our "veal Orloff days," and the quail preparation was as involved as we could make it. We would bone them, brown them, cook them with wild rice and mushrooms, and finally flame them with cognac we'd sneaked into my mother's Presbyterian kitchen. Delicious, but did you ever try boning a quail? Our butcher in Provence, the irrepressible Roland Henny, inspired this simpler grilled whole bird, with fresh coriander, lemon zest and cumin. It's better, too, because the bones of any fowl deliver so much flavor in the cooking. And Patricia adds coriander to the green beans to echo that essence from the quail.

And finally, to round out this meal, she indulged my passion for lemon with small portions of three lemon desserts. Small portions, but seconds were available.

As for the wine selection, since Patricia is so much better at picking wines than I am, she gets to do it. Both of us insist. Lately, though, the choice has been easy. Usually the only wine served after the aperitif glasses are emptied is our own Clos Chanteduc, a fledgling effort to produce a drinkable Côtes du Rhône from our tiny vineyard in Provence. We talk loud and we talk big, and we have a great time. (Why not? The Clos Chanteduc vineyard is the same size as La Tâche, and our investment so far means that drinking a bottle from our vineyard costs just about the same as a bottle of theirs.)

Other nights, happily alone, we have dinner in the kitchen, perched on our stools at the counter. "It's just terrible that we're letting our standards slip," Patricia says, affecting a Southern accent and quoting me mimicking a mother-in-law I no longer have.

On a day-to-day basis—in matters large and small—Patricia is invariably confronted with the French preoccupation with gastronomy. On a recent morning one of the titled neighbors in our building, a marquis who still lives off the income of his property in the Auvergne, stopped her in the street to ask about the state of affairs in Paris restaurants. An uptick in business there, he felt, would be the clearest sign that economic hope had returned to the French and the recession was ending. And our local dry cleaner, M. Lascar, has suggested that he be mentioned in Patricia's restaurant reviews as the best place to have sauce stains removed from blouses and ties. (It's true. He's a wizard.)

And we have frequent reason to call upon his services. At least three times a week, when I'm not obligated to remain at the paper until half-past midnight, Patricia and I meet at eight-thirty or nine o'clock and head for dinner. I may suggest a restaurant, but Patricia decides where we'll go, always looking for something new and undiscovered, a gem of a bistro that she can share with readers. The frequent assumption that restaurant critics save the really good places for themselves could not be further from the truth. There is so much more satisfaction in finding places for other people to enjoy.

"How can you eat so much and not be fat?" is one of the questions we are frequently asked. "My tailor is rich," is my quick reply.

In my first five years, I packed on twenty-five pounds, which seems about standard among American men my height and age who love French food and move here to eat it. Through flirtations with diet and discipline, I keep shuffling about the same amount of weight off and on. Patricia pays the price of her profession by taking morning runs in the Parc Monceau.

But the single most-asked question will always be about the fluency of our French. The language is a constant lesson in humility, a small unstructured study in the cognitive process.

And the answer is yes, our French is fluent, but fluent doesn't mean grammatical, and it certainly doesn't mean unaccented. For there is this truth about accents: the muscles you use to form words have been shaped by the time you are three. Just ask Schwarzenegger and listen to his answer.

There's a reason they call it a foreign language. I think that's why, in part, life here sometimes feels like a role, an exotic walk-on part. On a really terrific day it's even a cameo appearance in "The High Life."

To live in Paris is to be surrounded by texture and richness of all sorts, and I have friends who fix on one thing as the essence of the place, and they head for that symbol as soon as they get off the plane. One chum goes from the airport to lunch at La Coupole. Another times his arrival for dinner at L'Ami Louis, his reservation made long in advance.

Since we live here, when we return after an absence we usually feel more compelled to open the mail and get the laundry done. But one essential as we settle back in is a nonworking dinner at a favorite restaurant. Not one of the grands, but a homey spot like Le Petit Marguery in the 13th, or the Bistro de l'Étoile on rue Lauriston, or Benoît in the rue St.-Martin. We'll go late, and we'll choose basics like *blanquette de veau*. We'll talk and we'll dawdle, savoring the food and a bottle of Côtes du Rhône, but relishing even more the Parisian's favorite way of spending an evening.

As our life has evolved here, these are the experiences that have best served to give me a sense of place, to tell me that I'm home and that this hometown, too, is an accessible reality—even as much as McConnells, South Carolina, was in my boyhood.

Before our first trip to Paris together, a delayed honeymoon in the fall of 1979, I remember collecting addresses for days beforehand, writing them on index cards and arranging them by subject in a ring binder. Once here, I mostly left the addresses in the hotel room and thrived on wandering around, sometimes lost, always marveling, enjoying this beauty, this (please excuse me) vision of life.

A Truman Capote character in "Unspoiled Monsters" (one of the stories in *Answered Prayers* that actually did get published) dismisses Paris as just scenery after a while. I can't imagine plummeting to that level of ennui anywhere and especially not in Paris, a city that never fails to dazzle. But even as just scenery, it's not bad at all.

Oftentimes the mind fixes on a favorite place and calls it up at will, to relive pleasure or chase away anxiety. My own favorite visual mementos include Central Park at sunset from high above on Manhattan's West Side, a particular vista at a certain time of day on the Amalfi coast, and the kaleidoscope of Red Sea forms and colors from my only scuba adventure.

But what my mind's eye summons most often is the rose windows at Notre Dame, the sunlight streaming through. Just scenery, and I want it to illuminate all my days.

The Louvre Honors a Patron Saint of French Painting

BY JOHN RUSSELL

~~

editor's note

Charles Sterling was completely unknown to me before I read this piece, and I suspect he is unknown to a fair number of readers. Yet it is precisely because Sterling had such extraordinary talent—yet remains so little known outside art-history and museum circles—that I decided to include it. Students and museum-goers will, as John Russell notes, recognize many of the paintings Sterling was responsible for acquiring or identifying. Recently, I purchased the catalog that accompanied this Louvre exhibit. The catalog is the fortieth volume in the museum's own paperback series, *Les Dossiers du Département des Peintures.* Each volume is in French and is reasonably priced, with color and black-and-white reproductions. In addition to the art reproductions, *Hommage à Charles Sterling: Des Primitifs à Matisse* includes a photo of the Grande Galerie of the Louvre in 1939, after it was evacuated. Seeing the paintings Russell mentions together in this catalog made me appreciate Sterling even more and made me realize it was important to share his achievements, and his life, with others.

JOHN RUSSELL was for many years the chief art critic of *The New York Times* (to which he still contributes articles) and the London *Sunday Times.* He is the author of numerous books, including *Matisse: Father & Son* (1999), *Paris* (1983), and *Reading Russell: Essays 1941 to 1988 on Ideas, Literature, Art, Theater, Music, Places, and Persons* (1989), all published by Harry N. Abrams. Russell is also a Commander of the British Empire and an Officier of the Legion of Honor.

Not quite fifty years ago, when Fiorello La Guardia was mayor of New York, he went in his capacity as an ex officio trustee of the Metropolitan Museum to a meeting of its acquisitions committee. Not every mayor of New York makes the most of this opportunity, but on that afternoon La Guardia intervened in a way that those present did not forget.

Among the paintings proposed was the portrait of Guillaume Budé (1467–1540) by Jean Clouet. It had been brought forward by Charles Sterling, a Polish-born art historian and former member of the staff of the Louvre. Rescued from France in 1942 through the intervention of Francis Henry Taylor, the director of the Met at the time, Sterling had made himself indispensable.

It was Sterling's dearest wish that the Met should buy that Clouet. He went after it like a gundog. Budé had been one of the great European humanists. He knew more Greek than anyone else north of the Alps. He had helped to shape the future Collège de France in Paris. As for Clouet, he was the very apotheosis of a certain French style in portraiture.

In briefing Taylor as to what he should say at the meeting, Sterling added that Budé had been mayor of Paris and was responsible for paving some of its streets. The first lines of the brief did not strike sparks from the committee. The painting was and is a masterpiece, but even after nearly five hundred years Budé himself had the power to intimidate.

Progress was barely perceptible, therefore. But then Taylor mentioned, almost as an afterthought, that Budé had been an exemplary mayor of Paris. At that, La Guardia jumped to his feet, rapped on the table and said: "How about that? I'm a mayor, and this guy was a mayor! And he paved the streets of Paris! This is a picture we can't do without!"

And that is how the Met came by one of the great documents of the French Renaissance. It was not the only service Sterling rendered to New York. He was on the staff of the Met, part-time, until 1955 and did much of the work on the definitive catalog of its French paintings. Until 1972 he taught in New York for several months a year, first at Columbia and later at the New York University Institute of Fine Arts.

But his first and truest love was for the Louvre, and it is outside the Louvre that posters for the exhibition *Homage to Charles Sterling* can be seen today. The show that bears his name (and is on view through June 22) consists of exactly twenty-four paintings about which Sterling had something indispensable to say. They range in date from the celebrated fifteenth-century *Avignon Pietà* to the Matisse *Still Life With Oranges* that was one of Picasso's proudest possessions.

It would be no more than a distinguished anthology, were it not that every painting comes with a lengthy text drawn from Charles Sterling's published writings. Those texts reveal him not merely as a great archival scholar but as a connoisseur of the first rank who was also (and how rarely do the two go together!) a lord of language.

This is the more remarkable in that Sterling was in many ways a late beginner. He was twenty before he learned French. He was twenty-four when he arrived in Paris in 1925 as a lawyer, lately qualified in Warsaw, and decided to become an art historian. He was taught by Henri Focillon, who formed many a major art historian, and his gifts were immediately evident. But, even so, he regretted to the end of his life that in boyhood and young manhood he had never had the implacable education that had given a kick-start to so many a clever young Frenchman.

But it turned out that, in his use of French, Sterling was as attentive to the music of the word as he was to the music of the eye. He spoke true, and he spoke memorably well, with never a side step into gratuitous "fine writing."

It is fundamental to the show that every picture in it relates to a specific episode in Sterling's career. The Georges de La Tour reminds us that already in 1934 he gave the world a completely new idea of what he called the "painters of reality" in seventeenth-century France.

There are sublime and vastly varied still lifes by Luis Meléndez, Lubin Baugin, Jean-Siméon Chardin and Henri Matisse to remind us that Sterling pioneered the study of still life as an autonomous mode of painting that could take a high rank on its own merits. (As to that, nothing could be more cogent than the majestic exhibition of Picasso still lifes that will open next month at the Philadelphia Museum of Art.)

He also pioneered the scientific study of painting in France during the Middle Ages. (The first copy of volume two of his monumental study *Medieval Painting in Paris* was put into his hands as he lay dying last year, not far short of his ninetieth birthday.)

Thanks to his more than fifty years' research into this subject, we now know who painted what, and where, and when, in medieval France. On many occasions—and above all in the case of the *Avignon Pietà,* by general consent one of the finest European paintings of its date—Sterling was able to identify the artist concerned. The name of Enguerrand Quarton is never likely to be bandied about in the auction rooms, but as the author of the *Avignon Pietà* he has no need of other credentials.

Sterling was a colossal worker. In preparing a major exhibition, *Masterpieces of French Art,* in 1937, he dumbfounded his colleagues by his powers of endurance. (One of them, René Huyghe, remembers how Sterling once fell to the floor in a faint from exhaustion after a long day in the Alte Pinakothek in Munich that did not include a break for lunch.) In his working library, which he left to the Louvre, there were 12,155 books, most of them annotated by himself, and 38,000 photographs. Powered by a curiosity that knew no rest, he had as much to say about Cézanne as about the painters who had worked in Provence four hundred and more years earlier.

Who but he would have worked out exactly the effect upon Cézanne of the slow-moving little river Essonnes, not far from Paris, as distinct from the rivers near Aix-en-Provence?

In the Cézanne called *Le Pont de Maincy*, which is now in the Louvre, Sterling saw a paint structure "built with touch upon touch of solid and yet transparent enamel, like the blue-green ingredients of a mosaic." Looking at Rembrandt's famous painting of the skinned carcass of an ox, he noted that the dead meat had kept all the formidable energy of life and had become, in Rembrandt's hands, the rarest and most eloquent of all subjects for painting.

Faced with *Hercules and Omphale* in the Louvre, which was no more than a distinguished ruin in which Omphale gives Hercules' left ear a most terrible tweak, he coaxed it back into the canon of paintings by Rubens. No one had ever been able to give a name to the Maître de Moulins, who had surfaced in the 1480s as a major French artist. But long and close looking empowered Sterling to say once and for all, in association with archival research by his colleague Nicole Reynaud, that the Maître de Moulins was a painter called Jean Hey.

Like many another enthusiast for the subject who was not born in France, Sterling never tired of trying to define the Frenchness of French art. What was it, he asked himself, that distinguished a portrait of an old man by van Eyck, or Mantegna, from the portrait of the donor in the *Avignon Pietà*?

Now that Mantegna's portraits are present in force at the Met (through July 12), we can see exactly what Sterling meant when he said that with just a line or two, here and there, Mantegna could define the volumes of the head as if it were cast in bronze. Van Eyck, by contrast, worked with the wrinkled skin, and with an accumulation of every relevant detail, until the very hands of a senior subject would seem to tremble. Forty wrinkles to a cheek seemed to him none too many.

And Enguerrand Quarton, the painter of the *Pietà?* He mastered the structure of the skull as clearly as any Italian. But he also had a Flemish eye for the odd, important detail—the ill-shaven gray hairs on the face, for instance. Like many a French painter of his time, he had something of Flemish painting, and something of Italian painting, and something not easily defined that was specifically French.

In all Sterling's dealings, whether with works of art or with human beings, he thought first of others. He may have interrogated works of art (I quote here from René Huyghe) as an intelligence officer interrogates a prisoner of war. But he did it patiently and humanely, never taking advantage of his position.

In life, likewise, he was a model to us all. In October 1940, when Jews were forbidden by law to hold official positions in France, the Polish consulate in Marseilles told Sterling not to worry. "Drop by here any day," they said, "and we'll certify that your ancestors have been Aryans since the beginnings of time."

This could have saved Sterling from deportation and a terrible death. But he refused to do it. "If I had that piece of paper in my pocket," he said, "I should be ashamed to shake hands with my fellow Jews if I met them on the street."

He deserved as well of his fellow human beings as he did of the history of art, and I rejoice that he should be honored at the Louvre.

Janet Flanner

BY WILLIAM SHAWN

editor's note

I think this eloquent obituary on Janet Flanner reveals more of her than any full-length interview or biography. Somehow, in its succinctness and simplicity, it reveals precisely the sort of person she was.

Readers of *The New Yorker* before the 1990s know that it was the magazine's long-standing policy not to print bylines. Not until I requested permission to reprint this piece did I learn it had been written by WILLIAM SHAWN, distinguished editor of the magazine for nearly forty years. Though the obituary originally appeared without a byline, I have included it here. It was featured in the issue dated November 20, 1978.

Last week, at the end of a gentle, sunny day spent in characteristically witty, reflective talk with close friends and in an idyllic walk in Central Park during which she took in the autumn foliage with the eyes of a child and expressed astonishment and gratitude that it could be as beautiful as it was, Janet Flanner, at the age of eighty-six, died. The colors, the shapes, the sounds, and the textures of this earth, whether they were arranged by nature or by artists, enthralled her, just as words and the play of ideas enthralled her, and, finally and fundamentally, people, whoever they were. Her domain was spacious, and anyone lucky enough to come her way— friend, acquaintance, passerby—was warmly invited to share it. It is no wonder that she became a journalist, and that her journalism was transcendent.

On October 10, 1925, several months after the magazine was founded, Janet Flanner—under the name Genêt—wrote her first Paris Letter for *The New Yorker*. On September 29, 1975, she wrote her last Paris Letter. In the fifty years between them, she wrote more than seven hundred letters—hundreds of thousands of words—as our Paris correspondent: a journalistic effort without parallel. This might be a cheerless statistic were it not that each quality she had as a writer at the outset sharpened and deepened with the years. Her eye never became jaded, her ardor for what was new and alive never diminished, and her language remained restless. She was a stylist who devoted her style, bedazzling and heady in itself, to the subtle task of conveying the spirit of a subtle people. She loved the people of France among whom she lived so much of her life, and she loved no less the American people for whom she wrote. She was doubly, and openly, a patriot. True to her Quaker upbringing, whatever she wrote she imbued with moral concern. No matter how dark the prospect grew, she possessed an irreducible minimum of faith that somehow or other people would pull themselves together and extricate themselves from their predicament. She was an Indiana optimist perched in a small, cluttered room on the top floor of the Hôtel Continental in Paris, and when she looked down over her adored city she saw, even at the most unlikely moments, reason to hope.

Janet Flanner listened, as well, hearing vibrations too delicate for the ordinary ear, and recording them for the rest of us. Her estimates of people and events, her perceptions and illuminations, were rarely embarrassed by time. Her Paris Letters, which she supplemented prodigiously with scores of Profiles, Reporter at Large pieces, and letters from the various other capitals of Europe, constitute a vast contemporary report of historical events but of atmospheres, too, and of moods and states of mind. Her reporting methods were eccentric—seemingly haphazard. Facts came to her out of the air, and turned out to be the facts that she needed and that counted. As if by inadvertence, she wrote political, social, and cultural history of the first order. Disdaining ponderous analysis, she presented a running account of what was happening in France for half a century—and, along the way, she sketched memorable portraits of Mauriac, Cocteau, Gide, Valéry, Claudel, Malraux, Camus, Sartre, de Beauvoir, Colette, Sarraute, Gertrude Stein, Alice B. Toklas, Sylvia Beach, Picasso, Matisse, Utrillo, Braque, Léger, Stravinsky, Ravel, Poulenc, Milhaud, Piaf, Mistinguett, Josephine Baker, Yves Montand, Pétain, Laval, Daladier, Blum, Mendès-France, and, on the largest scale, the dominant figure of the era, de Gaulle. She caught history as it raced by and before others knew that it was history.

Silver-haired, highly charged, with virtuoso wit, with a strong, elegant face, with the diction and bearing of an actress in the grand manner, Janet Flanner was a stirring presence in any company. Her insistence, both as a conversationalist and as a writer, upon never saying anything in a predictable, or even a convenient, way, her compulsion to reach for unusual phrases and rhythms, reflected not simply a fondness for surprise and ornament—although that she had—but also a refusal to permit her thought to fall into molds or patterns. She had a dread of the commonplace, and she was a stranger to fatigue, boredom, cynicism. Nominally, she was a reporter, a journalist, but in the intensity of her response to what she observed, in her peculiar, all but explosive mixture of intuition and intelligence, in her imagery, in her verbal fun and audacity, in her inspired distillations, in her bizarre and marvelously controlled elisions, in her dependable gravitation toward the heart of the matter, she was a poet among journalists. She was also a tenderhearted, unstinting, protective, steadfast friend. Those of us who knew her well will miss her profoundly.

Bibliothèque

Madame de Sévigné: A Life and Letters, Frances Mossiker, Alfred A. Knopf, 1983. I had originally been interested to read Madame de Sévigné's letters for their historical value, and to read about the Hôtel Carnavalet (now the Musée Carnavalet) when she lived there; little did I realize that Marie de Rabutin-Chantal was a *really good,* passionate writer, who loved language and relaying the news of seventeenth-century Paris and Versailles (mostly to her daughter, but there were other lucky recipients of her missives as well). More than anyone else, perhaps, she appreciated the beauty and joys of writing and receiving handwritten, well-crafted letters. I find Mme. de Sévigné to be, even today, an inspiration to us all.

Napoléon Bonaparte, Alan Schom, HarperCollins, 1997. The only other biography of Napoléon I've read is Vincent Cronin's *Napoléon* (first published in hardcover in 1971 by Collins; published in paperback in 1973 by Penguin Books), which had been one of the leading biographies for a number of years. Cronin is not, however, referenced in either the index or bibliography of Alan Schom's book. I would still recommend Cronin's book to travelers looking for a general, paperback volume on Napoléon, but Schom's major book is *the* current, authoritative work. Historian Schom spent ten years researching this volume, and he is also the author of *One Hundred Days: Napoléon's Road to Waterloo; Trafalgar: Countdown to Battle, 1803–1805.* "History has always fascinated me," he writes in the preface, "but not the lifeless presentation of events of former times reduced to the dates of the reigns of kings and of battles and treaties, all but devoid of human association, of the men and women who actually created those events, and of the entire circumstances surrounding them. To correct such a myopic view and presentation one must introduce a sense of reality and understanding—in this case, the *full life* of Napoléon Bonaparte, whom the reader must see as a human being set in his own times." It was this paragraph that made me anxious to read this big (888 pages) book, in which Napoléon is presented in an extremely detailed and balanced manner. With maps and two black-and-white photo inserts.

The Horizon Book of the Age of Napoléon, American Heritage Publishing Company, distributed by Harper & Row, 1963. This out-of-print-but-worth-a-search-to-find book is perfect for family libraries as it's really more of an encyclopedia with hundreds of reproductions of paintings, drawings, photographs, caricatures, illustrations, and maps all presented in the inimitable Horizon style. The book begins with the French Revolution and features chapters on Napoléon's coronation, the Napoleonic wars, the British navy, Spain, America, Russia, the Czar, etc., and ends with a chapter entitled "History's Judgment," bringing the entire saga of Napoléon's life and times full circle. On the last page before the acknowledgments is a splendid picture entitled *Apotheosis of Napoléon* by Ingres, depicting Napoleon as emperor, crowned with laurels, ascending to heaven.

The Many Lives and Secret Sorrows of Josephine B. and *Tales of Passion, Tales of Woe,* both by Sandra Gulland, Scribner Paperback Fiction, 1999. I am aware that this planned trilogy is a work of historical fiction, but I decided to include it here because I thought it would not stand out properly among all the novels and fiction books listed in *"Des Belles Choses."* Gulland worked on this project—the life of Josephine Bonaparte—for twelve years, traveling extensively to the places Josephine lived and compiling a personal library of over three hundred related titles. I was somewhat skeptical that I would enjoy it as I prefer unadulterated nonfiction, but from the very first page of the first volume I was hooked. Written in the form of letters and diary entries, Josephine's amazing (and foretold) life unfolds and there is never a faltering moment. She emerges as a true heroine and role model, quite different from the image I previously had of Josephine. (At the time of this writing, the third volume in the trilogy, *The Last Great Dance on Earth,* was due to be published in the fall of 2000.)

The French Rothschilds: The Great Banking Dynasty Through Two Turbulent Centuries, Herbert Lottman, Crown, 1995. The only book I know of to focus exclusively on the French branch of the Rothschild family, by award-winning historian Lottman (also the author of *The Fall of Paris*—see *"Paris, Je T'Aime" bibliothèque*). While J. P. Morgan was famous in this country for providing loans to the U.S. government, the Rothschilds were "the single most important source of funds in Europe for governments in war and peace." How the family became the bankers to nobility and governments is a remarkable story. The passage of the law to nationalize wealth in 1981 under Mitterrand may have diminished the Rothschild holdings, but the family's wealth and position is still legendary. With a sixteen-page insert of black-and-white photos.

Zola: A Life, Frederick Brown, Farrar, Straus & Giroux, 1995. The first thing to notice about this book is its size—888 pages. However, Brown—also the author of a Jean Cocteau biography and books about Père Lachaise and the French stage—obviously felt his subject warranted this much ink. Brown draws mostly upon Zola's letters (which offer an extraordinary amount of detail) to present Zola's personal life, his fiction, and a history of Paris and France one hundred years ago. To read of Zola's famous *"J'accuse"* letter, his relationship with Cézanne, and the mysterious circumstances of his death is to read of a complex, committed man famous for going to battle against social injustice. Like other good biographies, this one is fascinating, and about much more than Émile Zola. With twenty-four pages of black-and-white photos.

Misia, Arthur Gold and Robert Fizdale, Alfred A. Knopf, 1980. When I first saw this book shortly after it was published, I had never heard of Misia, and I had no idea she was part of such a history-making crowd (Diaghilev, Coco Chanel, Toulouse-Lautrec, Renoir, Vuillard, Bonnard, Proust, etc.). This is the wildly entertaining but true story of the vivacious socialite Misia (who was born Marie Sophie Olga Zenaide Godebska), a Polish émigré living in Paris before and after World War I. She knew everybody who was anybody, and her third marriage was to Jose-Maria Sert, a Spanish painter who decorated such public buildings as Rockefeller Center and the grand ballroom of the Waldorf-Astoria in New York. Authors Gold and Fizdale had access to Misia's letters and those of her friends (including Stravinsky, Erik Satie, and Colette) and were thus able to bring us a vivid biography complete with black-and-white photographs and color reproductions of some portraits of Misia by all the great painters of the period.

Creating Colette, Volume 1: From Ingenue to Libertine, 1873–1913 and *Volume II: From Baroness to Woman of Letters, 1912–1954,* Claude Francis and Fernande Gontier, both Steerforth Press, both 1999. The story goes that in 1937, an interviewer pointed out to Colette that since she'd left her first husband, Henri Gauthier-Villars (Willy), she'd moved fourteen times. Colette's famous reply was that if she could only live in the Palais-Royal, she'd never move again. Sometimes we get what we ask for, and the occupant of No. 9 rue de Beaujolais vacated his apartment and Colette moved in. True to her word, she never moved again. Colette—the first woman writer to be honored with a state funeral in France—rarely returned to her native Burgundy once she became a Parisian; yet every year the number of *Colettolatres* (the French term for Colette devotees) who descend on the little Burgundian village of St.-Sauveur-en-Puisaye grows larger. I have very much enjoyed Colette's fiction, but I enjoy reading *about* her even more, and this two-volume, definitive biography is delicious in every respect. It seems that much of what the public perceived about Colette was fabricated—and promoted—by Colette herself, but it is still no surprise to discover that Colette led one vastly interesting life. Two other biographical Colette books of which I'm particularly fond are *Colette— Earthly Paradise: An Autobiography Drawn From Her Lifetime Writings* (1966) and *Belles Saisons: A Colette Scrapbook* (1978), both by Robert Phelps, both published by Farrar, Straus & Giroux. Additionally, Maurice Goudeket, Colette's second husband, whom she unsuccessfully hid from the Nazis (but successfully managed to free from deportation to Auschwitz), has written his own book about life with Colette: *The Delights of Growing Old* (A Common Reader edition; see "Bookstores" in *"Renseignements Pratiques"*).

Speak, Memory: An Autobiography Revisited, Vladimir Nabokov, Vintage International, 1989, with black-and-white photos. It's not accidental that there have been a number of Russian emblems in Paris: the Pont Alexandre III, Russian Orthodox cathedrals, and Sergey Diaghilev's *Ballets Russes*. Russian nobility spoke French and looked to France for the latest cultural trends. But after the Franco-Russian alliance of 1891 (forged after the Franco-Prussian war of 1870) and the Revolution of 1917, there was suddenly a large Russian community in Paris. Of the approximately fifty thousand émigrés, many were Jewish (prompting references to the "pletzl of Paris"), many never returned to Russia, and many reached their fullest potential during their Parisian sojourns. Although this Nabokov autobiography isn't limited to the years he lived in Paris, I think that it and Nina Berberova's autobiography (see below) are the best record we have of this vibrant community. *New Republic* hailed this as "the finest autobiography written in our time."

The Italics Are Mine, Nina Berberova, Vintage International, 1993, originally published in the U.S. in 1969 by Harcourt, Brace & World; in 1992, Alfred A. Knopf published an edition with an extensively revised translation. Berberova's autobiography recounts her journey from St. Petersburg to Berlin, Paris, and the U.S., the Paris years making up the majority of the book. She does not romanticize her life or the lives of other writers and artists—including Nabokov, Maxim Gorky, Ivan Bunin, Pasternak, and Aleksandr Kerensky—who fled Russia after the 1917 revolution; she openly writes of their collective poverty and depression, as well as the happier times. "The Black Notebook," the chapter about France under German occupation, is written entirely in the form of a diary, and at the end of the book she has compiled an alphabetical list of Russian names and biographical information. Berberova passed away in 1993 and is the subject of "Going On," an essay in Kennedy Fraser's wonderful book *Ornament and Silence* (Knopf, 1996).

The Unknown Matisse: A Life of Henri Matisse, 1869–1908, Hilary Spurling, Alfred A. Knopf, 1998. This biography is to Matisse what John Richardson's biography is to Picasso. Spurling's works—there are more volumes to come—will, *sans doute,* be the definitive biographic bible on Matisse for a long, long time. It is an absolutely first-rate accomplishment. Spurling maintains that this is a biography and not a work of art history, but it nonetheless has much value in the field of art history. In this first volume she uncovers a scandal known as the Humbert Affair, of which I knew nothing but which was just as sensational as the Stavisky Affair of the 1930s. As the case involved his in-laws, "Matisse was in no position to paint at all," Spurling writes. It was a dramatic, devastating affair but is no more interesting, really, than the rest of his early life. With twenty-four pages of color reproductions and 160 black-and-white illustrations/photographs, this is the bio to read if you are a serious fan of Matisse. You won't find one better.

A Life of Picasso: Volume I, 1881–1906 (1991); *Volume II: 1907–1917* (1996), John Richardson, both Random House. Positively the most definitive volumes on Picasso—and two more are to follow in the planned four-volume set. There are a few bigger Picasso books with more reproductions, but that's all they offer: more color plates. They are not accompanied by the meticulous, scholarly research of Richardson, distinguished author of books and magazine articles, exhibit organizer, and art professor. More importantly, he lived near Picasso in Provence for ten years and in that time became a trusted friend. After Picasso's death Richardson maintained a friendship with Picasso's widow, Jacqueline Roque, and was given access to previously inaccessible archives. The first volume takes Picasso to the age of twenty-five and features nine hundred illustrations. Volume II, equally as big, ends with the production of *Parade* by Jean Cocteau and Erik Satie, and Picasso about to depart for Rome. Richardson's magnum opus is not for casual fans, but for those with a serious interest in the life and work of Picasso.

Picasso: A Biography, Patrick O'Brian, W. W. Norton, 1994 (paperback); first published in 1976 by William Collins Sons & Co., London. I was surprised to discover this biography by the author of the popular Aubrey/Maturin novels, but as it turns out, I shouldn't have been. Not only is O'Brian a longtime admirer of Picasso but he's an accomplished nonfiction writer as well. If you decide that Richardson's multivolume biography is more than you desire, this is the book to pick up. O'Brian goes into much detail about Picasso's Spanish heritage and the impact this had on his work throughout his long life. He also successfully presents a balanced picture of the controversial artist.

The Success and Failure of Picasso, John Berger, Vintage International, 1993 (paperback); Pantheon, 1989 (hardcover); originally published in the U.S. and Great Britain by Penguin, 1965 and 1966. For yet another viewpoint, by novelist/critic/historian John Berger. Even more so than Patrick O'Brian, Berger delves deep into Picasso's Spanish heritage and into Spain itself. He has not exactly written a biography of Picasso, but something a little different: a fascinating critique of Picasso's paintings and drawings, simultaneously comparing them to works by, among others, Courbet, Poussin, Robert Delaunay, Brancusi, Delacroix, and Velázquez. Berger the historian also weaves social thought, political movements, and philosophy into the narrative. I found his thoughts on how the relationship between art and reality changed after 1914 particularly insightful. This is a great read for putting Picasso into the context of his times and will be of special interest to those planning to visit the Musée Picasso in the Marais.

Life With Picasso, Françoise Gilot and Carlton Lake, McGraw-Hill (hardcover), 1964; Anchor/Doubleday (paperback), 1989. In his introduction to this engaging book (once I began reading it I was incapable of putting it down), Carlton Lake says of Gilot, "I realized that she had an infinitely deeper and truer appreciation of Picasso's thought and work than anyone I had encountered." Lake certainly encountered enough people in Picasso's circle of friends and acquaintances to make such a statement. And judging from other works I've read about Picasso, I believe his observation is correct. Although Gilot and Picasso never married, they did have two children together, Paloma and Claude. I have great admiration for Gilot, who is an accomplished artist in her own right (for a complete look at her printmaking oeuvre, see *Stone Echoes: Original Prints by Françoise Gilot—A Catalogue Raisonné,* Mel Yoakum, Philip and Muriel Berman Museum of Art at Ursinus College, Collegeville, Pennsylvania, 1995; this book does not include her fifteen hundred oil paintings or over five thousand works on paper). In 1970, Gilot married Dr. Jonas Salk, who passed away some years ago. And so she has spent much of her life with two of the most influential people of the twentieth century. She is no less fascinating a figure.

Matisse and Picasso: A Friendship in Art, Françoise Gilot, Doubleday, 1990. Gilot, Picasso's companion from 1946 to 1954, was of course in a rare position to observe the friendship and rivalry between Matisse and Picasso. Much has been written about the ways in which they influenced each other but not from the personal perspective Gilot presents here. She shares previously unseen letters Matisse wrote to her as well as insights into the works of each artist.

Matisse, Picasso, Miró: As I Knew Them, Rosamond Bernier, Knopf, 1991, foreword by John Russell. Many people know Rosamond Bernier for the lively and interesting lectures she gives at the Metropolitan Museum of Art. Before she became a celebrated lecturer she spent twenty-plus years in France and cofounded the monthly art magazine *L'Œil.* Among the many artists she met were Matisse, Picasso, and Miró, and in this book she shares some of the memorable anecdotes and observations of her friendships with them. This is plentifully illustrated with color reproductions and black-and-white illustrations, with much that is fresh, and it's a joy to read.

Édouard Manet: Rebel in a Frock Coat, Beth Archer Brombert, Little, Brown and Company, 1996; University of Chicago Press, 1996, paperback. In a sea of books about Manet, this one stands out, and Brombert wrote it primarily for the general reader with an interest in Manet's art and the times in which he lived (as opposed to professional art historians). With thirty-two pages of black-and-white photos and reproductions of Manet's most famous and some lesser-known canvases.

Rodin: A Biography, Frederic V. Grunfeld, Da Capo Press, 1998; originally published by Henry Holt & Co., 1987. As he states in the preface, Grunfeld was writing an essay for *Horizon* on Rodin's *Balzac* and he tried to find a biography that reflected the literary aura of Rodin's time, an age with no shortage of notable writers on art (Goncourt, Zola, Maupassant, Gide, Mallarmé,

Apollinaire, etc.); but he couldn't find quite the book he was looking for, so he decided to write it himself. Grunfeld went on to note that the last Rodin biography based on original research was Judith Cladel's *Rodin, Sa vie glorieuse, sa vie inconnue,* published in 1936, so it was high time for a new, fresh biography. An authoritative, respected title.

Rodin: The Shape of Genius, Ruth Butler, Yale University Press, 1993. Also authoritative, and different from Grunfeld's book in that Butler draws for the first time on little-explored archives, letters, and unpublished anecdotes from the Musée Rodin. Not until 1973, when there was a change in chief curator at the museum, was she allowed access to the vast archives—apparently Rodin kept *everything:* publicity clippings, letters he wrote, letters he received. There are over five thousand dossiers in the archives, and Butler read only the ones containing letters *to* Rodin (those *from* him were unavailable because the staff was then preparing a four-volume publication of his letters), which is just as well or this book would surely not yet be published.

Toulouse-Lautrec: A Life, Julia Frey, Phoenix (a division of Orion Books), London, 1995; first published in Great Britain in 1994 by Weidenfeld and Nicolson. For this definitive biography, Frey had access to over one thousand of the family letters (previously unknown to historians), which helped to correct some widely believed myths. However, the essential facts of Toulouse-Lautrec's life still don't make a pretty picture: he was born an aristocrat but preferred spending time in cabarets, often in the company of prostitutes and the down-and-outs of society; he was also a dwarf, and an alcoholic. Still, this is an immensely fascinating book, and belle epoque Paris is evoked well. With a twenty-four-page insert of color art reproductions, and black-and-white photos throughout.

The Letters of Vincent van Gogh, edited and introduced by Mark Roskill, Atheneum, 1963; reprinted by arrangement with William Collins Sons & Co., London. Van Gogh's letters are often quoted, and though the quotes may be appealing by themselves, they reveal only the smallest portion of Vincent the painter, brother, and spiritual human being. The letters are essential in understanding van Gogh in full, but they also tell an unforgettable and heartbreaking story. Several good editions are available—I am fond of this one both for its comprehensiveness and small size; just be sure to avoid one that is too abridged. This edition also includes sixteen pages of black-and-white reproductions of van Gogh's canvases.

Henry Miller: The Paris Years, Brassai, originally published in France under the title *Henry Miller, grandeur nature,* published in the U.S. by Arcade Publishing (an imprint of Little, Brown and Company), New York, 1995. This work is photographer Brassai's memoir of Miller during the time they knew each other in Paris, 1930–39. What makes it unique is the generous use of extracts from Miller's letters and published works, and the neighborhood maps of Montparnasse and St.-Germain and Montmartre and Clichy, marked with numbers corresponding to passages in the text. With sixteen black-and-white photos by Brassai, this is a singular portrait of a writer—and sometimes painter—who lived, breathed, and devoured the city and became the original writer we know him to be during his years in Paris.

An Artful Life: A Biography of D. H. Kahnweiler: 1884–1979, Pierre Assouline, Fromm International Publishing Corporation, 1991, by arrangement with Grove Weidenfeld; originally published in French as *L'homme de l'art: D. H. Kahnweiler, 1884–1979* by Éditions André Balland, Paris, 1988. The biggest champion of many of the artists of the late 1800s and early 1900s was David-Heinrich Kahnweiler, possibly the greatest art dealer of the twentieth century. Among the painters he represented were Picasso, Braque, Juan Gris, Léger, André Derain, Paul Klee, and André Masson. De rigueur reading for an in-depth look at the French art world between the wars and the relationship between artists and dealers. With black-and-white photos.

Living Well Is the Best Revenge, Calvin Tomkins, Modern Library, 1998; originally published by Viking Press, 1971; *Everybody Was So Young,* Amanda Vaill, Houghton Mifflin, 1998, hardcover; Broadway Books, 1999, paperback. F. Scott Fitzgerald is one of my favorite writers, and *Tender Is the Night* is my favorite Fitzgerald book. When I first read it, I knew it was loosely based on the dazzling American expatriates Gerald and Sara Murphy, but I had no clue how much of it was fiction. I remained fascinated by the Murphys, and with the appearance of these two books, Murphy facts and fictions have been sorted out. The Modern Library edition, at 172 pages, is the smaller of the two, but is not a lesser book in any way. Tomkins, longtime art critic for *The New Yorker,* relates this story concisely and engagingly. Black-and-white reproductions of Gerald's paintings and sixty-nine photographs from the Murphys' family album are included (the color painting featured on the jacket, *Cocktail,* is also Gerald's and is part of the collection at the Whitney Museum of American Art). Amanda Vaill's book runs to 361 pages—plus a few pages for the author's note and acknowledgments—and also includes two inserts of black-and-white photos. This book is simply *more,* more detail, more background, more recent material (there are even a few photos from the forties and fifties, whereas in the Tomkins book a notation appears after the last photo: "The Murphys' family albums do not go beyond 1933, the year they came to America"). Initially, I wasn't sure what Gerald meant by his remark "Even though it happened in France, it was all somehow an American experience," but by the end I saw that this is very much an American tale, and a rather tragic one at that. If you're going to read one book, you might as well read them both. The slim hardcover can easily be devoured on the flight over, and you'll finish the paperback in the wee hours of the first or second night because you won't be able to resist.

The War Memoirs of Charles de Gaulle: The Call to Honor: 1940–1942, Collins, St. James Place, London, 1955; *Unity: 1942–1944,* Simon & Schuster, 1959; *Salvation: 1944–1946,* Simon & Schuster, 1960. Although it might seem appropriate for de Gaulle's war memoirs to appear in *"Le Kiosque,"* I chose to include them here because they are more closely associated with de Gaulle personally than as a definitive record of the war years in France. Truthfully, I was unaware until a few years ago that de Gaulle had written his war memoirs, and I bought them even though I was sure they would be so much puffery. It turned out I was only partially right—no one ever said de Gaulle was modest, after all—and I was quickly swept up in his *certaine idée de la France* (which included a certain place for him). It seems beside the point to debate whether his memoirs compare with Churchill's multivolume masterpiece on the Second World War; de Gaulle's memoirs stand alone, and his was the one true voice of occupied France during those dark years. Each edition contains good maps and black-and-white photographs. I found my three hardcovers at a used-book store, but there is now a single paperback volume available entitled *The Complete War Memoirs of Charles de Gaulle* (Carroll & Graf, 1998), which is a handy, if gigantic (over one thousand pages), book.

Saint-Exupery: A Biography, Stacy Schiff, Knopf, 1994. Everyone knows Saint-Ex as the author of *Le Petit Prince* (which continues to sell about three hundred thousand copies a year in France and over one hundred thousand copies in America; it's been translated into nearly eighty languages, making Saint-Ex the most translated author in the French language); some know him as the author of *Night Flight; Wind, Sand and Stars;* or *Flight to Arras;* but hardly anyone knows the private Saint-Exupery. Schiff has tried to bring him to us in this biography, and if Saint-Ex still remains somewhat enigmatic, I think that was an intentional part of how he chose to live his life. Schiff does not reveal any conclusive new evidence regarding his disappearance in 1944 (it's doubtful we'll ever know what happened on his flight from Corsica), but she does rule out some existing theories. It seems Saint-Ex was a controversial figure his entire life, and that life makes for captivating reading. With sixteen pages of black-and-white photographs.

A Chef's Tale: A Memoir of Food, France and America, Pierre Franey with Richard Flaste and Bryan Miller, Knopf, 1994. Born in Burgundy and trained in Paris, Franey was executive chef at two of the greatest French restaurants in

America: Le Pavillon and La Côte Basque, both in New York. He went on, of course, to write the "60-Minute Gourmet" column for *The New York Times* and became a cookbook author and television personality. But the less famous parts of his life story are just as interesting. This is a warm and heartfelt reminiscence—with a good selection of recipes at the end of the book—which is de rigueur for really understanding the respect accorded to food in Burgundy, and in all of France.

Reflected Glory: The Life of Pamela Churchill Harriman, Sally Bedell Smith, Simon & Schuster, 1996, with thirty-two pages of black-and-white photos. Pamela Digby Churchill Hayward Harriman (she was wife to Churchill's son, Randolph; Leland Hayward; and Averell Harriman) lived one of the twentieth century's more interesting lives. In 1993, she was nominated and confirmed as U.S. ambassador to France within four days. Pamela thus became the first woman to be named to this post. A group of us had the opportunity to meet her and tour the embassy residence and its pretty garden—which is just off the place de la Concorde—in 1995. It was a memorable visit, all the more so because she passed away just a few years later, in 1997 (her successor is Felix Rohatyn). Pamela declined interview requests for this book, but friends and associates were free to talk to Smith. As a result, it's hard to imagine that much else is missing from her life story.

French Lessons: A Memoir, Alice Kaplan, The University of Chicago Press, 1993. It is probably not accurate to refer to Kaplan as a "personality" outside of literary circles (her memoir was selected as a Notable Book of 1993 by *The New York Times Book Review* and was a National Book Critics Circle Award Nominee). However, I've included her book here both because it is a memoir and because Kaplan has spent portions of her life in France. It's an unusual memoir and an insightful work about language. I love the way she writes about learning and teaching French, her French summer camp in 1968 where if you were caught speaking one word of English you got a *mauvais point,* and her love affair with André on her junior year abroad. Also, I found her research on French Fascist intellectuals—and interview with the only one still living, Maurice Bardeche—unsettling and fascinating.

Les Musées, Jardins, et Monuments (Museums, Gardens, and Monuments of Note)

I threw myself on a bench and began to wonder if there was anything better in the world worth doing than to sit in an alley of clipped limes smoking, thinking of Paris and of myself.

—George Moore, "In the Luxembourg Gardens," MEMOIRS OF MY DEAD LIFE

I had never really wanted a photograph of a picture before I saw Millet's Man With the Hoe. *I was about twelve or thirteen years old, I had read* Eugénie Grandet *of Balzac, and I did have some feeling about what french country was like but* The Man With the Hoe *made it different, it made it ground not country, and France has been that to me ever since.*

—Gertrude Stein, PARIS FRANCE

The Domes of Paris

BY CARY MARRIOTT

∾

editor's note

....

The domes of Paris churches are among the city's little-known treasures, and in this piece Marriott highlights those of both famous buildings
such as the Dôme des Invalides, Val-de-Grâce, and the Panthéon as well as
the little-visited Temple de la Visitation Sainte-Marie, Saint-Joseph des
Carmes, and—my favorite—Saint-Paul–Saint-Louis.

Aside from Dalloyau and Pâtisserie Lerch, the restaurants mentioned in
the text may or may not still be as described. Their appearance in the piece
serves merely as a reminder, as you travel from dome to dome, to stop for
sustenance at the eating or drinking establishment of your choice.

D omes popped up on the skyline of Paris in the seventeenth
century much the way skyscrapers do in Manhattan today.
Though a number have been destroyed over the years, the domes
that remain add striking definition to the silhouette of the city, each
one a bauble on a necklace strung around the streets.

The story of the domes began for me when I was a student in
Paris. I was completing an art history paper that required me to race
around during a cold, rainy December in pursuit of these architectural emblems. Admittedly, at the start I was more interested in
semester break than I was in domes, but soon I became the captive
of kings and queens and cardinals and of the great architects of the
day. When I finished I was left with an impression I have not forgotten, one not of pediments and spires but of how seventeenth-
century Paris actually perceived itself. My work was like rustling
through the pages of the city's personal diary.

It was Paris's *grand siècle*, a time when the city blossomed into
the capital of France and became the hub of the world. By the end

of the century Paris had usurped Rome as the most important religious and artistic center, and politically France was challenging the long ascendancy of Spain.

The first domed church in Paris was not completed until after Henri IV's assassination in 1610, but he is integral to the story nonetheless. Taking the throne in 1589, Henri soon abjured his Protestant faith and thereby pulled France from the rubble of three decades of civil war between Protestants and Catholics. In 1598, the same year he signed a treaty with Spain, Henri gave equal rights to Huguenots with the Edict of Nantes. Peace established, he set about quickly to remodel Paris, using architecture to impose order on an unruly nation and to represent the power of his state. Among his triumphs were the place des Vosges, the place Dauphine, and the completion of the Pont Neuf; Louis XIII and Louis XIV were to follow his lead in urban planning.

The climate that Henri IV created—expressed in this building boom combined with architectural innovation and religious tolerance—gave rise to the domed church. Paris became prime missionary territory, as the Catholic Church—in the throes of the Counter-Reformation—saw a need to reassert itself: some sixty convents were built in the first forty years of the century.

The Church viewed architecture as a powerful tool as well, calculating decoration, lighting, and shape for maximum emotional effect. Churches of this time were meant for preaching and for defending the faith. A church with three naves separated by pillars did not allow everyone to see and hear the priest easily, and so a change of form was necessary. The addition of a dome both flooded the church with light and improved the acoustics. The Latin-cross pattern with a cupola above the crossing and a single aisle lined by chapels came directly from the mother church of the Jesuit order in Rome, Il Gesù, designed in 1568. Just as Louis Sullivan's first skyscraper had an enormous influence on city skylines for the following hundred years, this design affected church architecture for the following four hundred.

It makes sense to see the domes in chronological order. Each one endeavored to outdo those that came before it, and elements that started as purely functional motifs became more ornamental as time went by.

On a recent trip to revisit the domes, we chose as our base Le Sainte-Beuve, an impeccable little hotel at 9 rue Sainte-Beuve, a block-long street near the intersection of boulevards Raspail and Montparnasse. The hotel was central to many of the domes and a three-minute walk from the Luxembourg Gardens, my favorite Paris playground. Not yet two years old, the twenty-three-room hotel is as crisp and inviting as a freshly pressed shirt.

Our first stop was Saint-Joseph-des-Carmes, a modest church tucked away amid the bustle of the Saint-Germain quarter. Its cornerstone was laid in 1613 by Henri IV's widow, Marie de Médicis, and the crypt holds the bones of the 120 priests who were massacred here in the gardens during the Revolution. Originally part of a Carmelite monastery that stretched as far as the rues du Cherche-Midi and du Regard, the church now serves as a chapel to the Catholic Institute.

We entered through the Institute's impressive stone and brick facade on rue d'Assas, near the corner of rue de Vaugirard. I expected to find somber-looking people in dark robes but instead found a place animated with thoroughly modern-looking students of different nationalities. We came across the courtyard through a short, narrow passageway into the forecourt of the church, where the dome is hidden behind a two-tiered exterior.

Looking much like a small-scale version of Il Gesù, the church interior has a single aisle, lined with side chapels, that leads to center stage. The dome is made of wood and plaster and is less than thirty feet in diameter—quite different from the final dome built in the seventeenth century, at Les Invalides, which is made of stone and three times the size.

To convince the public that the transcendental was real, the artists of the Counter-Reformation mastered the art of optical illusion. The cupola fresco of Saint-Joseph-des-Carmes depicts Elijah on his way to heaven, riding in a chariot of fire surrounded by angels and followed by horses as he casts his mantle to his disciple. The artist, presumed to be Walthère Damery, a Flemish painter who worked in Paris after studying in Rome, achieved his goal of making the viewer feel a party to the event: as I stood beneath the cupola I felt that Elijah's cloak might actually float down into my arms. Don't be so distracted by this fresco that you overlook the marble statue of the Virgin and Child, sculpted after a model of Bernini's, in the transept.

After stopping around the corner on rue Cassette, which offers the best view of the dome's exterior (the incongruous lantern and bell tower were not part of the original building plan but were added much later), we made our way north to the place Saint-Sulpice, past the church of the same name, where the Café de la Mairie overlooks the fountain in the *place*. The café became a choice people-watching spot for this trip.

At the foot of the rue de Tournon we could see the domed portal of the Luxembourg Palace, now home to the Senate, looming like an exclamation point at the head of the street. It took us well over an hour to cover the two blocks that lead to it, stopping as we did in the most appealing stores, from Emmanuelle Khanh to Souleiado. We lingered in Allure, at No. 17. This aptly named shop carries an enticing array of all-white merchandise—from lamps to linens to teapots.

Upon her arrival in Paris, Marie de Médicis took up residence with her husband, King Henri IV, at the Louvre Palace. She continued to live there for a few years after she was widowed in 1610, but when her son the future King Louis XIII became engaged to Anne of Austria, Marie commissioned Salomon de Brosse to build the Luxembourg Palace for her retirement. The architect was instructed that the palace should be reminiscent of the queen regent's birthplace, the Pitti Palace, in Florence, but he took great liberty with his assignment: The statues, rusticated stone, ringed columns, and eight-sided dome reveal an Italian influence, but the building plan completely follows French tradition, evoking the sixteenth-century Hôtel Carnavalet, built between a courtyard and a garden.

In 1625 Marie settled into these sumptuous surroundings, which at the time bordered open countryside. However, she was not to remain there very long. In 1631, Louis XIII, who had had a quarrelsome history with his mother, banished her to Compiègne, in northern France.

With the Luxembourg Palace, Salomon de Brosse set the century's precedent of adapting Italian ideas to French tastes. But the French would never completely embrace the Italian baroque, a style synonymous with the Counter-Reformation; they would always temper it.

We stopped for dinner nearby at Bistro Henri, a cozy nook with a checkered floor and walls the color of dried apricots at 16 rue Princesse. The menu featured *gratin dauphinois* with all of the main courses, which was my cue to dine here. The cheesy potato dish deserved top billing and was perfect with a *tajine* of lamb and crisp roast duck. A small open kitchen adorned with copper pots, herbs in glass jars, and white ceramic bowls was commandeered by a young, mustached chef. "They should call me Marathon Man," declared the one waiter as he weaved and bobbed among a dozen tables.

The next day we joined a group for a tour of the unassuming Temple de la Visitation Sainte-Marie, on rue Saint-Antoine in the

Marais. Sponsored by Les Monuments Historiques, this was one of dozens of tours in French offered weekly for a nominal fee. Even for those who do not speak the language the tours are worthwhile because they afford access to places not generally open to the public. A brochure with information on the guided tours can be picked up at most historic monuments and museums and at the offices of Les Monuments Historiques in the Hôtel de Sully.

The name of our tour, "Cycle Couvents Parisiens du Grand Siècle II—La Visitation Sainte-Marie," seemed so esoteric that I was surprised to find a French group of more than thirty waiting when we arrived. Where else in the world would such a subject gather a crowd? It was clear testimony to the pride of the French in their capital city.

Sainte-Marie, built about 1632, had ties with the great families of this fashionable neighborhood. Jeanne de Chantal, Madame de Sévigné's grandmother, canonized in the eighteenth century, is buried in the crypt. Also buried here are Nicolas Foucquet, Louis XIV's minister of finance, and his family.

Historically, the church's architect, François Mansart, has been overshadowed by his great-nephew Jules Hardouin-Mansart, who designed the domed church at Les Invalides and completed the palace of Versailles, but without question the elder Mansart was the premier architect of his day. Little of his work has survived, so seek out this *chef d'oeuvre,* now a Protestant church, which is open only on Sunday mornings for services.

Breaking with tradition, Mansart expressed the dynamic new religious life of the kingdom in the architecture of the church. I stepped inside and took a deep breath, feeling for a moment as though I were inside a spinning top. The whole space turned and moved with circles, ellipses, and arches, creating an almost palpable energy. Once elaborately decorated, the church is now virtually bare, which is all the better, for the subtlety and harmony of

Mansart's design are emphasized. Outside, Mansart surmounted the huge dome—almost 108 feet high and 44 feet in diameter—with a lantern and a slender spire, giving it a sense of flight, and amplified the facade with pilasters and a grand curving fronton.

"The wars of religion had left the people with a sickness in their heads. Paris was undergoing a kind of spiritual rejuvenation," explained Monsieur Jacomet, the French scholar who led our tour. "This is where architecture and politics met." The style of this church, borrowing from but rejecting the excesses of the Italian baroque, would come to be called classicism.

"A monstrosity," "bizarre," and "disagreeably confused" are some of the words that have been used to describe the facade of Saint-Paul–Saint-Louis, the Jesuit church down the street from Sainte-Marie. Perhaps the most appropriate criticism is that it in no way reflects the building it announces. We walked around behind the church to the corner of rue Charlemagne and rue Jardins Saint-Paul to take in the simple lines of the roof and dome, a juxtaposition of geometric shapes—cone, triangle, circle, hexagon—that would make a perfect assignment for a beginner's drawing class. The rear view of the church is in sharp contrast to the ebullient front.

Part of the inconsistency may stem from the fact that the church had two architects. Étienne Martellange—a Jesuit father who was involved in no fewer than two dozen churches throughout France—patterned Saint-Paul–Saint-Louis after Il Gesù, incorporating a wide, barrel-vaulted nave lined with chapels; Corinthian pilasters; round-arch arcades, above which a low gallery extends; and a cupola, rising nearly 180 feet, that dominates the crossing. François Derrand, another Jesuit father, designed the facade and drew inspiration from Salomon de Brosse's Saint-Gervais–Saint-Protais, a few blocks away.

In 1641 Cardinal Richelieu consecrated the church with the first mass, given in the presence of Louis XIII. Saint-Paul–Saint-Louis enjoyed more than a golden century until 1762, when the Jesuits were outlawed from France.

The Jesuits wanted their followers literally to see the mysteries of the Catholic faith as a defense against false doctrines. Saint-Paul–Saint-Louis carried forth that idea in its sculptures and paintings representing the Eucharist and the cults of the Virgin, the angels, and the saints. A fine nineteenth-century painting by Delacroix, *Christ in the Olive Garden,* hangs in the left transept. Of the early artwork, a notable piece remains: the emotive statue of the Virgin by Germain Pilon, dating from 1586, in the chapel to the left of the altar. On the way out take note of the shell-shaped holy water basins at the entrance that were given by Victor Hugo, who lived nearby in the place des Vosges. Before I left I stood under the cupola, decorated with the medallions of the fathers of the Greek and Latin churches, in the abundant light of its tall, rounded windows and reflected on the importance of this church as the major source of inspiration and information that it was.

From here it's a short walk to the Picasso and Carnavalet museums and the place de la Bastille, but after all that divine meditation we were hankering after more worldly pursuits. We headed for a meal at Miravile, crossing the Île Saint-Louis, another pocketful of seventeenth-century architecture, to 25 quai de la Tournelle. Our plates arrived looking like sculptured works of art, and, fortunately, chef Gilles Epié's artful eye does not supersede his genius for flavor as he conjures up modern French food that emphasizes simplicity. My ratatouille-stuffed squash blossoms were followed by a Mediterranean fish that came atop a puree of potatoes and Niçoise olives—an unforgettable taste I couldn't wait to re-create at home.

With our coffee the next morning we enjoyed the superlative madeleines we'd bought around the corner from Miravile at Pâtisserie Lerch, on rue Cardinal-Lemoine, before heading across the Luxembourg Gardens toward the Latin Quarter. Few of the vestiges of the great seventeenth-century building boom remain in this neighborhood, but two lasting landmarks from that era are fine domed churches: the Sorbonne chapel and Val-de-Grâce. Unlike the functional domes that had come before, these were conceived completely with beauty in mind, leading the architects to modify the proportion of the dome to the nave. In the case of the Sorbonne, the dome is as tall as the church is long, about 130 feet.

Started as a theological college in about 1253, the Sorbonne was rebuilt in 1629 at Richelieu's expense by Jacques Lemercier, who like many of his contemporaries spent time in Rome, where he became familiar with Il Gesù, St. Peter's, and the Pantheon.

Completed in the mid-1600s, this building introduced the dome as ornament and symbol. Reminiscent of Italy's Pantheon, the Sorbonne is approached via a flight of fifteen broad steps climbing to the portico. The balance and proportion of the structure; the distinction between the three-dimensional elements and mere reliefs; and the abundance of sculptures, urns, and balustrades set this church apart from others built during this time in Paris and established a tradition for other great Parisian churches, including Val-de-Grâce. Inside is Richelieu's marble tomb, a masterpiece designed by Le Brun and sculpted by Girardon. Unfortunately I have seen it just in pictures because the chapel is open only during temporary exhibitions.

As I contemplated the statues of Victor Hugo and Louis Pasteur, watching over the chapel, I overheard some students engaged in heated conversation about upcoming elections. I thought to myself that three hundred years ago, when religion was the politics of the day, the same conversation would have taken place in Latin and the debate would have been over Jansenist and Jesuit doctrine.

We took a short eighteenth-century detour from here to the Panthéon. This dome, designed by Jacques-Germain Soufflot, bears little in common structurally with its seventeenth-century predecessors; however, it can hardly be overlooked. The building is perched on a hill and is one of the most visible in Paris. We were rewarded for our 250-step climb to the top—a suitable setting for Hitchcock's *Vertigo*—with a close-up look of the dome's interior and a good perspective of Paris's rooftops.

In need of a pick-me-up, we headed to Dalloyau, a civilized spot for tea and sweets, on boulevard Saint-Michel at the foot of the Luxembourg Gardens. From there, duly refreshed, it was a ten-minute walk to Val-de-Grâce.

The dome—posed on a drum surrounded by massive pillars that support sixteen male figures holding flaming urns and decorated with a frieze of fleur-de-lis and royal monograms—moves ever upward to a lantern encircled by a balustrade and is topped with an obelisk and a cross. It is a dome for a dome's sake; it lifts to the sky the images of Catholic and royal France and bears testimony to the status of the Church in the country. With its rich and abundant sculpture, the dome of Val-de-Grâce is reminiscent of the Roman baroque, and the church, inside and out, is one of the most noteworthy and best conserved buildings of the seventeenth century.

Val-de-Grâce was part of a convent built by Anne of Austria. In her midthirties, after twenty-one years of marriage, Anne, still without a child, promised to *"élever à Dieu un temple magnifique s'il lui envoyait un fils."* Her prayers were answered with the birth of the future King Louis XIV two years later, in 1638. After the death of Richelieu in 1642, which allowed her control of the treasury, and of her husband a year later, she had all the means necessary to realize her "temple." The church took twenty years to build and 3 million livres in silver.

Anne gave the commission to Mansart—she wouldn't have considered the also popular Lemercier, who had been architect to her archenemy Richelieu—and in 1645 the seven-year-old Louis laid the cornerstone. But, genius has its privilege only to a certain extent. Mansart, who had a tendency to draw up plans without regard to expense, tear down what he had started, and rebuild as he went along, spent so much on the foundations alone that the queen's finance minister fired him and hired Lemercier to take over the project in about 1647.

During the course of the church's construction French architects were being tempted by the idea of luxury. Richelieu's death seemed to spark an irrepressible desire for pleasure. That, combined with the great wealth accumulating from commerce in the colonies, manifested itself in art for art's sake. Characteristic of this time was Val-de-Grâce, which hesitated between the seductions of Italian baroque and French classicism.

The church interior is awash with color and light. I couldn't begin to take it all in at once—the architecture is as much a visual feast as a spatial experience. My eyes immediately lit on Gabriel Le Duc's sixty-foot baldachin with its twisted marble columns, designed after Bernini's in St. Peter's.

Credit for the divine array of sculpture—including the golden wooden angels of the baldachin, the marble nativity on the altar, the reliefs of allegories of the virtues above the chapels, and the four Evangelists on the pendentives of the crossing—goes to Michel Anguier, who clearly spent time in Rome. The cupola fresco is the only remaining decorative art of Pierre Mignard, who also probably studied in Rome. Completed in 1665, the fresco depicts Anne of Austria offering her crown and a maquette of Val-de-Grâce to God. An energetic swirl of prophets, kings, fathers of the Church, apostles, martyrs, and saints—two hundred in all and three times larger than life—spiral to the heavens. In his poem "The Glory of Val-de-Grâce," Molière speaks of the power in the tips of the artist's fingers and describes the dome as an "open school" revealing profound mysteries in full light.

A few years later, in 1663, Louis Le Vau—considered the chief of the baroque spirit in seventeenth-century France—developed plans for the most Roman church in Paris, at the Institut de France, in which he incorporated curved wings, square pavilions, and a dome. On our walk to the institute we dallied in some of the antiques shops on rue Bonaparte, taking particular note of the handsome silver and ivory baby rattles at Antiquités, near the École des Beaux-Arts. The institute, made up of the five royal academies—the French Academy, the Academy of Inscriptions and Belles Lettres, the Academy of Sciences, the Academy of the Fine Arts, and the Academy of Ethics and Political Science—overlooks the Seine on the edge of the Faubourg Saint-Germain. Its gold-ribbed dome, beautifully restored in 1962, is visible from many points along the *quais*.

The College of Four Nations, as the institute was known in the seventeenth century, owes its existence to Cardinal Mazarin. A few days before his death, in 1661, Mazarin willed 2 million livres in silver for the founding of a college for sixty gentlemen from the provinces annexed by recent military triumphs: Flanders with Artois, Alsace, Rousillon, and Piedmont. The planned site for the institute was near the Sorbonne, but Le Vau, who was working on the Louvre Palace, suggested the institute be built instead across from the Louvre because the domes intended for both buildings were designed with similar motifs. In the end, the plan for the Louvre's dome was never carried out.

We settled on a bench on the Pont des Arts, a bridge conceived by Le Vau but not built until 1802, and watched the river traffic. From here we walked behind the institute up the rue de Seine to the open-air market at Carrefour de Buci, always a visual delight of flowers and fruits, stopping in for a bite at Au Chai de L'Abbaye. This friendly wine bar with a simple menu offering, among other things, wonderful charcuterie with bread from Poilâne, was a perfect choice. As the waiter bellowed my order to the kitchen—*"Un croque-monsieur. Un Sancerre"*—I couldn't help but think the equivalent American experience would have taken place in a coffee shop with the waiter shouting to the counterman, "One grilled ham and cheese. One Coke." *Vive la différence!*

Fortified and rested, we took a long walk to the Dôme des Invalides, the culmination of a century of building bigger, better, more ornate domes. Rising up against a clear sky or illuminated against a black night in a calm and airy section of the capital, this monument is somber and rational. Louis XIV craved order and peace and saw architecture as a means of demonstrating the permanence of the monarchy. Taking building into his hands, as he did all aspects of the kingdom, he founded the Academy of Architecture in 1671 and through it established building guidelines based upon his personal tastes.

With the Hôtel des Invalides, a city within a city, Louis saw to the care of invalid and aged soldiers (a growing social problem due to frequent wars) and at the same time heightened his military prestige. Libéral Bruant won the competition held for the building's design, the king laid the cornerstone in 1671, and five years later almost six thousand soldiers had moved in.

When the king's minister, François Louvois, disapproved of Bruant's plans for the church that would be built within the complex, Hardouin-Mansart, the royal architect, was brought on the scene not only to build a church for the soldiers but to construct a mausoleum for the king. Between the south wings of the hotel, where there is now a not-to-be-missed military museum, Hardouin-Mansart erected a plain, narrow structure, the church of Saint-Louis, to serve as the soldiers' church. The king's chapel and mausoleum, the Dôme des Invalides, was then added, connected by a common chancel.

The dome rises 350 feet and is crowned by an elegant, open-work lantern, a spire, and a cross. It is decorated with twelve huge groups of arms and gilded lead military trophies, each several stories high and weighing four tons. The church has lost some of its luster with just six of the thirty-eight statues that once adorned the entire exterior still remaining.

What I saw first inside was the balustrade of the crypt, cut beneath the dome in the nineteenth century for Napoléon's tomb. We traced the floor plan to discover a Greek cross inscribed within a square. Huge Corinthian columns stand in front of the crossing pillars, and round chapels, topped by smaller cupolas, fill the corners of the square. I was most drawn to the simple Saint-Ambrose chapel with the tomb of World War I field marshal Ferdinand Foch, bathed as it was in an icy blue light.

Standing against the balustrade I looked up at the cupola, actually a double dome, a plan appropriated by Hardouin-Mansart from his great-uncle for the Bourbon mausoleum at Saint-Denis. Through a broad circular opening I could see a second dome, embellished by frescoes and lit by hidden attic windows: Saint Louis gives the sword with which he conquered the infidels to Christ in this mural by Charles de Lafosse.

Here, under the dome, as Napoléon received the first members of the Legion of Honor on July 15, 1804, the church resounded to the cry *"Vive l'empereur!"* Through the huge, round opening in the floor, which compromises the sense of space Mansart intended, I could see Napoléon's tomb. His body was interred here with much ado in 1840. It is a fitting place. As he said, "I want my body to rest by the Seine, among the French people who I love so much."

On the river side of the Hôtel des Invalides the esplanade boasts rows of trees and wide expanses of green lawns—being well used for a soccer game when we were there—extending to the Seine. It was at this entrance that the crowd on July 14, 1789, overwhelmed the guards and seized a storehouse containing some twenty thousand rifles.

Before heading for the Pont Alexandre III and the Right Bank, we turned back to take a look at the Hôtel's facade and the monumental door bearing a Latin inscription that translates: "Louis the Great in all his royal munificence for his soldiers and with prudent foresight for eternity founded this edifice in the year 1675." I felt certain he had written it himself.

Classicism was not a formula but a spirit, and the domed church was not so much a church as an image of French grandeur. Standing as the greatest example of French seventeenth-century religious architecture, just as Versailles does of civil architecture of the same period, the Dôme des Invalides marked at once an apogee and an end.

Our last night in Paris was rainy, and so we nipped into the restaurant next door to our hotel, recognizable only by the illuminated sign that reads "Couscous." It was the best Moroccan food I have ever eaten. The restaurant, actually named La Bonne Table de Fès, opened almost thirty years ago, and its quality assures it a continued long life. The cook, Zohra, who comes from Fès, and the amiable proprietress, Lilliane, make dining there a pleasure.

Before heading to the airport the next day we slipped into the pageantry of late Sunday mornings at the Luxembourg Gardens. We sat by the pond watching grandparents with grandchildren, boys sailing boats, and girlfriends chatting, and as if on cue a band struck up a waltz in the gazebo under the trees. It was one of those perfect moments when I was reassured that Paris has not really changed over the years since I lived there. It had become clear, too, as I made my way around the city and saw not just the domes but some of the more recent architectural works of Mitterrand's "Grands Projets," such as the Bastille Opera and the pyramid at the Louvre, that this governing leader is creating monuments to himself and his rule no differently than Henri IV or Louis XIV. Politics may have changed, but architecture as a symbol of power and permanence is firmly engrained in the French *esprit*.

Station to Station

BY BARBARA DINERMAN

～

editor's note

I prefer traveling by train above all other modes of transportation, and arriving in or departing from a grand train station is much more exciting to me than an airport. A tour of Paris's train stations is also a tour of the city in the years around the turn of the century. If you only have time to see one, you wouldn't be disappointed in choosing the Gare de Lyon, also home of the famed and beautiful restaurant Le Train Bleu.

BARBARA DINERMAN is a former resident of Paris and returns frequently. She writes regularly on architecture, interior design, and art for *Veranda, Robb Report, American Way,* and other magazines. In 1997, she won the annual Journalism Award from the Florida chapter of the American Society of Interior Designers.

～

We don't usually think of such utilitarian buildings as train stations when we plan our explorations of Paris. But the six great stations extant today are certainly worth our inspection. They're as much a history lesson as the noted monuments, as rewarding an architectural study as Baron Georges-Eugène Haussmann's facades of the *grands* boulevards, and as much fun as a visit to any of the flower-laden parks.

With the exception of the Gare Montparnasse, which soars eighteen stories in its familiar late-twentieth-century structural form, Paris's train stations reflect the exuberant faith in industrial progress that marked the end of the nineteenth century. The great architects of the day conceived these remarkable structures, and impressionist artists such as Édouard Manet, Claude Monet, Gustave Caillebotte, Jean Beraud and Norbert Goeneutte competed to properly record the dramatic impact of the stations on the Parisian landscape and its citizenry.

Just three years after the Paris Salon of 1874 (where Manet's *The Railway,* now known as *The Gare St.-Lazare,* brought down a storm of ridicule), Émile Zola took up the cause. "That is where painting is today," he wrote in defense of new paintings by Monet. "Our artists have to find the poetry in train stations, the way their fathers found the poetry in forests and rivers."

In fact, Monet's group of eleven works depicting the Gare St.-Lazare became the basis for an art exhibition titled *Manet, Monet and The Gare Saint-Lazare* at the Musée d'Orsay last spring. The successful exhibition moved to the National Gallery in Washington, D.C., in the summer. For modern-day audiences, these artistic efforts are powerful reminders that the trains, along with the cuttings and tracks that transformed their neighborhoods, were nothing less than a wondrous symbol of change.

As the stations made grand architectural statements, we can admire them today as a glimpse back at the turn of *that* century, and for what they still are today. Enter any station, and the crowds—not to mention the restaurant facilities and even the poster art—will amaze you. This dazzling network of railways is alive and well, despite the preponderance of air travel. Compare the SNCF (Société Nationale des Chemins de Fer) with Amtrak; not exactly a contest.

Of course, the sense of nostalgia is strong, and marketing efforts have been surprisingly aggressive. Having adopted the slogan *À*

Nous de Vous Faire Préférer Le Train on its brochures, schedules and ubiquitous ads, the company's officials are aware of the sentimental value of rail travel. Vintage posters show the legendary trains such as the 1925 Sud Express steaming out of the Gare de Lyon for the Riviera, and the La Boîte à Sel delivering elegantly dressed and coiffed passengers to the Gare d'Austerlitz from Biarritz.

With the stations recently cleaned up and vigorously updating their amenities, it can be richly rewarding to devote a few days to them. Think of them as a historical collection, a phenomenon unleashed by industrialization, and particularly as a glamorous symbol of mobility. For the first time, people could hop a train and ride in comfort to the south of France, the southwest, the north, the east. The possibilities seemed endless, and the opportunity to house these revolutionary steam railways gave architects a bold new form of expression.

At first, architects balked at the new engineering techniques, such as using iron beams or vaults to create the broad spans needed to construct the ticket halls and train sheds. As Anthony Sutcliffe notes in *Paris: An Architectural History,* an entirely new kind of structure was needed in nineteenth-century Paris—one that would accommodate "large-scale manufacturing, steam railways and high-volume commerce. These buildings started to appear in and around Paris in about 1840."

Iron and glass were becoming less expensive, but architects feared that aesthetic appeal might suffer. Respected names such as Labrouste, who designed the Ste.-Geneviève Library in 1842, made efforts to build with the new materials. In the 1850s, the Halles food market area (designed by eminent architect Baltard) pleased the emperor with its extensive system of roofs and clerestories. Still, the first two railway stations—Gare d'Orléans (1840), now Gare d'Austerlitz, and Gare du Nord (1846)—used modest railway architects. The Gare du Nord was originally an arcaded classical design "reflecting the horizontality of the trains and looking like *orangeries* or market buildings in the pre-Baltard style," notes Sutcliffe. But as the more fashionable architects showed that the new materials could be applied to fine architecture, the stations began to look like showplaces.

Gare du Nord

After its modest beginning as a railway-company design in a then remote area of the city, railway chairman Baron James de Rothschild took another look at the neoclassical structures that dotted the city—notably Jakob Ignaz Hittorff's nearby church of St.-Vincent-de-Paul. Rothschild commissioned the German-born architect to give the Gare du Nord a facelift in 1859. Hittorff created a neoclassical frontage with giant Ionic pilasters that define the central pavilion; the gables on the end pavilions reflect the wide pitched roof of the train shed. Huge statues stand on the facade, so that the structure "combined a practical design for a railway station and the classical features of a self-conscious Parisian public monument."

The interior is considered cathedral-like in its vastness, the original green columns supporting the roof of the train shed. Hittorff complained about a lack of "monumental street access," though Haussmann supplied two short approach streets. Access has further improved with the recent addition of a service road and drop-off area at the front entrance. From the upper level, you can see the bullet-shaped TGV trains to northern towns and the Thalys line to Belgium, Holland and Germany waiting to speed away.

The Gare du Nord is also the starting point for Eurostar, the Channel Tunnel line, and the upper level has been transformed into a plush service-area-cum-waiting lounge. To inaugurate the Euro Tunnel in May 1994, François Mitterrand commissioned a sculpture. Europa Operanda's futuristic bronze figures of an adult and child dominate the parapet overlooking the Grandes Lignes.

Built three years after the original Gare du Nord, this station inspired all the others. As Sutcliffe notes, the stations "offered the chance to create completely new spaces and circulation systems, using iron and glass in a more creative way than was normally possible in Parisian architecture." Stations also had "monumental potential at the head of the approach streets." Architect F. A. Duquesney emphasized the semicircular vault of the train shed, "which sprang above an arcaded frontage and was flanked by two three-story pavilions, topped by a balustrade, in the formal style of railway offices of the day." The large, glazed arch had radiating iron tracery and glass that formed a striking wheel symbol. As in the Gare du Nord, statues graced the facade, each representing a town served by the network.

The boulevard de Strasbourg, linking the Gare de l'Est and the *grands* boulevards, would not be completed until the early 1850s, but Duquesney designed the structure with the future vista in mind. Although—or perhaps because—the immediate neighborhood today is a bit down-at-the-heel, the station makes an imposing sight as it dominates place Napoléon III.

What is perhaps most striking about the Gare de l'Est, however, is its haunting history as the point of departure for the Nazi concentration camps of World War II. If you don't have this history in mind at first (as you contemplate such eastern destinations as Strasbourg and Bâle, plus the newly completed TGV line to Strasbourg and Germany), you will soon be reminded by at least four large plaques. *"N'oublions jamais,"* the plaques implore visitors, *"de cette gare partirent des milliers des patriotes français pour le tragique voyage,"* and so on.

Gare St.-Lazare

Farther west and serving the western region of the country, including Normandy as well as extensive Paris suburbs, this more centrally located station didn't stand at the head of a great vista. Sutcliffe dismisses the Gare St.-Lazare as "a conforming Parisian facade architecture, virtually unrecognizable as a station." However, in its newly sandblasted state, connected by a blue filigreed skywalk from the Hôtel Concorde St.-Lazare, this mid-nineteenth-century structure has a definite glamour; its neighbors include the splendid Second Empire department stores Au Printemps and Galeries Lafayette.

The Gare St.-Lazare was redesigned in the 1860s as the Second Empire made its mark under Napoléon III. Haussmann's street improvements were in full swing, and the Hôtel Terminus (now the Concorde St.-Lazare) coincided with the remodeling of the station. Today, this bustling area is entertaining. The 1895 seafood restaurant Mollard is across the street, decorated with fabulous mosaic murals, and the posh 1889 Paul Boulangerie is located at boulevard Haussmann and rue Tronchet (where lines form for turtle-shaped loaves and gourmet sandwiches).

The most striking feature of the Gare St.-Lazare is the range of its amenities. On the ground floor is the vast Galerie Marchande, open from 7:30 A.M. to 7 P.M. This ultra-mall sells everything from fresh vegetables to Swarovski crystal. You can get your umbrella repaired at Maroquinerie à la Pierrette. (*"Même les plus malades,"* a sign promises.) And when was the last time you were in a station that had an antique shop? Oh, yes, you can get glasses in an hour and your photos developed at the same time.

The Galerie Marchande is undergoing a massive renovation. According to the manager of the new SNCF Boutique—where you can buy tickets for all trains—completion is expected in late 1999. This is also the site of the future RER Haussmann-St.-Lazare station. Meanwhile, up the escalator to the main ticket hall, two huge brasseries are doing a brisk business, and the hot-dog-shaped stainless-steel stands on rubber tires—a whimsical presence in every station—serve all sorts of refreshments to go.

While renovations proceed, signs boast that "in August 1998, on your Paris-St.-Lazare-Caen-Cherbourg line, 97 percent of the trains arrived at their terminus with a delay of under ten minutes." And *wagons-lits* posters exhort us to "discover the new cuisine on board—for the pleasure of the taste and the trip."

Gare d'Austerlitz

After our virtual journeys to the north, east and west from these Right Bank stations, let's move south to the Left Bank for the southern routes. If the Gare St.-Lazare and its environs recall city life in the late nineteenth century, the Gare d'Austerlitz reflects the era of travel to the posh watering holes of the southwest, notably Biarritz and St.-Jean-de-Luz.

Though the station itself is rather nondescript due to its early origins, it offers a fine glimpse into a leisurely era, when travelers disported themselves in the formal restaurant upstairs, seen from outside as a row of bright blue awnings over flowered window boxes. In the restaurant, Le Grenadier, you will be given its history (named for a neighborhood soldier in Napoléon's army) and a daily changing menu offered with private-label wine. Salons display paintings of the campaigns.

In the ticket hall, banners announce a new link with the city of Bourges. Travelers can buy packages that include guided visits to the Cathédral St.-Étienne and other sights. Plans call for the TGV to serve the station by next summer. In the early 1990s, Jacques Chirac launched the Seine-Rive-Gauche project, a pleasant riverside strip that runs southeast from the station.

Many Parisians dismiss the Gare d'Austerlitz as architecturally dull. However, the sight of the metro trains entering on an overpass (the huge archway on the upper level of the station) is compelling, like watching a train disappear into a mountain.

Just across the Seine (technically the Right Bank), the station's fanciful clock tower dominates the rue de Bercy area, which is being revitalized, particularly with the Bibliothèque Nationale de France. But when the Gare de Lyon was being built, in 1902, the area was poor and the site awkward.

The Paris Exposition of 1900 had created a climate for change. Railway companies felt "a strong obligation to enhance the cityscape," notes Sutcliffe. Both the Gare de Lyon and the Gare d'Orsay (now the Musée d'Orsay) were "variants of the classical style, though the Gare de Lyon, standing at the gateway to the East End, was more daring, using symbolism, the picturesque, expressionism and height. . . . [It] epitomizes public architecture in Paris at the height of the belle epoque."

Architect Marius Toudoire created, says Sutcliffe, "languorous sculpture springing directly from the walls, and the colorful decoration recalled the architecture of luxury hotels and casinos on the Côte d'Azur." For present-day visitors, the legendary Train Bleu restaurant is "the world's most palatial station restaurant in a lush neo-rococo." Lunch or dinner is a feast for the senses, and though reviews of the cuisine vary, I found the food to be delicious, and the service elegant (*pommes gaufrettes* served in a silver bowl). The rack of lamb arrives on a Christofle slicing-trolley, which has a hood of embossed silver.

The Train Bleu's fabulous murals of high society enjoying themselves in Lyon and the Riviera, its richly carved moldings, crystal chandeliers and velvet drapes make even a cup of coffee memorable in the adjoining bar, Le Club Américain. The restaurant is listed as a historic site. In an elegant glass case are mementos, from the signature china to the Train Bleu watch.

This startlingly modern station on boulevard Montparnasse was rebuilt to serve the TGV to the Atlantic coast, including Nantes and Quimper as of 1990. It forms a glass-and-concrete complex with the 1973 Tour Montparnasse, which soars to fifty-nine stories over the once-Bohemian district. Sutcliffe calls the Gare Montparnasse nothing more than a "modest practicality," but it appeals with its broad arched views of the surrounding area, its restaurants judiciously placed on the perimeter of the upper level.

Whether or not the charms and unexpected comforts of the train stations persuade you to *"préférer le train,"* you can savor the pleasures of the journey—past and present—simply by visiting the stations themselves. For precise schedules, phone Rail Europe at 800-438-7245 and it will send you an immediate fax; or place an Internet order at www.sncf.fr.

The Carousels of Paris

BY SUSAN HACK

∽

editor's note

First-time visitors to Paris may not think of carousels as an intrinsic part of the city's landscape, but as residents and those who have visited the city before know, carousels are ubiquitous in Paris. They share room on my short list of sights that are uniquely and immediately identifiable as Parisian. In addition to the carousels highlighted in this piece, there are countless others in parks all around the city. One I particularly like is in the Parc Monceau, where on a Sunday morning, amidst the joggers and lovers, the carousel is filled to capacity. You can hear it long before you see it, and the squeals of young children and the faces of their delighted parents and grandparents is a French spectacle not to be missed.

SUSAN HACK lives in Paris and Cairo and is a contributing editor at *Condé Nast Traveler.*

It's called the City of Light, but as my husband, young daughter and I discovered when we moved here three years ago, Paris is also a city of carousels. One of our favorites spins in a corner of the Champ de Mars, the old military parade ground, between a playground and a small refreshment stand. On Wednesday afternoons and weekends, two dozen hand-painted wooden horses bearing names like "Baba" and "Bijou" emerge from their "stable" (actually a locked green shed) to be suspended from hooks off a circular wooden frame. Built in 1913, this antique carousel remains powered by a simple hand crank. Pint-sized riders can request a wooden stick or "baguette" to joust with the ring man, who stands on a platform loading dozens of tin circles into a medieval-looking feeder.

Visit the *Mona Lisa* in the Louvre or all those impressionist masterpieces in the Musée d'Orsay? Our six-year-old daughter, Sophie, still prefers the ring game. Fortunately, almost every park and public square in the French capital features a *"manège,"* or merry-go-round, including at least a dozen survivors from the belle epoque. We've evolved a family quid pro quo: An afternoon of museum time or other culturally enlightening indoor fare, or simply a long, lingering Paris walk, earns a side trip to a carousel.

We like the *manège* in Luxembourg Garden, whose turn-of-the-century, weathered wooden menagerie includes a camel, an antlered reindeer and a solemn gray elephant, none much larger than a golden retriever. While my husband and I munch sugar crepes and keep lookout for French movie stars and their offspring, Sophie buckles a leather safety strap around her waist and concentrates on spearing rings at high speed (an electric motor has replaced the carousel's original hand crank). In the leafy Jardin des Plantes, we'll follow a tour of the newly renovated Natural History Museum, the Mineral Museum or the dinosaur-filled Hall of Paleontology with a turn on a contemporary merry-go-round of extinct and endangered creatures featuring a wistful Dodo, a bright green Tyrannosaurus Rex and a leaping phalanx of proto-giraffes. At the foot of the Eiffel Tower, flower-draped donkeys cavort with palanquin-bearing lions under a midnight-blue canopy painted with golden stars. Just across the Iena bridge, not far from the Trocadero and the Museum of Mankind, we sometimes find newlyweds posing on a double-decker carousel of prancing horses, wooden swings and rocking sea-scallop carriages.

At eight to ten francs (about $1.30–$1.60) per ride, an afternoon of Paris carousel-hopping isn't cheap, especially when all three of us want multiple spins. But just as on the metro, you can usually buy a packet of tickets at a discount. On our outings my backpack is a jumble of plastic tokens. Just as spearing rings has gotten easier with practice for Sophie (current record: seventeen), I've developed a system of color-coded envelopes that help me keep track of which ticket goes with which merry-go-round in which arrondissement.

Our carousel expeditions brighten the long, gray winters, and Christmas brings a special treat: The Mairie of Paris, which allocates citywide merry-go-round concessions to private owners, offers a week of unlimited free rides between Christmas and New Year's as a holiday gift to *les citoyens*. Foregoing museums altogether, we head for the place Willette, at the foot of the Sacre Coeur steps, to line up for free turns on an Italian-built carousel, whose painted ceiling features Venetian canals, but whose stampeding horses (made of plastic) boast pink and blue eagle feathers and an American Wild West theme. In the place Saint-Sulpice, Philippe

Campion, head of an amusement park dynasty, sets up a merry-go-round built in England in 1871, at the beginning of the steam era, a precursor of the giant "salon" carousels popular at the end of the nineteenth century. The elaborately decorated wooden chargers have wild, flaring eyes and double-seated saddles, and they rotate clockwise, contrary to their continental counterparts. This summer, as always, this migrating merry-go-round has reappeared in the Tuileries Garden, site of an annual July–August carnival called the Foire du Trone.

American cities have one or two merry-go-rounds, if any. In Paris, carousels are so much a part of the landscape that you find them not just in parks and squares but inside supermarkets and fast-food restaurants like McDonald's. When our list of outdoor favorites reached twenty-five, I began to wonder, why such a cornucopia? The answer, it turns out, has to do with a constellation of factors, including France's reverence for tradition, a clement Parisian climate, a habit of indulging small children and, of course, history.

Jardins du Luxembourg

BY CATHARINE REYNOLDS

〜

editor's note

Paris has no shortage of lovely parks, but Les Jardins du Luxembourg are a favorite of many visitors and residents alike, perhaps because, as Catharine Reynolds notes in this piece, they serve two very different communities: bourgeois and *bohème*. The gardens are certainly a favorite of mine, for a variety of reasons, one of which has to do with my astonishment at discovering a mini Statue of Liberty one day when I was wandering the pathways. I had no idea it was there, and to come upon it suddenly when I was missing family and friends in the U.S. made the park a special place.

One reason Parisian parks are so well-groomed is that walking on the grass is *interdit* (forbidden). This seems to me to illustrate a fundamental difference in French and American philosophies about parks and gardens. In Paris in particular—and in other French cities as well—parks serve as integral parts of daily life: urban dwellers walk across them or saunter through them every day, to and from work or en route to here and there. It's as if they are a pleasant reminder that gardens are a beautiful part of life, a daily tonic as important as a good meal. Few parks in the U.S. are designed for daily use—New York's Central Park and Boston's Public Garden are two notable exceptions—and indeed most Americans are accustomed to think of parks as places where you show up in sweatpants for a game of football or to toss around the Frisbee. If Parisian gardens seem a bit formal, it does not mean they are not welcoming—you just can't frolic on the grass!

CATHARINE REYNOLDS, who was introduced in the *"Renseignements Pratiques"* section, is a contributing editor at *Gourmet*. This piece was featured in April 1988.

R eturn visitors to Paris decry the changes wrought by recent decades. Yet, as marked as those alterations may be, I find even more striking the things that haven't changed. Take for example the Jardins du Luxembourg. In April of 1644, the English diarist John Evelyn wrote:

> I went to see . . . the fine Palace of Luxembourg, in the Faubourg St.-Germain, built by Marie de Médicis, and I think one of the most noble, entire, and finished piles that is to be seen, taking it with the garden and all its accomplishments. . . .
> The gardens are near an English mile in compass, enclosed with a stately wall, and in a good air. The parterre is indeed of box, but so rarely designed and accurately kept cut, that the

embroidery makes a wonderful effect to the lodgings which front it. . . .

In sum, nothing is wanted to render this palace and gardens perfectly beautiful and magnificent; nor is it one of the least diversions to see the number of persons of quality, citizens and strangers, who frequent it, and to whom all access is freely permitted, so that you shall see some walks and retirements full of gallants and ladies; in others, melancholy friars; in others, studious scholars; in others, jolly citizens, some sitting or lying on the grass, others running and jumping; some playing at bowls and ball, others dancing and singing; and all this without the least disturbance, by reason of the largeness of the place.

Nigh on 350 years have changed things little. The gardeners' lobby has ruled the grass out of bounds, persons of quality perchance often look less like it, chairs that a hundred years ago were rented under a three-tier price system like continental railway seats are now free, but, for the rest, the Luxembourg remains the preeminent resort of the Quartier Latin. Where else can (and do) residents of the Left Bank's 5th and 6th Arrondissements wolf a *cornet* of ice cream; gaze at the nodding beds of petunias; knit; complete a crossword; research a treatise (yes, I've seen zealous sun-worshipping scholars with books gathered around their knees); nap; exercise the dog; grasp the brass ring on a carousel; play *boules,* chess, and checkers; squeal at the marionettes; push a pram and air its occupant; exalt in sentimental sculpture; discuss politics; and discover love—all activities that have flourished under the garden's chestnuts, lindens, and planes for at least a century.

As the most Parisian of gardens, the Jardins du Luxembourg are a place of engaging contrasts. The rigid parterres of the *jardin à la française* set off what has been called "the most perfect of all late-

Renaissance buildings in Paris." Marshaled flowers form a foil to the shady intimacy of the spiraling paths of the *jardin à l'anglaise,* just as the garden's own greenery sets off the dome of the Panthéon. The atmosphere is calm yet animated, mirroring the two principal communities it serves, bourgeois and *bohème.* Demure behavioral standards are upheld by the *surveillants* (watchmen), who enforce regulations banning drunks, beggars, the indecently attired, and all attempts to kick footballs. On the other hand, they do little to discourage what Victor Hugo called the *"école buissonnière,* that school for lovers under the sky which will endure as long as there are trees and novices." A tacit agreement reserves the western half of the garden for children and the pensive and the eastern half for more boisterous students. With more than fifty of its sixty-four acres open to the public, there's space for all comers.

First-time visitors and habitués alike find the Luxembourg haunting and haunted. Sticky-fingered toddlers, gripped by scolding nursemaids, are direct descendants of the young Louis XIII, who gallivanted in the shadow of the palace more than three centuries ago.

The Palais du Luxembourg wasn't always there. In the beginning there was a Roman military encampment. After it was abandoned in the fifth century the area was forgotten for six hundred years until the excommunicated king Robert the Pious retreated from the Île de la Cité and built the Château Vauvert on the site. On his death, the château was deserted and its ruin reputedly occupied by an evil spirit. More likely, the said spirit was a band of brigands, cashing in on the legend. Whatever the case, terrified Parisians came to equate the Château Vauvert with the wilds, and many a Frenchman still characterizes a trip to the back-of-beyond as *"aller au diable Vauvert,"* though few may be aware of the allusion.

Such superstition no doubt offended the sainted Louis IX, who therefore took up the Carthusian monks' offer to exorcise the spirit in return for the grant of the lands. The good friars built a monastery on what is now the southern end of the Jardins du Luxembourg, which was soon famed for its nursery and vegetable garden.

Early in the seventeenth century the clean air rustling the monastic vines attracted a less than salubrious character: Marie de Médicis, the scheming widow of the assassinated Henri IV and wholly incompetent regent for her son Louis XIII. On April 2, 1612, she purchased nearly twenty acres on the northern side of the Carthusians' property and commissioned Salomon de Brosse to build her a residence reminiscent of the Pitti Palace. His bold, masculine plans suited her admirably, even if the Florentine details were only skin-deep; Marie was thrilled with the rusticated stone and committed a fortune to the project, even, it is said, authorizing the substitution of silver glazing bars for common lead on the windows of her own apartment.

Marie also cozened Peter Paul Rubens into illustrating her apotheosis in a series of twenty-four allegorical canvases in which he cast her as Juno to Henri IV's Jupiter. To the synonyms *Junoesque* and *Rubenesque* should truly be added *Mariesque*—as anyone who has tarried before the results, now hung in the Louvre, would agree.

With a dwelling worthy of her Florentine youth, Marie also commissioned de Brosse to devise gardens after the Boboli. He secured help from Boyceau de la Baraudière, a man noted for his *parterres en broderie* outlined in yew and box and *jets d'eau,* which in the case of the Luxembourg were fed by an aqueduct that extended miles south to Rungis. The Florentine engineer Thomas Francini designed the ornamental pond and the terrace, both of which were arrayed against a backdrop of hornbeams, chestnuts, and two thousand elms. The whole was enclosed within a stone wall.

But Marie could not barricade herself beyond political events. On November 10–11, 1631, the Journée des Dupes, she was definitively outmaneuvered by her loathed former protégé, Cardinal Richelieu. Her son banished her, installing Richelieu as prime minister. In July of the following year she fled to Cologne, where, eleven years later, she died penniless and friendless.

The Luxembourg was not to remain vacant long. Marie's second son and favorite, the intriguing Gaston d'Orléans, installed himself and his spectacular collection of books there. His daughter Anne Marie Louise d'Orléans, whom history rightly knows as La Grande Mademoiselle, is thought to have been her century's richest woman. Only impetuosity scotched her projected marriages to Louis XIV and Charles II; eventually she wedded the worthless Duc de Lauzun, much against Louis XIV's will—who offered her little consolation when Lauzun's arrogant foppery got the better of her good nature and she locked him out of the Luxembourg.

Her sister Elisabeth d'Orléan's subsequent tenancy was more sedate, which couldn't be said for the Duchesse de Berry's in the following century. That woman of letters felt constrained to close the garden to the public, better to "pass summer nights . . . with a liberty that had more need of correspondents than witnesses." The gouty Comte de Provence was the Luxembourg's last occupant before the Revolution, when he stole away to England.

The Terror converted the Luxembourg into the Maison Nationale de Sûreté, where prisoners like Camille Desmoulins, Danton, Thomas Paine, Louis David, and Joséphine de Beauharnais were incarcerated. Desmoulins's wife stood with their child in the gardens, hoping to glimpse him by the flickering light of the forges casting cannons, while the irrepressible Danton harangued passersby in the rue de Vaugirard from his window. In the end both mounted the scaffold. Others were more fortunate. Joséphine, for example, survived to live (and dance) in the Luxembourg as wife of the first consul.

Prussians and Cossacks were to bivouac in the gardens, sealing the end of Napoléon I's empire, but the allure of the Luxembourg endured. In 1826 Henry Wadsworth Longfellow described the "very extensive and beautiful garden—with long, shady gravel walks over which the tall old trees, which are all regularly planted, form perfect arches—and directly in the center, a valley or lower level of the ground in which are little plats of flowers—rows of orange trees, and a little pond with two beautiful white swans."

Under the July Monarchy the palace was altered for the Chambre des Pairs, which convened there, counting Victor Hugo among its members. Fondly he was to write of the gardens in *Les Misérables*:

The flower beds shed forth balm and dazzling beauty into the sunlight. The branches, wild with the brilliant glow of midday, seemed endeavoring to embrace. In the sycamores there was an uproar of linnets, sparrows triumphed, woodpeckers climbed along the chestnut trees, administering little pecks to the bark. The flower beds accepted the legitimate royalty of the lilies; the most august of perfumes is that which emanates from whiteness. . . . The sun gilded, empurpled, set fire to and lighted up the tulips, which are nothing but all the varieties of flame made into flowers. All around the banks of tulips the bees, the sparks of those flame flowers, hummed.

William Makepeace Thackeray was more somber in his sketch, telling of walking in the Luxembourg "where bonnes, students, grisettes, and old gentlemen with pigtails love to wander in the melancholy, quaint old gardens." A few Prussian shells fell on outbuildings in 1870, but Fédérés spared the Luxembourg the torch by occupying the area during the Commune.

The Third Republic was the Luxembourg garden's heyday and the era when it entered the fabric of French life, with velocipede races and concerts, balloon ascensions and promenades. Honoré de Balzac, George Sand, Sainte-Beuve, Théodore de Banville, Charles Baudelaire, and Paul Verlaine all frequented its *allées*. So did Oscar Wilde and André Gide.

This century saw the Jardins du Luxembourg penetrate the folklore of American literature with Ernest Hemingway, who lived over a sawmill in the adjacent rue Notre-Dame-des-Champs. He captured an essence of Paris in the twenties when he recounted how he would flesh out the family diet by wheeling his infant son Bumby through the Luxembourg, waiting for a moment when the watchman's back was turned, and capturing unsuspecting pigeons, which he secreted under Bumby's blanket.

Hemingway would also meet Gertrude Stein in the Luxembourg, walking her poodle Basket. There, according to Humphrey Carpenter's *Geniuses Together*, she explained to him how she managed to amass her fabled collection of paintings, which she kept in her nearby apartment. "You can either buy clothes or pictures," she said. "It's simple. No one who is not very rich can do both." Looking at the strange clothes she wore, Hemingway could well believe it. Surely Isadora Duncan, who delighted in dancing through the gardens just after their dawn opening, was easier on the eye.

World War II brought German airmen to the green alleys of the Luxembourg. The palace was headquarters for the Third Luftwaffe, who positioned blockhouses amid the trees. Generalfeldmarschall Hugo Sperrle's care for the plantations throughout the Occupation was largely undone after his headquarters was shifted to Reims on August 16, 1944; after mining the palace with seven tons of TNT, the SS arrayed themselves and their tanks on the lawns. The Luxembourg was the first German strongpoint in Paris to be attacked by the Forces Françaises de l'Intérieur—and the last to fall. The damage was severe but repairable.

Today the palace is the home of the French Sénat, which, through the Conservation des Jardins du Luxembourg, is responsible for the maintenance of the gardens. As the president of the Sénat lives on the spot, he takes a vigorous interest, which helps explain the high standard of upkeep. Rivalry rages between the Luxembourg's gardeners and those of the Ville de Paris, who care for the rest of the city's parks. As well as maintaining the portions of the gardens open to the public and providing flowers for the state rooms of the palace, the Conservation also tends the Sénat's private gardens. These include the dazzling Petit Parterre de la Reine Mère and two thousand square feet of greenhouses, which shelter a precious collection of at least four hundred species of *Paphiopedilum* orchids, known in French as *sabots de Vénus,* or Venus's clogs.

The Conservation fills flower beds and borders for each season of bloom: in spring, with pansies, forget-me-nots, tulips, and stock; in summer, with geraniums, petunias, calceolarias, ageratums, dahlias, and sage; and in autumn with a splendid show of chrysanthemums. These colorful displays require a total of 160,000 bedding and herbaceous plants annually, many of which are raised from seed in the Conservation's hothouses. The gardeners must also care for the aucubas, laurels, palms, privets, and laurustines that are the basic background shrubs of the gardens and keep the trees trimmed in the best Cartesian fashion.

In these gardens the plants must be assertive to make themselves seen, because more than the ghosts of garden visitors from the past people its alleys: Statues have nearly taken over parts of the garden since the time of Louis-Philippe. The Third Republic's "commemorative mania" is nowhere better seen. Ronald Searle and Kaye Webb's *Paris Sketchbook* recounts how "one night the painter Degas and a companion stumbled against some . . . [small railings in the Luxembourg]. His friend cursed, demanded why they should

be there at all. Explained Degas, 'It is because they are afraid someone will come in the night and deposit another statue.'"

Nearly a hundred stone likenesses (metal ones were melted during World War II) greet people. They do not fail to stir us, even if
they touch our funny bone sooner than our hearts. The most overwrought are probably those of Paul Verlaine, who deserves better,
and Gabriel Vicaire, with subjects like *Joie de la Famille* in torrid
contention. The finest is probably Jules Dalou's monument to
Eugène Delacroix, located in the Sénat's private gardens. To me the
most ticklesome is that to the Comtesse de Ségur, whose sickly
sweet tales were the joy of my governess—and the bane of my
childhood. Most arresting is probably Auguste Bartholdi's scaled-
down *Liberté*, her feet shrouded in shrubs rather than obscured by
ferries.

Perhaps the most romantic monument in the garden is the
Fontaine de Médicis, which, though dramatically remodeled by
Alphonse de Gisors in the nineteenth century, still manages to
draw on the aesthetic of the originator of the palace and gardens.
What Salomon de Brosse likely designed as a grotto in 1620 was
transformed into a fountain in 1864 to disguise a section of the
garden Baron Georges Haussmann was excising. The artistic
merit of Auguste Ottin's bronze Cyclops Polyphemus, doing violence to the marble shepherd Acis in pursuit of the nymph
Galatea, is not overwhelming, but its lush setting under arching
trees and ivy-garlanded, flower-filled urns, all mirrored in gold-
fished still water, makes it one of Paris's most fabulous retreats.
And, as a fillip, Achille Valois's neo-Renaissance bas-relief of
Leda and the swan on the reverse is a masterpiece of charm and
elegance.

The fountain is just one of the multitude of features that attract
generation after generation to the Luxembourg. What Parisian

child has not launched his dreams on the octagonal sailboat basin? There is no excuse not to, as an obliging man rents a marinaful from his bicycle display. The prizes at the weekend regattas are as sharply contested as mere silverware was off Perth. Equally hard-fought are the tricycle races. Younger sisters and brothers content themselves with outdoing one another in castle building at the sandboxes. And nearly every Paris child must have begged an ever-so-tall papa for a donkey ride, astride or in a cart, since the rides were instituted in 1900. Equally enticing are the Punch-and-Judy and carousel on the west terrace. Though the plans for the latter were drafted by Charles Garnier, architect of the Opéra, the carousel is slightly ascetic and rather *sage*—like the children who patronize it. And even the most indulged and solemn twentieth-century child seems to delight in *saute-mouton* and *cheval fondu,* two variations of leapfrog.

Adults are no less well served, with tennis, *boules, pétanque,* and organized checkers and chess. More esoteric, though equally popular, are the beekeeping and horticultural courses that are a direct outgrowth of the preceptive agricultural vocation of the Carthusians, who tilled these very acres centuries ago. In fact, the Rucher-École, or "beehive-school," is run by an Esperanto-speaking Dominican friar. Cached behind a hedge on the western side of the gardens, it offers theoretical and practical courses; curiously, the bees rarely bite the public. The Cours du Luxembourg, or horticultural courses, were instituted in 1809 and each year attract about 350 students, who study either fruit-growing or landscape design. Students of the former can draw on a peculiar resource: the rows of espaliered fruit trees, all barbered with military precision and emblazoned with Latin tags, which border the rue Auguste-Comte.

If exertion leads to hunger, the Luxembourg is well equipped. Eleven green-painted kiosks, which date from 1880, dispense treats like licorice shoelaces, aniseed-flavored sweets, and *barbe à papa* (papa's beard, or, less metaphorically, cotton candy), not to mention tops, skipping ropes, and the occasional (hula) hoop. Upscale, there are ice creams from Dalloyau, whose vitrines face the northeast gates of the gardens at 2 place Edmond-Rostand. If a fond grandmother is in tow, one can even aspire to China tea with chocolate macaroons or éclairs or, best of all, a *gâteau Opéra,* served in starchy style by a firm that originated in 1802.

Fortified, one can then proceed to luxuriate in the Luxembourg's greatest pleasure, to *flâner* in its bowers toward sunset, perhaps until the *surveillants* ring the closing bell and the gates shut for yet another day. The miracle of the Jardins du Luxembourg is that they ease one into a continuum, where childhood gently melds with youthful romance and reflective old age and where change ebbs into history. As George Moore mused, is there "anything better in the world worth doing than to sit in an alley of clipped limes . . . thinking of Paris and of myself?"

The best way to cap off a visit to the Luxembourg was discovered long ago, 188 years, to be precise. Throughout those years habitués of the gardens have beaten a path up the hill, past that most wondrous of monuments, *La Fontaine des Quatre Parties du Monde,* to that *café par excellence,* the Closerie des Lilas at 171 boulevard du Montparnasse. *The Imperial Paris Guide* in 1867 intoned:

> . . . the far-famed *grisette* . . . known to every reader of a certain class of French novel . . . can only be seen in full feather in the Quartier Latin, where the students live, and particularly at the Closerie des Lilas, near the Jardin du Luxembourg. There also a glimpse may occasionally be obtained of the cancan, a far more expressive than elegant

way of dancing, which only the presence of the police can keep within the bounds of decency.

Eighties clients go more in search of cultural nostalgia than the cancan, and the management respects this appetite by inserting brass plaques inscribed with the names of some of the famous who have paused there: Paul Verlaine; Charles Baudelaire; Paul Fort; Dominique Ingres; Leon Trotsky; Pablo Picasso; Guillaume Apollinaire; Henry Miller; August Strindberg; Oscar Wilde; Lenin; Amedeo Modigliani; André Gide, who was a pupil at the neighboring École Alsacienne; and, of course, Hemingway, who wrote much of *The Sun Also Rises* seated over a *café crème*.

The upstairs dining room is altogether disappointing, but, notwithstanding the departed lilacs, tables still line the boulevard under the awning in fair weather. Meals there tend to be expensive, though the *pigeon de Bresse rôti* (not, may I hasten to interject, from Mr. Hemingway's source) rarely deceives. More gratifying still is a meal of oysters and steak tartare, taken on one of the moleskin banquettes in the brasserie-like *"bateau,"* accompanied by piano tunes alumnus George Gershwin would recognize. The intellectual-at-ease bent of the clientele is still another thing about Paris that is little changed. See? Perhaps it was this scene that prompted Gertrude Stein's famous dictum: *"L'Amérique c'est mon pays, Paris c'est chez moi."*

Closerie des Lilas, 171 boulevard du Montparnasse, 6ème. Telephone: 43.26.70.50 and 40.33.21.68.

This article originally appeared in *Gourmet*. Copyright © 1988 by Catharine Reynolds. Reprinted by permission of the author.

Toy Boats and Pony Rides in the Heart of Paris

BY RICHARD REEVES

~~

editor's note

....

Due to the popularity and variety of the Luxembourg, another piece seems not at all indulgent. Writer David Downie, whose work appears elsewhere in this book, once wrote that a day spent in the Luxembourg Gardens "teaches you more about Paris and its inhabitants than a dozen scholarly tomes."

RICHARD REEVES is an award-winning American journalist who lived for a number of years in Paris. In addition to writing for publications such as *Travel & Leisure, Islands,* and *The New York Times,* he is the author of several books, including *President Kennedy: Profile of Power* (Simon & Schuster, 1993), *American Journey* (Simon & Schuster, 1982), and *Family Travels* (Andrews & McMeel, 1997).

When Napoléon escaped from Elba in 1815 and marched to Paris to rule again for the Hundred Days, one of the first things he did was to go to the Luxembourg Gardens to check on the plantings and construction he had ordered before his exile.

An emperor has to have priorities, and I agree with Napoléon's. Without quite his entourage, I used to do the same thing each year when I visited Paris: check in at a hotel and then walk or ride over to the Luxembourg. I wanted to make sure that the rows of chestnut trees were still straight, that little boys were still there to guide sailboats across the basin, that the same old men were playing *boules*—and that Napoléon's iron fence of black and gold was being kept up.

Now, living two blocks away, I do it every day. "My" park (like everyone else around here, I think of it that way) is always the same, always different.

Les Jardins du Luxembourg, the great green patch of Paris's Left Bank neighborhoods, has looked about the same since Napoléon took it over at the end of the eighteenth century. He lived in the Luxembourg Palace after taking power and, like any new tenant, began playing around with its fifty-two-acre yard, which Maria de' Medici, at the beginning of the seventeenth century, had tried to model after the Boboli Gardens of Florence.

Marie, as she was called in France, had bought the property from the duke of Luxembourg after the death of her husband, Henry IV. She spent almost twenty years planning and building the gardens, but they never came to be known by her name, for a very simple reason: Parisians hated her. And why not? When a new aqueduct was built to increase Parisian water supplies (each citizen had been getting only a quart a day), she took more than half the Left Bank's supply to water her new gardens and their fountains. Soon enough, there was intrigue and dissension; she died in exile in Germany, and the gardens became public property.

Today, under the administration of the French Senate, the gardens alter every day in a very French way. The central idea of French gardening is to improve on nature. So the flower beds are redone daily with some of the 160,000 plants and 35,000 bushes stored in warehouses on the outskirts of Paris. The Luxembourg is literally what God would do if He had the money.

The mood of the gardens changes constantly from dawn to dusk. In the early hours, my wife and I walk the winding, English-style paths at the perimeter of the gardens. Our few companions are usually students from the Sorbonne, reading alone, and the city's firefighters, the *sapeurs-pompiers,* running their required daily laps in blue sweatsuits.

By late morning, the students have taken over, studying in sunlight now, but also gossiping and flirting around the octagonal basin and fountain at the center of the gardens, where little boys in short pants are wrestling sailboats as big as themselves into the water. At lunchtime, secretaries and bosses from Left Bank offices come to join the students, eating sandwiches, reading their papers and ignoring each other in the Parisian manner. Then, in the afternoon, the children come, with mothers and baby-sitters—and me—in tow. I have a two-year-old daughter who gives me entry to the small area of sandboxes and wading pools in front of the Orangerie. On the other side of the Luxembourg, the side bounded by the boulevard St.-Michel, Ernest Hemingway might once have stalked the pigeons. He wrote later that he was so hungry in those days that he used to come with his baby son to the grand fountain built by Marie de Médicis and strangle pigeons to take home for dinner.

The Luxembourg has always attracted Americans. Isadora Duncan danced here alone. Tom Paine, leaving our revolution for theirs, was a prisoner in the palace for eleven months during 1793–94. Thirty years later, after Napoléon had done his work, Henry Wadsworth Longfellow wrote this to his brother:

You descend from the higher grounds to this little vale, which is an amphitheater, open towards the palace—by flights of stone steps, which here and there interrupt the stone balustrade around the brink. On the higher grounds, and in an oval, parallel to this balustrade, are placed the marble statues of the garden, each placed upon a high pedestal in a niche cut from the boughs of the trees. This part of the garden is the general lounge and promenade—and it is full of rush-bottomed chairs! Not to an absolute plenum—but a row or two on each side of the walk, where the ladies sit to be looked at—and the gentlemen to look at them.

It is all the same still, except that the chairs are now steel-bottomed. The ninety statues, it must be said, are only a touch better than they were then—forgettable works, many of forgettable people. The exception is Aimé-Jules Dalou's memorial to Delacroix, with its allegorical figures representing Poetry, Philosophy, Rhetoric and Science. The group stands in front of the Petit Luxembourg, a smaller palace facing rue de Vaugirard that serves as an art museum. Two others move me, though, whatever their artistic merit. One is a nine-foot model of the Statue of Liberty, cast by Frédéric-Auguste Bartholdi, whose studio was nearby. The other is a small, very calm bronze of a former French premier, Pierre Mendès-France. Perhaps I just like statues of politicians with their mouths shut.

Louis Philippe put in most of the statues in the 1840s, and there are people who are still mad at him. That, after all, is fairly recent history in the gardens. Gallo-Roman villas once covered the area. When they fell into ruin, a highwayman named Vauvert used the place as his camp sometime in the tenth century. He must have been a very fierce fellow because, for the next two hundred years or so, Parisians wouldn't go near the place; they believed he haunted it. Finally, in 1257, the Carthusians, the ghostbusters of their day, built a monastery on what is now the rue Auguste Comte, and people began building in the vicinity again.

During the German occupation of 1940–44, the Germans used the Luxembourg Palace as Luftwaffe headquarters, and pillboxes and trenches were dug in the gardens before a small but very destructive battle in August 1944. After the war, the French Senate, which now meets in the palace, had a good deal of rebuilding to do.

It's astounding how many things are tucked away in the nooks and crannies of my gardens. There is the puppet theater and the merry-go-round designed and built in 1879 by Garnier, the architect of the Paris Opera. There are six tennis courts and as many *boules* courts—and what I call "the American field" because of its old basketball hoop and the boys who play a clumsy version of baseball or American football there. There are playgrounds, large and small, pony rides for the young and pavilions where their fathers and grandfathers silently play chess. There is a small restaurant and café, stands that sell waffles and cotton candy, balloon vendors, a day school for children under six—and I'm not sure I've mentioned everything or even seen everything.

But I have seen Paris. On Sunday, the Luxembourg *is* Paris. Everybody is there: grandparents and babies, workers and their families in from the suburbs, students and immigrants and the BCBG—the *bon chic, bon genre*—upper class from the Right Bank. Where else on earth would anyone want to be?

The Shape of a Rodin Tour

BY FREDERIC V. GRUNFELD

editor's note

The French family I lived with as a student lived in the rue de Grenelle, just a few blocks away from the Musée Rodin in the rue de Varenne. As I was also an au pair, I was permitted to wander the garden of Rodin's Hôtel Biron gratis when I had two-year-old Laurent with me. (This is a little-publicized fact of gardens attached to museums or historical sites. Adults accompanied by young children are admitted free to the grounds only, so if there are at least two adults, they can take turns visiting the museum. The kids are infinitely happier on the grounds—which are stroller-friendly—and at the Musée Rodin there is a popular sandbox at the back of the garden.) As pleasant as the garden is, the museum is on the short list of many people's favorites in all of Paris. It not only displays works by Rodin but also works he collected by others.

FREDERIC GRUNFELD (1929–87) was an art critic and author. His published works include *Rodin: A Biography* and *Prophets Without Honor: A Background to Freud, Kafka, Einstein and Their World* (both published by Henry Holt). Grunfeld was also a contributing editor of *Connoisseur* and a roving editor of *Horizon*.

The obvious Rodinophile's rendezvous in Paris is the Musée Rodin, one of the most popular museums in France. For decades—at least until Picasso got his museum in the Marais—it had no rival among one-man galleries anywhere in the world. A young Parisian friend and I used the museum, on rue de Varenne, as the starting point for a Rodin tour of Paris, a tour on foot, metro and train that led to churches, tenement and mansion, to both banks of the Seine and to a suburban vantage point.

In the museum are *The Kiss, The Thinker, The Burghers of Calais* and many other of the sculptor's works as well as casts of originals, and furniture, pictures and antiquities that belonged to Rodin. After gazing our fill at the busts and statues indoors we strolled around the almost deserted garden, with its formidable array of bronzes and marbles scattered around a fountain and among the trees, paths and neatly trimmed shrubbery. Sheltered by a high wall from the traffic of the boulevard des Invalides, the garden of the Rodin Museum is still one of the quietest places in the center of Paris.

When Rodin discovered this remarkable sanctuary in 1908, both the house and the garden were in a semiderelict state. During the eighteenth century it had been one of the great mansions of Paris—after the Maréchal-Duc de Biron moved in, it became known as the Hôtel Biron—and during the nineteenth century it had housed a convent school for aristocratic girls. But when Rodin found it the property had been taken over by the government and was scheduled for demolition. A liquidator was renting rooms at bargain rates to temporary tenants, mainly artists and writers such as Jean Cocteau, who wrote of the tangled garden as a fairy-tale realm: "Did Paris really live, walk, drive, and work around such a pool of silence?"

The young German poet Rainer Maria Rilke was also briefly a tenant (the plaque on the outer wall that claims he lived here from 1908 to 1911 is pure wishful thinking), and it was he who called Rodin's attention to the house. Although Rodin already had free use of two government-owned studios in the nearby Marble Depot in the rue de l'Université (the modern building on the site now belongs to French television), he fell in love with the Hôtel Biron and was soon installed as its principal tenant. At sixty-eight he was then at the height of his fame as the *grand maître* of contemporary sculpture, and he told Rilke that he wanted his suite of rooms as a secret hideaway. In fact, it quickly became his favorite place to receive visitors and meet the press, which played a considerable part in persuading the government to preserve the house as a museum.

During the years when Rodin's business affairs were managed by the American-born Duchesse de Choiseul, née Claire Coudert, she used part of the main floor as a showroom and was able to boast of having raised his yearly income from sixty thousand to four hundred thousand francs. In a sunny room upstairs he did hundreds of the one-minute figure drawings that became a preoccupation in his later years.

On our jaunt, however, our main purpose was to retrace the footsteps of the younger Rodin, and so we set off in a southerly direction toward less fashionable districts of the Left Bank: geographically and psychologically, Rodin was a Left Bank person virtually all his life. We went underground at the Varenne metro station, which has been turned into a sort of poor man's Rodin museum, with casts of *Balzac* and *The Thinker* looming above the platforms. We changed trains at Duroc and emerged at Maubert-Mutualité to begin a not very steep ascent to the Montagne Ste.-Geneviève, where we wanted to visit the Panthéon. Rodin spent his boyhood in the crowded streets behind this immense neoclassical temple; his mother took him to mass there in the days when it was still a church. About thirty years later his portrait appeared on its walls—because his friend Jean-Paul Laurens had used Rodin as a model for one of the Merovingian warriors in a historical fresco.

By then the government had converted the building into a republican hall of fame, for which Rodin was supposed to create a Victor Hugo monument. But the selection committee rejected his original maquette, which became the nude Victor Hugo that now reposes in the Hôtel Biron garden, and the Panthéon never did acquire a Rodin monument. Instead, his friends organized a public subscription to install a monumental cast of *The Thinker* in front of the Panthéon in 1906, an event that Rodin regarded as one of his crowning achievements. But Paris is fickle in its enthusiasms and *The Thinker* no longer occupies his post in front of the rather forlorn-looking temple; years ago he was packed off to the rue de Varenne.

A few steps farther stands the far older church of St.-Étienne-du-Mont, and we spent half an hour admiring what is surely one of the most fascinating buildings in Paris. Rodin also sat in these pews as a boy, amid a shiplike interior that was begun the year Columbus discovered America. Perhaps the boy's impressions of these high, slender pillars with their gravity-defying gallery planted the seed that flowered into Rodin's passion for Gothic churches. His book, *Les Cathédrales de France,* is one long love letter to buildings like this one, illustrated with his spidery drawings of just such details as the rib-vaulting of St.-Étienne's ceiling.

We descended the hill along the narrow rue Mouffetard in search of the sculptor's birthplace. Crossing the street at right angles is the rue de l'Arbalète (Crossbow Street), in the center of what in the nineteenth century was once a most notorious slum. Rodin was born November 12, 1840, in the house that is now No. 7 rue de l'Arbalète, a nondescript tenement building in which his parents and sister occupied a fifth-floor apartment. Rodin's father was then a minor functionary in the Paris police.

We climbed up the ancient staircase and looked out of the fifth-floor window at what is still a bare, sunless courtyard. Understandably, the Rodins moved away from here as soon as they could afford less depressing quarters. No plaque marks the building as the birthplace of one of the great artists of France, but a boutique recently installed downstairs serves notice that the whole neighborhood is in the throes of gentrification. Indeed, the Quartier de la Mouffe, once famous for its ragpickers and footpads, has come up in the world, and as we walked farther down the street it was the smell of herbs and spices, of freshly baked patisserie and expensive cheeses that greeted our nostrils.

Rodin was christened in the medieval church of St.-Médard, just around the corner. We had been squeezed into narrow lanes and had even walked single file through the street market of the rue Mouffetard, but at St.-Médard the constricted street suddenly widens into a great open space, and we felt like a cork coming out of a bottle. Now we were headed uphill again, along the spacious avenue des Gobelins, to the old royal tapestry factory, the Manufacture des Gobelins, where Rodin, as an apprentice sculptor, attended free evening classes. Little has changed here in the last two hundred years except the patterns of the tapestries. The baroque buildings of the factory, a quiet corner alongside a bustling avenue, are still occupied by artists and craftsmen living in a privileged enclave with cobbled courtyards and a private park. Rodin's classes included his first regular life class, which was held in what had been the dining room of Charles Le Brun, the director of the Manufacture under Louis XIV. (The Petite École, Rodin's first art school, was meant for artisans on whom a life class was deemed to be wasted.)

Farther along the avenue des Gobelins, across the street at No. 73, is the Théâtre des Gobelins, now a movie house. On the second floor, above an arched loggia, rise two elongated figures in high relief that turn out to be Rodin's largest sculptures of the 1860s. Even now they're very impressive. The female figure, holding a jester's staff and a pair of classic Greek castanets, symbolizes comedy. Her male companion, brandishing a torch and a sword, personifies the spirit of tragedy. Rodin, in his late twenties, received one hundred francs for the pair. But if you want to study the sculptures properly as an unheralded work of the young Rodin, you'd do best to take binoculars and stand on the other side of the street.

Fifteen minutes after going underground at Métro Gobelins we emerged across the river at Franklin Roosevelt and the Champs-Élysées. We had decided to make a digression to the Right Bank to see something of the work that Rodin had done for his employer, the architectural sculptor Carrier-Belleuse—before the Franco-Prussian War sent them both into exile in Brussels. At 25 Champs-Élysées stands the exclusive Travellers' Club, once a neo-Renaissance mansion, built by the German mine owner Count Henckel von Donnersmarck, for the femme fatale Marquise de Païva, who was born Esther Lachmann in a Russian ghetto. Carrier-Belleuse was one of La Païva's principal suppliers of decorative sculpture, and Rodin was then working as his chief assistant molder. In later years Rodin used to enjoy showing his friends the ornamental heads on the facade of the Hôtel de Païva that he had produced at piece rates for Carrier-Belleuse. They're still there, but again we needed our binoculars to see them properly.

Our next stop was at the Opéra, where we explored the most sumptuous of Second Empire environments. Carrier-Belleuse was an old friend of Charles Garnier, the architect of this stupendous theater, and he contributed the elaborate torchères that hold the candelabra illuminating the grand staircase. His gifted assistant, however, is more likely to have had a hand in the making of the two large caryatids, *La Comédie* (with mask) and *La Danse* (with tambourine) that flank the east chimney of the grand foyer. On most afternoons the Opéra is pleased to sell sight-seeing tickets for about $3 to curiosity seekers like ourselves, so we were able to view the two sculptures at close range, wondering whether their toes and fingers might have been the work of Rodin, who often did the hands and feet of his patron's figures.

To conclude our search for such Carrier-Rodins we went to the Church of St.-Vincent-de-Paul, near the Gare du Nord, to see one of Carrier-Belleuse's finest works, a Virgin and Child called *Le Messie* (the Messiah). We walked to the far end of the cavernous neoclassical church to find this forgotten sculpture, dimly lighted, in the chapel at the back of the choir. It is an unusual image, for the Virgin holds the Child aloft in a gesture of fierce maternal pride. Rodin is said to have worked on this figure as well.

From the Gare du Nord we made our way back across the Seine to the city's new treasure trove of nineteenth-century art, the Musée d'Orsay. Here, under the steel-and-glass canopy of Victor Laloux's onetime railroad station, Rodin's sculptures soar out into space and take on far more life than they can in the intimate surroundings of the Hôtel Biron. The d'Orsay galleries, moreover, allowed us to see Rodin in perspective, together with his teachers, colleagues and rivals. We paused in front of the still astonishing plaster cast of the *Balzac,* the very one that caused such an uproar at its debut in 1898, and a no less remarkable plaster cast of the unfinished *Whistler Monument.* The catalog fails to mention that this is a nude portrait of Gwen John, the unhappiest of Rodin's mistresses and, unbe-known to him, one of the great British painters of the twentieth century. It was a case of entertaining an angel unawares. Against one wall stand the Gates of Hell in plaster, more or less the way Rodin knew them—he never saw a bronze cast of his great unfin-ished symphony. It was for this site on the quai d'Orsay that the Gates of Hell was commissioned in the first place. In 1880 there were plans to build a museum of applied arts in place of the ruins of the old Cour des Comptes, which had burned down during the Paris Commune. But the government lost interest and the land was acquired by the Paris-Orléans Railroad.

For forty years the Gare d'Orsay accommodated up to two hun-dred trains a day, until electrification made it obsolete—its plat-forms proved too short for the longer trains. That set the stage for its conversion into the world's most sumptuous museum of Salon and anti-Salon art, in a setting that still preserves something of the nerve-tingling excitement of a railroad station. There are some trains that continue to run beneath the quai d'Orsay: on Line C of the suburban RER Railroad. We bundled ourselves into the next train in the direction of Versailles and alighted a quarter of an hour later at Meudon-Val Fleury. Rodin moved to this suburb in 1896 after buying a house there, the Villa des Brillants, which had been built for a painter.

From the station to the house is a distance of a little more than half a mile. We knew, as we trudged up the avenue Paul-Bert, that the Villa des Brillants, now a branch of the Rodin Museum, is closed from October through March (the rest of the year it is open on Saturdays, Sundays and Mondays from 1 to 7 P.M.). Yet we didn't mind finding the gates firmly shut, since a path skirts the fence, allowing us to descend past the deserted house and the ancient chestnut trees to the spot where another *Thinker* sits brooding over Rodin's grave. It was very quiet on this hillside where Rodin lived for twenty years with his ever-growing collection of Greek and Roman antiquities, his pavilion-museum (long since replaced by another), his assistants, ranging from the composer Edgar Varèse to the sculptor Carl Milles. We looked out over the view of distant Paris that gave him so much pleasure.

We retraced our steps; it was growing dark and we still had one more stop on our whirlwind tour. We got off the train at the Javel station, on the banks of the Seine, and walked to the Pont de Grenelle, where we crossed over to the Île des Cygnes, the narrowest and least known of the city's islands. A single path runs down the spine of the island and there are trees on either side, but a hundred years ago there were buildings here, including a storehouse where Rodin kept some of his sculptures. When Edmond de Goncourt went to see them in 1886 he was enthralled by the sculptor's "admirable torsos of small women" because he was so good at modeling the curve of the back "and, as it were, the beating wings of their shoulders."

All traces of Rodin have disappeared from the Île des Cygnes but at one end of the island stands the work of a slightly older contemporary with whom he was acquainted, Bartholdi's *Liberty Enlightening the World*—yes, the Bedloe's Island Liberty, though in a scaled-down version. Sculpture, indeed, is an art of multiples.

"The Shape of a Rodin Tour" by Frederic V. Grunfeld. Copyright © 1988 by Frederic V. Grunfeld.

Père-Lachaise:
A Historic Resting Place

BY CATHARINE REYNOLDS

∽

editor's note

The reason for my first visit to Père-Lachaise was no different from that of any other American college student: to see Jim Morrison's grave. I only owned one album by The Doors, so I didn't even consider myself a proper fan; but it seemed like the thing to do, and anyway, the wine that was passed around was pretty good. Only later did I read that so many other famous people were buried there, and that, taken together, they represented a broad cross-section of French personalities.

Père-Lachaise is more than just personalities, however; as noted in this piece, which was featured in July 1987, it "evokes *civilisation française*—for citizen and foreigner alike." I think the "dramatic monuments" referred to in the eastern half of the cemetery are those honoring the victims of Nazi persecution. They are the most moving memorials I have ever seen, anywhere. I once took my friend Sarah to Père-Lachaise, and we came across one that was simply footprints leading into a large, dark structure. Sarah cried out while pointing to it, and we were reduced to tears.

A more recent article about Père-Lachaise—but very different from this one—is "A Still Wind" by Mark Mordue (*Madison*, April 1999), which is a personal view of the cemetery. Whenever I tell friends and colleagues to include Père-Lachaise on their itinerary, they always tell me it was the surprise of their trip, that it was their favorite site to see in all of Paris.

CATHARINE REYNOLDS, a longtime contributing editor of *Gourmet,* has spent much of her life in Paris. She has also written about the cemeteries of Montmartre and Montparnasse (*Gourmet,* April 1998).

T he nineteenth century has suddenly come into its own in Paris. Certainly the hoopla over the new Musée d'Orsay has catalyzed the fashion, but *antiquaires,* historians, and other heralds had seen that its time had come. The fever pitch of sentiment holds a curious attraction for a country treading a cohabitation tightrope. Are Parisians caught up in a new era of what Stendhal saw as the essential character of the last century, "an increasing thirst for strong emotions"?

Whether or not we choose to argue that issue around café tables, we can certainly enjoy one of the shrines of nineteenth-century emotion, the Cimetière du Père-Lachaise. Visitors to London flock to Westminster Abbey's memorials; only the very squeamish should neglect what Henry Wadsworth Longfellow considered its Parisian equivalent, which has the fillip of a sylvan setting and a view that stretches across the city.

The largest necropolis within the metropolis is neither lugubrious nor ghostly. "Friendship and glory are the only inhabitants of the tombs," observed Honoré de Balzac, before his bones and debts were laid to rest there. Glory is virtually commonplace, with Frédéric Chopin, Eugène Delacroix, Alfred de Musset (all lovers of George Sand's), Dominique Ingres, Georges Seurat, Sarah Bernhardt, Oscar Wilde, and Louis David present and accounted for, along with illustrati who spanned this and that century, people like Marcel Proust, Colette, and Edith Piaf. Their friendships seem to reach out from their graves. Is not painter Camille Corot, the "St. Vincent de Paul of the art world," buried only yards from Honoré Daumier, the multitalented artist whose blind old age he succored? Ironic, on the other hand, that Daumier should be buried amid the bourgeois he excelled at caricaturing.

Little wonder, then, that eight hundred thousand celebrity-chasing tourists troop to Père-Lachaise annually, making it Paris's fourth most visited site. Many find more life in those stony sepulchers than they might in dusty biographies. At Père-Lachaise imperial marshals jostle composers, artists lie by industrialists, burghers meet Bohemians, and fame struggles against obscurity. The monuments, simple slabs or architect-designed chapels drawn from

Egyptian, classical, Gothic, or mongrel sources, with and without taste, stretch across more than a hundred acres, split among ninety-seven segments called *divisions,* each marked by green-painted, cast-iron street signs.

The Cimetière de l'Est, as Père-Lachaise is properly called, was created, along with the Cimetières du Nord (Montmartre) and du Sud (Montparnasse), by a Paris prefect called Nicolas Frochot under the Consulate in answer to the pressing needs of a growing capital. The initial forty-four acres were laid out as a park under the supervision of Alexandre Théodore Brongniart and received their first tenant May 21, 1804.

But who was Père Lachaise? My imagination conjured visions of a kindly parish priest who accompanied the cortege of that first grieving family. None of it. In fact, he was a long-dead Jesuit, a power in the land in the seventeenth century, who had lived in a splendid country house at the crest of the hill where the chapel now stands. Louis XIV had been introduced to François de La Chaise d'Aix by the wily Cardinal Mazarin, who brought the fourteen-year-old king to this clergyman's country hideaway to watch the civil skirmishes between the royal troops and a rebellious faction. Boy king and prelate got on so well that Lachaise became the monarch's confessor. His power never rivaled Richelieu's or Mazarin's, but he is judged to have had considerable influence on the king's policies toward Jansenists and Protestants, as well as having urged the dismissal of Mistress Montespan in favor of the Madame of the Moment, *La Maintenon,* to whom he is widely believed to have secretly married the king on the night of October 9–10, 1683.

This quick-witted, able psychologist also managed to live very well indeed. His younger brother, a lieutenant in the king's bodyguard, was ostensibly responsible for the parties given at this country house.

On the heels of pleasure followed beauty,
Opulence and idleness.
On these laughing slopes, in these joyous groves,
Not long ago reigned love with pleasure

the verse recounts, but such fetes did little to improve the reputation
of the Jesuits. Père Lachaise did not live to see his order's expulsion
from France in 1763. He succumbed to the harsh winter of 1709 and
was buried in the Marais's Église St.-Paul–St.-Louis.

The property changed hands repeatedly until it was purchased
by the Baron family, who held it until the Revolution ruined them.
They were pleased indeed to exchange it for Préfet Frochot's 180,000
francs and even chose to be buried in their former demesne.

The new municipal burial ground was not a *succès fou*. To make
it more glamorous, authorities decided to transfer some of the land's
more glorious dead to its precincts, choosing Héloïse and Abelard,
Molière, and Jean de La Fontaine as star attractions. Abbess and the-
ologian have always been France's favorite star-crossed lovers, and so
their romance was served up under a trefoiled, canopied monument
composed of medieval remains. Molière's selection was more ironic:
Having collapsed playing the title role in *Le Malade Imaginaire*,
hadn't he first been buried by night without benefit of clergy as
penance for his evil play-acting life? La Fontaine was every
Frenchman's favorite, recalling the singsong of *"Maître Corbeau, sur
un arbre perché. . . ."*

The public relations stunt worked, and Père-Lachaise was soon
adopted as "the grandest address in Paris." Success was so great
that the city repeatedly acquired adjacent land, nearly trebling the
original area. Père-Lachaise became the ceremonial coda for lives of
accomplishment. The rhythm of the seasons took over, punctuated
by state funerals, only occasionally shattered by more earthshaking

events. Temporary havoc reigned when the Russians bivouacked there, chopping down trees during the occupation of 1814.

In the last week of May 1871, Père-Lachaise played a more central role on the political stage as the scene of the Commune's heroic last gasp. Two hundred National Guards holed up there with two batteries of guns. Bullets ricocheted off the family vaults in hand-to-hand combat against Adolphe Thiers's government troops, and one of the cemetery's last defenders was finally killed near Balzac's tomb. Defeat was compounded by infamy when 147 captured Communards were lined up against the eastern wall and shot. Others were similarly slain as the last rebels were winkled out of the neighborhood. The futility of the carnage made martyrs of these Fédérés, and their memorial along that eastern wall, the Mur des Fédérés, remains a rallying point for French left-wing radicals.

On the whole, city cemeteries possess little charm for me; I hold with the earthy serenity of New England country churchyards, and so I had lived in Paris nearly a year before I focused on Père-Lachaise. My Spanish cleaning lady asked for a late-October afternoon off to clean her "morning lady's" family mausoleum in preparation for Jour de la Toussaint, or All Saints' Day, on November 1. When she explained that this was an all-day task—scrubbing walls and floor and polishing stained glass and bronze—the status of her morning employer ballooned in my estimation and piqued my curiosity. I did not then realize that the majority of French families who can afford to be buried at Père-Lachaise have over the generations invested substantially in stone and mortar way stations to the hereafter.

So one blowy mid-November day I betook myself to the 20th Arrondissement and discovered the nineteenth century, intact, showing off its beauty and its excesses. But the first thing that struck me was the size of Père-Lachaise. The grand ceremonial gate on the boulevard de Ménilmontant straddles the western side of the cemetery at the foot of the Colline de Charonne. Street upon lane upon avenue of memorial chapels stretch to left and right, twisting amid the trees. Fortunately, the guard at the gate pressed a map upon me (in return for three francs), or I would soon have been overwhelmed by the kaleidoscope before me. No standardized headstones for most of these worthies: instead, equestrian statues, shrouded widows, castles, busts, plaques, lighthouses, overwrought epitaphs, porcelain flower arrangements, and genuflecting angels sure to win a nod from Saint Pierre. The less creative settled for tiny family chapels, large enough to contain a prie-dieu or two for relations come to pray.

At Père-Lachaise I unlocked within a bustling city an enclave that attracts local denizens as much as visitors from afar. Some come to call on their dead. Others bring their children to skip rope and play hide-and-seek. Old ladies arrive equipped to feed the hundreds of cats who make Père-Lachaise their home. The cats lie in wait for the other recipients of the old ladies' largesse, the colonies of blackbirds, jays, magpies, woodpeckers, and nightingales that warble in the cemetery's twelve thousand trees. Couples, too, come to bill and coo; not all are young, nor is it clear whether all are legally free to woo, but even those whose amours are perforce clandestine find that love blooms along the paths of Père-Lachaise. Solitary philosophers saunter through the bowers, musing on the fate of nations. All commune with the seasons and survey the chestnut "candles" and bluebells of spring, the flowering morning glories of summer, and the bright leaves of autumn. Père-Lachaise is best enjoyed on dry days, as the byways grow muddy with rain, and the cobblestones are perilous to those wearing high heels.

Père-Lachaise draws one back, and I have returned often. Map in hand, one soon masters the geography, discovering that the western half, which clings to the hill, is more romantic, with its sinuous paths and ancient trees. The eastern half, at the top of the hill, stretches flat and more stark, suitable for the sometimes very dramatic monuments that dot it. What endless discoveries, the odd name or date under the ivy mantle, the panache of a sculpture, which free-associate into a diorama of the city's and nation's past. Père-Lachaise provides an aperçu of the interior decor of a well-educated Frenchman's mind, untidy cupboards and all, and evokes *civilisation française*— for citizen and foreigner alike.

On the one hand, there is Gustave Doré, whose illustrations created our images of Balzac's *Contes Drolatiques,* La Fontaine's *Fables,* and Dante's *Inferno* even when we couldn't grasp the text. On the other is Louis David, who made Jean-Paul Marat die and Napoléon live in our imaginations. His pupil, Dominique Ingres, isn't far away. The Romantics, Théodore Géricault and Eugène Delacroix, inhabit the same western side of Père-Lachaise, Géricault reclining, palette in hand, atop a bas-relief of his masterpiece, *Le Radeau de la Méduse,* Delacroix beneath an austere black lava classical sarcophagus that is strangely at odds with his dramatic canvases. Antoine Louis Barye, author of the bronze animals that were a delight of my childhood, lurks behind him, and sculptor Pierre Jean David d'Angers has duly come to rest in Père-Lachaise, for which he created several of the finest memorials.

Many of Père-Lachaise's residents devoted themselves to politics; some of their honorifics ring hollow today. Other *hommes politiques* have been assured a curious immortality. For example, Third Republic president Félix Faure rests under the cypresses of the avenue Principale. His slightly smutty place in every French adolescent's theogony was guaranteed by his death in active proximity to his mistress. One daren't inquire if those same *lycéens* recall his policies toward the Dreyfus Affair.

More idealistic were the Comte de St.-Simon and his quondam colleague Auguste Comte, who, having laid the foundations of sociology, drove himself nearly mad. Less idealistic was Pierre-Augustin Caron de Beaumarchais, that jack-of-all-trades from watchmaking to espionage, whom Americans should acknowledge for the part he played in supplying the Continental army. And the world can thank him for the tale of Figaro, the intrigue in whose life was the stuff of Beaumarchais's.

Gioacchino Rossini fans must content themselves with their hero's memorial chapel, as the onetime director of the Théâtre Italien's remains were removed to Florence. His composing contemporary Esprit Auber is best remembered among Parisians for the metro stop named after him and the prominence of his name on the facade of the Opéra. Auber's teacher Luigi Cherubini languishes, eclipsed by his neighbor Frédéric Chopin, whom George Sand described as a "high-flown, consumptive, and exasperating nuisance" (how's that for spite?). Chopin's grave, with its bust by Jean-Baptiste Clésinger surmounted by a white marble muse of music overcome by grief, is almost invariably garlanded: it remains a mail drop for illicit lovers. Romance wafts like a woodwind among the composers: Didn't Georges Bizet die of a broken heart because of the critical failure of *Carmen*? How was he to know that those same critics' comments about the immorality of the plot would bring the public in droves? How would he have responded to the condemnation of generations of "toreadors," a noun he compounded out of *torero* and *matador* to make up his rhythm?

In death Père-Lachaise's performers seem to have lost little of their following. "The divine Sarah"'s canopied granite tomb still attracts many an enthusiast too young to have ever seen her in *L'Aiglon*.

Edith Piaf's simple black gravestone is considered Père-Lachaise's biggest draw. The violet-eyed "little sparrow" was truly an *enfant du pavé*, born "on a cop's cape under a lamppost in front of 72 rue de Belleville," little over a mile away. Forty thousand devotees, including a detachment of legionnaires, came to mourn her on a sunny day in October 1963. Simone Signoret has recently joined her.

A younger crowd congregates around the graffiti-strewn bust of Jim Morrison, lead singer and songwriter for The Doors. Mystery shrouds his supposed death at twenty-eight, and fans stand vigil at Père-Lachaise, hoping the author of the lyric "No one here gets out alive" will walk back into their lives.

Unlike the Panthéon, Père-Lachaise is not the exclusive preserve of the famous. Its *allées* are peopled mostly by the bourgeoisie; after all, it drew chiefly on the populations of the 5th, 6th, 7th, and 8th Arrondissements, *quartiers* both artistic and fashionable. Victor Hugo wryly observed that "to be buried in Père-Lachaise is like having mahogany furniture." Their substantial monoliths are the warp and woof of the cemetery's tapestry, whether they belong to families named Rothschild or Dupont (the French Smith or Jones).

Sandwiched among them are the odd surprises, like the grave of Jean-François Champollion, Egyptologist, the mastery of the spelling of whose name and the "hi-ero-glyph-ics" he deciphered from the Rosetta stone was one of the accomplishments of my eighth year. Or then the doughty philosopher of Belley, whose words have a savor all their own, Anthelme Brillat-Savarin, whose *La Physiologie du Goût* was published only three weeks before his death.

Antoine-Augustin Parmentier's shrine, decorated with plow, alembic, ears of corn and wheat, and the essential basket of potatoes, is a place of pilgrimage to *frite*-o-philes. And there are unmitigated curiosities, like the baroque monument to Jean Pezon, animal tamer, portrayed riding his lion Brutus, who, history records, devoured him; chronicles fail to reveal whether Brutus, too, is buried at Père-Lachaise.

Other monuments cast aside all humor and strike chords of a

common humanity—like the sandstone figure in the ninety-fourth *division* to a fatality of Verdun, carved to resemble the sandbags of the trenches ringed with barbed wire, the young soldier's laureled helmet cast aside.

Equally affecting are the memorials to the victims of Nazi concentration and labor camps opposite the Mur des Fédérés. The gigantic, emaciated copper figure of a man, destroyed by his own existence, recalls the dead of Oranienburg and Sachsenhausen. Farther down the hill stand memorials to France's Resistance heroes.

Though quintessentially a French *campo santo*, Père-Lachaise welcomes foreigners, among them Sir Richard Wallace, whose drinking fountains still grace many Paris streets. "Good Americans, when they die, go to Paris," incanted Oliver Wendell Holmes, and both Isadora Duncan and Loie Fuller, whose dancing galvanized Europe, slumber in the Columbarium, with Gertrude Stein not far away. Stein was friend and patron of the Lost Generation she baptized. "Tiny, nimble, and mustachioed" Alice B. Toklas, whose cookbook still tickles, effaces herself in death as in life behind Gertrude's stone.

Oscar Wilde's mausoleum is no shrinking violet—through no fault of his own. He died as he had lived, beyond his means, and so the generosity of a lady admirer funded the grand Assyrian figure by Jacob Epstein. One senses that a man who, asked by a New York customs officer if he had anything to declare, replied, "No, I have nothing to declare—except my genius," would have been pleased. Though a deathbed convert to Catholicism, Wilde retained his verve, tweaking his friend Robbie Ross with "When the last trumpet sounds, and you and I are couched in our purple and porphyry tombs, I shall turn and whisper, 'Robbie, dear boy, let us pretend we do not hear it.'"

Another notorious eccentric litterateur, this time native, Gérard de Nerval, is probably better known in the English-speaking world for walking his lobster on a leash than for his sonorous sonnets, *Les Chimères*. On the other hand, Marcel Proust is probably less esteemed in France than in America, where the spindly asthmatic stands tall beside Joyce and James on the prose podium. His black tombstone rarely lacks a tiny bunch of violets, their stems wrapped in foil.

Colette's black granite slab always sports flowers. Legend has it that cats replenish the roses; certainly they bask in the sun there. Close by lies Alfred de Musset, precocious schoolboy Romantic and man-about-town, who expressed his funerary desires lyrically in "Lucie":

> Mes chers amis, quand je mourrai,
> Plantez un saul au cimetière.
> J'aime son feuillage éploré,
> La pâleur m'en est douce et chère,
> Et son ombre sera légère
> À la terre où je dormirai

—little heeding that Père-Lachaise's loamy soil is less than hospitable to willows. The authorities struggle against nature to comply, replanting periodically.

Balzac, France's Dickens, remains for me the figurehead of the literary community on the Colline de Charonne. The two thousand characters of *La Comédie Humaine* are indeed a complete society, rather like that of Père-Lachaise. And Balzac's hero, Eugène Rastignac, buries Père Goriot there and hurls forth from the heights his challenge to the dusk-bound city below, *"Paris, à nous deux"* (Paris, it's between you and me now), the summons to make one's way, to fulfill one's dream, the reply to which has been the creation of this cultural universe.

P.S. If I've omitted your favorite hero or tomb, please forgive me. Père-Lachaise overwhelms me, and it will you, too.

Cimetière du Père-Lachaise, boulevard de Ménilmontant, 20éme.

All Alone in Paris

BY JEAN BOND RAFFERTY

∽

editor's note

Everyone who lives in Paris ends up having a "favorite" garden, park, café, bar, museum, bakery, bridge, street, etc., mostly because friends and visitors always *expect* you to have favorites. As a student living with a family in the 7th Arrondissement, I rarely set foot in the gardens of the Palais-Royal. "Too formal, too quiet," I sniffed, preferring the impromptu gatherings of guitar-playing young people in the little park next to St.-Julien-le-Pauvre. Returning to Paris over the years, however, I have come to prefer the Palais-Royal, and it has unequivocally become my "favorite."

JEAN BOND RAFFERTY lived in Paris for over twenty-five years and writes about a wide variety of topics for a wide variety of publications, including *Town & Country, Departures,* and the former *European Travel & Life,* where this piece originally appeared.

S o you think you know Paris. You've tracked down the perfect bistro and the most charming small hotel, discovered the address of the manufacturer's outlet where Saint Laurent is half-price. The metro is no mystery, and you've even located the side door of the Louvre so you can thumb your nose at the long lines waiting at the Pyramid. Ah, but do you know the Palais-Royal? Even native Parisians fail this ultimate test for connoisseurs.

"Paris is not very familiar with Paris," wrote Colette when she first moved here in 1927. "Thus, the gardens are known and frequented only by riverside dwellers and immediate neighbors." Then, as now, the crowds of the bustling avenue de l'Opéra simply surged by without even suspecting the existence of this beautiful backwater whose aristocratic architecture and serene greenery are secreted just steps away, between the rue St.-Honoré and the rue des Petits-Champs.

The Palais-Royal is a quadrangle with gardens at the center, the palace at one end, and arcades along the other three sides, with shops and restaurants at ground level and apartments above. "It's an island, an enclave. People think they haven't the right to come in," says France's minister of culture, Jack Lang, whose offices overlook his own controversial contemporary contribution to the Palais-Royal's eighteenth-century decor: striped columns by modern sculptor Daniel Buren. To help passersby know how to enter, Lang introduced explanatory signs on the place Colette, named for its most famous resident.

Colette called it *"ma province à Paris."* Waking to the sound of the gardener raking the gravel beneath her window, she wrote, "My first morning at the Palais-Royal, eyes still closed, gave the illusion of a fine day in the country."

The enchantment that preserves the Palais-Royal still holds sway. Residents find themselves unimaginably rich in the rarest of twentieth-century luxuries—silence. The splash of a fountain, the rustle of the breeze through the leaves, the songs of birds and cooing of pigeons, the clack of the gardener's shears as he trims the hedges, and, later, the boisterous cries of children freed from school are the only sounds that accompany the play of sun and shadow in the dreaming arcades.

"The splendor of opening your window onto the garden in the morning is like living in a château in the middle of Paris," says Inès de la Fressange, France's most famous model, who until her marriage last year lived in an apartment overlooking the fountain. "I have a collection of old engravings of the Palais-Royal. Very, very little has changed. You still see the same lanterns in the arcades, the old-fashioned shops selling stamps, military decorations, and lead soldiers. One senses the past. And even the French don't know it. Very few people come except on Sunday afternoons."

Palais-Royalists find other parts of Paris pale in comparison. "It was very difficult to leave," admits de la Fressange. "I adored it." Colette was also a convert. She lived here twice, first in the entresol of 9 rue de Beaujolais, where she could reach up and touch the ceiling with her hand. "Take care not to jump for joy there," advised a witty friend, "or you'll fracture your skull." She loved her lair—"like living in a drawer," she wrote—but lack of sun and chronic bronchitis forced her to move on. Almost ten years later, she jumped at the chance to move into the second-floor apartment of the same building. She spent the rest of her life there, writing *Paris de ma fenêtre* while reclining on a divan overlooking the gardens, and her final book, *Le Fanal bleu,* named for the blue-shaded lamp that shone from her window at night like the beacon of a literary lighthouse.

The patchwork of people who inhabit this secret spot today— actors and bankers, antiques dealers and artists, writers and scions of such famous French names as Citroën, Taittinger, and Rothschild—reflects the influence of the powerful institutions that surround it: the Bibliothèque Nationale, the Banque de France, the Louvre, and the Comédie Française. Its daytime inhabitants include the employees of the Ministry of Culture, the Conseil d'État (a sort of supreme court), and the Conseil-Constitutionnel, which occupy parts of the extended former palace.

For the last seven years, Jacques Grange, decorator to the beau monde of Paris, has had the view from Colette's window. "The beauty of the architecture, the proportions, and the rhythm are magnificent. And at night the silence is extraordinary," he says.

In the apartment, photographs of Colette glimmer here and there like a benediction. Grange likes to stretch out on a chesterfield chaise longue, placed in the magic spot by the window, but says, "I respect her, but I'm not obsessed by her. I'm not stepping into her shoes. I have invested this house with my 'moi.'"

"Moi" is never minimalist for Grange, whose baroque romanticism will be on show in the remake of the Barbizon Hotel in New York and the new Torrente couture house in Paris. It is currently starring in the latest mecca for the fashionable avenue Montaigne crowd: Bernard Arnault's new restaurant, L'Avenue.

Grange has also been prolific right at home, in part because of the dining room's glass ceiling, which seems to be continually undergoing repairs. At the Association Arcades Colette in the Galerie Valois, Jean-Claude Saladin, who lived in the apartment for sixteen years with Colette de Jouvenal, the writer's daughter, smiles. "Some things never change. That glass roof has always leaked. Colette wrote about it in her books." Colette de Jouvenal hoped to establish the apartment as a museum to her mother, but it was not to be so, and she died in 1981. Saladin then formed the association, which arranges Colette exhibitions, to finance the reproduction of the decor for the Musée Colette, which will be located in St.-Sauveur-en-Puisaye, the writer's native village.

The sleeping-beauty image of the Palais-Royal today is a far cry from its racy, royal, and revolutionary past when it was more renowned for temptations than tranquillity. Cardinal Richelieu built the first palace in the 1630s, leaving it to the French royal family. Louis XIV was brought up here, playing king and queen in the palace kitchens with a servant's daughter and almost drowning, as the story goes, in the fountain. Cardinal Mazarin organized educational entertainments for young Louis in the gardens (a miniature hunt with hare, stag, and wild boar, for example) and built a small fort for royal exercises in warfare. Later, Louis conducted his first (historically recorded) liaison with Louise de La Vallière here, setting a regal romantic precedent, followed more than a hundred years later by Lieutenant Napoléon Bonaparte, who supposedly made his first conquest in the gardens on November 22, 1787.

When Philippe d'Orléans became regent in 1715, he instituted the notorious private suppers in company with his dissolute *Roués*— called thus because for their vices they deserved to be broken on the wheel (*roue*)—that firmly established the Palais-Royal's risqué reputation. During the Restoration, the licentious ladies and gambling dens got so out of hand that Louis-Philippe closed them down.

Today, social life here is more subdued. "The Palais-Royal is a little bit like an English club," says Patrick Guerrand-Hermès, who has had an apartment here for almost thirty years. "We see each other, but we don't stop and talk. We smile from a distance."

Guerrand-Hermès, who lives mostly in Morocco, keeps the apartment as a family pied-à-terre. His son Olaf married Olga Rostropovich, daughter of the celebrated cellist and a musician herself, in the French wedding of the year in Paris and Marrakech; they left for the airport from the Palais-Royal.

Dominique Paramythiotis lives in the entresol above the Manufacture du Palais-Royal, which sells antiques and his own designs of hand-painted porcelain. He gives summer dinner parties under the arcades or puts down a rug in the gardens for a picnic. "People are so surprised to see it in the middle of Paris," he says.

The elegant arcaded quadrangle we see today, designed by Victor Louis in 1780, was the happy result of Duc Louis-Philippe d'Orléans's (later Philippe Égalité) unhappy penchant for profligacy. The duke cut a dashing figure, dallying with such a myriad of mistresses (fifteen aristocratic *amoureuses* are listed in one account) and so chronically short of funds that he decided to replace the wooden arcades in the gardens with rentable apartments and boutiques. He named the three new streets that surrounded them after his sons, Montpensier, Beaujolais, and Valois.

"It was the first royal real estate deal," says Guerrand-Hermès. "After that, the English copied us by turning royal gardens into residential squares."

At Versailles, the duke's cousin, Louis XVI, retorted, "Now that you're running a shop, no doubt we'll see you only on Sundays." The cousins didn't get on, and, encouraged by Orléans, the Palais-Royal became a hotbed of the Revolution. It was from the top of a café table in the gardens that Camille Desmoulins raised the call to storm the Bastille.

Victor Louis was also the architect of the Théâtre Français, which became the new home of the Comédie Française, inaugurated with a performance of Corneille's *Le Cid* on May 30, 1799. By then, Victor Louis's former patron, the duke, who had voted his cousin's death, had met his fate, like the king and Desmoulins, on the guillotine.

"Just before the Revolution, the Palais-Royal was very chic and infamous at the same time. One had to be seen there," says Jean Taittinger, whose family company owns Le Grand Véfour restaurant, as well as the most perfect private perspective of the gardens. The Taittinger's dramatic duplex on the rue de Beaujolais has the full center view of the fountain and former palace beyond. In the summer, when the linden trees are clipped flat on top, other residents have surprising scenery. "It's like looking out onto a lawn," says one.

There is some dissent in this palatial paradise. Outright outrage was the reaction when Jack Lang became the highest-profile—and most successful—cultural minister since André Malraux and decided to commission contemporary sculptures for the garden's Cour d'Honneur. Silver ball fountains by Pol Bury and especially the striped, truncated columns by Daniel Buren caused furious protests. "Only good for dogs," sniffs one resident, while antiques dealer Paramythiotis fumes, "It's a disfiguration, like putting stripes on the Mona Lisa." But M. Leopold of the Librarie de Valois points out the columns were "an advantageous replacement of a parking lot," and even critics admit the controversy has drawn many people to the Palais-Royal for the first time. On a Wednesday afternoon, half-day off for French schools, the columns' magnetic appeal is apparent as children slalom through them on skateboards and shimmy up to strike antic poses in the manner of comic statues. And Buren's handiwork served as the backdrop for an unconventional birthday party. The birthday girl set candles out on the columns and invited her family and friends for champagne.

Jean Cocteau and Colette used to stroll the *allées* and sit gossiping on garden chairs next to the rose parterre. But one must be lucky to snag a seat today. French designer Jean-Michel Wilmotte's contemporary green garden chairs have found such fervent favor that, despite being weighted down and chained together at night, only a handful have survived the attentions of modern design collectors. "I think they hook them up into the apartments," laughs the designer, who delivers fifty new chairs every year.

As the gardens, unlike most Parisian public spaces, belong to the federal government, not the city, Jack Lang is their uncrowned king. When he wishes to avoid irate demonstrations under his office window, for example, he can order the iron gates closed, sealing the Palais-Royal off as effectively as pulling up the bridges over a moat. Gallery, restaurant, and shop owners find that this equally effectively dissuades their clients. Comte Jean de Rohan-Chabot is the president of the Comité du Palais-Royal, formed to convince the public powers to "take us seriously into consideration."

Rohan-Chabot, who opened his La Vie de Château shop two years ago, is part of the mini-renaissance taking place at the Palais-Royal. The shop specializes in eighteenth-to-twentieth-century tableware—ravishing tea and coffee services, drawers full of silver flatware, tables of glassware and majolica—"What you might find in the cupboards of a château," he says. It came about after the count dined one night with the governor of the Banque de France. The bank, which owns one-third of the Palais-Royal arcades—the Galerie Valois, where the governor has an apartment—seems ready to bring new life to the Palais by granting leases to a host of new shops. Mireille Haguel and Yves Gastou opened a gallery devoted to contemporary design furniture; Muriel Grateau, a former stylist, has introduced her own stunning "fundamentals" in a boutique that carries tableware and fashion; and the rumor is that the Japanese giant Shiseido plans a boutique here devoted to its cosmetic line. On the corner of the rue de Beaujolais, the new L'Espace Champagne, a restaurant bar open until 2 A.M., sells bubbly by the glass and uses it liberally in its cuisine.

Just outside the gates, on the rue des Petits-Champs, designer Chantal Thomas has earmarked a former café as the site of her new boutique. When Jean-Charles de Castelbajac opened his shop recently on the same street, he replaced the back wall with glass to give a view of the arcades and gardens.

The completion of the renovation of the Grand Louvre, due at the end of next year, may bring the Palais-Royal a wider public. When the parking lots in the place Palais-Royal disappear, the Conseil d'État has promised to open its two iron gates to allow direct access to the gardens. One will be able to walk directly from I. M. Pei's twentieth-century Pyramid to eighteenth-century elegance at the Palais-Royal, then to a glimpse of the Bibliothèque Nationale's glorious Second Empire reading room. The august library has opened its first-ever boutique in the strikingly renovated

Passage Colbert, carrying unusual editions and rare-book facsimiles. One may wish to pause for tea or chocolate (and some delicious pastry) at the fin de siècle Café Colbert before confronting the future at Jean Paul Gaultier's boutique on the rue Vivienne. There, the avant-garde designs of Madonna's favorite couturier are revealed in a spectacular "new baroque" art-deco-meets-science-fiction setting.

Cities have their seasons, but life in the Palais-Royal is circumscribed by the clock. Outsiders may enter this regal rectangle only when the heavy iron gates open at 7 A.M. in the summer, 7:30 A.M. in the winter. Closing times vary from 8:30 P.M. in winter to 9:30 P.M., 10:15 P.M., and 11 P.M. in fall, spring, and summer. Mornings are delicious. One can discover this palatial province in almost solitary serenity. The shops here are as special as the atmosphere. At L'Oriental, a sign proclaims: NONSMOKERS ARE TOLERATED. Raymond Crohin, whose clients write fan letters to the "artist of the pipe," handcrafts such famous models as the Pasha, made of bordeaux-tinted meerschaum with an amberlite stem.

In the Galerie Valois, Alain de Grolée-Virville's antiquarian bookshop is even older than the arcades, established by the engraver to Louis XV in 1761. It specializes in genealogy and heraldry and engraves now for the Republic. The Librarie de Valois stocks local books (Colette's novels and memoirs) and plays of the Comédie Française. Ask about the miniature jars of the pale local honey, which the owner says is produced by bees who feast on the flowers of the Palais-Royal and is harvested on the roof of the Paris Opéra.

Shopping here can be charmingly civilized. One American husband gratefully sank down into a chair in the garden while his wife modeled vintage Chanel suits from Didier Ludot. Ludot's sumptuous secondhand couture (starring Chanel suits and Hermès bags) is to a thrift shop as Harry Winston is to Woolworth.

You'll know when it's midday. At the stroke of noon, a man from

Paris's oldest gunsmith, Fauré Le Page on the rue de Richelieu, sets off the astonishing loud report of the tiny bronze cannon behind the statue in the rose parterre. The cannon, which dates from 1786, was positioned on the Paris meridian to sound at midday from May to October, triggered by the sun through a magnifying glass. The cannon broke down in 1914 but has been back in service since 1975.

At lunchtime, one can look forward to the most pleasurable outdoor eating in Paris, with nary a gasoline fume. Stroll across the garden to Le Gaudriole, where on sunny days tables are laid in the garden. The luncheon menu—which can include a refined monkfish salad, salmon with lobster sauce, and crème brûlée—is a great value at 150 francs ($24.60). But one must be prepared to savor it slowly. A gentle request for service met with a sharp rebuke from the owner: "I'm not a fast food." The Muscade offers a lighter and faster lunch as well as tasty cakes and tarts served at teatime. Or one can hop around the corner to Willi's Wine Bar, named partly in honor of Colette's first husband, where preppy stockbrokers from the Bourse merge with the *branché* fashion crowd of the place des Victoires and journalists from nearby newspapers. At Armand, on the rue de Beaujolais, in the lovely vaulted rooms that once housed the carriages of Armand-Jean du Duplessis, Duc de Richelieu, the chef's imaginative fish dishes—and his raspberry soufflé—draw plaudits.

On a matinee day, one can choose between the classics of the Comédie Française and the comedies of the Théâtre de Palais-Royal, which started in 1784 as the Duc de Beaujolais's marionette theater and launched the smash hit *La Cage aux folles* in 1973.

When it comes to dinner, there is only one perfect Palais-Royal finale. "The good news is there is a new chef at Le Grand Véfour," says Patrick Guerrand-Hermès. "It's again *the* place to eat."

The great gastronomic restaurants, as we know them today, were born at the Palais-Royal at the end of the eighteenth century. Le Grand Véfour, with its dazzling Directoire decor, is the only survivor of that epoch. Everyone from Napoléon and Josephine to Jean Paul Gaultier and Madonna have eaten here. Balzac and George Sand came often, as did Colette and Cocteau, another Palais-Royal resident, whose drawing graces the menu, and whose sculptures (of Sand's hands) serve as ashtrays. The new man in the chef's toque, Gérard Fouché, has given classic cuisine the twist of his native southwest France: lobster salad with truffle and champagne vinaigrette, for example, Bresse chicken breasts in white truffle sauce, chicken thighs flavored with black truffles, and divine fried eggs with foie gras and *sauce suprême*. Save room for the deep-chocolate soufflé.

As the day ends and you walk home through the lantern-lit arcades and detect the heady fragrance of the linden trees in blossom, you may discover you've become a Palais-Royalist yourself.

Passages

BY CATHARINE REYNOLDS

editor's note

If the remaining few *passages* in Paris are said to be predecessors of our shopping malls of today, we have much to be thankful for in that there are at least some left, but much to lament in that their modern versions are such poor imitations.

I find it fascinating to visit these old *passages*, beautiful shopping arcades built of iron and glass in the mid-1800s. Each *passage* has its own character—no two are alike—and I've found some of the contemporary shops to be among the most enticing in Paris. (Visitors may also recognize Galerie Vivienne from Luis Buñuel's *That Obscure Object of Desire*.) Try to include a walk through at least one *passage* as you explore Paris—we really do not have an equivalent in the States.

CATHARINE REYNOLDS went to live in Paris as a student, in 1964, and has lived and traveled there, off and on, ever since. In 1972, she began editing Joseph Wechsberg's (*Blue Trout and Black Truffles: The Peregrinations of an Epicure*) Paris letters for *Gourmet,* where she has been a contributing editor for many years. This piece was featured in January 1988.

W inter *will* come, and then Paris is the devil," lamented the Irish poet Thomas Moore in 1820. His moan remains relevant: Last winter brought ample evidence of just how filthy January weather in Paris could get—it took the army, equipped with trench spades, to dig the city out of the snow. Yet for visitors and residents all is not forlorn if the weather turns nasty. No need to lock oneself in, deprived of the city's pleasures. Clearly Moore didn't, for he went on to write:

> *Where shall I begin with the endless delights*
> *Of this Eden of milliners, monkies* [sic] *and sights—*
> *This dear busy place, where there's nothing transacting*
> *But dressing and dinnering, dancing and acting?*

Together with affluent Parisians of his time, Moore would have taken refuge from the weather in the *passages* that were lacing together Restoration Paris. The *Petit Larousse* tells us that a *passage* is "a covered walkway where only pedestrians go," a definition that disregards the narrow boutiques that have traditionally lined the *passages* of Paris and excludes the glazed roofs that were and are essential to the enchantment of Paris's *passages.*

Paris is hardly alone in possessing such glassed-in commercial walkways. Milan and Naples have their *gallerie,* London has its arcades, Brussels has its *galeries;* so do Leningrad and Moscow. All are the ancestors of our modern shopping malls, but Paris's nineteenth-century *passages* possess bags more charm.

The origins of the *passages* are not clear. The commercial success of Philippe-Égalité's late-eighteenth-century wooden arcades in the Palais-Royal no doubt attracted the attention of speculators. Inspiration may have come from descriptions of Oriental bazaars by veterans returning from Napoléon's Egyptian campaign. Demand coincided with technology, for engineers had perfected systems that permitted economical overhead glazing of large, long areas.

The money-spinning appeals of the *passages* were obvious: Post-Napoléonic France was reveling in the fruits of her belated Industrial Revolution. Her citizens were all too delighted to be able to spend their money in the dry warmth of the *passages,* sheltered from the hurly-burly of unwieldy carriages, fractious horses, and earthy odors. Developers were not slow to see the opportunities; between the battles of Waterloo and Sedan *passages* mushroomed in the area from the Palais-Royal north to the Grands Boulevards.

In their heyday the *passages* were places to see and to be seen. Most were located near coach transport depots and theaters. *Mondaines* hastened there to visit their glovemakers, engravers, milliners, and jewelers, and then to gush over their prizes at the nearby cafés and restaurants. As time went on the attractions were multiplied with the growth of the entertainments of the Boulevards. As John Russell says so aptly, "a hundred years ago . . . the Grands Boulevards were Cosmopolis itself," and the *passages* functioned as a vital element in that sophistication. Where else were the boulevardier's wife and mistress to buy their fripperies?

Then came the nearly fatal hiatus. In the intervening century the epicenter of the city moved west, and trains altered the transport habits of the capital, leaving the Boulevards to molder—often not very genteelly. Baron Haussmann mercilessly cut streets through some of the finest *passages,* like the Passage de l'Opéra. Fashionable Third Republicans deserted the small, specialized shops of the *passages* for the *grands magasins.*

Of the 137 *passages* enumerated by the *Véritable Conducteur Parisien* of 1828 only about twenty worthy of the name remain. Until just a few years ago even the handsomest of those were tenanted chiefly by sex shops, cut-rate clothes outlets, unpedigreed stamp dealers and numismatists, pedicurists, cobblers, printers, and a handful of old-fashioned deluxe *commerçants,* who were bravely determined to rise above the rainwater spilling through the broken panes of the skylights that had once been the glory of these very *passages.*

All that is changing. Demand for central-Paris real estate has made it increasingly attractive to restore and refurbish many of the city's nineteenth-century *passages.* Fueled by the prosperity of Paris's born-again Bourse, renovation is rife, and the *passages* nearest the stock exchange have been the first to benefit. What with this pressure on central-Paris real-estate values, many of the city's nineteenth-century *passages* are undergoing a resurrection—which is a boon to the nostalgic; the curious; students of urbanism; admirers of nineteenth-century cast-iron architecture; chronic *léche-vitrines,* that is, those suffering from that most extreme, Gallic form of window shopping; and Parisian and visitor alike caught by winter's weather. Rain or shine, an expedition, map in hand, through the three kilometers of Paris's *passages* (which need not be undertaken of a piece!) offers a seasonable opportunity to see what's old and new in Paris.

Just to the east of the Palais-Royal, running off the tiny rue du Bouloi behind a tree-bedecked square, lies one of the lesser-known *passages,* the Galerie Véro-Dodat, developed in 1826 by a pair of savvy pork butchers, who built opposite the terminus of the Messageries-Générales, the line of horse-drawn carriages that brought provincials to Paris from all of eastern France. Messrs. Véro and Dodat must have been tasteful butchers as well, for the identical mahogany shop fronts, with narrow, brass-framed windows outlined with *faux marbre* columns topped with gilded bronze capitals and cherubs, are a model of grace and sobriety.

A dally along the diagonal black-and-white checkerboard-floored *passage* overhung with ivies dangling from the second-story window boxes can yield all manner of surprises. The bright, chic hats and trendy sweaters at Jean-Claude Brousseau catch the eye immediately. His is an address treasured by misses in search of a turban or an outrageously oversize velvet beret that will turn the heads of race-goers at Chantilly and Gauloises-puffing Breton fishermen alike. Il Bisonte at the other end of the Galerie can provide the same misses with solid Florentine-made handbags and satchels. In between are the specialist *antiquaires,* dealers like Robert Capia, Paris's leading expert on antique dolls and the very man to see for those in search of a doll marked Bru, Jumeau, Steiner, or Schmitt. M. Capia is equally pleased to take on repairs or simply to chat about the history of the *passage.* His neighbors, Alain Fassier, R. and F. Charles, Eric Philippe, and Bernard Gauguin, trade in nineteenth-century rustic furniture, stringed instruments, early-twentieth-century furniture, and books respectively. M. Gauguin has some particularly fine old cookbooks, which are said to attract Alain Senderens, who is forever on the lookout for new dishes for Lucas-Carton. Nor is the *passage* without its restaurant, Le Véro-Dodat, behind whose lace curtains chef Yannick Ouvrard serves up tempting fare.

A few blocks to the northeast a pair of linked *passages* runs off the rue des Petits-Champs. The Galerie Vivienne and the Galerie

Colbert are perhaps the best-restored and most lively of Paris's *passages*. They share neoclassical decors, though in fact the Vivienne was built in 1823, three years before the Colbert. Goddesses and nymphs disport themselves under the Vivienne's arched roof and around its rotunda, while young models people its length below. They wander across the swirling pastel mosaics from shops like Catherine Vernoux, run by a former casting director with a penchant for colorful geometric knits; to Yuki Torii, a bold Japanese designer who seems to have broken away from the somber palette of most of his countrymen; to Camille Blin, a lady given to shapely jersey dresses and daring jewelry; to Jean Paul Gaultier, whose clothes an exhibitionist can wear with confidence. The more domestic then tuck into Casa Lopez to ogle its splendid custom-made rugs or Si Tu Veux for a magician's hat or an old-fashioned wooden pull toy for a godchild. Then they collapse into one of the wicker chairs spread before A Priori Thé, a tea shop started by three Americans, which explains the superiority of the brownies and pecan pie.

The more pensive can stop at the Librairie Petit-Siroux, founded in 1826 and still redolent of the provincial, timeless atmosphere that has long drawn writers to the *passages*. Surrealist Louis Aragon was a regular there and a great champion of the outright louche and secret aura of the *passages,* eloquently limning their spell in *Le Paysan de Paris*. Small wonder that this bookshop does a good business in volumes about Paris.

A door leads into the glittering rotunda of the Galerie Colbert, which has just undergone a total face-lift. The Bibliothèque Nationale owns the Colbert and has recently installed its comely Musée des Arts du Spectacle and the Musée Charles Cros between the *faux marbre* columns, along with the winning boutique Colbert, selling well-reproduced postcards and posters drawn from the library's collection. The museums mount changing exhibits of posters and costumes related to theater, opera, and dance and a dazzling collection of antique phonographs.

The Passage Choiseul stands five blocks down the rue des Petits-Champs. Restoration is more of an intention than a reality there, yet the Choiseul merits a visit. Betwixt the neon bedizenments, general sleaze, and shops selling unlabeled clothes purported to come from leading manufacturers, one can enjoy the graceful tribune supported on Ionic columns and savor what Paul Verlaine calls *"les passages Choiseul aux odeurs de jadis. . . ."*

This is the most literary of the *passages,* for here Alphonse Lemerre, the publishing genie of the Parnassiens, had his offices at Nos. 27–31 from the 1860s onward. Paul Verlaine, Sully Prudhomme, Leconte de Lisle, and José-Maria de Heredia met in his shop regularly. Louis-Ferdinand Céline, author of *Mort à Crédit,* lived there also. His mother kept a lace shop, over which he spent sixteen years, inhabiting "three rooms linked by a corkscrew." The nineteenth-century atmosphere is extended by the captivating office and artists' suppliers Lavrut, whose oaken drawers overflow with pastels and a bounteous selection of my favorite Clairefontaine notebooks with ultrasmooth paper designed for those who appreciate the pleasures of writing with a fountain pen. Not to break the spell, one can slip into the café-au-lait box called Pandora to sip some of Paul Corcellet's ethereally flavored teas, perhaps accompanied by the house's poppy-seed-studded quiche lorraine and a salad.

The Passage des Princes, running off the rue de Richelieu to the north, was another hangout of the Parnassiens, whose poetry magazine, the *Revue Fantaisiste,* published works of Charles Baudelaire, Catulle Mendès, and others. Built in 1860, the elbow-shaped Passage des Princes is the last subsisting Second Empire *passage,* yet it looks very tired, which seems a terrible pity, especially when one reflects on the glitter its airy, lantern-hung coral arches once knew as the home of Peter's restaurant. French gastronome Courtine credits the eponymous Pierre Fraysse, who had worked in Chicago, with naming *homard à l'américaine,* a variation on a lobster preparation of his native Sète, to flatter a table of late-arriving Americans.

Today the Passage des Princes' most visitable shop is Sommer, a pipe-making concern five years older than the Passage itself and long-standing supplier to serious smokers like Georges Simenon. Even the most dedicated antitobacco lobbyist cannot help but admire the workmanship in the antiques for sale or stand fascinated before the craftsmen creating small works of art in the window, using brier and the firm's specialty, *écume de mer,* a silicate said to purify the noxious elements in tobacco.

Perhaps the most evocative if not the tidiest of Paris's *passages* are the three spanning the boulevard Montmartre, the Passage des Panoramas, the Passage Jouffroy, and the Passage Verdeau. The oldest, the Panoramas, is named for the two giant panoramas that were installed to either side of its entrance by an American speculator named James Thayer. Thayer had purchased the French patent for painted perspectives, or panoramas, from countryman Robert Fulton, who used the proceeds to fund his experiments with steamboats. Meanwhile Thayer developed the *passage* to cash in on the crowds come to see the sixty-two-foot-high canvases of Paris and Toulon.

And his success was great. The Passage des Panoramas was a center of fashionable shopping right up to the fall of the Second Empire. *Modistes* vied with stylish cafés. Jean Marie Farina perfumed the air with his *véritable* eau de Cologne. Marquis's chocolate brought top-hatted dandies sprinting. There the *antiquaire* Susse sold Alexandre Dumas *père* Eugène Delacroix's *La Tasse de la Prison des Fous* for six hundred francs, little suspecting that the wily Dumas would go on to sell it for fifty thousand.

The Passage des Panoramas was extended repeatedly, eventually providing access to the stage door of the Théâtre des Variétés, the theater where Zola's Nana held men spellbound. Here is Zola's description of the Panoramas, where poor Comte Muffat waited.

Under the glass panes, white with reflected light, the *passage* was brilliantly illuminated. A stream of light emanated from white globes, red lanterns, blue transparencies, lines of gas-jets, and gigantic watches and fans outlined in flame, all burning in the open; and the splash of window displays, the gold of the jewelers, the crystal jars of the confectioners, the pale silks of the milliners, glittered in the shock of mirrored light behind the plate-glass windows.

However bogus Nana's art, real talent was encouraged there after 1868, when the Académie Julian was installed in the Passage des Panoramas. The Académie tutored many painters, including Americans Childe Hassam and Charles Dana Gibson.

Today the Passage des Panoramas has more memories than glamour, but it seems to be bootstrapping its way up, led in no small part by Stern, the capital's grandest *graveur,* which since 1840 has served a clientele of emperors, grandees, miscellaneous aristocrats, diplomats, and just plain folk with painstakingly engraved *bristols* (calling cards), bookplates, signet rings, invitations, and letterheads from its ravishing shop paneled with dark oak heavy with caryatids and curlicues.

The neighborhood is mixed. The less said about the Sauna Hamman Euro Men's Club the better. The food shops are generally fast, though L'Arbre à Cannelle serves an amiable tea amid potted palms; the stamp dealers tout themselves as *maisons de confiance,* which always leaves me wondering; and the newer shops—like Maknorth, the outlet for a Cambodian designer of the bold school, and Trompe l'Oeil, the place for obelisks and for fruit not intended for eating—are signs that things are looking up.

Across the boulevard Montmartre the Passage Jouffroy, dating from 1845, beckons from beneath the weight of the Hôtel Ronceray. It has an Oriental flavor, thanks to two of its largest shops, the Palais Oriental and La Tour des Délices. The former is ideal if you have to cancel a trip to Marrakech, stocking almost everything to be found in the souks. The latter is full of delectable sweetmeats made of honey and almonds and coconut, which it serves up with mint tea.

France takes over farther down under the skylight with Pain d'Épice, a shop specializing in tiny, shiny toys to fill a stocking as well as the miniature *batterie de cuisine* and provisions for the larder of a dollhouse Cordon Bleu. Galerie 34 and Abel are treasure-houses of parasols, umbrellas, walking sticks, and canes, dating from the seventeenth century to the end of World War II. And I never fail to stop at La Boîte à Joujoux at the bend of the *passage* opposite the exit of the Musée Grévin to select a fifteen-franc bag of *bonbons à l'ail* (garlic hard candies) from among the jokes.

The Librairie Vulin operates in a more serious vein, promising "*toujours de belles occasions*" (always good bargains). The shop's bins of books line the *passage*, making Vulin a *bouquiniste* without the hazards of Seine-side rainstorms. Opposite stands Cinédoc, a mecca for film fanatics questing for posters, postcards, magazines, black-and-white studio stills, and books, including biographies of stars from Bud Abbott to Loretta Young.

Across the rue de la Grange-Batelière the Passage Verdeau entices from between Corinthian columns. Its skylights, divided into small squares, its peeling cream paint, and its stony floor make the *passage* seem more tenebrous and bleak, but its restaurant and specialist shops assure it a following. Most prominent among the boutiques is Photo Verdeau, the source for rare cameras. Its ample stock of nineteenth-century matériel—objects like stereopticons— is complemented by a selection of silent films starring Harold Lloyd and Charlie Chaplin. Cheek by jowl, two good bookstores, the Librairie Farfouille and the Librairie La Comédien, offer delicious scents to the bookhound. Postcard collectors flock to La France Ancienne. A good postsearch lunch is available at either the Restaurant Martin Malburet (aka Drouot Verdeau) or Les Menus Plaisirs. The first is more ambitious, with its collection of enameled promotional signs spread over two stories. I spied one vaunting Brasseries du Katanga while enjoying the *gigotin d'agneau en croûte* (lamb in pastry) and the *marquise au chocolat extra bitter et moka* (dense bitter chocolate and mocha mousse).

Another day I sampled Les Menus Plaisirs, a restaurant name with a double entendre, referring to both the pleasures of the *carte* and the small pleasures enjoyed by a king when he ruled the land. In the case of this small restaurant the pleasures take the form of such offerings as good salads and pastas with smoked salmon, foie gras, basil, or garlic.

The fate of some of the other *passages* has been less happy. Some, like the Passage du Caire and the Passage du Havre, have capitulated to the worst excesses of commerce. In the case of the Passage du Caire this is a shame, for it is the oldest extant, with an exceptionally elegant, bright glass skylight. Its entrance on the rue du Caire still bears three stylized *retour d'Egypte* pharaohs. Unfortunately the wholesale garment district seized the neighborhood, and today the poor *passage* is hostage to neon-lit tenants who supply display wares, mannequins, and wrapping materials to small shops across France. I have long bought Christmas wrapping paper in hundred-meter rolls there. One need only brave the lack of service in this wholesale world; the shopkeepers always seem pleased enough to deal in cash if one is prepared to purchase in bulk.

The Passage du Havre, located near the Gare Saint-Lazare, is even more honky-tonk, with the three well-stocked boutiques of La

Maison du Train its only redeeming features. Little boys of all ages journey there to purchase rolling stock and to obtain spare parts and repairs.

Sadder still are those *passages,* like the Brady and the Prado, that have been grossly misused and not maintained, their identities swallowed up by neighborhoods grown tacky around them. The Brady was truncated by the cutting of the boulevard de Sébastopol and never really recovered. Today its name is hardly discernible in the broken floor tiles, and holes in the glazing gush rainwater on the merchants of ginger and manioc. The only shop front worth a pause—for the young and brave—is Allô-stop, a unique organization that for a minimal fee introduces would-be hitchhikers to drivers who are bound in the same direction.

But there is hope. With the examples of the Galerie Colbert and the Galerie Vivienne to inspire them, Paris's architectural watchdogs appear to have persuaded the Assistance Publique, which owns the boarded-up Passage du Grand Cerf, to restore this once lovely, airy *passage* located near the Forum des Halles. Its glass will be renewed and its aerial walkways under the skylights will again survey healthy *commerces.* Improvements in its neighbor, the Passage Bourg-l'Abbé, now chiefly devoted to wholesale underwear manufacture, will surely follow, because late-twentieth-century urbanists have awakened to the amenity value of the *passage.*

But beware! There are *passages* and *passages.* Paris's contemporary property developers have appropriated the name but spurned the extravagance of the glazed roof. However glitzy the boutiques that line the *passages* and *galeries* of the Champs-Élysées, they cannot compete with the haunted and haunting charms of the nineteenth-century *passages.*

Affordable Gothic Thrills

BY ANNE PRAH-PEROCHON

〜

editor's note

"How to Look at a Gothic Cathedral" would be a good subtitle for this piece. For the uninitiated, the three major elements of Gothic architecture are the *l'arc brise* (pointed arch), *voûte sur croisées d'ogives* (vaulted arches which cross diagonally), and *les arcs boutants* (flying buttresses).

If you read a little French and have a passion for architecture, look for the *Grammaire des Styles* series in Latin Quarter bookstores (*Gibert Jeune* is the best known). The series, published by Flammarion and popular among students, covers architectural styles from all over the world; the three most useful for France are *L'Art Roman, L'Art Gothique,* and *La Renaissance Française.* Each volume is an inexpensive, slender paperback and features black-and-white photos and drawings.

ANNE PRAH-PEROCHON is an art historian, lecturer, and the editor in chief of *France Today* and *Journal Français.* She has been decorated by the French government as a Chevalier de la Légion d' Honneur and Officier des Palmes Académiques.

The sheer number of major churches that rose in France between 1170 and 1270 (six hundred of them!) is awe-inspiring. Even more impressive is the fact that they are still standing to this day, through numerous wars and hundreds of years. It is impossible to visit France without stumbling upon these lofty monuments in which you can appreciate, for free, masterpieces of just about any art form.

However, you might sometimes be perplexed about the best way to visit these awesome buildings. I hope the following tips and recommendations, based on personal experience, will contribute to your enjoyment.

Take along warm clothing—even in the middle of summer, a cathedral is usually chilly and drafty (the crypts are particularly icy). Also, wear comfortable shoes, because you will probably be doing a lot of pacing in one spot as you admire your surroundings. Inside the church, beware of uneven flagstones, worn over many centuries by millions of feet. Because you walk most of the time with your eyes up, it is easy to make a misstep or even twist your ankle.

If you are tempted to climb the stairs leading to the towers or the steeple to enjoy a panoramic view, remember that there are hundreds of them—narrow, hollowed in the center, very steep, and in spirals. Climbing cathedral steps is not for the weak of heart; Notre-Dame de Paris, for one, counts 387 steps in its northern tower!

Sunlight streaming through the *verrières* (stained-glass windows) of large cathedrals such as Chartres, Amiens, and Bourges offers a kaleidoscopic effect, so select a sunny day for your visit if possible. If not, try to visit each cathedral at its optimal time of day. For example, Notre-Dame de Paris is very dark inside, so if you must visit on an overcast day, do so at midday. Chartres and Amiens, on the other hand, are naturally bright, so you can visit them later in the day. Different parts of the churches—all oriented the same way—are also best seen at particular moments of the day: The light through the windows of the apse (behind the altar) is at its most joyous in the morning, whereas the sunset light creates very dramatic effects on the rose windows of the western facade.

Even if you are not religious, you will have an enriching experience if you attend high mass on Sunday mornings, because a cathedral is fully alive during mass. Attend a service to experience the organ music, the vapors of the incense, the flowers and the liturgical chants. Times are posted at the entrance or marked in your Michelin guidebook. In summer, large cathedrals offer free concerts of sacred music on Sunday afternoons. Until his death a few years ago, the celebrated organist Cochereau was often rehearsing or performing in Notre-Dame de Paris.

A guided tour is only as interesting as its guide. If you spot a priest or a monk explaining the details of the church, follow him! They are the best guides, because they live on the premises, take part in local excavations, and often have authored scholarly books on their church; in short, they are passionately in love with their topic. In the absence of a tour guide, your region-specific Michelin guidebook (with the green cover) offers a good balance of explanations and useful tips.

Before entering the cathedral, walk around it to appreciate its architecture and the relationship of the steeple and the towers to the rest of the building. Remember that builders always started with the choir (where the altar stands), because without a choir the church was useless. Because it often took several generations to build, a cathedral could become a stylistic hodgepodge as architects of different eras came and went. The average building time was about eighty years and life expectancy was thirty years, so a child born in Reims around 1210, when its cathedral was begun, could hardly have hoped to see it finished. This privilege was reserved for the child's great-grandchildren. This hodgepodge effect can be seen in Chartres cathedral, although it was built remarkably fast. On the north portal of Chartres, the statues have stylized hieratic heads seemingly stuck on stiff candlelike bodies, whereas the statues of the Royal Portal are graceful and free, representative of a later style.

When looking at a Gothic cathedral, you are at a disadvantage over your medieval counterpart, who, upon entering a church, automatically knew where to find a symbolic scene and the reason for its placement. Keep in mind that all cathedrals, at least until the sixteenth century, were enormous compasses oriented from the rising to the setting sun, a custom dating from early Christian days. It was customary to enter from the western side, which is where sculptors lavished their creativity, particularly on the tympanum above the main portal. Medieval theologians and artists confused the meaning of the word *occidens* (the western side) with the verb *occidere,* meaning "to kill," so it seemed natural to them to represent the end of the world on the western facade (the western facades of many cathedrals, including Notre-Dame de Paris, La Sainte-Chapelle, Bourges and Chartres depict Last Judgment or Apocalypse scenes).

Once inside, look at the relationship between the length of the church, the height of its ceiling vault and the dominating presence of windows. Before looking at the numerous details of the interior, take a quick tour of the cathedral, following the *bas-côté* (right aisle) all the way to the *abside* (apse) and then come back to the main portal by the left aisle. Stop at the *croisée du transept* (transept crossing), where the north-south and east-west axes meet. This is the best place from which to evaluate the daring of the medieval engineers and architects, who erected vaults up to 140 feet high. Leaning against one of the four angle pillars, look up to the vault or the tower in the transept. It is dizzying, especially in Bourges or Amiens. Try to imagine the cathedral as it looked originally, when every inch of space was covered with color—paint, tapestry, embroidery, Byzantine brocades or Oriental rugs.

Depending on the time you have and the interest you feel for details of architecture and iconography, you may want to tour the cathedral again, this time following the description of Michelin or a more specialized book. To better appreciate the beauty and picturesque details of the pillars and tall stained-glass windows, bring a pair of binoculars. Without them, you might not realize that the beautiful stained-glass windows are not just displays of color, but long narrations that usually can be read from bottom to top and from left to right. In Chartres, the famous Charlemagne window (on the left in the ambulatory, behind the main altar) traces Charlemagne's story from the vision of Emperor Constantine to Charlemagne's deliverance of Jerusalem through Roland's battle with the Infidels and subsequent death.

Chartres's windows also reflect the wide range of donors, those individuals with sufficient power and wealth to make donations independently of the ecclesiastical authorities. A full panorama of medieval society (some four thousand royalty, nobility, tradesmen and craftsmen) is shown in figurative medallions depicting seventy guilds or corporations (bakers, shoemakers, water carriers, butchers, money changers, wine merchants and tailors, among others) hard at work.

The Charlemagne window was paid for by the corporation of fur merchants, whose "signature" stands at the bottom, where a merchant shows a fur-lined cloak to his customer. Some signatures were displayed in prominent locations (the medieval equivalent of advertising): The newly baked bread of the bakers who donated the window of the Prodigal Son can be seen in the central window of the central chapel, whereas the portrait of another donor, Thibault, Count of Chartres, was put in a dark corner next to the Notre-Dame de la Belle Verrière window to the right of the choir.

The art of identifying seemingly anonymous characters or saints in stained-glass windows or other art forms lies in the recognition of their distinctive emblems, used in art since the sixth century C.E. These clear and expressive images enabled even illiterate people to understand abstract ideas. Not only do we recognize them because of their appropriate dress (bishops in robes, kings crowned and robed, soldiers in armor) but also by the instrument of their death (the wheel for Saint Catherine, the knife for Saint Bartholomew, stones for Saint Stephen, arrows for Saint Sebastian . . .).

Equally important is the relative position of the saints in relation to Christ, because the closer to God, the saintlier the character is assumed to be. On the portal of the Last Judgment in Notre-

Dame de Paris, the saints are presented in orderly concentric bands below the patriarchs, prophets, confessors, martyrs and virgins surrounding the figure of Christ.

Symmetry was also regarded as the expression of heaven's inner harmony, so artists juxtaposed the twelve patriarchs of the Old Testament with the twelve apostles of the New Testament (each with the emblem of his former occupation, such as the fish for Peter, the fisherman, and a purse for Matthew, the tax gatherer) and the four major prophets (Isaiah, Ezekiel, Daniel and Jeremiah) with the four evangelists (Matthew, Mark, Luke and John). In the saintly hierarchy, next came the four archangels. Naturally, Mary held the prime location, very close to Christ on the right-hand side.

Once you have identified the carved scenes in one cathedral, you will be able to apply this knowledge to most churches, because no medieval artist would be rash enough to modify the appearance of figures and the arrangement of the great scenes from the Gospels or to group figures according to individual fancy. Similarly, you won't need long to identify the church iconography and to recognize many characters and scenes, even if you weren't born into the Christian religion. King David is always shown playing the harp, and the three magi are invariably wearing crowns, even while they sleep! Seeing a tiny naked child, you will recognize the image of a soul; seeing a mature woman clasping a young girl, you'll know it is Anne, holding her daughter, the Virgin Mary.

Now, after arming yourself with the appropriate clothing, a good guidebook, binoculars and a little knowledge and endurance, you can fully appreciate this free and edifying pastime of visiting cathedrals.

To Refresh Your Memory

So many great books have been written about Gothic cathedrals that they form an inexhaustible supply. Two of the oldest studies remain the best:

Henry Adams, *Mont-Saint-Michel and Chartres,* Boston, Houghton Mifflin Co., 1933.

Allan Temko, *Notre-Dame de Paris,* Viking Press, 1959.

The Road to Discovery

Paris

Notre-Dame de Paris, place du Parvis Notre-Dame, 4e, Métro Cité. Tel.: 01.42.34.56.10 www.pariscope.fr/visiterparis/monuments/notredame/ NOTREDAM.HTM. Open every day 8 A.M.–6:45 P.M.

Crypt of Notre-Dame de Paris. Tel.: 01.43.29.83.51. Open Apr.–Sept., daily 10 A.M.–5:30 P.M.; Oct.–Mar., 10 A.M.–4:30 P.M. The crypt contains vestiges of two-thousand-year-old houses.

Musée de Notre-Dame de Paris, 10 rue du Cloître Notre-Dame, 4e, Métro Cité. Tel.: 01.43.25.42.90. This museum retraces the great moments in the history of the cathedral.

La Sainte-Chapelle, 4 boulevard du Palais, 4e, Métro Saint-Michel or Cité. Tel.: 01.53.73.78.50. Open Apr.–Sept., 9:30 A.M.–6:30 P.M.; Oct.–Mar., 10 A.M.–5 P.M.

Amiens (Somme)

Cathédrale Notre-Dame, place Notre-Dame. Tel.: 03.22.91.79.28. www. u-picardie.fr/~patrick/Cathedrale/visite.html. Open Apr.–Oct., 8:30 A.M.–noon, 2–7 P.M.; Nov.–Mar., 8:30 A.M.–noon, 2–5 P.M. Its nave rises 138 feet (42 m) with the support of 126 slender pillars.

Beauvais (Oise)

Cathédrale Saint-Pierre. Tel.: 03.44.45.08.18.

Bourges (Cher)

Cathédrale Saint-Étienne. Tel.: 02.48.24.75.33. This is the widest Gothic French cathedral and the most similar to Notre-Dame de

Paris. Its western facade has five sculpted portals. Beautiful stained-glass windows.

Chartres (Eure-et-Loir)
Cathédrale Notre-Dame, place de la Cathédrale. Tel.: 02.37.21.75.02. www1.pitt.edu/~medart/menufrance/chartres/charmain.html.

Reims (Marne)
Cathédrale Notre-Dame, place du Cardinal Luçon. Tel.: 03.26.47.55.34. Open 7:30 A.M.–7 P.M. This cathedral has been the backdrop of French kings' coronations from medieval times to 1825 (King Charles X). Its western facade has two thousand statues. In its apse, there is a lovely Chagall window showing the Crucifixion and the sacrifice of Isaac.

Rouen (Seine-Maritime)
Cathédrale Notre-Dame, place de la Cathédrale. Tel.: 02.35.71.41.77. www.ndrouen.simplenet.com/ndrouen.hts. This Gothic master-piece was painted thirty times by Monet in the 1890s; several of the paintings are in the Orsay Museum in Paris.

Bibliothèque

Little-Known Museums in and Around Paris, Rachel Kaplan, Harry N. Abrams, 1996. If you are a museum-goer, you'll want and need this handy book. It's doubtful visitors would ever learn of many of these less popular museums without this guide; even though some of them are listed in the *Plan de Paris,* there is no description, so you have no idea if you might find any worth your while. Museum summaries are thorough and interesting, and there's really not a one that wouldn't be rewarding. Over thirty museums—including six just outside of Paris, such as the wonderful Musée National de la Renaissance—le Château d'Ecouen and Le Domaine du Château de Monte Cristo—are highlighted and accompanied by ample color photographs.

Knopf Guides: The Louvre, Alfred A. Knopf, 1995, originally published in France by Nouveaux-Loisirs, a subsidiary of Gallimard, Paris, 1994. This is a great book to bring along because it's comprehensive and compact, if a bit thick. Some sections include "The Louvre Through Visitors' Eyes," "Conservation and Display," and "Origin of the Name *Louvre,*" and then there are sections on the collections: Oriental antiquities, Islamic art, Egyptian art, Greek antiquities, decorative arts, furniture, European painting . . . all the things that have made it the largest museum in the world. An added feature of this guide is the section on "Itineraries Around the Louvre Quarter," and the "Practical Information" section is especially useful as it contains such features as "Finding Your Way Around the Museum," tours, lectures, activities, shopping, "The Louvre for the Visitor in a Hurry," and "The Louvre for Children." There are several foldouts, including one showing the entire Grand Louvre.

Paintings in the Louvre, Sir Lawrence Gowing, Stewart, Tabori & Chang, 1994. This gigantic book is a companion volume of sorts to *Paintings in the Musée d'Orsay* (see below). Like the d'Orsay edition, there really is no better, more complete book for viewing the museum's paintings in a single volume.

Art Treasures of the Louvre: One Hundred Reproductions in Full Color, Abrams, 1951; text translated and adapted from the French of Rene Huyghe, with a brief history of the Louvre by Milton S. Fox. This book—and the other editions in the Library of Great Museums series—is not meant to be comprehensive. It's a selective, special collection of a variety of objects in the Louvre's permanent collection. I love this volume and had to include it here because there is not another book like it. Out of print, but it still turns up at garage sales and in used-book stores.

Paintings in the Musée d'Orsay, Robert Rosenblum, foreword by Françoise Cachin (former director, Musée d'Orsay, and current director of the Musées de France and president of the Réunion des Musées Nationaux), Stewart, Tabori & Chang, 1989. I was in awe of the architectural transformation that took place when the turn-of-the-century Gare d'Orsay became a museum. I'm less in awe of the museum itself and still maintain that the impressionists—and visitors—were better served in the more intimate Jeu de Paume. The d'Orsay is the repository for art from the Revolution of 1848 up to World War I, and for a sneak preview, there is no other book like this (gigantic) one. The quality of the reproductions is excellent, and the book is divided into seven sections that mirror the permanent collection.

General Art Reference

History of Art, H. W. Janson, Anthony F. Janson, fifth revised edition, Harry N. Abrams, 1999. Still enormous, still a fixture on college and university campuses, and still a classic for your home library.

The Story of Art, E. H. Gombrich, Phaidon Press, London, sixteenth edition, 1995. Although Sir Ernst Gombrich has authored numerous volumes on art, this is the one that really established his reputation. To quote from the jacket, "*The Story of Art* is one of the most famous and popular books on art ever published. For forty-five years it has remained unrivaled as an introduction to the whole subject . . ." Though a comprehensive book, French artists and those who worked in France are well represented.

The Voices of Silence, André Malraux, translated by Stuart Gilbert, Doubleday, 1953. An unusual and appealing discourse on art from all around the world, by former cultural minister Malraux. I really love this beautiful book, and French artists are well represented. It's out of print, sadly, but very worth the search.

The Oxford Companion to Christian Art and Architecture: The Key to Western Art's Most Potent Symbolism, Peter and Linda Murray, Oxford University Press, 1998. A thorough reference guide with color plates; general background to the Old and New Testaments and Christian beliefs; a glossary of architectural terms; and a detailed bibliography.

From Abacus to Zeus: A Handbook of Art History, James Smith Pierce, Prentice-Hall, 1977. Pierce has keyed the A–Z entries in this useful guide to the second edition of H. W. Janson's *History of Art,* which I mention only to illustrate the extent to which this is an extremely thorough and indispensable reference. Entries are presented alphabetically within five chapters: "Art Terms, Processes, and Principles"; "Gods, Heroes, and Monsters"; "Christian Subjects"; "Saints and Their Attributes"; and "Christian Signs and Symbols."

Angels A to Z: A Who's Who of the Heavenly Host, Matthew Bunson, Crown Trade Paperbacks, 1996. *Not* just another angel book. This is a fascinating and useful reference you'll be glad to have. From "abaddon" to "zutu'el" and with numerous black-and-white reproductions, this is really a great resource for looking at art. In his foreword, Bunson gives several reasons for the popularity of angels, and he states that "Finally, and perhaps most important, throughout history one thought has proven powerfully constant and nearly universally accepted by Jewish writers, Christian saints, Muslim scholars, and followers of the New Age: The angel is one of the most beautiful expressions of the concern of God for all of his creations, an idea beautifully expressed by Tobias Palmer in *An Angel in My House:* 'The very presence of an angel is a communication. Even when an angel crosses our path in silence, God has said to us, "I am here. I am present in your life." '"

French Styles and Movements

French Art: Prehistory to the Middle Ages; The Renaissance, 1430–1620; and *The Ancien Régime: 1620–1775,* all by André Chastel, translated from the French by Deke Dusinberre, Flammarion, 1995, 1996. Chastel was adviser to André Malraux, founder of the French Inventory of Historical Monuments, editor of the prestigious *Revue de l'Art et de l'Archéologie,* and a professor at the Sorbonne and the Collège de France. With over four hundred exquisite color illustrations, these are simply the most detailed, most beautiful, and therefore the best books available on French art, unmatched in their thoroughness.

The Barbizon School & the Origins of Impressionism, Steven Adams, Phaidon Press, London, 1994. An important book highlighting some of the still relatively unknown painters who greatly influenced the impressionists: Charles-Émile Jacque, Theodore Rousseau, Narcisse Diaz de la Pena, and Georges Michel. These landscape painters, followed by Corot, Courbet, Daubigny, and Millet, had been coming to Barbizon (a small village on the edge of the Forest of Fontainebleau, about forty miles southwest of Paris) nearly fifty years before the word *impressionniste* was first uttered in Paris.

The Origins of Impressionism, Gary Tinterow and Henri Loyrette, The Metropolitan Museum of Art/Harry N. Abrams, 1994; published to accompany the exhibit of the same name.

The History of Impressionism (first edition copyright 1946; revised editions 1955, 1961, and 1973) and *Post-Impressionism: From van Gogh to Gauguin* (1956), John Rewald, both The Museum of Modern Art. Of the hundreds of books published about these popular art movements, Rewald's have long been the leading and acclaimed volumes. With the exception of *Impressionism: Reflections and Perceptions* (Meyer Schapiro, George Braziller, 1997), I wouldn't bother with any other general impressionist books.

Impressionists Side by Side: Their Friendships, Rivalries, and Artistic Exchanges, Barbara Ehrlich White, Knopf, 1996. A beautiful book and an original project. Art historian White compares the personal friendships and professional relationships between seven pairs of painters: Degas and Manet; Monet and Renoir; Cézanne and Pissarro; Manet and Morisot; Cassatt and Degas; Morisot and Renoir; and Cassatt and Morisot. These artists often painted canvases of the same subjects, which are here presented side by side, many for the first time since they were created over a century ago. Only a handful of the paintings are in Paris museums, but this is an absolutely fascinating study to read before you go.

Art Books of Related Interest

Pleasures of Paris: Daumier to Picasso, Barbara Stern Shapiro, Museum of Fine Arts, Boston, in association with David R. Godine, 1991; published to accompany the exhibit of the same name held at the Museum of Fine Arts (June 5–September 1, 1991) and the IBM Gallery of Science and Art, New York (October 15–December 28, 1991). This show, one of the best I've ever seen, was organized to investigate the second half of the nineteenth century in Paris, famous as a time of frivolity and pleasure. But as we know, this image is somewhat distorted, the Second Empire also being a time of social injustice and political and military boondoggles. Though the works of art—by Manet, Daumier, Tissot, Toulouse-Lautrec, Degas, Renoir, Forain, Mucha, Vuillard, Cheret, Cézanne, Pissarro, Bonnard, Picasso, and others—were chosen to document some of the more pleasant aspects of the period, they nonetheless also illustrate the harsher realities of the times.

The Artist in His Studio, Alexander Liberman, Random House, 1988. A splendid record of Liberman's visits to a number of artists—thirty-one of them, nearly all of whom were French or worked in France—in the 1940s after the war. He felt compelled to personally meet these artists and take photos in their studios because he feared if he didn't, there would be no trace of the remarkable flowering of painting and sculpture the first half of the twentieth century had witnessed. No doubt he was also moved to do so by World War II's annihilation and destruction. A unique and special book, filled with color and black-and-white photographs and the text of Liberman's conversations with each artist.

The Banquet Years: The Origins of the Avant-Garde in France, 1885 to World War I, Roger Shattuck, Vintage Books, 1968. An original and thoroughly fascinating book linking playwright Alfred Jarry, painter Henri Rousseau, musician Erik Satie, and poet Guillaume Apollinaire as a group of artists representing significant aspects of fin de siècle Paris. Shattuck believes that this group reveals the period better than a single individual, and in this book he explores how the avant-garde took the arts into a period of "astonishingly varied renewal and accomplishment," which was to change after the First World War. I've always loved the title of this book, and although Shattuck doesn't say so, he may have been inspired by the famous *banquet Rousseau* organized by Picasso in his *bateau lavoir* studio. This banquet, as Shattuck writes, "cele-

526 · P a r i s

brated a whole epoch," one for which our appetite seems inexhaustible. With thirty-two pages of photos, illustrations, and reproductions of artwork.

Portrait of Dr. Gachet: The Story of a van Gogh Masterpiece, Money, Politics, Collectors, Greed and Loss, Cynthia Saltzman, Penguin Books, 1999; published in hardcover by Viking Penguin, 1998. A remarkable tale about van Gogh, a particular (and very famous) painting, collecting, the art market, and much more (such as how the Third Reich confiscated "degenerate" works of art from German museums, behind the scenes at Christie's and Sotheby's, etc.). Although *Portrait of Dr. Gachet* is not the first work of art to have an interesting and many-layered provenance, surely it has one of the most complex. (Note that the *Portrait of Dr. Gachet* that hangs in the Musée d'Orsay—and was lent to the Metropolitan Museum of Art for its 1999 exhibit *The Collection of Dr. Gachet*—is not the subject of this book. Van Gogh's usual practice was to paint two versions of his portraits, and the canvas at the center of this book was sold from the artist's estate in 1897, found homes with thirteen owners—one of whom was Hermann Göring, who had it for a brief time in 1938—and was eventually bought at auction in 1990 by Ryoei Saito of Tokyo for $82.5 million, the highest price ever paid at auction for a work of art.) Postscript to the book's ending: In August 1999, it was revealed that the *Portrait of Dr. Gachet* had left Japan, but reports that the painting had been sold to an American investor were unconfirmed.

A Day with Picasso: Twenty-Four Photographs by Jean Cocteau, Billy Kluver, The MIT Press, 1997; a version of this book was published in Germany by Editions Cantz under the title *Ein tag mit Picasso* (1993) and in French by Éditions Hazan under the title *Un jour avec Picasso* (1994). This is an amazing project: Kluver (coauthor of *Kiki's Paris* and coeditor of *Kiki's Memoirs*) was collecting photographs of the Montparnasse artists' community, and he discovered that some previously unassociated photos were, indeed, very much associated. He noticed that the people *in* the photos—Picasso, Max Jacob, Moise Kisling, Modigliani, and others—were all wearing the same clothes, and the shots appeared to have been taken on the same day. Twenty-four photos in all were found, but Kluver didn't know who the photographer was. After exhaustive, meticulous research, he pinpointed the summer of 1916 as the most likely time the photos were taken. He then measured buildings and plotted the angles and lengths of shadows in the photos to narrow the date down even further. He eventually identified Cocteau as the photographer and concluded that the photos were taken on August 12, 1916. With the help of computer printouts of the sun's position on that date, coupled with the length of the shadows, he was able to put the pictures in proper sequence. What a brilliant investigation, and what an unexpected treat for us! The black-and-white photos are great and the book also includes other photos and drawings, short biographies of all the subjects, and a section on the Montparnasse art world at that time.

Baudelaire's Voyages: The Poet and His Painters, Jeffrey Coven with an essay by Dore Ashton, Bulfinch Press (Little, Brown and Company), 1993. Companion volume to an exhibit of the same name that was mounted at the Heckscher Museum (Huntington, New York) and the Archer M. Huntington Gallery (University of Texas at Austin). A unique package that allows for reading Baudelaire's poetry and viewing the art of his contemporaries together (it's the only time I've ever seen Matisse's *Luxe, Calme et Volupté* side by side with Baudelaire's *L'Invitation au Voyage*). With sixty-five color and forty-nine black-and-white reproductions featuring Manet, Seurat, Rodin, Gauguin, Daumier, Delacroix, Jongkind, Goya, Munch, Whistler, etc.

Matisse: Father & Son, John Russell, Abrams, 1999. The subtitle says it all: "The story of Pierre Matisse, his father, Henri Matisse, his gallery in New York, and the artists that he introduced to America, among them, Joan Miró, Alberto Giacometti, Balthus, and Jean Dubuffet," based on unpublished correspondence.

Series

Discoveries (originally published in France by Gallimard, English translation copyright by Abrams and Thames & Hudson). These paperback books are a terrific value: they're jammed with information; the quality of the reproductions is good; they're lightweight and easy to pack (approximately five by seven inches); and the price is right. Titles in the series that are appropriate for France include *Cézanne: Father of 20th Century Art; Chagall: The Art of Dreams; Corot: Extraordinary Landscapes; Degas: The Man and His Art; Gauguin: The Quest for Paradise; Manet: The Influence of the Modern; Matisse: The Wonder of Color; Monet: The Ultimate Impressionist; Picasso: Master of the New Idea; Renoir: A Sensuous Vision; Rodin: The Hands of Genius; Toulouse-Lautrec: Scenes of the Night; and Van Gogh: The Passionate Eye.*

World of Art (Thames & Hudson, London, New York). Also a paperback series, not quite as portable as Discoveries titles—each book will fit nicely inside a handbag but not a pocket. Appropriate titles include *Fauvism, The Impressionists at First Hand, Art Nouveau, Post-Impressionism, Romanticism and Art, Marcel Duchamp, Mary Cassatt, Picasso, Rodin, Toulouse-Lautrec, Gauguin, Bonnard, Cézanne, Van Gogh, Magritte, Seurat, Matisse,* and *Manet.*

Pegasus Library (Prestel, Munich, London, New York). Pegasus is similar to Discoveries and World of Art but is a hardcover imprint (only four are published in paperback) and a little more scholarly. The books are not pocket-sized but are still slender, lightweight, and packable. Appropriate titles include *Edgar Degas: Dancers and Nudes; Paul Gauguin: Images From the South Seas; Édouard Manet: Images of Parisian Life; Monet at Giverny* (also available in paperback);

Picasso's World of Children; Renoir: Paris and the Belle Epoque; Auguste Rodin and Camille Claudel (also available in paperback); *Henri Rousseau: Dreams of the Jungle;* and *Toulouse-Lautrec: The Soul of Montmartre.*

Single-Artist Books and Museum Catalogs

The following are definitive volumes (some are comprehensive catalogs that accompanied museum exhibitions) and are worth a special effort to track down. I've only included titles that represent an artist's full oeuvre (as opposed to specialized subjects or periods, unless the subject or period is inseparable from the artist's style; for example, *Fernand Léger, 1911–1924: The Rhythm of Modern Life,* is thirteen years of his work, but "the rhythm of modern life" so completely defines Léger that I felt it would not serve any purpose to exclude it) or are related to Paris in some way.

Max Beckmann and Paris, edited by Tobia Bezzola and Cornelia Homburg,. Taschen, 1998; published on the occasion of the exhibition *Max Beckmann and Paris,* Kunsthaus Zurich (September 25, 1998–January 3, 1999) and the Saint Louis Art Museum (February 6–May 9, 1999). Beckmann lived in Paris for fifteen years, from 1925 to 1939.

Bonnard, essays by Sarah Whitfield and John Elderfield, catalog by Sarah Whitfield, Harry N. Abrams, 1998; published to accompany the exhibition *Bonnard,* organized by the Tate Gallery, London (February 12–May 17, 1998), in conjunction with the Museum of Modern Art, New York (June 17–October 13, 1998).

Bonnard, Nicholas Watkins, Phaidon Press, London, 1994.

Bonnard: The Late Paintings, published to accompany the exhibition of the same name organized by the Musée National d'Art Moderne, Paris (February 23–May 21, 1984); the Phillips Collection, Washington, D.C. (June 9–August 25, 1984); and the Dallas Museum of Art, Texas (September 13–November 11, 1984). John Russell notes in the introduction, "If I stress the Parisian aspect of Bonnard, it is because he is too often thought of as someone who lived his life in country places and was happy to ignore the climate of the age . . . for personal reasons Bonnard came to live more and more in the country, whether in the Île-de-France, in Normandy, or latterly in the Midi. The open countryside, not the streets of Paris, lay beneath his windows. But Bonnard was a Parisian to the end of his days."

Gustave Caillebotte: Urban Impressionist, Anne Distel and others, introductory essay by Kirk Varnedoe, chief curator of painting and sculpture, the Museum of Modern Art (New York), the Art Institute of Chicago, and Abbeville Publishing Group, 1995; French edition published under the title *Gustave Caillebotte, 1848–1895.* Published in conjunction with the exhibition of the same name held at the Galeries Nationales du Grand Palais (Paris, September 1994–January 1995); the Art Institute of Chicago (February–May 1995); and the Los Angeles County Museum of Art (June–September 1995).

Calder's Universe, Jean Lipman, Running Press, Philadelphia, in conjunction with the Whitney Museum of American Art, 1976, 1987. Originally a Philadelphian, Alexander Calder worked for many years in France, and I find him to be as talented as Picasso in many respects.

Calder at Home: The Joyous Environment of Alexander Calder, Pedro E. Guerrero, foreword by Alexander S. C. Rower, Archetype Press (distributed in the U.S. by Stewart, Tabori & Chang), 1998. Alexander Rower is a grandson of Calder and director of the Alexander and Louisa Calder Foundation in Woodstock, New York.

Mary Cassatt: Modern Woman, organized by Judith A. Barter with contributions by Erica Hirshler, George T. M. Shackelford, Kevin Sharp, Harriet Stratis, and Andrew Walker, the Art Institute of Chicago in association with Harry Abrams, 1998; published in conjunction with the exhibition *Mary Cassatt: Modern Woman,* organized by the Art Institute of Chicago (October 10, 1998–January 10, 1999) in collaboration with the Museum of Fine Arts, Boston (February 14–May 9, 1999), and the National Gallery, Washington, D.C. (June 6–September 6, 1999).

Cézanne, Abrams, 1996. Published in conjunction with the exhibition *Cézanne* held at the Galeries Nationale du Grand Palais (September 25, 1995–January 7, 1996), the Tate Gallery in London (February 8–April 28, 1996), and the Philadelphia Museum of Art (May 30–August 18, 1996).

The Paintings of Paul Cézanne: A Catalogue Raisonné, John Rewald, Harry Abrams, 1996. Large, boxed hardcover set in two volumes, the texts (volume I) and the plates (volume II).

Paul Cézanne: Letters, edited by John Rewald, translated by Seymour Hacker, Hacker Art Books, 1984.

Chagall: A Retrospective, edited by Jacob Baal-Teshuva, Hugh Lauter Levin Associates, 1995.

Corot, Gary Tinterow, Michael Pantazzi, Vincent Pomarede, Metropolitan Museum of Art, 1996; published to accompany the exhibit of the same name.

Image of the People: Gustave Courbet and the 1848 Revolution, T. J. Clark, University of California Press, Berkeley, 1973, 1982, and 1999.

Honoré Daumier, Bruce Laughton, Yale University Press, 1996.

David and Neo-Classicism, Sophie Monneret, Pierre Terrail (the art-books division of Bayard Presse SA), Paris, 1999; English translation by Chris Miller with Peter Snowdon.

Delacroix, Barthelemy Jobert, Princeton University Press, 1998; original French edition published by Éditions Gallimard, 1997.

Delacroix: The Late Work, Philadelphia Museum of Art, 1998; published to accompany the exhibit of the same name, held at the Galeries Nationales du Grand Palais (April 7–July 20, 1998) and the Philadelphia Museum of Art (September 15, 1998–January 3, 1999).

The Complete Works of Marcel Duchamp, Arturo Schwarz, Thames & Hudson, 1997; first published in Great Britain in 1969. A beautiful boxed set in two volumes, text (volume I) and plates (volume II).

Marcel Duchamp, edited by Anne d'Harnoncourt and Kynaston McShine, the Museum of Modern Art and the Philadelphia Museum of Art, Prestel, first published in 1973, reprinted 1989.

Gauguin and The Nabis: Prophets of Modernism, Arthur Ellridge, Éditions Pierre Terrail, 1995.

Georges de La Tour and His World, Philip Conisbee, with essays by nine other writers, Yale University Press, 1996; published to accompany the exhibit of the same name held at the National Gallery of Art, Washington, D.C. (October 6, 1996–January 5, 1997) and the Kimbell Art Museum, Fort Worth, Texas (February 2–May 11, 1997).

Fernand Léger, Carolyn Lanchner, with essays by Carolyn Lanchner, Jodi Hauptman, and Matthew Affron, and contributions by Beth Handler and Kristen Erickson, the Museum of Modern Art (distributed by Harry Abrams); published in conjunction with the exhibition *Fernand Léger* at the Museum of Modern Art, New York (February 15–May 12, 1998).

Fernand Léger, 1911–1924: The Rhythm of Modern Life, Prestel (Munich, New York), 1994; published on the occasion of the exhibition *Fernand Léger, 1911–1924, Le rythme de la vie moderne,* Kunstmuseum Wolfsburg (May 29–August 14, 1994) and Kunstmuseum Basel (September 11–November 27, 1994).

Henri Matisse: A Retrospective, John Elderfield, the Museum of Modern Art, 1992.

Matisse and Picasso, Yve-Alain Bois, foreword by Joachim Pissarro, Flammarion, 1998; accompanied the exhibition *Matisse and Picasso: A Gentle Rivalry* at the Kimbell Art Museum, Fort Worth, Texas (January 31–May 2, 1999). The Matisse-Picasso relationship is well documented (see the memoirs of Françoise Gilot and Rosamond Bernier in *"Les Personalités" bibliothèque*), but this beautiful book is the best of its kind in comparing and contrasting their artwork.

Jean-François Millet: Drawn into the Light, Alexandra Murphy, Yale University Press, the Sterling and Francine Clark Art Institute (Williamstown, Massachusetts) in association with the Frick Art & Historical Center (Pittsburgh, Pennsylvania), 1999.

Monet or the Triumph of Impressionism, Daniel Wildenstein, Taschen/

Wildenstein Institute, 1999. This coffee-table-sized biography is a revised version of the first volume of the four-volume catalogue raisonné, also published by Taschen. Wildenstein is a world authority on impressionism and also edited catalogues raisonnés of Manet and Gauguin.

Pissarro, Harry N. Abrams, 1989; this edition is a concise version of a previous book, *Pissarro,* by John Rewald, which Abrams published in 1963.

The Impressionist and the City: Pissarro's Series Paintings, Richard R. Brettell and Joachim Pissarro, Royal Academy of Arts, London/Yale University Press, 1992. Published in conjunction with an exhibit at the Dallas Museum of Art, Philadelphia Museum of Art, and the Royal Academy of Arts in London, this book concentrates on Pissarro's urban-view painting, which he devoted his attention to in the last decade of his life, 1893–1903. I have always been immensely fond of Pissarro's *grands boulevards* canvases, but the surprise of this book to me were the scenes of Rouen (although unfortunately the city as we see it in Pissarro's paintings bears no resemblance to its appearance today). In addition to a catalog of Pissarro's eleven urban series (seven of Paris, one of Rouen, two of Dieppe, and one of Le Havre), authors Brettell and Joachim Pissarro (Camille Pissarro's great-grandson) also contributed chapters on the tradition of painting urban scenes during and prior to impressionism, and Pissarro's conceptualization and interpretation of urban views.

Nicolas Poussin: 1594–1665, Richard Verdi, Zwemmer, in association with the Royal Academy of Arts, London, 1995; first published on the occasion of the exhibition of the same name at the Galeries Nationales du Grand Palais, Paris (September 27, 1994–January 2, 1995) and the Royal Academy of Arts, London (January 19–April 9, 1995).

Pierre-Paul Prud'hon, The Metropolitan Museum of Art, distributed by Harry N. Abrams, 1998; published in conjunction with the exhibition of the same name held at the Galeries Nationales du Grand Palais, Paris (September 23, 1997–January 5, 1998), and the Metropolitan Museum of Art, New York (March 10–June 7, 1998).

Georges Seurat: 1859–1891, Robert L. Herbert, The Metropolitan Museum of Art, 1991; published to accompany the exhibit of the same name.

Soutine: Catalogue Raisonné, Taschen, 1993. A two-volume, hardcover boxed set on Chaim Soutine.

Van Gogh: The Complete Paintings, Part I: April 1881–February 1888, Ingo F. Walther and Rainer Metzger, Taschen, 1997. This comprehensive book, which is almost the size of a small coffee table, is nearly eight hundred pages, so the $50 price is not unreasonable. Taschen published a boxed set of two smaller hardcovers titled *The Complete Paintings* by the same authors, 1993. Although not quite as impressive as the bigger van Gogh volume, the boxed set is beautiful and the quality of the reproductions is excellent.

Van Gogh, A. M. and Renilde Hammacher, Thames & Hudson, 1982.

Vincent: A Complete Portrait, Bernard Denvir, Running Press, Philadelphia, Pennsylvania, 1994. A terrific idea for a book: all of van Gogh's self-portraits, with excerpts from his writings, and a beautiful package.

Monuments and Gardens

Notre-Dame of Paris: The Biography of a Cathedral, Allan Temko, Viking, 1952. "The road—every road—has led to this moment and this place. Paris in the thirteenth century was one of the main stopping points in history, like Athens in the fifth century before Christ, and Byzantium in the sixth century after. Each had a social and political lesson for the world; each made the world a gift of architecture: the Parthenon, Sancta Sophia, the western facade of Notre-Dame." So opens one of the chapters in the most definitive book ever written on Paris's most famous cathedral. With black-and-white photographs, a fold-out of the cathedral's plan and various cross sections, and a great bibliography.

French Gardens: A Guide, Barbara Abbs, photographs by Deidre Hall, Sagapress, Sagaponack, New York, 1994. For easy reference, the author divides this book into four sections: north, the Paris region, the center, and the south. There are forty-one garden and park listings for Paris and the Île-de-France. Each entry includes a phone number, address, and directions with reference to the Michelin road atlas. The author notes that many private gardens are open to the public in June and sometime during the first weekend of the month. These events—known as *journées des portes d' ouvertes*—are listed in brochures produced by each region and should be available at local tourist offices (you may have to ask for them). Additionally, there is a day in September reserved for notable architecture, which provides another opportunity to view any adjoining gardens not generally open to the public. Last year, the Fêtes des Jardins de Paris was held on September 12, and the secluded gardens of eight convents and monasteries in the city were open to the public.

The Garden Lover's Guide to France, Patrick Taylor, Princeton Architectural Press, 1998. This book is undoubtedly a prettier package than *French Gardens,* above, although I don't find it quite as detailed. Still, the color photographs help present the beauty and unique highlights of the over one hundred private and public gardens featured in the book. Taylor has organized the gardens by five regions: northern France, Île-de-France, central Paris, central and southwestern France, and southeastern France. There are thirty-five gardens featured in Normandy, Brittany, and the Loire Valley; thirteen in central Paris; and thirty-five in Île-de-France. A serviceable map is found at each chapter opener, and there is a glossary of French garden terms at the back of the book.

Plaisir d'Offrir

675422
MODRE FRANCE
II70PT
Réunion des Musées Nationaux
ENTRÉE 04. 39 F
RÉUNION
DES MUSÉES NATIONAUX
ENTRÉE
PLEIN TARIF
39 F
675422
MODRE FRANCE
II70PT

Des Belles Choses
(Good Things, Favorite Places)

Doubtless you have your own Paris. It's not geographical; it's the place where life first came vividly to bloom for you, where you couldn't believe the exquisite beauty of the buildings or the clouds, or the sun that shone after the rain.

—Don George,
"PARIS ON MY MIND," salon.com

French Twist

༄

LAUREL DELP is a features writer whose work has appeared in a wide
variety of newspapers and magazines. She is also a contributing editor for
Travel Holiday, where this piece originally appeared. Additionally, Laurel
has just completed a novel, which is set in Laos at the end of the 1950s. I
neglected to ask her if she's still tying scarves like a pro, but my own skills
improved dramatically with a little book small enough to fit in your purse
called *Sensational Scarfs: 44 Ways to Turn a Scarf into a Fabulous Fashion
Look* (Carol Straley, Three Rivers Press, 1995).

Early dusk and chill winds off the Seine had driven me into the
deco bar at the Hôtel Lutétia in St.-Germain-des-Prés, which
was jam-packed with people lounging in overstuffed, jewel-hued
chairs, talking and laughing in the amber lamplight that glinted off
glasses and teacups and warmed the patina of polished wood.
Suddenly an elegant woman with regal cheekbones dropped her
shopping bags and sank into one of the seats opposite mine, absent-
mindedly shrugging off her coat. She was dressed very plainly in an
olive sweater and skirt, but somehow the black, red and gold scarf
twisted around her neck transformed the outfit into something inef-
fably chic. It might have been the artful slash of color against the
dull background, but more, it was the way she had tied the scarf, so
that it had become a twisted rope of silk sculpture.

I couldn't help leaning over to ask her how she'd done it. She
laughed, loosened the scarf, held it out like a magician, then without looking looped it back around her neck and retied it with a few
deft flicks.

536   P a r i s

So many Parisian women have style that it's tempting to think they're born with it. The rest of the world has always been a bit intimidated by their chic. But what is the secret? It's certainly not money, nor is it age or conventional beauty. When pressed, most Parisiennes say it's nothing more than a gift for accessories, an ability to put on just the right thing to finish a look. And if accessories are the key to chic, then the scarf is the linchpin of the look.

In fact, walking the streets of Paris is like having a scarf epiphany. Parisiennes collect scarves the way Imelda collected shoes. The big three department stores, Galeries Lafayette, Au Printemps and Au Bon Marché, have scarf sections that rival entire accessory departments in their American counterparts. At the Kenzo counter at Galeries Lafayette, bold flowers are printed on chiffon. Down the the way at Idea Plus, rust-colored Indian silks are folded neatly beside metallic kerchiefs. When the store is busy, counters are buried in brilliant mounds of silk, and women line up at mirrors, scarves held to their cheeks as salesgirls squint in appraisal and pull out more samples. The scarf section is a tumble of colors, a mad garden of clashing blooms, the occasional square fluttering off the counter like a butterfly descending for a drink.

Of course, the great virtue of the scarf is its democracy—unlike the rest of high fashion, the scarf exists outside the exclusive realm of the wealthy. Men and women have been wearing scarves since the dawn of weaving; from the Assyrians to Mme. de Pompadour to Isadora Duncan. They've come in and out of style, grown into shawls and shrunk into kerchiefs. They've warmed necks, softened décolletages and distinguished military rank. The scarf's contemporary history dates from the late twenties into the thirties, when French couturiers began producing signature scarves to go with their collections. Suddenly, even if you could not afford a Schiaperelli gown, you could at least wear one of her scarves.

During World War II, women working in factories in Europe

and America tied their hair into scarves for protection against the heavy machinery. Then in the postwar years, as fashion grew progressively more informal, the scarf came to replace the hat. The fifties and sixties were a golden age for the scarf. Queen Elizabeth and Princess Margaret wore them. So did Grace Kelly, Audrey Hepburn, and Elizabeth Taylor. Diana Vreeland was a fervent believer. In the seventies they had a brief resurgence as part of Saint Laurent's luxe peasant look. Now, in the nineties, they're once again an essential part of any stylish woman's wardrobe.

"Scarves are having a revival," concurs Corinne Delattre, a marketing director at Kenzo, sitting in one of the fashion house's warren of offices on the place des Victoires. "We sell a lot, both with the collection and on their own. People buy more accessories now because you can change them more easily to adapt to the latest trend. For me, to use a scarf to create your look is the difference between following fashion and having style."

"Accessories make the difference," said Chantal Jacob firmly, dismissing the idea there's any mystery to French chic. "You don't have to spend a lot of money, just a good scarf, a good belt, and good jewelry with a simple dress." Jacob, one of only five female hotel managers in France, is a woman with great personal style. During one of Paris's coldest winters in memory, she went out and bought scarves to protect her female desk clerks from the arctic blasts that swept in from the streets with the guests.

Scarves are also the universal gift in France. During the Christmas season the Hermès flagship store on the rue du Faubourg St.-Honoré sells a scarf every fifty seconds. Customers line up three deep at the counter, and a bank of salesclerks unfurl scarf after scarf in swirling flashes of color.

Hermès scarves, like all designer scarves, are made in Lyons, France's silk capital, and the elaborate color schemes can take up to forty-eight separate silk screens to achieve. They are then hand-rolled and stitched. In 1995 the company sold 950,000 of them. And twice a year, in the third weeks of January and June, Parisiennes toting folding chairs and picnic breakfasts start gathering on the sidewalk at 4 A.M., waiting for the doors of Hermès to open for the sales.

I love scarves, but I can't bring myself to spend $260 on an Hermès *carré* (as they call their scarves) even though the words *Hermès* and *scarf* have long been synonymous. In Paris, designer scarves can run anywhere from $80 to $300. But if you have doubts about making this kind of investment, you can visit one of a dozen stores on the rue de Rivoli opposite the Louvre, or one of the couple of souvenir shops on the place de la Madeleine, where you'll find knockoffs of designer scarves priced anywhere from $10 to $30. These scarves won't be silk, and their edges won't be hand-rolled and stitched, but they're a good way to start practicing your tying techniques before you take the big plunge.

There's no better place for learning how to tie a scarf than the imposing Hermès headquarters on rue du Faubourg St.-Honoré. Stephanie Peigne, who travels Europe demonstrating the proper technique for tying Hermès scarves, gave me a few quick pointers. She draped one of the oversized square *carrés* over the counter, then folded two diagonally opposite corners in so that they formed triangles that met at the center. She continued folding each of the sides to the center until the scarf had become a neat four-inch-wide oblong. Then she carefully tied a loose flat knot in the center, placed the knot at her throat, and wound the ends around her neck, tucking each end through the knot. Voilà! The scarf looked at once flowing, shapely and devil-may-care. Why hadn't I thought of that? Next she folded the scarf in half and seized diagonally opposite corners in her fingers. She held the scarf behind her neck, then tied the ends together. At once the scarf formed a neat square across her chest, the ends of the knot at her collar.

I ran back down the rue du Faubourg St.-Honoré to my room at the Hôtel Bristol, where I lined up my own scarf collection and began practicing. Already some of my notes were incomprehensible (do what?), but I mastered enough so that for the first time my scarves, rather than hanging limply from my throat, had become a statement. As I wore them in the days that followed, French people began coming up to me in the street to ask for directions.

Inside the temples of couture on the Right Bank—Dior, Lacroix, Saint Laurent, Ungaro, Chanel—colorful squares of silk hold pride of place, and outside the passing parade of women is a demonstration in imaginative ways of wearing them. On the more relaxed Left Bank and in the yuppified Marais, young women wrap themselves in ethnic silk, chiffon, velvet, or flea-market finds.

"Commercially speaking, accessories are a really good item," said Philippe Bonan, co-owner of Idea Plus, a fast-growing scarf and accessory design firm with counters in all of the big French department stores. "People keep their clothes and change accessories—change the scarf and you change the whole look."

We wandered through Bonan's warehouse in the Bastille area. Scarves drooped off shelves and fell in heaps on the floor, a mix of colors and styles from the most elegant to the wildest and most playful. Deep wholesale bins were filled with the previous year's designs. Bonan held up a scarf from the spring line dotted with big artificial flowers. "We have no limit," he laughed. He and his partner began their business importing ethnic scarves from India, then started designing. Now their line is a favorite of European fashion magazines.

Like so many of the Parisiennes I met, Claire Hubert, a manager and part-owner in designer Marcel Marongiu's atelier on the rue Scribe by the Paris Opera, has a monumental scarf collection. Her partner, on the other hand, is a minimalist.

"For me the garment is much more important," he said, as

Claire stood in the doorway, arms crossed, one eyebrow raised indulgently. "Accessories make boring items look better," he added. "That's a bit like cheating, isn't it?"

I watched as Claire prepared to go out to lunch by wrapping an exquisite Indian scarf around her neck. "This way of tying came from polo players," she explained. The silk fabric now framed her face, the fine gold threads in the deep maroon shimmering like a necklace.

Suddenly it all started to make sense. Tied properly, a scarf can transform any outfit into a statement of personal style. Now I understood why the souvenir shops on the rue de Rivoli were packed with imitation designer scarves. In addition to the mini Eiffel Towers and the Mona Lisa T-shirts, that thirty-five-inch-square of silk is part of the national psyche.

People go to Paris for many reasons. They go because they love architecture, because they love food. They go for the fashion collections, or for business. They go for the museums. You may go for all those reasons, or for none, but whatever you do, don't forget your scarf.

Des Belles Choses

Granted, it's quite personal, but this is my list—in no particular order and subject to change on any day of the week—of some favorite things to see, do, and buy. A note about stores: I have a particular knack for "discovering" shops that a year or so later end up in books and articles; therefore, I think it would be redundant to list some of my favorite retailers which are also featured in the books listed below under "Shopping/*Les Souvenirs.*" I have only listed a few of these stores if I had something extra to say about their wares.

~The grave of Victor Noir in Père-Lachaise: I first saw a photo of Noir's unusual grave in John Berger's *Keeping a Rendezvous,* and I was so intrigued I had to go and take a look at it myself. The story goes that in 1870, Prince Pierre Bonaparte, cousin to Emperor Napoléon III, wrote an article in a reactionary Corsican journal that criticized *La Revanche,* a radical Paris newspaper. The editor of *La Revanche* sent Noir and another journalist to Corsica to ask for an apology, but Prince Bonaparte shot Noir instead. The grave portrays Noir, just twenty-two, dead on the ground moments after he was shot.

~Deyrolle (46 rue du Bac, 7th): Reached by climbing up a flight of stairs, this dusty shop—which is more like a natural-history museum—is where you can find those good-quality posters of botanical and agricultural drawings (I have three on fruit, wine, and olive oil). Deyrolle (printed at the bottom of each poster) is their home, and they're more expensive everywhere else in the city.

~Musée Carnavalet (23 rue de Sévigné, 3rd): Devoted to the history of Paris, the Carnavalet—in a beautiful *hôtel particulier* in the Marais—is an absolute must for *all* visitors, whether Paris is new or familiar. In addition to the collections representing every age in the history of the city, there are replicas of Proust's bedroom, an Art Nouveau storefront, a model of the city when its bridges had shops and houses on them and paintings of the St. Bartholomew Day's Massacre and Léon Gambetta escaping Paris in a balloon in 1870.

~The Pont Alexandre III, especially seen at night while on a Seine cruise.

~The four remaining *barrières* (tollhouses), built by Claude-Nicolas Ledoux in the late 1700s. Approximately fifty-five *barrières* were constructed as customs offices to regulate and collect taxes on food and wine brought into Paris. Each was strategically placed along the wall around the city (now destroyed), and the four that visitors can still see are at place Denfert-Rochereau, place de la Nation, place de Stalingrad, and Parc Monceau.

~There are other cities farther north than Paris, but somehow its particular quality of light and atmosphere, and its palette of silver, gray, and slate-blue, is only found here.

~Musée Marmottan (2 rue Louis-Boilly, 16th), and especially its painting *Impression, Soleil Levant* (Impression, Sunrise) by Monet: this groundbreaking painting—an art critic who saw the work in 1875 referred to Monet and his colleagues as "impressionists"—was stolen from the Marmottan in 1987 (along with eight other impressionist works from the collection). It was found on Corsica and returned to the museum in 1991.

~The Grand Bassin of the Jardins du Luxembourg.

~Boutiques Correspondances: These are the two shops of the Musée de la Poste. I have never seen such an imaginative array of individual postage stamps and stamp gift sets, stationery, jewelry, albums, etc., all having to do with *la poste*. Two locations: 34 boulevard de Vaugirard, 15th, and allée du Grand Louvre, 1st.

~The Musée Jacquemart-André (158 boulevard Haussmann, 8th).

~Paris et Son Patrimoine: This is my favorite bookstore in the entire city, in a tiny shop on the Île St.-Louis (25 rue St.-Louis-en-l'Île). There are only a few titles in English, but if you read some French and are a history buff, you'll want every book in the store. The books are published by Éditions Action Artistique de la Ville de Paris and feature the streets, neighborhoods, monuments, architecture, painting, music, theater, etc., of Paris. The store also stocks cards, prints, and maps worthy of framing.

~A *citron pressé* (fresh-squeezed lemon juice served in a tall glass with ice, with a pitcher of water on the side), at any café.

~Le Pont Neuf: Most everyone knows the Pont Neuf was the first bridge built without buildings on it, but what is perhaps less well-known is that the bridge is not symmetrical, and no two of its arches are exactly alike.

~The dome of Galeries Lafayette department store (40 boulevard Haussmann, 9th).

~The little park of St.-Julien-le-Pauvre (1 rue St.-Julien-le-Pauvre, 5th). I'm a great fan of Joni Mitchell, and as a student I decided it was my mission to determine which park she was referring to when she sang, "Sittin' in a park in Paris, France." I am not exaggerating when I say that I visited every park in my *Plan de Paris,* and I concluded this was it. More attractive parks can certainly be found in Paris, but I was *certaine* this was where she hung out (I have no idea if she really did).

~The Cour Carrée of the Louvre.

~La Tour Eiffel: Standing underneath it is so impressive, and not at all the same as seeing it from a distance, even from the Trocadéro, and in case you were wondering, it's 986 feet, the ninth-tallest tower in the world. (I found this fact in a nifty book called *Skyscrapers: A History of the World's Most Famous and Important Skyscrapers,* by Judith Dupre, introductory interview with Philip Johnson, Black Dog & Leventhal, 1996, which is published in a vertical format measuring 18″ by 7¾″, the only way, of course, to view skyscrapers short of standing in front of them yourself.) La Tour has evoked strong reactions, as the following accounts attest: "The merit of the Eiffel Tower is that he shows you not only Paris to the ultimate edges in every direction save on the northern slopes of Montmartre, but he shows you (almost) France too. How long the Eiffel Tower is to stand I cannot say, but I for one shall feel sorry and bereft when he ceases to straddle over Paris. For though he is vulgar he is great, and he has come to be a symbol. When he goes he will make a strange rent in the sky" (E. V. Lucas, *A Wanderer in Paris*, 1909). And: "Maupassant often lunched at the restaurant in the tower, though he didn't care much for the food: *It's the only place in Paris*, he used to say, *where I don't have to see it*" (Roland Barthes, *The Eiffel Tower and Other Mythologies*, Farrar, Straus and Giroux, 1979).

~Musée Picasso (Hôtel de Sale, 5 rue de Thorigny, 3rd).

~The fountain created by Niki de Saint Phalle and Jean Tinguely in place Igor Stravinsky.

~*Les Journées du Patrimoine:* Check with the tourist office for the dates of this annual Heritage Weekend, when many of France's architectural gems normally closed to the public are open. It's a not-to-be-missed opportunity to see the interiors of palaces, mansions, ministries, and embassies (in 1999, I was able to walk inside the Palais-Royal offices of the Ministère de la Culture et de la Communication and the Conseil d'État). Now in its seventeenth year, Heritage Weekend is usually scheduled in September, and in Paris alone there are approximately thirty buildings to tour—and it's all *gratuit*.

~Musée Rodin (77 rue de Varenne, 7th).

~The Gallery of the Kings and Le Pilier des Nautes (both in the Musée National du Moyen Age at the Hôtel de Cluny, 6 place Paul-Painleve, 5th): Le pilier was built by the Nautae Parisiaci, the corporation of water merchants, who carved it with the names of both their own gods and those of Rome; one inscription dates from the reign of Emperor Tiberius, making it the oldest sculpture in Paris.

~The Canal St.-Martin (19th).

~Val-de-Grace (1 place Alphonse-Laveran, 5th), not only for the story of how it was built (as a thank-you to God for producing a son to Louis XIII and Anne of Austria) or its beauty, but also for its being a supreme example of the divine right of kings. The Hebrew letters carved into the stone walls of the interior should not surprise anyone, as Ina Caro notes in her wonderful book *The Road From the Past:* "Charlemagne was called David by his courtiers and the King of France considered himself both 'the successor of the Caesars' and 'heir to the power of David and Solomon, anointed of God.'"

~Having a drink at the bar at La Coupole (102 boulevard du Montparnasse, 14th).

~L'Institut du Monde Arabe (1 rue des Fossees St.-Bernard, 5th), especially the view from its outdoor terrace.

~The Jeu de Paume when it housed the impressionists. It may seem pointless to mention something one can't really experience anymore, and although we can still see the impressionist paintings in the d'Orsay (thankfully), there is something very special about viewing art in a small museum. Thinking about how compact the Jeu de Paume was—I can still remember the exact placement of each painting in every room—reminds me of a passage from Hemingway's *A Moveable Feast,* in which he speaks of the small museum of *his* day: "There you could always go to the Luxembourg Museum and all the paintings were sharpened and clearer and more beautiful if you were belly-empty, hollow-hungry. I learned to understand Cezanne much better and to see truly how he made landscapes when I was hungry. I used to wonder if he were hungry too when he painted; but I thought possibly it was only that he had forgotten to eat. It was one of those unsound but illuminating thoughts you have when you have been sleepless or hungry. Later I thought Cezanne was probably hungry in a different way" (from the chapter "Hunger Was Good Discipline"). I was hungry often in Paris too, which is undoubtedly one reason why I am so fond of Hemingway; but I will never forget how standing and looking in the Jeu de Paume made me feel about art, my life, and the extraordinary place which is Paris. So I mention all this to encourage visitors not to overlook Paris's wealth of small museums, where, in any one of them, you may very well have your own illuminating thoughts.

~Every inch of the Île St.-Louis.

~The grand staircase and the Marc Chagall ceiling of the Opéra de Paris Garnier (place de l'Opéra, 9th).

~St.-Eustache and *l'Écoute,* the sculpted head by Henri de Miller (place du Jour, 1st).

~The art deco La Samaritaine department store (10 rue de la Monnaie, 1st) and the unbeatable view of Paris's rooftops from its Building 2 outdoor terrace on the Toupary restaurant level.

~Les Arènes de Lutèce (rue de Navarre, 5th), the remains of a Roman arena dating from the second century not far from the rue Mouffetard, where you can buy provisions at the daily *marché* (one of the oldest street markets in Paris) and enjoy your feast on one of the arena's stone tiers.

~The Musée Nissim de Camondo (63 rue de Monceau, 8th).

~The original, art nouveau *métropolitain* entrances designed by Hector Guimard (only a few remain) and the facade of the synagogue at 10 rue Pavee (4th), also designed by Guimard.

Bibliothèque—
Companion Reading

Classics

Italo Calvino in his thoughtful book *Why Read the Classics?* (Pantheon, 1999) notes, "Classics are books which, the more we think we know them through hearsay, the more original, unexpected, and innovative we find them when we actually read them." Don't postpone joy, then! Here's a selection to choose from, to read or reread, poetry included. These are available in several different publishing series (Modern Library, Plume, etc.) in both hardcover and paperback.

Charles Baudelaire—poems.

La Bête Humaine, Émile Zola.

The Charterhouse of Parma, Stendhal; referred to by André Gide as the greatest of all French novels, and by Henry James as "among the dozen finest novels we possess." The Modern Library edition of last year features a new translation by Richard Howard.

Cousin Bette, Honoré de Balzac.

Eugenie Grandet, Honoré de Balzac.

Germinal, Émile Zola.

The Hunchback of Notre Dame, Victor Hugo.

In Search of Lost Time: Swann's Way, Within a Budding Grove, The Guermantes Way, Sodom and Gomorrah, The Captive & The Fugitive, Time Regained & A Guide to Proust, Marcel Proust, Modern Library, hardcover and paperback volumes. I've specifically endorsed the Modern Library version because this set—by Andreas Mayor and Terence Kilmartin, revised by D. J. Enright—is considered *the* translation by scholars.

Madame Bovary, Gustave Flaubert.

Les Misérables, Victor Hugo.

Nana, Émile Zola.

The Red and the Black, Stendhal.

Arthur Rimbaud—poems.

The Stranger, Albert Camus.

A Tale of Two Cities, Charles Dickens.

Fiction, Short Stories, and Spy Novels

Across the Bridge (1993), *The Collected Stories of Mavis Gallant* (1996), and *Overhead in a Balloon: Twelve Stories of Paris* (1985), all by Mavis Gallant, all Random House. Many of Gallant's stories are set in Paris or are about Parisians or both, and her characters and scenes are unforgettable.

Babylon Revisited, F. Scott Fitzgerald, Scribner, 1996 (paperback reprint edition).

Birdsong (Random House, 1996, hardcover; Vintage, 1997, paperback), *Charlotte Gray* (Random House, 1999, hardcover; Vintage paperback, 2000), *The Girl at the Lion d'Or* (Vintage, 1999), the French trilogy by Sebastian Faulks.

The Château, William Maxwell, Vintage International, 1995; originally published in hardcover by Alfred A. Knopf, 1961.

City of Darkness, City of Light: A Novel, Marge Piercy, Fawcett Columbine (Ballantine Books), 1996.

The Club Dumas, Arturo Perez-Reverte, Vintage International, 1998.

Fields of Glory, Jean Rouaud, translated by Ralph Manheim, Arcade Publishing (a Little, Brown company), 1990 by Les Éditions de Minuit; 1992 translation copyright. This slender little novel is beautifully written and won the 1990 Prix Goncourt for best work of fiction in France.

French Folktales, Henri Pourrat, selected by C. G. Bjurstrom, translated and with an introduction by Royall Tyler, Pantheon Books, 1989. 105 legends culled from the rural provinces of France, which are, as Tyler writes in the introduction, "stories to eat with your pocketknife, among friends. They are delicious, and the days they taste of will never come again."

Le Divorce, Diane Johnson, Dutton, 1997, hardcover; Plume, 1998, paperback.

The Mark of the Angel, Nancy Huston, Steerforth Press, 1999.

Mayhem (1999), *Salamander* (1998), *Sandman* (1997), and *Stonekiller* (1997), all by J. Robert Janes, all published by Soho Press.

A Moveable Feast, Ernest Hemingway, Scribner hardcover, 1996; Touchstone paperback, 1996, both reprinted editions. Though it may be trite to say so, I will never forget how reading Hemingway made me feel when I was a student in Paris. Years later, I came across the following quote by writer Gene Bourg, and was relieved that someone could set things straight: "In *A Moveable Feast* Hemingway postulated that once a man has been young and happy in Paris, he can never be truly happy again. Agreeing with him would be very dangerous indeed. But agreeing and understanding are entirely different things." (*Gourmet,* October, 1998)

Reckless Appetites: A Culinary Romance, Jacqueline Deval, The Ecco Press, 1993. One of my favorite, quirky, delicious books, blending the fictional story of Pomme and Jeremy with literary history and almost one hundred recipes.

Scaramouche: A Romance of the French Revolution, Rafael Sabatini, originally published in 1921; Buccaneer Books hardcover (1997) and Regnery Publishing paperback (1999).

Shadows of a Childhood: A Novel of War and Friendship, Elisabeth Gille, translated from the French by Linda Coverdale, The New Press, 1999.

Somewhere in France, John Rolfe Gardiner, Alfred A. Knopf, 1999.

The Tattered Cloak and Other Novels, Nina Berberova, translated from the Russian by Marian Schwartz, Vintage, U.K., 1992. Each of these six short novels is set in Paris, the characters all Russian émigrés. Berberova also provides one of the most memorable passages of Paris I've ever read: "Paris, Paris. There is something silken and elegant about that word, something carefree, something made for a dance, something brilliant and festive like champagne. Everything there is beautiful, gay, and a little drunk, and festooned with lace. A petticoat rustles at every step; there's a ringing in your ears and a flashing in your eyes at the mention of that name. I'm going to Paris. We've come to Paris."

The World at Night: Paris 1940 (1996), and its sequel, which begins in 1941, *Red Gold* (1999), both by Alan Furst, both published by Random House.

French Style and Decorating

Pierre Deux's Paris Country: A Style and Source Book of the Île-de-France (Linda Dannenberg, Pierre Levec, and Pierre Moulin, photographs by Guy Bouchet, Clarkson Potter, 1991) is a beautiful coffee-table book that also contains useful tips for visitors. Though some of the restaurant and hotel information may be dated, information about them—as well as shops, antique fairs, museums, and festivals—can be confirmed with the tourist office.

Bringing France Home, Cheryl MacLachlan, photographs by Ivan Terestchenko, Clarkson Potter, 1995.

Living in Paris, Jose Alvarez, photographs by Christian Sarramon and Nicholas Bruant, Flammarion, 1996; translated from the French by Deke Dusinberre, originally titled *L'Art de Vivre à Paris*. In addition to beautiful photos of Paris indoors and out, the visitor's guide at the back of the book provides information on some unusual guided tours, such as those offered by the government organization Visites-Conférences des Monuments Historiques (La Caisse Nationale des Monuments Historique, 62 rue Saint-Antoine, 4th; 01.44.61.21.69). Lecture tours allow you to see private monuments and interiors, such as those in embassies.

Country Houses of France, Barbara and Rene Stoeltie, Taschen.

Shopping/Les Souvenirs

I am not much into shopping as a general rule, but I enjoy buying gifts for other people, especially when I'm traveling. Most of what I purchase—even for myself—falls into the food and wine category, and I have found that even supermarkets sell beautifully packaged items of yummy stuff that's hard to find, expensive, or both in the U.S. Occasionally, I look for other types of singular gifts, so I've enjoyed consulting *Through the Windows of Paris: Fifty Unique Shops* (photographs and text by Michael Webb, Balcony Press, Glendale, California, 1999) and *The Paris Shopping Companion: A Personal Guide to Shopping in Paris for Every Pocketbook* (by Susan Swire Winkler, Cumberland House Publishing, Nashville, Tennessee, 1998).

The most thorough book I've seen—although it's not exclusively for Paris—is *The Riches of France: A Shopping and Touring Guide to the French Provinces* (by Maribeth Clemente, St. Martin's Press, 1997). The first section includes real nuts-and-bolts information on exchange rates, VAT, customs and duties, shopping hours, returns, discount shopping, sizes, mailing purchases home, packing tips, etc. For visitors planning to make trips outside of Paris, this book is especially helpful as Burgundy, Île-de-France, the Loire Valley, and Normandy are covered in separate chapters. Instead of presenting a roundup of stores in Paris, Clemente has given the chapter a theme, "The Provinces in Paris," and lists appropriate stores alphabetically by region or type of product. Clemente's recommendations are very helpful in purchasing unique gifts for business clients, colleagues, and friends.

~Additionally, see these *Gourmet* articles by Catharine Reynolds: "Hermès" (February 1987); "The Great Department Stores" (Le Bon Marché, BHV, Au Printemps, Galeries Lafayette; October 1993); and "Discount by Design" (fashion and jewelry bargains all around the city; October 1994). Good vocabulary words to know (especially if you're in Paris in January and August) are *soldes* (sales); *dégriffes* (refers to clothing where the labels have been cut out); *moitié-prix* (half-price); *coin des affaires* (refers to the bargain section of a large store); *deuxième choix* (seconds); and *tout doit disparaître* (everything must go!). Also, *je regarde* (I'm just looking) is useful for any type of shopping or browsing.

Travel Anthologies

Edith Wharton Abroad: Selected Travel Writings, 1888–1920, edited by Sarah Bird Wright with a preface by Shari Benstock, St. Martin's Press, 1995, 1996. Included in this selection of seven essays are three on France: "A Motor-Flight Through France," "Dunkerque to Belfort," and "French Ways and Their Meaning." Wharton lived in Paris from 1911 to 1937, when she died, and she traveled widely until World War I (the other essays in this collection are on Algiers, Tunis, Greece, Turkey, Italy, and Morocco). With twenty black-and-white photos and illustrations, and a glossary of foreign words and phrases.

Travels With Alice, Calvin Trillin, Avon, 1989. Not all of the fifteen essays in this witty and entertaining book are about Paris or France, but I couldn't resist including it here because Calvin Trillin is on my short list of favorite writers. The "Prix du Hamburger" is the only piece with Paris as backdrop (there are also three in the south of France: "Hanging Around in Uzes," "Damp in the Afternoon"—my favorite—and "Full Basket"), but it doesn't matter—Trillin is irresistible, and a traveling companion par excellence.

L'Île-de-France
et d'Ailleurs
(The Île-de-France
and Beyond—Short Trips
from Paris)

To understand *French landscape one must visit the* Île-de-France, *that region northwest of Paris where small villages nestle in gently rolling hills covered with fruit trees and flowers. The human scale of the land, the humbleness of the steeple of every village church evoke another age.*
— Alexander Liberman,
THE ARTIST IN HIS STUDIO

Secret Versailles

BY SUSAN HACK

~

The Galerie des Glaces (Hall of Mirrors) is my favorite feature of Versailles, or so I think until I'm outside walking around looking at the vistas, or picnicking, and then I decide that the grounds are really the jewel of the château. Indoors or out, crowds or not, Versailles does not disappoint. It can't be beat for a short trip (by RER, SNCF, or car, the journey is under an hour), and you'll feel a million miles away from Paris. Connoisseurs often mention other *châteaux* as their favorites—Vaux-le-Vicomte, for example, which I happen to prefer as well, but I wouldn't see it without also seeing Versailles. (However, as Vaux was the inspiration for Versailles, I enthusiastically recommend a visit, and the best article I've read on it is "Vaux-le-Vicomte: A Perfect Château Envied by a King," by Simon Schama, "The Sophisticated Traveler" edition of *The New York Times Magazine,* October 20, 1991.)

This piece on Versailles, which appeared in September 1997, highlights even more reasons to be awed by it. For a related detour, combine a visit there with a guided tour of the Potager du Roi, the chateau's kitchen garden of vegetables and fruit. A ten-minute walk from the château's entrance, the twenty-three-acre *potager* is administered by the École Nationale Supérieure d'Horticulture and École Nationale du Paysage. Ninety-minute tours, conducted in French, are offered from April to November (Wednesday–Sunday, 2:30) and meet at 6 rue Hardy (phone: 01.39.24.62.00/fax: 01.39.24.62.01). On Tuesday and Friday, produce from the gardens is sold at No. 4 rue Hardy. See "Where Versailles Grew Its Veggies," by Catharine Reynolds, *The New York Times* travel section, September 11, 1994, for more historical background. As Reynolds notes of the *potager,* "If we are what we eat, a visit there can offer as much insight into the court of the Sun King and his successors as a jostle around the State Apartments."

To do justice to the château of Versailles and its vast grounds requires at least a day, and if one hasn't planned for a picnic, a good meal to either break up a visit or provide a suitable ending to one is essential. A decent meal is not that easy to find in the vicinity of the château, however, but a good source for some recommendations is "Hard by the Château, Royal

Eating" by Jacqueline Friedrich (*The New York Times* travel section, January 24, 1999), in which she reviews four restaurants within a fifteen-minute walk of the château.

SUSAN HACK lives in Paris and Cairo. She is a contributing editor at *Condé Nast Traveler*.

W e are wandering through an attic of Versailles, arguably the world's most famous palace, indisputably the most visited château in France. One floor down, an international babel of language is rising toward the vaulted ceiling of the Hall of Mirrors, where painted allegories depict Louis XIV in all his Apollonian glory. More than the gold brocade in his canopied bedroom, the very titles of the Sun King's paintings (*The Young King Turning Away from Pleasure and Sports to Contemplate the Crown of Immortality Proffered Him by Glory, to Which Mars, the God of War, Is Pointing*, and so on) convey the grandeur and pretension of his residence. It's harder to imagine now, because revolutionaries auctioned off the furniture, all seventeen thousand lots, in 1793. But once upon a time, before the era of monolithic tour groups, Versailles was a universe of plumed courtiers and solid-silver chairs, where even the overdressed horses lived in palace-size stables.

Up here in the attic of the North Wing, away from the tourist mob, I'm exploring an altogether different treasure trove—one that the French, in all their eccentric glory, have chosen to keep half-hidden from the public for more than a century. Elbowing their way through 120 rooms of restored seventeenth- and eighteenth-century royal apartments they have been able to enter, few visitors realize that Versailles has another 125 rooms, containing six thousand paintings and two thousand sculptures celebrating fifteen centuries of French history. It was because of these rooms, collectively known as the Museum of the History of France, that the Sun King's

Versailles survives as anything more than a description in a book or an illustration in a gilt-framed painting. The museum opened in 1837, the creation of another king of France, Louis Philippe. Although it closed in 1871, the museum remains perfectly preserved in the realm of the real. But to the French, it's a distant memory.

And that's the paradox, the great Gallic Conundrum. Despite the last, furious decade of museum- and monument-building in Paris (latest tally: ninety-two museums), the Museum of the History of France, the most important history museum in Europe, remains guillotined off from the rest of Versailles. The château's annual 3.2 million visitors see only the Hall of Mirrors, Louis XIV's state rooms, and a few royal apartments. From the Crusades to the colonization of Africa, the galleries assembled by Louis Philippe recount vast and uncomfortable swaths of France's extraordinary past. Many exceptional works by David, Delacroix, Girodet, and Gros provide an instructive window on pre-impressionist French art. Bits and pieces of the unique collection have been fleetingly on display at Versailles since the 1960s. But no one, except a handful of curators, has seen the museum as a contiguous whole for 126 years.

As you read this, Versailles's authorities are opening twenty-one rooms devoted to the history of seventeenth-century France, a sort of companion volume to the standard tour of Louis XIV's state apartments. But much of the rest of the Museum of the History of France will remain off-limits—unless you're willing to fork over a hefty $238 (1,440 francs) for a truncated ninety-minute private tour. The tours are difficult to arrange, as I found when I tried to book one early last June, only to learn that the guides were all tied up giving talks entitled "A Day in the Life of the Sun King." I ruled out the $990 (6,000 francs) option of a "prestige visit" with a senior curator. Finally, Versailles officials agreed to let me explore the Museum of the History of France, at no charge, in the company of a security guard. My "guide," Frédéric Maguin, lacked a Ph.D. in art history. But he did pack an impressive ring of eight-inch skeleton keys.

Greeting me at the appointed hour with a curt *bonjour,* Frédéric leads the way to an attic in Versailles's North Wing. There's no electricity—just the echo of our footsteps and the creak of window shutters opened to let in some light. The air is stale, yet the smell of pine and the shine on the parquet indicate that the floors have recently been waxed. Exquisitely covered in flowers of fine wool needlepoint, the cushioned benches that once invited footsore visitors to rest have now become antiques.

Over a fireplace hangs a haunting tour de force, a posthumous portrait by the French master Jean-Auguste-Dominique Ingres of Ferdinand-Philippe, the Duke of Orléans, who died in 1842 after being thrown from a carriage. In the next room there's a painting of the duke's bereaved father, Louis Philippe, self-styled king of the French from 1830 to 1848, who failed to realize his dream of establishing an Orléanist dynasty. I've prepared for my visit by reading biographies of Louis Philippe, and it's a lucky thing, because the paintings lack descriptive labels. Surveying the unfamiliar faces of this royal household, I'm stopped short by a portrait of a voluptuous young woman with black hair and an olive complexion, exotic in her black lace mantilla. This is Princess Françoise of Brazil, who married into the French royal family and debuted at court in 1838. She made a lasting impression at her very first state dinner, contemptuously sending back the chicken consommé. "Take this away," she commanded, "and bring me parrot soup!"

We walk the length of the attic and double back, emerging on a silent marble staircase. Frédéric leads the way down, unlocking a giant double door on the ground-floor landing. As he walks ahead opening more windows, I try to get my bearings in the sudden light.

There's an optical illusion: Marble doorframes and garish flocked-velvet walls seem to stretch to infinity.

Accustomed to information-age audio guides, info-boards, and brochures, I'm struck again by the alienness of this nineteenth-century museum. There's no context—just personalities distilled in portraits. In the sea of painted wigs and silks, the Marquis de Dangeau stands out because he's literally lost under his getup of brocaded silver and green silk robes. His face is a tiny oval amid the excessive cascade of a brown wig that falls, Howard Stern–like, halfway down his chest. It's painter Hyacinthe Rigaud's private joke. By emphasizing the clothes over the man, he has visually labeled the marquis a vain and fatuous jerk. Pierre Mignard, another master of seventeenth-century French portraiture, has done an infinitely gentle job on Mademoiselle de Blois, love child of Louis XIV and one of his mistresses, Madame de Montespan. In an age when youngsters were invariably cast as cherubs or miniature adults, she is charmingly childlike, curled up on two red pillows, blowing bubbles.

Three and a half hours later, we're still on the move. We pass through the Crusades Room, a neo-Gothic time capsule decorated with coats of arms, giant Orientalist canvases, and the original bronze and carved-cedar door of the Hospital of the Knights of St. John of Jerusalem in Rhodes. In the stuffy Chimay and Midi attics, the collection takes my breath away: Hundreds of hidden artworks, originally commissioned by Napoléon Bonaparte, hang on walls of bright gold, black, and maroon silk. I immediately spot two famous paintings featured in every art-history textbook. Jacques-Louis David's personal copy (he painted five) of *The First Consul Crossing the Alps* ennobles Napoléon, placing him on a rearing stallion rather than on his foot-sure donkey. By contrast, Antoine-Jean Gros's *General Bonaparte on the Bridge of Arcola* makes use of gritty realism. Long-haired and skinny, his Napoléon in a dirty uniform has an edgy charisma and a modern rock star's sex appeal.

Our last stop is the Hall of Battles, Louis Philippe's pièce de résistance, whose main entrance intersects the tourist throng at the end of the queen's state apartment. Catching my eye, Frédéric wordlessly draws me aside. Skirting a gate into a deserted stone corridor, we stop by an ordinary-looking wall. Frédéric slips in an eight-inch skeleton key and a fourteen-foot slice of the "wall" swings open. Suddenly we're dwarfed in a vast room, two stories high, whose architecture mimics the marble columns and arched skylight of the Grand Gallery at the Louvre. The 380-foot-long Hall of Battles features thirty-three giant canvases documenting French military victories from the year 496 to 1809. With the exception of Eugène Delacroix's *Battle of Taillebourg,* the writer William Makepeace Thackeray once dismissed these works as "the worst pictures that eye ever looked on," an opinion that may have been influenced by the profusion of French victories over the British. I'm a neutral party, with no specialist knowledge, but I admit the content is repetitive. Every king of France, and every snorting steed, seems straight out of the nineteenth-century equivalent of central casting.

It's curious, though, how the past throws its reflection on the present. Walking through the Hall of Battles, I begin thinking about the hype and sniping that greeted a more recent attempt to improve the face of glory: François Mitterrand's decision to erect a glass pyramid at the Louvre.

Picture the inaugural gala of the Museum of the History of France, which took place in the Hall of Battles on the evening of June 10, 1837. Concerned for the safety of the head of state, a special task force of Paris firemen make sure the new museum is secure. Cooks prepare a vast banquet, enlisting two hundred soldiers and five hundred valets to lay tables for fifteen hundred VIPs. Actors from the Comédie Française perform extracts from Molière's *Misanthrope* before a celebrity crowd of painters, sculptors, poets, and European royalty. The entertainment ends after midnight. The chief curator—King Louis Philippe himself—finally rises from his chair and leads guests on a candlelit tour of the galleries. The last guest rolls out the door at two in the morning. Badly behaved journalists gossip and take notes.

Drawn by the publicity, twelve thousand people turned up the next day for the general opening. There was debate, but most visitors applauded Louis Philippe's audacious decision to erect a new monument in Versailles's central courtyard. It wasn't a glass pyramid. It was a bronze equestrian statue of Louis XIV, the Sun King.

The museum enjoyed continued popularity, judging by the handwritten nineteenth-century admissions log preserved in the Versailles archives, which tallies the arrival of the three-millionth visitor on September 7, 1845. At the inaugural reception, Louis Philippe had cornered Victor Hugo to ask his opinion. "The century of Louis XIV has written a beautiful book, but the King has just given this beautiful book a magnificent cover," the writer sputtered diplomatically. Hugo praised the decision to turn a royal monument into a national one. But he knew as well as anyone that Louis Philippe needed to shore up his fragile legitimacy, that the king sought to ensure his own succession even as he walked the streets of Paris wearing a gray top hat and carrying an ordinary umbrella. "Millions from the civil list," wrote Hugo, outraged at the fortune Louis Philippe spent on Versailles. "The gray hat and umbrella of the bourgeois king have cost more than the crown of Charlemagne!"

"All I want to do is to give employment to workers, to encourage the arts, and leave beautiful monuments behind me for France," Louis Philippe told his chief minister, François-Pierre Guizot, in a remark that could have come straight from Mitterrand's lips. But a few decades later, tastes had changed; the curator king had become a Philistine. After 1871, the mob of critics declared a revolution.

Close the doors. Off with his head. The architect I. M. Pei completed Mitterrand's pyramid to almost universal acclaim in 1988. Given Louis Philippe's experience, maybe the late French president shouldn't rest so easily in his grave.

It would take days, if not weeks, to do justice to six thousand paintings and two thousand sculptures. By now I'm a little numb with sensory overload. While not everything's a masterpiece, there's still enough here to fill several major art galleries in the United States and Great Britain. The Museum of the History of France, however, was never intended to represent the heights of artistic achievement.

Louis Philippe, France's only constitutional monarch, was summoned to the throne at the end of the Bourbon Restoration. He'd grown up at the court of Versailles and, as a sixteen-year-old, had watched his godparents, Louis XVI and Marie Antoinette, be hauled off by the mob. To escape execution under the Terror, he spent years in exile, often disguised, in places as far-flung as Switzerland, Lapland, and a Cherokee village in Tennessee. Returning from England to Paris after Napoléon's 1815 defeat at Waterloo, Louis Philippe eventually replaced Charles X, a political anachronism who believed in the divine right of kings and who provoked a second revolution in July 1830 by curbing the press and trying to curtail the right to vote.

The head of the liberal Orléans branch of the Bourbon family, Louis Philippe had been a member of the Jacobin Club and briefly fought in the Revolutionary army. He was therefore a unifying figure in the whirlwind of political forces destabilizing France in the wake of 1789, a "bourgeois" monarch who understood the necessity of placating republicans, Bonapartists, and two royalist factions. Eager to prove his love of the common man, he sent his sons to public school and often invited commoners and chance acquaintances to dinner. His spin-control monarchy (he called himself king of the French, rather than king of France) didn't win everyone over: He survived no less than seven assassination attempts.

In running the country, Louis Philippe found that his hands were tied by his three-man cabinet. But in restoring Versailles, he enjoyed free rein. In 1802 there'd been a halfhearted attempt to turn the abandoned château into a museum of the school of French painting. But in 1830 there was talk of tearing down the rotting hulk, which had been stripped of all its art and furniture, and which Bonaparte and the two Bourbon kings had refused to live in. Although it was not politically expedient to move in himself, Louis Philippe nonetheless poured 23 million francs of his own money into fixing it up, directing the reappointment of Louis XIV's bedroom from memory. A dossier kept by the chief architect, Frédéric Nepveu, reveals the king as a control freak who patterned himself, at least as a Versailles project manager, after Louis XIV. The Sun King devoted thirty-three years to expanding his father's hunting lodge, riding herd over three famous architects, Louis LeVau, Jules Hardouin Mansart, and André Le Nôtre. Starting in 1833, Louis Philippe made 398 visits to Versailles just to make sure his own workmen were getting things right.

His motive was propaganda. By turning Versailles into a public museum, Louis Philippe wanted to transform it from a symbol of the ancien régime into a symbol of national unity. Exempting only the Louvre, he requisitioned from châteaux across the country paintings and sculptures that illustrated great events and figures from the past. The best-known artists of the time, including Eugène Delacroix, were commissioned to fill in any historical gaps. In an era of nascent European nationalism, and before the emergence of professional historians, Louis Philippe believed his galleries complemented the restored royal apartments. Like illustrations for a giant school textbook, they were intended to demonstrate that monarchy, not just revolution, played a role in the emergence of modern France.

Louis Philippe's reign suddenly ended in February 1848, when a new revolution brought in Napoléon Bonaparte's nephew, Louis-Napoléon Bonaparte, first as elected president and then as emperor. Fearing for his safety, Louis Philippe abdicated, fled Paris in a cab, and boarded a Channel steamer at Le Havre disguised as a "Mr. Smith."

Deprived of its royal patron, and falling out of fashion amid the advent of impressionism and photography, the Museum of the History of France closed in 1871. That year, an occupying Prussian army declared the creation of the German Empire in the Hall of Mirrors and billeted wounded troops in the Hall of Battles. Weeks later, the uprising of the Paris Commune prompted the new French government to take over Versailles as its headquarters.

For most of this century, Louis Philippe's history galleries have been shrouded in the discredit attached to "official" nineteenth-century painting. The standard line, taken by generations of Baedekers, Michelins, and Blue Guides, was that Louis Philippe had bad taste and viewed history through rose-tinted glasses. He cut down important canvases to fit fancy gilded frames. He destroyed priceless examples of seventeenth-century decorative art by gutting the apartments of lesser nobles to make way for his museum, filling it with inferior paintings from successive Paris Salons, the annual event that Édouard Manet and his friends famously rejected in 1863. Today, however, nineteenth-century art is enjoying a reappraisal. And Louis Philippe is credited with influencing the creation of national institutes across Europe, including London's National Portrait Gallery.

Versailles's curators included Louis Philippe's museum in the program of post–World War I restorations that began with a massive injection of funds by John D. Rockefeller. But they focused attention on the royal apartments and kept the history galleries out of public view. As a result of all this secrecy, practically no French person today has ever heard of the Museum of the History of France—despite the presence of its motto, A TOUTES LES GLOIRES DE LA FRANCE, chiseled in huge letters across Versailles's pediments. It's the ultimate irony, given the past decade's museum mania in Paris, just twelve miles from Versailles, where crowds line up for the new Richelieu Wing at the restored Grand Louvre, the Musée d'Orsay, and the Picasso Museum, as well as for every special exhibition at the Pompidou Center and the Grand Palais.

Continuing the monument-building tradition of his predecessors, President Jacques Chirac has announced a plan for a new museum at the Trocadéro to house masterpieces of tribal art. The past year alone has seen the opening of the Museum of Music at the Parc de la Villette, the restoration of treasures such as the Delacroix Museum, and the inauguration of Mitterrand's last big project, the new National Library on the Left Bank.

Happily, the devaluation of Louis Philippe's museum is coming to an end. In 1992 Versailles and the French luxury group Louis Vuitton Moët Hennessy (LVMH) announced a multimillion-dollar project to fund restoration of the seven Africa Rooms, in recognition of "their great value, not only for the light they cast on the sense of history in the time of the Citizen King but also for the quality of the paintings themselves." This year, France's biggest newspaper, *Le Figaro,* recruited famous historians in a campaign to reopen Louis Philippe's museum in its entirety. The head of the old National Library, the historian Emmanuel Le Roy Ladurie, mourned the abandonment of "this genre of national treasure" during the program of "Great Works" undertaken by Mitterrand during two presidential terms. Contemplating the punishing cost of Mitterrand's pyramid, the new library, and the overhaul of the shoddily built Beaubourg, the historian Henri Amouroux was blunt. "I find it particularly distressing," he told *Le Figaro*, "that we have invested so abundantly in cement."

"Versailles has always been the poor cousin of the national museum system," sighs Hubert Astier, president of the Château and Domain of Versailles, when I ask for explanations in his office overlooking the royal stables. A spinmeister himself, Astier has deflected all the bad press from Versailles to the Ministry of Culture, focusing the debate on a chronic shortage of security guards. Astier says that Versailles needs 140 additional guards to open all the history galleries without closing any of the rooms pertaining to Louis XIV. That would seem a fairly easy matter to resolve, except that in France's bureaucratic labyrinth, the guards are civil servants who work for the Ministry of Culture, which hires and assigns guards to all the national museums and monuments. The French government has embarked on an austerity plan to qualify for monetary European union, and there's a drive on to reduce the total number of state employees. Consequently, the ministry is being stingy. Astier managed to wrangle thirty guards from the allocation for the new National Library, permitting the August opening of the seventeenth-century history rooms.

The first noncurator ever to head Versailles, Astier was brought over, amid much controversy, from his number two post at the Ministry of Culture in 1995 to unite the château's diverse departments under a single management for the first time. A graduate of the elite École Normale d'Administration, like practically all of France's top politicians and CEOs, he envisions Versailles as a mixed corporation—part château, part museum, part park, part performance center. His ambitious ten-year, $200-million plan to boost revenue includes the possible construction of a Louvre-influenced glass roof over the central courtyard, the creation of a sculpture museum in the royal stables, the international marketing of the Versailles logo, and the reopening of Louis XIV's seven-hundred-seat Opéra.

In addition to the seventeenth-century rooms, Astier this year decided to open the Hall of Battles daily on an ad hoc basis, depending on the number of extra guards on the morning roster. If things go well, all of the history galleries in the North Wing will open by the end of 1998, giving visitors unprecedented contiguous access to a large section of the château. Astier hopes that the Napoleonic galleries on the ground floor and in the attics of the South Wing will follow suit by the end of 1999. In the meantime, he's investigating the development of a sophisticated handheld video guide to assist the many visitors unfamiliar with the gyrations of French history.

A weakness of the plan, in the eyes of the bean counters, is that the galleries lag behind the top-notch Parisian museums in terms of the ratio of outright masterpieces per square foot. But Astier, like the editors of *Le Figaro,* is convinced that the ensemble has importance and relevance far beyond the market price of individual paintings.

"France today is searching for its roots," he tells me, as we discuss France's persistent 12.8 percent unemployment rate and the anxiety many French people are feeling about their future and national identity in a federated Europe. "This is a very simple museum presenting a story of battles and great events, not our current story of economic and social problems.

"I find the rooms very beautiful," he says finally. "It's very much like going back in time."

Despite Hubert Astier's enthusiasm, I detect ambivalence on the part of other senior château employees about following his plan. Claire Constans, chief curator for nineteenth-century paintings, notes that it will be extremely difficult to bridge "the intellectual gap" between the history rooms and the royal apartments, and that the huge size of the château and gardens ultimately remains the main impediment to appreciation of Versailles.

"There's not one reason the history galleries have been closed, there are twenty-five," she tells me as we stand in front of one of Girodet's masterpieces, *The Revolt in Cairo,* during another of my visits. "Tourists come to Versailles to see the Hall of Mirrors. They look at the apartments and the gardens for two hours and they're done. It's crowded, and they're tired. To visit these galleries on top of that—well, you can judge how difficult that is. It's not a problem with the museum but a problem with the nature of tourism."

Even if Louis Philippe's Museum of the History of France eventually opens in its entirety, it will undoubtedly confound modern visitors. Louis XIV's Versailles is far easier to digest, requiring no special knowledge of French history or appreciation of historical genre painting. Indeed, to the millions who make the pilgrimage, a tour of royal Versailles plays like an episode of *Lifestyles of the Rich and Famous,* with Louis XIV's famed insistence on living in full public view providing grist for the mill. For example, Versailles's five thousand resident courtiers considered admission to the spectacle of Louis XIV defecating a special privilege; the inner circle also got to watch the king remove his dirty boots after hunting, a ceremony called *le débotter.* One of the best-sellers in the Versailles gift shop, the comic book version of "A Day in the Life of the Sun King," contains the complete lowdown on seventeenth-century court ritual, including the information that Louis XIV ate eighteen-course dinners with his fingers.

Past attempts to reopen the history galleries have proved short-lived, either because money ran out or, in one notorious case, because their contents proved too explosive for public consumption.

The only terrorist attack on Versailles in its history occurred in July 1978, two months after curators decided to reopen the ground-floor Napoléon rooms for the first time since 1871. A powerful time bomb left in a camera bag along the outer wall during a fireworks display blew a huge hole in the floor of the Hall of Battles and shredded sixteen Napoleonic canvases in the ground-floor galleries. Police said the bomb was the work of Breton separatists protesting French "imperialism" in Brittany.

The rooms themselves are works of art, the walls painted with Napoleonic icons such as lions and eagles, as well as miniature scenes repeating the themes and historical content of the large canvases. Restored, the ground-floor Napoleonic galleries remain closed to this day. (The attic trove, restored in 1970, was last on public view for three short months in 1989.)

It is unlikely that 160-year-old canvases depicting France's colonial conquest of Algeria would have a similar effect on today's armed Islamic extremists. But given the sensitivity of Algeria as a political issue in France, the paintings in the Africa Rooms are downright embarrassing. The issue is so touchy that I am denied official permission to visit these rooms, currently under restoration and devoted to France's imperial wars in North Africa, Belgium, the Crimea, and Mexico. I fret about how I can possibly cajole my laconic security-guard friend into using one of his skeleton keys in an unofficial manner. As it turns out, I needn't have worried. Some restorers had left a door open. When I throw Frédéric a questioning glance, he shrugs and nonchalantly stares off into space. In France, it seems, an official "no" actually means "maybe." Without exchanging compromising words, I slip inside.

The so-called Smalah Room, while out of sync with seventeenth-century architecture, strikes me as being among the most astonishing places at Versailles. Diffused light from the skylight illuminates the robin's-egg blue walls and bestows upon the gilt and painted frieze of cannon and soldiers an eerie and almost classical stillness. But the centerpiece, Horace Vernet's *Taking of Smalah*, is a mass of politically incorrect gore, its flag-draped French soldiers mercilessly slaughtering North African natives. The rooms remind me a bit of South Africa's Boer Monument, on a hilltop outside Pretoria, where the bas-relief of Zulu-fighting Afrikaners now plays like an apartheid version of the Elgin marbles.

The painting I remember most vividly from my tour is an 1846 Vernet portrait that hangs on a wall of the stone corridor facing the Crusades Room. It shows Louis Philippe, flanked by his five sons, riding a white horse out the gilded front gate of Versailles. A bronze equestrian statue of Louis XIV stands behind him in the palace courtyard. Louis XIV's royal symbol, the fleur-de-lis, emblazons the gate overhead. One of the last official portraits of Louis Philippe's reign, this is by no means the most beautiful painting in the collection. It's forced and stodgy, yet it speaks volumes. Whatever prideful dynastic ambitions he had, Louis Philippe believed that a link existed between himself and Louis XIV and that it was possible to bridge the intellectual and emotional canyons between divine right and democracy, revolution and national reconciliation.

The Sun King died in 1715, having ruled France for seven prosperous decades. He died in agony, of gangrene, but at least he died happy, knowing that his great-grandson Louis XV had peacefully inherited the throne. Louis Philippe was born under absolute monarchy and saw his own father executed during the French Revolution. He managed to hold on to his throne for eighteen years, so sensitive to his people's nostalgia for glory that he repatriated Napoléon's ashes from St. Helena and laid them under the golden dome of the Invalides in Paris. He died at seventy-six, in miserable exile, his fortune confiscated, his vision of succession dashed. Dedicated to France's national achievements, his forgotten museum is an uneasy monument to glory's fleeting nature. It's a lesson for any of us. If only we could see it.

Versailles's Hidden Treasures

A guide to the collections France has concealed for over a century:

The standard Versailles tour covers the King's State Apartment, the Hall of Mirrors, and the Queen's State Apartment, which form a contiguous whole on the first floor. At the end of the Queen's quarters you'll find the Coronation Room, created by Louis Philippe to mark the glory of Napoléon Bonaparte's ascension as well as his disastrous retreat from Egypt just before the Battle of Aboukir.

Hubert Astier, Versailles's president, has pledged to open the rest of the Museum of the History of France, except for the Africa Rooms, by the end of 2004. Until then, you need to book a private tour to see the Hall of Crusades and the rooms devoted to the nineteenth century (see below). Eighteenth-century rooms are incorporated into the recently restored apartments of the Dauphin and Dauphine.

The Hall of Crusades, off a stone corridor on the ground floor, between the Chapel and the Opéra, seems inspired by Sir Walter Scott's *Ivanhoe*. Ornate neo-Gothic woodwork and ubiquitous coats of arms complement paintings of knights in armor that read like Romantic illustrations—not accurate depictions—of such historic events as the capture of Jerusalem in 1099.

The more interesting rooms on the ground and second floors of the South Wing illustrate the meteoric military career and brief empire of Napoléon Bonaparte. On the ground floor, where oversize canvases are gathered, Orientalist portraits of Muslim potentates, painted en route during the 1798 Egyptian campaign, complement Girodet's masterwork *The Revolt in Cairo*.

Small scenes depicting the battle of the Pyramids are painted directly on the walls near the windows. The winding South and

Chimay attics house works by Jacques-Louis David and his atelier, among them David's personal copy of *The First Consul Crossing the Alps,* his brilliant, unfinished *Tennis Court Oath,* and an atelier copy of *The Death of Marat.* Other remarkable canvases include Antoine-Jean Gros's *General Bonaparte on the Bridge of Arcola,* Andrea Appiani's *General Desaix,* and Girodet's *Jean-Baptiste Belley,* a powerful portrait of the black deputy of Santo Domingo and an important visual document of the slave rebellion in Haiti.

Versailles Revealed

Apart from the seventeenth-century history galleries and the Hall of Battles, the only access to Louis Philippe's Museum of the History of France is with a specialist guide. Available June through October, the ninety-minute thematic tours cost $238 per person (for individuals or groups of up to thirty) and must be booked at least a month in advance (tour reservations and information, 30.84.76.18, fax, 30.84.75.64; the château and grounds are closed on Monday).

If you intend to spend only a few hours at Versailles, try to arrive at three-thirty. The crowds will have left, admission is half-price, and you'll be able to cover the seventeenth-century history galleries, the state apartments, and the Hall of Mirrors, as well as dip into the gardens—all before the six o'clock closing time. If you arrive in the morning, skip the long line at the general admission desk at entrance A and head directly to entrance C or D, where with no wait you can book an audio guide or a guided tour to one or more private royal apartments, as well as get your ticket for the state apartments and the Hall of Mirrors.

Reading

The bookstore in the Princes' Courtyard, around the corner from entrance C, has the biggest selection of Versailles literature. Pierre

Lemoine's *Versailles and Trianon: Guide to the Museum and National Domain* is the best overall guidebook and contains a description of the Museum of the History of France (Réunion des Musées Nationaux, $16). Also look for *The Sun King,* Nancy Mitford's witty 1966 biography of Louis XIV (out of print) and the interactive CD-ROM *Versailles: Complot à la Cour du Roi Soleil,* which faithfully re-creates Versailles as it existed in the seventeenth century.

Your local library may have copies of two out-of-print books. In Louis Philippe's translated *Diary of My Travels in America,* the twenty-three-year-old future king describes frontier democracy during three years on the run from the Paris Directory. And biographer Agnes de Stoeckl obviously can't forgive Louis Philippe for betraying Charles X, but her 1957 *King of the French* provides priceless details about his childhood at Versailles, his experiences during the French Revolution, his exile, and his eighteen-year reign.

Also recommended is Rachel Kaplan's nifty paperback guide *Little-Known Museums In and Around Paris* (Abrams, $20).

Seeing the Light in Chartres

BY JOAN GOULD

∿

editor's note

I had once read that the only way to see Notre-Dame de Chartres was on a brilliantly sunny day, when the light streamed in the stained-glass windows, which I'd also read were vastly more beautiful than those in Notre-Dame de Paris. The day my classmates and I set out with our architecture professor, it was gray and overcast, and I thought the excursion might be canceled. It wasn't, and the cathedral surpassed my expectations—there was, even with cloud cover, enough light to see the deep blue in the stained glass, a shade completely unlike any other, and there was something satisfying about having to use my imagination to visualize what the cathedral would have looked like in full sunlight.

After this piece appeared in *The New York Times,* it was the subject of a number of letters from readers, several of whom wrote to praise the services of Malcolm Miller, an Englishman who has been leading tourists through and around the cathedral for over forty years. Miller's tours—in English, for about 30 francs—are offered at noon and 2:45 P.M. every day *almost* without exception (he does take some days off). Inquire at the Office de Tourisme (place de la Cathédrale/02.37.21.50.00) or check the cathedral bulletin board. One reader also suggested trying to convince Mr. Miller to agree to a tour longer than an hour—she suggests a half hour more and notes it would be worth the money. Readers may also be interested in Miller's book, *Chartres Cathedral* (Riverside Book Company, 1997, with color photographs by Sonia Halliday and Laura Lushington). Inquire, too, about the free organ recitals, which have typically been offered Sunday afternoons from July to October. Though one could see the cathedral and be back in Paris in time for lunch (Chartres is only an hour away by train), it would be a shame to miss the other interesting features of the town. Visitors may want to consider an overnight stay, or plan a full day's excursion, stopping in Chartres en route to Fontainebleau, for example.

JOAN GOULD is the author of *Spirals: A Woman's Journey Through Family Life* (Random House, 1988).

I t looms through a fog above the flat farmland known as the Beauce, this Cathedral of Chartres, looking impossibly big, bigger than anything built by man, as I drive my car west on Route N10. Isolated and improbable on its hilltop, the mass of stone looks like a whale on a beach, or like the Ark on the first day after the flood waters receded. When I come close and park my car, the Ark shrinks to half its size.

Tourists are clustered in front of the Royal Portal with its row of twelfth-century statues, only half-freed from their columns, that Henry Adams called the Elgin marbles of French art. But I'm not ready for statues yet, nor for the south tower, which the architect Eugène Viollet-le-Duc called "the greatest and surely the most beautiful monument of this kind that we possess in France." I'm about to take a trip through time, back to the beginning, when this hilltop, this Mound, as it was called, was still forest and grottoes. And so I walk through a small doorway in the side of the cathedral with my guide and go down a flight of stairs, at the bottom of which I step into time past.

I'm escaping from beauty, because beauty is the trap that waits for tourists here. Abbot Suger, who built the first of all Gothic churches at St.-Denis, near Paris, foresaw the trouble and put an inscription on his gilded bronze door, warning us visitors not to be dazzled by what we see. We should let the radiance—which includes the light streaming through the stained-glass windows inside—turn us away from the dense matter of the everyday world and light our minds on their flight upward toward the nature of God: "Through palpable, visible beauty, the soul is elevated to that which is truly beautiful."

To philosophers of the twelfth century like Abbot Suger, God is light, and the light reflected on earth is the closest thing we know to the divine. Light is the least material substance, the source of growth, the mediator between bodies and the bodiless. It is the way in which we apprehend the universe, but, at the same time, the light that strikes our eyes is dense compared to the inner light that it is supposed to kindle.

But how am I supposed to look at Gothic light streaming through Gothic windows inside a Gothic space with twentieth-century eyes, accustomed to the scale of skyscrapers and color television? On earlier trips here, I admired each statue on the portals and spent hours inspecting the stained-glass windows through my binoculars, but that doesn't mean that I measured up to the cathedral's challenge. Maybe pilgrims can only find what they've learned to seek. In the twelfth and thirteenth centuries, pilgrims came here looking for God, and in the twentieth century for beauty, but we're approaching the twenty-first century now, and what I want smacks of both.

On this trip I decided to tour the cathedral in a radically different way, moving through time rather than space, starting so far back in history that I might manage to see a Gothic cathedral—for a few minutes, anyway—through Gothic eyes. This meant starting with what was below my feet: the crypt, still the largest in France, which contains an underground church of its own. Quite by accident, I'd stumbled onto an old mystical tradition that claims that Chartres— not the cathedral but the geographic spot, specifically this hill with its subterranean grottoes—was holy ground long before the first Christian arrived here.

According to this tradition, prehistoric Chartres was exactly what it remains today: a patch of earth sacred to a mother goddess, a Black Virgin, but a patch that is holy ground in the literal sense, where (according to mystics like Louis Charpentier) powerful currents come out of the earth itself.

And now I'm inside the belly of the whale, in the oldest portion of the cathedral, the subterranean chamber known as the Crypt of St. Lubin. In front of me stretches a long, low tunnel, which is the Chapel of Notre-Dame de Sous-Terre, Our Lady of the Crypt, a church beneath a church, dimly lit by hanging lamps up front near the altar, but growing darker and darker toward the rear.

I've reached the foundation of the cathedral in every sense. The weight of the building rests on these walls, which don't show a crack, being built of the fine, hard ashlar of the region that literally bears responsibility for the marvels of Gothic engineering.

(Normandy lacks this quality of stone, and so Norman vaults, which are usually made of rubble, have to be twice as thick and heavy as their counterparts in the region around Paris known as the Île-de-France.)

Facing me, I see a Gallo-Roman wall, which is easy to identify because of the thin layers of red brick alternating with white mortar, looking very much like ancient Oreo cookies. This Gallo-Roman wall, dating from the third or fourth century, may or may not mean that a Roman temple stood on this spot, but Julius Caesar himself places the Druids in the vicinity.

In his account in *The Gallic Wars,* he reports: "At a certain season, the Druids meet at a sacred spot in the country of the Carnutes, the reputed center of all Gaul. . . . The whole Gallic race is addicted to religious ritual; consequently, those suffering from serious maladies or subject to the perils of battle sacrifice human victims or vow to do so." (Chartres derives its name from its ancient inhabitants, the Carnutes.)

The Druids couldn't have found a more suitable spot than this one for rites that required a grotto, such as those that lie under the Mound, along with a source of pure water, like that in the Gallo-Roman well in front of me, now known as the Puits des Saints-Forts. Near their sacred water, according to the scholar Émile Mâle, the Gauls during that period often put up statues of protective goddesses known as The Mothers, usually in groups of three, but sometimes only one, a solitary goddess seated with an infant on her knees. Could such an image have inspired the medieval legend that turned the Druids of this region into miraculous heralds of Christianity, like the Magi? According to this legend, before Mary was born a prophetic spirit informed the Druids that one day a virgin would give birth to a child, and so they erected an altar here to a *virgo paritura,* a virgin about to give birth. No connection with a statue can be proved—in fact, there are scholars who deny that such images ever existed. In any case, there's no record of a statue in the crypt until the twelfth century at the earliest, and the legend itself doesn't appear until the fourteenth, and yet this place seems to have belonged to a madonna, an earth goddess at home beneath the earth, at least as far back as history extends.

The pillar that I'm leaning against is square, a strange sight under the gracefully curved vaults, but the pillar was here first, dating from the ninth century.

In this crypt in the year 876, Charles the Bald, who was the grandson of Charlemagne, gave the gift that made this cathedral a focal point for the worship of the Virgin: a piece of Middle Eastern cloth, reputed to be the tunic or chemise worn by Mary, either on the day of the Annunciation or the night of the Nativity, depending on the version.

One miracle after another was credited to this garment, which used to be stored in the crypt directly under the high altar. (It's now kept in the cathedral treasury.) When the Normans attacked Chartres in the tenth century, the bishop stood on top of the city gates and waved the tunic, the Sancta Camisia, until the Normans fled in panic.

By the year 1000 the worship of the Virgin had reached such a pitch that soon afterward Bishop Fulbert consecrated a great Romanesque cathedral, including the crypt in which I'm standing, which was as wide as the Gothic cathedral above my head and not much shorter. It was built in a U around the ninth-century chapel so that pilgrims could walk around the holy relic, carrying candles and offering up prayers—unless it was designed in a U, as the mystics suggest, because no one dared disturb the buried altar of the Druids.

This section, which is really a second church, had its own shrine, with a twelfth-century statue of a Black Madonna, one of those mysterious images whose blackness has never been fully explained, credited with working wonders, especially for women.

The pilgrims who flocked here were bedded down and the sick were nursed on straw spread out both in the crypt and the cathedral itself. Big as it was, the crypt wasn't big enough: around 1144 it had to be made even longer, in order to meet two new towers that were being constructed in front of Fulbert's church.

Never before or since was a building job undertaken in such a frenzy of devotion, it seemed. As Haimon, abbot of St.-Pierre-sur-Dives, wrote at the time, "Has anyone ever seen or heard of powerful lords and mighty princes . . . and even women of noble birth bowing their necks to the yoke and harnessing themselves to cart?" Robert de Torigny, the abbot of Mont-St.-Michel, added that men and women dragged wagons loaded with wood, stone, and grain "through deep swamps on their knees, beating themselves with whips, numerous wonders occurring everywhere, canticles and hymns being offered to God. One might say that the prophecy was being fulfilled: 'The breath of life was in the wheels.' (Ezekiel 1:20)"

And then, on June 10, 1194, a fire broke out that destroyed most of the town of Chartres as well as the entire cathedral, except for the two new towers with the Royal Portal between them and the crypt. It was assumed that the tunic was lost in the ashes. The wrathful Virgin had abandoned her shrine because of the sins of her people. In response, the inhabitants could think of nothing but abandoning the town, which was indefensible without the tunic and had nothing left in it worth defending in any case. Not only was the devastation spiritual; it was economic as well. Without the relic, there would be no pilgrims, which meant no customers and none of the fairs that were the lifeblood of the economy.

The cardinal of Pisa, who happened to be in Chartres at the time, addressed the people on the next feast day and begged them to rebuild their cathedral. In the middle of his plea, the bishop

appeared carrying the tunic, which had apparently just been discovered in a secret hiding place in the crypt—a sign that the Virgin
not only favored Chartres still but also wanted her people to build
a new and more glorious church in her honor.

Everything overhead, in other words—the nave and choir and
the stained-glass windows that illumine them—rose from this
crypt, just as the architect of the Gothic cathedral used the crypt's
floor plan as the basic outline of his structure.

And now at last, as I climb the stairs that lead out of Fulbert's
church, I move from the eleventh century and its antecedents to the
thirteenth, and from Romanesque to Gothic.

But I also move out of the belly of the whale, out of the dusky
tunnel with its ribs and walls, which were formerly painted, into
space that seems to have no walls at all, only openings of colored
light under arches that lift me upward like rocket ships.

For the first time in my life I become conscious of inner space
and outer light, not light in the twentieth-century sense of showing
us a view, but light for its own sake, seen through windows that fil-
ter the colorless air of day and make the rainbow inside it visible to
our eyes.

Chartres has done its job. It has made me see the light.

On the floor of Chartres Cathedral, the paving stones trace a
pattern that spans the entire width of the central nave, yet Michelin
does not mention this pattern and tourists rarely see it. A labyrinth,
or maze, shaped like a spiral, has been hidden from view in modern
times by tourists' feet and rows of flimsy chairs.

The symbol, more than forty feet in diameter, is at least as old
as ancient Egypt and Crete: a path that twists and turns upon itself
in apparent confusion until it eventually reaches its center. In
Chartres, however, the labyrinth takes on a mystical significance so
profoundly medieval in spirit that it has been literally overlooked

for hundreds of years. Lying under our feet like a shadow of the western rose window over our heads, the circle on the floor repeats the stained-glass circle in the wall, which is almost exactly the same diameter, each circle with a flower at its center.

This sort of analogy, as the medieval builders called it, was essential to the thinking of the mathematicians and mystics who made up the School of Chartres. In the view of these Platonic philosophers, whatever existed on earth could be only a dim reflection of a higher reality that existed on another plane, but the reflection must remain true to the original in number and proportion.

The rose window, the jewel of the cathedral, symbolizes Heaven with Christ at its center surrounded by four rings with twelve circles in each, twelve symbolizing the church with its apostles. When this heavenly rose, which is composed of nothing denser than colored light, casts its image down to earth, however, it is transformed into a maze, a place of confusion and suffering for a pilgrim who struggles to follow the path to its center. Everything on earth is doomed to be incomplete; the flower on the floor has only six petals.

According to tradition, penitents who were unable to go on distant pilgrimages wound their way on their knees to the center of the labyrinth and out again. This is not the sort of labyrinth in which a person can get lost, which is another message in the stones: the path is laid down for us. Once we start, we have no choice. Round and round the path goes, first right, then left, in inexorable loops that lead us toward the central stone, which was known as Jerusalem, except when it was called Le Ciel, or Heaven.

Others call the center Troy, after the account mentioned in Virgil of the Troy game, which may or may not have been the round dance performed by Theseus before he entered the labyrinth in Crete to kill the Minotaur. In support of this theory, the central stone at Chartres used to bear the legend: "This stone represents the

Cretan's labyrinth. Those who enter cannot leave unless they be helped, like Theseus by Ariadne's thread." Entering the labyrinth and reaching the center might be difficult but it was not enough. Finding one's way out again was what mattered; it was the process of rebirth. Similar mazes existed in such cathedrals as Amiens and Lucca, and mazes made of turf can be seen in England.

Even today there are visitors to Chartres who take off their shoes and tread as much of the labyrinth as they can reach in spite of the chairs. Some swear that when they stand on the central stone they feel a force that passes through the soles of their feet, a force that seems to rise from the earth itself, but no one can say what lies beneath the labyrinth that might create such a force. The central portion of the crypt below the cathedral is filled with rubble; the guidebooks label it "unexplored."

Chantilly

BY ALEXANDER LOBRANO

editor's note

I still wonder how it is possible that I never visited Chantilly the entire time I lived in Paris as a student (it is, after all, a mere thirty miles north). Not until sixteen years later did I finally find myself there, looking at the paintings in the Musée Condé, and feeling extraordinarily fortunate that I now had this opportunity to see such a memorable, beautiful collection. The château and gardens—landscaped by Le Nôtre—are also wonderful, and I dallied so long I never made it into town to try the Chantilly.

ALEXANDER LOBRANO lives in Paris and writes a weekly dining column for *Paris Time Out*. He is also editor of the *Zagat Survey of Paris* and is one of the "endearingly picky know-it-alls" Fodor's chose to write its *Paris 2000* guide. Lobrano also writes for a variety of other publications, including *Departures, France Discovery Guide, Bon Appétit, Food & Wine,* and *FRANCE Magazine.*

C hantilly offers yet another enviable French paradox. Only in a country as gloriously rich with museums as France could a magnificent château less than thirty minutes from Paris and housing one of the world's most exquisite small art collections remain relatively obscure.

Here, visitors can still relish the rare and wonderful experience of standing alone before a great work of art. The Musée Condé, as the château's collection is called, is one of only two French museums—the other is the Louvre—to boast three Raphaels. These magnificent canvases, along with the 140 gorgeous miniature paintings from the fifteenth-century *Book of Hours of Étienne Chevalier,* are reason enough to make the journey. But there is much, much more: 819 paintings, more than 3,000 drawings, hundreds of engravings, furniture, objets d'art, tapestries, sculptures and a library second only to the Bilbiothèque Nationale in terms of value and prestige. This is, quite simply, a superb museum.

And this year, a lot of people are going to find out about it. To celebrate the centennial of the Duc d'Aumale's bequest of this fabulous property to the Institut de France, the château has organized a number of special events and is working hard to get the word out about them. "Chantilly is not a national museum, so we don't benefit from the kind of advertising that the Ministry of Culture can afford," says Nicole Garnier, curator of the Musée Condé. "But we've put together some wonderful exhibitions this year and we're hoping a lot of people, especially foreigners, will discover the château for the first time."

Anniversary events officially began in May when Cardinal Lustiger of the Académie Française said a mass at the château chapel in memory of the man who was single-handedly responsible for Chantilly as we know it today: Henri d'Orléans, the Duc d'Aumale (1822–97), the fifth son of King Louis Philippe and Queen Marie-Amélie. D'Aumale inherited the château from his uncle in 1830 but didn't live there until after his marriage in 1844. Four short years later, however, the Orléans family was forced into exile. The duke would not return until 1871.

By then, he had lost his wife and five of his six children; his last son died the year after his return to France. The sorrowful duke turned his energies to rebuilding the château and amassing a private art collection that would perpetuate his family name and serve as a monument to his love for France. He commissioned architect Honoré Daumet to renovate the château and instructed him to include two large galleries, the nucleus of today's museum. (It was always the duke's intention that his collections be displayed to the public.)

Daumet's design was Chantilly's last major renovation, but it was certainly not its first. Records of the estate's history date back to the tenth century, and it is known that in the twelfth century the Bouteiller de Senlis family built a stronghold there. Nothing remains of that edifice, but the triangular shape of the château today is explained by the fact that it rests on the fourteenth-century foundations of a subsequent castle, which eventually belonged to the constable Anne de Montmorency (1493–1567), one of the most dashing figures of Renaissance Europe and the man largely responsible for Chantilly's present grandeur.

Anne engaged architect Jean Bullant to build the Capitainerie, a separate château on an adjacent island that originally housed the château's military command. The Capitainerie was originally linked to the large château by a walkway, but the channel separating them was filled in during the nineteenth century. Displaying a characteristic Renaissance architectural idiom (often seen in the Loire Valley), the walls of the Capitainerie, also known as the Petit Château, are reflected in the pool that surrounds it. Anne was also responsible for adding the impressive Galerie des Cerfs, several chapels scattered throughout the park, and a number of other improvements.

In 1632, Anne's grandson and heir, Henri II de Montmorency, was beheaded—he had rebelled against Cardinal Richelieu—and King Louis XIII seized the property. A decade later, however, Chantilly was back in the Montmorency family, thanks to Louis XIII's wife, who gave the domain to Charlotte-Marguerite de Montmorency, Princesse de Condé. This inaugurated the Condé era, when some of the most spectacular changes were made at Chantilly.

The family notably commissioned André Le Nôtre, who later landscaped Versailles, to design a new park for the château. His plans included the monumental Grand Degré, a massive granite staircase linking the château with the gardens. Le Nôtre also oversaw ambitious engineering projects that drained the surrounding watercourses and created the ingenious and impressive network of canals, basins, streams and ponds that is one of the most distinctive aspects of the estate today.

But perhaps the Condés' greatest contribution to Chantilly is the Grandes Écuries, one of the architectural masterpieces of eighteenth-century France. Today these magnificent stables house the Musée Vivant du Cheval, a "living equine museum" featuring some thirty different breeds of horses. Also dating from the eighteenth century is the charming Hamlet, a group of seven thatched-roofed country cottages (five survive today) that inspired Marie Antoinette's famous hamlet at the Trianon in Versailles.

The French Revolution was not kind to Chantilly. The owners went into exile, and during their absence much of the château was destroyed and the rich art collections transferred to the Central Museum of Arts, later known as the Louvre. When the family returned to Chantilly in 1815, they restored the château and recovered some of the art, and in 1830 bequeathed the estate to the eight-year-old Duc d'Aumale.

"Fortunately, Chantilly was protected during the duke's own exile," says Garnier. "In 1864 the duke willed the property to the Institut de France, but two years later, he was forced into exile yet again. Fearing that the property would be confiscated by the state during his absence, he immediately gave it to the Institut, with the provision that once he returned, he could live there for the rest of his life." The Institut has since inherited a number of other properties and collections, but Chantilly was the first and largest donation.

Collecting art was practically in the duke's genes. His father, King Louis Philippe, was a renowned collector, having notably created the historic galleries at Versailles. The duke reputedly began amassing art when he was still a student at Paris's Lycée Henri IV. Using his allowance, he purchased Bellangé's *Porte-drapeau de la République.* He continued to purchase works during his long exile in England, but it was after his return in 1871 that he became truly serious about his pursuit of art. "He would seek the advice of the best consultants of the day when buying paintings," says Garnier, "but when it came to books, he was himself a respected specialist. He wrote a catalog that remained an authoritative work for years."

Often, the duke would buy entire collections, such as the six-teenth- and seventeenth-century portraits belonging to the duke of Sutherland and forty canvases purchased from Frédéric Reiset, the director of national museums. Among the Reiset canvases are some of the Condé Museum's greatest treasures—works by Piero di Cosimo and Lippi as well as French painters Poussin and Ingres. This diverse assortment was hung in the dense and random "academic" style of the day in the skylit Grand Gallery. It may seem curious to find Poussin and Horace Vernet (Louis Philippe's favorite painter, who often depicted military or hunting scenes) not only side by side but nearly frame-to-frame, since the walls are practically paved with paintings. "It was a condition of d'Aumale's will that the installation never be altered," explains Garnier. "Nor are we allowed to lend out any of the artwork. That is why, when there is, say, a big Poussin exhibit in Paris, we hold a parallel exhibit here."

Visiting the museum today, one gains a keen sense of the duke's personality. He was first and foremost a soldier, as is evident from the great number of paintings commemorating battles. At twenty-one, he became a national hero when he captured the *smalah*, or caravan of riches, belonging to the Emir Abd-el-Kadar, who had revolted against the French presence in Algeria. The Musée Condé still has the emir's weapons and a number of other objects seized in the desert.

But the duke was also an ambitious aesthete, who was at once proud, sensitive, highly cultivated and academic. The atmosphere of the museum has more in common with a grand Napoléon III–era private home than an institution. Putting aside the remarkable quality of Chantilly's collections, it is perhaps this peaceful and intimate gallery experience in such a personalized and historic setting that makes a visit so memorable, especially in a time when big-city museums are becoming ever larger and more crowded.

A self-guided tour begins with the Galerie des Cerfs, conceived by architect Daumet as a place for the Duc d'Aumale to honor the hunting traditions of Chantilly and to display trophies. Here, eight

Gobelin tapestries depict states of the hunt and astrological signs. Ringing the room are twelve dramatic bronze hands grasping torches—Chantilly was one of the first châteaux in France to be lit by gas-burning sconces. The coats of arms decorating the coffered ceiling belong to the different families who have owned the château—note the monogram H.O., for Henri d'Orléans, Duc d'Aumale. In the 1880s, the duke often used this room for banquets, inviting such cultural luminaries as the novelist Alexandre Dumas and the playwright Pierre Loti.

After dinner, the duke delighted in ushering his guests into the adjacent grand Picture Gallery, where one wall is covered with Italian paintings and another with French artwork. Two of the more unusual canvases in this room are *Le Déjeuner d'Huîtres* by J. F. de Troy and *Le Déjeuner de Jambon* by Nicolas Lancret, both commissioned by Louis XV for his apartments at Versailles, and both showing bawdy gatherings amid tables laden with food. (Gourmets will be interested to learn that *Le Déjeuner d'Huîtres* contains one of the earliest depictions of champagne in French art.)

Continuing on there are thirty-four more rooms to visit, each holding some wonderful surprise, whether it be the beautiful self-portrait of Ingres or the duke's personal collection of objects excavated at Pompeii. The Psyche Gallery is a tour de force, with forty-two different grisaille stained-glass windows made between 1542 and 1544 for the Château d'Ecouen, today the French Museum of the Renaissance. Beyond the delicate quality of the work, what's especially interesting about this sequence is that it's a rare example of a profane subject—the myth of Psyche—in medieval glass.

Perhaps the most impressive gallery, however, is the Sanctuario, conceived as a quiet place where visitors could contemplate what the Duc d'Aumale considered to be the greatest masterpieces in his collection. The dim lighting of the room (for conservation reasons) creates a certain drama, drawing you immediately to Raphael's *The*

Three Graces and the *Virgin of the House of Orleans*. There's also a fine Filippino Lippi, *Esther and Assuerus,* and truly exquisite pages from the *Book of Hours of Étienne Chevalier.*

Across the way in the Petit Château, the Great Apartments house a fantastic collection of decorative arts and are particularly rich in eighteenth-century decorative paneling and woodwork. The Grand Cabinet, with its elegant ormolu woodwork, boasts rare pieces of furniture by Jean-Baptiste Sené and the amusing Singerie—always a favorite with visitors. Here, in typical eighteenth-century style, are painted panels of monkeys behaving like humans in chinoiserie settings. The allegorical motifs include war, hunting, music, alchemy and architecture.

The Private Apartments of the duke and his wife offer an intriguing chronology of nineteenth-century decorative styles from the 1840s to the 1880s. The only eighteenth-century room here is the whimsical Petite Singerie, or little monkey room, with an aristocratic calendar of pleasures and events being enjoyed by monkeys. The most important items in the apartment are some fine Sèvres porcelain and furniture by the Grohe Brothers, cabinetmakers to King Louis Philippe. In the duchess's boudoir, note the curved piano designed especially to fit the oval room.

With so much to discover inside the château, don't forget to leave plenty of time to enjoy the splendid grounds. A unique way to get a sense of the sixteen-thousand-acre forest surrounding Chantilly is to go up in the Aérophile, a tethered hot-air balloon that rises five hundred feet and is the largest of its kind in the world. Aloft, you can get a wonderful visual definition of the difference between the formal French and rambling English approaches to landscape architecture. You can also see the famous stables and the racetrack, where two of the most prestigious races in France—the Prix de Diane and the Prix du Jockey-Club—are held annually. Another way to take in Chantilly is aboard the

Kydrophile, which plies the château's watercourses. During the seventeenth century, these channels were the setting for the mock naval battles shown in paintings hanging in the Musée Condé—the canals and basins here had both an ornamental and recreational function.

Though Chantilly is a mere forty-five-minute drive from central Paris or a twenty-five-minute train ride from the Gare du Nord, you'll doubtless have the impression that it's a world away from the capital. This is perhaps because the real genius of Chantilly is that it so subtly provokes and guides your historical imagination, allowing you to easily grasp nearly the entire history of France in terms of several great families, the fabulous château they lived in, and the magnificent art they collected.

"Chantilly," by Alexander Lobrano, *FRANCE Magazine,* Summer, 1997.

Loire Valley—
Royal Châteaux Country

BY DAVID DOTY

editor's note

The Loire Valley is often referred to as the "Garden of France" as it produces a profusion of fruits and vegetables—and game, fish, goat cheese, and wine—in every season. Visitors to the *centre de la France* will be greatly rewarded by taking in more than the *grands châteaux* and wandering a bit off the well-beaten path, as David Doty did for this piece.

The Maison de la France received an enormous response to this piece after it appeared, and the Loire Valley remains the second most popular place people want to visit in France (after Paris; Normandy's Mont-St.-Michel is the most popular *monument* people want to see).

DAVID DOTY is founder and president of Flatiron Communications, a publishing company that produces magazine articles, books, Web sites, and custom media. He is editor of *France Insider's News,* a quarterly publication available at the three French Government Tourist Offices in the U.S. (for a complimentary subscription, contact the office nearest you, or write to French Government Tourist Office, P.O. Box 386, Bohemia, New York, 11716). Doty has written for numerous national magazines, including *Departures, Travel & Leisure, Food & Wine, GQ,* and *Wired,* and was also the author of *Frommer's Guide to New York City* from 1996 to 1999. Additionally, he teaches the history of Paris at the New School in New York and holds a master's degree in French literature from the University of Michigan.

The only sounds were my footsteps and faint rumbles from the tiny, waking village of Montoire-sur-le-Loir. On this brisk autumn morning, I carried two long, well-worn keys down a winding lane flanked by rough stone walls. Arriving at a pair of whitewashed doors, I slid one of the keys into the lock, pushed back the door, and found what I had been looking for.

A green lawn, a garden of red and yellow flowers, and a pear tree heavy with ripe fruit encircled the squat, rounded apse of the thousand-year-old Chapelle St.-Gilles. I closed and locked the door behind me. No one, no noise could disturb my meditation here.

I made my way past four spiraling yew trees and pulled out the second key. The chapel's bulky front door opened to reveal a fortresslike space. Sunlight made golden slits on bright white walls. Byzantine murals depicting a majestic Christ of the Apocalypse heightened the sense of mystery that came from being all alone in this ancient, vaulted space.

Nearly five hundred years ago, the great French poet Pierre de Ronsard was prior of St.-Gilles. Enclosed in a time so silent men thought they heard the music of the heavens, he, too, must have sat alone in this very garden to write his urgent love poems.

Memorable, quiet moments like this were what I'd hoped to find in the Loire Valley. I had come to marvel at the Loire's grand sights, of course, but more important I wanted to divine its ineffable spirit, to encounter great historical figures, Ronsard and his contemporaries, and to meet the people who inhabit *la douce France* today.

Surely the grand royal châteaux that dominate the Loire Valley—graceful Chenonceaux, stately Villandry with its exquisite gardens, elegantly proportioned Azay-le-Rideau—are among the world's great architectural treasures. But I planned to go off the familiar paths and discover the lesser-known châteaux, some of which have been occupied by the same families for hundreds of years.

I anticipated dinners *en famille* in châteaux that welcomed guests, and leisurely bicycle trips through the Loire's well-groomed forests. Instead of traipsing like a schoolboy on a homework assignment from important sight to important sight, I would follow a route of my own design, guided by those whom I chanced to meet.

My travels would not take me, regrettably, to every corner of the region. I did not return to the magnificence of the Gothic cathedral at Chartres. And while I enjoyed its wines I missed visiting the wineries of Touraine. The great marshes of Brenne, now a natural park and bird sanctuary, will also have to wait for another trip.

Orleans and Blois

The great and fertile Beauce Plain meets the Loire River at the city of **Orléans,** renowned as the site of Joan of Arc's first defeat of the English. This is the gateway to France's center. Outside Orléans, pretty small towns punctuate the flat, open rural landscape. Near **Beaugency,** with its medieval bell tower, narrow streets, and lively Saturday-morning market, I made my first discovery: often overlooked by tourists, **Château de Talcy** is a moody edifice, more Gothic than Renaissance despite its having been built in the sixteenth century by an Italian merchant. Full of atmosphere and built on a human scale, it is a welcoming place filled with furniture chronicling French taste from the time of Charles VIII to Louis XV. **Blois** is a food-lover's town. Fresh breads and game can be found in abundance at the market on Saturday mornings. The Loire's asparagus is the finest in the world. The colorful market in Blois sprawls over the cobbled alleyways of the town's old quarter and flourishes as if in defiance of the château, a durable curmudgeon that casts a forbidding shadow over the sounds and smells of commerce. First erected in the thirteenth century, the château at Blois encompasses six hundred years of French architecture, from the Middle Ages to the neoclassical period.

The Loir River Valley

Just north of the Loire a much smaller river, also called the Loir (without the final *e*), wends meekly through lovely countryside. I followed it to the medieval town of **Trôo,** where, as the guest of Messieurs Clays and Venon at **Château de la Voûte,** a seventeenth-century castle with tasteful antique-filled rooms, I received a warm introduction to châteaux that offer *chambres d'hôtes* (bed-and-breakfasts).

M. Venon suggested that the best way to know Trôo is to walk the hills above the château. Here people still live as troglodytes, in cave dwellings carved out of soft rock. Their homes are by no means primitive, however. Though they have been inhabited since prehistoric times, the caves today are distinctly modern. The unmistakable sounds of television and, even more incongruous, rock music emanate from within.

Along the sunflower-clustered road to **Montoire-sur-le-Loir,** sheep and cattle kept their timeless vigil in the fields. After discovering the haunting intimacy of the Chapelle St.-Gilles, I followed the road as it weaves south and came to **Lavardin,** which has been called *"le plus français des villages de France,"* owing to its picturesque, flower-decked houses and winding streets that eventually lead to another wonderful sanctuary, the mural-lined church of St.-Genest.

Farther east were the ruins of a medieval castle set high above **Vendôme** and decorated with a surprising trio of flags—one from Vendôme itself, one from France, and right next to them, Old Glory. Why the Stars and Stripes? Maréchal de Rochambeau, whose troops defeated the British during the War of Independence at Yorktown in 1781, comes from the region. His statue stands in the middle of the town square near L'Abbaye de la Trinité, a remarkable example of Flamboyant Gothic architecture.

From Vendôme, the well-marked route Touristique du Val du Loir winds north with two "must" stops along the way. The impressive **Château of Montigny-le-Gannelon** once housed two of the grandest families of France, the Montmorency-Lavals and, later, the Lévis. Insightful and fascinating, Mme. de la Motte St.-Pierre guided me through the castle, then suggested other sites to visit along the Loir, particularly the castle at Châteaudun. It combines medieval, Gothic, and Renaissance architecture. I arrived at sundown—as advised—and found a brooding and shimmering vision, just as she had promised.

The Sologne

Unlike the well-tended farmlands of the Loir Valley, the Sologne, south of the Loire River and north of the Cher River, is a misty land of birch and pine forests. Abundant wildlife—duck, partridge, pheasant, and hare—make it a paradise for hunters. Its many ponds and rivers attract the patient fisherman. Its footpaths and flat roads are ideal for hikers and bicyclists.

A few miles east of Blois sits the restful **Manoir de Clénord,** run with graceful ease by Mme. Renauld. Built mainly in the eighteenth century (though a wing remains from earlier times), its cozy down-stairs salon with family photographs displayed around the fireplace and its antique-furnished upstairs bedrooms are the essence of country charm. Rustic in appearance only, the Manoir offers every modern comfort, including business equipment (a group of executives from Paris came for a meeting the day I was there).

I rented a bicycle to explore the quiet (and blessedly flat) country roads that corkscrew through the forests and lead to some of the best châteaus of the Loire Valley. Just a short ride south, the Renaissance **Château de Beauregard** sits grandly at the end of a majestic *allée* and boasts a unique and stunning achievement: a gallery of over three hundred historical portraits of kings, queens, courtiers, Joan of Arc, and other important French and foreign contemporaries, painted at the beginning of the seventeenth century.

Ride east through the forest toward **Mont-Près-Chambord,** where you can stop to pick up your picnic lunch on the way to the underappreciated architectural jewel **Château de Villesavin,** built in 1537 with a courtyard so well-proportioned that it puts you at peace with the world.

Take your lunch with you to the great forest park that surrounds **Chambord,** the extravagant riot of sculpted stone that loudly proclaims the arrival of the Renaissance château in France. It is the combined inspiration of Leonardo da Vinci and his royal patron, François Ier. Walk the parapet that surrounds the château to appreciate its placement in the center of a great and bountiful forest.

If you're very fit, I suggest you pedal on to two more châteaux, quite unlike in their demeanor—and not far away.

In the town of **Fougères-sur-Bièvre** is an extraordinary edifice that goes by the same name. More castle than château, it was built after the Renaissance had made its mark on local architecture but its owner preferred the look of a fortified medieval dwelling. Empty of furniture and devoid of decoration, the cavenous rooms hint at the rigor of life centuries ago, allowing me to imagine an interior alive with all the comings-and-goings of daily life when construction here was begun in 1470.

Cheverny, on the edge of the Sologne Forest, is a splendidly classical château, built in 1604 by the same two men responsible for Chambord and Blois. Its sumptuous interiors are graced with paintings by the likes of Titian and Raphael. Its balanced and bright white stone facade startles the visitor by its beauty. Still privately occupied but open to visitors, the château remains dedicated to the hunt, with all its trappings, from baying hounds to redingotes.

Farther east, L'Hostellerie des Chênes Rouges in Villeny is a most welcome and unlikely combination of cool efficiency and warm country charm. It is owned by Mme. Lambert de Loulay, who, having tired of the urban rat race, retreated to her country property. She has built a delightful hotel complete with a pool and a man-made lake stocked with fish that might be dinner—for those lucky enough to catch one.

Berry and Sancerre

The medieval city of Bourges is a warren of pedestrian streets and the capital of Berry, the southernmost part of central France. Besides the famous Palais de Jacques Cœur, the city's other not-to-be-missed treasure is the cathedral of St.-Étienne, whose stained-glass windows are surely, with those in Chartres, the most beautiful in the world.

I was fortunate to arrive on a sunny day. As I strolled around the crimson-and-violet-illuminated apse of the cathedral, I could examine the windows in detail from very close range. Unlike many such masterpieces, these windows do not tower high above you but are situated almost at eye level.

The countryside of Berry is enchanting. Charolais cattle graze on gentle hillsides crisscrossed by woods and streams. One soon recognizes this peaceful, lolling land as the backdrop for the marvelous miniatures of *Les Très Riches Heures du Duc de Berry*.

Berry is home to some of the most intriguing châteaux in all of France. Just south of Bourges, on the route Jacques Cœur, lies **Meillant,** its richly decorated rooms carefully kept by the discerning Mme. de Mortemart. The château's Lion Tower and chapel are worth any detour and testify to an illustrious history dating from the fourteenth century.

Seldom do châteaux still possess their original exterior, or "curtaining," walls. Happily, **Ainay-le-Vieil** is the exception. Medieval towers and walls, parts of which were erected in the twelfth century, surround a gracious courtyard that gives access to the Renaissance wing. After walking along crenellated walls, you can keep the view of a knight or princess from one of the watchtowers. The striking beauty of its rooms completes Ainay-le-Vieil as one of the truly fairy-tale châteaux in France.

Here, in the heart of *la France profonde,* life moves at a pleasantly slow pace in villages like **Saint-Amand-Montrond, Bruère-Allichamps,** and **Farges-Allichamps,** some of which vie for the distinction of geographic center of France, an amusing though somewhat mystifying competition for the outsider. Nearby, in **Bannegon,** the Auberge du Moulin de Chaméron, owned by the friendly Candoré family, who spent twenty years in San Francisco, serves gourmet food to rival any you are likely to have in the French countryside.

For the quintessential château experience I suggest a room or suite at the elegantly furnished Château de la Commanderie, owned by Comte et Comtesse de Jouffroy-Gonsans. This exquisitely civilized couple make excellent dinner companions, and the sound of Madame's bell brings on succulent Charolais from the best local butcher. Lively conversation is offered, in English or French.

Just a short drive but a world away from the luxurious Commanderie is the Cistercian Abbey of **Noirlac**. The abbey is austere but elegant, and astonishingly well-preserved, the most complete structure of its kind in all of Europe.

Hillier terrain lies to the northeast, and nestled among its folds are the vineyards of **Sancerre**. A tour of the town of Sancerre is an exhilarating hike past medieval fortifications and up narrow stone streets. Naturally, I wanted to taste the local wine and followed signs to one of the area's finest producers of the flinty white Sancerre, Domaine Vacheron, still run by the founding family.

In summer, the city fathers hold regular Vacheron tastings in the town square. There is no better perspective for watching the people of the region go about their daily business, which almost certainly has something to do with wine.

In Search of Proust

BY ANDRÉ ACIMAN

∽

editor's note

Marcel Proust may be more celebrated now than he ever was, and many a visitor to Paris makes time for a pilgrimage to Illiers-Combray, just south of Chartres. The popularity of recent books such as *How Proust Can Change Your Life: Not a Novel* by Alain de Botton (Pantheon, 1997) and *The Year of Reading Proust* by Phyllis Rose (Scribner, 1997) has helped keep Proustomania alive and well. The depth to which Proust inspires people is explored well in this piece, which was featured in *The New Yorker*'s December 21, 1998, issue.

ANDRÉ ACIMAN is the author of *Out of Egypt: A Memoir* (Farrar, Straus & Giroux, 1995, hardcover; Riverhead Books, 1996, paperback) and editor of *Letters of Transit: Reflections on Exile and Memory* (The New Press, 1999). He is also associate professor of French at Bard College.

It was by train that I had always imagined arriving in Illiers-Combray—not just any train but one of those drafty, pre–World War, rattling wagons which I like to think still leave Paris early every morning and, after hours of swaying through the countryside, squeak their way into a station that is as old and weather-beaten as all of yesteryear's provincial stops in France. The picture in my mind was always the same: the train would come to a wheezing halt and release a sudden loud chuff of steam; a door would slam open; someone would call out, "Illiers-Combray"; and, finally, like the young Marcel Proust arriving for his Easter vacation just over a century ago, I would step down nervously into the small, turn-of-the-century town in Eure-et-Loir which he described so lovingly in *À la Recherche du Temps Perdu*.

Instead, when I finally made my way to Illiers-Combray, late last year, I arrived by car with Anne Borrel, the curator of the Proust Museum there, who had offered to pick me up at my Paris hotel that morning. In my pocket was a cheap and tattered Livre de Poche edition of *Swann's Way*, which I had brought in the hope that I'd find a moment to read some of my favorite passages on holy ground. That was to be my way of closing the loop, of coming home to a book I had first opened more than thirty years before.

I had bought it with my father, when I was fifteen, one summer evening in Paris. We were taking a long walk, and as we passed a small restaurant I told him that the overpowering smell of refried food reminded me of the tanneries along the coast road outside Alexandria, in Egypt, where we had once lived. He said he hadn't thought of it that way, but, yes, I was right, the restaurant did smell like a tannery. And as we began working our way back through strands of shared memories—the tanneries, the beaches, the ruined Roman temple west of Alexandria, our summer beach house—all this suddenly made him think of Proust. Had I read Proust? he asked. No, I hadn't. Well, perhaps I should. My father said this with a sense of urgency, so unlike him that he immediately tempered it, for fear I'd resist the suggestion simply because it was a parent's.

The next day, sitting in the sun on a metal chair in Lamartine Square, I read Proust for the first time. That evening, when my father asked how I had liked what I'd read, I feigned indifference, not really knowing whether I intended to spite a father who wanted me to love the author he loved most or to spite an author who had come uncomfortably close. For in the eighty-odd pages I had read that day I had rediscovered my entire childhood in Alexandria: the impassive cook, my bad-tempered aunts and skittish friends, the buzz of flies on sunny afternoons spent reading indoors when it was too hot outside, dinners in the garden with scant lights to keep mosquitoes away, the "ferruginous, interminable" peal of the garden bell announcing the occasional night guest who, like Charles Swann, came uninvited but whom everyone had nevertheless been expecting.

Every year, thousands of Prousto-tourists come to the former Illiers, which extended its name in honor of Proust's fictional town Combray, in 1971, on the centennial of his birth. The town knows it, proclaims it, milks it. Today, Illiers-Combray sells around two thousand madeleine pastries a month. The shell-shaped cakes are displayed in the windows of pastry shops like propitiatory offerings to an unseen god and are sold by the dozen—in case one wants to take some home to friends or relatives, the way pilgrims take back holy water from the Jordan or an olive twig from Gethsemane.

For the reader on a Proustian pilgrimage, tasting a madeleine is the supreme tribute to Proust. (As no patisserie fails to remind the tourists, it was on tasting a madeleine, now the most famous sponge cake in the history of world literature, that the adult narrator of Proust's novel was transported to his boyhood days in Combray.) It is also a gesture of communion through which readers hope, like Proust, to come home to something bigger, more solid, and ultimately, perhaps, truer than fiction itself. Anne Borrel often tells these Proust groupies that the cult of the madeleine is blasphemous, as are the claims made by one of the *pâtissiers* that members of the *famille* Proust used to purchase their madeleines on his premises. (In earlier drafts of the novel, Proust's madeleines may have been slices of melba toast, which evolved into toasted bread, only later to metamorphose into the sponge cakes.) But no one listens. Besides, going to Illiers-Combray and not tasting a madeleine would be like going to Jerusalem and not seeing the Wailing Wall or to Greenwich and not checking your watch. Luckily, I was able to resist temptation: during my visit, on a Sunday just a few days before Christmas, all the pastry shops were closed.

Before going to the Proust Museum, Anne Borrel and I had lunch at a tiny restaurant called Le Samovar. Plump and middle-aged, Borrel is the author of a cookbook and culinary history titled *Dining with Proust*. She told me that some of the tourists come from so far away and have waited so long to make the trip that as soon as they step into Proust's house they burst into tears. I pictured refugees getting off a ship and kneeling to kiss the beachhead.

I asked about Proust's suddenly increasing popularity.

"Proust," Borrel replied, "is a must." (She repeated these four words, like a verdict, several times during the day.) She reminded me that there were currently six French editions of *À la Recherche du Temps Perdu* in print. I told her that a fourth English-language edition was due to appear in 2001. And that wasn't all: trade books on Proust and coffee-table iconographies were everywhere; in Paris, I had seen at least half a dozen new books that bore Proust's name or drew on Proustian characters occupying precious space on the display tables of bookstores and department stores. Even Proust's notes, manuscripts, and publishing history had been deemed complicated enough to warrant a book of their own, called *Remembrance of Publishers Past*. Add to that T-shirts, watches, CDs, concerts, videos, scarves, posters, books on tape, newsletters, and a comic-strip version, entitled *Combray*, whose first printing, of twelve thousand copies, sold out in three weeks. Not to mention the 1997–98 convention in Liège celebrating the seventy-fifth anniversary of Proust's death, with sessions on music and Proust, eating and Proust, a writing competition (on the subject of "Time Lost and Time Regained"), and a colloquium on asthma and allergies.

This kaleidoscope of Proustophernalia is matched by as many testimonials and tributes to Proust, in which he takes many forms. There is Proust the elitist and high-society snob; Proust the son of a Jewish mother; Proust the loner; Proust the dandy; Proust the analytical aesthete; Proust the soulful lovelorn boy; Proust the tart, the dissembling coquette; the belle epoque Proust; the professional whiner; the prankster; the subversive classicist; the eternal procrastinator; and the asthmatic, hypochondriac Proust.

But the figure who lies at the heart of today's Proust revival is the intimate Proust, the Proust who perfected the studied unveiling of spontaneous feelings. Proust invented a language, a style, a rhythm, and a vision that gave memory and introspection an aesthetic scope and magnitude no author had conferred on either before. He allowed intimacy itself to become an art form. This is not to say that the vertiginous spate of memoirs that have appeared recently, with their de rigueur regimens of child, spouse, and substance abuse, owe their existence, their voice, or their sensibility to Proust—clearly, they owe far more to Freud. But it does help to explain why Proust is more popular today, in the age of the memoir, than he has been at any other time in the century.

Like every great memoirist who has had a dizzying social life and a profoundly lonely one, Proust wrote because writing was his way of both reaching for an ever elusive world and securing his distance from it. He was among the first writers in this century to disapprove of the critics' tendency to seek correspondences between an artist's work and his private life. The slow, solitary metamorphosis of what truly happened into what, after many years, finally emerges in prose is the hallmark of Proust's labor of love.

Proust is at once the most canonical and the most uncanonical author, the most solemnly classical and the most subversive, the author in whom farce and lyricism, arrogance and humility, beauty and revulsion, are indissolubly fused, and whose ultimate contradiction reflects an irreducible fact about all of us: we are driven by something as simple and as obvious as the desire to be happy, and, if that fails, by the belief that we once have been.

My conversation with Anne Borrel was interrupted by the arrival of customers outside Le Samovar. "Take a look at those four," Borrel said, pointing to the two couples dawdling at the entrance. "I'll bet you anything they're *proustiens*." She referred to all tourists as *proustiens*—meaning not Proust scholars but individuals whom the French like to call *les amis de Proust*, Proustologues, Proustolaters, Proustocentrics, Proustomaniacs, Proustophiles, Proustophiliacs, Proustoholics . . . or *fidèles* (to use a term dear to Proust's malevolent arch-snob, Mme. Verdurin).

One of the four opened the door of the restaurant and asked in a thick Spanish accent whether lunch was still being served. "*Pintades*"—guinea hens—"are all that's left," snapped the owner of Le Samovar. Borrel and I exchanged a complicitous glance, because talk of fowl immediately brought to mind a discussion we'd had in the car about Proust's servant, Françoise, who in *Swann's Way* butchers a chicken and then curses it for not dying fast enough.

The four tourists were shown to a table. One asked the proprietor what time the Proust Museum would open that afternoon, and he regretfully informed them that the museum was closed for the holidays. They were crestfallen. "What a pity! And we've come all the way from Argentina."

Anne Borrel had heard every word of the exchange. She reminded me of a teacher who with her back turned to the class while she's writing on the blackboard knows exactly who's whispering what to whom. She leaned over and told one of the Argentines, "You may have come to the right place."

Overjoyed, the Argentine blurted out, "You mean Marcel Proust used to eat here, in this restaurant?"

"No," Borrel answered, smiling indulgently. She told them that an improvised tour of the house could be arranged after coffee, and the Argentines went back to talking softly about Proust, staring every once in a while at our table with the thrilled and wary gaze of people who have been promised a miracle.

By the time our coffee was served, we had also acquired two English and three French *proustiens,* and a warm, festive mood permeated Le Samovar. It was like the gathering of pilgrims in Chaucer's Tabard Inn. Introductions were unnecessary. We knew why we were there, and we all had a tale to tell. By then, some of us would have liked nothing more than a fireplace, a large cognac, and a little prodding to induce us to recount how we had first come to read Proust, to love Proust, how Proust had changed our lives. I was, it dawned on me, among my own.

After dessert, Borrel put on her coat. "*On y va?*" she asked, rattling a giant key chain that bore a bunch of old keys with long shafts and large, hollowed oval heads. She led us down the rue du Docteur

Proust, named after Proust's father, who by the turn of the century had helped to halt the spread of cholera in Europe. The sidewalks and streets were empty. Everyone seemed to be away for the holidays. Franco-jazz Muzak emanated from loudspeakers, mounted on various lampposts, that were apparently intended to convey a festive yule spirit, but otherwise Illiers-Combray was deserted and gray—a dull, cloying, humdrum, wintry, ashen town, where the soul could easily choke. Small wonder that Marcel developed asthma, or that he had the heebie-jeebies on returning home after long evening walks with his parents, knowing that by the time dinner was served life would hold no surprises—only the inevitable walk up the creepy staircase and that frightful drama called bedtime.

Borrel stopped at one of many nondescript doors along the empty street. She stared at it for a moment, almost as though she were trying to remember whether this was indeed the right address, then took out her keys, inserted one into the lock, and suddenly gave it a vigorous turn, yanking the door open.

"*C'est ici que tout commence,*" she said.

One by one, we filed into Proust's garden. Fortunately, no one cried. Borrel pointed to a little bell at the top of the gate. I couldn't contain myself. "Could this be the ferruginous bell?" I asked. It was a question she'd heard before. She took a breath. "You mean not the large and noisy rattle which deafened with its ferruginous, interminable, frozen sound any member of the household who set it off by coming in 'without ringing,' but the double peal, 'timid, oval, gilded,' of the visitor's bell, whereupon everyone would exclaim, 'A visitor! Who on earth could it be?'" (She was quoting from memory, and every time one of us asked a question after that she would recite the answer.)

Next she led us into the restored, relatively humble middle-class house—by no means the large villa I'd always imagined. The kitchen, where I'd envisaged Françoise cooking the chicken she had viciously butchered, was a sunless alcove. The dining room, with a small round table and dark wood paneling, was a depressing melee of browns. Then we came to Marcel's bedroom, with its tiny Empire-style bed, the magic lantern that kept him company at night when he dreaded sleep, and nearby the George Sand novel bound in red. In another room was the sofa that Proust had given to his maid, Céleste Albaret, and which her daughter had donated to the museum—and which was perhaps the inspiration for the fictional sofa that Marcel inherited from his Tante Léonie, made love on, and eventually passed along to the owner of a brothel.

When Borrel indicated another room, on the second floor, I interrupted her to suggest that it must surely be the room where, under lock and key, Marcel discovered the secret pleasures of onanism. Borrel neither confirmed nor denied my allegation. She said only, "The little room that smelt of orrisroot . . . [where] I explored, across the bounds of my own experience, an untrodden path which I thought was deadly." In this way, I was summarily put in my place—for presuming to show off and for implying that I could make obvious what Proust's oblique words had made explicit enough.

Back in the garden, I told her that the way she had opened the main door had reminded me of the moment in the novel when, after a long, moonlit family walk, Marcel's father pretends to be lost. Everyone in our group suddenly remembered the episode, and, excited, one of the Englishmen described it to his friend, explaining that it was only after making everyone else panic in the dark that Marcel's father had finally taken a key out of his pocket and quietly inserted it in what the others until then had failed to see was the back gate to their very own house. According to the Englishman, Marcel's admiring mother, stunned by her husband's ability to save the day, had exclaimed, *"Tu es fantastique!"*

"Tu es extraordinaire!" Borrel corrected him.

I had always liked that scene: the family wandering in the moonlight, the boy and his mother convinced that they're lost, the father teasing them. It reminded me of the way Proust's sentences roam and stray through a labyrinth of words and clauses, only to turn around—just when you are about to give up—and show you something you had always suspected but had never put into words. The sentences tell you that you haven't really drifted far at all, and that real answers may not always be obvious but aren't really hidden, either. Things, he reminds us, are never as scary as we thought they were, nor are we ever as stranded or as helpless as we feared.

Borrel left us for a moment to check on something inside the museum, and we spent some time discussing our favorite Proust passages. We all wondered which gate Swann's prototype would come through in the evenings, and where the aunts had been sitting when they refused to thank him for his gift but finally consented to say something so indirect that Swann failed to realize that they actually were thanking him.

"It all seems so small," said the Englishman, who was visibly disappointed by the house.

My thoughts drifted to a corner of the garden. The weather was growing colder, and yet I was thinking of Marcel's summer days, and of my own summer days as well, and of the garden where, deaf to the world, I had found myself doing what Proust described in his essay "On Reading":

> giving more attention and tenderness to characters in books than to people in real life, not always daring to admit how much I loved them . . . those people, for whom I had panted and sobbed, and whom, at the close of the book, I would never see again, and no longer know anything

about. . . . I would have wanted so much for these books to continue, and if that were impossible, to have other information on all those characters, to learn now something about their lives, to devote mine to things that might not be entirely foreign to the love they had inspired in me and whose object I was suddenly missing . . . beings who tomorrow would be but names on a forgotten page, in a book having no connection with life.

The guided tour took more than two hours. It ended, as all guided tours do, in the gift shop. The guests were kindly reminded that, despite the impromptu nature of today's visit, they shouldn't forget to pay for their tickets. Everyone dutifully scrambled to buy Proust memorabilia. I toyed with the idea of buying a Proust watch on whose dial were inscribed the opening words of *À la Recherche du Temps Perdu: "Longtemps, je me suis couché de bonne heure."* But I knew I'd never wear it.

The visitors began talking of heading back to Paris. I was almost tempted to hitch a ride with one of them, but Borrel had promised to take me for a night walk through the streets of Illiers-Combray and then accompany me to the train station. The others stood idly about in the evening air, obviously reluctant to put Illiers-Combray behind them. They exchanged addresses and telephone numbers. "Proust is a must," I heard the Argentine say, an infatuated giggle in his voice. When Borrel left the shop to lock the back door, I was suddenly alone.

As I looked out the window at the garden where the Proust family had dined on warm summer evenings, I was seized with a strange premonition of asthma. How could Marcel have ever loved such a place? Or had he never loved it? Had he loved only the act of returning to it on paper, because that was how he lived his life—first by wanting to live it, and later by remembering having wanted to, and ultimately by writing about the two? The part in between—the actual living—was what had been lost.

Proust's garden was little more than a place where he had once yearned to be elsewhere—never the primal scene or the ground zero. Illiers itself was simply a place where the young Proust dreamed of a better life to come. But, because the dream never came true, he had learned to love instead the place where the dream was born. That life did happen, and happened so intensely, to someone who seemed so reluctant to live it is part of the Proustian miracle.

This is the irony that greets all Proust pilgrims: they go in search of things that Proust remembered far better than he had ever really known them, and which he yearned to recover more than he had ever loved them. In the end, like the boy mentioned by Freud who liked to lose things because he enjoyed finding them, Proust realized that he couldn't write about anything unless he thought he had lost it first. Perhaps I, too, had come here in order to lose Combray, if only to rediscover it in the pages I knew I would read on the way home.

My train wasn't due for an hour and a half, and Anne Borrel invited me to have a cup of tea at her house before our walk. We closed the door to the museum and set off down dark and deserted alleys.

"Illiers gets so empty," she said, sighing.

"It must be lonely," I said.

"It has its plusses."

Her house was bigger than Proust's and had a far larger garden and orchard. This seemed odd to me—like finding that the gate-keeper owns a faster car and has better central heating than the owner of the palace.

As we headed back to the train station after our tea, I walked quickly. Borrel tried to stop long enough to show me the spot where the Prousts had returned from their Sunday promenades, but I didn't want to miss my connection to Paris. It seemed a shame that, after so many years, this longed-for moonlit walk, so near at hand, should be the very thing I'd forfeit. But the last thing I needed was to be sentenced to a sleepless night in Proust's boyhood town. I alluded to a possible next time. Borrel mentioned spring, when Proust's favorite flower, the hawthorn, would be in bloom. But I knew, and perhaps she knew, too, that I had no plan to return.

On my way to Paris, I skimmed through the pages of "Combray," the first chapter of *In Search of Lost Time*. As I read about the steeples of Martinville or Tante Léonie, eternally perched in her bedroom, on the first floor, overlooking rue Saint-Jacques, it occurred to me that I had rushed back to the book not to verify the existence of what I had just seen but to make certain that those places I remembered and loved as though my own childhood had been spent among them had not been altered by the reality of the dull, tile-roofed town shown to me by Anne Borrel.

I wanted to return to my first reading of Proust—the way, after seeing a film based on a novel, we struggle to resurrect our private portrait of its characters and their world, only to find that the images we've treasured for so long have vanished, like ancient frescoes exposed to daylight by a thoughtless archaeologist. Would my original image of a stone villa with a spacious dining room and a wide staircase leading to the child's solitary bedroom be able to withstand the newly discovered little house with its squeaky wooden stairwell and drab, sunless rooms? And could this tawdry garden really be the glorious place where Marcel read away entire afternoons on a wicker chair under a chestnut tree, lost to the voices of those calling him inside and to the hourly chime of the church of Saint-Hilaire—whose real name, as I had found out that day, was

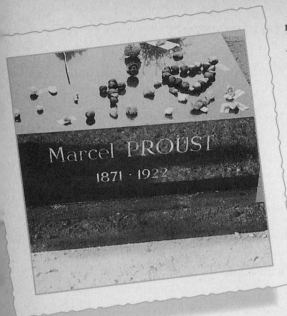

not Saint-Hilaire but Saint-Jacques, which, moreover, was not really the name of the street watched over by Tante Léonie, who, it turned out, was herself more likely to have been an uncle.

Inside the sepia cover of *Swann's Way* I searched also for the sense of wonder I had brought to it that summer evening more than thirty years before, when I'd had the good fortune to be with a man who was the first person to mention Proust to me and who, because he was unable to give me so many things then, had only this to give me, and gave it tentatively, self-consciously, as though he were giving part of himself, as he told me about Proust—how Proust remembered things that everyone else seemed to forget, how he saw through people though they still managed to fool him, and how he did all those things in sentences that were ever so long—and steered me, as we rushed to buy the first volume before the stores closed, to a writer I have since loved above all others, not just because of who he was and what he wrote, or because of who I became the more I read him, but because on that late-summer evening I already knew I had just received, perhaps without my father's knowing it, his dearest, most enduring gift of love.

Bibliothèque

Île-de-France

A Guide to the Impressionist Landscape: Day Trips from Paris to Sites of Great Nineteenth-Century Paintings, Patty Lurie, Bulfinch Press (an imprint and trademark of Little, Brown and Company), 1990. The French, unlike Americans, are not anxious to tear down old buildings and replace them with new ones, which Lurie discovered firsthand when she set out to find the exact sites where the impressionist painters set up their easels outside of Paris. It is really an amazing thing that this is so. As Lurie says in the preface, the only site that is drastically different today is the suburb of Argenteuil. This guide leads you to painting sites of Boudin, Cézanne, Monet, Pissarro, Renoir, Sisley, and van Gogh. Each "tour" is planned as an outing of no more than one day, mostly via SNCF trains departing from the Gare St.-Lazare. Details about the train trip, address of the tourist office, a map, specific directions to the site, and color photographs of the particular painting(s) and its present view are included for each entry. A few painting-site matchups were a stretch (*Seven Cows in a Meadow, Woman with a Parasol on the Beach at Trouville*), but nearly all are remarkably accurate.

The Sun King: Louis XIV at Versailles, Nancy Mitford, Crescent Books, 1982; originally published by Harper & Row, 1966. Nancy Mitford, who passed away at her home in Versailles in 1973, was a successful novelist (*The Pursuit of Love*, 1945; *Love in a Cold Climate*, 1949) and biographer (*Madame de Pompadour*, 1954; *Voltaire in Love*, 1957). In this book she has presented Versailles from its rather humble beginnings as the Sun King's father's hunting lodge to its glory days as "the hub of the universe." There is no other book on Versailles I've seen that is as comprehensive; amply illustrated with color and black-and-white reproductions of artwork, maps, and building plans; and entertainingly written. A visit to the château will mean so much more—especially since even the best tours are not as thorough as this book—by reading Mitford's classic.

Loire Valley

Loire Valley guidebooks include *Cadogan France: The Loire* (which is authored by Philippe Barbour, who thankfully has the same discriminating taste as Dana Facaros and Michael Pauls); *Michelin: Châteaux of the Loire; Knopf Guides: The Loire Valley;* and *Eyewitness Travel Guides: Loire Valley.*

Loire Valley: A Wine and Food Guide to the Loire, Jacqueline Friedrich, Henry Holt and Company, 1996. In combination with whichever guidebook you choose, you need this book if you're going anywhere at all along the Loire.

American journalist Jacqueline Friedrich lives in France and has written extensively about Loire wines for French publications. She also spent two years traveling along the river to research this book, which is a practical, interesting, and mouthwatering guide. The first part is about the river, wine history, climate, soil, grapes, etc. Then there is a chapter on foods of the Loire Valley, followed by a wine route, which takes the traveler through the Nantais, Anjou and Saumur, Touraine, the Sancerrois, and the Auvergne. At the end of the book are four appendixes, which feature specific suggestions for restaurants, markets, wine shops, regional specialties, fairs, and festivals; a glossary of French terms; suggested temperatures for serving Loire wines; and conversion tables (for hectares, hectoliters, and Celsius and Fahrenheit). De rigueur—do not hesitate for a second before putting this hardcover in your carry-on bag.

The Châteaux of the Loire, Pierre Miquel, photographs by Jean-Baptiste Leroux, Penguin, 1999. Of all the books I've ever seen on Loire Valley châteaux, this is is the most magnificent. The photos of the twenty-five castle-fortresses along the Loire are elegant and gorgeous, and if you've never seen the châteaux, this book will make you ache to do so; if you already love the Loire Valley, this is the keepsake book to have (it goes without saying that it makes a beautiful gift, but I don't see how you could refrain from keeping it yourself).

Further Afield

Célestine: Voices From a French Village, Gillian Tindall, first published in Great Britain, 1995, by Sinclair-Stevenson; published in the U.S. in hardcover (1996) and paperback (1997) by Henry Holt. I bought this book at The Travel Bookshop in London because I was intrigued by the cover photograph—a misty, pinkish, serene image—and I was unable to determine the time of day it was taken. I didn't get around to reading the book for several years, and when I did, I got no further than the opening quotations when it dawned on me that I was about to read a very special book of the sort one rarely encounters. This is not a tragic or terrible story, yet it is somehow inestimably sad, in a way I am utterly incapable of explaining. Tindall and her family, who are English, bought an old house in the village of Chassignolles in the very center of France, which is sometimes referred to as *la France profonde*. Just how *profonde* is illustrated by Tindall's description of a present-day bus trip to a town about thirteen miles from Chassignolles: "It begins with seven kilometers into La Chatre on foot or by bicycle to catch one of the infrequent buses that run to Châteauroux today from the moribund railway station. The bus does not take the direct route but, impersonating the branch-line train that it has replaced, it makes its way circuitously for an hour or so through half a dozen villages in the valley of the Indre before finally surfacing onto the modernity of the main road into Châteauroux. There it gets up a sudden speed, past the new sheet-metal hangars called Mammouth and Bricomarche and Jardiland, graceless as pink elephants, before its triumphant arrival at the station with minutes to spare to catch a train to Paris or Toulouse. The same gathering crescendo has to be executed in reverse for the return journey . . ." After the house was cleaned out, Tindall discovered a cardboard case containing seven letters dating from the 1860s, all of which were addressed to a Célestine, who was the former owner's grandmother. This book is Tindall's attempt to re-create the life of Célestine and her contemporaries, as well as the history of the village, the province of Berry, and indeed the history of vanishing rural France. She has succeeded in providing us with a work of great value, tracing events of the nineteenth and twentieth centuries while observing every nuance of French provincial life. We come to understand the great significance of the coming of the railroad, and we come to know her neighbors and friends as if they are ours, too. A curious expression used frequently by her country neighbors is *à présent*, as in *Je suis vieux, à présent* (I am old, at present) or *mort à present* (so-and-so is dead, at present). Tindall reveals that this is a technically correct but slightly archaic French phrase that apparently suggests a more temporary state rather than the more permanent one we know as "now," as if a person could be old at the present time but may one day be young again. Tindall's book is filled with little observations like this, and beautifully written passages, and it is unquestionably a masterpiece. I also learned that in this part of France, dusk is characterized by a "pinkish, theatrical light," and I knew this was the precise moment the cover photo was taken.

Articles

The following articles are good sources for trip planning outside Paris: "A Weekend Interlude: Imperial Pleasures North of Paris," Catharine Reynolds, *Gourmet,* November 1996 (includes hotels, restaurants, museums, and theaters around Compiègne—where the hugely symbolic 1918 armistice was signed—about sixty miles from Paris); "The Best Hotels in the North of France," Christopher Petkanas, *Travel & Leisure,* September 1996 (features eight country accommodations, from simple to luxurious, in Burgundy, Île-de-France, Normandy, and Brittany); and "Riverside Rendezvous," Catharine Reynolds, *Gourmet,* July 1994 (features seven *guinguettes*—rustic riverside restaurants, the most famous of them, Maison Fournaise, captured so magnificently in Renoir's breathtaking painting *Déjeuner des canotiers*—in suburban Paris.

Additional Credits

Page 1: Quotation from "PARIS" by Julian Green, translated by Jim Underwood, published by Marion Boyars Publishers Inc., 1991.

Introduction: From FRAGILE GLORY: A PORTRAIT OF FRANCE & THE FRENCH by Richard Bernstein, Copyright © 1990 by Richard Bernstein. Reprinted by permission of Alfred A. Knopf, Inc.

Renseignements Pratiques: Quote from *Paris: Places & Pleasures* reprinted by permission of International Creative Management, Inc., Copyright © 1971, Kate Simon.

Le Kiosque: James Baldwin, *No Name in the Street,* Dial Press, 1972.

La Seine: Mort Rosenblum, *The Secret Life of the Seine,* a William Patrick Book, Addison-Wesley Publishing Company, 1994.

Paris, Je T'Aime: John Berger, "Imagine Paris," *Keeping a Rendezvous,* Vintage, 1992.

Les Quartiers: From FRAGILE GLORY: A PORTRAIT OF FRANCE & THE FRENCH by Richard Bernstein, Copyright © 1990 by Richard Bernstein. Reprinted by permission of Alfred A. Knopf, Inc. Quote from *Paris: Places & Pleasures* reprinted by permission of International Creative Management, Inc., Copyright © 1971, Kate Simon.

Saveurs Françaises: Waverly Root, *The Food of France,* Vintage Books, 1992; originally published in hardcover by Alfred A. Knopf, 1958.

À Table!: George Moore, *Confessions of a Young Man,* Swan Sonnenschein, London, 1889.

Les Personalités: Rosamond Bernier, from the introduction to *Paris,* John Russell, Harry N. Abrams, 1983.

Des Belles Choses: Don George, "Paris on My Mind," salon.com, 2 June, 1999. Ernest Hemingway, "Hunger Was Good Discipline," *A Moveable Feast,* Scribner, 1964.

L'Île-de-France et d'Ailleurs: Alexander Liberman, *The Artist in His Studio,* Random House, 1998.